EVOLUTION OF LEARNING AND MEMORY MECHANISMS

Evolution of Learning and Memory Mechanisms is an exploration of laboratory and field research on the many ways that evolution has influenced learning and memory processes, such as associative learning, social learning, and spatial, working, and episodic memory systems. This volume features research by both outstanding early-career scientists as well as familiar luminaries in the field. Learning and memory in a broad range of animals are explored, including numerous species of invertebrates (insects, worms, sea hares), as well as fish, amphibians, birds, rodents, bears, and human and nonhuman primates. Contributors discuss how the behavioral, cognitive, and neural mechanisms underlying learning and memory have been influenced by evolutionary pressures. They also draw connections between learning and memory and the specific selective factors that shaped their evolution. *Evolution of Learning and Memory Mechanisms* should be a valuable resource for those working in the areas of experimental and comparative psychology, comparative cognition, brain–behavior evolution, and animal behavior.

Mark A. Krause is Professor of Psychology at Southern Oregon University. He has served as Associate Editor of *Animal Behavior and Cognition*, and is co-author of *Introduction to Psychological Science* (2020).

Karen L. Hollis is Professor Emerita of Psychology at Mount Holyoke College. She served as President of APA's Divisions 3 and 6 and has received the Comparative Cognition Society Research Award for contributions to the field.

Mauricio R. Papini is Professor of Psychology at Texas Christian University. He was Editor of the *International Journal of Comparative Psychology* and is the author of *Comparative Psychology: Evolution and Development of Brain and Behavior, Third Edition* (2021).

EVOLUTION OF LEARNING AND MEMORY MECHANISMS

Edited by

MARK A. KRAUSE
Southern Oregon University

KAREN L. HOLLIS
Mount Holyoke College

MAURICIO R. PAPINI
Texas Christian University

CAMBRIDGE
UNIVERSITY PRESS

CAMBRIDGE
UNIVERSITY PRESS

University Printing House, Cambridge CB2 8BS, United Kingdom

One Liberty Plaza, 20th Floor, New York, NY 10006, USA

477 Williamstown Road, Port Melbourne, VIC 3207, Australia

314–321, 3rd Floor, Plot 3, Splendor Forum, Jasola District Centre, New Delhi – 110025, India

103 Penang Road, #05-06/07, Visioncrest Commercial, Singapore 238467

Cambridge University Press is part of the University of Cambridge.

It furthers the University's mission by disseminating knowledge in the pursuit of education, learning, and research at the highest international levels of excellence.

www.cambridge.org
Information on this title: www.cambridge.org/9781108487993
DOI: 10.1017/9781108768450

First published 2022

A catalogue record for this publication is available from the British Library.

ISBN 978-1-108-48799-3 Hardback
ISBN 978-1-108-73831-6 Paperback

CONTENTS

INTRODUCTION: PERSPECTIVES ON THE EVOLUTION OF LEARNING
AND MEMORY MECHANISMS   1
Mark A. Krause, Karen L. Hollis, and Mauricio R. Papini

PART I EVOLUTION OF LEARNING PROCESSES

1   LEARNING AND MEMORY IN THE NEMATODE *CAENORHABDITIS*
ELEGANS   15
Alex J. Yu and Catharine H. Rankin

2   ADAPTIVE EVOLUTION OF LEARNING AND MEMORY
IN A MODEL LINEAGE   33
William G. Wright

3   LEARNING IN INSECTS: PERSPECTIVES AND POSSIBILITIES   52
Alexis Lillian Kriete and Karen L. Hollis

4   EXPERIMENTAL EVOLUTION AND MECHANISMS FOR
PREPARED LEARNING   71
Aimee S. Dunlap and Andreia F. Dexheimer

5   EVOLUTIONARY PROCESSES SHAPING LEARNING ABILITY
IN INSECTS   89
Maartje Liefting

FIGURES

TABLES

CONTRIBUTORS

Tamara del Águila, Laboratory of Psychobiology, University of Sevilla, Spain

Patrick Anselme, Faculty of Psychology, Department of Biopsychology, Ruhr-University Bochum, Germany

Michael J. Beran, Department of Psychology and Language Research Center, Georgia State University, USA

Scott Center for Neuroscience, Mind and Behavior, Bowling Green State University, USA

Aaron P. Blaisdell, Department of Psychology, University of California–Los Angeles, USA

Barbara A. Church, Language Research Center, Georgia State University, USA

Nicola S. Clayton, Department of Psychology, University of Cambridge, UK

Michelle E. Coverdale, Department of Psychological Sciences, Purdue University, USA

Jonathon D. Crystal, Department of Psychological and Brain Sciences, Indiana University, USA

Andreia F. Dexheimer, Department of Biology, University of Missouri–Saint Louis, USA

Marie C. Diquelou, School of Psychology, University of Newcastle, Australia

Michael Domjan, Department of Psychology, University of Texas at Austin, USA

Aimee S. Dunlap, Department of Biology, University of Missouri–Saint Louis, USA

Magnus Enquist, Centre for Cultural Evolution and Department of Zoology, Stockholm University, Sweden

Michael S. Fanselow, Department of Psychology, University of California–Los Angeles, USA

Stefano Ghirlanda, Department of Psychology, Brooklyn College, USA and Centre for Cultural Evolution, Stockholm University, Sweden

Antonia Gómez, Laboratory of Psychobiology, University of Sevilla, Spain

Andrea S. Griffin, School of Psychology, University of Newcastle, Australia

Ji-Song Guan, School of Life Science and Technology, Shanghai Tech University, China

Robert R. Hampton, Psychology Department and Yerkes National Primate Research Center, Emory University, USA

Karen L. Hollis, Department of Psychology and Interdisciplinary Program in Neuroscience and Behavior, Mount Holyoke College, USA

Brooke N. Jackson, Language Research Center, Georgia State University, USA

Rachel L. Kendal, Department of Anthropology, Durham University, UK

Mark A. Krause, Department of Psychology, Southern Oregon University, USA

Alexis Lillian Kriete, Department of Entomology and Plant Pathology, College of Agriculture and Life Sciences, North Carolina State University, USA

Meike Kroneisen, Department of Psychology, University of Koblenz-Landau, Germany

Kevin Laland, School of Biology, St Andrews University, UK

Maartje Liefting, Applied Zoology and Animal Ecology, Freie Universität Berlin, Germany

Johan Lind, Centre for Cultural Evolution, Stockholm University, Sweden

Rubén N. Muzio, Comparative Learning and Cognition Group, Biology of Behavior Laboratory, IBYME-CONICET, and Faculty of Psychology, University of Buenos Aires, Argentina

James S. Nairne, Department of Psychological Sciences, Purdue University, USA

Francisco M. Ocaña, Laboratory of Psychobiology, University of Sevilla, Spain

Thomas Oudman, School of Biology, St Andrews University, UK

Mauricio R. Papini, Department of Psychology, Texas Christian University, USA

Audrey E. Parrish, Department of Psychology, The Citadel, USA

Catharine H. Rankin, Department of Psychology, University of British Columbia, Canada

Fernando Rodríguez, Laboratory of Psychobiology, University of Sevilla, Spain

Cosme Salas, Laboratory of Psychobiology, University of Sevilla, Spain

Alexandra K. Schnell, Department of Psychology, University of Cambridge, UK

Benjamin M. Seitz, Department of Psychology, University of California–Los Angeles, USA

Francisco J. Silva, Department of Psychology, University of Redlands, USA

Kathleen M. Silva, Department of Psychology, University of Redlands, USA

J. David Smith, Department of Psychology, Georgia State University, USA

Wataru Toyokawa, School of Biology, St Andrews University, UK; now at Social Psychology and Decision Sciences, University of Konstanz, Germany

Jennifer Vonk, Department of Psychology, Oakland University, USA

William G. Wright, Life and Environmental Sciences, Schmid College of Science and Technology, Chapman University, Orange, California, USA

Alex J. Yu, Djavad Mowafaghian Centre for Brain Health, University of British Columbia, Canada

PREFACE

Volumes like this one often come about because scholars with a shared scientific interest agree that the time has come to synthesize the current status of their field of study. Here, that scientific interest centers on understanding how evolutionary processes influence the ways in which organisms learn and remember. Although a common theme is shared, the approaches taken are quite varied. Researchers examining Pavlovian conditioning in worms, cultural transmission of behavior in chimpanzees, and episodic memory in humans, for example, each pursue answers to questions of both *how* and *why* learning and memory processes have evolved, although their approaches to doing so are widely different. In addition, researchers of these topics may rarely interact, even though their subject matter shares a common theme. The purpose of this volume is to feature the diverse ways in which scientists have approached this topic, and, hopefully, in so doing provide readers with solid grounding on current methods and results from both laboratory and field experiments on learning and memory in animals, including humans.

We have been fortunate to assemble an amazing group of contributors to this volume. Each has discovered something fascinating about the evolution of learning and memory, and has something important to share. We are grateful that the authors of each chapter of this book agreed to collaborate on the effort, and we appreciate their hard work. When we proposed the project to Cambridge University Press, and as we began inviting authors to contribute, we received feedback that was music to our ears. People told us that this book was one of a kind, which naturally is exactly what we, and Cambridge University Press, wanted to hear. Our colleagues had positive remarks on the mixture of scientific backgrounds represented (e.g., within psychology and biology). The comment "I wish a book like this was available when I was starting out" certainly resonated with us, and we hope that a new generation of scientists-in-training will find inspiration in these pages.

Despite our early success in securing contributors to the book, the next steps in our path were not easy. Of course, one always expects challenges to major undertakings such as this. But at the outset we would have hardly expected a global pandemic to be among them. It is hard for us to sufficiently express our gratitude to the contributors to this volume. The coronavirus pandemic hit right in the middle of the project timeline. We all abruptly found ourselves in quarantine, worrying about our health and that of our loved ones, fighting to keep laboratories running, pivoting to online teaching, homeschooling children, protecting vulnerable friends and family members, and absorbing the pain and frustration of watching a large segment of the public refusing to acknowledge science. One of us (MK) lost his home and entire neighborhood to a wildfire in September 2020. We all watched helplessly, forced to the sidelines, as friends and colleagues contracted the virus; although many, thankfully, recovered, others did not.

So, it is with our utmost pleasure and pride that we have seen this project to completion. We sincerely thank Stephen Acerra and Emily Watton at Cambridge University Press for their editorial assistance and consultation throughout the course of this project; too often the rigor and feedback that go into creating an edited volume like this are overlooked. We are grateful to the anonymous reviewers of our proposal for their helpful comments and suggestions, as well as members of the Academic Press Board at Cambridge who decided that our proposal merited our efforts to make this book happen. Mark A. Krause thanks Gordon Burghardt (University of Tennessee–Knoxville) and Michael Domjan (University of Texas–Austin) for the wonderful years of collaboration and mentorship on the topics of learning, behavior, and evolution. Karen L. Hollis thanks Bruce Overmier (Professor Emeritus, University of Minnesota–Minneapolis) for more than 50 years of wise and caring mentorship, unshakable support, and deep and enduring friendship. Mauricio R. Papini thanks Jeff Bitterman (University of Hawaii–Manoa) and Bruce Overmier for their mentorship, guidance, support, and friendship.

INTRODUCTION

Perspectives on the Evolution of Learning and Memory Mechanisms

Mark A. Krause, Karen L. Hollis, and Mauricio R. Papini

The capacity to learn and remember exists in most known animal species, which raises fascinating questions about the role of evolutionary processes. Logic suggests that processing and storing information for future use is likely to be fundamental for an animal's survival and reproductive success. Foraging for food requires capacities to respond to cues that signal its availability and location, and store memories for future excursions; successful reproduction requires capacities to locate and choose a suitable mate; and, evading predators requires learning about and remembering cues associated with survival threats, such as the presence and location of predators; all of these capacities, either directly or indirectly, enhance reproductive success. Although logical deduction plays an important role in science, empirical tests are needed to confirm, in this case, evolutionary hypotheses about learning and memory. This book is about the ways in which evolutionary hypotheses inform the design of experiments on learning and memory, the empirical methods and tests that have been developed, and the knowledge derived from research programs that reveal relationships between learning, memory, and evolution. The contributors to each chapter provide unique insights into how evolution has influenced a broad array of learning and memory mechanisms across a diverse representation of invertebrate and vertebrate species.

How learning and memory work has been at the center of inquiry in comparative psychology since the earliest days of the field. However, comparative psychologists and biologists share an interest in *why* learning and memory occur. As a result, we find approaches that converge on Tinbergen's four aims of inquiry (Tinbergen, 1963). That is, to understand the capacity for learning and memory fully, researchers have explored its underlying neural and molecular mechanisms (causation), its genetic and developmental bases (ontogeny), its adaptive function (survival and reproductive fitness), and its phylogenetic distribution across species (evolution). Although no single approach will tell us *why* learning and memory evolved, their integration gives us fascinating clues. And, as it turns out, approaching learning and memory from an evolutionary perspective has yielded important insights that further our understanding of the fundamental questions of *how* they occur. Each contributor to this volume (whose names are cited in **bold**) offers an important empirical and theoretical view toward advancing our understanding of the relationships between learning, memory, and evolution.

We assembled this volume because so much fascinating research on the evolutionary basis of learning and memory has been conducted by psychologists and biologists. We felt it was time to bring together researchers approaching evolutionary questions from diverse viewpoints, behavior systems, and study species, and, in doing so, create a single volume that represents not only how the field has changed in recent decades, but also the directions in which it is headed. Our aim in this introduction is to provide a brief overview of the major questions and issues that provide context for the book, and, hopefully, offer a rationale for why we believe such a book is an important contribution to our field.

I.1 GENERAL PROCESS, ADAPTIVE SPECIALIZATION, OR BOTH?

Adaptation by natural selection is a major concept driving our understanding of learning and memory. As an evolutionary concept, adaptation is usually invoked when a character exhibits a complexity in organization that defies alternatives, such as other forces of nature or the product of random processes. Williams (1966) warned that adaptation should not be invoked when more basic processes provide an explanation. To use his own example, it is apparently adaptive for flying fish to return to water because they cannot survive outside of it; however, an adaptive explanation is not needed because the return to the water can be explained more parsimoniously by gravity. Some clues that a character is an adaptation, when measures of reproductive success are not available, involve the complexity of the character and the presence of intermediate forms of that character. For example, the eye of vertebrates can be traced to a basal form in living lampreys from which the complex eye of jawed classes evolved over the last 500 million years (Lamb et al., 2007). Regarding learning and memory, the intricacies of processes involved in the encoding and retrieval of information strongly suggest that their evolution was shaped by natural selection. Moreover, studies on animals with few neurons may help us understand how these components have evolved to produce the complexity that we observe today in terms of incentive representations, spatial mapping, episodic memories, and metacognition, to name some functions described in this volume. But how is adaptation to be incorporated into our understanding of learning and memory in an evolutionary context?

Since the 1960s, comparative psychologists have been struggling with these two questions: Are learning and memory all-purpose mechanisms common to many species? Or has selection acted upon learning and memory mechanisms such that they are either constrained or specialized by the attentional, sensory/perceptual, or learning capacities of the study species? The answer to which alternative best summarizes the current state of knowledge regarding the evolution of learning and memory may depend on the scope of the question. At a macro level, Pavlovian conditioning, for example, occurs across a wide range of organisms (Ginsberg & Jablonka, 2010; Hollis, 1997; Hollis & Guillette, 2011, 2015; Krause & Domjan, 2017; Papini, 2021). Signature effects such as acquisition and extinction are found across species, and across aversive and appetitive response systems. However, unique ecological and evolutionary circumstances may give rise to adaptively specialized forms of this learning, and empirical findings of this effect have laid challenges for the principle of *equipotentiality*. According to this tenet of the general process view of learning, learning is unaffected by the nature of the stimuli that organisms experience, and responses to stimuli are unaffected by stimulus properties. This principle is contradicted in various Pavlovian conditioning phenomena (**Blaisdell & Seitz**), including taste aversions (Garcia & Koelling, 1966; Miller & Domjan, 1981), antipredator behavior (Griffin et al., 2001), and sexual responses (Domjan & Krause, 2017; **Krause & Domjan**). The behavior systems framework synthesizes disparate "anomalies" that contradict general process theories of learning into a coherent structure (**Silva & Silva**). But even when equipotentiality does not apply, the efficient stimuli and reinforcers for learning seem to exhibit some familiar phenomena, including acquisition, extinction, discrimination, generalization, and others.

The capacity to learn can lead to adaptive outcomes; the question is how general the trait is. The tension between general processes and adaptive specializations applies to other traits beyond learning and memory, as demonstrated by the following example involving temperature regulation in vertebrates (Bicego et al., 2007). Within some limits, living birds and mammals are endothermic, that is, they are able to maintain a constant internal temperature by means of behavioral and physiological mechanisms. Living reptiles, however, are ectothermic, able to regulate their internal temperature only by behavioral means. This ability to regulate temperature, albeit by different means, is true for these classes of vertebrates despite adaptations to a broad range of environments (think of penguins in the Antarctic and ostriches in the African savannah). Occasionally, however, some animals have evolved mechanisms for endothermy, including some fish species of the family Scombroidei, like tuna and mackerel (Block & Finnerty, 1994), and temperature regulation may underlie the evolution of fish species with large body size, like some sharks, as well as sea turtles (Ferrón, 2017;

Sato, 2014). A high surface-to-volume ratio in large animals makes preserving constant core temperature more likely. Similarly, as far as we know, all animals with neurons exhibit habituation, sensitization, and conditioning phenomena, with similar behavioral properties and similar mechanisms of synaptic plasticity. The type of functional and neural stability exhibited by the role of the hippocampus in spatial learning in vertebrates, and perhaps epigenetic mechanisms, warn us of the limits of adaptation as a local process. One way to understand these stable properties of learning and memory is that the selective pressures behind their evolution are factors common to a wide range of ecological conditions, such as time and space (Dickinson, 1980). But examples of local adaptations in learning and memory also are possible, and may be restricted to a relatively small set of species, as illustrated in this volume in such research areas as sexual conditioning and metacognition. General adaptations would be consistent with a general-process view, whereas local adaptations would be consistent with constraints on learning, associative selectivity, or preparedness (Papini, 2002). This framework leads to a treatment of all forms of learning as adaptations, namely, the products of natural selection.

1.2 EVOLUTION AND GENERAL LEARNING PROCESSES

Since the advent of the modern synthesis of evolution (Huxley, 1942) – a unification of Mendelian genetics and Darwinian theory – evolution has been recognized as an opportunistic process affecting gene frequencies, a process that was sometimes interpreted as leading to constant change, even at the genetic level. For example, as Mayr (1963, p. 609) proposed, "Much that has been learned about gene physiology makes it evident that the search for homologous genes is quite futile except in very close relatives." However, in an insightful article, Simpson (1964, pp. 1536–1537) suggested that

> Behavior is subject to particularly strong selection, and it is probably farthest removed from the genes and also most elaborately polygenic as a rule. [...] Convergence to the point of identity or of seriously confusing similarity would appear to be more likely in a single kind of molecule, even one as complicated as a protein, than in such phenotypic characters of a very large number of such molecules.

These passages, produced by two major proponents of the modern synthesis, illustrate the tension between the notion that natural selection is constantly changing the genome (so that similarities, when found, are unlikely to be examples of homologies) and the notion that deep similarities in complex biological characters are likely to be the result of homology, rather than homoplasy. But these evolutionary biologists also recognized character stability, without which taxonomy would be impossible. As we emphasize in greater detail later in this introduction, this same tension in the study of learning and memory, namely, between local adaptations and deep homologies, forms the background to the constraints-on-learning debate, the question of whether all learning must be an evolutionary response to local selective pressures or a result of a more general learning process.

During the past few decades, advances in evolutionary developmental biology have uncovered an impressive degree of conservation in gene sequence and function, again emphasizing general mechanisms. Hox genes provide a striking example (e.g., Ferrier, 2016; Raff, 1996). First discovered in *Drosophila*, they are present in every animal studied thus far and are characterized by a sequence of 180 bases, the *homeobox*, that is stable across vertebrates, arthropods, annelids, nematodes, and flat worms. Hox genes are expressed in the anterior-posterior axis in the same sequence across animal phyla that have evolved independently at least since the Cambrian Period, about 640 million years ago. This stability at the cellular-molecular level across widely divergent lineages also provides a basis for general process views of learning and memory. For example, the role of CREB (the cAMP response-element-binding protein) in gene expression, which is related to synaptic plasticity and important for learning and long-term memory, has been identified in species from at least four animal phyla: nematodes, mollusks, arthropods, and vertebrates (e.g., Bozorgmehr et al., 2013; Kandel 2012). Such stability is so specific that explaining it in terms other than homology is difficult. Of course, learning and memory go beyond this cellular-molecular level, also involving neurochemical (synaptic transmission) and neurobiological (circuit architecture) levels, which provide room for further homologies, but also for homoplasy (parallel and convergent evolution) and divergent evolution.

Although learning and memory are nearly ubiquitous across animal taxa, the early decades of comparative psychology, in particular, yielded discoveries about a relatively small number of study species. The reason that species diversity in studies of learning and memory has historically been low is not exclusively because rats and pigeons, for example, are just easier to acquire and keep in a laboratory. It is also because researchers were pursuing the types of questions that would not necessitate comparing multiple species. Clearly, a single "model" species and some good hypotheses to test have made significant contributions to the field. Similar concentrations on a few species were a common research strategy in other experimental disciplines, including *Drosophila* in genetics, the sea urchin and chick embryo in developmental biology, and currently mice in cellular and molecular studies. However, in recent decades comparative psychologists and biologists have greatly expanded the diversity of study species. Studying multiple species enables researchers to test adaptive hypotheses about the evolution of behavioral and physical traits, for example, to determine whether a mechanism of learning and memory is restricted to a particular taxonomic group, or whether it is common to a group of species because of homoplasy (common function independently evolved) or homology (common function inherited from common ancestors) (**Schnell & Clayton; Kriete & Hollis**). Pavlovian conditioning, for example, is widely distributed across all major animal lineages (Hollis, 1997; Hollis & Guillette, 2011, 2015; Papini, 2021). By contrast, episodic memory may occur only within a relatively small group of animals. Depending on one's definition, particularly if that definition includes the capacity for language, episodic memory may be restricted to humans (Suddendorf & Corballis, 2007), or alternatively exists in a mosaic of species (Clayton, 2017; Crystal, 2018; Krause, 2015a) (**Crystal**).

Exploration of the neurobiological basis that supports learning and memory has been particularly useful to comparative evolutionary analyses, and again emphasizes the evolution of general processes. For example, habituation and sensitization to chemical cues in nematode worms (*Caenorhabditis elegans*) involve acquired changes in behavior that can be accomplished with a subset of the 302 total available neurons (**Yu & Rankin**). Spatial cognition in amphibians, as in animals of other taxa, is accomplished using egocentric, beacon-guided cues, as well as, quite possibly, "cognitive mapping" involving activation of the medial pallium (hippocampus) in toads (**Muzio & Bingman**). We see a similar neurobiological approach to the hippocampus in studies of the hippocampal pallium and its role in relational memory in teleost fish (**Gómez, Ocaña, del Águila, Rodríguez, & Salas**) and in research exploring the phylogenetic distribution of neural processes supporting nonassociative learning and Pavlovian conditioning in gastropod mollusks (**Wright**) and incentive learning in vertebrates (**Papini**). Finally, researchers continue to reveal what are still much underappreciated epigenetic mechanisms that contribute to long-term memory consolidation (**Guan**). Ultimately, we need a combination of a broader comparative base and systematic research on specific model species to test for general learning and memory capacities. To this end, we have invited contributors who work with a wide diversity of animal species, including nematodes, gastropod mollusks, insects, amphibians, actinopterygian fish, birds, and mammals, including rats, bears, monkeys, apes, and humans, among others.

I.3 EVOLUTION AND ADAPTIVE SPECIALIZATIONS

The term "adaptive specialization" represents an empirical claim about the evolution of a trait, in this case learning. Thus, if the term is used to explain empirical data derived from learning experiments, then we should expect that an adaptive hypothesis has been tested using established methods. Testing the adaptive nature of a trait, physical or behavioral, requires that certain methods have been employed to rule out alternative explanations (e.g., random mutation, exaptation, or by-product). We all recognize that spinning a story about how data fit an evolutionary interpretation based on local adaptations is not sufficient as a scientific practice (e.g., Gould & Lewontin, 1979). Specific methods must first be implemented and put to empirical test. Current evolutionary theory provides several options for testing adaptive hypotheses. Traditional methods include, but are not limited to, comparative methods (e.g., systematics), measures of reproductive success, quantitative and molecular genetics, common garden survival experiments, and examination of fossil specimens and records. The late twentieth century witnessed a surge of additional methodologies, such as genomics, bioinformatics, and evolutionary developmental biology (Pigliucci, 2009; Rose & Oakley, 2007). Krause (2015b) examined the degree to which traditional methods for testing adaptive hypotheses have been applied to studies reporting adaptively specialized fear learning in primates (e.g., "prepared" conditioning to biological threats, Öhman & Mineka, 2003) and conditioned sexual behavior in birds (Domjan et al., 2004), and reports that both research programs have made significant efforts to formally test adaptive hypotheses of Pavlovian conditioning. Moreover, in each program, experimental results confirm adaptive hypotheses.

Direct tests of how prepared – and, thus, adaptively specialized – learning can evolve over multiple generations are possible in laboratory experiments (Dunlap & Stephens, 2014) and reveal evidence that natural selection acting on free-living organisms can result in altered phenotypic expression of learning (**Dunlap & Dexheimer**). Indeed, free-living organisms show measurable phenotypic change, including learning capacity, in response to environmental changes (**Griffin & Diquelou**), and both laboratory and naturalistic studies of species that are less represented tell us about the complex ways in which selection can act upon learning and memory (**Vonk**). However, as behavioral ecologists discovered many years ago, just because something is specialized does not mean it performs at a theoretical optimum (**Anselme**).

This same issue concerning adaptive specialization versus general mechanism closely parallels ongoing debate in the field of human memory, where many researchers have been addressing evolutionary questions. A major issue concerns the *survival processing effect* (**Nairne & Coverdale**). The survival processing effect, a phenomenon that involves episodic memory, refers to repeatable observations of superior recall for words evoking survival scenarios in comparison to scenarios that are matched on all characteristics but survival. A central theme in research on the survival processing effect, which also carries through much of the literature on animal learning and memory, concerns whether the effect is an outcome of evolutionary processes, thus making it adaptive memory, or whether general memory processes can account for it without requiring an evolutionary interpretation (Nairne & Pandeirada, 2016). A similar contrast of views on the evolution of human memory concerns other potentially adaptive functions, such as enhanced memory for cheaters (**Kroneisen**). The lively debate over the evolutionary implications of human memory processing made it clear to us that this volume needed to represent researchers from this sphere.

Related to the question of adaptive specializations is why animals appear to possess so many separate types of learning and memory mechanisms, each adaptively specialized for a particular function, given that such mechanisms are behaviorally and physiologically costly. One possibility is that learning and memory capacities are fine-tuned because such fine-tuning is more efficient, in evolutionary terms, than highly generalized capacities (**Lind, Ghirlanda, & Endquist**). In addition, social learning, yet another form of learning and memory, may be favorable, in evolutionary terms, when the benefits of learning from others outweigh the costs. However, contemporary research on social learning (**Kendal**) suggests that we should not overstate its uniqueness as a separate mechanism. That is, both domain-specific and domain-general capacities underlie social learning, and these may not be distinct from the same associative processes that also guide individual learning. One advantage of a mechanism for social learning is that it can afford rapid and widespread changes in behavior among populations. The plasticity that allows widespread changes to occur can itself be selected upon through genetic accommodation. Furthermore, culturally transmitted behavior can result in environmental changes that actually alter the effects of natural selection on populations (**Laland, Oudman, & Toyokawa**). Thus, learning has a bidirectional relationship with natural selection.

The capacity for explicit-declarative cognition in humans, yet another capacity that appears to be adaptively specialized, particularly when examined in tasks that require symbolic language, creates a sense that humans are qualitatively unique in some aspects of learning and memory. For example, studying episodic memory in nonhumans would be a dead end if it was universally held that it cannot exist without language (e.g., Tulving, 2005). This view has changed among many researchers of animal behavior (Krause & Sanz, 2019). The challenge for comparative psychologists and biologists has been to devise tests for memory and cognition that circumvent the need for language. In so doing, complex cognition can appear in surprising ways (**Schnell & Clayton**). For example, both implicit and explicit rule-following in dimensional categorization can occur in monkeys as well as humans and, although monkeys require a multitude of trials to learn explicit rules, the capacity nonetheless exists (**Church, Jackson, & Smith**). Moreover, monkeys appear to know *that* they know, exhibiting what is called *meta-memory*, a capacity that has been cleverly demonstrated by offering monkeys the opportunity to opt out of taking a challenging test, which they readily choose to do (**Hampton**). Further evidence of complex learning and memory processes in nonhumans comes from studies of choice, namely, situations in which animals can exercise self-control by choosing to wait, or expend greater effort, to acquire a more valuable reward at a later time (**Beran & Parrish**).

Laboratory studies allow researchers to test specific hypotheses about the underlying processes involved in learning and memory (**Fanselow**). A fundamental issue concerns learning and memory as they occur naturally among free-living organisms. Although adaptive specializations of learning and memory promote survival and reproduction in numerous species, testing hypotheses about how they might have evolved in natural populations is a difficult endeavor, involving quantifying phenotypic variation, its heritable basis, and the direction and strength of selection on that trait. Phenotypic variation in learning and memory capacities has been documented extensively, though mostly on captive animals (see Morand-Ferron, 2017, for a review). Heritable performance of learning ability in wild populations is challenging to measure for a variety of logistical reasons, including the challenge of calculating repeatability. However, although heritability estimates may apply only to the population from which they are drawn, they still provide key background information about how learning for a given species is under selective pressures within corresponding natural populations, especially if the cognitive capacities of individuals in natural populations are quantified. An experimental evolutionary approach, in which the reliability of biologically relevant cues is manipulated directly, demonstrates the evolution of specialized learning phenotypes in *Drosophila* (**Dunlap & Dexheimer**). Similarly, phenotypic change in associative learning in parasitic wasps (*Nasonia*) also responds to selective pressures (**Liefting**). Indeed, ontogenetic change that occurs through learning does not work in opposition to generational change through natural selection. Their interaction is dynamic, complex, and merits a volume of its own in which to explore it.

1.4 ORGANIZATION OF THE BOOK

The organization of this book has taken us on a long road of individual contemplation and collaborative discussion, a road with many twists and turns. Because in many categorical schemes, three is often a magical number, we began with a three-part scheme in mind. However, as the chapters arrived and we attempted to group them, placing each one into its appropriate section, the three themes began to shift, and then reform and shift again. Our organizational road seemed to be made of beach sand. At some point, however, a point that was disconcertedly near our publisher's deadline, we made the final decision to divide the book into two sections, one emphasizing basic conditioning processes and another emphasizing memory. Readers might be tempted to think that they recognize this dichotomy as the same one that many older texts follow, an unfortunate, and scientifically flawed, dichotomy that separates "animal learning" from "human memory." However, as we hope to have already convinced readers in the previous pages of this introduction, many of the same questions – for example, homology vs. homoplasy, general process vs. adaptive specialization – drive research in both learning and memory. Our organizational goal, then, has not been to separate human and nonhuman animal research but, rather, to emphasize researchers' similar focus on the ways in which animals, both human and nonhuman alike, learn and remember. We describe these sections thusly:

* Part I: **Evolution of Learning Processes.** Chapters in this part examine the evolution of learning based on conditioning and basic associative processes. Chapters focus on functional considerations, such as learning and its relationship to survival, reproduction, and ecological adaptation, and also on the underlying mechanisms, whether at the psychological, neurobiological, neurochemical, or cellular-molecular level.
* Part II: **Evolution of Memory Processes.** Chapters in this part examine the evolution of learning based on different memory processes, including spatial, emotional, episodic, prospective, recognition, and working memory, as well as metamemory. Whereas most of these chapters deal with behavioral data, the seeds for an understanding of memory at lower levels of analysis are also present.

REFERENCES

Bicego, K. C., Barros, R. C. H., & Branco, L. G. S. (2007). Physiology of temperature regulation: Comparative aspects. *Comparative Biochemistry and Physiology, Part A: Molecular & Integrative Physiology, 147*, 616–639. https://doi.org/10.1016/j.cbpa.2006.06.032

Block, B. A., & Finnerty, J. R. (1994). Endothermy in fishes: A phylogenetic analysis of constraints, predispositions, and selection pressures. *Environmental Biology of Fishes, 40*, 283–302. https://doi.org/10.1007/BF00002518

Bozorgmehr, T., Ardiel, E. L., McEwan, A. H., & Rankin, C. H. (2013). Mechanisms of plasticity in a *Caenorhabditis elegans* mechanosensory circuit. *Frontiers in Physiology, 4*, 88. https://doi.org/10.3389/fphys.2013.00088

Clayton, N. S. (2017). Episodic-like memory and mental time travel in animals. In J. Call (Ed.), *Handbook of comparative psychology: Vol 2. Perception, learning, and cognition* (pp. 227–243). American Psychological Association Press.

Crystal, J. D. (2018). Animals models of episodic memory. *Comparative Cognition and Behavior Reviews, 13*, 105–122. http://doi.org/10.3819/CCBR.2018.130012

Dickinson, A. (1980). *Contemporary animal learning theory*. Cambridge University Press.

Domjan, M., Cusato, B., & Krause, M. (2004) Learning with arbitrary versus ecological conditioned stimuli: Evidence from sexual conditioning. *Psychonomic Bulletin & Review, 11*, 232–246. https://doi.org/10.3758/BF03196565

Domjan, M., & Krause, M. A. (2017). Adaptive specializations and the generality of the laws of classical and instrumental conditioning. In R. Menzel (Ed.), *Learning theory and behavior, Vol. 1 of Learning and memory: A comprehensive reference* (2nd ed., pp. 180–201) J. H. Byrne (Ed.). Academic Press. http://dx.doi.org/10.1016/B978-0-12-809324-5.21012-2

Dunlap, A. S., & Stephens, D. W. (2014). Experimental evolution of prepared learning. *Proceedings of the National Academy of Sciences, 111*(32), 11750–11755. https://doi.org/10.1073/pnas.1404176111

Ferrier, D. E. K. (2016). Evolution of homeobox gene clusters in animals: The giga-cluster and primary vs. secondary clustering. *Frontiers in Ecology and Evolution, 4,* 36. https://doi.org/10.3389/fevo.2016.00036

Ferrón, H. G. (2017). Regional endothermy as a trigger for gigantism in some extinct macropredatory sharks. *Plos One, 12,* e0185185. https://doi.org/10.1371/journal.pone.0185185

Garcia, J., & Koelling, R. A. (1966). Relation of cue to consequence in aversion learning. *Psychonomic Science, 4,* 123–124. https://doi.org/10.3758/BF03342209

Ginsburg, S., & Jablonka, E. (2010). The evolution of associative learning: A factor in the Cambrian explosion. *Journal of Theoretical Biology, 266,* 11–20. https://doi.org/10.1016/j.jtbi.2010.06.017

Gould, S. J., & Lewontin, R. C. (1979). The spandrels of San Marco and the Panglossian paradigm: A critique of the adaptationist programme. *Proceedings of the Royal Society of London B: Biological Sciences, 205,* 581–598. https://doi.org/10.1126/science.24.602.58

Griffin, A. S., Evans, C. S., & Blumstein, D. T. (2001). Learning specificity in acquired predator recognition. *Animal Behaviour, 62*(3), 577–589. https://doi.org/10.1006/anbe.2001.1781

Hollis, K. L. (1997). Contemporary research on Pavlovian conditioning: A "new" functional analysis. *American Psychologist, 52,* 956–965. https://doi.org/10.1037/0003-066X.52.9.956

Hollis, K. L., & Guillette, L. M. (2011). Associative learning in insects: Evolutionary models, mushroom bodies, and a neuroscientific conundrum. *Comparative Cognition and Behavior Reviews, 6,* 24–45. https://psycnet.apa.org/doi/10.3819/ccbr.2011.60004

(2015). What associative learning in insects tells us about models for the evolution of learning. *International Journal of Comparative Psychology, 28,* 1–18. https://escholarship.org/uc/item/3v15313t

Huxley, J. (1942). *Evolution: The modern synthesis.* George Alien & Unwin Ltd.

Kandel, E. R. (2012). The molecular biology of memory: cAMP, PKA, CRE, CREB-1, CREB-2, and CPEB. *Molecular Brain, 5,* 14. https://doi.org/10.1186/1756-6606-5-14

Krause, M. A. (2015a). Adaptive memory in humans from a comparative perspective. *International Journal of Comparative Psychology, 28.* https://escholarship.org/uc/item/6v66z8x1

(2015b). Evolutionary perspectives on learning: conceptual and methodological issues in the study of adaptive specializations. *Animal Cognition, 18*(4), 807–820. https://doi.org/10.1007/s10071-015-0854-4

Krause, M. A., & Domjan, M. (2017). Ethological and evolutionary perspectives on Pavlovian conditioning. In J. Call (Ed.), *Handbook of comparative psychology: Vol 2: Perception, learning and cognition* (pp. 247–266). American Psychological Association. https://doi.org/10.1037/0000012-012

Krause, M. A., & Sanz, C. M. (2019). The evolution of human learning and memory: Comparative perspectives on testing adaptive hypotheses. In T. B. Henley, M. J. Rossano, & E. P. Kardas (Eds.), *Handbook of cognitive archaeology: Psychology in prehistory* (pp. 174–195). Routledge.

Lamb, T. D., Collin, S. P., & Pugh, E. N. Jr. (2007). Evolution of the vertebrate eye: Opsins, photoreceptors, retina, and eye cup. *Nature Reviews Neuroscience, 8,* 960–976. https://doi.org/10.1038/nrn2283

Mayr, E. (1963). *Animal species and evolution.* Harvard University Press.

Miller, V., & Domjan, M. (1981). Selective sensitization induced by lithium malaise and footshock in rats. *Behavioral & Neural Biology, 31*(1), 42–55. https://doi.org/10.1016/S0163-1047(81)91050-5

Morand-Ferron, J. (2017). Why learn? The adaptive value of associative learning in wild populations. *Current Opinion in Behavioral Sciences, 16,* 73–79. https://doi.org/10.1016/j.cobeha.2017.03.008

Nairne, J. S., & Pandeirada, J. N. S. (2016). Adaptive memory: The evolutionary significance of survival processing. *Perspectives on Psychological Science, 11*, 496–511. https://doi.org/10.1177/1745691616635613

Öhman, A., & Mineka, S. (2003). The malicious serpent: Snakes as a prototypical stimulus for an evolved module of fear. *Current Directions in Psychological Science, 12*, 5–9. https://doi.org/10.1111/1467-8721.01211

Papini, M. R. (2002). Pattern and process in the evolution of learning mechanisms. *Psychological Review, 109*, 186–201. https://doi.org/10.1037/0033-295X.109.1.186

(2021). *Comparative psychology: Evolution and development of brain and behavior.* Taylor & Francis.

Pigliucci, M. (2009). An extended synthesis for evolutionary biology. *Annals of the New York Academy of Sciences, 1168*, 218–228. https://doi.org/10.1111/j.1749-6632.2009.04578.x

Raff, R. A. (1996). *The shape of life.* University of Chicago Press.

Rose, M. R., & Oakley, T. H. (2007) The new biology: Beyond the modern synthesis. *Biology Direct 2*, 30. https://doi.org/10.1186/1745-6150-2-30

Sato, K. (2014). Body temperature stability achieved by the large body mass of sea turtles. *Journal of Experimental Biology, 217*, 3607–3614. https://doi.org/10.1242/jeb.109470

Simpson, G. G. (1964). Organisms and molecules in evolution. *Science, 146*, 1535–1538.

Suddendorf, T., & Corballis, M. C. (2007). The evolution of foresight: what is mental time travel and is it unique to humans? *Behavioral and Brain Sciences, 30*, 299–313. https://doi.org/10.1017/S0140525X07001975

Tinbergen, N. (1963). On aims and methods in ethology. *Zeitschrift für Tierpsychologie, 20*, 410–433. https://doi.org/10.1111/j.1439-0310.1963.tb01161.x

Tulving, E. (2005). Episodic memory and autonoesis: Uniquely human? In H. S. Terrace & J. Metcalfe (Eds.), *The missing link in cognition: Origins of self-reflective consciousness* (pp. 3–56). Oxford University Press. https://doi.org/10.1093/acprof:oso/9780195161564.003.0001

Williams, G. C. (1966). *Adaptation and natural selection.* Princeton University Press.

PART I

EVOLUTION OF LEARNING PROCESSES

1

LEARNING AND MEMORY IN THE NEMATODE *CAENORHABDITIS ELEGANS*

Alex J. Yu and Catharine H. Rankin

Organisms encounter various challenges in their surroundings and they need to adjust their behaviors to better survive in ever-changing environments. Learning and memory enable animals to navigate the environment and avoid danger. This capacity is not only true for large, complex mammals, but also for microscopic short-lived invertebrates such as *Caenorhabditis elegans*. Learning and memory are such important contributors to the survival of most animals that they might be considered a defining feature of the animal kingdom. With only 302 neurons, *C. elegans* shows a broad range of forms of learning and many of the behavioral rules and patterns are the same across phylogeny. Understanding the mechanisms of learning and memory in *C. elegans* will help us understand the evolution of this amazing behavioral ability.

C. elegans is a free-living, microscopic nematode that was first adopted as a model to study genetics and development by Brenner (1974). A growing body of research on this nematode has greatly expanded our knowledge of the biology of *C. elegans*, making it arguably the best-understood multicellular organism. A fully mapped connectome of its 302 identified neurons (White et al., 1986); a fully sequenced genome (The C. elegans Sequencing Consortium, 1998); and abundant, well-developed genetic tools and resources, along with its convenience for laboratory work (e.g., it cultures on Petri dishes and a library of mutant strains are available), have allowed the rapid advance in the research on the cellular and molecular mechanisms of learning and memory in *C. elegans*.

It was originally believed that, because *C. elegans* shows deterministic development with an invariant cell lineage (Sulston et al., 1983) and a similar pattern of nervous system connectivity between individuals (White et al., 1986), it would be incapable of learning. Additionally, learning and memory did not appear to be necessary for the worm, as its reproductive cycle is merely three days long. Rankin et al. (1990) were the first to demonstrate that worms could learn and remember earlier training. Since this first report, researchers have observed various types of learning and elucidated many underlying mechanisms of learning and memory in this nematode.

Although the nervous system of *C. elegans* has only 302 neurons, the worms' behaviors and the underlying cellular and molecular mechanisms are remarkably complex. The studies reviewed in this chapter are discussed from an ethological and evolutionary perspective. These observations provide insights into the evolutionary advantages of learning and suggest that adaptive modification of behavior promotes survival.

1.1 NONASSOCIATIVE LEARNING

There are two major forms of nonassociative learning: habituation is the response decrement produced by repeated stimuli; sensitization is the response facilitation produced by novel, intense, and/or noxious stimuli. Nonassociative learning is observed in virtually all animal species, and it modulates innate behavior, helping organisms to selectively and efficiently distribute their cognitive resources and/or attention (Groves & Thompson, 1970; Lorenz, 1981, see pp. 264–266; Rankin et al., 2009).

In *C. elegans*, habituation was the first form of learning demonstrated (Rankin et al., 1990); later, habituation and its underlying mechanisms have been studied in several paradigms and conditions. This research shows that the simplest form of learning in a simple organism is not really so simple and that changes in multiple behavioral components are coordinated for this learning to be expressed.

HABITUATION

In habituation, response decrement occurs when stimuli are repeatedly presented; this decreasing response to recurring stimuli allows filtering out redundant information and freeing up attention for higher cognitive functions (Ramaswami, 2014; Rankin et al., 2009). The behavioral rules for habituation are conserved across phylogeny (Groves & Thompson, 1970; Rankin et al., 2009); however, this conservation does not mean its mechanisms are also conserved. Studies with the gill-withdrawal reflex in *Aplysia*, a mollusk, found that habituation was mediated by depression of an excitatory synapse (Pinsker et al., 1970), while studies of olfactory habituation in *Drosophila*, an arthropod, indicated it was mediated by enhancement of an inhibitory synapse (Das et al., 2011). These contrasting findings emphasize how little we understand the cellular and molecular mechanisms for habituation in any organism (Rankin et al., 2009).

Although many responses habituate in *C. elegans*, habituation to mechanosensory stimuli has been the most thoroughly scrutinized. A tap to the side of a Petri dish on which worms are cultured typically elicits backward movement; the magnitude of this reversal response decreases over repetition of stimuli (Rankin et al., 1990). Detailed analyses of how different factors influence habituation has led to insights into its cellular mechanisms.

Timbers et al. (2013) varied tap intensity and observed faster habituation to weaker taps and slower to stronger taps. Furthermore, older worms habituated to taps of the same intensity faster than younger worms. Interestingly, when the touch receptor neurons were activated with blue light by genetically engineering the expression of light-gated cation channels channelrhodopsin-2 (ChR2), and mechanosensory transduction was bypassed, older and younger worms did not differ in habituation rate. Timbers et al. (2013) hypothesized that older worms experience stimuli as weaker, possibly because aging-related cuticle thickening decreases the sensitivity of the mechanoreceptors, and habituation is consequently altered.

Habituation is also affected by interstimulus interval (ISI). Worms trained at shorter ISIs habituated, and spontaneously recovered from habituation, more rapidly than worms trained at longer ISIs (Rankin & Broster, 1992). This led to the hypothesis that habituation at different ISIs may be mediated, at least in part, by different processes. This hypothesis was substantiated by studies showing that there are genes differentially mediating habituation at different ISIs (Ardiel et al., 2018). Two genes, *cmk-1* and *ogt-1*, the *C. elegans* orthologs of human CAMK1 (calcium/calmodulin-dependent protein kinase I) and OGT (O-linked N-acetylglucosamine transferase), function in the touch receptor neurons to modulate habituation in an ISI-dependent manner: *cmk-1* and *ogt-1* mutants habituated faster than wild-type worms at a 10 s ISI, and slower than wild-type worms at a 60 s ISI. Thus, different molecular signaling cascades may be involved in short- and long-ISI habituation. It may be that habituation at long ISIs is more energetically costly and so it is better to retain the memory for longer durations, while habituation at short ISIs may be energetically less expensive.

Historically, habituation has been viewed as an equivalent decrement of all components of a response, however, this is not always the case. Timbers et al. (2013) compared habituation for response probability and distance travelled, and found that aging differentially affected habituation of these two components. Ardiel et al. (2018) further dissected "distance" into speed and duration components. Worms with mutations in *cmk-1* and *ogt-1* had similar habituation curves for response distance; however, examining speed and duration separately revealed that *cmk-1* mutants had a higher response speed and a lower response duration than *ogt-1* mutants, and the two components showed different habituation dynamics. These findings suggest that the response components of habituation might be modulated by different underlying mechanisms.

Consistent with findings in other species, long-term memory (LTM) is most effectively produced by spaced/distributed training. LTM for habituation was observed 24 hours after 4 blocks of 20 taps at a 60 s ISI separated by 1 hour resting periods (Beck & Rankin, 1995; Rose et al., 2002). In a later study, memory from this training lasted at least 48 hours, a remarkably long time given the short lifespan of *C. elegans*. By contrast, massed training with the same number of stimuli, 80 taps, at a 60 s ISI with no rest periods produced an intermediate-term memory of habituation that was exhibited 12 hours but not 24 hours later (Li et al., 2013).

Distinct molecular mechanisms underlie memories for habituation lasting different durations and produced by different training protocols. In short-term habituation, the mechanosensory neurons and the sensory-interneuron synapses were hypothesized to be the major cellular sites of habituation (Wicks & Rankin, 1995), and, because the mechanosensory neurons are glutamatergic, a role for glutamate at this locus was implicated (Rankin & Wicks, 2000). Intermediate-term memory for habituation was hypothesized to be caused by an increase in FLP-20, a FMRFamide-like neuropeptide, released by the mechanosensory neurons; this intermediate-term memory was correlated with an increase in synaptic vesicle density in the so-called PLM mechanosensory neurons (and likely the ALM neurons; Li et al., 2013), suggesting an increase in FLP-20-containing vesicles recruited to the pre-synaptic terminals. By contrast, the molecular mechanisms for LTM, as in many other species, involves protein-synthesis-dependent changes in glutamate signaling (Rose et al., 2003) and activity of a transcription factor, cAMP response element-binding protein (CREB; Timbers & Rankin, 2011). This memory is eliminated by protein synthesis inhibition (heat shock; Beck & Rankin, 1995) and reconsolidation blockade (Rose & Rankin, 2006). These data indicate that there is not a single "memory" process, but that memory for short-, intermediate-, and long-term habituation can be produced with different paradigms and are mediated by nonoverlapping cellular and molecular signaling pathways, perhaps to minimize interference among different forms of memory.

Environmental factors also affect mechanosensory habituation. Kindt et al. (2007) found that *C. elegans* habituated more rapidly and to a greater degree when trained without food (*E. coli* patches) on the Petri plates. This occurs because food texture triggers dopamine release, which activates a dopamine D1-like receptor DOP-1 in the touch receptor neurons to modulate mechanosensation and delay habituation. One possible explanation is that the presence of food helps worms remain alert to incoming stimuli, and the absence of food reduces responding to save energy and prioritize foraging.

Environmental contextual cues can add an associative component to habituation. Worms habituated with a distinct chemosensory cue, either the taste of salt or the odor of a volatile chemical, retained the memory better if they were rehabituated later in the same context (Lau et al., 2013). The effect of the context on habituation memory is mediated by an NMDA-type glutamate receptor subunit NMR-1, as *nmr-1* mutants showed normal short- and long-term habituation, but failed to display enhanced memory in the presence of the contextual reminder. Thus, nonassociative learning can have associative components, suggesting that the configuration of environmental cues and stimulation patterns may convey specific information that animals store in memory for future use.

Habituation has also been studied in chemosensation in *C. elegans*. Decreased responding to repeated chemosensory stimuli could depend on habituation, sensory adaptation, or both. Response decrement by adaptation only recovers over time; this sensory fatigue is mediated by different cellular processes than habituation. Habituation is an attentional process that can be differentiated from adaptation by testing for dishabituation and by determining the rate of spontaneous recovery after training (Rankin et al., 2009).

Bernhard and van der Kooy (2000) dissociated chemosensory adaptation and habituation in *C. elegans*. Preexposure to 0.001% or to 100% diacetyl led to a decreased approach response to diacetyl (normally an attractant). If this exposure was followed by being spun in a centrifuge, only worms preexposed to 0.001% diacetyl showed dishabituation, suggesting the decreased approach was habituation, whereas worms preexposed to 100% diacetyl did not dishabituate, suggesting the decrement was adaptation. Thus, habituation primarily mediated decrement at low concentration, whereas adaptation occurred at high concentration. Habituation to diacetyl smell is *glr-1* dependent (Bernhard & van der Kooy, 2000); by contrast, habituation to benzaldehyde smell is not (Morrison & van der Kooy, 2001). Additionally, worms habituated to benzaldehyde could be dishabituated by centrifugation, and this phenomenon was also glutamate dependent, as mutants lacking a vesicular glutamate transporter do not exhibit dishabituation (Nuttley et al., 2001).

Like mechanosensory habituation, chemosensory habituation is also affected by the presence of food. Nuttley et al. (2002) found that habituation to benzaldehyde was inhibited in the presence of food. Exogenous serotonin mimicked the inhibitory effect of food on habituation to benzaldehyde, and the presence of food had no effect on the habituation in serotonin-deficient *cat-4* and *tph-1* mutants. These studies illustrate that convergent and divergent molecular mechanisms underlie habituation within and across sensory modalities.

SENSITIZATION

Sensitization is facilitation of a response when the animal faces unexpected, often intense stimuli. The facilitated response may serve to enhance the success of avoidance or escape behaviors. In *Aplysia* and leeches, the neuromodulator serotonin was found to play a key role in sensitization (Byrne & Hawkins, 2015). Research in *C. elegans*, however, showed that other molecular mechanisms underlie sensitization.

In *C. elegans*, the pair of polymodal nociceptor ASH neurons in the head of the worm detect aversive stimuli, including harsh touch, volatile chemicals, and osmotic pressure. Detection of these stimuli causes the worm to crawl backward away from the source of stimulation. Transgenic worms with genetically encoded ChR2 in ASH respond to photoactivation of ASH by reversing. If a worm experienced a tap stimulus followed by optogenetic stimulation of the ASH neurons, the ASH-mediated escape response shows sensitization (Chew et al., 2018). Intriguingly, FLP-20, the same neuropeptide implicated in intermediate-term habituation, also regulates this form of sensitization. Mechanosensory neuron-released FLP-20 binds to FRPR-3 neuropeptide receptors to mediate ASH response sensitization. One major cellular site of action of FRPR-3, the neuroendocrine interneuron RID, was identified.

Chemosensory responses can also be sensitized by previous experience. Avoidance of the noxious odor of 2-nonanone can be sensitized if worms are preexposed to it (Yamazoe-Umemoto et al., 2015). This form of sensitization is also neuropeptide dependent, as mutations in genes encoding key components of neuropeptide biosynthesis *egl-3* (proprotein convertase) and *egl-21* (carboxypeptidase E) showed no increased avoidance in this paradigm. Interestingly, although dopamine is not involved in producing sensitization, it contributes to maintaining the movement direction away from the source of aversive stimuli (Yamazoe-Umemoto et al., 2015). Together, neuropeptides and dopamine interact to increase the effectiveness of the avoidance response.

HABITUATION TO NOCICEPTIVE STIMULI AS A WAY TO SHIFT BEHAVIORAL STRATEGY

C. elegans habituates to repeated stimulation of the ASH nociceptor neurons (Ardiel et al., 2016; Hart et al., 1999). Why do animals habituate to potentially dangerous nociceptive stimuli? Additional studies examined behavioral changes of different response components during habituation as well as assessed the behavior during the ISI. Habituation to repeated optogenetic activation of ASH occurs differently in components of the reversal response: pronounced decrement was observed in duration and latency, whereas the probability of responding showed very little decrement (Ardiel et al., 2016). While habituating to the stimuli, worms also displayed a previously uncharacterized sensitization of forward locomotion between stimuli (Ardiel et al., 2017). With repeated stimulation, locomotion during the ISI gradually decreased backward movement and increased fast forward movement. Thus, integration of a suite of coordinated behavioral changes occurred during repeated optogenetic activation of ASH neurons such that worms remained fairly responsive to ensure an escape response to a potentially toxic stimulus; meanwhile, worms reduced the magnitude of the response and increasingly engaged in accelerated forward locomotion to evacuate from where they repeatedly encountered aversive stimuli. The coordination of response habituation and locomotion sensitization is mediated by a family of neuropeptides, Pigment-Dispersing Factors PDF-1 and PDF-2, that are orthologs of a neuropeptide previously implicated in arousal in arthropods (Ardiel et al., 2017). Without these peptides or their receptor PDFR-1, the forward locomotion sensitization did not occur. Thus, habituation of components of the response to aversive stimuli combined with sensitization in other behaviors serves to adaptively alter the behavioral strategy to help animals respond to, and disperse away from, potential danger.

SUMMARY OF NONASSOCIATIVE LEARNING

The behavioral characteristics of nonassociative learning in *C. elegans* largely align with those in other species; although some of the underlying molecular mechanisms appear to be conserved, others showed divergence. Based on studies of habituation in *C. elegans*, behavioral responses are made up of multiple components (probability, duration, speed, latency, and ongoing behaviors) that undergo differential plasticity to produce a large range of behaviors. Habituation and sensitization independently modify innate responses, as well as synergistically increase the effectiveness of behavior in the experimental context. These results show that nonassociative learning is not a single, global phenomenon that governs all behavioral aspects; rather, different behavioral changes may occur in one or several behavioral components, depending on the animal's experience, to produce optimal responses for specific situations.

1.2 ASSOCIATIVE LEARNING

C. elegans flourishes in habitats encompassing rich environmental features in which a multitude of sensory experiences modulate its behavior (Shulenberg & Félix, 2017). *C. elegans* exhibits stereotypic, goal-directed, taxis behaviors to a variety of stimuli, in which it migrates along gradients toward the source of positive cues or away from the source of negative cues (Gray et al., 2005). Studies have demonstrated that these unconditioned responses can be modified based on learned associations between a variety of stimuli through classical conditioning. The most studied classical conditioning protocols using *C. elegans* involve sensory cues (CS) that predict either the presence or absence of bacterial food (US). The well-characterized nervous system in *C. elegans* also provides a unique opportunity to uncover the neural substrates underlying associative learning.

GUSTATORY LEARNING

C. elegans is innately attracted to NaCl. Na+ and Cl− ions are mainly detected by the pair of ASE gustatory neurons in an asymmetrical way: the left ASE neuron, ASEL, primarily senses Na+ and the right one, ASER, primarily senses Cl− (Pierce-Shimomura et al., 2001). Wen et al. (1997) found that untrained worms showed equal preference for Na+ and Cl− in a choice test; however, if one of the ions was paired with the presence of food and the other ion with a repulsive substance, or with the absence of food during training, their choice was biased toward the ion paired with food and away from the ion paired with the repulsive substance.

Worms placed on a Petri dish with NaCl and no food later avoided NaCl; this avoidance could be reversed by exposure to NaCl and food together or starvation without NaCl (Saeki et al., 2001). Similarly, if NaCl was paired with repulsive chemicals, worms then avoided NaCl (Hukema et al., 2008). NaCl avoidance can be impaired by drugs disrupting transcription and translation or by mutations affecting CREB, suggesting that memory for salt avoidance is protein synthesis dependent, and perhaps long-lasting (Peymen et al., 2019). Thus, worms can promptly modify their response to salt based on their recent experience and retain LTM for salt avoidance.

Three parallel neuropeptide signaling pathways are involved in salt avoidance. Tomioka et al. (2006) showed that an insulin signaling pathway is critical for learned NaCl avoidance. The insulin-like peptide INS-1 acts on DAF-2 insulin receptor specifically in ASER to mediate salt learning. By contrast, the vasopressin/oxytocin-related neuropeptide NTC-1 signals through its receptor, NTR-1, in the ASEL sensory neuron, to facilitate salt conditioning (Beets et al., 2012). Myoinhibitory peptide MIP-1/NLP-38 mediates learned salt avoidance by functioning in several neurons (Peymen et al., 2019). Taken together, peptidergic neuromodulation functions in parallel in different cells to underlie salt avoidance learning. Such collaborative molecular actions may ensure that the learned avoidance is strong enough to counteract unconditioned appetitive behavior and allow for tuning of learned behavior at different cellular sites.

In mammals, an important mediator of associative learning is the NMDA-type glutamate receptor. In *C. elegans*, Kano et al. (2008) showed that NMDA receptors were involved in the maintenance of salt conditioning memory. Learned salt avoidance diminished faster in worms with mutations in NMDA receptor subunits *nmr-1* and *nmr-2*. NMDA receptors gate Ca+ influx, and CMK-1, a calcium/calmodulin-dependent kinase, function in the ASE sensory neurons to induce salt avoidance (Lim et al., 2018). Lau et al. (2013) showed that *nmr-1* was critical for context conditioning, suggesting a critical role of NMDA receptors in mediating classical conditioning across paradigms and phylogeny.

OLFACTORY LEARNING

C. elegans is attracted to odors of volatile chemicals such as diacetyl produced by bacteria (food). Conditioning worms with diacetyl paired with aversive acetic acid led to avoidance of diacetyl odor (Morrison et al., 1999). Using the same paradigm, Morrison and van der Kooy (2002) found that worms missing a *glr-1* AMPA type glutamate receptor subunit failed to learn avoidance, suggesting a role for glutamate. Worms also learned to avoid an attractant, 1-propanol, when it was paired with HCl, a repulsive acid (Amano & Maruyama, 2011). Short-lived memory (less than 3 hours) for conditioned propanol avoidance is produced in a massed-training paradigm, whereas LTM lasting at least 24 hours is produced in a spaced-training paradigm. Mutations in NDMA receptor subunit *nmr-1* impaired both short-term memory and LTM for conditioned propanol aversion, whereas worms with a mutation in the transcription factor CREB, *crh-1*, showed a selective deficit in LTM. The role of glutamate signaling and CREB in learning and memory in animals ranging from worms to humans shows the evolutionarily ancient role of these molecules in experience-dependent plasticity.

Experience-dependent changes in unconditioned chemosensory avoidance have also been observed. Worms normally avoid butanone. However, exposure to butanone and food leads to approach toward butanone (Torayama et al., 2007). Two AWC olfactory neurons (labelled AWC^{ON} and AWC^{OFF}) have distinct gene expression patterns and sense different volatile chemicals; butanone is detected by the AWC^{ON} neuron (Bargmann, 2006). *C. elegans* homologs of Bardet–Biedl syndrome genes, *bbs-1*, *osm-12/bbs-7*, and *bbs-8*, function specifically in AWC^{ON} to mediate butanone appetitive learning (Torayama et al., 2007). Using this odor–food pairing, Kauffman et al. (2010) showed that spaced training with butanone produced LTM that required CRH-1/CREB. Nishijima and Maruyama (2017) showed that after aversive 1-nonanol and appetitive KCl were presented together, worms switched their response to the odor from avoidance to approach. This appetitive olfactory memory shared features with aversive olfactory memory. Memories last for different time periods depending on massed or spaced training protocols. They were affected similarly by *nmr-1* and *crh-1* mutations suggesting that shared molecular mechanisms mediate both aversive and appetitive olfactory learning. Overall, this research shows that *C. elegans* modifies unconditioned chemosensory preferences as a result of experience: a compound that predicts food becomes attractive, one that predicts lack of food or something unpleasant becomes repulsive. Thus, chemosensory responses are sculpted by experience in ways that enhance the worm's ability to successfully find food and avoid environments without food.

Worms are attracted to the smells of some pathogenic bacteria, but they learn to avoid the pathogen after they have experienced illness produced by the bacteria; thus, they learn an association between the odors and pathogenicity. When given a choice between *E. coli* OP50, the laboratory food for *C. elegans*, and *Pseudomonas aeruginosa* PA14, a pathogenic bacterium that infects the worm's intestine and releases toxins, naïve worms initially showed a preference for PA14; however, a four-hour exposure to PA14 caused worms to lose this attraction (Zhang et al., 2005). Zhang et al. (2005) showed that the learned pathogen avoidance is dependent on serotonin synthesized in the ADF neurons and a serotonin-gated chloride channel, MOD-1. Pathogen aversive learning in *C. elegans* is regulated by a complex insulin signaling network, and at least five insulin-like neuropeptides, including INS-6, INS-7, INS-4, INS-16, and INS-11 (Chen et al., 2013; Lee & Mylonakis, 2017; Wu et al., 2019), have been shown to mediate learned pathogen avoidance. Interestingly, insulin has also been implicated in conditioned taste aversion in *Lymnaea* snails (Mita et al., 2014). Additionally, sites outside of the nervous system have been found to participate in this form of learning. INS-11, an intestine-secreted neuropeptide, regulates this learned avoidance. Zhang and Zhang (2012) found that DBL-1, a TGF-β homolog, acting on its receptor in the hypodermis, was necessary for learned avoidance. Collectively, olfactory aversive learning to pathogens is mediated by multiple neuromodulators, and the mechanisms identified suggest that learning can be modulated by tissues both inside and outside of the nervous system.

THERMOSENSORY LEARNING

Temperature regulates essential biological processes, including circadian rhythm and metabolism in *C. elegans*. Mori and Ohshima (1995) found that the neural circuit required for thermotaxis was comprised of the pair of AFD thermosensory neurons and interneurons AIY, AIZ, and RIA. Additionally, AWC olfactory neurons were found to be secondary thermosensory neurons (Biron et al., 2008; Kuhara et al., 2008). Well-fed worms learned the association between a specific temperature and the presence of food and will thermotax toward their previous cultivation temperature (Hedgecock & Russell, 1975; Mori & Oshima, 1995). AFD responds to temperature increase and decrease from a baseline set by previous cultivation, and interestingly, the memory for previous cultivation temperature is stored in these sensory neurons, as laser-ablating AFD dendrites disrupted thermosensory memory (Clark et al., 2006). Ohnishi et al. (2011) demonstrated that AFD-released glutamate inhibits AIY through a glutamate-gated inhibitory receptor and causes worms to migrate toward a colder temperature, whereas AWC-released glutamate activates AIY through an excitatory glutamate receptor and causes worms to migrate toward a warmer temperature. Thus, the learned temperature preference is regulated by the balance between AFD-AIY and AWC-AIY synaptic signaling. Perhaps having two reciprocal cellular sites to encode thermotaxis allows worms to differentiate the response to relative cold and warm temperatures based on their thermal experience rather than on absolute temperatures.

Mohri et al. (2005) observed that worms thermotaxed toward temperatures paired with food and away from temperatures paired with starvation and showed that the effect of feeding state on thermosensory associative learning is mediated by monoamines, as exogenous serotonin and octopamine mimicked the effects of on- and off-food, respectively. Kodama et al. (2006) showed that INS-1 antagonizes DAF-2 in AIZ, and this insulin signaling pathway modulates temperature-feeding state conditioning by downregulating AIZ activity. It is interesting to note that although insulin signaling is important for both salt starvation conditioning and thermotaxis to cultivation temperature, it plays opposite roles in these processes. By contrast, TAX-6, a homolog of calcineurin, is critical for both thermosensory and gustatory associative learning (Kuhara & Mori, 2006).

LEARNING OF OTHER FEATURES

C. elegans also learns about other environmental features. For example, although worms have a natural preference for a specific level of oxygen in the environment, that oxygen preference can be altered by experience (Cheung et al., 2005). When allowed to freely roam in an 0%–21% oxygen gradient, naïve worms prefer 5%–12% oxygen; however, worms previously maintained at 1% oxygen with food sought low oxygen (0%–7%), suggesting that worms learn the association between oxygen level and food, and use oxygen level as a cue for food. Prior experience with high or low levels of oxygen also reprograms the response to pheromones (Fenk & de Bono, 2017). The same pheromone attracted worms maintained at 21% oxygen, but repelled worms maintained at 7% oxygen, and this cross-modal behavioral modification is thought to be mediated by the RMG interneurons.

Worms can also integrate multiple sensory experiences in learning. Normally, both male and hermaphrodite worms exhibit learned salt avoidance after salt-starvation conditioning. Surprisingly, male worms showed a form of sex-specific learning in this paradigm. If there were hermaphrodites nearby during conditioning, male worms continued to be attracted to salt even after it was paired with starvation, suggesting that they used salt as a cue to find mates, perhaps to prioritize reproductive success (Sakai et al., 2013). Sammut et al. (2015) found that the neuropeptide PDF-1 in a pair of male-specific interneurons, MCM, regulates sex-specific conditioning.

SUMMARY OF ASSOCIATIVE LEARNING

Research has shown that worms can learn and remember a wide range of environmental features that predict the presence or absence of food or danger and modulate their behavior according to their experience in a way that allows them to find optimal environments and escape from adversity.

Various forms of associative learning are mediated by both shared and distinct neural and molecular pathways, and a number of genes and molecules show functional convergence between worms and other species (see Kriete and Hollis, Chapter 3; Guan, Chapter 25), suggesting that many learning and memory mechanisms may be evolutionarily conserved.

1.3 OLFACTORY IMPRINTING AND TRANSGENERATIONAL LEARNING

Olfactory imprinting is a form of learning that occurs during early life stages and produces a permanent memory. Remy and Hobert (2005) first observed that worms that were exposed to benzaldehyde during the L1 larval stage exhibited an enhanced appetitive response to benzaldehyde in adulthood compared to naïve worms or worms exposed to the odor at other postembryonic stages. Imprinting memory was produced only by chemicals that were sensed by the pair of AWC olfactory neurons and showed odorant selectivity. Imprinting was sensitive to food cues, as starvation disrupted imprinting memory in L1 worms, suggesting that olfactory imprinting may serve to help worms remember favorable conditions. Remy and Hobert (2005) discovered that a G protein-coupled seven-transmembrane receptor, SRA-11, functions in the AIY interneurons to mediate imprinting memory. Jin et al. (2016) found that exposing L1 worms to the pathogen PA14 caused increased avoidance of PA14 odors in adult worms. The neuromodulator tyramine was implicated in this aversive imprinting. Similarly, worms exposed to a pheromone that signals overcrowding (ascr#3) in L1 showed greater avoidance of the pheromone in adulthood (Hong et al., 2017). In both cases of aversive imprinting, the enduring behavioral effect required exposure to aversive stimuli during the L1 larval stage, suggesting a critical period is necessary for imprinting. Thus, this early experience confers a life-long advantage for worms to steer away more effectively from spots associated with infection and overcrowding.

Perhaps the most surprising observations of memory are those inherited from previous generations. Transgenerational memory may be adaptive as it allows critical information to be passed on to progeny. Moore et al. (2019) found that the offspring of adult worms exposed to PA14 that learned to avoid the bacterial odors also observed avoidance to PA14 in the offspring of these worms through four generations, even though the offspring themselves were never exposed to the pathogen. Levels of DAF-7, a TGF-β ligand, in the ASI sensory neurons were correlated with the transgenerational memory, and expression of *daf-7* in ASI was regulated by a PIWI Argonaute homolog, PRG-1. PIWI is a family of RNA-binding proteins, and PIWI-interacting RNAs (piRNAs) have previously been shown to regulate transgenerational epigenetics in *C. elegans* and *Drosophila*, and at least one piRNA is involved in LTM in *Aplysia* (reviewed in Landry et al., 2013). This transgenerational learning suggests that some experiences may alter the behavior not only of the animal that experiences the stimulation, but also the offspring of that individual for several generations. Surely this would give the conditioned offspring an advantage over worms lacking this conditioning.

1.4 CONCLUDING REMARKS

C. elegans shows many forms of learning and memory that enable complex behavioral modifications in a simple worm to promote fitness. The *C. elegans* nervous system only has 302 neurons, and understandably was originally thought to rely on innate behaviors; however, research over the past 30 years has shown a remarkable catalogue of types of learning and memory. Memory allows *C. elegans* to adjust its behavior to navigate favorable and unfavorable environments, and even prepare offspring for environmental challenges. The genetic and molecular mechanisms of learning discovered in *C. elegans* show similarities with those in other species, suggesting that the building blocks of learning and memory play a significant role in the success of an animal's abilities to adapt to changing environments. With its compact nervous system, *C. elegans* offers the research opportunity to bring us closer to a better understanding of the fundamental cellular and molecular processes underlying learning and memory.

ACKNOWLEDGMENTS

This work is supported by an NSERC PGS-D scholarship to AJY and an NSERC project grant NSERC RGPIN-2019-05558 and a CIHR project grant CIHR PJT 165947 to CHR.

REFERENCES

Amano, H., & Maruyama, I. N. (2011). Aversive olfactory learning and associative long-term memory in *Caenorhabditis elegans*. *Learning & Memory*, *18*, 654–665. https://doi.org/10.1101/lm.2224411

Ardiel, E. L., Giles, A. C., Yu, A. J., Lindsay, T. H., Lockery, S. R., & Rankin, C. H. (2016). Dopamine receptor DOP-4 modulates habituation to repetitive photoactivation of a *C. elegans* polymodal nociceptor. *Learning & Memory*, *23*, 495–503. https://doi.org/10.1101/lm.041830.116

Ardiel, E. L., McDiarmid, T. A., Timbers, T. A., Lee, K. C. Y., Safaei, J., Pelech, S. L., & Rankin, C. H. (2018). Insights into the roles of CMK-1 and OGT-1 in interstimulus interval-dependent habituation in *Caenorhabditis elegans*. *Proceedings of the Royal Society B: Biological Sciences*, *285*, 20182084. https://doi.org/10.1098/rspb.2018.2084

Ardiel, E. L., Yu, A. J., Giles, A. C., & Rankin, C. H. (2017). Habituation as an adaptive shift in response strategy mediated by neuropeptides. *npj Science of Learning*, *2*, 9. https://doi.org/10.1038/s41539-017-0011-8

Bargmann, C. I. (2006). Chemosensation in *C. elegans. WormBook*, ed. The *C. elegans* research community. https://doi.org/10.1895/wormbook.1.123.1, www.wormbook.org.

Beck, C. D., & Rankin, C. H. (1995). Heat shock disrupts long-term memory consolidation in *Caenorhabditis elegans. Learning & Memory*, 2(3–4), 161–177. https://doi.org/10.1101/lm.2.3-4.161

Beets, I., Janssen, T., Meelkop, E., Temmerman, L., Suetens, N., Rademakers, S., . . . Schoofs, L. (2012). Vasopressin/oxytocin-related signaling regulates gustatory associative learning *in C. elegans. Science, 338*, 543–545. https://doi.org/10.1126/science.1226860

Bernhard, N., & van der Kooy, D. (2000). A behavioral and genetic dissection of two forms of olfactory plasticity in *Caenorhabditis elegans*: Adaptation and habituation. *Learning and Memory, 7*, 199–212. https://doi.org/10.1101/lm.7.4.199

Biron, D., Wasserman, S., Thomas, J. H., Samuel, A. D. T., & Sengupta, P. (2008). An olfactory neuron responds stochastically to temperature and modulates *Caenorhabditis elegans* thermotactic behavior. *Proceedings of the National Academy of Sciences, 105*, 11002–11007. https://doi.org/10.1073/pnas.0805004105

Brenner, S. (1974). The genetics of Caenorhabditis elegans. *Genetics, 77*(1), 71–94. www.ncbi.nlm.nih.gov/pubmed/4366476

Byrne, J. H., & Hawkins, R. D. (2015). Nonassociative learning in invertebrates. *Cold Spring Harbor Perspectives in Biology, 7*, a021675. https://doi.org/10.1101/cshperspect.a021675

The *C. elegans* Sequencing Consortium. (1998). Genome sequence of the nematode *C. elegans*: A platform for investigating biology. *Science, 282*, 2012–2018. https://doi.org/10.1126/science.282.5396.2012

Chen, Z., Hendricks, M., Cornils, A., Maier, W., Alcedo, J., & Zhang, Y. (2013). Two insulin-like peptides antagonistically regulate aversive olfactory learning in *C. elegans. Neuron, 77*, 572–585. https://doi.org/10.1016/j.neuron.2012.11.025

Cheung, B. H. H., Cohen, M., Rogers, C., Albayram, O., & De Bono, M. (2005). Experience-dependent modulation of *C. elegans* behavior by ambient oxygen. *Current Biology, 15*, 905–917. https://doi.org/10.1016/j.cub.2005.04.017

Chew, Y. L., Tanizawa, Y., Cho, Y., Zhao, B., Yu, A. J., Ardiel, E. L., . . . Schafer, W. R. (2018). An afferent neuropeptide system transmits mechanosensory signals triggering sensitization and arousal in *C. elegans. Neuron, 99*, 1233–1246.e6. https://doi.org/10.1016/j.neuron.2018.08.003

Clark, D. A., Biron, D., Sengupta, P., & Samuel, A. D. T. (2006). The AFD sensory neurons encode multiple functions underlying thermotactic behavior in *Caenorhabditis elegans. Journal of Neuroscience, 26*, 7444–7451. https://doi.org/10.1523/JNEUROSCI.1137-06.2006

Das, S., Sadanandappa, M. K., Dervan, A., Larkin, A., Lee, J. A., Sudhakaran, I. P., . . . Ramaswamia, M. (2011). Plasticity of local GABAergic interneurons drives olfactory habituation. *Proceedings of the National Academy of Sciences, 108*(36): E646–E654. https://doi.org/10.1073/pnas.1106411108

Fenk, L. A., & de Bono, M. (2017). Memory of recent oxygen experience switches pheromone valence in *Caenorhabditis elegans. Proceedings of the National Academy of Sciences, 114*, 4195–4200. https://doi.org/10.1073/pnas.1618934114

Gray, J. M., Hill, J. J., & Bargmann, C. I. (2005). A circuit for navigation in *Caenorhabditis elegans. Proceedings of the National Academy of Sciences, 102*, 3184–3191. https://doi.org/10.1073/pnas.0409009101

Groves, P. M., & Thompson, R. F. (1970). Habituation: A dual-process theory. *Psychological Review, 77*(5), 419–450. www.ncbi.nlm.nih.gov/pubmed/4319167

Hart, A. C., Kass, J., Shapiro, J. E., & Kaplan, J. M. (1999). Distinct signaling pathways mediate touch and osmosensory responses in a polymodal sensory neuron. *Journal of Neuroscience, 19*, 1952–1958. https://doi.org/10.1523/jneurosci.19-06-01952.1999

Hedgecock, E. M., & Russell, R. L. (1975). Normal and mutant thermotaxis in the nematode *Caenorhabditis elegans. Proceedings of the National Academy of Sciences, 72*, 4061–4065. https://doi.org/10.1073/pnas.72.10.4061

Hong, M., Ryu, L., Ow, M. C., Kim, J., Je, A. R., Chinta, S., ... Kim, K. (2017). Early pheromone experience modifies a synaptic activity to influence adult pheromone responses of *C. elegans. Current Biology, 27*, 3168–3177.e3. https://doi.org/10.1016/j.cub.2017.08.068

Hukema, R. K., Rademakers, S., & Jansen, G. (2008). Gustatory plasticity in *C. elegans* involves integration of negative cues and NaCl taste mediated by serotonin, dopamine, and glutamate. *Learning and Memory, 15*, 829–836. https://doi.org/10.1101/lm.994408

Jin, X., Pokala, N., & Bargmann, C. I. (2016). Distinct circuits for the formation and retrieval of an imprinted olfactory memory. *Cell, 164*, 632–643. https://doi.org/10.1016/j.cell.2016.01.007

Kano, T., Brockie, P. J., Sassa, T., Fujimoto, H., Kawahara, Y., Iino, Y., ... Maricq, A. V. (2008). Memory in *Caenorhabditis elegans* is mediated by NMDA-type ionotropic glutamate receptors. *Current Biology, 18*, 1010–1015. https://doi.org/10.1016/j.cub.2008.05.051

Kauffman, A. L., Ashraf, J. M., Corces-Zimmerman, M. R., Landis, J. N., & Murphy, C. T. (2010). Insulin signaling and dietary restriction differentially influence the decline of learning and memory with age. *PLoS Biology, 8*, e1000372. https://doi.org/10.1371/journal.pbio.1000372

Kindt, K. S., Quast, K. B., Giles, A. C., De, S., Hendrey, D., Nicastro, I., ... Schafer, W. R. (2007). Dopamine mediates context-dependent modulation of sensory plasticity in *C. elegans. Neuron, 55*, 662–676. https://doi.org/10.1016/j.neuron.2007.07.023

Kodama, E., Kuhara, A., Mohri-Shiomi, A., Kimura, K. D., Okumura, M., Tomioka, M., ... Mori, I. (2006). Insulin-like signaling and the neural circuit for integrative behavior in *C. elegans. Genes and Development, 20*, 2955–2960. https://doi.org/10.1101/gad.1479906

Kuhara, A., & Mori, I. (2006). Molecular physiology of the neural circuit for calcineurin-dependent associative learning in *Caenorhabditis elegans. Journal of Neuroscience, 26*, 9355–9364. https://doi.org/10.1523/JNEUROSCI.0517-06.2006

Kuhara, A., Okumura, M., Kimata, T., Tanizawa, Y., Takano, R., Kimura, K. D., ... Mori, I. (2008). Temperature sensing by an olfactory neuron in a circuit controlling behavior of *C. elegans. Science, 320*, 803–807. https://doi.org/10.1126/science.1148922

Landry, C. D., Kandel, E. R., & Rajasethupathy, P. (2013). New mechanisms in memory storage: PiRNAs and epigenetics. *Trends in Neurosciences, 36*, 534–542. https://doi.org/10.1016/j.tins.2013.05.004

Lau, H. L., Timbers, T. A, Mahmoud, R., & Rankin, C. H. (2013). Genetic dissection of memory for associative and non-associative learning in *Caenorhabditis elegans. Genes, Brain and Behavior, 12*, 210–223. https://doi.org/10.1111/j.1601-183X.2012.00863.x

Lee, K., & Mylonakis, E. (2017). An intestine-derived neuropeptide controls avoidance behavior *in Caenorhabditis elegans. Cell Reports, 20*, 2501–2512. https://doi.org/10.1016/j.celrep.2017.08.053

Li, C., Timbers, T. A., Rose, J. K., Bozorgmehr, T., McEwan, A., & Rankin, C. H. (2013). The FMRFamide-related neuropeptide FLP-20 is required in the mechanosensory neurons during memory for massed training in *C. elegans. Learning & Memory, 20*, 103–108. https://doi.org/10.1101/lm.028993.112

Lim, J. P., Fehlauer, H., Das, A., Saro, G., Glauser, D. A., Brunet, A., & Goodman, M. B. (2018). Loss of CaMKI function disrupts salt aversive learning in *C. elegans. Journal of Neuroscience, 38*, 6114–6129. https://doi.org/10.1523/JNEUROSCI.1611-17.2018

Lorenz, K. Z. (1981). *The foundations of ethology*. Springer Vienna. https://doi.org/10.1007/978-3-7091-3671-3

Mita, K., Yamagishi, M., Fujito, Y., Lukowiak, K., & Ito, E. (2014). An increase in insulin is important for the acquisition conditioned taste aversion in *Lymnaea. Neurobiology of Learning and Memory, 116*, 132–138. https://doi.org/10.1016/j.nlm.2014.10.006

Mohri, A., Kodama, E., Kimura, K. D., Koike, M., Mizuno, T., & Mori, I. (2005). Genetic control of temperature preference in the nematode *Caenorhabditis elegans. Genetics, 169*, 1437–1450. https://doi.org/10.1534/genetics.104.036111

Moore, R. S., Kaletsky, R., & Murphy, C. T. (2019). Piwi/PRG-1 Argonaute and TGF-β mediate transgenerational learned pathogenic avoidance. *Cell, 177*, 1827–1841.e12. https://doi.org/10.1016/j.cell.2019.05.024

Mori, I., & Ohshima, Y. (1995). Neural regulation of thermotaxis in *Caenorhabditis elegans*. *Nature, 376*(6538), 344–348. https://doi.org/10.1038/376344a0

Morrison, G. E., & van der Kooy, D. (2001). A mutation in the AMPA-type glutamate receptor, glr-1, blocks olfactory associative and nonassociative learning in *Caenorhabditis elegans*. *Behavioral Neuroscience, 115*, 640–649. https://doi.org/10.1037/0735-7044.115.3.640

Morrison, G. E., Wen, J. Y. M., Runciman, S., & van der Kooy, D. (1999). Olfactory associative learning in *Caenorhabditis elegans* is impaired in *lrn-1* and *lrn-2* mutants. *Behavioral Neuroscience, 113*, 358–367. https://doi.org/10.1037//0735-7044.113.2.358

Nishijima, S., & Maruyama, I. N. (2017). Appetitive olfactory learning and long-term associative memory in *Caenorhabditis elegans*. *Frontiers in Behavioral Neuroscience, 11*, 80. https://doi.org/10.3389/fnbeh.2017.00080

Nuttley, W. M., Atkinson-Leadbeater, K. P., & van der Kooy, D. (2002). Serotonin mediates food-odor associative learning in the nematode *Caenorhabditis elegans*. *Proceedings of the National Academy of Sciences, 99*, 12449–12454. https://doi.org/10.1073/pnas.192101699

Nuttley, W. M., Harbinder, S., & van der Kooy, D. (2001). Regulation of distinct attractive and aversive mechanisms mediating benzaldehyde chemotaxis in *Caenorhabditis elegans*. *Learning and Memory, 8*, 170–181. https://doi.org/10.1101/lm.36501

Ohnishi, N., Kuhara, A., Nakamura, F., Okochi, Y., & Mori, I. (2011). Bidirectional regulation of thermotaxis by glutamate transmissions in *Caenorhabditis elegans*. *EMBO Journal, 30*, 1376–1388. https://doi.org/10.1038/emboj.2011.13

Peymen, K., Watteyne, J., Borghgraef, C., Van Sinay, E., Beets, I., & Schoofs, L. (2019). Myoinhibitory peptide signaling modulates aversive gustatory learning in *Caenorhabditis elegans*. *PLOS Genetics, 15*, e1007945. https://doi.org/10.1371/journal.pgen.1007945

Pierce-Shimomura, J. T., Faumont, S., Gaston, M. R., Pearson, B. J., & Lockery, S. R. (2001). The homeobox gene lim-6 is required for distinct chemosensory representations in *C. elegans*. *Nature, 410*, 694–698. https://doi.org/10.1038/35070575

Pinsker, H., Kupfermann, I., Castellucci, V., & Kandel, E. (1970). Habituation and dishabituation of the gill-withdrawal reflex in *Aplysia*. *Science, 167*, 1740–1742. https://doi.org/10.1126/science.167.3926.1740

Ramaswami, M. (2014). Network plasticity in adaptive filtering and behavioral habituation. *Neuron, 82*, 1216–1229. https://doi.org/10.1016/j.neuron.2014.04.035

Rankin, C. H., Abrams, T., Barry, R. J., Bhatnagar, S., Clayton, D. F., Colombo, J., … Thompson, R. F. (2009). Habituation revisited: An updated and revised description of the behavioral characteristics of habituation. *Neurobiology of Learning and Memory, 92*, 135–138. https://doi.org/10.1016/j.nlm.2008.09.012

Rankin, C. H., Beck, C. D., & Chiba, C. M. (1990). *Caenorhabditis elegans*: A new model system for the study of learning and memory. *Behavioural Brain Research, 37*, 89–92. https://doi.org/10.1016/0166-4328(90)90074-O

Rankin, C. H., & Broster, B. S. (1992). Factors affecting habituation and recovery from habituation in the nematode *Caenorhabditis elegans*. *Behavioral Neuroscience, 106*, 239–249. https://doi.org/10.1037/0735-7044.106.2.239

Rankin, C. H., & Wicks, S. R. (2000). Mutations of the *Caenorhabditis elegans* brain-specific inorganic phosphate transporter *eat-4* affect habituation of the tap-withdrawal response without affecting the response itself. *Journal of Neuroscience, 20*, 4337–4344.

Remy, J. J., & Hobert, O. (2005). Neuroscience: An interneuronal chemoreceptor required for olfactory imprinting in *C. elegans*. *Science, 309*, 787–790. https://doi.org/10.1126/science.1114209

Rose, J. K., Kaun, K. R., Chen, S. H., & Rankin, C. H. (2003). GLR-1, a non-NMDA glutamate receptor homolog, is critical for long-term memory in *Caenorhabditis elegans*. *Journal of neuroscience, 23*, 9595–9599. https://doi.org/10.1523/JNEUROSCI.23-29-09595.2003

Rose, J. K., Kaun, K. R., & Rankin, C. H. (2002). A new group-training procedure for habituation demonstrates that presynaptic glutamate release contributes to long-term memory in *Caenorhabditis elegans*. *Learning and Memory, 9*, 130–137. https://doi.org/10.1101/lm.46802

Rose, J. K., & Rankin, C. H. (2006). Blocking memory reconsolidation reverses memory-associated changes in glutamate receptor expression. *Journal of Neuroscience, 26*, 11582–11587. https://doi.org/10.1523/JNEUROSCI.2049-06.2006

Saeki, S., Yamamoto, M., & Iino, Y. (2001). Plasticity of chemotaxis revealed by paired presentation of a chemoattractant and starvation in the nematode Caenorhabditis elegans. *Journal of Experimental Biology, 204*(10), 1757–1764. https://doi.org/10.1242/jeb.204.10.1757

Sakai, N., Iwata, R., Yokoi, S., Butcher, R. A., Clardy, J., Tomioka, M., & Iino, Y. (2013). A sexually conditioned switch of chemosensory behavior in *C. elegans*. *PLoS ONE, 8*(7): e68676. https://doi.org/10.1371/journal.pone.0068676

Sammut, M., Cook, S. J., Nguyen, K. C. Q., Felton, T., Hall, D. H., Emmons, S. W., . . . Barrios, A. (2015). Glia-derived neurons are required for sex-specific learning in *C. elegans*. *Nature, 526*(7573), 385–390. https://doi.org/10.1038/nature15700

Schulenburg, H., & Félix, M. A. (2017). The natural biotic environment of *Caenorhabditis elegans*. *Genetics, 206*, 55–86. https://doi.org/10.1534/genetics.116.195511

Sulston, J. E., Schierenberg, E., White, J. G., & Thomson, J. N. (1983). The embryonic cell lineage of the nematode *Caenorhabditis elegans*. *Developmental Biology, 100*, 64–119. https://doi.org/10.1016/0012-1606(83)90201-4

Timbers, T. A., Giles, A. C., Ardiel, E. L., Kerr, R. A., & Rankin, C. H. (2013). Intensity discrimination deficits cause habituation changes in middle-aged *Caenorhabditis elegans*. *Neurobiology of Aging, 34*, 621–631. https://doi.org/10.1016/j.neurobiolaging.2012.03.016

Timbers, T. A., & Rankin, C. H. (2011). Tap withdrawal circuit interneurons require CREB for long-term habituation in *Caenorhabditis elegans*. *Behavioral Neuroscience, 125*, 560–566. https://doi.org/10.1037/a0024370

Tomioka, M., Adachi, T., Suzuki, H., Kunitomo, H., Schafer, W. R., & Iino, Y. (2006). The Insulin/PI 3-Kinase pathway regulates salt chemotaxis learning in *Caenorhabditis elegans*. *Neuron, 51*, 613–625. https://doi.org/10.1016/j.neuron.2006.07.024

Torayama, I., Ishihara, T., & Katsura, I. (2007). *Caenorhabditis elegans* integrates the signals of butanone and food to enhance chemotaxis to butanone. *Journal of Neuroscience, 27*, 741–750. https://doi.org/10.1523/JNEUROSCI.4312-06.2007

Wen, J. Y. M., Kumar, N., Morrison, G., Rambaldini, G., Runciman, S., Rousseau, J., & Van Der Kooy, D. (1997). Mutations that prevent associative learning in *C. elegans*. *Behavioral Neuroscience, 111*, 354–368. https://doi.org/10.1037/0735-7044.111.2.354

White, J. G., Southgate, E., Thomson, J. N., & Brenner, S. (1986). The structure of the nervous system of the nematode *Caenorhabditis elegans*. *Philosophical Transactions of the Royal Society of London. Series B, Biological Sciences, 314*, 1–340.

Wicks, S. R., & Rankin, C. H. (1995). Integration of mechanosensory stimuli in *Caenorhabditis elegans*. *Journal of Neuroscience, 15*, 2434–2444.

Wu, T., Duan, F., Yang, W., Liu, H., Caballero, A., Fernandes de Abreu, D. A., . . . Zhang, Y. (2019). Pheromones modulate learning by regulating the balanced signals of two insulin-like peptides. *Neuron, 104*, 1095–1109.e5. https://doi.org/10.1016/j.neuron.2019.09.006

Yamazoe-Umemoto, A., Fujita, K., Iino, Y., Iwasaki, Y., & Kimura, K. D. (2015). Modulation of different behavioral components by neuropeptide and dopamine signalings in non-associative odor learning of *Caenorhabditis elegans*. *Neuroscience Research*, *99*, 22–33. https://doi.org/10.1016/j.neures.2015.05.009

Zhang, X., & Zhang, Y. (2012). DBL-1, a TGF-β, is essential for *Caenorhabditis elegans* aversive olfactory learning. *Proceedings of the National Academy of Sciences USA*, *109*, 17081–17086. https://doi.org/10.1073/pnas.1205982109

Zhang, Y., Lu, H., & Bargmann, C. I. (2005). Pathogenic bacteria induce aversive olfactory learning in *Caenorhabditis elegans*. *Nature*, *438*, 179–184. https://doi.org/10.1038/nature04216

2

ADAPTIVE EVOLUTION OF LEARNING AND MEMORY IN A MODEL LINEAGE

William G. Wright

The ethological traditions of Konrad Lorenz, Nikolaas Tinbergen, and others seek to understand natural behavior at the developmental, mechanistic, ecological, and evolutionary levels (Carew, 2000). Here, I describe how examining new research questions across multiple levels has helped us develop a more informed understanding of the evolution of learning and memory in a model lineage.

2.1 MECHANISMS OF SENSITIZATION IN IDENTIFIED NEURONS IN *APLYSIA*

The stage for this multilevel analysis was set by the long and remarkably rich effort to understand mechanisms of learning and memory in the gastropod sea hare, *Aplysia californica* (Kandel, 1976, 2012; Owen & Brenner, 2012; Walters, 1994). Much of this research has focused on *sensitization* (Marcus et al., 1988), considered a key component of the study of learning and memory (Kandel, 2012) as well as pain (Walters, 1994, 2018). Sensitization is a behavioral phenotype; it refers to an increase in amplitude (e.g., duration) of a withdrawal response to a mild tactile stimulus after delivery of an intervening strong noxious stimulus.

The great advantage of *Aplysia* as a model species is its relatively large size and reduced number of neurons (Kandel, 2012). This advantage allows *Aplysia* researchers to use intracellular recordings to investigate the neural underpinnings of sensitization: How are neurons that underlie behavioral reflex withdrawals in *Aplysia* changed (modulated) by a noxious experience that increases reflex response (sensitization)? Here, I focus on two key neuromodulatory changes observed in the identified mechanosensory neurons (SNs) that initiate withdrawal reflexes (Byrne & Kandel, 1996).

Spike broadening (SB) is a prolongation of each individual action potential (Figure 2.1a) in a SN. This prolongation in turn extends the influx of calcium caused by each action potential, thereby increasing transmitter release from

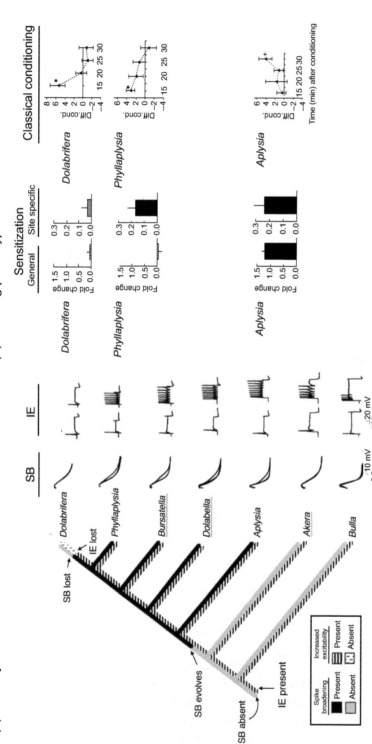

FIGURE 2.1. Evolution of neuromodulatory traits is correlated with behavioral (learning) phenotypes. (a) Sensory-neuron modulation. Cladogram of genera in the order Aplysiida (plus outgroup genus *Bulla*). Shown by the pattern of the evolutionary branches is the most parsimonious evolution of spike broadening (SB) (gray line: absent; black line: present) and increased excitability (light-striped line: absent; dark-striped line: present). Column SB: Spikes before and after 5-HT are superimposed. SB, when present (e.g., *Phyllaplysia*), is seen as a narrower spike before and a broader spike after 10^{-5} M 5-HT, and increased excitability (IE); when present, second panel (all but *Dolabrifera*) shows multiple spikes. (b) Sensitization: Vertical axis shows the "fold change" from pre-shock reflex duration. General sensitization: Left bar for each genus. Site-specific sensitization: right bar for each genus. Differential classical conditioning: Difference in withdrawal duration(s) between the tactile stimulus site that is paired with noxious stimuli during training, versus the stimulus site unpaired with noxious stimuli (positive difference indicates conditioning).
(a) Adapted from Wright et al. (1996), Erixon et al. (1999), and Wright (2000); (b) adapted from Wright (1998), Erixon et al. (1999), Marinesco et al. (2003), and Hoover et al. (2006).

SNs onto interneurons and motor neurons of the withdrawal reflex, thus leading to the stronger postsynaptic response that contributes to a sensitized reflex.

Increased excitability (IE) is an increase (following an electric shock) in the number of action potentials elicited by a given tactile stimulus (Figure 2.1a), resulting in more transmitter release from SNs, again enhancing (sensitizing) reflex withdrawal.

To measure SB, one first establishes an intracellular recording in a SN, and then injects a short (ca. 1 ms) pulse of depolarizing current to elicit an action potential and thereby establish the baseline spike duration. Following a noxious stimulus, one elicits a second spike and measures its increased duration (SB). To measure IE with the same intracellular electrode, one adjusts the current amplitude of a longer (500 ms) depolarizing pulse to produce a single action potential; IE is measured as the increase in the number of action potentials to the same depolarizing pulse after the noxious stimulus.

Instead of a noxious stimulus, one can directly apply serotonin (5-hydroxytryptamine, or 5-HT), a monoamine transmitter released throughout the central nervous system by noxious stimuli (Marinesco & Carew, 2002) that is likely an important component of sensitization (Glanzman et al., 1989). The application of 5-HT in lieu of an electric shock causes robust SB and IE in *Aplysia* (Figure 2.1a, third genus from bottom; Wright et al., 1996). The hallmark of experiments on 5-HT-elicited SB and IE is that they are easy to perform and very reliable.

2.2 EVOLUTION OF THE NEURAL MECHANISMS OF SENSITIZATION

Evolutionary analysis of SB and IE in the gastropod order Aplysiida (all genera in Figure 2.1 except *Bulla*) brings two distinctive advantages, in addition to those mentioned earlier for *Aplysia*. First, SNs, especially those that innervate the tail, are uniquely identifiable across the entire cladogram by their characteristic anatomical location and size (Erixon et al., 1999; Marinesco et al., 2003; Wright et al., 1996). Second, there is a well-resolved phylogeny for the sea hare clade (Aplysiida; Bouchet et al., 2017), which allows for deduction of the evolutionary pathway from a trait's distribution across the species of that phylogeny.

Wright et al. (1996) demonstrated marked variation in SB and IE across the phylogeny in Figure 2.1, thus allowing the following most parsimonious evolutionary deductions for both processes (Figure 2.1a): SB was likely absent in the ancestral Aplysiida (as deduced by its absence in *Bulla* and *Akera*, Figure 2.1a), and first evolved in the ancestor of the rest of the sea hares. Much later, it was lost after the split with *Phyllaplysia* in the lineage leading to *Dolabrifera* (Figure 2.1a). IE was likely present in all the earliest Aplysiida, but was also lost in the lineage leading to *Dolabrifera* after its split from *Phyllaplysia* (Papini, 2002; Wright, 2000; Wright et al., 1996; see Blaisdell and Seitz, Chapter 26).

Perhaps the most significant discovery of this evolutionary analysis was the complete loss of *both* neuromodulatory traits in the lineage leading to *Dolabrifera* (top of Figure 2.1a). Much of the subsequent neurophysiological, behavioral, ecological, and evolutionary analyses focused on this "phylogenetic lesion" (Himstead & Wright, 2018; Hoover et al., 2006; Marinesco et al., 2003; Takagi et al., 2010; Wright, 1998, 2000; Wright et al., 1996).

2.3 REDUCTIONISTIC QUESTIONS

Where has the intracellular signal leading to SB and IE in *Aplysia* been blocked in *Dolabrifera*? The most likely locus to investigate is the well-studied intracellular pathway in sensory neurons that leads in multiple steps from the noxious stimulus to SB and IE (Kandel, 2012). In *Aplysia*, noxious stimuli cause the release of 5-HT from interneurons. 5-HT binds to receptors on sensory neurons, activating a G_s-protein in the SN membrane, thereby stimulating adenylyl cyclase, which increases the level of cyclic adenosine monophosphate (cAMP) in SNs. Increased cAMP activates an A-kinase that closes (or slows the opening of) potassium channels throughout the SN, thereby broadening action potentials and increasing excitability (Byrne & Kandel, 1996; Kandel & Schwartz, 1982; Owen & Brenner, 2012). Thus, activation of this pathway by 5-HT ensures that subsequent tactile stimuli elicit larger reflex withdrawal.

There are myriad approaches (e.g., biophysical, pharmacological, molecular) to a reductionistic research pathway to identify the *specific* intracellular change that eliminates SB and IE in *Dolabrifera*. As interesting and important as this reductionistic program is, circumstances have allowed only a single experiment: Bath application of membrane-permeable cAMP caused IE in the same *Dolabrifera* SNs that are unresponsive to 5-HT (Wright, 2000). This result suggests a disabled component of the cAMP cascade upstream from cAMP (i.e., adenyl cyclase, G proteins, and/or 5-HT receptors). Clearly, the scientific journey to pinpoint the cellular locus/loci of the phylogenetic lesion has yet to be completed.

2.4 WHOLISTIC QUESTIONS: BEHAVIOR, ECOLOGY, AND EVOLUTION

In addition to reductionistic questions, the loss of SB and IE in *Dolabrifera* invites us to investigate more wholistic, integrative questions.

BOTTOM-UP APPROACH

First, I will discuss the wholistic questions that flow from the bottom up. Each of these questions asks in different ways, "What are the consequences of the loss of SB and IE for the biology of *Dolabrifera*?"

TESTING PREDICTIONS FROM NEURAL HYPOTHESES At the behavioral level, 5-HT-elicited SB and IE in *Aplysia* have been shown to contribute to several forms of learning (Byrne & Kandel, 1996; Kandel et al., 1987; Owen & Brenner, 2012). Thus, we expect that their loss in *Dolabrifera* should impact those learning phenotypes and testing these predictions should shed light on the utility of the neural hypotheses. Most directly, evolutionary loss of SB and IE predicts a sharp decrease in all forms of sensitization in *Dolabrifera*. Behavioral experiments using the same protocols that reliably produce short- and long-term sensitization in *Aplysia* (Figure 2.1b, bottom) failed to produce either short-term sensitization (Figure 2.1b, top; Wright, 1998) or long-term sensitization (reflex increase that lasts more than 24 hours; Wright, 1998). Dishabituation (enhancement of a reflex that has been habituated prior to the noxious stimulus) was also missing (Wright, 1998). Finally, site-specific sensitization – sensitization of a withdrawal reflex to a particular location on the body (e.g., tail) after a noxious stimulus near that site (Walters, 1987) – was missing as well (Figure 2.1b; Marinesco et al., 2003). The complete absence of sensitization in *Dolabrifera* supports the critical role of 5-HT-induced SB and IE in behavioral sensitization, and sheds rare light on how evolution of a learning phenotype may be supported by changes to its underlying mechanisms.

Interestingly, serotonergic fibers similar to those in *Aplysia* are clearly present in the same (homologous) ganglia of *Dolabrifera* (Marinesco et al., 2003; Wright et al., 1995). Furthermore, chronoamperometric electrode recordings in these ganglia in *Dolabrifera* showed that 5-HT is released in response to noxious stimuli, much as it is in *Aplysia* (Marinesco et al., 2003). This evolutionary conservation of 5-HT release suggests that modulation of other behaviors by 5-HT (e.g., locomotion; Mackey & Carew, 1983; Stopfer & Carew, 1988) may still be part of *Dolabrifera*'s response to noxious stimuli.

What is the phylogenetic lesion's effect on *associative* learning in *Dolabrifera*? In classical conditioning (a form of associative learning), the subject learns that an innocuous tactile stimulus to one anatomical location (e.g., one side of the tail) will be followed by a noxious stimulus, such as a strong electric shock, applied elsewhere. Once trained, the subject demonstrates associative learning by responding more strongly to the particular tactile stimulus that was temporally paired with shock during training, relative to a different tactile stimulus (applied to a different anatomical location, e.g., opposite side of the tail) that was not paired with the shock (Carew et al., 1983; Jami et al., 2007). Learning that a *specific* stimulus is dangerous is categorically different from general sensitization (a nonassociative form of learning), in which the subject learns that the world has become a nonspecifically dangerous place, and thus amplifies defensive responses to *many different* sensory stimuli.

Given the phylogenetic lesion of SB and IE, how do we expect associative learning in *Dolabrifera* to be altered? Interestingly, models of classical conditioning in *Aplysia* (Bailey et al., 2000), birds (Ding & Perkel, 2004), and mammals (Almaguer-Melian et al., 2005; LeDoux, 2000) agree that the *persistence* of associative memory that is formed between two different paired stimuli is very sensitive to neuromodulatory activity during that formation. For example, memories formed when the brain is flooded with epinephrine last far longer than those formed in the absence of epinephrine (Almaguer-Melian et al., 2005). At the physiological level, a barrage of action potentials in presynaptic neurons enhances their postsynaptic connections. This form of plasticity, known as long-term potentiation (LTP), is widely considered to be the neural basis for the formation of associative memory (Glanzman, 2010; Lynch, 2004; Martin et al., 2000). Interestingly, the duration of LTP is greatly lengthened when the barrage of action potentials is administered simultaneously with release of a neuromodulatory transmitter such as epinephrine (Harley, 2007), dopamine (Schultz, 1998), or, in *Aplysia*, 5-HT (Bailey et al., 2000; Eliot et al., 1994).

Consideration of this memory-prolonging role of neuromodulatory transmitters predicts that the loss of the SN response to the neuromodulatory transmitter 5-HT may not eliminate classical conditioning in *Dolabrifera*, but instead shorten its memory. In support of this prediction, Hoover et al. (2006) found significant classical conditioning in *Dolabrifera*, but the memory was much briefer (Hoover et al., 2006; Figure 2.1b, top panel, Classical Conditioning) than that of *Aplysia* (Figure 2.1b, bottom right panel; Carew et al., 1983; Jami et al., 2007).

TESTING PREDICTIONS FROM ECOLOGICAL HYPOTHESES At the ecological level, if we assume that sensitization is adaptive (a reasonable assumption), then the evolutionary loss of sensitization in *Dolabrifera* should correlate with changes in its ecology. The question of how individuals of *Dolabrifera* compensate for their lack of sensitization is difficult to answer, inasmuch as we know almost nothing about the adaptive advantage of sensitization in the sea hares that do express it. We barely even know which natural stimuli in a sea hare's world can *cause* sensitization!

Perhaps the closest natural stimulus to the painful electrical shock used to train *Aplysia* in the lab is the painful attack of a predator (Walters, 1991).

Aplysia has a fierce and ubiquitous predator in the California spiny lobster, *Panulirus interruptus*. Watkins et al. (2010) sought to test the hypothesis that lobster attack causes sensitization in *Aplysia*. Unfortunately, although lobsters readily attack and eat thawed squid or shrimp in captivity, they do not attack *Aplysia* unless deprived of food for two to four weeks. This is almost certainly due to *Aplysia*'s arsenal of chemical defenses, including those passively incorporated into their body wall, as well as the ink and opaline actively released upon attack (Bornancin et al., 2017; Derby, 2007; Derby & Aggio, 2011; Pennings et al., 1999). Thus, the Watkins team deprived lobsters of food, and then measured the effects of lobster attack on reflex withdrawal in *Aplysia*. They found that a single lobster attack sensitized sea hares in the same way an electric shock does (Watkins et al., 2010; see also *Nature Research Highlights*, 2010). Furthermore, multiple lobster attacks, like multiple electric shocks, caused long-term sensitization lasting more than 24 hours (Mason et al., 2014; Figure 2.2a and b). Finally, SNs of long-term sensitized sea hares had significantly lower thresholds for evoked action potentials (Figure 2.2b; Mason et al., 2014). These findings by Watkins et al. (2010) and Mason et al. (2014) parallel those when *Aplysia* is sensitized by an electric shock (reviewed in Walters, 1991), and are the first to document a *natural* noxious stimulus that causes equivalent neural and behavioral changes produced by an electric shock in *Aplysia*.

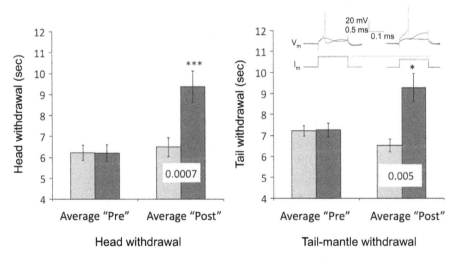

FIGURE 2.2. Long-term sensitization (lasting more than 24 hours) and neural correlates after four lobster attacks. (Left) Head withdrawal and (right) tail withdrawal in response to tactile stimuli were significantly enhanced in sea hares that experienced lobster attacks (dark bars: post), relative to their own pre-attack reflexes (average "pre"; asterisks indicate probability for paired *t*-test, ***p < 0.005; *p < 0.05; *N* = 14 each for shocked and unshocked), and relative to the reflexes of control sea hares that experienced no attacks (light bars: average "post"; *p*-values of two-sample *t*-tests span bars). In addition, inset shows (representative example experiment) that SNs of long-term sensitized sea hares required less current (inset: square pulses in bottom right panel) to initiate a spike (top right traces), relative to SNs from unattacked control animals (control superimposed traces on left).

Where in nature might we find this "natural stimulus" (i.e., food-deprived lobsters that attack *Aplysia*)? Berriman et al. (2015) showed that foraging lobsters in most coastal waters will not attack proffered *Aplysia*, most likely because they are deterred by *Aplysia*'s ample chemical defenses (Bornancin et al., 2017; Derby, 2007; Derby & Aggio, 2011; Pennings et al., 1999). However, Berriman et al. (2015) found a strikingly different response in lobsters tested in "no-take reserves" where lobster fishing has been barred for 20–30 years. In such reserves, lobsters attain much greater size and abundance (Berriman et al., 2015; Tetreault & Ambrose, 2007), which results in their depleting the stock of otherwise abundant preferred prey species (e.g., sea urchins; Berriman et al., 2015). Berriman et al. (2015) found that when these hungry lobsters in reserves were proffered sea hares in the field, they attacked and consumed them. These findings suggest that sensitization in *Aplysia* has its evolutionary roots in the predator–prey regime found in coastline conditions prior to the depletion of lobsters by modern human fishing pressure.

Furthermore, they also identified a heretofore underappreciated ecological consequence of marine reserves: When sizes and densities of crustacean (and fish) predators are allowed to grow to pre-fishing levels in no-take reserves, the increase in competition can turn a species' ecological role from that of a scavenger in fished ecosystems, into a keystone predator, ready to attack and eat the most abundant prey species, thereby enhancing the overall diversity of that ecosystem (Berriman et al., 2015; Paine, 1966).

Given that lobsters can cause sensitization of *Aplysia* in the wild, what then is the adaptive value of sensitization? The most direct hypothesis posits that sea hares with stronger post-attack withdrawal reflexes are better protected against further attacks (cf. squid, Crook et al., 2014; amphipod, Perrot-Minnot et al., 2017), as their bodies are transformed in the minutes to days following the attack into small, tight, inaccessible balls. Berriman, Goldstein, and Wright (unpublished observations) performed an *in situ* pilot study to test this hypothesis in the reserve on Santa Catalina Island off the coast of California. They caged hungry lobsters from the surrounding reserve *in situ* with tagged sea hares. Half of the tagged sea hares had been "previously sensitized" with electric shock, the other half left untouched as controls. If the caged lobster had been deterred from eating the sensitized *Aplysia*, and only ate unsensitized controls, our hypothesis would have strong support. Instead we found *more* pre-sensitized *Aplysia* eaten by caged lobsters. We surmise that this is because the previously sensitized sea hares had ejected all of their active chemical defenses (ink and opaline) when they received the electric shock, thereby losing their frontline protection against the enclosed lobster. An additional, perhaps more compelling, hypothesis for the adaptive advantage of sensitization is that it protects injured tissue from further damage and facilitates healing (Walters, 1994). We might call this hypothesis a "bandage" benefit, rather than an "anti-predator" benefit. This bandage effect, by redu-cing the release of chemicals from inside the sea hare's body in the hours and days following attack, may reduce the chance of post-attack predation by lobsters that would otherwise detect these chemicals (Walters, 2019).

It appears that the effectiveness of chemical protection in *Aplysia* depends critically on the strength of the predator's motivation. Outside the reserve, predators such as lobster and sheepshead have abundant prey and reduced competition. There, they do not attack chemically protected sea hares at all. However, inside reserves, competition and hunger appear to drive crustacean and fish predators to attack *Aplysia* (videos of these behaviors can be found under the research tab on sites.chapman.edu/wwright/). Nevertheless, the fact that Berriman et al. (2015) found that not all lobsters in reserves strongly attack sea hares suggests that *Aplysia* can coexist with lobster, if the latter are not too hungry. It is likely in this broad middle ground of predator hunger that sea hares experience the value of the combination of chemical protection and post-attack behavioral change, including, but not limited to, sensitization (Gillette, 2006; Jing et al., 2008; Mackey & Carew, 1983; Marinesco et al., 2004). Nevertheless, in the most protected no-take reserve on Santa Catalina Island, where large lobsters have sufficiently depleted their food, some 30% of lobsters tested were not at all deterred by *Aplysia* chemical defenses, and vigorously attacked and consumed proffered sea hares (Berriman et al., 2015).

Given the assumption that sensitization in sea hares is related to preda-tion, we return to the ecology of *Dolabrifera*. The tropical near-shore habitats of *Dolabrifera* have even more predator pressure than in temperate waters (Palmer, 1979; Vermeij, 1994, 2013). How, then, can *Dolabrifera*, which lacks all forms of sensitization, protect itself from predators?

Perhaps *Dolabrifera* increases its level of chemical protection beyond that of sea hares from temperate waters to *compensate* for its lack of sensitization. Takagi et al. (2010) tested this hypothesis by performing feeding assays with standardized pellets of the ground-up body wall of both *Aplysia* and *Dolabrifera*, as well as the fully palatable squid. They fed the pellets to the hermit crab, *Pagurus samuelis*, an omnivorous crustacean, chosen for its bold behavior, broad diet, and easy husbandry. As expected from other experi-ments with the chemically protected *Aplysia* (Pennings & Paul, 1993), hermit crabs ate *Aplysia* pellets much more slowly (~2 mg per half hour) than they did squid pellets (~10 mg per half hour). The hypothesis of Takagi et al. (2010) predicted that consumption of pellets made from the *Dolabrifera* would be even slower than that of pellets made from *Aplysia*. That hypothesis was destroyed by finding (Takagi et al., 2010) that hermit crabs ate *Dolabrifera* pellets several times *faster* (9 mg per half hour) than they did *Aplysia* pellets, and nearly as fast as they ate squid pellets. Clearly, these results left entirely unresolved the question of how *Dolabrifera* copes with predators.

An alternative hypothesis is that *Dolabrifera* avoids its predators. *Dolabrifera* typically rests under boulders or inside cracks when not foraging (Kay, 1979). Himstead and Wright (2018) found that individual *Dolabrifera* emerge very precisely from these cryptic habitats to graze on benthic micro-algae only after the ebbing tide has isolated their pool, and only in the heat of the day (see videos of these behaviors under the research tab on sites .chapman.edu/wwright/). No individuals emerged when the tide was high enough to wash the pools, nor during nighttime low tides (Figure 2.3, left panel). The time of day that the first *Dolabrifera* emerged from its pool was strikingly correlated with the time the pool was first isolated by the ebbing tide (Figure 2.3, right panel; Himstead & Wright, 2018).

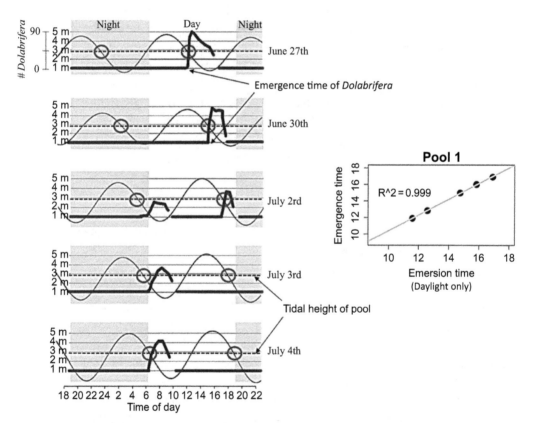

FIGURE 2.3. Individuals of *Dolabrifera* emerge immediately upon the daytime ebbing tide dropping below their pool level. (Left panel) Data from one representative pool (Pool 1) of seven studied. The height of the oscillating tide (m, relative to mean lower low water, solid thin line) and the elevation of the pool (dashed horizontal line) are superimposed on the number of visible sea hares (thick solid line). Circles indicate when the pool is isolated by the ebbing tide (*emersion time*). (Right panel) The time of day that the first individual *Dolabrifera* emerged into the open tide pool was strikingly correlated (range of R^2 of seven similar pools: 0.984–0.999) with the time of day the pool was emersed (and thereby isolated from the ocean). Data from June 28 and 29 are not shown on the left panel but are represented in the right panel, which is limited exclusively to emergences occurring from midday to afternoon (Himstead & Wright, 2018).

This exceptionally precise foraging behavior suggests, albeit indirectly, that *Dolabrifera* in Panama *is* avoiding both nocturnal benthic crustaceans (caridean shrimp, spiny lobsters, crabs) during nighttime low tides, as well as subtidal piscine predators (puffer fish, wrasses, etc.) that encroach on their pools during high tides (Bertness et al., 1981). Himstead and Wright (2018) further explored this hypothesis by tethering individual *Dolabrifera* outside their tidepool cracks during nighttime low tides. Not a single tethered *Dolabrifera* (of 18) was eaten. They attributed this result to very heavy local fishing (Panama City, ca. 3 km distance) of crustaceans (primarily lobster and crab) by humans. Other tests of the predator avoidance hypothesis, such as proffering individual *Dolabrifera* to predators or adding predator scent to pools to inhibit foraging in *Dolabrifera*, remain to be executed.

Why has *Dolabrifera* traded in chemical protection and sensitization for precise predator avoidance? Cimino and Ghiselin (2009) reported that three genera of sea hares, including *Dolabrifera*, have "changed their diet." Most sea hares cheaply extract deterrent molecules from their food, whether from macro-algae (as in *Aplysia* and *Dolabella*) or cyanobacteria (as in *Bursatella* and *Stylocheilus*), and then redeploy those chemicals for predator defense at a relatively low energetic cost (Cimino & Ghiselin, 2009). By contrast, the diet of *Dolabrifera* is comprised exclusively of diatoms, which have very low levels of available secondary metabolites (Cimino & Ghiselin, 2009). Consequently, any defensive chemicals in *Dolabrifera* must be synthesized *de novo*. This is likely a more expensive process (M. Ghiselin, personal communication), which may explain the comprehensive shift in anti-predator adaptations of *Dolabrifera* from chemical defense and sensitization in its Aplysiida ancestor to a precisely constrained cryptic habitat and habit.

This hypothesis predicts that any other genus with a diatom diet should show similarly cryptic behavioral ecology with little or no chemical protection/sensitization. It turns out that the sister genus of *Dolabrifera*, *Phyllaplysia* (Figure 2.1a), also consumes diatoms. As predicted, its habitat is also very specialized and cryptic, blades of sea grass in shallow estuaries, where it lies camouflaged off the substratum. Furthermore, Takagi et al. (2010) confirmed that the chemical protection in the body wall of *Phyllaplysia* is nearly as low as that of *Dolabrifera*. Thus, *Phyllaplysia* seems to be ecologically similar to *Dolabrifera*. How then can we explain that its SNs still show SB and IE in response to 5-HT (Figure 2.1a)? Does this weaken the "change in diet" hypothesis? Not necessarily. That hypothesis predicts *behavioral* phenotype (sensitization), not underlying mechanisms. When *Phyllaplysia* behavior was directly tested for general sensitization, none was found (Figure 2.1b; Erixon et al., 1999; Marinesco et al., 2003). Thus, *Phyllaplysia*'s behavioral phenotype (no general sensitization) *does* support the "change in diet" hypothesis. Because *Phyllaplysia* expresses SB and IE (Erixon et al., 1999), its loss of general sensitization is likely due to change in a *different* mechanism. Previous research in *Aplysia* has identified multiple candidate mechanisms, one or more of which might be lost in *Phyllaplysia*, including: (1) different processes in SNs that increase transmitter release without SB or IE (Byrne & Kandel, 1996), (2) interposed excitatory and inhibitory interneurons in the reflex circuits that are modulated by 5-HT to increase the overall signal to motor neurons (Cleary et al., 1995, 1998; Frost et al., 1988; White et al., 1993), and (3) 5-HT-sensitive post-synaptic processes in motor neurons that increase their response to synaptic inputs (Chitwood et al., 2001; Glanzman, 1995, 2008).

In principle, natural selection could reduce sensitization in *Phyllaplysia* by reducing/eliminating changes at any of these neural loci, or others not yet discovered, without affecting SB or IE. Furthermore, in *Dolabrifera*, it is still possible that additional sensitization mechanisms are disabled and thereby contribute to the total loss of sensitization.

Finally, even though *Phyllaplysia* expresses no general sensitization, the fact that it still expresses SB and IE suggests that its loss of learning may not be as complete as that of *Dolabrifera*. Further support for this idea comes from the following observations:

(1) Unlike *Dolabrifera*, *Phyllaplysia* still expresses site-specific sensitization (Figure 2.1b; Marinesco et al., 2003).
(2) IE of SNs in *Phyllaplysia* after strong shock to peripheral pedal nerves is intermediate between that of *Aplysia* and the null response in *Dolabrifera* (Marinesco et al., 2003).
(3) 5-HT release in response to peripheral-nerve stimulation in *Phyllaplysia* is intermediate between that of *Aplysia* and *Dolabrifera* (Marinesco et al., 2003).
(4) Memory of classical conditioning is intermediate between that of *Aplysia* and *Dolabrifera* (Hoover et al., 2006; Figure 2.1b).

Dolabrifera and *Phyllaplysia* are sister genera, i.e., more closely related to each other than either is to any other genus. Cimino and Ghiselin (2009) identified a third genus, *Petalifera*, which has also switched to a diatom diet. Molecular work by A. Valdes (personal communication) places *Petalifera* as a more distant relative of *Dolabrifera/Phyllaplysia*, suggesting it switched independently to a diatom diet. This makes future studies of the neurobiology of sensitization in *Petalifera* particularly interesting as an independent test of the "change-in-diet" hypothesis.

TOP-DOWN APPROACH

The adaptive evolutionary narratives described above are the result of a "bottom up" scientific process, with each new question arising directly from new discoveries. In addition, however, science also makes progress when scientists propose general sweeping hypotheses, setting the stage for myriad tests of those hypotheses. There are at least two general evolutionary hypotheses that relate to the evolutionary patterns described above.

ADAPTIVE DEGRADATION OF PHENOTYPES IS VARIABLE How do phenotypes change when new selective pressures cause a phenotype to lose its adaptive advantage? One view (Byers, 1997; Lahti et al., 2009) holds that the trajectory of phenotypic loss is expected to be unpredictable (i.e., variable), relative to the steady incremental process of phenotypic gain. Vestigial structures often reflect this unpredictable consequence of relaxed selection (e.g., Senter, 2010). They remind us that the original adaptation may well have evolved pleiotropic connections to other critical functions in positive, unpredicted ways, substantially slowing down or even halting its disappearance (Blumstein, 2006; Byers, 1997). Our growing understanding of the evolutionary losses of sensitization in the sister genera, *Dolabrifera* and *Phyllaplysia* detailed above, suggests that the process is, indeed, quite variable. *Dolabrifera* has lost sensitization completely, at least partly due to the loss of the neuromodulatory effects (SB and IE) of 5-HT on SNs. By contrast, the loss of sensitization in *Phyllaplysia* is incomplete (Figure 2.1), and not at all due to loss of SB and IE, both of which are still expressed. The question of whether SB and IE observed in *Phyllaplysia* (Figure 2.1a; Marinesco et al., 2003; Wright et al., 1996) are vestigial nonadaptive processes, or in fact part of a more muted but still adaptive behavioral plasticity, will require careful study at both behavioral and neurobiological levels. Finally, the investigation of *Petalifera* mentioned above, including testing for SB and IE, general, and site-specific sensitization, will improve the evaluation of this "variable loss" hypothesis, as will behavioral testing of all the genera in Figure 2.1.

GENERALIST ANCESTORS SPAWN SPECIALIST DESCENDANTS This theory proposes that generalist ancestors can use their phenotypic plasticity to fill multiple niches, including narrow "specialist" niches. In these narrow niches, rapid speciation can give rise to new canalized (phenotypically "hardened") species in place of the ancestral generalist (Baldwin, 1896; Futuyma & Kirkpatrick, 2017; West-Eberhard, 1989, 2003). Does our "model lineage" of sea hares support this theory? *Aplysia* and *Dolabella* appear to fit the description of phenotypically plastic generalist source lineages (Carefoot, 1987). Adults forage for many hours a day in virtually all habitats (sand and hard substrate, protected and exposed coasts, to 20 m depth), and feed on a wide variety of macro-algae (Carefoot, 1987; Pennings et al., 1993). In addition, *Aplysia* is routinely found in much narrower "safe zones," such as intertidal pools, shallow lagoons, and shallow fronds of near-shore macro-algae (Ricketts et al., 1992; D. Reed, personal communication). It is easy to imagine these zones as refuges for evolution of narrow-niche specialists, especially if the founding generalist species is thinned out by evolving ecological challenges, such as increased predation (Palmer, 1979; Vermeij, 1994, 2013; Walker & Brett, 2002), or competition with herbivorous fish (Estes & Steinberg, 1988). Such thinning out would likely increase speciation by the usual allopatric mechanisms in mainstream habitats (; Futuyma & Kirkpatrick, 2017, but see Krug, 2011), leaving multiple descendent species of *Aplysia*. In addition, and critical for this idea, this thinning could leave descendant lineages isolated in rarified specialist niches, where they would be under strong selective pressure for specialist traits that are more finely tuned to their niche, as well as reduced selective pressure for phenotypic plasticity, which no longer serves as an adaptive function in this unchanging narrow niche.

Although the data are still sparse, the patterns are promising: Multiple relatively narrow niches appear to be filled by genera that have evolved morphologically away from the ancestral *Aplysia* form. A. Valdes (personal communication) has recently analyzed molecular sequence data from multiple aplysiid species and finds two very well-distinguished sister clades:

(1) A clade of *Aplysia* species that closely resemble each other morphologically, but which are clearly (by molecular analysis) different species.
(2) A sister clade consisting of one generalist genus (*Dolabella*; Pennings et al., 1993) and five specialist genera (*Petalifera, Bursatella, Stylocheilus, Phyllaplysia,* and *Dolabrifera*), each of which has its own narrow diet (exclusively cyanobacteria or diatoms) and distinct cryptic ecology: in predator-free microhabitats, such as shallow/intertidal habitats, including cracks, or on algae, surfgrass, or cyanobacteria patches).

The idea that generalist ancestors with a plastic phenotype should spawn specialist descendants with reduced plasticity (Baldwin, 1896; Futuyma & Kirkpatrick, 2017; West-Eberhard, 1989, 2003) predicts that learning should be reduced in all five of the specialist opistobranchs. We already know that two of these species (*Dolabrifera* and *Phyllapysia*) have reduced or eliminated two forms of learning, i.e., sensitization (Erixon et al., 1999; Wright, 1998), and classical conditioning (Hoover et al., 2006). The remaining three (*Petalifera, Bursatella, Stylocheilus*) of these specialists need to be tested for sensitization and classical conditioning before we can comprehensively discuss the evidence for or against this theory. Importantly, the prediction of reduced learning among the five specialists is critical: If, for example, the phenotype of even one of them includes robust sensitization, the theory would be significantly weakened. On the other hand, reduced sensitization in all five would lend ample support to the idea that these genera have lost the phenotypic plasticity of their generalist ancestor (*Aplysia/Dolabella*), as part of their evolution into a narrower habitat and habit. Note that this prediction of evolutionary losses of sensitization in all five specialist genera diverges from the "change in diet" hypothesis (Cimino & Ghiselin, 2009), which does *not* predict loss of sensitization in *Bursatella* and *Stylocheilus*, because their cyanobacterial diet has ample defensive metabolites, which can be cheaply redeployed for their own defenses, in concert with behavioral plasticity (e.g., sensitization). Divergent predictions like these make future research on sensitization in these sea hares particularly attractive.

2.5 CONCLUSION

This chapter illustrates how, starting with neural underpinnings of learning and memory, we have assembled an interacting series of questions, hypotheses, and tests that have begun to clarify at multiple levels how learning in sea hares likely evolved. An emerging feature of this clarity is that learning, like any other phenotype, is an adaptation with benefits and costs, and its heterogeneity of expression is rich and illuminating at multiple levels.

ACKNOWLEDGMENTS

I would like to thank Emilie Marcus, Deborah Bird, John Christy, Mary Jane West-Eberhard, John Byers, Walter Piper, and Terry Walters for their invaluable comments on earlier drafts of this chapter.

REFERENCES

Almaguer-Melian, W., Rojas-Reyes, Y., Alvare, A., Rosillo, J. C., Frey, J. U., & Bergado, J. A. (2005). Long-term potentiation in the dentate gyrus in freely moving rats is reinforced by intraventricular application of norepinephrine, but not oxotremorine. *Neurobiology of Learning & Memory, 83,* 72–78. https://doi.org/10.1016/j.nlm.2004.08.002

Bailey, C. H., Giustetto, M., Huang, Y. Y., Hawkins, R. D., & Kandel, E. R. (2000). Is heterosynaptic modulation essential for stabilizing Hebbian plasticity and memory? *Nature Reviews Neuroscience, 1,* 11–20. https://doi.org/10.1038/35036191

Baldwin, J. M. (1896). A new factor in evolution. *American Naturalist, 30,* 441–451.

Berriman, J. S., Kay, M. C., Reed, D. C., Rassweiler, A., Goldstein, D. A., & Wright, W. G. (2015). Shifts in attack behavior of an important kelp forest predator within marine reserves. *Marine Ecology Progress Series, 522,* 193–201. https://doi.org/10.3354/meps11157

Bertness, M. D., Garrity, S. D., & Levings, S. C. (1981). Predation pressure and gastropod foraging: A tropical-temperate comparison. *Evolution, 35,* 995–1007. https://doi.org/10.2307/2407870

Blumstein, D. T. (2006). The multipredator hypothesis and the evolutionary persistence of antipredator behavior. *Ethology, 112,* 209–217. https://doi.org/10.1111/j.1439-0310.2006.01209.x

Bornancin, L., Bonnard, I., Mills, S., & Banaigs, B. (2017). Chemical mediation as a structuring element in marine gastropod predator–prey interactions. *Natural Product Reports, 34,* 644–676. https://doi.org/10.1039/C6NP00097E

Bouchet, P., Rocroi, J.-P., Hausdorf, B., Kaim, A., Kano, Y., Nützel, A., Parkhaev, Pavel, Schrödl, Michael, & Strong, E. E. (2017). Revised classification, nomenclator and typification of gastropod and monoplacophoran families. *Malacologia, 61,* 1–526. https://doi.org/10.4002/040.061.0201

Byers, J. A. (1997). *American pronghorn: Social adaptations and the ghosts of predators past.* University of Chicago Press.

Byrne, J. H., & Kandel, E. R. (1996). Presynaptic facilitation revisited: State and time dependence. *Journal of Neuroscience, 16,* 425–435. https://doi.org/10.1523/JNEUROSCI.16-02-00425

Carefoot, T. H. (1987). *Aplysia*: Its biology and ecology. *Oceanography & Marine Biology, 25,* 167–284. <Go to ISI>://WOS:A1987K531000005

Carew, T. J. (2000). *Behavioral neurobiology: The cellular organization of natural behavior.* Sinauer.

Carew, T. J., Hawkins, R. D., & Kandel, E. R. (1983). Differential classical conditioning of a defensive withdrawal reflex in *Aplysiida californica. Science, 219,* 397–400. https://doi.org/10.1126/science.6681571

Chitwood, R. A., Li, Q., & Glanzman, D. L. (2001). Serotonin facilitates AMPA-type responses in isolated siphon motor neurons of Aplysia in culture. *Journal of Physiology-London, 534,* 501–510. https://doi.org/10.1111/j.1469-7793.2001.00501.x

Cimino, G., & Ghiselin, M. T. (2009). Chemical defense and the evolution of opisthobranch gastropods. *Proceedings of the California Academy of Sciences, 60,* 175.

Cleary, L. J., Byrne, J. H., & Frost, W. N. (1995). Role of interneurons in defensive withdrawal reflexes in *Aplysia. Learning & Memory, 2,* 133–151. https://doi.org/10.1101/lm.2.3.133

Cleary, L. J., Lee, W. L., & Byrne, J. H. (1998). Cellular correlates of long-term sensitization in *Aplysia. Journal of Neuroscience, 18,* 5988–5998. https://doi.org/10.1523/JNEUROSCI.18-15-05988

Crook, R. J., Dickson, K., Hanlon, R. T., & Walters, E. T. (2014). Nociceptive sensitization reduces predation risk. *Current Biology, 24,* 1121–1125. https://doi.org/10.1016/j.cub.2014.03.043

Derby, C. D. (2007). Escape by inking and secreting: Marine molluscs avoid predators through a rich array of chemicals and mechanisms. *Biological Bulletin, 213,* 274–289. https://doi.org/10.2307/25066645

Derby, C. D., & Aggio, J. F. (2011). The neuroecology of chemical defenses. *Integrative & Comparative Biology, 51,* 771–780. https://doi.org/10.1093/icb/icr063

Ding, L., & Perkel, D. J. (2004). Long-term potentiation in an avian basal ganglia nucleus essential for vocal learning. *Journal of Neuroscience, 24,* 488–494. https://doi.org/10.1523/JNEUROSCI.4358-03.2004

Eliot, L. S., Hawkins, R. D., Kandel, E. R., & Schacher, S. (1994). Pairing-specific, activity-dependent presynaptic facilitation at *Aplysia* sensory-motor neuron synapses in isolated cell-culture. *Journal of Neuroscience, 14,* 368–383. https://doi.org/10.1523/JNEUROSCI.14-01-00368

Erixon, N. J., Demartini, L. J., & Wright, W. G. (1999). Dissociation between sensitization and learning-related neuromodulation in an aplysiid species. *Journal of Comparative Neurology, 408,* 506–514.

Estes, J. A., & Steinberg, P. D. (1988). Predation, herbivory, and kelp evolution. *Paleobiology, 14,* 19–36. https://doi.org/10.1017/S0094837300011775

Frost, W. N., Clark, G. A., & Kandel, E. R. (1988). Parallel processing of short-term memory for sensitization in *Aplysia. Journal of Neurobiology, 19,* 297–334. https://doi.org/10.1002/neu.480190402

Futuyma, D., & Kirkpatrick, M. (2017). *Evolution.* Sinauer.

Gillette, R. (2006). Evolution and function in serotonergic systems. *Integrative & Comparative Biology, 46,* 838–846. https://doi.org/10.1093/icb/icl024

Glanzman, D. L. (1995). The cellular basis of classical conditioning in *Aplysia californica*: It's less simple than you think. *Trends in Neurosciences, 18,* 30–36. https://doi.org/10.1016/0166-2236(95)93947-V

(2008). New tricks for an old slug: The critical role of postsynaptic mechanisms in learning and memory in *Aplysia*. In W. S. Sossin, J. C. Lacaille, V. F. Castellucci, & S. Belleville (Eds.), *Essence of memory* (Vol. 169, pp. 277–292). Elsevier. https://doi.org/10.1016/S0079-6123(07)00017-9

(2010). Common mechanisms of synaptic plasticity in vertebrates and invertebrates. *Current Biology*, 20(1), R31–R36.

Glanzman, D. L., Mackey, S. L., Hawkins, R. D., Dyke, A. M., Lloyd, P. E., & Kandel, E. R. (1989). Depletion of serotonin in the nervous system of *Aplysia* reduces the behavioral enhancement of gill withdrawal as well as the heterosynaptic facilitation produced by tail shock. *Journal of Neuroscience*, 9, 4200–4213. https://doi.org/10.1523/JNEUROSCI.09-12-04200.1989

Harley, C. W. (2007). Norepinephrine and the dentate gyrus. In H. E. Scharfman (Ed.), *Dentate Gyrus: A Comprehensive Guide to Structure, Function, and Clinical Implications* (Vol. 163, pp. 299–318). Elsevier. https://doi.org/10.1016/S0079-6123(07)63018-0

Himstead, A., & Wright, W. G. (2018). Precise foraging schedule in an intertidal euopistho-branch mollusk. *Marine & Freshwater Behaviour and Physiology*, 51, 131–141. https://doi.org/10.1080/10236244.2018.1505430

Hoover, B. A., Nguyen, H., Thompson, L., & Wright, W. G. (2006). Associative memory in three aplysiids: Correlation with heterosynaptic modulation. *Learning & Memory*, 13, 820–826. https://doi.org/10.1101/lm.284006

Jami, S. A., Wright, W. G., & Glanzman, D. L. (2007). Differential classical conditioning of the gill-withdrawal reflex in *Aplysia* recruits both NMDA receptor-dependent enhancement and NMDA receptor-dependent depression of the reflex. *Journal of Neuroscience*, 27, 3064–3068. https://doi.org/10.1523/jneurosci.2581-06.2007

Jing, J., Vilim, F. S., Cropper, E. C., & Weiss, K. R. (2008). Neural analog of arousal: Persistent conditional activation of a feeding modulator by serotonergic initiators of locomotion. *Journal of Neuroscience*, 28, 12349–12361. https://doi.org/10.1523/jneurosci.3855-08.2008

Kandel, E. R. (1976). *Cellular basis of behavior: An introduction to behavioral neurobiology.* Freeman.

(2012). The molecular biology of memory: cAMP, PKA, CRE, CREB-1, CREB-2, and CPEB. *Molecular Brain*, 5: 14. https://doi.org/10.1186/1756-6606-5-14.

Kandel, E. R., Klein, M., Hochner, B., Shuster, M., Siegelbaum, S. A., Hawkins, R. D., Glanzman, D. L., Castellucci, V. F., and Abrams, T. W. (1987). Synaptic modulation and learning: New insights into synaptic transmission from the study of behavior. In G. Edelman & W. E. Gall (Eds.), *Synaptic function* (pp. 472–518). John Wiley & Sons. https://doi.org/10.1002/hup.470050111

Kandel, E. R., & Schwartz, J. H. (1982). Molecular biology of learning: Modulation of transmitter release. *Science*, 218, 433–443. https://doi.org/10.1126/science.6289442

Kay, A. (1979). *Hawaiian marine shells.* Bernice Pauahi Bishop Museum.

Krug, P. J. (2011). Patterns of speciation in marine gastropods: A review of the phylogenetic evidence for localized radiations in the sea. *American Malacological Bulletin*, 29, 169–186. https://doi.org/10.4003/006.029.0210

Lahti, D. C., Johnson, N. A., Ajie, B. C., Otto, S. P., Hendry, A. P., Blumstein, D. T., Coss, R. G., Donohue, K., and Foster, S. A. (2009). Relaxed selection in the wild. *Trends in Ecology & Evolution*, 24, 487–496. https://doi.org/10.1016/j.tree.2009.03.010

LeDoux, J. E. (2000). Emotion circuits in the brain. *Annual Review of Neuroscience*, 23, 155–184. https://doi.org/10.1146/annurev.neuro.23.1.155

Lynch, M. A. (2004). Long-term potentiation and memory. *Physiological Reviews*, 84, 87–136. https://doi.org/10.1152/physrev.00014.2003

Mackey, S., & Carew, T. J. (1983). Locomotion in *Aplysia*: Triggering by serotonin and modulation by bag-cell extract. *Journal of Neuroscience*, 3, 1469–1477. https://doi.org/10.1523/JNEUROSCI.03-07-01469.1983

Marcus, E. A., Nolen, T. G., Rankin, C. H., & Carew, T. J. (1988). Behavioral dissociation of dishabituation, sensitization and inhibition in *Aplysia*. *Science*, 241, 210–213. https://doi.org/10.1126/science.3388032

Marinesco, P., & Carew, T. J. (2002). Serotonin release evoked by tail nerve stimulation in the CNS of *Aplysia*: Characterization and relationship to heterosynaptic plasticity. *Journal of Neuroscience, 22,* 2299–2312. https://doi.org/10.1523/JNEUROSCI.22-06-02299.2002

Marinesco, S., Duran, K. L., & Wright, W. G. (2003). Evolution of learning in three aplysiid species: Differences in heterosynaptic plasticity contrast with conservation in serotonergic pathways. *Journal of Physiology-London, 550,* 241–253. https://doi.org/10.1113/jphysiol.2003.038356

Marinesco, S., Wickremasinghe, N., Kolkman, K. E., & Carew, T. J. (2004). Serotonergic modulation in Aplysia. II. Cellular and behavioral consequences of increased serotonergic tone. *Journal of Neurophysiology, 92,* 2487–2496. https://doi.org/10.1152/jn.00210.2004

Martin, S. J., Grimwood, P. D., & Morris, R. G. M. (2000). Synaptic plasticity and memory: An evaluation of the hypothesis. *Annual Review of Neuroscience, 23,* 649–711. https://doi.org/10.1146/annurev.neuro.23.1.649

Mason, M. J., Watkins, A. J., Wakabayashi, J., Buechler, J., Pepino, C., Brown, M., & Wright, W. G. (2014). Connecting model species to nature: Predator-induced long-term sensitization in *Aplysia californica*. *Learning & Memory, 21,* 363–367. https://doi.org/10.1101/lm.034330.114

Nature Research Highlights (2010) Animal behaviour: Lobster shock. *Nature 467,* 8.

Owen, G. R., & Brenner, E. A. (2012). Mapping molecular memory: Navigating the cellular pathways of learning. *Cellular & Molecular Neurobiology, 32,* 919–941. https://doi.org/10.1007/s10571-012-9836-0

Paine, R. T. (1966). Food web complexity and species diversity. *American Naturalist, 100,* 65–75. https://doi.org/10.1086/282400

Palmer, A. R. (1979). Fish predation and the evolution of gastropod shell sculpture: Experimental and geographic evidence. *Evolution, 33,* 697–713. https://doi.org/10.2307/2407792

Papini, M. R. (2002). Pattern and process in the evolution of learning. *Psychological Review, 109,* 186–201. https://doi.org/10.1037/0033-295X.109.1

Pennings, S. C., Nadeau, M. T., & Paul, V. J. (1993). Selectivity and growth of the generalist herbivore, *Dolabella auricularia* feeding upon complementary resources. *Ecology, 74,* 879–890. https://doi.org/10.2307/1940813

Pennings, S. C., & Paul, V. J. (1993). Sequestration of dietary secondary metabolites by 3 species of sea hares-location, specificity, and dynamics. *Marine Biology, 117,* 535–546. https://doi.org/10.1007/BF00349763

Pennings, S. C., Paul, V. J., Dunbar, D. C., Hamann, M. T., Lumbang, W. A., Novack, B., & Jacobs, R. S. (1999). Unpalatable compounds in the marine gastropod *Dolabella auricularia*: Distribution and effect of diet. *Journal of Chemical Ecology, 25*(4), 735–755. Retrieved from <Go to ISI>://WOS:000080123000005

Perrot-Minnot, M. J., Banchetry, L., & Cézilly, F. (2017). Anxiety-like behaviour increases safety from fish predation in an amphipod crustacea. *Royal Society Open Science, 4,* 171558. https://doi.org/10.1098/rsos.171558

Ricketts, E. F., Calvin, J., & Hedgpeth, J. W. (1992). *Between Pacific tides* (5th ed.). Stanford University Press.

Schultz, W. (1998). Predictive reward signal of dopamine neurons. *Journal of Neurophysiology, 80,* 1–27. https://doi.org/10.1152/jn.1998.80.1.1

Senter, P. (2010). Vestigial skeletal structures in dinosaurs. *Journal of Zoology, 280,* 60–71. https://doi.org/10.1111/j.1469-7998.2009.00640.x

Stopfer, M., & Carew, T. J. (1988). Development of sensitization in the escape locomotion system in *Aplysia*. *Journal of Neuroscience, 8,* 223–230. https://doi.org/10.1523/JNEUROSCI.08-01-00223.1988

Takagi, K. K., Ono, N., & Wright, W. G. (2010). Interspecific variation in palatability suggests cospecialization of antipredator defenses in a sea hare. *Marine Ecology Progress Series, 416,* 137–144. https://doi.org/10.3354/meps08738

Tetreault, I., & Ambrose, R. F. (2007). Temperate marine reserves enhance targeted but not untargeted fishes in multiple no-take maps. *Ecological Applications, 17*, 2251–2267. https://doi.org/10.1890/06-0161.1

Vermeij, G. J. (1994). The evolutionary interaction among species: Selection, escalation, and coevolution. *Annual Review of Ecology & Systematics, 25*, 219–236. https://doi.org/10.1146/annurev.es.25.110194.001251

(2013). On escalation. *Annual Review of Earth & Planetary Sciences, 41*, 1–19. https://doi.org/10.1146/annurev-earth-050212-124123

Walker, S. E., & Brett, C. E. (2002). Post-Paleozoic patterns in marine predation: Was there a Mesozoic and Cenozoic marine predatory revolution? *Paleontological Society Papers, 8*, 119–194. https://doi.org/10.1017/S108933260000108X

Walters, E. T. (1987). Site-specific sensitization of defensive reflexes in *Aplysia:* A simple model of long-term hyperalgesia. *Journal of Neuroscience, 7*, 400–407. https://doi.org/10.1523/JNEUROSCI.07-02-00400.1987

(1991). A functional, cellular, and evolutionary model of nociceptive plasticity in *Aplysia. Biological Bulletin, 180*, 241–251. https://doi.org/10.2307/1542394

(1994). Injury-related behavior and neuronal plasticity: An evolutionary perspective on sensitization, hyperalgesia, and analgesia. *International Review of Neurobiology, 36*, 325–427. https://doi.org/10.1016/S0074-7742(08)60307-4

(2018). Nociceptive biology of molluscs and arthropods: evolutionary clues about functions and mechanisms potentially related to pain. *Frontiers in Physiology, 9*, 1049.

(2019). Adaptive mechanisms driving maladaptive pain: How chronic ongoing activity in primary nociceptors can enhance evolutionary fitness after severe injury. *Philosophical Transactions of the Royal Society B-Biological Sciences, 374*, 20190277. https://doi.org/10.1098/rstb.2019.0277

Watkins, A. J., Goldstein, D. A., Lee, L. C., Pepino, C. J., Tillett, S. L., Ross, F. E., Wilder, E. L., and Wright, W. G. (2010). Lobster attack induces sensitization in the sea hare, *Aplysia californica. Journal of Neuroscience, 30*, 11028–11031. https://doi.org/10.1523/JNEUROSCI.1317-10.2010

West-Eberhard, M. J. (1989). Phenotypic plasticity and the origins of diversity. *Annual Review of Ecology and Systematics, 20*(1), 249–278.

(2003). *Developmental plasticity and evolution.* Oxford University Press.

White, J. A., Ziv, I., Cleary, L. J., Baxter, D. A., & Byrne, J. H. (1993). The role of interneurons in controlling the tail-withdrawal reflex. *Journal of Neurophysiology, 70*, 1777–1786. https://doi.org/10.1152/jn.1993.70.5.1777

Wright, W. G. (1998). Evolution of nonassociative learning: Behavioral analysis of a phylogenetic lesion. *Neurobiology of Learning & Memory, 69*, 326–337. https://doi.org/10.1006/nlme.1998.3829

(2000). Neuronal and behavioral plasticity in evolution: Experiments in a model lineage. *Bioscience, 50*, 883–894. https://doi.org/10.1006/nlme.1998.3829

Wright, W. G., Jones, K., Sharp, P., & Maynard, B. (1995). Widespread anatomical projections of the serotonergic modulatory neuron, CB1, in Aplysia. *Invertebrate Neuroscience 1*, 173–183. https://doi.org/10.1007/bf02331914

Wright, W. G., Kirschman, D., Rozen, D., & Maynard, B. (1996). Phylogenetic analysis of learning-related neuromodulation in molluscan mechanosensory neurons. *Evolution, 50*, 2248–2263. https://doi.org/10.1111/j.1558-5646.1996.tb03614.x

3

LEARNING IN INSECTS: PERSPECTIVES AND POSSIBILITIES

Alexis Lillian Kriete and Karen L. Hollis

As recent reviews of insect learning (Giurfa, 2015; Hollis & Guillette, 2011, 2015; Perry et al., 2013) demonstrate, an increasingly voluminous body of research confirms the broad associative infrastructure on which insects rely to find food, locate hosts, avoid danger, and secure mates. Although most of that research focuses on but 2 of the approximately 30 orders of insects, namely, Hymenoptera (bees, wasps, and ants) and Diptera (flies, including *Drosophila* spp.), our current search reveals that many new species have recently been added to the record (see Table 3.1). We agree with Perry et al. (2013) that a true comparative study of learning in invertebrates is wanting, especially in light of so many other noninsect invertebrates missing from the learning literature, for example species from other arthropod classes (e.g., millipedes and barnacles) as well as from other invertebrate phyla, such as microscopic rotifers and cnidarians (jellyfish and anemones). Nonetheless, as our review of insect learning makes clear, newly studied insect species appear to rely on associative learning to solve ecological problems in much the same way as previously studied species, an observation that potentially can begin to illuminate – and raise new questions about – the underlying mechanisms of learning, to which we return later in this chapter. We begin with a brief review of the insect learning literature, focusing on the role of learning in insects' behavioral ecology.

3.1 THE ROLE OF LEARNING IN THE BEHAVIORAL ECOLOGY OF INSECTS

FINDING FOOD

Of the approximately 30 insect orders – large groupings that contain anywhere from fewer than 100 to more than 350,000 different species (Resh & Cardé, 2003) – only 14 are represented in the learning literature (Table 3.1). However, across many of those orders, the use of learned cues to find food

TABLE 3.1. *Associative learning in insects (Class: Insecta)*

Insects are a single class of organisms within the superclass Hexapoda (from the Greek for "six feet"). Here we list all families in which the associative learning capacity of at least one species in that family has been studied; rows in which no family name is listed (and that are not shaded for easy identification) are those in which, to our best knowledge, no one has claimed to demonstrate associative learning in any member of that insect order. The list is nonexhaustive, designed simply to expand the information in this text and reveal research gaps. Species marked with asterisks represent a newly studied (<5 years) family of insect (**) or a newly studied species (*) in a family already represented in the literature. References can be found in the text or in Hollis and Guillette (2015).

Order name (Common name)	Number of families/species	Families studied	Selected examples of associative learning
Archaeognatha (bristletails)	2		
Zygentoma (silverfish)	5	Lepismatidae	• *Lepisma saccharina* (silverfish)
Ephemeroptera (mayflies)	40		
Odonata (dragonflies, damselflies)	3,100		
	5,600	Calopterygidae	• *Calopteryx splendens* (damselfly)**
	33	Coenagrionidae	• *Enallagma* spp. (damselfly)
Blattodea (cockroaches)	5	Blaberidae	• *Leucophaea maderae* (Madeira cockroach)
	4,000	Blattidae	• *Periplaneta americana* (American cockroach)
Mantodea (mantids)	8	Mantidae	• *Tenodera ardifolia* (mantid)
	1,800		
Isoptera (termites, white ants)	7		
Grylloblattodea (rock crawlers)	1		
	2,500		
Dermaptera (earwigs)	7		
	75		
Plecoptera (stoneflies)	16	Perlidae	• *Paragnetina media* (stonefly)
	2,000		
Embiidina (web spinners)	8		
	300		
Orthoptera (grasshoppers, katydids)	29	Acrididae	• *Melanoplus sanguinipes* (grasshopper)
	24,000		• *Shistocerca americana* and *S. gregaria* (desert locusts)
		Gryllidae	• *Gryllus bimaculatus* (field cricket)
Phasmida (walking sticks)	2		
	3,000		
Mantophasmatodea (gladiators, heel-walkers)	1		
	16		

53

TABLE 3.1. (cont.)

Order name (Common name)	Number of families/species		Families studied	Selected examples of associative learning
Zoraptera (angel insects)	1	32		
Psocoptera (booklice, barklice)	17	4,400		
Phthiraptera (biting lice, sucking lice)	24	4,900		
Hemiptera (true bugs)	104	55,000	Cicadellidae	• *Homalodisca vitripennis* (glassy-winged sharpshooter)
			Liviidae	• *Diaphorina citri* (Asian citrus psyllid)**
			Reduviidae	• *Rhodnius prolixus* (triatomid bug)
Thysanoptera (thrips)	9	6,000		
Megaloptera (alderflies, dobsonflies)	2	328		
Raphidioptera (snakeflies)	2	215		
Neuroptera (antlions)	17	6,000	Myrmeleontidae	• *Myrmeleon crudelis* (antlion)
			Chrysopidae	• *Ceraeochrysa cubana* (common lacewing)**
Coleoptera (beetles, weevils)	135	350,000	Bothrideridae	• *Dastarcus helophoroides* (parasitoid beetle)**
			Chrysomelidae	• *Callosobruchus maculatus* (seed beetle)**
			Elateridae	• *Limonius canus* (Pacific Coast wireworm)
			Tenebrionidae	• *Tenebrio molitor* and *T. obscurus* (mealworm beetles)
Strepsiptera (twisted-wing parasites)	8	550		
Mecoptera (scorpion flies)	9	570		
Diptera (flies)	117	150,000	Calliphoridae	• *Lucilia cuprina* and *Phaenicia sericata* (walking blowflies)
			Culicidae	• *Anopheles gambiae* (malaria mosquito)
				• *Culex quinquefasciatus* (filariasis mosquito)
			Drosophilidae	• *Drosophila melanogaster* (fruit fly)
			Muscidae	• *Musca domestica* (house fly)
			Tachinidae	• *Exorista mella* and *Drino bohemica* (tachinid flies)
			Tephritidae	• *Rhagoletis pomonella* (apple maggot fly)

Order			Family	Species
Siphonaptera (fleas)	15	2,600	Pulicidae	*Xenopsylla conformis* (rat flea)
Lepidoptera (moths, butterflies)	120	160,000	Arctiidae	*Diacrisia virginica* (wooly bear caterpillar)
			Nymphalidae	*Bicyclus anynana* (bush brown butterfly)*
				Danaus plexippus (monarch butterfly)
			Papilionidae	*Battus philenor* (pipevine swallowtail)
			Pieridae	*Pieris brassicae* and *P. rapae* (cabbage white butterflies)
			Sphingidae	*Manduca sexta* (tobacco hornworm)
			Tortricidae	*Cydia pomonella* (codling moth)
Trichoptera (caddisflies)	46	13,000	Limnephilidae	*Hesperophylax occidentalis* (caddisfly)
Hymenoptera (ants, bees, wasps)	73	150,000	Apidae	*Apis mellifera* (European honey bee)
				Bombus terrestris (bumblebee)
				Eucera berlandi (solitary bee)*
			Braconidae	*Psyttalia concolor* (parasitoid wasp)*
			Eucoilidae	*Leptopilina heterotoma* (parasitoid wasp)
			Eulophidae	*Tamarixia triozae* (parasitoid wasp)**
			Figitidae	*Leptopilina boulardi* (parasitoid wasp)
			Formicidae	*Acromyrmex ambiguus* (leafcutter ant)*
				Formica spp. (ant)
			Ichneumonidae	*Lissopimpla excelsa* (orchid dupe wasp)*
				Pimpla disparis (parasitoid wasp)*
			Pteromalidae	*Lariophagus distinguendus* (parasitoid wasp)*
				Nasonia giraulti* and *N. vitripennis* (parasitoid wasps)
			Vespidae	*Polistes fuscatus* (paper wasp)**
			Trichogrammatidae	*Trichogramma deion* and *T. sathon* (egg parasitoids)**

Adapted with permission from Hollis and Guillette (2015).

appears ubiquitous. Moreover, whenever investigators have explored the function of learning, individuals' ability to rely on learned cues appeared to dramatically increase the efficiency of their search – and, in turn, their reproductive fitness – as has been known in vertebrates for many years (Hollis, 1982, 1997). For example, a now-classic study demonstrates that grasshoppers (*Schistocerca americana*, Order Orthoptera) are able to rely on previously learned cues to help guide their search for a particular source of high-quality food. They not only grow faster than grasshoppers denied the benefit of such cues but also pupate into adulthood sooner, a nearly direct fitness benefit (Dukas & Bernays, 2000). Similarly, locusts (*Locusta migratoria*), another orthopteran, are able to use learned color cues to guide their discriminative choice of a food source that contains the specific nutrient that they lack (Raubenheimer & Tucker, 1997), and guide them to drinking water (Raubenheimer & Blackshaw, 1994).

Cockroaches (*Periplaneta americana*, Order Blattodea) are capable of an even more sophisticated discrimination task than locusts, namely, *context-dependent* discrimination learning (Matsumoto et al., 2012). In this task, different background contexts signaled which of two different – and conflicting – discrimination problems would be rewarded: A flickering light context signaled that one odor (CS_1) would be reinforced with sucrose, but a second odor (CS_2) would not; and when, instead, a steady light signaled the context, the reverse discrimination operated. That is, CS_2 would be reinforced with sucrose, but CS_1 would not. Not only are cockroaches able to solve this complex task successfully, but also crickets and honeybees are capable of solving context-dependent learning tasks (see Perry et al., 2013, for a review).

Among the hymenopterans, the role of associative learning in honeybees' search for sources of nectar and pollen on the basis of learned cues is long established – and continues to be intensely studied at multiple levels by comparative psychologists, behavioral ecologists, and neuroscientists (e.g., Bitterman, 2000; Giurfa, 2013; North & Greenspan, 2007; Srinivasan, 2010). More recently, however, hymenopterans have displayed much more complex forms of learning, including reversal learning, contextual learning, numerosity, and the ability to form abstract concepts (Perry et al., 2013). For example, bumblebees (*Bombus terrestris*) can learn to associate a complex color pattern – a 4 × 4 matrix of two colors in which only a single spatial arrangement of those 16 color patches is correct – to guide their search for food (Blackawton et al., 2011).

Together with hymenopterans, Diptera, which includes flies and mosquitoes, has been the most extensively studied order of insects, beginning with the groundbreaking demonstrations of appetitive associative learning in fruit flies (*Drosophila melanogaster*; Quinn et al., 1974) and blowflies (*Phormia regina*; Nelson, 1971). Relative newcomers to the list – valuable additions not only to the associative learning literature but also to potential biological control programs – are several mosquito species, namely, *Anopheles gambiae*, an especially efficient malaria vector (Chilaka et al., 2012); *Aedes aegypti*, a dengue and yellow fever vector (Menda et al., 2013; Vinauger et al., 2018); and *Culex quinquefasciatus*, a vector of West Nile, and possibly Zika, viruses (Tomberlin et al., 2006), all of which are capable of associating learned cues with blood meals. In the case of *A. gambiae*, this information can be retained for at least 72 hours (Chilaka et al., 2012).

Within three different families of dipteran flies (Table 3.1), their search for food is also facilitated by associative learning (Campbell & Strausfeld, 2001; Fukushi, 1989; McGuire, 1984; Prokopy et al., 1998; Sokolowski et al., 2010). An interesting exception among these dipterans is a Batesian mimic of honeybees, namely, hoverflies (*Eristalis tenax*), which have a seemingly immutable preference for yellow flowers from which they obtain both nectar and pollen; this preference, at least so far, does not seem to be altered by extensive conditioning (Lunau et al., 2018). Whether *E. tenax* is capable of learning in other behavioral contexts, however, remains to be determined.

Unlike research with grasshoppers and locusts, with which we began this section, relatively few studies have explored exactly how learning contributes to insects' feeding efficiency and fitness. However, research with pit-digging larval antlions (Order Neuroptera, Family Myrmeleontidae) is an exception, as well as an important addition to the insect-learning literature. Unlike other species, which are forced to depend on an active search for food sources, a lifestyle facilitated by associative learning and once thought critical to the ability to learn (Bernays, 1993), larval antlions are sit-and-wait predators that excavate pits in sandy soils and wait for prey to stumble inside. Nonetheless, learned cues benefit antlions, too: Reliable signals of food's imminent arrival enable them to increase both the rate and the efficiency with which they extract the nutritive contents of prey, which in turn enable them to grow faster and pupate into adults sooner, thus shortening their highly vulnerable larval stage (Guillette et al., 2009; Hollis et al., 2011; see Hollis et al., 2015, for a review).

LOCATING HOSTS

Hymenopterans, studied extensively for their ability to use learned signals to find food, are also capable of using learned signals to locate hosts, a form of learning found within several families of parasitoid wasps. Among the Braconidae family, *Microplitis croceipes*, a parasitoid of pest caterpillars – and thus an important biological control among its myriad other uses as a biosensor (Rains et al., 2006) – can learn to discriminate between food and host cues while under food deprivation and then transfer this discriminative ability to a situation in which it is well fed but needs a host (Lewis & Takasu, 1990). Another wasp, *Aphidus ervi*, which parasitizes aphids and, like

M. croceipes, is sometimes used in biological pest control, is able to retain a preference for a particular host odor learned as a larva and then, as an adult, exhibit this preference when searching for a host on which to deposit eggs (Gutiérrez-Ibáñez et al., 2007). *Biosteres arisanus*, a wasp parasitoid of tropical fruit fly eggs, also shows long-term retention of learned host cues, which enables it to locate and parasitize the host's eggs, increasing both the number of eggs that it can lay and, importantly, the number of offspring that reach adulthood (Dukas & Duan, 2000). Table 3.1 lists several other hymenopteran parasitoids that use learned cues to locate hosts.

AVOIDING DANGER

Although early studies of aversive learning typically employed electric shock as the negative reinforcer (e.g., Aceves-Piña & Quinn, 1979; Goldsmith et al., 1978), later emphasis on the *function* of learned aversions demonstrated that locusts can learn to avoid poisons (Lee & Bernays, 1990), and larval fruit flies can learn to avoid predation (Dukas, 1999). A more recent example of a learned aversion is from a study of hymenopteran leafcutter ants (*Acromyrmex ambiguous*), which accept or reject leaves from plants based on learned odor cues they experience either in their fungus garden, where plants suitable for growing fungus are found, or in their colony waste, where plants harmful to their fungus garden are dumped (Arenas & Roces, 2018).

In another hymenopteran, nest-founding paper wasp queens (*Polistes fuscatus*), called foundresses, are better able to learn and remember the individual faces of conspecifics than are workers (Tibbetts et al., 2018). Individual recognition is critical to dominance interactions among foundresses; thus, face recognition is presumably a strategy to circumvent repeated aggressive interactions.

Finally, the suggestion of learned avoidance behavior in two hymenopterans makes an interesting transition to the next section on reproduction. Male solitary bees (*Eucera berlandi*) rapidly approach *Ophrys* flowers, which mimic the visual and olfactory signals of female bees, and attempt to mate with these sexually deceptive orchids; after an unsuccessful copulation attempt, however, the male bees hover above the flower for up to a minute, visually scanning the unique flower pattern on the orchid's labellum. Follow-up experiments with honeybees, whose visual system is similar to that of solitary bees, demonstrated that honeybees could easily learn the labellum patterns of different plants, suggesting, at least preliminarily, that the solitary bees' distinctive hovering behavior is an attempt to learn and subsequently avoid sexually deceptive orchids (Stejskal et al., 2015). In another deceived pollinator, a hymenopteran wasp (*Lissopimpla excelsa*), an unsuccessful copulation attempt with orchids results in decreased frequency of attempted copulation with those flowers (Weinstein et al., 2016). In both studies, in which the focus was orchid pollination systems rather than avoidance learning *per se,* the obvious learning control groups are missing; nonetheless, the results suggest that learning may well operate to help hymenopteran pollinators avoid sexually deceptive orchids.

SECURING MATES

In several studies reminiscent of early experiments that explored the function of learned reproductive behavior in fish (Hollis et al., 1997) and Japanese quail (see Krause and Domjan, Chapter 7, this volume), individuals representing multiple species from different orders have been shown to exhibit learned preferences for particular mate characteristics following some aspect of mating experience. These include damselflies (*Calopteryx splendens*, Order Odonata) (Verzijden & Svensson, 2016); butterflies (*Bicyclus anynana*, Order Lepidoptera) (Westerman & Monteiro, 2013); and a hemipteran psyllid fly (*Diaphorina citrii*) (Stockton et al., 2017), a carrier of the bacterium that causes citrus greening disease, which threatens citrus groves worldwide.

While exploring the difficult mating system of male parasitoid wasps (*Pimpla disparis*, Order Hymenoptera), Danci et al. (2013) found that male wasps learn to visit pupa locations that they have previously associated with the presence of a developing female about to emerge from her host. Because the competition for newly emerging females is intense in this species – and because males are forced to reproduce sexually while haplodiploid females can reproduce without mating – males that learn the location of newly emerging females would likely gain fitness benefits.

As this brief review of insect learning reveals, insects from multiple species, families, and orders appear to rely on associative learning in much the same way as do vertebrates. Not surprisingly, then, the view that all vertebrates should be capable of associative learning now applies to the study of insects – indeed, all invertebrates, a topic to which we now turn.

3.2 TO LEARN OR NOT TO LEARN: PLASTICITY AND VARIATION IN LEARNING

3.2.1 LEARNING AS AN EMERGENT PROPERTY OF NERVOUS SYSTEMS

For over a decade, behavioral researchers have joined those who study neuronal architecture and development in arguing that learning may be universal in *all* animals with a nervous system, including many noninsect invertebrates (e.g., Dukas, 2008; Greenspan, 2007; Hollis & Guillette, 2015; Raine, 2009). That is, the capacity for associative learning may be an emergent property of nervous systems – a "fundamental principle of brain functionality" (Greenspan, 2007, p. 649) – such that, whenever selection pressures favor the evolution of a nervous system, for whatever reason, the capacity for associative learning follows *ipso facto* (see Hollis & Guillette, 2015, for a detailed analysis). Of course, this view does not preclude situations in which particular insect species, like their vertebrate counterparts, rely on hard-wired responses in some contexts – nor does it preclude situations in which some individuals in the colony are better able to learn than others. Elsewhere, Hollis and Guillette (2011) argued that learning is simply the default of neural circuitry and that, where fitness would benefit more from a hard-wired response, evolution acts to suppress the default.

CONSTRAINTS ON LEARNING

As is true in vertebrates, learning in insects is highly context dependent. Genetic, social, developmental, temporal, and environmental factors have all been shown to modulate learning – or simply the performance of learned tasks (see Silva and Silva, Chapter 12, and Blaisdell and Seitz, Chapter 26, this volume). For example, several recent studies have shown that circadian rhythms affect insects' learning capabilities, often dramatically. Kissing bugs (*Rhodinus prolixus*) trained in an aversive operant conditioning task during the day performed worse than individuals trained at night (Vinauger & Lazzari, 2015). Similarly, Decker et al. (2007) found that cockroaches, *Rhyparobia maderae*, could learn to associate two odors in a classical conditioning task if trained at night, but not if trained during the day; because performance depended on the time of training, not testing, circadian rhythms clearly modulate learning acquisition rather than recall. Surprisingly, *R. maderae* could successfully learn a nearly identical – albeit *operant* conditioning – task at any time of day (Garren et al., 2013), although they were worse at recalling learned associations when tested during the day. Circadian rhythms also affect learning in fruit flies, which performed best in an aversive conditioning task if they were trained four hours after nightfall (Fropf et al., 2014). Although these studies focused on the role of insects' circadian clocks on long-term learning, circadian rhythms also modulate short-term learning in honeybees (Lehmann et al., 2011) and fruit flies (Lyons & Roman, 2009). Taken together, these experiments clearly indicate that learning ability can be tightly coupled with a circadian clock. One might expect insects to be better learners – able to form and remember associations more readily or accurately – during their active period, when they forage, court, or travel, and the available research generally supports this notion.

In addition to plasticity arising from circadian rhythms, insects' learning abilities may be constrained by developmental stage or, in eusocial insects, caste. A developmental example comes from solitary parasitoid wasps (genus *Trichogramma*), which are capable of learning olfactory cues as adults, but not as pupae (Wilson & Woods, 2016). Caste-based learning differences have been demonstrated in eusocial Hymenoptera, including ants (Perez et al., 2013), bees (Gong et al., 2018), and wasps (Tibbetts et al., 2018).

Environmental context, including both biotic and abiotic factors, also affects insects' learning abilities. The literature on environmental modulation of learning is extensive, although again heavily biased toward Hymenoptera. Among the many factors that have been shown to impair learning in honeybees and bumblebees are low rearing temperatures (Jones et al., 2005), viral or parasitic infection (Iqbal & Mueller, 2007; Kralj et al., 2007), immune activity (Alghamdi et al., 2008), and pesticide exposure (Piiroinen & Goulson, 2016). In fruit flies, learning is impaired by heat stress (Wang et al., 2007) and sleep deprivation (Seugnet et al., 2011). Somewhat surprisingly, however, and despite the theoretical appeal of early environmental enrichment on later learning ability, training fruit flies to learn about food choices as larvae appears not to enhance their adult learning ability (Durisko & Dukas, 2013).

Intra- and interspecific genetic differences also contribute to variability in learning. Within-species genetic variation has been linked to the ability to learn odor cues in two species of parasitoid wasps (Froissart et al., 2017; König et al., 2015). Studies using fruit flies have identified numerous naturally occurring allelic variants that affect learning, memory, and forgetting (Reaume et al., 2011; Williams-Simon et al., 2019), and have shown that flies from inbred populations are worse at learning than outbred flies (Nepoux et al., 2015). Evidence consistent with genetic differences also comes from studies of different species within the same genus; for example, *Nasonia vitripennis* wasps formed long-term memories after a single odor conditioning trial, while closely related *Nasonia giraulti* females required multiple trials to form long-term memories (Hoedjes & Smid, 2014). Similarly, a parasitic wasp, *Cotesia glomerata*, required four hours to form long-term memories in an olfactory learning task, whereas a congeneric species, *Cotesia rubecula*, required three days (Smid et al., 2007).

Another factor that influences learning in insects, as it does in vertebrates, is sex. For example, female Asian citrus psyllids (*Diaphorina citri*) can learn to distinguish individual components of an odor blend, while males cannot (Stockton et al., 2016). Similarly, in a study in which *Nasonia vitripennis* wasps were artificially selected for improved visual learning capabilities, female wasps, but not males, also gained improved olfactory learning capabilities (Liefting et al., 2018; see Liefting, Chapter 5, this volume). In another wasp species, *Polistes fuscatus*, females learned to discriminate between pairs of facial images more accurately than males (DesJardins & Tibbetts, 2018).

Finally, social context is an important source of variation in insect learning. The use of social learning (see Kendal, Chapter 14, this volume) in foraging within various bee and ant species is especially well documented (Grüter & Leadbeater, 2014). Moreover, bumblebees are even capable of using social information to learn how to manipulate artificial objects, such as strings (Alem et al., 2016) and balls (Loukola et al., 2017). A growing body of evidence shows that non-eusocial insects also learn from each other. In fruit flies, social learning has been shown to play a role in mate choice (Nöbel et al., 2018), song learning (Li et al., 2018), and parasitoid avoidance (Kacsoh et al., 2018). Studies of orthopterans demonstrate the importance of social learning in this group as well; wood crickets, *Nemobius sylvestris*, use social information to hide from predaceous wolf spiders (Coolen et al., 2005), and field crickets, *Teleogryllus oceanicus*, modulate their reproductive behavior based on social experience (Bailey & Zuk, 2009).

In sum, a large and expanding body of evidence demonstrates the same kinds of plasticity and variation in learning in insects as in vertebrates. In addition, diverse insect taxa are capable of sophisticated forms of learning once thought to be restricted to higher vertebrates, such as numerosity, concept learning, and contextual learning (see Perry et al., 2013; Giurfa, 2013, for reviews). In light of insects' performance with a minuscule neural architecture, it is tempting to speculate how organisms with even smaller, simpler nervous systems – or no organized nervous systems at all – compare to insects in their ability to learn.

3.3 LEARNING IN OTHER INVERTEBRATES AND SINGLE-CELLED ORGANISMS

The best-studied species with a small nervous system is the nematode, *Caenorhabditis elegans*, whose 302 neurons, and the synaptic connections between them, have been mapped. Like many insects, *C. elegans* displays several forms of both associative and nonassociative learning (see Yu and Rankin, Chapter 1, this volume). Yet, despite the breadth of its learning repertoire, *C. elegans* appears unable to learn to perform operant conditioning tasks, in contrast to many insect species (Perry et al., 2013).

Organisms with even smaller nervous systems also are capable of some forms of learning. Rotifers, microscopic animals with about 200 neurons, can learn to habituate to tactile stimuli (Applewhite, 1968). Sea anemones, which lack a centralized nervous system altogether, are capable, not only of habituation but also of associative learning (Haralson et al., 1975). Unfortunately, in the nearly half-century since these studies were published, no follow-up work has been done to elucidate a mechanism for nonneural learning in these species.

What about organisms that lack neurons entirely? A slime mold, *Physarum polycephalum*, a unicellular protist, is an interesting case study. It can habituate to caffeine or quinine after repeated exposures to either chemical (Boisseau et al., 2016); it can also habituate to salt, evidently by absorbing it and using it as a circulating cytoplasmic memory (Boussard et al., 2019). Salt habituation in *P. polycephalum* not only is long-lasting, persisting through the slime mold's month-long dormant phase, but also can be transferred to conspecifics via cytoplasmic exchange (Vogel & Dussutour, 2016). Still unclear is whether other chemical stimuli can be learned and transferred using the same cytoplasmic storage mechanism. The ability of slime molds to remain habituated to salt after emerging from their dormant phase – during which time most of the proteins and nucleic acids in the cell are destroyed – raises intriguing parallels to the ability of holometabolous insects (possessing four developmental stages) to retain learned associations after metamorphosis, a process that breaks down and remodels neural tissue (Blackiston et al., 2008; Ramírez et al., 2016). The fact that both groups store memories across life stages points to shared selection pressures: It is likely as advantageous for a slime mold to emerge from dormancy having retained old information, as it is advantageous for insects to remember larval associations.

Slime molds diverge from insects in that they may be incapable of associative learning. Although one study demonstrated that *Physarum* can learn to associate cooler temperatures with a food reward, this conclusion must be interpreted cautiously, as the authors did not include controls to rule out sensory adaptation (Shirakawa et al., 2011). Similarly, an earlier study showed that slime molds anticipate a recurrent, periodic event, apparently associating a time interval with the unconditioned stimulus, but the study design could not disentangle sensitization from associative learning (Saigusa et al., 2008). Although associative learning has not been observed in living bacteria, it has been demonstrated *in vitro* by Zhang et al. (2014) using an artificial, four-component genetic circuit that caused *E. coli* to produce a fluorescent signal after learning to associate a conditioned and an unconditioned stimulus. The simplicity of the circuit raises questions about why associative learning appears not to have arisen naturally in any prokaryote. In contrast, a single-celled eukaryote, *Paramecium caudatum*, is capable of associative learning, as it can learn to avoid a light or dark area paired with an electric shock (Armus et al., 2006; Mingee, 2013). Additionally, plants are capable of habituation, sensitization, and associative learning (Abramson & Chicas-Mosier, 2016; Gagliano et al., 2016) through an unknown mechanism, possibly involving epigenetic modifications acting as a form of memory (Thellier & Lüttge, 2012). Interestingly, epigenetic modifications are required for certain forms of learning in at least some insect species (Kramer et al., 2011; Li et al., 2018), which raises the possibility that epigenetic mechanisms for learning and memory predate the evolution of the nervous system (see Guan, Chapter 25, this volume).

Aside from these epigenetic modifications as the potential evolutionary precursor of behavioral change, the nagging question remains: To what extent do the underlying mechanisms of learning – across all taxa – represent homology or homoplasy? Obviously, if we are to include animals without a nervous system, the answer cannot lie in synaptic plasticity; however, possible mechanisms at a more basic, molecular level – which modulate synaptic plasticity in animals that possess synapses – offer tantalizing possibilities: For example, cyclic adenosine monophosphate (cAMP) signaling is involved in both vertebrate and insect learning (Louis et al., 2018); in the slime mold, *Dictyostelium discoideum*, cAMP acts as a chemotactic signal that causes cells to aggregate (Loomis, 2014), and cAMP also plays an important role in bacteria (Perlman & Pastan, 1971). Might cAMP signaling – or any other intracellular communication system – be a homologous mechanism of learning at the molecular level? Of course, just because animals across multiple taxa share a particular molecular signal does not mean it is a homologous *learning* mechanism.

3.4 CONCLUSIONS

Additional studies of learning in insects will facilitate comparative analyses of learning in general. Many insect orders are still entirely unrepresented in the learning literature, including groups with interesting ecologies that could be used to test hypotheses about learning. For example, soil-dwelling insect larvae share an ecological niche with nematodes, protists, annelids, and bacteria, and presumably encounter many of the same chemical and physical cues. In insects, these cues are recognized at the periphery of the nervous system, transduced by signaling neurons, and translated into altered neuronal properties and organization in the mushroom body. In all other organisms that can learn, environmental cues must also be recognized and processed. How do different organisms, equipped with vastly different cellular and neural hardware, solve the common problem of sensing and integrating signals in their environment? With the advent of species-agnostic genome editing using CRISPR-Cas, improved imaging technology, and high-throughput or automated behavioral analysis, researchers can come closer than ever before to answering this question – as well as perplexing questions of homology in the evolution of learning and memory mechanisms.

REFERENCES

Abramson, C. I., & Chicas-Mosier, A. M. (2016). Learning in plants: Lessons from *Mimosa pudica*. *Frontiers in Psychology, 7*, 417. https://doi.org/10.3389/fpsyg.2016.00417

Aceves-Piña, E. O., & Quinn, W. G. (1979). Learning in normal and mutant *Drosophila* larvae. *Science, 206*, 93–96. https://doi.10.1126/science.206.4414.93

Alem, S., Perry, C. J., Zhu, X., Loukola, O. J., Ingraham, T., Søvik, E., & Chittka, L. (2016). Associative mechanisms allow for social learning and cultural transmission of string

pulling in an insect. *PLoS Biology, 14*(10), e1002564. https://doi.org/10.1371/journal.pbio
.1002564

Alghamdi, A., Dalton, L., Phillis, A., Rosato, E., & Mallon, E. B. (2008). Immune response
impairs learning in free-flying bumble-bees. *Biology Letters, 4*, 479–481. https://doi.org/
10.1098/rsbl.2008.0331

Applewhite, P. B. (1968). Non-local nature of habituation in a rotifer and protozoan. *Nature,
217*, 287–288. https://doi.org/10.1038/217287a0

Arenas, A., & Roces, F. (2018). Appetitive and aversive learning of plants odors inside
different nest compartments by foraging leaf-cutting ants. *Journal of Insect Physiology,
109*, 85–92. https://doi.org/10.1016/j.jinsphys.2018.07.001

Armus, H. L., Montgomery, A. R., & Gurney, R. L. (2006). Discrimination learning and
extinction in Paramecia (*P. caudatum*). *Psychological Reports, 98*, 705–711. https://doi
.org/10.2466%2Fpr0.98.3.705-711

Bailey, N. W., & Zuk, M. (2009). Field crickets change mating preferences using
remembered social information. *Biology Letters, 5*, 449–451. https://doi.org/10.1098/rsbl
.2009.0112

Bernays, E. A. (1993). Aversion learning and feeding. In D. R. Papaj & A. C. Lewis (Eds.),
Insect learning (pp. 1–17). Routledge, Chapman & Hall. https://doi.org/10.1007/978-1-
4615-2814-2_1

Bitterman, M. E. (2000). Cognitive evolution: A psychological perspective. In C. Heyes & L.
Huber (Eds.), *The evolution of cognition* (pp. 61–80). The MIT Press.

Blackawton, P. S., Airzee, S., Allen, A., Baker, S., Berrow, A., Blair, C., Churchill, M., Coles, J.,
Cumming, R. F.-J., Fraquelli, L., Hackford, C., Hinton Mellor, A., Hutchcroft, M.,
Ireland, B., Jewsbury, D., Littlejohns, A., Littlejohns, G. M., Lotto, M., McKeown, J., . . .
Lotto, R. B. (2011). Blackawton bees. *Biology Letters, 7*, 168–172. https://doi.org/10.1098/
rsbl.2010.1056

Blackiston, D. J., Casey, E. S., & Weiss, M. R. (2008). Retention of memory through metamorphosis: Can a moth remember what it learned as a caterpillar? *PLoS ONE, 3*(3), e1736.
https://doi.org/10.1371/journal.pone.0001736

Boisseau, R. P., Vogel, D., & Dussutour, A. (2016). Habituation in non-neural organisms:
Evidence from slime moulds. *Proceedings of the Royal Society B, 283*, 20160446. https://
doi.org/10.1098/rspb.2016.0446

Boussard, A. Delescluse, J., Pérez-Escudero, A., & Dussutour, A. (2019). Memory inception
and preservation in slime moulds: The quest for a common mechanism. *Philosophical
Transactions of the Royal Society B, 374*, 20180368. https://doi.org/10.1098/rstb.2018
.0368

Campbell, H. R., & Strausfeld, N. J. (2001). Learned discrimination of pattern orientation in
walking flies. *Journal of Experimental Biology, 204*, 1–14.

Chilaka, N., Perkins, E., & Tripet, F. (2012). Visual and olfactory associative learning in the
malaria vector *Anopheles gambiae sensu stricto*. *Malaria Journal, 11*, 27. https://doi.org/
10.1186/1475-2875-11-27

Coolen, I., Dangles, O., & Casas, J. (2005). Social learning in noncolonial insects? *Current
Biology, 21*, 1931–1935. https://doi.org/10.1016/j.cub.2005.09.015

Danci, A., Hrabar, M., Ikoma, S., Schaefer, P. W., & Gries, G. (2013). Learning provides
mating opportunities for males of a parasitoid wasp. *Entomologia Experimentalis et
Applicata, 149*, 229–240. https://doi.org/10.1111/eea.12129

Decker, S., McConnaughey, S., & Page, T. L. (2007). Circadian regulation of insect olfactory
learning. *Proceedings of the National Academy of Sciences, 104*, 15905–15910. https://doi
.org/10.1073/pnas.0702082104

DesJardins, N., & Tibbetts, E. A. (2018). Sex differences in face but not colour learning in
Polistes fuscatus paper wasps. *Animal Behaviour, 140*, 1–6. https://doi.org/10.1016/j
.anbehav.2018.03.012

Dukas, R. (1999). Ecological relevance of associative learning in fruit fly larvae. *Behavioral
Ecology and Sociobiology, 45*, 195–200. https://doi.org/10.1007/s002650050553

(2008). Evolutionary biology of insect learning. *Annual Review of Entomology, 53*, 145–160. https://doi.org/10.1146/annurev.ento.53.103106.093343

Dukas, R., & Bernays, E. A. (2000). Learning improves growth rate in grasshoppers. *Ecology, 97*, 2637–2640. https://doi.org/10.1073/pnas.050461497

Dukas, R., & Duan, J. J. (2000). Potential fitness consequences of associative learning in parasitoid wasps. *Behavioral Ecology, 11*, 536–543. https://doi.org/10.1093/beheco/11.5.536

Durisko, Z., & Dukas, R. (2013). Effects of early-life experience on learning ability in fruit flies. *Ethology, 119*, 1067–1076. https://doi.org/10.1111/eth.12168

Froissart, L., Giurfa, M., Sauzet, S., & Desouhant, E. (2017). Cognitive adaptation in asexual and sexual wasps living in contrasted environments. *PLoS ONE,12*(5), e0177581. https://doi.org/10.1371/journal.pone.0177581

Fropf, R., Zhang, J., Tanenhaus, A. K., Fropf, W. J., Siefkes, E., & Yin, J. C. P. (2014). Time of day influences memory formation and dCREB2 proteins in *Drosophila*. *Frontiers in Systems Neuroscience, 8*, 43. https://doi.org/10.3389/fnsys.2014.00043

Fukushi, T. (1989). Learning and discrimination of coloured papers in the walking blowfly, *Lucilia cuprina*. *Journal of Comparative Physiology A, 166*, 57–64. https://doi.org/10.1007/BF00190210

Gagliano, M., Vyazovskiy, V. V., Borbély, A. A., Grimonprez, M., & Depczynski, M. (2016). Learning by association in plants. *Scientific Reports, 6*, 38427. https://doi.org/10.1038/srep38427

Garren, M. V., Sexauer, S. B., & Page, T. L. (2013). Effect of circadian phase on memory acquisition and recall: Operant conditioning vs. classical conditioning. *PLoS ONE 8*(3), e58693. https://doi.org/10.1371/journal.pone.0058693

Giurfa, M. (2013). Cognition with few neurons: Higher-order learning in insects. *Trends in Neurosciences, 36*, 285–294. https://doi.org/10.1016/j.tins.2012.12.011

(2015). Learning and cognition in insects. *Wiley Interdisciplinary Reviews: Cognitive Science, 6*, 383–395. https://doi.org/10.1002/wcs.1348

Goldsmith, C. M., Hepburn, H. R., & Mitchell, D. (1978). Retention of an associative learning task after metamorphosis in *Locusta migratoria migratorioides*. *Journal of Insect Physiology, 24*, 737–741. https://doi.org/10.1016/0022-1910(78)90071-9

Gong, Z., Tan, K., & Nieh, J. C. (2018). First demonstration of olfactory learning and long-term memory in honey bee queens. *Journal of Experimental Biology, 221*, jeb177303. https://doi.org/10.5281/zenodo.1148794

Greenspan, R. J. (2007). Afterword: Universality and brain mechanisms. In G. North & R. J. Greenspan (Eds.), *Invertebrate neurobiology* (pp. 647–649). Cold Spring Harbor Laboratory Press.

Grüter, C., & Leadbeater, E. (2014). Insights from insects about adaptive social information use. *Trends in Ecology & Evolution, 29*, 177–184. https://doi.org/10.1016/j.tree.2014.01.004

Guillette, L. M., Hollis, K. L., & Markarian, A. (2009). Learning in a sedentary insect predator: Antlions (Neuroptera: Myrmeleontidae) anticipate a long wait. *Behavioural Processes, 80*, 224–232. https://doi.org/10.1016/j.beproc.2008.12.015

Gutiérrez-Ibáñez, C., Villagra, C. A., & Niemeyer, H. M. (2007). Pre-pupation behaviour of the aphid parasitoid *Aphidius ervis* (Haliday) and its consequences for pre-imaginal learning. *Naturwissenschaften, 94*, 595–600. https://doi.org/10.1007/s00114-007-0233-3

Haralson, J. V., Groff, C. I., & Haralson, S. J. (1975). Classical conditioning in the sea anemone, *Cribrina xanthogrammica*. *Physiology & Behavior, 15*, 455–460. https://doi.org/10.1016/0031-9384(75)90259-0

Hoedjes, K. M., & Smid, H. M. (2014). Natural variation in long-term memory formation among Nasonia parasitic wasp species. *Behavioural Processes, 105*, 40–45. https://doi.org/10.1016/j.beproc.2014.02.014

Hollis, K. L. (1982). Pavlovian conditioning of signal-centered action patterns and autonomic behavior: A biological analysis of function. *Advances in the Study of Behavior, 12*, 1–64. https://doi.org/10.1016/S0065-3454(08)60045-5

(1997). Contemporary research on Pavlovian conditioning: A "new" functional analysis. *American Psychologist, 52,* 956–965. https://psycnet.apa.org/doi/10.1037/0003-066X.52.9 .956

Hollis, K. L., Cogswell, H., Snyder, K., Guillette, L. M., & Nowbahari, E. (2011). Specialized learning in antlions (Neuroptera: Myrmeleontidae), pit-digging predators, shortens vulnerable larval stage. *PLoS ONE, 6*(3), e17958. https://doi.org/10.1371/journal.pone .0017958

Hollis, K. L., & Guillette, L. M. (2011). Associative learning in insects: Evolutionary models, mushroom bodies, and a neuroscientific conundrum. *Comparative Cognition & Behavior Reviews, 6,* 24–45. https://psycnet.apa.org/doi/10.3819/ccbr.2011.60004

(2015). What associative learning in insects tells us about models for the evolution of learning. *International Journal of Comparative Psychology, 28,* 1–18.

Hollis, K. L., Harrsch, F. A., & Nowbahari, E. (2015). Ants vs. antlions: An insect model for studying the role of learned ad hard-wired behavior in coevolution. *Learning & Behavior, 50,* 68–82. https://doi.org/10.1016/j.lmot.2014.11.003

Hollis, K. L., Pharr, V. L., Dumas, M. J., Britton, G. B., & Field, J. (1997). Classical conditioning provides paternity advantage for territorial male blue gouramis (*Trichogaster trichopterus*). *Journal of Comparative Psychology, 111,* 219–225. https://psycnet.apa.org/doi/10 .1037/0735-7036.111.3.219

Iqbal, J., & Mueller, U. (2007). Virus infection causes specific learning deficits in honeybee foragers. *Proceedings of the Royal Society B, 274,* 1517–1521. https://doi.org/10.1098/rspb .2007.0022

Jones, J. C., Helliwell, P., Beekman, M., Maleszka, R., & Oldroyd, B. P. (2005). The effects of rearing temperature on developmental stability and learning and memory in the honey bee, *Apis mellifera. Journal of Comparative Physiology A, 191,* 1121–1129. https://doi.org/ 10.1007/s00359-005-0035-z

Kacsoh, B. Z., Bozler, J., & Bosco, G. (2018). Drosophila species learn dialects through communal living. *PLoS Genetics, 14*(7), e1007430. https://doi.org/10.1371/journal.pgen .1007430

König, K., Krimmer, E., Brose, S., Gantert, C., Buschlüter, I., König, C., Klopfstein, S., Wendt, I., Baur, H., Krogmann, L., & Steidle, J. L. M. (2015). Does early learning drive ecological divergence during speciation processes in parasitoid wasps? *Proceedings of the Royal Society B, 282,* 20141850. https://doi.org/10.1098/rspb.2014.1850

Kralj, J., Brockmann, A., Fuchs, S., & Tautz, J. (2007). The parasitic mite Varroa destructor affects non-associative learning in honey bee foragers, *Apis mellifera* L. *Journal of Comparative Physiology A, 193,* 363–370. https://doi.org/10.1007/s00359-006-0192-8

Kramer, J. M., Kochinke, K., Oortveld, M. A. W., Marks, H., Kramer, D., de Jong, E. K., Asztalos, Z., Westwood, J. T., Stunnenberg, H. G., Sokolowski, M. B., Keleman, K., Zhou, H., van Bokhoven, H., & Schenck, A. (2011). Epigenetic regulation of learning and memory by *Drosophila* EHMT/G9a. *PLoS Biology, 9*(1), e1000569. https://doi.org/10 .1371/journal.pbio.1000569

Lee, J. C., & Bernays, E. A. (1990). Food tastes and toxic effects: Associative learning by the polyphagous grasshopper *Schistocerca americana* (Drury) (Orthoptera: Acricicae). *Animal Behaviour, 39,* 163–173. https://doi.org/10.1371/journal.pbio.1000569

Lehmann, M., Gustav, D., & Galizia, C. G. (2011). The early bee catches the flower – Circadian rhythmicity influences learning performance in honey bees, *Apis mellifera. Behavioral Ecology and Sociobiology, 65,* 205–215. https://doi.org/10.1007/s00265-010-1026-9

Lewis, W. J., & Takasu, K. (1990). Use of learned odours by a parasitic wasp in accordance with host and food needs. *Nature, 348,* 635–636. https://psycnet.apa.org/doi/10.1038/ 348635a0

Li, X., Ishimoto, H., & Kamikouchi, A. (2018). Auditory experience controls the maturation of song discrimination and sexual response in *Drosophila. eLife, 7,* e34348. https://doi.org/ 10.7554/eLife.34348

Liefting, M., Hoedjes, K. M., Le Lann, C., Smid, H. M., & Ellers, J. (2018). Selection for associative learning of color stimuli reveals correlated evolution of this learning ability across multiple stimuli and rewards. *Evolution, 72*, 1449–1459. https://doi.org/10.1111/evo.13498

Loomis, W. F. (2014). Cell signaling during development of Dictyostelium. *Developmental Biology, 391*, 1–16. https://doi.org/10.1016/j.ydbio.2014.04.001

Louis, T., Stahl, A., Boto, T., & Tomchik, S. M. (2018). Cyclic AMP-dependent plasticity underlies rapid changes in odor coding associated with reward learning. *Proceedings of the National Academy of Sciences, 115*, E448–E457. https://doi.org/10.1073/pnas.1709037115

Loukola, O. J., Perry, C. J., Coscos, L., & Chittka, L. (2017). Bumblebees show cognitive flexibility by improving on an observed complex behavior. *Science, 355*, 833–836. https://doi.org/10.1126/science.aag2360

Lunau, K., An, L., Donda, M., Hohmann, M., Sermon, L., & Stegmanns, V. (2018). Limitations of learning in the proboscis reflex of the flower visiting syrphid fly *Eristalis tenax. PLoS ONE 13*(3), e0194167. https://doi.org/10.1371/journal.pone.0194167

Lyons, L. C., & Roman, G. (2009). Circadian modulation of short-term memory in *Drosophila. Learning and Memory, 16*, 19–27. https://doi.org/10.1101/lm.1146009

Matsumoto, C. S., Matsumoto, Y., Watanabe, H., Nishino, H., & Mizunami, M. (2012). Context-dependent olfactory learning monitored by activities of salivary neurons in cockroaches. *Neurobiology of Learning and Memory, 97*, 30–36. https://doi.org/10.1016/j.nlm.2011.08.010

McGuire, T. R. (1984). Learning in three species of Diptera: The blow fly *Phormia regina*, the fruit fly, *Drosophila melanogaster*, and the house fly, *Musca domestica. Behaviour Genetics, 14*, 479–526. https://doi.org/10.1007/BF01065445

Menda, G., Uhr, J. H., Wyttenbach, R. A., Vermeylen, F. M., Smith, D. M., Harrington, L. C., & Hoy, R. R. (2013). Associative learning in the dengue vector mosquito, *Aedes aegypti*: Avoidance of a previously attractive odor or surface color that is paired with an aversive stimulus. *Journal of Experimental Biology, 216*, 218–223. https://doi.org/10.1242/jeb.074898

Mingee, C. M. (2013). Retention of a brightness discrimination task in Paramecia, *P. caudatum. International Journal of Comparative Psychology, 26*, 202–212. https://escholarship.org/uc/item/5428c5xn

Nelson, M. C. (1971). Classical conditioning in the blowfly (*Phormia regina*): Associative and excitatory factors. *Journal of Comparative and Physiological Psychology, 77*, 353–368. https://psycnet.apa.org/doi/10.1037/h0031882

Nepoux, V., Babin, A., Haag, C., Kawecki, T. J., & Le Rouzic, A. (2015). Quantitative genetics of learning ability and resistance to stress in *Drosophila melanogaster. Ecology and Evolution, 5*, 543–556. https://doi.org/10.1002/ece3.1379

Nöbel, S., Allain, M., Isabel, G., & Danchin, E. (2018). Mate copying in *Drosophila melanogaster* males. *Animal Behaviour, 141*, 9–15. https://doi.org/10.1016/j.anbehav.2018.04.019

North, G., & Greenspan, R. J. (2007). *Invertebrate neurobiology*. Cold Spring Laboratory Press.

Perez, M., Rolland, U., Giurfa, M., & d'Ettorre, P. (2013). Sucrose responsiveness, learning success, and task specialization in ants. *Learning & Memory, 20*, 417–420. https://doi.org/10.1101/lm.031427.113

Perlman, R. L., & Pastan, I. (1971). The role of cyclic AMP in bacteria. *Current Topics in Cellular Regulation, 3*, 117–134.

Perry, C. J., Barron, A. B., & Cheng, K. (2013). Invertebrate learning and cognition: Relating phenomena to neural substrate. *WIREs Cognitive Science, 4*, 561–582. https://doi.org/10.1002/wcs.1248

Piiroinen, S., & Goulson, D. (2016). Chronic neonicotinoid pesticide exposure and parasite stress differentially affects learning in honeybees and bumblebees. *Proceedings of the Royal Society B, 283*, 20160246. https://doi.org/10.1098/rspb.2016.0246

Prokopy, R. J., Reynolds, A. H., & Ent, L.-J. van der (1998). Can *Rhagoletis pomonella* flies (Diptera: Tephritidae) learn to associate presence of food on foliage with foliage colour? *European Journal of Entomology, 95,* 335–341.

Quinn, W. G., Harris, W. A., & Benzer, S. (1974). Conditioned behavior in *Drosophila melanogaster. Proceedings of the National Academy of Sciences, 71,* 708–712. https://doi .org/10.1073/pnas.71.3.708

Raine, N. E. (2009). Cognitive ecology: Environmental dependence of the fitness costs of learning. *Current Biology, 19,* R486–R488. https://doi.org/10.1016/j.cub.2009.04.047

Rains, G. C., Utley, S. L., & Lewis, W. J. (2006). Behavioral monitoring of trained insects for chemical detection. *Biotechnology Progress, 22,* 2–8. https://doi.org/10.1021/bp050164p

Ramírez, G., Fagundez, C., Grosso, J. P., Argibay, P., Arenas, A., & Farina, W. M. (2016). Odor experiences during preimaginal stages cause behavioral and neural plasticity in adult honeybees. *Frontiers in Behavioral Neuroscience, 10,* 1–14. https://doi.org/10.3389/fnbeh .2016.00105

Raubenheimer, D., & Blackshaw, J. (1994). Locusts learn to associate visual stimuli with drinking. *Journal of Insect Behavior, 7,* 569–575. https://psycnet.apa.org/doi/10.1007/ BF02025450

Raubenheimer, D., & Tucker, D. (1997). Associative learning by locusts: Pairing of visual cues with consumption of protein and carbohydrate. *Animal Behaviour, 54,* 1449–1459. https://doi.org/10.1006/anbe.1997.0542

Reaume, C. J., Sokolowski, M. B., & Mery, F. (2011). A natural genetic polymorphism affects retroactive interference in *Drosophila melanogaster. Proceedings of the Royal Society B, 278,* 91–98. https://doi.org/10.1098/rspb.2010.1337

Resh, V. H., & Cardé, R. T. (Eds.). (2003). *Encyclopedia of insects.* Elsevier Science, Academic Press.

Saigusa, T., Tero, A., Nakagaki, T., & Kuramoto, Y. (2008). Amoebae anticipate periodic events. *Physical Review Letters, 100,* 018101. https://doi.org/10.1103/PhysRevLett.100 .018101

Seugnet, L., Suzuki, Y., Donlea, J. M., Gottschalk, L., & Shaw, P. J. (2011). Sleep deprivation during early-adult development results in long-lasting learning deficits in adult *Drosophila. Sleep, 34,* 137–146. https://doi.org/10.1093/sleep/34.2.137

Shirakawa, T., Gunji, Y.-P., & Miyake, Y. (2011). An associative learning experiment using the plasmodium of *Physarum polycephalum. Nano Communication Networks, 2,* 99–105. https://doi.org/10.1016/j.nancom.2011.05.002

Smid, H. M., Wang, G., Bukovinszky, T., Steidle, J. L. M., Bleeker, M. A. K., van Loon, J. J. A., & Vet, L. E. M. (2007). Species-specific acquisition and consolidation of long-term memory in parasitic wasps. *Proceeding of the Royal Society B, 274,* 1539–1546. https:// doi.org/10.1098/rspb.2007.0305

Sokolowski, M. B. C., Disma, G., & Abramson, C. I. (2010). A paradigm for operant conditioning in blow flies (*Phormia terrae novae* Robineau-Desvoidy, 1830). *Journal of the Experimental Analysis of Behavior, 93,* 81–89. https://doi.org/10.1901/jeab.2010.93-81

Srinivasan, M. V. (2010). Honey bees as a model for vision, perception, and cognition. *Annual Review of Entomology, 55,* 267–284. https://doi.org/10.1146/annurev.ento .010908.164537

Stejskal, K., Streinzer, M., Dyer, A., Paulus, H. F., & Spaethe, J. (2015). Functional significance of labellum pattern variation in a sexually deceptive orchid (*Ophrys heldreichii*): Evidence of individual signature learning effects. *PLoS ONE, 10*(11), e0142971. https://doi.org/10 .1371/journal.pone.0142971

Stockton, D. G., Martini, X., Pratt, J. M., & Stelinski, L. L. (2016). The influence of learning on host plant preference in a significant phytopathogen vector, *Diaphorina citri. PLoS ONE, 11*(3), e0149815. https://doi.org/10.1371/journal.pone.0149815

Stockton, D. G., Pescitelli, L. E., Martini, X., & Stelinski, L. L. (2017). Female mate preference in an invasive phytopathogen vector: How learning may influence mate choice and fecundity in *Diaphorina citri*. *Entomologia Experimentalis et Applicata*, *164*, 16–26. https://doi.org/10.1111/eea.12590

Thellier, M., & Lüttge, U. (2012). Plant memory: A tentative model. *Plant Biology*, *15*, 1–12. https://doi.org/10.1111/j.1438-8677.2012.00674.x

Tibbetts, E. A., Injaian, A., Sheehan, M. J., & Desjardins, N. (2018). Intraspecific variation in learning: Worker wasps are less able to learn and remember individual conspecific faces than queen wasps. *American Naturalist*, *191*, 595–603. https://doi.org/10.1086/696848

Tomberlin, J. K., Rains, G. C., Allan, S. A., Sanford, M. R., & Lewis, W. J. (2006). Associative learning of odor with food- or blood-meal by *Culex quinquefasciatus* Say (Diptera: Culicidae). *Naturwissenschaften*, *93*, 551. https://doi.org/10.1007/s00114-006-0143-9

Verzijden, M. N., & Svensson, E. I. (2016). Interspecific interactions and learning variability jointly drive geographic differences in mate preferences. *Evolution*, *70*, 1896–1903. https://doi.org/10.1111/evo.12982

Vinauger, C., Lahondère, C., Wolff, G. H., Locke, L. T., Liaw, J. E., Parrish, J. Z., Akbari, O. S., Dickinson, M. H., & Riffell, J. A. (2018). Modulation of host learning in *Aedes aegypti* mosquitoes. *Current Biology*, *28*, 333–344. https://doi.org/10.1016/j.cub.2017.12.015

Vinauger, C., & Lazzari, C. R. (2015). Circadian modulation of learning ability in a disease vector insect, *Rhodinus prolixus*. *Journal of Experimental Biology*, *218*, 3110–3117. https://doi.org/10.1242/jeb.119057

Vogel, D., & Dussutour, A. (2016). Direct transfer of learned behavior via cell fusion in non-neural organisms. *Proceedings of the Royal Society B*, *283*, 20162382. https://doi.org/10.1098/rspb.2016.2382

Wang, X., Green, D. S., Roberts, S. P., & de Belle, S. (2007). Thermal disruption of mushroom body development and odor learning in *Drosophila*. *PLoS ONE*, *2*(11), e0177581. https://doi.org/10.1371/journal.pone.0001125

Weinstein, A. M., Davis, B. J., Menz, M. H. M., Dixon, K. W., & Phillips, R. D. (2016). Behaviour of sexually deceived ichneumonid wasps and its implications for pollination in Cryptostylis (Orchidaceae). *Biological Journal of the Linnean Society*, *119*, 283–298. https://doi.org/10.1111/bij.12841

Westerman, E. L., & Monteiro, A. (2013). Odour influences whether females learn to prefer or to avoid wing patterns of male butterflies. *Animal Behaviour*, *86*, 1139–1145. https://doi.org/10.1016/j.anbehav.2013.09.002

Williams-Simon, P. A., Posey, C., Mitchell, S., Ng'oma, E., Mrkvicka, J. A., Zars, T., & King, E. G. (2019). Multiple genetic loci affect place learning and memory performance in *Drosophila melanogaster*. *Genes, Brains and Behavior*, *18*, e12581. https://doi.org/10.1111/gbb.12581

Wilson, J. K., & Woods, H. A. (2016). Innate and learned olfactory responses in a wild population of the egg parasitoid Trichogramma (Hymenoptera: Trichogrammatidae). *Journal of Insect Science*, *16*(1), 1–8. https://doi.org/10.1093/jisesa/iew108

Zhang, H., Lin, M., Shi, H., Ji, W., Huang, L., Zhang, X., Shen, S., Gao, R., Wu, S., Tian, C., Yang, Z., Zhang, G., He, S., Wang, H., Saw, T., Chen, Y., & Ouyang, Q. (2014). Programming a Pavlovian-like conditioning circuit in *Escherichia coli*. *Nature Communications*, *5*, 3102. https://doi.org/10.1038/ncomms4102

4

EXPERIMENTAL EVOLUTION AND MECHANISMS FOR PREPARED LEARNING

Aimee S. Dunlap and Andreia F. Dexheimer

Evolved preparedness, the notion that a species' evolutionary history can make animals more prepared for some combinations of stimuli, responses, and reinforcers is a powerful and useful approach to thinking about animal learning in nature. Highly biologically relevant learning about danger and sex have enabled strong predictions about learning in these contexts. In practice, studies of preparedness have suffered from a lack of knowledge of that evolutionary history. Investigators have been able to recognize the "biological constraints" imposed by natural selection only after the fact, leaving this commonsense hypothesis about the historical connectedness of associations testable only through *post hoc* approaches. This limitation has made progress in testing ideas of evolutionary preparedness difficult, as biologists and comparative psychologists avoid the trap of "just-so stories" about why an observed case of learning is adaptive, and we lack a time machine to directly observe an animal's evolutionary past. However, recent work on a tractable theoretical framework allows for prospective predictions of preparedness that can then be empirically tested. The technique of experimental evolution allows for directly testing preparedness through the manipulation of variables across evolutionary time (e.g., Garland & Rose, 2009). Methodological advances in genomics and transcriptomics are now widely available, and an expanding toolbox is accessible in neurobiology, allowing the field to connect genotype to phenotype. In this chapter, we discuss the role of changing environments on theory of when preparedness should evolve, demonstrate what we can learn from experimental evolution, provide testable predictions for how mechanisms may evolve, and outline some exciting future directions.

4.1 MANY MECHANISMS CAN RESULT IN BIOLOGICAL PREPAREDNESS

An important concept to consider is that for behavior to be adaptive (i.e., affect fitness), the specific mechanisms underlying the learning that is employed do not matter as much as the end result of that cognitive process (Domjan et al., 2004). For instance, evolution can select for some associations to be more readily learned than others, although selection may not be acting directly on associative learning processes. Although preparedness is often taken as shorthand for prepared learning specifically, what makes that learning "prepared" doesn't necessarily come as a result of changes in associative learning alone. Despite a critique of prepared learning hinging on the specifics of selective association (Dwyer, 2015), preparedness functionally encompasses a wide range of mechanisms. In his original work on preparedness, Seligman (1970) acknowledged that evolution could prepare animals on levels from perception to the rules of learning themselves. Natural selection ultimately acts upon function, which then evolves through changes in mechanism; thus, thinking of biological preparedness more broadly than just biological preparedness of associative learning is useful. Nonassociative learning, such as increased sensitization and less habituation, can serve to enhance the associative learning of a prepared stimulus. Interactions between multiple stimuli can also affect the strength of learning.

We know that some experiences affect behavior more than others. The term salience is often used to connote that a stimulus or situation is simply important in some way. Over the years, the term "salience" has often been used vaguely to explain why some stimuli are more important than others in the learning process. It is a slippery word that is applied across a number of disciplines. Rescorla and Wagner (1972) used the salience of a stimulus as a parameter in their classic learning model, in which salience could influence the rate of conditioning. Salience can occur as a result of evolutionary effects, without experience, but can also be modified with learning: Experience with a paired association can cause a stimulus to acquire salience (Mackintosh, 1974). The salience of a given stimulus in the absence of experience is often a result of evolution, and, in a subset of cases, we argue it is a type of preparedness (see Silva and Silva, Chapter 12; Blaisdell and Seitz, Chapter 26). An animal's evolutionary history directs what it attends to and what it ignores. This connection between salience and preparedness is useful, and encourages us to consider preparedness broadly rather than preparedness as being limited to a particular type of learning. A full understanding of the evolution of preparedness must take sensory changes, attention, and bias, as well as learning and memory, into account. This understanding requires a clear knowledge of the selective history of a population. Despite being a section in nearly every textbook of animal learning, the evolutionary processes behind preparedness are still not well studied, either empirically or theoretically.

4.2 EVOLUTION OF BIOLOGICAL PREPAREDNESS

Early thoughts on preparedness were primarily conceptual rather than mathematical, but the key framing remains that patterns across evolutionary time of the connectedness of stimuli and responses would lead to the evolution of preparedness. Associative learning is based on causal relationships, and if one stimulus is more likely to be coupled with a given reward, then it might be advantageous to learn this association better than other not-so-common or unreliable associations. In other words, evolution should select for some associations to be more readily learned than others. And stronger correlations, either positive or negative, over evolutionary time should result in stronger preparedness or contrapreparedness.

RELIABILITY AS A KEY PREDICTIVE VARIABLE

The connectedness of stimuli and responses can be described in terms of reliability: how reliably are specific unconditioned stimulus (US) and conditioned stimulus (CS) pairings (or stimulus and response pairings, etc.) connected across evolutionary time? Reliability has long been considered an important component of animal learning. In behavioral ecology, there are rich theoretical frameworks for understanding the role of environmental change on the evolution and function of information use (e.g., Dall et al., 2005). Broadly, reliability is a key component of models of information use because it determines the value of information (e.g., Koops, 2004): Information that is more reliable better enables an animal to predict the future state of the environment, thus matching its behavior to that anticipated state. Reliability is important in predicting when learning generally should evolve in theoretical space and when it actually evolves in experimental evolution studies (Dunlap & Stephens, 2009).

ROLE OF MULTI-STIMULUS INTERACTIONS IN THE ADAPTIVE VALUE OF LEARNING

Learning about multicomponent stimuli in a stimulus-rich natural world is a major area of current work. We describe just a few interesting aspects of this work, because the ideas developed previously scale quite well to evolutionary time. When multiple stimuli are present, the most reliable stimulus is typically learned. For instance, bumble bees switch between social and floral cues based on their relative reliability (Dunlap et al., 2016), and blue jays show similar patterns for learning about color and shape (Rubi & Stephens, 2015). In both cases, a bias is evident when both cues are perfectly reliable, with bees favoring social cues and jays favoring color cues. Work in the area of receiver psychology has developed these ideas in the context of co-evolving communication systems, with a special focus on the evolution of multicomponent signals. Two recent insights from this work highlight intriguing points. First, the impact of reliability on following a signal can interact with the frequency of those events, resulting in the evolution of signal-following for rare events (Rubi & Stephens, 2016). A second point comes from work on the role of learning in the evolution of Batesian mimicry, namely, that, in both theory and experiment, the learning that evolves may not be optimal but rather what is "just good enough" to gain fitness (e.g., Kikuchi & Pfennig, 2013).

FROM RELIABILITY TO THE EVOLUTION OF PREPAREDNESS

To create tractable tests for the evolution of preparedness, we first need specific hypotheses about how different selective histories can create different levels of preparedness to learn from different types of experience. The conceptual basis of the evolution of preparedness was first formalized as a mathematical model by Dunlap and Stephens (2014) and was based on a general model of behavioral plasticity, known as the "flag model" (e.g., Dunlap & Stephens, 2016). The flag model, so named because its basic shape resembles a naval flag, was successful in applications involving the reliability of signal-following and learning in the bee and jay examples described earlier. The preparedness model is logically similar in framing and outcome to within-lifetime reliability models. In describing this model, it might be useful to think in terms of a behavior occurring in its natural context.

Let's imagine a foraging bee that encounters flower types that either provide pollen or nectar, both equally important resources. Each of the pollen-providing and nectar-providing flowers creates a different foraging condition (C1 and C2, respectively) that requires a different foraging pattern. For instance, scrabbling and grooming for collecting pollen (C1) and extending the proboscis and probing to collect nectar (C2). We can call these two possible alternative actions, Action 1 and Action 2, in which Action 1 is better if Condition 1 is true and Action 2 is better if Condition 2 is true. Finally, we can imagine that two forms of experience about flowers are possible, for instance color and odor, and these can be arbitrarily represented by S and T. When we say forms of experience (color and odor), we mean that alternatives exist. For instance, in a simple case of two alternatives, color (S) might be blue or violet and, similarly, odor (T) might be the floral volatiles, geraniol or linalool.

We can then incorporate the concept of statistical reliability, using the conditional probability that a cue available for learning reliably predicts the best action for an animal to take. We imagine that the occurrence of these different states says something, statistically speaking, about the underlying situation. We represent this statistical information via two conditional probabilities, $q = P(S_a|C_1) = P(S_b|C_2)$, so that when q is 1.0, encountering S_a means that Condition C_1 must be true, and encountering S_b means that C_2 must be true; alternatively, a q value of ½ means that S (a or b) has no informational value. We call q the reliability of S. Similarly, the reliability of experience T is defined as $r = P(T_a|C_1) = P(T_b|C_2)$. The simplest version of the preparedness problem asks: Should you learn S or should you learn T?

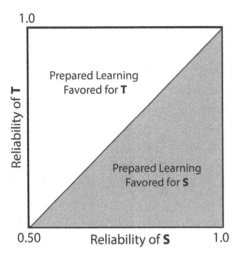

FIGURE 4.1. A subset of predictions for the flag model of preparedness. The axes run from 0.50, completely unreliable, to 1.0, completely reliable. Evolution should favor prepared learning of the most reliable stimulus. Where reliability is equal for each experience, the predictions are neutral: both experiences are equally favored. The model also applies to values that are below 0.50 and reliably predictive in the opposite direction. The function becomes a mirror image across the axis and is where we would predict contrapreparedness to evolve. (Adapted with permission from Dunlap and Stephens (2014). Experimental evolution of prepared learning. *Proceedings of the National Academy of Sciences, 111*(32), 11750–11755. https://doi.org/10.1073/pnas.1404176111.)

The answer for a broad range of conditions is that you should follow the most reliable of the two experience types (Figure 4.1). In terms of prepared-ness, then, our hypothesis is that animals should be more prepared to respond to experiences that have been reliable in applying the correct action to the appropriate condition, and, conversely, they should not be prepared to respond to experiences that have been unreliable over generational time.

The benefit of the flag model for preparedness is that it is extremely amenable to experimentation. The variables are tractable across a range of applications and can be manipulated across generations. Because the model makes no predictions about which specific mechanisms will evolve, no *a priori* constraints need to be invoked. Although a few models might incorp-orate selected aspects of preparedness into simulations as decision rules, theoretical work for preparedness remains underdeveloped. An extension of the flag model by Rubi and Stephens (2016) actually suggests that the preparedness model may form a special case of a larger theoretical space where the interaction of reliabilities of S and T also interact with how frequently events that are important to fitness occur. Additional predictions of this model are situations in which both S and T experiences should be used to inform behavior, rather than the single most reliable experience, and areas where both S and T should be always accepted or always rejected.

4.3 EMPIRICAL TESTS OF THE EVOLUTION OF PREPAREDNESS

To rigorously test these hypotheses, we must control or measure the selective histories that are, after all, the putative causal factors in the evolution of prepared learning. Experimental evolution is a powerful technique for creating and understanding how phenotypes evolve in response to our theoretical predictions. Experimental evolution thus solves the classic "time machine" problem of evolution because we can both control and observe the patterns of experience across generations, producing populations with different behaviors assumed to reflect cognitive attributes. Once populations have evolved, other important hypotheses remain about evolution with tests of life history trade-offs, economics of choices, and adaptive and functional aspects of evolved responses. In experimental evolution, we are not selecting directly on a specific discrete phenotype, for instance, a learning ability above 90% accurate. Instead, we are selecting for any behavior consistent with the selection landscape we have created, and a suite of traits may evolve.

A single experimental evolution study, thus far, directly tests predictions about how patterns of reliability influence the evolution of preparedness. Using fruit flies (*Drosophila melanogaster*), Dunlap and Stephens (2014) were able to evolve prepared learning for color cues over odor cues, and vice versa, as predicted by their relative reliabilities. To do this, they used an oviposition preference procedure originally developed by Mery and Kawecki (2002). This experimental paradigm is based upon a female fruit fly's decision of where to lay her eggs, which involves attending to many aspects of potential substrates, including color, taste, odor, density, texture, and any conspecifics present. Two dishes of egg-laying media are presented to populations of flies in two separate presentations: an experience phase and a consequence phase. In all cases the dishes are "labeled" with different colors and different odors so that one dish will be, for instance, blue+almond-scented and the other will be aqua+cherry-scented. In the first presentation, the "experience" phase, one dish is also marked with an aversive chemical, quinine; thus, flies experience one media that is favorable and one that is aversive. In the second phase, the consequence phase, the colors and odors are present but quinine is absent. The name "consequence phase" derives from the fact that eggs are reared from only one of the plates. The reliability of this predictiveness of the cue pairing in the consequence phase is manipulated through the conditional probabilities in which the aversive quinine-color and quinine-odor associations indicate which plates should then be avoided. The preparedness problem arises because the flies can avoid the color that was previously paired with quinine, or they can avoid the odor that was previously paired with quinine. Populations of flies are then assigned to a treatment in which color-quinine associations are reliable, and odor-quinine

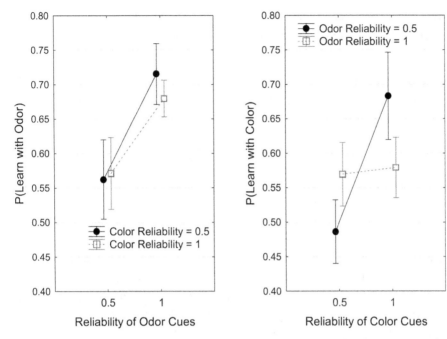

FIGURE 4.2. Data from Dunlap and Stephens (2014) showing the results of learning tests for fly lines within each treatment after 40 generations of selection, from which we calculate the proportion of choices consistent with learning. The left panel shows the strength of learning for odor cues alone, and the right panel shows learning for color cues alone. Each of the four treatments is depicted in each graph, but are arranged to emphasize the focal stimulus modality of each panel.

(Adapted with permission from Dunlap and Stephens (2014). Experimental evolution of prepared learning. *Proceedings of the National Academy of Sciences*, 111(32), 11750–11755. https://doi.org/10.1073/pnas.1404176111.)

associates are unreliable across many generations of selection; while assigning others to treatments where the reverse is true. After 40 generations of selection, all the lines of flies are assessed for learning about color cues alone and then learning about odor cues alone.

Figure 4.2 shows the major results of this first experimental study of the evolution of preparedness. After 40 generations of selection, fly lines that experienced reliable odor cues but unreliable color cues across their experimental evolution history show better learning for odor cues than lines where odor cues are unreliable. A similar result is found for lines which experienced reliable color cues and unreliable odor cues: Here color reliability predicts learning about color as long as odor was unreliable across time. However, this effect disappears once odor cues are reliable. The results for these cases in which both types of cues are equally reliable are analogous to tests of the flag model for reliability within generations. As with bees and jays, when both experiences are equally reliable or equally unreliable, one experience is favored over the other. Over the course of the experiment, flies evolved to favor learning about odor in the equal reliability treatments. Although much care was taken to balance stimuli, this outcome may reflect in part the importance for odor cues generally across hundreds of thousands of years in making oviposition decisions.

4.4 GENERAL INSIGHTS FROM EXPERIMENTAL EVOLUTION AND ARTIFICIAL SELECTION STUDIES OF LEARNING

A handful of studies in the past 20 years have used experimental evolution or artificial selection approaches to look broadly at the evolution of learning. Although none of these studies explicitly tested prepared learning specifically, a few conclusions can be drawn about preparedness. In the groundbreaking work of Mery and Kawecki (2002), flies that evolved enhanced learning also showed enhanced learning abilities to novel stimuli not encountered during experimental evolution, which is evidence for a general learning mechanism. This generalized learning process was further shown with enhanced learning and memory for a different task, and different stimuli (Mery et al., 2007). The evolved learning presented life history trade-offs for flies, with effects on life span and larval competitive ability (Burger et al., 2008; Mery & Kawecki, 2003). In producing these flies, a cue for learning was always completely reliable, but the reliability of individual stimuli was not manipulated in a way that would allow preparedness to evolve for one cue or modality over another. In a later study, Mery and Kawecki (2004) produced both enhanced learning and innate bias in completely fixed environments with perfect reliability. Dunlap and Stephens (2009) manipulated reliability and environmental certainty to evolve enhanced learning, as well as innate bias without learning, showing that unreliability was necessary for innate bias alone to evolve. Thus, high reliability is undoubtedly important in the evolution of learning generally, but reliability of forms of experience are necessary for preparedness to evolve.

Whereas experimental evolution experiments focus on the process of evolution and can allow for any strategy to evolve that can be successful in the manipulated environmental conditions, artificial selection experiments select directly for a specific trait based on a chosen performance threshold. Two recent research programs shed light on the evolution of learning generally. In work by Liefting et al. (2018; see Liefting, Chapter 5), parasitoid wasps were artificially selected to associate color with a food reward. They found enhanced learning to novel stimuli, but they also found enhanced learning for females across another sensory modality, olfaction, as well as enhanced learning for males under a different behavioral context, namely, mating. Selection quickly acted upon gene areas and networks known to be involved in cognition (Kraaijeveld et al., 2018). Again, reliability for learning generally begets a generalized learning ability without evidence of a specific preparedness.

Selecting directly on the brain yields slightly different responses. Kotrschal et al. (2013) artificially selected guppies for large and small relative brain size, finding correlated differences in learning performance. Further tests of their lines uncovered correlated differences in cognition between the sexes. For instance, large-brained females learned better on numerical assays (Kotrschal et al., 2013), while large-brained males learned better on mazes testing for spatial search of mates (Kotrschal et al., 2014). These studies are useful in thinking about the generalization of learning and of constraints generally, but studies involving artificial selection on prepared learning will be particularly valuable in elucidating the evolved mechanisms responsible, as well as their correlated traits.

Finally, we highlight another promising approach for testing the evolution of preparedness: digital evolution. Digital evolution consists of a virtual environment in which digital, self-replicating beings are subject to evolutionary forces, such as mutation and natural selection (e.g., Adami et al., 2000). This approach is important for two reasons. First, it allows for the exploration of *de novo* behaviors, with the digital beings as a true *tabula rasa*, which is, of course, impossible to do with animals. Second, it allows for tests of repeatability of mechanism within evolution. Recent work by Pontes et al. (2020) tested *de novo* digital evolution of associative learning across four different experimental environments, finding that associative learning repeatedly arose through the recurrent evolution of the same building blocks, but also that nonassociative strategies arose and performed well. These findings echo experimental evolution in that many mechanisms can evolve to solve the same environmental problem.

4.5 LIMITATIONS AND CHALLENGES OF AN EXPERIMENTAL EVOLUTION APPROACH

Of course, not everything selected for will evolve in a predictably tidy way. Our laboratory found that, while attempting to evolve a response to a supernormal color stimulus, we instead produced female flies with increasing fecundity because they chose every option by allocating increasing numbers of eggs in each population (Marcus et al., 2017). The reasons for this specific result remain unexplored, but many examples in experimental evolution for noncognitive traits demonstrate constraints and unexpected results due to developmental and pleiotropic effects, or unanticipated solutions to the evolutionary problem posed (like increasing fecundity). Rather than being a nuisance for testing theory, these effects are themselves important insights into the variables that affect evolution in natural systems. An additional issue is that our animals are already the product of a long evolutionary past and finding neutral stimuli can be incredibly difficult, if not impossible (e.g., Silva, 2018; see Silva and Silva, Chapter 12). In experimentally evolving preparedness in flies, lengthy psychophysics titration trials were needed to find stimuli that were equally attractive and would not overshadow each other from the start of the experiment, approximating neutrality as much as possible. Practical aspects can also constrain which species can be used for experimental approaches; smaller animals with faster development times have been the traditional choice for good reasons. However, the use of vertebrates is common in the experimental evolution literature, and manipulating reliability over evolutionary time is absolutely possible (Garland & Rose, 2009).

Experimental evolution is a powerful, but extremely time-consuming, approach, and more studies are needed to clarify the weighty remaining questions. A full understanding of the evolution of preparedness must take into account each of the mechanistic/physiological levels in which evolution can act upon to produce biologically prepared behavior. This requires a clear knowledge of the selective history of a population, but does not require experimental evolution (Morand-Ferron 2017). Well-chosen natural populations with known selective histories can be valuable in these tests. To make these comparisons stronger, we need a framework of predictions for mechanisms resulting in biological preparedness.

4.6 PREDICTIONS FOR EVOLVED MECHANISMS IN BROAD BIOLOGICAL PREPAREDNESS

The evolutionary theory of preparedness is agnostic with regards to the mechanisms that may evolve to accomplish prepared learning. Although Dunlap and Stephens (2014) showed differential learning responses, the full mechanisms underlying these evolved differences remain unexamined. Many untested questions remain concerning how the evolved prepared learning is accomplished and how it functions in a multi-stimulus world. In this section, we present some predictions, as well as explanations, for how evolution can prepare an animal to make choices about its environment.

SELECTIVE ASSOCIATIONS

A special and relatively well-studied case of prepared learning is selective associations. In selective associations, there is an interaction between a stimulus and a reinforcer that results in faster acquisition of a conditioned response (CR) with one CS than another, but an opposite effect with a different reinforcer (e.g., Linwick et al., 1981; LoLordo, 1979). A crucial part of the definition of a selective association is that these differences in acquisition must be due to that interaction and not to any particular feature of the stimuli, such as salience or intensity. As with the textbook example of the Garcia effect, evolved preference can result in classic selective associations (Garcia & Koelling, 1966).

SENSORY AND PERCEPTUAL BIAS

Stimuli interact with an animal's sensory systems and each sensory system may favor some stimuli over others. Salience is often invoked in this context, in which animals focus on stimuli that are more prominent in some way. These effects can be influenced by an animal's perception, which can be affected by physiological changes, such as a change in receptor function, or by changes in cognitive processes, such as stimulus filtering and tuning (Hauser & Chang, 2017). One way in which preparedness can evolve is through constraints in the sensory and cognitive systems by favoring (or hindering) some stimuli over others. But sensory and perceptual biases are not necessarily context dependent, and may be co-opted from their original evolutionary context to their current use. For example, what are called sensory exploitation and sensory drive models in the sexual selection litera-ture suggest that females have preexisting biases that evolved in a context outside of mating (e.g., foraging for food), and these evolved preferences can play a role in the perception of mating signals (e.g., Stevens, 2013). Thus, preparedness that has evolved in one setting may influence multiple contexts across an animal's behavior.

ATTENTIONAL PROCESSES AND SAMPLING

Stimuli that have been evolutionarily prepared should elicit increased atten-tion. Once perception of a stimulus is possible, selective attention can have strong effects on what is learned, with the assumption that animals attend to more salient information (e.g., Knudsen, 2007). Although attention can be mediated at a perceptual level, the salience of cues can also be motivationally informed, as well as modified by learning. The general logic of this assertion is that when a predictive cue is found, attention is increasingly committed to that cue while attention to irrelevant stimuli decreases. The probability of encountering a given stimulus and forming an experience is itself affected by both attention and perceptual bias, and this basic environmental sampling affects experiential learning (e.g., Snell-Rood & Steck, 2015). Thus, prepared-ness can function, through innate preference and enhanced attention, to shape learning occurring by both enhancing and inhibiting the tendency to sample a given resource (Maharaj et al., 2018).

NONASSOCIATIVE LEARNING: HABITUATION
AND SENSITIZATION

Habituation and sensitization, which describe changes in responsiveness to repeated stimulation are ubiquitous and important forms of learning, espe-cially in narrowing down which of the abundant stimuli in the world are relevant to fitness. Habituation is typically stimulus specific and not due to simple sensory adaptation outside of the brain. Sensitization is not stimulus specific, but can reflect a change in state that then allows reactivity to increase for a number of cues. Preparedness/salience should result in the evolved salient stimulus becoming more resistant to habituation and result in enhanced sensitization.

INTERACTING STIMULI: BLOCKING AND OVERSHADOWING

Two relevant paradigms address how multiple stimuli may interact: If multiple stimuli are contiguously presented during learning, the more salient stimulus can overshadow potential learning of another stimulus (overshadowing); prior exposure to a stimulus can then block the learning of future presentations of a different stimulus (blocking). Effects of blocking and overshadowing are well described in classical conditioning, are a predicted consequence of selective associations, and can be a predicted consequence of evolutionary preparedness. With preparedness, an animal's evolutionary history of reliability of stimuli can result in enhanced salience of a stimulus. These effects are biologically significant for learning, but have not always been considered by behaviorists working on multi-stimulus treatments of learning in ecological settings. More salient stimuli are assumed to be the stimuli that block and/or overshadow the learning of other stimuli. Overshadowing has long been described as being affected by the relative intensities of stimuli (e.g., Pavlov, 1927). In this case, evolved salience or sensory changes can mediate overshadowing. But it has long been known that one stimulus can overshadow another, even when both are relatively salient (e.g., Mackintosh, 1974). Prepared learning should show classic blocking effects: Prepared stimuli will be more likely to block learning of less prepared stimuli, and also less likely to be blocked by other stimuli (Köksal et al., 1994). Prepared learning should also show classic overshadowing effects: Prepared stimuli and pairings will overshadow learning of other stimuli present (Oberling et al., 2000).

EXTINCTION

In extinction, the animal retains the learned information, but no longer responds in the absence of the US. However, the learned response quickly returns upon the restoration of the US. Early work by Garcia and Koelling (1966) showed that prepared learning in the form of taste aversions was extremely resistant to extinction. Conceptually, any learned association important enough across evolutionary time to become prepared should also be more robust to patterns of non-reward once acquired (Krause et al., 2003). Extinction, like forgetting, to which we turn next, is a crucial part of the puzzle in determining how reversible or malleable prepared learning is within the lifetime of an animal.

FORGETTING

The basic predictions of adaptive forgetting follow from the value of information: Because the value of information is specifically tied to its ability to predict future states of the environment, more important information will be remembered for longer periods of time (e.g., Dunlap et al., 2009; McNamara & Houston, 1987). Empirical work in both psychology and behavioral ecology demonstrates that valuable information is remembered longer, and that forgetting will be adaptive for certain stimuli and experiences, for instance, according to patterns of change in the environment (e.g., Dunlap & Stephens, 2012; Kraemer & Golding, 1997), as well as for learning about evolutionarily important events like predation (e.g., Ferrari et al., 2012). A number of neural mechanisms for active forgetting are being identified (e.g., Davis & Zhong, 2017), placing theory on adaptive forgetting squarely in the range of physiological possibility. Prepared learning should be associated with longer memories. Less clear are predictions for contraprepared learning, since for that learning to actually occur, many more trials will have happened, increasing practice, and, potentially, memory length. These predictions again relate to the question of reversibility and malleability of prepared learning within single lifetimes.

4.7 TOWARD THE FUTURE

The study of preparedness lies at the confluence of the psychology of animal learning, and ecology and evolution. After decades of slow development, we now have the techniques to answer questions about preparedness, from evolution to molecular mechanism. Now is an exciting time to be thinking about biological preparedness! Why animals learn some things better than others is at the heart of what can make behavior adaptive. By working from relatively simple theory, it is possible to directly test these hypotheses and to observe what should be evolving with prepared learning. Two approaches to the experimental study of behavioral phenotype are especially promising. One is using experimental and digital evolution to create an evolutionary history across populations and directly test theory. Another is using natural populations, continuing to move from *post hoc* explanations to using observed differences in patterns of change to propose testable predictions about preparedness.

Theoretical treatments of how preparedness will evolve are still in early stages and more work is needed. For instance, extensions of the flag model framework can be used to make predictions about stimulus specificity as well as within- and between-modality effects for groups of stimuli. This approach is particularly interesting when considering the role of sensory constraints and is a fascinating direction for testing the mechanisms of evolution for preparedness broadly. We also need further theory on how preparedness will affect decision-making. Decision-making is typically not considered in the preparedness framework, but evolved preparedness can influence decision-making in many ways. For example, we can consider how different experiences are integrated and how innate aspects like salience will be weighted with experience. Finally, decision rules themselves can evolve to influence preparedness (e.g., Fawcett et al., 2014), and these predictions can be tested through experimental evolution (Burnham et al., 2015).

Although the first experimental evolution test of basic theory on when prepared learning would evolve was successful (Dunlap & Stephens, 2014), many questions remain untested. For instance, how prepared learning was accomplished evolutionarily, and how it then functions in a multi-stimulus world. Other important questions remain about the evolved phenotype with tests of life history trade-offs, economics of choices, the adaptive and functional aspects of evolved responses, and the importance of context in preparedness. Malleability and reversibility of evolved responses both in a single lifetime and across evolutionary time remain unaddressed. Large swathes of theoretical space remain empirically untested. For instance, a continuum of reliability remains untested, as does the evolution of contrapreparedness, and an evolutionary test of the flag model extension by Rubi and Stephens (2016), which suggests that rare events are important in the evolution of preparedness.

For both experimentally evolved populations of animals and natural populations, rich and detailed tests of mechanism remain possible. But investigations of mechanisms can also go deeper, from using new techniques in genomics for understanding the genetic and evolutionary underpinnings of phenotypic change in gene expression and the regulation of gene networks, to newly tractable aspects of neurophysiology. The development of powerful genomics tools opens many possibilities. For instance, we can predict allelic differences in genes involved in the sensory system, in learning and memory, and also across some life history traits. We can also use transcriptomic approaches to look at changes in gene expression during the lifetime in response to exposure to prepared stimuli and associations, and during learning and memory consolidation processes. We have described some results of these techniques for artificial selection, but work on natural populations is also resulting in new insights. For instance, recent population genomics work on facial learning in wasps has shown evidence of hard selective suites of novel mutations on genes associated with a range of cognitive traits, instead of only adaptation on existing genetic variation, testing an important question in cognitive evolution (Miller et al., 2020). Tractable tools in neuroscience allow us to analyze how the observed behavior is being accomplished, as well as the relative contributions of sensory systems versus learning and memory. Enhanced learning for one stimulus modality versus another could be accomplished through innate bias mediated through sensory processes in the peripheral nervous system, for instance, at the level of receptors. The enhanced learning could also be accomplished within central processing in the brain, as information from stimuli are integrated, as learning is occurring, as memories are being consolidated, and as the decision is made using that prior experience. We can look for physical investment into different brain and sensory areas (e.g., Farris & Schulmeister, 2011), and changes in sensory receptors and filtering can be directly measured through neuroanatomical approaches as well as assessed through gene expression and evolutionary genomics (e.g., Brand & Ramírez, 2017; Riffell, 2020). Finally, new techniques allow for the measurement of neuromodulation within learning circuits by monoamines and peptides, allowing us to directly assess how unconditioned stimuli are received in the brain (e.g., Van Damme et al., 2021).

With more applications of new and growing techniques, both in experimental evolution and in genomics and neurobiology, we are poised as a field to fully address long-standing questions about the evolution of cognition, from preparedness to adaptive specializations. We may find that learning, long assumed to be special, like social learning (see Kendal, Chapter 14), is simply a specialized adaptation of generalized learning and preparedness for stimuli, a view that is growing among some practitioners of social learning in animals (Leadbeater & Dawson, 2017; Reader, 2016). And preparedness can shed light on important co-evolved signaling systems, such as that within plant-pollinator dynamics, in which plants evolved floral cues to manipulate pollinators, while pollinators evolved a suite of mechanisms to allow for better collection of resources. Decades of work on biologically relevant learning has shown the power of thinking in a preparedness framework. Continuing these studies, along with developing more theory, conducting more experimental evolution studies, and pursuing the genetic and neurological underpinnings, will help us understand the many fascinating ways in which nature has prepared animals for learning.

REFERENCES

Adami, C., Ofria, C., & Collier, T. C. (2000). Evolution of biological complexity. *Proceedings of the National Academy of Sciences*, 97(9), 4463–4468. https://doi.org/10.1073/pnas.97.9.4463

Brand, P., & Ramírez, S. R. (2017). The evolutionary dynamics of the odorant receptor gene family in corbiculate bees. *Genome Biology and Evolution*, 9(8), 2023–2036. https://doi.org/10.1093/gbe/evx149

Burger, J. M. S., Kolss, M., Pont, J., & Kawecki, T. J. (2008). Learning ability and longevity: A symmetrical evolutionary trade-off in *Drosophila*. *Evolution*, 62(6), 1294–1304. https://doi.org/10.1111/j.1558-5646.2008.00376.x

Burnham, T. C., Dunlap, A. S., & Stephens, D. W. (2015). Experimental evolution and economics. *Sage OPEN* (October–December) 1–17. https://doi.org/10.1177/2158244015612524

Dall, S., Giraldeau, L., Olsson, O., McNamara, J., & Stephens, D. W. (2005). Information and its use by animals in evolutionary ecology. *Trends in Ecology & Evolution, 20*(4), 187–193. https://doi.org/10.1016/j.tree.2005.01.010

Davis, R. L., & Zhong Y. (2017). The biology of forgetting – A perspective. *Neuron, 95*(3), 490–503. https://doi.org/10.1016/j.neuron.2017.05.039

Domjan, M., Cusato, B., & Krause, M. (2004). Learning with arbitrary versus ecological conditioned stimuli: Evidence from sexual conditioning. *Psychonomic Bulletin & Review, 11*(2), 232–246. https://doi.org/10.3758/bf03196565

Dunlap, A. S., McLinn, C. M., MacCormick, H. A., Scott, M. E., & Kerr, B. (2009). Why some memories do not last a lifetime: Dynamic long-term retrieval in changing environments. *Behavioral Ecology, 20*(5), 1096–1105. https://doi.org/10.1093/beheco/arp102

Dunlap, A. S., Nielsen, M. E., Dornhaus, A., & Papaj, D. R. (2016). Foraging bumble bees weigh the reliability of personal and social information. *Current Biology, 26*(9), 1195–1199. https://doi.org/10.1016/j.cub.2016.03.009

Dunlap, A. S., & Stephens, D. W. (2009). Components of change in the evolution of learning and unlearned preference. *Proceedings of the Royal Society B: Biological Sciences, 276* (1670), 3201–3208. https://doi.org/10.1098/rspb.2009.0602

(2012). Tracking a changing environment: optimal sampling, adaptive memory and overnight effects. *Behavioural Processes, 89*(2), 86–94. https://doi.org/10.1016/j.beproc.2011.10.005

(2014). Experimental evolution of prepared learning. *Proceedings of the National Academy of Sciences, 111*(32), 11750–11755. https://doi.org/10.1073/pnas.1404176111

(2016). Reliability, uncertainty, and costs in the evolution of animal learning. *Current Opinion in Behavioral Sciences, 12,* 73–79. https://doi.org/10.1016/j.cobeha.2016.09.010

Dwyer, D. M. (2015). Experimental evolution of sensitivity to a stimulus domain alone is not an example of prepared learning. *Proceedings of the National Academy of Sciences, 112*(5), E385. https://doi.org/10.1073/pnas.1420871112

Farris, S. M., & Schulmeister, S. (2011). Parasitoidism, not sociality, is associated with the evolution of elaborate mushroom bodies in the brains of hymenopteran insects. *Proceedings of the Royal Society B: Biological Sciences, 278*(1707), 940–951. https://doi.org/10.1098/rspb.2010.2161

Fawcett, T. W., Fallenstein, B., Higginson, A. D., Houston, A. I., Mallpress, D. E. W., Trimmer, P. C., & McNamara, J. M. (2014). The evolution of decision rules in complex environments. *Trends in Cognitive Sciences, 18*(3), 153–161. https://doi.org/10.1016/j.tics.2013.12.012

Ferrari, M. C. O., Vrtělová, J., Brown, G. E., & Chivers, D. P. (2012). Understanding the role of uncertainty on learning and retention of predator information. *Animal Cognition, 15*(5), 807–813. https://doi.org/10.1007/s10071-012-0505-y

Garcia, J., & Koelling, R. A. (1966). Relation of cue to consequence in avoidance learning. *Psychonomic Science, 4*(1), 123–124. https://doi.org/10.3758/bf03342209

Garland, T., & Rose, M.R. (2009). *Experimental evolution: Concepts, methods, and applications of selection experiments* (1st ed.). University of California Press.

Hauser, F. E., & Chang, B. S. W. (2017). Insights into visual pigment adaptation and diversity from model ecological and evolutionary systems. *Current Opinion in Genetics & Development, 47,* 110–120. https://doi.org/10.1016/j.gde.2017.09.005

Kikuchi, D. W., & Pfennig, D. W. (2013). Imperfect mimicry and the limits of natural selection. *The Quarterly Review of Biology, 88*(4), 297–315. https://doi.org/10.1086/673758

Knudsen, E. I. (2007). Fundamental components of attention. *Annual Review of Neuroscience, 30*(1), 57–78. https://doi.org/10.1146/annurev.neuro.30.051606.094256

Köksal, F., Domjan, M., & Weisman, G. (1994). Blocking of the sexual conditioning of differentially effective conditioned stimulus objects. *Animal Learning & Behavior, 22,* 103–111.

Koops, M. A. (2004). Reliability and the value of information. *Animal Behaviour, 67*(1), 103–111. https://doi.org/10.1016/j.anbehav.2003.02.008

Kotrschal, A., Corral-Lopez, A., Amcoff, M., & Kolm, N. (2014). A larger brain confers a benefit in a spatial mate search learning task in male guppies. *Behavioral Ecology, 26*(2), 527–532. https://doi.org/10.1093/beheco/aru227

Kotrschal, A., Rogell, B., Bundsen, A., Svensson, B., Zajitschek, S., Brännström, I., Immler, S., Maklakov, A. A., & Kolm, N. (2013). Artificial selection on relative brain size in the guppy reveals costs and benefits of evolving a larger brain. *Current Biology, 23*(2), 168–171. https://doi.org/10.1016/j.cub.2012.11.058

Kraaijeveld, K., Oostra, V., Liefting, M., Wertheim, B., de Meijer, E., & Ellers, J. (2018). Regulatory and sequence evolution in response to selection for improved associative learning ability in *Nasonia vitripennis*. *BMC Genomics, 19*(1), 1–15. https://doi.org/10 .1186/s12864-018-5310-9

Kraemer, P. J., & Golding, J. M. (1997). Adaptive forgetting in animals. *Psychonomic Bulletin & Review, 4*(4), 480–491. https://doi.org/10.3758/bf03214337

Krause, M. A., Cusato, B., & Domjan, M. (2003). Extinction of conditioned sexual responses in male Japanese quail (*Coturnix japonica*): Role of species typical cues. *Journal of Comparative Psychology, 117*, 76–86.

Leadbeater, E., & Dawson, E. H. (2017). A social insect perspective on the evolution of social learning mechanisms. *Proceedings of the National Academy of Sciences, 114*(30), 7838–7845. https://doi.org/10.1073/pnas.1620744114

Liefting, M., Hoedjes, K. M., Le Lann, C., Smid, H. M., & Ellers, J. (2018). Selection for associative learning of color stimuli reveals correlated evolution of this learning ability across multiple stimuli and rewards. *Evolution, 72*(7), 1449–1459. https://doi.org/10.1111/ evo.13498

Linwick, D., Patterson, J., & Overmier, J. B. (1981). On inferring selective association: Methodological considerations. *Animal Learning & Behavior, 9*(4), 508–512. https://doi .org/10.3758/bf03209782

LoLordo, V. M. (1979). Selective associations. In A. Dickinson and R. A. Boakes (Eds.), *Mechanisms of learning and motivation: A memorial volume to Jerzy Konorski* (pp. 367–398). Lawrence Erlbaum..

Mackintosh, N. J. (1974). *The psychology of animal learning.* Academic Press.

Maharaj, G., Horack, P., Yoder, M., & Dunlap, A. S. (2018). Influence of preexisting preference for color on sampling and tracking behavior in bumble bees. *Behavioral Ecology, 30* (1), 150–158. https://doi.org/10.1093/beheco/ary140

Marcus, M., Burnham, T. C., Stephens, D. W., & Dunlap, A. S. (2017). Experimental evolution of color preference for oviposition in *Drosophila melanogaster*. *Journal of Bioeconomics, 20*(1), 125–140. https://doi.org/10.1007/s10818-017-9261-z

McNamara, J. M., & Houston, A. I. (1987). Memory and the efficient use of information. *Journal of Theoretical Biology, 125*(4), 385–395. https://doi.org/10.1016/s0022-5193(87) 80209-6

Mery, F., & Kawecki, T. J. (2002). Experimental evolution of learning ability in fruit flies. *Proceedings of the National Academy of Sciences, 99*(22), 14274–14279. https://doi.org/10 .1073/pnas.222371199

(2003). A fitness cost of learning ability in *Drosophila melanogaster*. *Proceedings of the Royal Society of London B Biological Sciences, 270*, 2465–2469. https://doi.org/10.1098/rspb .2003.2548

(2004). The effect of learning on experimental evolution of resource preference in *Drosophila melanogaster*. *Evolution, 58*(4), 757. https://doi.org/10.1554/03-540

Mery, F., Pont, J., Preat, T., & Kawecki, T. J. (2007). Experimental evolution of olfactory memory in *Drosophila melanogaster*. *Physiological and Biochemical Zoology, 80*(4), 399–405. https://doi.org/10.1086/518014

Miller, S. E., Legan, A. W., Henshaw, M. T., Ostevik, K. L., Samuk, K., Uy, F. M., & Sheehan, M. J. (2020). Evolutionary dynamics of recent selection on cognitive abilities. *Proceedings*

of the National Academy of Sciences, 117(6), 3045–3052. https://doi.org/10.1073/pnas
.1918592117

Morand-Ferron, J. (2017). Why learn? The adaptive value of associative learning in wild
populations. *Current Opinion in Behavioral Sciences, 16*, 73–79.

Oberling, P., Bristol, A. S., Matute, H., & Miller, R. R. (2000). Biological significance attenuates
overshadowing, relative validity, and degraded contingency effects. *Animal Learning &
Behavior, 28*, 172–186.

Pavlov, I. P. (1927). *Conditioned reflexes.* Oxford University Press.

Pontes, A. C., Mobley, R. B., Ofria, C., Adami, C., & Dyer, F. C. (2020). The evolutionary
origin of associative learning. *The American Naturalist, 195*(1), E1–E19. https://doi.org/
10.1086/706252

Reader, S. M. (2016). Animal social learning: Associations and adaptations. *F1000Research,
5*, 2120. https://doi.org/10.12688/f1000research.7922.1

Rescorla, R. A. & Wagner, A. R. (1972). A theory of Pavlovian conditioning: Variations in the
effectiveness of reinforcement and nonreinforcement. In A. H. Black & W. F. Prokasy
(Eds.), *Classical conditioning II: Current research and theory* (pp. 64–99). Appleton-
Century-Crofts.

Riffell, J. (2020). The neuroecology of insect-plant interactions: The importance of physiological state and sensory integration. *Current Opinion in Insect Science, 42*, 118–124.
https://doi.org/10.1016/j.cois.2020.10.007

Rubi, T. L., & Stephens, D. W. (2015). Should receivers follow multiple signal components?
An economic perspective. *Behavioral Ecology, 27*(1), 36–44. https://doi.org/10.1093/
beheco/arv121

(2016). Why complex signals matter, sometimes. In M. Bee & C. Miller (Eds.), *Psychological
mechanisms in animal communication. Animal signals and communication* (Vol. 5,
pp. 119–136). Springer. https://doi.org/10.1007/978-3-319-48690-1_5

Seligman, M. E. (1970). On the generality of the laws of learning. *Psychological Review, 77*(5),
406–418. https://doi.org/10.1037/h0029790

Silva, F. J. (2018). The puzzling persistence of "neutral" conditioned stimuli. *Behavioural
Processes, 157*, 80–90. https://doi.org/10.1016/j.beproc.2018.07.004

Snell-Rood, E. C., & Steck, M. (2015). Experience drives the development of movement-
cognition correlations in a butterfly. *Frontiers in Ecology and Evolution, 3*, 63–73. https://
doi.org/10.3389/fevo.2015.00021

Stevens, M. (2013). *Sensory ecology, behaviour, and evolution* (Illustrated ed.). Oxford
University Press.

Van Damme, S., De Fruyt, N., Watteyne, J., Kenis, S., Peumen, K., Schoofs, L., & Beets, I.
(2021). Neuromodulatory pathways in learning and memory: Lessons from invertebrates.
Journal of Neuroendocrinology, 33(1), e1291. https://doi.org/10.1111/jne.12911

5

EVOLUTIONARY PROCESSES SHAPING LEARNING ABILITY IN INSECTS

Maartje Liefting

Evolution does not necessarily increase complexity, but it is at its most fascinating when it does. Evolutionary biologists strive to understand how complex traits like cognition (in particular our own) arise through evolutionary processes. Yet, for decades the cognitive capabilities of small organisms have been greatly underestimated because of their much smaller brains. This oversight is unfortunate since small brains like that of insects can actually be of great help in answering complex questions on the evolution of cognitive abilities like learning. It is in this light vital to realize that although insect brains are *small*, they are not *simple* (Perry et al., 2017). Even though the number of neurons in the average insect brain is infinitely small compared to large-brained birds and mammals, insects can perform cognitive tasks that require considerable computational power. Insects can plan ahead based on internal predictive modelling, demonstrate an ability for selective attention, solve the travelling salesman problem by finding the shortest route while visiting floral patches, and adjust their behavior based on information acquired in the past through learning and memory (see Haberkern & Jayaraman, 2016; Perry & Chittka, 2019; Perry et al., 2017, and references therein; see Yu and Rankin, Chapter 1; Kriete and Hollis, Chapter 3; Dunlap and Dexheimer, Chapter 4).

I refer to both cognition and learning ability in this chapter, and it is important to note the difference. The term cognition covers a broad range of mental capacities such as perception, categorization, spatial navigation, numerosity, and learning. The ability to learn, that is, the process of integrating information from experience into memory that can be accessed at a later point in time, underlies many cognitive processes and is an extremely common feature in animals. Any type of behavioral plasticity involves the effects of experience in the past on current behavior (Stamps, 2016), and for this reason learning has been suggested to be one of the fastest ways to respond plastically to environmental variation in a reversible manner. The ability to learn and memorize is predicted to be beneficial under certain levels of predictable variation (Dunlap & Stephens, 2016; Ernande & Dieckmann, 2004). If there is no variation in information value of a certain cue, there is also no need to learn about it because an innate preference or fixed behavior is likely to be more efficient. Conversely, if relevant cues or the reward value vary too strongly to anticipate, there is also no potential for learning to evolve. Between these two extremes is a range of conditions in which learning can be beneficial, in particular when environments change between generations, but within-generation predictability is high (Stephens, 1991). Although learning is often cited as being an adaptation to change, it is as much an adaptation to predictability. Variation in patterns of predictability in relation to an animal's life history can subsequently lead to variation in learning ability. However, due to a lack of empirical data, we are just beginning to understand how learning ability evolves in the wild and how natural variation for this ability is maintained.

In this chapter, I focus on the evolutionary processes that shape learning ability in insects on a relatively short timescale. I address long-standing questions in this field and the extent to which they have been answered through empirical work, as well as identify the gaps in our knowledge and how these gaps outline future research. For learning ability to evolve under direct natural selection, the following requirements must be met: (1) there is variation in learning ability between individuals, (2) this variation is heritable, and (3) this variation is related to variance in fitness in specific environments. This chapter follows these three requirements of the evolutionary process in this same order.

5.1 VARIATION IN LEARNING

Hence I look at individual differences, though of small interest to the systematist, as of high importance for us, as being the first step towards such slight varieties as are barely thought worth recording in works on natural history.

Origin of Species – Chapter II, page 51 (Darwin, 1859).

QUANTIFYING VARIATION BEYOND SPECIES-LEVEL LEARNING CAPACITIES

A range of behavioral experiments and comparative studies have demonstrated collectively that there is ample genetically based variation in learning ability among insect species (reviewed in Dukas, 2008a; Hoedjes et al., 2011; Mery, 2013). Insight into the nature of this variation is crucial to understanding how cognitive abilities like learning ability respond to environmental factors and how they evolve.

Research on variation in cognition in a broad sense, including different forms of learning, has traditionally focused on comparative methods at the species level. This species-level approach tends to ignore individual variation and places a focus on a subset of high-performing individuals as a demonstration of the cognitive capabilities of a species. In a meta-analytic review of individual variation in cognition, Thornton and Lukas (2012) argue that relying on such small sample sizes impedes drawing robust conclusions about individual cognitive abilities as well as inter- and intraspecific differences. The rise of the research field of animal personality, namely, the study of consistent individual differences in an animal's behavior across time or contexts, has also resulted in an increased effort in exploring individual variation in cognition because of its close relationship with behavior (Griffin et al., 2015). However, although this research field includes many different species (Gosling, 2001), the average sample size is still relatively small (Dougherty & Guillette, 2018).

Working with an insect model system can be a useful approach to overcome issues with sample sizes and repeated measuring of the same individual, because it is possible to observe genetically identical siblings in multiple settings. For this reason, learning ability is extensively studied in the parasitic wasps of the genus *Nasonia* that have demonstrated both visual and olfactory learning capabilities. Their broad behavioral repertoire, combined with an expanding array of genomic and transcriptomic resources, makes *Nasonia* exceptionally well suited for evolutionary studies on natural variation in learning and memory (Hoedjes et al., 2014; Kraaijeveld et al., 2018; Werren et al., 2010). The genus encompasses four species of small gregarious wasps that parasitize fly pupae, with partly overlapping distributions and host ranges (Werren & Loehlin, 2009).

Empirical work on inter- and intraspecific differences in associative learning ability in these wasps also clearly demonstrates the caveats when determining species-level differences based on small sample sizes. For example, studies of olfactory learning in two species reported distinct interspecific variation: *Nasonia vitripennis* forms long-term memories that last for at least five days after a single associative learning trial, whereas the memory retention of *N. giraulti* sharply declines within two days after the same learning experience (Hoedjes et al., 2012; Hoedjes & Smid, 2014). However, the reported differences in memory formation were based on the behavior of a single, highly inbred strain in each of the two species. In a follow-up study, the memory retention patterns for both olfactory and visual learning of the original isogenic strains and two additional genetically variable (outbred) strains in each species were measured. The typical short-term memory of the *N. giraulti* isogenic strain originally demonstrated after olfactory learning was also found after color learning, and therefore the memory pattern was robust and independent of the learned stimulus (olfactory or visual). By contrast, the two outbred strains of the two species both demonstrated long-term memory formation after the same learning experience and

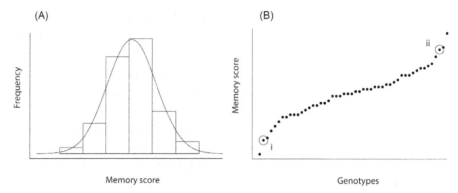

FIGURE 5.1. Simulated population data for variation in learning ability measured with a memory score, assuming a normal distribution of phenotypes. (A) If we randomly draw 50 individuals from this population, the majority of individuals (or genotypes) would exhibit an average memory score. (B) However, at the extremes (circled points i and ii) we can expect phenotypes with memory scores that can be significantly different.

therefore do not differ as dramatically as did the two isogenic strains (Liefting et al., 2020).

In other words, the memory retention pattern of these two *Nasonia* isogenic strains is not necessarily representative for the species in general, although more strains need to be studied to fully characterize inter- versus intraspecific variation in these particular species. Finding such dramatic differences among phenotypes not only serves as a caution against extrapolating characteristics measured on single genotypes to interspecies differences (van Grunsven & Liefting, 2015; Harvey et al., 2015), but also emphasizes the need to adopt a broader approach in studying variation in cognitive abilities. The isogenic phenotypes, whether rare or common in natural populations, are most likely part of the natural phenotypic range of the species studied and they are not "abnormal" like some learning mutants. Consider the simulated data in Figure 5.1: Extreme phenotypes (indicated with i and ii in Figure 5.1B) can differ from each other either within a species or between species, even when the range of learning phenotypes for both species overlaps to a large extent. The current shift away from species-level cognitive abilities toward an approach in which changes in the relative frequencies (or lack thereof) of phenotypes within a species or population are explored in response to environmental factors should prove to be insightful.

MAINTAINING GENETIC VARIATION IN LEARNING ABILITY

Darwin's fascination with variation in traits between and within species undoubtedly contributed to his ideas about evolution through natural selection. How and why this variation is maintained in natural populations has been the subject of numerous studies ever since (Hallgrímsson & Hall, 2005).

Based on findings from quantitative genetic studies and artificial selection studies, a pattern of continuous genetic variation in learning and memory appears quite common (e.g., Chandra et al., 2001). In addition to random processes like mutation and drift, genetic variation can also be maintained through natural selection. Natural selection can be stabilizing, disruptive, directional, or balancing, and each of these modes of selection can have an effect on phenotypic variation. Under stabilizing selection, there is selection toward the mean trait value and against more extreme phenotypes. Disruptive selection is the opposite of stabilizing selection, with selection toward the more extreme phenotypes. Under directional selection the frequency of a particular allele is increased as a result of its effect on the phenotype. Lastly, balancing selection refers to several different processes, for example, frequency-dependent selection and temporal or spatial variation in selection, that can maintain polymorphism within a population.

Some of these modes of selection are likely to be more relevant to maintaining variation in cognition in natural population than others (Mitchell-Olds et al., 2007). However, hardly any of these selective processes have been tested empirically in the context of cognitive traits. There is good evidence that balancing selection can maintain substantial heritability in phenotypic traits, but, to my knowledge, there is only one well-documented case that is related to learning behavior. In *Drosophila melanogaster*, a behavior polymorphism that affects foraging behavior is caused by two alleles of the *foraging* gene. This polymorphism is maintained through negative frequency-dependent selection, a specific case of balancing selection, as either genotype has their highest fitness when rare (Fitzpatrick et al., 2007). Flies carrying the so-called "rover" allele (for^R) move more while feeding than those homozygous for the "sitter" allele (for^s). Mery, Belay et al. (2007) demonstrated that this natural polymorphism also affects behavior through associative learning. The rover flies learned faster but forgot sooner than the sitter flies, while the sitter flies learned more slowly but demonstrated better long-term memory. This inverse relationship between the two memory types is hypothesized to be linked to the different lifestyles of rovers and sitters. Rover adults may be more likely to encounter new environments as they are moving more actively, and learning new information rapidly could be advantageous. Sitters, on the other hand, are more likely to remain in the same environment for longer and would hypothetically benefit more from accurately learned information that is relevant for a longer period of time.

Other modes of selection can also affect phenotypic variation: If there is a strong (dis)advantage to fitness of a certain learning phenotype in a population, directional selection should target traits that are associated with this phenotype. Several studies report a positive relation between learning performance and fitness (Dukas & Duan, 2000; Pasquier & Grüter, 2016; see also Madden et al., 2018, and references therein), which implies that directional selection can target more extreme learning phenotypes and associated abilities. These findings raise the question of why variation in learning abilities is maintained in natural populations. Instead of directional selection, given the costs that certainly are involved in learning and memorizing information (see below), stabilizing selection might actually be of greater importance under natural conditions than is generally assumed (Boogert et al., 2018, but see Kingsolver et al., 2001).

5.2 HERITABILITY OF COGNITIVE TRAITS AND LEARNING ABILITY

ESTIMATING HERITABILITY

For cognitive traits like learning ability to be available to selection, variation in learning between individuals also needs to be heritable. Heritability is a concept in evolutionary biology that summarizes how much of the observed variation in a trait is due to variation in genetic factors. This requires partitioning of variance introduced by environmental and genetic factors by means of repeated measurements either within or between generations. Estimating heritability of life-history and behavioral traits is notoriously difficult because many nongenetic effects are involved and values of heritability for such traits are typically low (Price & Schluter, 1991). Croston et al. (2015) provide an overview of what is known about heritability estimates of cognitive and neural traits and how this knowledge can advance our understanding of cognitive trait evolution. Still, it is challenging to accurately collect repeatable measures of cognitive ability (Morand-Ferron et al., 2016; Rowe & Healy, 2014) and, in addition to these practical difficulties, interpreting heritability estimates is far from straightforward because of the strong dependence on the environment in which they were measured (Boogert et al., 2018).

HERITABILITY THROUGH SELECTION

Another way to establish whether behavioral or cognitive traits are heritable is through artificial selection, and insects are particularly well suited for this type of experimental design because of their short generation time and high fecundity. One of the earliest selection studies on learning ability reported a response to directional selection in blow flies (Hirsch & McCauley, 1977). Holliday and Hirsch (1986) later questioned these results because the better performance of the "bright" strains could also have been caused by higher levels of sensitization. This demonstrates the necessity of proper control procedures to assess whether the artificial selection regime indeed targeted some form of learning ability and not another factor that contributed to the changed performance like, for example, motivation and perception. Since then, several studies have demonstrated the presence of (selectable) genetic variation in learning in insects (Brandes, 1988; Ferguson et al., 2001; Lofdahl et al., 1992). More recently, evolutionary change in learning ability has been demonstrated in several invertebrate species in the context of both artificial selection (Liefting et al., 2018; Zwoinska et al., 2016) and experimental evolution (see Dunlap and Dexheimer, Chapter 4; Dunlap & Stephens, 2014; Mery & Kawecki, 2002, 2002).

In a study of experimental evolution (Mery & Kawecki, 2002), *Drosophila melanogaster* populations were exposed to two differently flavored oviposition substrates so that adult flies could form an association between a flavor and oviposition opportunity. One substrate also contained a deterring chemical cue (quinine) during the exposure phase. Several hours after this initial exposure, the flies were again offered the choice between the two substrates with the deterring cue removed. The substrates that had previously contained quinine were then discarded, so only flies that learned to avoid the substrate previously containing quinine contributed to the next generation. This design thereby favored associative learning of chemical cues, and within 15 generations the experimental populations indeed realized a better ability to learn to avoid certain substrates compared to the control populations. To make sure that the flies were indeed selected for improved chemosensory avoidance learning and not because they simply became more sensitive to detecting chemicals in their medium, the flies from the selected lines were also tested in other learning assays, where they demonstrated improved aversive learning with other types of cues (Mery, Pont et al., 2007).

Parasitoid wasps, *Nasonia vitripennis*, also responded quickly to an artificial selection regime involving visual associative learning (Liefting et al., 2018). Female wasps learned to associate a host reward with a colored background during the conditioning phase. In the selected lines, only the wasps that demonstrated a learned preference for a color when offered a choice in a T-maze 24 hours after the initial experience were allowed to reproduce. The visual associative learning ability was enhanced within 10 generations of selection and also extended to the learning of odors. Similarly, although the associative learning assay was specifically tailored to the learning behavior of females, the learning ability of males was also affected even though there had never been any selection for male learning. Besides confirming that there was indeed selection for associative learning ability and not sensitization to the conditioned stimuli, this finding touches upon another interesting feature of evolution of cognitive traits, namely, co-evolutionary effects. That is, selection on visual associative learning in *Nasonia* females targeted a more general associative learning ability that also improved learning of odor stimuli and learning in both sexes. Understanding the effects of co-evolution is important as they may restrain independent evolution of other traits and also affect the interpretation of heritability of cognitive traits. As many cognitive processes depend on shared neurological pathways, the evolution of one aspect of learning cannot be understood in isolation from other cognitive abilities (Ellers & Liefting, 2015).

HERITABILITY IN NATURAL POPULATIONS

To extend these findings to the naturally occurring evolution of learning processes, we need to understand the level of heritable variation in learning in wild populations. To assess the genetic variation component of a heritability estimate, it is necessary to control the environmental variation, so experiments under controlled laboratory conditions are sometimes unavoidable. This shift to laboratory experimentation also means that heritability estimates of cognitive traits will differ from those measured in wild populations. The majority of studies that explore variation in learning ability use laboratory populations or strains with unknown or ancient field origin, or commercially reared cultures. These practices are reasons for concern as inbreeding, and adaptation to laboratory circumstances can also affect learning ability (Népoux et al., 2010; Sepúlveda et al., 2017). Our understanding of how genetic variation is maintained and how it responds to selection will greatly benefit from studies of natural populations in the wild (Hoppitt et al., 2012; Quinn et al., 2016; Raine et al., 2006) or from studies that bring samples of wild populations to the laboratory for assessment (Versace & Reisenberger, 2015). It would be naïve to ignore the trade-off between the possible level of control in a laboratory setting and the level of ecological realism of field-based studies, but researchers' choice for either setting needs to be justified. After all, researchers should be concerned not only with answering questions correctly, but also with answering the correct questions (van Grunsven & Liefting, 2015).

5.3 FITNESS: COSTS AND BENEFITS OF LEARNING

IS FASTER BETTER?

The idea that fast and flexible learning is beneficial has dominated the thinking of both laypeople and researchers for a long time. It is both intuitive and reassuring in that it suggests a plausible evolutionary direction in increasing cognitive complexity and flexibility. Even though there has always been a general awareness of pitfalls in this kind of logical reasoning, that awareness did not prevent the authors of one of the earliest bidirectional artificial selection experiments on learning to use the terms "dull" and "bright" for the different selected lines (Hirsch & McCauley, 1977). The benefits to learning *per se* seem obvious, since daily challenges like searching for food and mates while avoiding predators and poisonous food are nearly impossible to overcome if faced perpetually naïve. But that does not automatically lead to the conclusion that learning is always preferable over not learning, or that faster or more flexible cognitive abilities are always "better." As we have already seen, there is ample variation found in learning phenotypes, which suggests that besides implied benefits, there are also costs involved in the ability to learn and memorize information. To understand the evolution of phenotypic plasticity of traits like learning ability, we need to understand the balance between the benefits and these costs (Callahan et al., 2008; DeWitt et al., 1998).

BENEFITS OF LEARNING AND ITS RELATION TO FITNESS

Let us consider first the potential benefits to learning, because selection would favor learning only if this ability is indeed able to promote reproduction. These benefits seem intuitive and, indeed, foraging efficiency of fruit flies and parasitoid species in complex habitats improved after individuals had the opportunity to learn about their environments (Kruidhof et al., 2015; Zrelec et al., 2013). In addition, fruit flies that had the ability to learn about the unresponsiveness of heterospecific females were better at directing their courtship to suitable partners (Dukas, 2008b), and growth rates in grasshoppers were increased when information about diet quality was predictable enough to be learned (Dukas & Bernays, 2000). These studies all demonstrate how learning, under certain conditions of predictability, can be beneficial.

There are also reports of a linear positive relationship between enhanced learning abilities and fitness. For example, the individual learning ability of ants is linked to foraging success at the colony level (Pasquier & Grüter, 2016), and bumblebee (*Bombus terrestris*) colonies whose foragers are better at forming associations between artificial flower colors and food presence are also better at food collection in the wild (Raine & Chittka, 2008). These correlations imply that learning ability can be targeted by directional selection, which begs the question why such "enhanced" learning phenotypes are not more common in natural populations. The fact that this remains such an open question is not in the least caused by the fact that we simply do not understand very well what is actually beneficial under natural conditions. For one thing, fast learning can also be a disadvantage, for example, when it leads to less efficient foraging in bumblebees (Evans et al., 2017). Even making foraging errors is not necessarily a setback, as long as such costs are outweighed by the benefit of discovering new food sources (Evans & Raine, 2014). These insights should urge researchers to be very careful when addressing the presumed fitness benefits of learning, especially when learning ability is assessed based on lab-designed cognitive puzzles that do not necessarily reflect natural situations, or when they are based on a single proxy of fitness that may not reflect overall fitness outcomes. Rather than trying to find a positive relation between enhanced cognitive performance and some measure of fitness, the more interesting question might be why such extreme learning phenotypes (as represented in Figure 5.1B) are rare in natural populations in the first place.

THE COSTS OF LEARNING AND MEMORY

An important factor at play here are the costs involved in learning and memory. Costs can be paid on an energetic and physiological level or on the level of misdirected behavior and missed opportunities. The first category stems from the high energetic costs involved in generating and maintaining neurological tissues and structures. These costs typically become apparent through trade-offs with developmental, physiological, and life-history traits (Dunlap et al., 2019). In insects, studies on the energetic costs of learning have revealed that the activity of learning, or just having the ability for enhanced learning, can lead to lower fecundity (Snell-Rood et al., 2011), delayed juvenile development (Christiansen et al., 2016), decreased longevity (Burger et al., 2008; Lagasse et al., 2012), and reduced larval competitive ability (Mery & Kawecki, 2003). In addition, different types of memory, like short-term and long-term memory, can also trade off with each other (Lagasse et al., 2012), which suggests that resources for consolidating and storing memories are limited.

Energetic costs associated with enhanced learning ability were also assessed in *Nasonia vitripennis* lines that were selected for fast associative learning (Liefting et al., 2018). Because the fast learning phenotype was relatively rare in the starting population, it was expected that one or more possible trade-offs as identified in previous studies would also be relevant in these selected lines. However, fast learning ability did not appear to trade-off with longevity, brain size, or several fitness-related traits (Liefting et al., 2018, 2019). Also, no trade-off between short- and long-term memory was identified, although the learning ability of the selected lines did slowly revert back over time to the level of the control lines when selection was completely relaxed. This return to baseline learning ability implies that some costs might be involved. A likely explanation for the apparent lack of energetic costs is that there are ecological costs to be paid under natural conditions. Because these costs are not relevant under laboratory conditions, there appear to be no costs involved in the fast learning ability.

Ecological or economic costs are caused by suboptimal behavior while learning about something new or when unreliable information is learned that results in misdirected behavior (Dunlap & Stephens, 2016; Eliassen et al., 2017). Such ecological costs could be relevant for the *Nasonia* wasps from the artificial selection experiment (Liefting et al., 2018), as the wasps of these selected lines form long-term memory based on a single associative learning event. Such fidelity to an association based on a single encounter is likely only profitable under very stable conditions. A similar explanation has been suggested in the study of *Drosophila* rover versus sitter phenotypes in which rover flies learned faster but forgot sooner compared to the sitter flies (Mery, Belay et al., 2007). Forgetting may be beneficial for individuals like rovers, which often find themselves in new environments because of their more active lifestyle (McNamara & Houston, 1987). Outdated memories in the wrong environment may lead to mismatched behavior and they can possibly also interfere with new memories (Cheng & Wignall, 2006).

Ecological costs have been approached mainly through modelling studies and need more attention in empirical studies given their predicted importance. For example, bumblebees with fast learning abilities collected food at the same rate in the field as slow learning bumblebees but also foraged for fewer days, which suggests that some ecological cost was involved when these bumblebees foraged in the wild (Evans et al., 2017). Similarly, a recent study on information use in the parasitoid wasp *Cotesia glomerata* explored possible ecological costs associated with persisting unreliable memory (de Bruijn et al., 2018). During an experience phase, wasps learned to associate herbivore-induced plant volatiles with host presence (in contrast to control wasps that had no such experience). Both experienced and control wasps were subsequently allowed to forage in a wind-tunnel environment where either suitable or unsuitable hosts were located on the plants that previously had only suitable hosts. The searching efficiency of the control wasps was not strongly affected by the presence of unsuitable hosts since the induced volatiles did not have any specific meaning to them. However, wasps that had learned to associate certain plant volatiles with host presence during the prior experience phase remained strongly attracted to these plants even though the volatiles were produced by an unsuitable host. In this study, persistent memories led to maladaptive foraging behavior when the learned information became unreliable. These results demonstrate that ecological costs could be of pivotal importance in defining the adaptive value of learning ability and these costs should therefore be better included in future empirical studies.

5.4 CONCLUSIONS

Progress in the study of the evolution of insect learning will continue to take place on multiple fronts. I have attempted to provide an overview of what we know about evolutionary processes relevant to learning in insects. Knowledge of these processes is incomplete and I have provided ideas on what topics should be further explored. For one, we need to better acknowledge the variation in learning ability between individuals, for example, by considering the distribution of learning phenotypes in (natural) populations and monitoring changes in frequency in these phenotypes in response to different environments. We should also strive to better understand what selective processes (e.g., directional and stabilizing selection or migration between populations) are important in maintaining genetic variation in learning ability in the wild. Empirical studies on the costs of learning should also include the ecological costs of learning in natural populations that affect fitness. There are obvious constitutive and operating costs involved in learning and memory, but being misinformed or holding on to obsolete memories can be even more costly. Perhaps "dull" phenotypes can realize a higher fitness because they will not be hindered by having learned arbitrary information. This idea is not new but really needs to be tested under natural conditions. It is telling that Daniel Papaj and Alcinda Lewis (1993) in the afterword of the influential book *Insect Learning* stated that "First and foremost, we need to document better the actual significance of learning in nature." I guess there is no time like the present.

REFERENCES

Boogert, N. J., Madden, J. R., Morand-Ferron, J., & Thornton, A. (2018). Measuring and understanding individual differences in cognition. *Philosophical Transactions of the Royal Society B*, 373(1756), 1–10. http://dx.doi.org/10.1098/rstb.2017.0280

Brandes, C. (1988). Estimation of heritability of learning behavior in honeybees (*Apis mellifera capensis*). *Behavior Genetics*, 18(1), 119–132. https://doi.org/10.1007/BF01067081

de Bruijn, J. A. C., Vet, L. E. M., & Smid, H. M. (2018). Costs of persisting unreliable memory: Reduced foraging efficiency for free-flying parasitic wasps in a wind tunnel. *Frontiers in Ecology and Evolution*, 6(160), 1–9. https://doi.org/10.3389/fevo.2018.00160

Burger, J. M. S., Kolss, M., Pont, J., & Kawecki, T. J. (2008). Learning ability and longevity: A symmetrical evolutionary trade-off in *Drosophila*. *Evolution*, 62(6), 1294–1304. https://doi.org/10.1111/j.1558-5646.2008.00376.x

Callahan, H. S., Maughan, H., & Steiner, U. K. (2008). Phenotypic plasticity, costs of phenotypes, and costs of plasticity: Toward an integrative view. *Annals of the New York Academy of Sciences*, 1133, 44–66. https://doi.org/10.1196/annals.1438.008

Chandra, S. B. C., Hunt, G. J., Cobey, S., & Smith, B. H. (2001). Quantitative trait loci associated with reversal learning and latent inhibition in honeybees (*Apis mellifera*). *Behavior Genetics*, 31(3), 275–285. https://doi.org/10.1023/A:1012227308783

Cheng, K., & Wignall, A. E. (2006). Honeybees (*Apis mellifera*) holding on to memories: Response competition causes retroactive interference effects. *Animal Cognition*, 9(2), 141–150. https://doi.org/10.1007/s10071-005-0012-5

Christiansen, I. C., Szin, S., & Schausberger, P. (2016). Benefit-cost trade-offs of early learning in foraging predatory mites *Amblyseius swirskii*. *Scientific Reports*, 6(23571), 1–11. https://doi.org/10.1038/srep23571

Croston, R., Branch, C. L., Kozlovsky, D. Y., Dukas, R., & Pravosudov, V. V. (2015). Heritability and the evolution of cognitive traits. *Behavioral Ecology*, 26(6), 1447–1459. https://doi.org/10.1093/beheco/arvo88

Darwin, C. (1859). *On the origin of species*. John Murray.

DeWitt, T. J., Sih, A., & Wilson, D. S. (1998). Costs and limits of phenotypic plasticity. *Trends in Ecology & Evolution*, 13(2), 77–81. https://doi.org/10.1016/S0169-5347(97)01274-3

Dougherty, L. R., & Guillette, L. M. (2018). Linking personality and cognition: A meta-analysis. *Philosophical Transactions of the Royal Society B: Biological Sciences, 373* (1756), 1–12. https://doi.org/10.1098/rstb.2017.0282

Dukas, R. (2008a). Evolutionary biology of insect learning. *Annual Review of Entomology, 53*, 145–160. https://doi.org/10.1146/annurev.ento.53.103106.093343

(2008b). Learning decreases heterospecific courtship and mating in fruit flies. *Biology Letters, 4*(6), 645–647. https://doi.org/10.1098/rsbl.2008.0437

Dukas, R., & Bernays, E. A. (2000). Learning improves growth rate in grasshoppers. *Proceedings of the National Academy of Sciences, 97*(6), 2637–2640. https://doi.org/10.1073/pnas.050461497

Dukas, R., & Duan, J. J. (2000). Potential fitness consequences of associative learning in a parasitoid wasp. *Behavioral Ecology, 11*, 536–543. https://doi.org/10.1093/beheco/11.5.536

Dunlap, A. S., Austin, M. W., & Figueiredo, A. (2019). Components of change and the evolution of learning in theory and experiment. *Animal Behaviour, 147*, 157–166. https://doi.org/10.1016/j.anbehav.2018.05.024

Dunlap, A. S., & Stephens, D. W. (2014). Experimental evolution of prepared learning. *Proceedings of the National Academy of Sciences, 111*(32), 11750–11755. https://doi.org/10.1073/pnas.1404176111

(2016). Reliability, uncertainty, and costs in the evolution of animal learning. *Current Opinion in Behavioral Sciences, 12*, 73–79. https://doi.org/10.1016/j.cobeha.2016.09.010

Eliassen, S., Jørgensen, C., Mangel, M., & Giske, J. (2017). Exploration or exploitation: Life expectancy changes the value of learning in foraging strategies. *Oikos, 116*(3), 513–523. https://doi.org/10.1111/j.2007.0030-1299.15462.x

Ellers, J., & Liefting, M. (2015). Extending the integrated phenotype: Covariance and correlation in plasticity of behavioural traits. *Current Opinion in Insect Science, 9*, 31–35. https://doi.org/10.1016/j.cois.2015.05.013

Ernande, B., & Dieckmann, U. (2004). The evolution of phenotypic plasticity in spatially structured environments: Implications of intraspecific competition, plasticity costs and environmental characteristics. *Journal of Evolutionary Biology, 17*(3), 613–628. https://doi.org/10.1111/j.1420-9101.2004.00691.x

Evans, L. J., & Raine, N. E. (2014). Foraging errors play a role in resource exploration by bumble bees (*Bombus terrrestris*). *Journal of Comparative Physiology A, 200*(6), 475–484. https://doi.org/10.1007/s00359-014-0905-3

Evans, L. J., Smith, K. E., & Raine, N. E. (2017). Fast learning in free-foraging bumble bees is negatively correlated with lifetime resource collection. *Scientific Reports, 7*(1), 1–10. https://doi.org/10.1038/s41598-017-00389-0

Ferguson, H. J., Cobey, S., & Smith, B. H. (2001). Sensitivity to a change in reward is heritable in the honeybee, *Apis mellifera*. *Animal Behaviour, 61*(3), 527–534. https://doi.org/10.1006/anbe.2000.1635

Fitzpatrick, M. J., Feder, E., Rowe, L., & Sokolowski, M. B. (2007). Maintaining a behaviour polymorphism by frequency-dependent selection on a single gene. *Nature, 447*(7141), 210–212. https://doi.org/10.1038/nature05764

Gosling, S. D. (2001). From mice to men: What can we learn about personality from animal research? In *Psychological Bulletin* (Vol. 127, Issue 1, pp. 45–86). https://doi.org/10.1037/0033-2909.127.1.45

Griffin, A. S., Guillette, L. M., & Healy, S. D. (2015). Cognition and personality: An analysis of an emerging field. *Trends in Ecology & Evolution, 30*(4), 207–214. https://doi.org/10.1016/j.tree.2015.01.012

van Grunsven, R. H. A., & Liefting, M. (2015). How to maintain ecological relevance in ecology. *Trends in Ecology & Evolution, 30*(10), 563–564. https://doi.org/10.1016/j.tree.2015.07.010

Haberkern, H., & Jayaraman, V. (2016). Studying small brains to understand the building blocks of cognition. *Current Opinion in Neurobiology, 37*, 59–65. https://doi.org/10.1016/j.conb.2016.01.007

Hallgrímsson, B., & Hall, B. K. (2005). *Variation – A central concept in biology* (B. Hallgrímsson & B. K. Hall (eds.)). Elsevier. https://doi.org/10.1016/B978-0-12-088777-4 .X5000-5

Harvey, J. A., Malcicka, M., & Ellers, J. (2015). Integrating more biological and ecological realism into studies of multitrophic interactions. *Ecological Entomology*, *40*(4), 349–352. https://doi.org/10.1111/een.12204

Hirsch, J., & McCauley, L. A. (1977). Successful replication of, and selective breeding for, classical conditioning in the blowfly *Phormia regina*. *Animal Behaviour*, *25*(3), 784–785. https://doi.org/10.1016/0003-3472(77)90130-0

Hoedjes, K. M., Kruidhof, H. M., Huigens, M. E., Dicke, M., Vet, L. E. M., & Smid, H. M. (2011). Natural variation in learning rate and memory dynamics in parasitoid wasps: opportunities for converging ecology and neuroscience. *Proceedings of the Royal Society B*, *278*(1707), 889–897. https://doi.org/10.1098/rspb.2010.2199

Hoedjes, K. M., & Smid, H. M. (2014). Natural variation in long-term memory formation among *Nasonia* parasitic wasp species. *Behavioural Processes*, *105*, 40–45. https://doi.org/ 10.1016/j.beproc.2014.02.014

Hoedjes, K. M., Smid, H. M., Vet, L. E. M., & Werren, J. H. (2014). Introgression study reveals two quantitative trait loci involved in interspecific variation in memory retention among *Nasonia* wasp species. *Heredity*, *113*(6), 542–550. https://doi.org/10.1038/hdy.2014.66

Hoedjes, K. M., Steidle, J. L. M., Werren, J. H., Vet, L. E. M., & Smid, H. M. (2012). High-throughput olfactory conditioning and memory retention test show variation in *Nasonia* parasitic wasps. *Genes, Brain and Behavior*, *11*(7), 879–887. https://doi.org/10.1111/j .1601-183X.2012.00823.x

Holliday, M., & Hirsch, J. (1986). A comment on the evidence for learning in diptera. *Behavior Genetics*, *16*(4), 439–447. https://doi.org/10.1007/BF01074263

Hoppitt, W., Samson, J., Laland, K. N., & Thornton, A. (2012). Identification of learning mechanisms in a wild meerkat population. *PLoS ONE*, *7*(8), e42044. https://doi.org/10 .1371/journal.pone.0042044

Kingsolver, J. G., Hoekstra, H. E., Hoekstra, J. M., Berrigan, D., Vignieri, S. N., Hill, C. E., Hoang, A., Gibert, P., & Beerli, P. (2001). The strength of phenotypic selection in natural populations. *The American Naturalist*, *157*(3), 245–261. 0003-0147/2001/15703-0001$03.00

Kraaijeveld, K., Oostra, V., Liefting, M., Wertheim, B., Meijer, E. de, & Ellers, J. (2018). Regulatory and sequence evolution in response to selection for improved associative learning ability in *Nasonia vitripennis*. *BMC Genomics*, *19*, 892. https://doi.org/doi.org/10 .1186/s12864-018-5310-9

Kruidhof, H. M., Roberts, A. L., Magdaraog, P., Muñoz, D., Gols, R., Vet, L. E. M., Hoffmeister, T. S., & Harvey, J. A. (2015). Habitat complexity reduces parasitoid foraging efficiency, but does not prevent orientation towards learned host plant odours. *Oecologia*, *179*(2), 353–361. https://doi.org/10.1007/s00442-015-3346-y

Lagasse, F., Moreno, C., Preat, T., & Mery, F. (2012). Functional and evolutionary trade-offs co-occur between two consolidated memory phases in *Drosophila melanogaster*. *Proceedings of the Royal Society B*, *279*(1744), 4015–4023. https://doi.org/10.1098/rspb .2012.1457

Liefting, M., Hoedjes, K. M., Le Lann, C., Smid, H. M., & Ellers, J. (2018). Selection for associative learning of color stimuli reveals correlated evolution of this learning ability across multiple stimuli and rewards. *Evolution*, *72*(7), 1449–1459. https://doi.org/10 .1111/evo.13498

Liefting, M., Rohmann, J. L., Le Lann, C., & Ellers, J. (2019). What are the costs of learning? Modest trade-offs and constitutive costs do not set the price of fast associative learning ability in a parasitoid wasp. *Animal Cognition*, *22*(5), 851–861. https://doi.org/10.1007/ s10071-019-01281-2

Liefting, M., Verwoerd, L., Dekker, M. L., Hoedjes, K. M., & Ellers, J. (2020). Strain differences rather than species differences contribute to variation in associative learning ability in *Nasonia*. *Animal Behaviour*, *168*, 25–31. https://doi.org/10.1016/j.anbehav.2020.07.026

Lofdahl, K. L., Holliday, M., & Hirsch, J. (1992). Selection for conditionability in *Drosophila melanogaster*. *Journal of Comparative Psychology*, *106*(2), 172–183. https://doi.org/10.1037/0735-7036.106.2.172

Madden, J. R., Langley, E. J. G., Whiteside, M. A., Beardsworth, C. E., & Van Horik, J. O. (2018). The quick are the dead: Pheasants that are slow to reverse a learned association survive for longer in the wild. *Philosophical Transactions of the Royal Society B*, *373*(1756), 1–9. https://doi.org/10.1098/rstb.2017.0297

McNamara, J. M., & Houston, A. I. (1987). Memory and the efficient use of information. *Journal of Theoretical Biology*, *125*(4), 385–395. https://doi.org/10.1016/S0022-5193(87)80209-6

Mery, F. (2013). Natural variation in learning and memory. *Current Opinion in Neurobiology*, *23*(1), 52–56. https://doi.org/10.1016/j.conb.2012.09.001

Mery, F., Belay, A. T., So, A. K.-C., Sokolowski, M. B., & Kawecki, T. J. (2007). Natural polymorphism affecting learning and memory in *Drosophila*. *Proceedings of the National Academy of Sciences*, *104*(32), 13051–13055. https://doi.org/10.1073/pnas.0702923104

Mery, F., & Kawecki, T. J. (2002). Experimental evolution of learning ability in fruit flies. *Proceedings of the National Academy of Sciences*, *99*(22), 14274–14279. https://doi.org/10.1073/pnas.222371199

(2003). A fitness cost of learning ability in *Drosophila melanogaster*. *Proceedings of the Royal Society of London B*, *270*(1532), 2465–2469. https://doi.org/10.1098/rspb.2003.2548

Mery, F., Pont, J., Preat, T., & Kawecki, T. J. (2007). Experimental evolution of olfactory memory in *Drosophila melanogaster*. *Physiological and Biochemical Zoology*, *80*(4), 399–405. https://doi.org/10.1086/518014

Mitchell-Olds, T., Willis, J. H., & Goldstein, D. B. (2007). Which evolutionary processes influence natural genetic variation for phenotypic traits? *Nature Reviews Genetics*, *8*(11), 845–856. https://doi.org/10.1038/nrg2207

Morand-Ferron, J., Cole, E. F., & Quinn, J. L. (2016). Studying the evolutionary ecology of cognition in the wild: A review of practical and conceptual challenges. *Biological Reviews*, *91*(2), 367–389. https://doi.org/10.1111/brv.12174

Népoux, V., Haag, C. R., & Kawecki, T. J. (2010). Effects of inbreeding on aversive learning in *Drosophila*. *Journal of Evolutionary Biology*, *23*(11), 2333–2345. https://doi.org/10.1111/j.1420-9101.2010.02094.x

Papaj, D. R., & Lewis, A. C. (1993). *Insect learning: Ecology and evolutionary perspectives* (D. R. Papaj & A. C. Lewis (eds.)). Chapman & Hall.

Pasquier, G., & Grüter, C. (2016). Individual learning performance and exploratory activity are linked to colony foraging success in a mass-recruiting ant. *Behavioral Ecology*, *27*(6), 1702–1709. https://doi.org/10.1093/beheco/arw079

Perry, C. J., Barron, A. B., & Chittka, L. (2017). The frontiers of insect cognition. *Current Opinion in Behavioral Sciences*, *16*, 111–118. https://doi.org/10.1016/j.cobeha.2017.05.011

Perry, C. J., & Chittka, L. (2019). How foresight might support the behavioral flexibility of arthropods. *Current Opinion in Neurobiology*, *54*, 171–177. https://doi.org/10.1016/j.conb.2018.10.014

Price, T. D., & Schluter, D. (1991). On the low heritability of life-history traits. *Evolution*, *45*(4), 853–861. https://doi.org/10.2307/2409693

Quinn, J. L., Cole, E. F., Reed, T. E., & Morand-Ferron, J. (2016). Environmental and genetic determinants of innovativeness in a natural population of birds. *Philosophical Transactions of the Royal Society B*, *371*(1690), 1–14. https://doi.org/10.1098/rstb.2015.0184

Raine, N. E., & Chittka, L. (2008). The correlation of learning speed and natural foraging success in bumble-bees. *Proceedings of the Royal Society B*, *275*(1636), 803–808. https://doi.org/10.1098/rspb.2007.1652

Raine, N. E., Ings, T. C., Ramos-Rodriguez, O., & Chittka, L. (2006). Intercolony variation in learning performance of a wild British bumblebee population (Hymenoptera: Apidae:

Bombus terrestris audax). *Entomologia Generalis*, *28*(4), 241–256. https://doi.org/10
.1127/entom.gen/28/2006/241

Rowe, C., & Healy, S. D. (2014). Measuring variation in cognition. *Behavioral Ecology*, *25*(6), 1287–1292. https://doi.org/10.1093/beheco/aru090

Sepúlveda, D. A., Zepeda-Paulo, F., Ramírez, C. C., Lavandero, B., & Figueroa, C. C. (2017). Loss of host fidelity in highly inbred populations of the parasitoid wasp *Aphidius ervi* (Hymenoptera: Braconidae). *Journal of Pest Science*, *90*(2), 649–658. https://doi.org/10
.1007/s10340-016-0798-8

Snell-Rood, E. C., Davidowitz, G., & Papaj, D. R. (2011). Reproductive tradeoffs of learning in a butterfly. *Behavioral Ecology*, *22*(2), 291–302. https://doi.org/10.1093/beheco/arq169

Stamps, J. A. (2016). Individual differences in behavioural plasticities. *Biological Reviews*, *91* (2), 534–567. https://doi.org/10.1111/brv.12186

Stephens, D. W. (1991). Change, regularity, and value in the evolution of animal learning. *Behavioral Ecology*, *2*, 77–89. https://doi.org/https://doi.org/10.1093/beheco/2.1.77

Thornton, A., & Lukas, D. (2012). Individual variation in cognitive performance: Developmental and evolutionary perspectives. *Philosophical Transactions of the Royal Society B*, *367*(1603), 2773–2783. https://doi.org/10.1098/rstb.2012.0214

Versace, E., & Reisenberger, J. (2015). Large-scale assessment of olfactory preferences and learning in *Drosophila melanogaster*: behavioral and genetic components. *PeerJ*, *3*, e1214. https://doi.org/10.7717/peerj.1214

Werren, J. H., & Loehlin, D. W. (2009). The parasitoid wasp *Nasonia*: An emerging model system with haploid male genetics. *Cold Spring Harbor Protocols*, *4*(10), 1–10. https://doi
.org/10.1101/pdb.emo134

Werren, J. H., Richards, S., Desjardins, C. A., Niehuis, O., Gadau, J., Colbourne, J. K., Beukeboom, L. W., Desplan, C., Elsik, C. G., Grimmelikhuijzen, C. J. P., Kitts, P., Lynch, J. A., Murphy, T., Oliveira, D. C. S. G., Smith, C. D., van de Zande, L., Worley, K. C., Zdobnov, E. M., Aerts, M., . . . Gibbs, R. A. (2010). Functional and evolutionary insights from the genomes of three parasitoid *Nasonia* species. *Science*, *327*(5963), 343–348. https://doi.org/10.1126/science.1178028

Zrelec, V., Zini, M., Guarino, S., Mermoud, J., Oppliger, J., Valtat, A., Zeender, V., & Kawecki, T. J. (2013). *Drosophila* rely on learning while foraging under seminatural conditions. *Ecology and Evolution*, *3*(12), 4139–4148. https://doi.org/10.1002/ece3.783

Zwoinska, M. K., Lind, M. I., Cortazar-Chinarro, M., Ramsden, M., & Maklakov, A. A. (2016). Selection on learning performance results in the correlated evolution of sexual dimorphism in life history. *Evolution*, *70*(2), 342–357. https://doi.org/10.1111/evo.12862

6

BRAIN AND SPATIAL COGNITION IN AMPHIBIANS

Stem Adaptations in the Evolution of Tetrapod Cognition

Rubén N. Muzio and Verner P. Bingman

This chapter offers a selective review of the spatial cognitive abilities of amphibians as manifest under natural conditions and in the laboratory, and the importance of the medial pallium, the hippocampus homologue in amphibians, for those abilities. We explore questions surrounding the evolution of the hippocampus, variation in hippocampal organization among vertebrate classes, and the functional consequences of such variation. Field data suggest that anurans and salamanders often display extraordinary navigational abilities associated with breeding behavior and the caring of young. Analysis of experimental data on learning strategies in amphibians has shown that, as in other vertebrate classes, they are capable of navigating to goal locations using either an egocentric turn strategy or a beacon-guidance strategy. When visual landmarks are used to locate a goal, it is notable that increasing the distance between a visual cue and the reward impairs learning. Additionally, the experimental manipulation of two or more visual landmark cues revealed evidence for blocking, overshadowing, and latent inhibition. But of most importance, amphibians have been shown to learn map-like representations of goal locations that resemble so-called "cognitive maps." Assuming some similarity between the medial pallium of extant amphibians and the medial pallial-hippocampal homologue of the stem tetrapods (the ancestors of modern amniotes, that is, reptiles, birds, and mammals), we hypothesize that the evolution of the hippocampus of modern amniotes began with a medial pallium characterized by a relatively undifferentiated cytoarchitecture and a broad role in associative learning and memory processes that included the map-like representation of space. However, any meaningful reconstruction of hippocampal evolution will require more robust comparative investigations into the neurobiological and functional properties of the nonmammalian hippocampus. We hope this chapter makes clear the crucial role amphibians would play in such a comparative analysis.

6.1 AMPHIBIAN EVOLUTION

Living amphibians (Lissamphibia) are a diverse group of anamniotes (i.e., species that lay their eggs in water) divided into three orders: Urodela (Caudata), the salamanders; Anura (Salientia), the frogs and toads; and Apoda (Gymnophiona), the caecilians. From a comparative perspective, amphibians, more than any other vertebrate class, are assumed to most resemble a group of stem tetrapods (i.e., ancestors of all four-limbed verte-brates), likely the Temnospondyli (Schoch, 2014), of some 335 million years ago. As such, amphibians offer a window into the brain organization and cognitive abilities of the ancestral tetrapod condition. However, the stem tetrapods as a whole were a highly diverse group of organisms, and modern amphibians and amniotes likely evolved from different lineages of stem tetrapods (Schoch, 2014). Therefore, modern amphibians are not necessarily more similar to stem tetrapods than are amniotes, although we will adopt this heuristically useful, but unsupported, assumption in the narrative later in this chapter. The reconstruction of lissamphibian evolution is not straight-forward (Carroll, 2009; Schoch, 2014), but fossils of all three orders are found in Jurassic deposits, some 160 million years ago. Anurans and urodeles are often considered to belong to the same clade with their separate lineages having diverged perhaps during the mid-Permian, about 260–300 million years ago (Anderson et al., 2008; Schoch, 2014). This evolutionary recon-struction is generally supported by molecular-genetic analysis (San Mauro, 2010; Figure 6.1).

As noted, it is often casually and perhaps misleadingly assumed that extant amphibians are the closest living relatives to the ancestral species that left the boundaries of freshwater habitats and were the basis of tetrapod evolution. The questionable validity of this assumption notwithstanding, understanding the relationship between spatial cognition and brain organiza-tion in living amphibians likely still offers the best opportunity to gather insight into the brain and cognition of those ancestral life forms. This in turn may offer a baseline for understanding the evolution of more complex brain organizations, including that of the medial pallium or hippocampus, and cognitive abilities in birds and mammals, whose brain organizations substan-tially differ from ancestral forms. In the construction of this chapter, we will use the slippery assumption of modern amphibians more closely resembling some stem tetrapod groups to help the narrative flow. But what should be gleaned from the brief summary presented earlier is that modern amphibians and amniotes should be seen as derived and not as faithful replicates of their ancestral lineages (Hodos & Campbell, 1969). This last point is made clear by the notable morphological divergence of anurans from the ancestral, stem tetrapod body form, which resembles more that of extant salamanders.

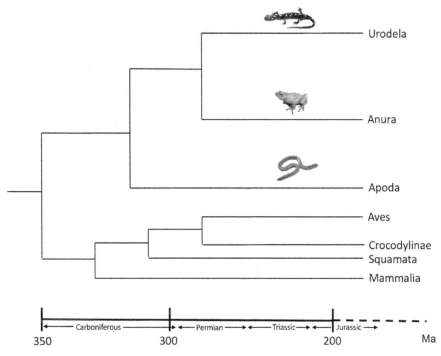

FIGURE 6.1. Evolutionary reconstruction of the three amphibian orders (Anura, Urodela, and Apoda) in relation to amniotes. Note the suspected sister ancestry of anurans and urodeles and that the stem tetrapod origin of amphibians is not that same as that of amniotes.
Adapted from San Mauro (2010). Figure prepared by Kaylyn A. S. Flanigan.

6.2 SPATIAL COGNITION IN THE FIELD: NAVIGATION AND SPATIAL MEMORY

Amphibians are rarely discussed among the great navigators of the animal kingdom, likely because of their limited spatial ranges. Foremost, amphibians need to stay near a body of water to manage the challenges of breeding, water balance, and thermoregulation. Amphibians do not navigate thousands of kilometers, something observed among migratory birds, sea turtles, and cetaceans. In anurans, distance traveled may be limited to about 15 km (Sinsch, 1990). But in the context of their smaller spatial ranges, they often display impressive navigational ability and robust spatial memory. Many amphibian species are faithful to breeding sites (Sinsch, 2014) and regularly move between breeding and nonbreeding locations; experiments with frogs, toads, and salamanders (newts) have shown an ability to navigate to breeding sites and other goal locations after experimental displacements (Sinsch, 1990; Twitty et al., 1964). For example, common toads, *Bufo bufo*, routinely migrate to breeding ponds that can be more than 3 km away and they can do so when experimentally displaced (Sinsch, 1987). As a curious observation, Boland (2004) reported that invasive cane toads (*Rhinella marina*) in

Australia could relocate the nests of a bee-eater bird species (*Merops ornatus*; cane toads eat the eggs and young of this bird) after displacements of up to 1.2 km. Two species of European newts (*Triturus cristatus, Lissotriton vulgaris*) were found to successfully orient their movements in an experimental arena toward their breeding ponds where they were captured, but only up to displacement distances of less than 1 km (Sinsch & Kirst, 2016). By contrast, Phillips et al. (1995) reported successful breeding-pond orientation in Eastern red-spotted newts (*Notophthalmus viridescens*) when displaced more than 40 km away and tested in an enclosed arena. In this study, newts were sensory deprived during displacement, but it is worth noting that similar navigational ability was observed in newts that were not sensory deprived (Phillips, 1987).

The local, albeit relatively short-distance, navigational ability of amphibians raises the question of underlying sensory mechanisms and spatial representations. In his review, Sinsch (1990) summarized the evidence for visual, olfactory, and geomagnetic cues playing a prominent role in guiding anuran navigation and proposed that it supports both a positional "map sense" and a directional "compass sense" of different sensory modalities in anurans. For example, there is evidence for a geomagnetic map in Eastern red-spotted newts, *Notophthalmus viridescens* (Fischer et al., 2001), and either a geomagnetic compass or a map in the common toad, *Bufo bufo* (Landler & Gollmann, 2011). By contrast, Grant et al. (1968) reported that navigation in another species of newts, *Taricha rivularis*, was dependent on olfactory inputs.

In the context of spatial cognition, poison frogs of the family Dendrobatidae are of particular interest because of their unusual reproductive behavior and use of space (e.g., Summers & Tumulty, 2013). Many species deposit the eggs in trees or on leaves on the forest floor and parents need to return regularly to the eggs to hydrate them. After hatching, small numbers of young are separately transported to different pools of water, essentially scattering their offspring in the local environment. Clearly, the reproductive behavior of many poison frogs reveals strong selective pressure for a robust spatial memory and spatial navigational ability. In many ways, from a spatial cognitive perspective, poison frogs resemble food-storing birds (Sherry, 2017), that also need to remember many spatially distinct locations and how to navigate among them. The importance of space in shaping the behavioral ecology of poison frogs is nicely highlighted by the use of spatial information by strawberry poison frogs (*Oophaga pumilio*). These frogs faithfully return to the same holding-cup location to provision their young even if the young were moved to a separate holding cup just 2 cm away (Stynoski, 2009). More striking are their navigational abilities. Like many better-known navigators, the movement of brilliant-thighed poison-arrow frogs (*Allobates femoralis*) through their local range enables them to successfully orient to a goal location when displaced up to 400 m in their familiar space. However, outside that familiar space and at similar displacement distances, that navigational ability is lost (Pašukonis et al., 2014). Using artificial pools, Pašukonis et al. (2016) showed that navigation was based on spatial memory as frogs returned to pool *locations* while the artificial pools themselves had been displaced.

In birds and mammals, navigational ability of the kind described here is often thought to imply a so-called "cognitive map" (O'Keefe & Nadel, 1978), dependent on the hippocampus (in mammals) or the dorsomedial pallium (in birds; see later). A critical adaptive value of a cognitive map is that it would allow goal-directed navigation even from places an animal has never been before as long as the animal has sensory contact with familiar landmarks or landscape features. Recent research in poison frogs points to the use of a spatial representation with the properties of a cognitive map. In the field, three-striped poison frogs (*Ameerega trivittata*) were found to successfully navigate back to their home range after displacement of up to 800 m to areas outside of the zones they would encounter during their routine movements (Pašukonis et al., 2018). Working with the green and black poison dart frog (*Dendrobates auratus*), Liu et al. (2019) used a water-maze design to demonstrate "cognitive map-like abilities" under controlled laboratory conditions. In a subsequent study, Liu et al. (2020) observed that *D. auratus* is characterized by a greater reliance on the *spatial* representation of associative outcomes compared to the túngara frog (*Physalaemus pustulosus*), which is more reliant on the feature properties of stimuli for its associative memory. These cognitive differences co-occurred with different transcriptomic activation of the medial pallium (the amphibian homologue of the mammalian hippocampus; Northcutt & Kicliter, 1980; Northcutt & Ronan, 1992) in the two species. Interestingly, many of the genes upregulated in *D. auratus* are often discussed in the context of synaptic plasticity and the network construction of memories.

6.3 SPATIAL COGNITION UNDER CONTROLLED LABORATORY CONDITIONS

The mostly field evidence of amphibian navigational ability described so far, inspired by the traditions of ethology, has naturally led to experiments designed to investigate the spatial cognitive abilities of amphibians under controlled experimental conditions inspired by the traditions of comparative psychology.

An experimental paradigm frequently used to study spatial orientation under controlled laboratory conditions in a wide variety of animals, including different species of Anura, relies on T-mazes. The T-maze requires subjects to learn an egocentric turn response to locate a goal without any beacon, such as a visual cue, near the goal (Daneri & Muzio, 2013a). For example, Greding

(1971) studied the ability of six species of anurans (toads and frogs) to escape from a weak electric shock delivered in the stem-axis and left arm of the T-maze. Animals were faced with the choice of turning to the left (where the electric shock would continue) or to the right (where there was no discharge). Although the results were characterized by considerable variability, the six species of anurans displayed at least a modest learning ability. By contrast, Brattstrom (1990) showed that the oriental fire-bellied toad (*Bombina orientalis*) can quickly learn the correct response in a T-maze, using water as reward in partially dehydrated animals. Using the terrestrial toad *Rhinella arenarum*, Muzio and colleagues have also demonstrated that partially dehydrated subjects are able to learn an appropriate turn response in a T-maze with water as reward (Daneri et al., 2011). These results are consistent with previous experiments in an open field with green frogs (*Rana clamitans*) indicating they can use memorized paths to orient themselves in space (Adler, 1980). In the Adler study, the subjects in the test arena were able to form a memory representation of the successful paths previously traveled and repeatedly used them to reach the reward in the goal box.

Another type of memory-based spatial behavior that has been routinely studied in a variety of species is the so-called cue guidance. In cue guidance response, a visual or some other sensory cue works as a beacon to indicate a goal location and animals have to detect and approach it to reach the goal. This type of navigation is based on associative mechanisms and has been observed in many species of phylogenetically older vertebrate groups, including turtles (Grisham & Powers, 1990; López et al., 2001), fish (López et al., 1999), and amphibians (Daneri et al., 2011; Lüddecke, 2003; Sotelo et al., 2015). For example, in a seminal study, Daneri et al. (2011) observed that, in addition to performing a turn response, terrestrial toads have the ability to use a visual cue adjacent to a reward as a goal beacon in a plus maze. In fish, Ingle and Sahagian (1973) showed that goldfish can learn to swim in a constant direction in relation to a reference visual cue located in a small, enclosed environment. They can even do so if they approach the decision point to reach the goal from the opposite direction and they are able to alternate the direction of their turns in different tests to track the beacon (for additional evidence, see Salas et al., 1996). The turtle, *Pseudemys scripta*, is also able to use a visual beacon cue to locate a reinforced feeder in an open field (López et al., 2001).

Spatial navigation to a goal based on learning egocentric turn and beacon guidance responses are readily understood in the context of associative learning theory. Learning an egocentric turn response can be described as a form of instrumental conditioning, while a beacon guidance response can be described as a form of classical or Pavlovian conditioning (Mackintosh, 2002). The properties of these two systems have been extensively studied in mammals (Nadel, 1991; O'Keefe & Nadel, 1978) and birds (Bingman, 1990;

Bingman et al., 1989), which can quickly learn to solve a spatial task using either goal-representational strategy. But as noted, both types of spatial learning mechanisms are found in older vertebrate groups, such as amphibians, suggesting that this ability arose early during vertebrate evolution (see Daneri et al., 2011, 2015).

Muzio and colleagues have initiated a systematic laboratory study of the spatial abilities of terrestrial toads, *Rhinella arenarum*, using several experimental settings (plus maze, circular and rectangular arenas) and water as reward (e.g., Daneri et al., 2011, 2015; Sotelo et al., 2015). These experiments showed that terrestrial toads can use the information provided by visual cues and boundary features that characterize an environment, as well as proprioceptive information, to locate a goal.

In a first experimental series, toads were trained to execute a turn or guidance response in a plus maze to access water (Daneri et al., 2011). In each training trial, only three arms were used in a T-maze arrangement (using one of two opposites arm as a starting point, randomly alternated, and the two "cross arms" as potential goals). First, three groups of toads were trained to perform a turn response to locate the rewarded goal arm: Right turn, Left turn, and Control (random relationship between turn and reward). Toads received 20 acquisition sessions and then another 10 reversal sessions. During reversal, the reward was located by turning in the opposite direction with respect to the start point set in the acquisition. Results showed that animals were able to readily learn the correct egocentric turn response to locate the goal. Moreover, reversal proceeded rapidly, indicating that animals potentially had learned a rule they could apply to a new condition thus enabling a faster learning rate than that observed in the initial acquisition. In addition, using the same plus maze arena, trained toads were also able to locate the goal in another experimental setting that required a guidance response, using a visual beacon cue above the rewarded location (Daneri et al., 2011).

In a second experimental series, toads were trained in a circular arena: (1) to study the effect of distance between a reference visual cue and the goal on navigational performance (Daneri et al., 2015) and (2) to investigate for the first time the presence of three basic learning phenomena in amphibians: blocking, overshadowing, and latent inhibition between visual cues. These phenomena have been widely observed in several classes of vertebrates, including mammals, and only recently demonstrated in amphibians (Daneri & Muzio, 2013b; Daneri et al., in prep.). To study the effect of distance between a visual cue and the goal, each of three groups of toads were trained with the visual cue either Above, Near (10 cm away), or Far (30 cm away) from the reward location. Results showed that learning rate declined as distance increased, with a significant correlation between distance and the number of training sessions needed to reach the learning criteria

(Daneri et al., 2015). To investigate the presence of blocking and over-shadowing, four water containers distributed crosswise were placed in the circular arena (only one was rewarded). Different visual cues were placed on the internal wall of the circular arena that could be used to approach the goal. For the study of blocking, experimental toads in the first phase of training had the rewarded container indicated by a single visual cue, located near (10 cm away) to one side. In a second phase, another visual cue was added on the other side of the reward (the cue predicted to be blocked). Control toads were trained only in this second phase, where the rewarded container was always indicated by the two visual cues together. Results of the test trials with only the cue added in the second phase in the experimental group revealed that previous training with one of the visual cues blocked the toads' associ-ation between the added cue and the reward. This was demonstrated by a lower percentage of correct responses to the second cue in the experimental group compared to the control group (Daneri & Muzio, 2013b). For the study of overshadowing, experimental toads in the first phase had the rewarded container indicated by two visual cues, one nearby (located 10 cm to the right of the rewarded container) and a second, more distant one (placed 70 cm to the left on the wall between adjacent and opposite containers). Control toads had the reinforced container indicated by a distant visual cue only (also located on the left, on the wall between the adjacent container and opposite to the rewarded container). After acquisition, the results of test trials showed that the location of a visual cue located far from the reward was overshadowed by the presence of the nearby cue. Indeed, experimental toads displayed a lower percentage of correct responses to the more distant cue than controls (Daneri & Muzio, 2013b). Finally, for the study of latent inhibition, toads were preexposed for five sessions to a visual cue without reward. In a second phase, this visual cue indicated the location of the reward. Comparison of the average number of sessions to reach the learning criterion of the preexposed group with respect to a control, non-preexposed group showed that preexposed animals needed more training sessions to reach learning asymptote. Thus, nonrewarded preexposure to a visual cue delayed acquisition (Daneri et al., in prep.). These findings dem-onstrated for the first time that amphibians are capable of displaying these basic learning phenomena, suggesting that these learning abilities, and their underlying neural mechanisms, originated early in vertebrate evolution. In support of this idea, besides our recent data from amphibians, there is evidence of blocking and overshadowing in other nonmammalian verte-brates, such as goldfish (Tennant & Bitterman, 1975; Wolach et al., 1977), although the evidence for latent inhibition is not yet conclusive (Chivers et al., 2014; Mitchell et al., 2011; Shishimi, 1985).

In another experimental series, toads were trained in a geometric rect-angular arena to study the properties of spatial learning by contrasting the use of boundary geometry and visual cues. There is a long research history of studying the relative importance of environmental geometry and visual cues for locating a goal in different species of vertebrates, such as mammals (e.g., rats, Cheng, 1986; Gallistel, 1990; humans, Newcombe et al., 2010; Sturz et al., 2011), birds (e.g., pigeons, Bingman et al., 2006; Nardi & Bingman, 2007; chicks, Pecchia & Vallortigara, 2010), reptiles (e.g., turtles, López et al., 2003), and fish (e.g., goldfish, Vargas et al., 2004, 2006). But only recently has this research interest extended to amphibians, work that has been carried out mostly in the Muzio laboratory. In one study, Sotelo et al. (2015) trained toads either in a white rectangular arena (Geometry Only group) or in the same arena with a removable panel with horizontal-colored stripes on one of the short walls (Geometry-Feature group). Four water containers were placed in each of the corners of the arena, but only one was rewarded (accessible water) for animals trained in the Geometry-Feature condition, while two were rewarded in geometrically equivalent corners for animals trained in the Geometry-Only condition. After the acquisition phase, the underlying learning representation was assessed in different types of nonrewarded test trials interspersed among training trials. For the Geometry Only group, a single type of test trial was administered, as the rectangular geometry was transformed by adding two white panels that changed the shape of the arena to a square. In this case, all corners were geometrically the same and, because of the absence of other information, the expected behavior was random choices among the four water containers (i.e., 25% of choices directed toward each of the four corners of the arena). Results of the test trials confirmed that the toads chose all four corners close to the equal probability of 25%. For the Geometry-Feature group, three types of test trials were carried out: (1) Geometry Test, in which the striped panel (the visual/feature cue) was removed and only the rectangular geometry was kept. (2) Feature Test, in which the shape of the arena was changed to a square (all "short walls") and the feature cue, the striped panel, was present on one of the walls. (3) Conflict Test, in which the rectangular geometry of the arena was maintained, but the visual feature cue was substituted by a larger one (maintaining the same stripe pattern) placed on one of the long walls of the arena. Therefore, in Conflict Tests, the correct containers indicated by the boundary geometry of the arena differed from the correct container indicated by the new location of the visual cue. Consequently, if the animals had learned the location of the goal using both sources of information, it was expected that (1) they would be able to choose the two correct containers with respect to geometry when the visual cue was not present on the Geometry-Only test trials; (2) they would be able to correctly choose the rewarded container when only the visual cue was present on the Feature-Only test trials; and (3) as the Conflict test trials were designed to determine which of the two sources of information held greater control over the behavior of the subjects, no a priori

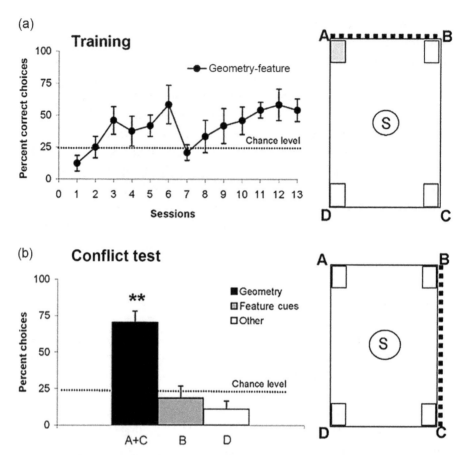

FIGURE 6.2. Summary of results contrasting the importance of boundary geometry and visual feature cues for the goal navigation behavior of the Terrestrial toad *Rhinella arenarum*.
(a) Left, learning as indicated by the percentage of correct responses by the Geometry-Feature group during training. Right, for a representative test subject, the goal (here at corner "A") could be located in relation to the boundary geometry or feature cue (dotted squares). S, trial start location. (b) Percentage of responses to the different corners during the unrewarded Conflict-test trials (note that the feature cue has been translocated to a long wall). When the two sources of information are set in conflict, toads preferentially relied on boundary geometry (corners A and C) to locate the goal. Asterisks indicate significant differences between conditions (**: $p < 0.01$).
Adapted from Sotelo et al. (2015).

prediction was offered. Results of these test trials revealed that toads can use both the boundary geometry of the arena and the visual cue (striped panel) to locate a goal, but geometry had more control over navigation behavior as "geometry choices" were overwhelmingly preferred over "feature choices" when the two were set in conflict (Figure 6.2). Additional studies with terrestrial toads using a rectangular arena to enable locating a goal by boundary geometry also showed: (1) slope-based encoding of a goal location (Sotelo et al., 2017) and (2) transfer of spatial learning between geometrically different shaped environments (Sotelo et al., 2020).

6.4 THE AMPHIBIAN MEDIAL PALLIUM/HIPPOCAMPUS

Among vertebrates, any conversation about the neural basis of spatial cognition begins with the mammalian hippocampus and its medial/dorsomedial pallial homologues in other tetrapod classes. The binding functional descriptor of the tetrapod hippocampus, as well as its presumptive homologue in the lateral pallium of teleost fish (Rodríguez et al., 2002), is that it plays some role in the map-like representation of space supporting navigation and provides a spatial context to support memory (see later, also Bingman & Muzio, 2017; Bingman et al., 2009, 2017; Herold et al., 2015). Given the considerable variation in tetrapod hippocampal organization (see Bingman & Muzio, 2017; Bingman et al., 2017; González et al., 2017), the binding functional descriptor of a role in spatial cognition across tetrapods is perhaps somewhat surprising. The question raised then is how might the organization of the amphibian medial pallium, so different from the dorsomedial pallium of birds and the hippocampus of mammals, implement spatial representations capable of supporting their often-remarkable spatial cognitive abilities described earlier?

Depicted in Figure 6.3 are Nissl-stained images through the telencephalon of a frog, a toad, and a salamander highlighting the medial pallium (caecilians are not included, but see González et al., 2002; Northcutt & Kicliter, 1980). What is striking comparing the anurans with the salamander is the remarkable similarity in the cytoarchitectural organization of their medial pallium region, despite the dramatic difference in body form and as much as 300 million years of independent evolution. The cytoarchitectural similarity of the medial pallium notwithstanding, not all aspects of anuran and salamander brain organization should be considered identical (e.g., Marín et al., 1997). Traditionally, the pallium of amphibians (Figure 6.3) has been subdivided into lateral, dorsal, and medial regions (Northcutt & Kicliter, 1980; Neary, 1990), with the medial pallium considered homologous to the mammalian hippocampus (Bruce & Neary, 1995; Northcutt & Ronan, 1992; Wang et al., 2007). Although the amphibian medial pallium is large relative to other pallial regions, it has a number of seemingly primitive features compared to the dorsomedial pallium/hippocampus of amniotes. Cytoarchitecturally, the amphibian medial pallium displays little organization in the distribution of cell types, revealing little or no laminar structure. Also, rather than projecting lateral dendritic processes bidirectionally to intersect fibers of passage, the principal cells of the amphibian medial pallium project their dendrites in only one direction (Westhoff & Roth, 2002). Also, in contrast to the dorsomedial pallium/hippocampus of amniotes, which receive most of their sensory inputs after some processing in other portions of the telencephalon (e.g., the dorsal ventricular ridge or neocortex), the amphibian medial pallium receives more direct olfactory inputs and direct visual, auditory, and

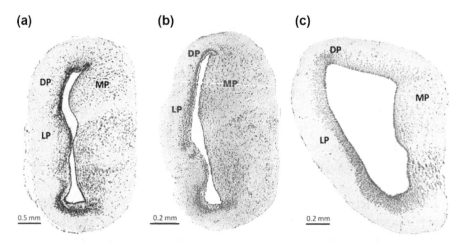

FIGURE 6.3. Nissl-stained coronal sections through the telencephalon of a representative (a) frog (*Xenopus laevis*, African clawed frog), (b) toad (*Rhinella arenarum*, terrestrial toad) and (c) salamander (*Pleurodeles wartl*, the Iberian ribbed newt) highlighting the location and cytoarchitecture of the homologue of the mammalian hippocampus, the medial pallium.
Frog image courtesy of Loreta Medina, Toad image courtesy of María Inés Sotelo and Rubén N. Muzio, salamander image courtesy of Agustín González.

somatosensory thalamic inputs (González & López, 2002; Northcutt & Ronan, 1992; Westhoff & Roth, 2002). Despite these apparently primitive characteristics, one feature that is shared between the amphibian medial pallium and mammalian hippocampus is a septo-hippocampal cholinergic projection, which has been observed in anurans (González et al., 2002).

6.5 MEDIAL PALLIUM AND SPATIAL COGNITION

Not surprisingly, a considerable amount of research has investigated the role of the amphibian medial pallium in spatial cognition. The functional profile of the medial pallium confirms a role of this hippocampal homologue in spatial cognition, but with some unexpected differences. Muzio and colleagues have investigated the relationship between spatial cognition and the amphibian medial pallium. This research included: (1) an evaluation of medial pallial neural activity as toads were engaged in a beacon-guidance task in a circular arena and a boundary-geometry learning task in a rectangular arena and (2) an assessment of the disruptive effect of medial pallial lesions when toads were challenged with an egocentric-turn or beacon-guidance task in a plus maze, as well as a boundary-geometry learning task in a rectangular arena. For example, Sotelo et al. (2015, 2016) demonstrated in the terrestrial toad that finding a goal location using the boundary geometry of a rectangular arena resulted in an upregulation of the immediate-early gene c-Fos in the medial pallium. This medial pallium-boundary geometry coupling found in the terrestrial toad reinforces an inferred ancestral role of the hippocampus in spatial vertebrate cognition. Based on this neural activation finding, in a subsequent study it was predicted and confirmed that medial pallial lesions would interfere with goal navigation using the same boundary geometry task (Figure 6.4a; Sotelo et al., in prep.). Relevant here is the observation of an upregulation of neuronal activity in the medial pallium of poison frogs when engaged in parental care, which includes the transport of young to remembered pools of water (Fischer et al., 2019).

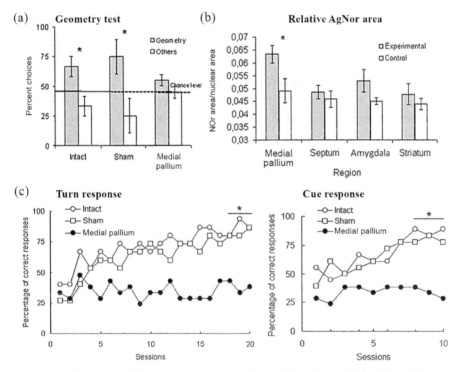

FIGURE 6.4. Summary of the more important results involving the medial pallium of the Terrestrial toad *Rhinella arenarum* originating from recent experiments carried out in the Muzio laboratory. (a) Percentage distribution of first choices recorded during a test of geometric learning in three groups of toads (intact, sham operated, and medial pallium lesioned) trained in a rectangular arena (Sotelo et al., in prep.). Asterisks indicate statistically significant, preferential responding to geometrically correct corners ($p < 0.05$), and the impairment associated with medial pallium lesion is apparent; (b) Relative AgNOR activity area of several brain regions for two groups of toads trained to approach a beacon to locate a reward in a circular arena (Daneri et al., in prep.). The AgNOR technique stains cell nucleoli and provides an index of neural activity. Asterisk indicates statistically significant upregulation of AgNOR activity in the medial pallium of toads trained to the beacon ($p < 0.05$); (c) Percentage of correct choices during the acquisition of an egocentric turn response (Left) or a beacon guidance response (Right) in three groups of toads (intact, sham operated, and medial pallium lesioned) trained in a plus maze (chance at 25%; Daneri & Muzio, in prep.). Again, the impairment associated with medial pallium lesion is apparent. Asterisks indicate statistically significant correct responding in the two control groups as well as a statistically reliable difference between the control groups and the toads with medial pallial lesions ($p < 0.05$).

The now demonstrated relationship between the amphibian medial pallium and boundary geometry is perhaps not a surprise. But what is striking about the medial pallium in amphibians is that its role in cognition extends well beyond the map-like representation of space as revealed by the neural activation and lesion studies described earlier. Using the histological marker AgNOR, which stains cell nucleoli providing an index of cell activation, upregulated neuronal activity in the medial pallium was also observed when toads were trained in a circular arena to rely on a visual beacon to locate a reward (Figure 6.4b; Daneri et al., in prep.). The behavioral performance of terrestrial toads trained in the previously described plus-maze task to locate a goal using egocentric, non-map-like turn (turn left or right) and beacon (move toward a visual cue) strategies (Daneri et al., 2011) was also impaired after lesions of the medial pallium (Figure 6.4c Left: egocentric-turn response; Figure 6.4c Right: beacon-guidance response; Daneri & Muzio, in prep.). Thus, the medial pallium of amphibians appears to be broadly involved in controlling spatial behavior regardless of the underlying representational/behavioral strategy and supporting associative mechanisms. Importantly, neither the hippocampal formation of birds nor the hippocampus of mammals would be necessary to guide goal navigation based on learning a simple egocentric turn or approaching a beacon cue (Bingman & Muzio, 2017). In this sense, and again in contrast to hippocampal function in birds and mammals, it is also remarkable that medial pallial lesions in the terrestrial toad have been found to impact instrumental behavior in a simple runway apparatus, including impairing extinction learning (Muzio et al., 1993), as well as increasing perseveration after partial reinforcement learning (Muzio et al., 1994), and after a downshift in reward magnitude (i.e., under conditions of incentive contrast; Papini et al., 1995; see Papini, Chapter 10).

6.6 FINAL REMARKS

Based on the examination of the medial pallium of extant amphibians, we hypothesize that the ancestral hippocampus of modern tetrapods was characterized by a less differentiated cytoarchitectural organization, more direct/less processed sensory inputs, and a functional profile that, although including the map-like representation of space, also extended to other aspects of cognition that would be considered more basic/less complex, such as egocentric spatial responses and aspects of instrumental learning (although we should note that the mammalian hippocampus has also been reported to support nonspatial, associative learning; e.g., MacDonald et al., 2013; Sakimoto & Sakata, 2018; Yoshida et al., 2019).

Comparative psychologists and neurobiologists continue to be confronted with trying to reconcile the following observations with respect to the evolution of the tetrapod hippocampus/medial pallium: (1) that the hippo-campus/medial pallium/hippocampal formation plays a central role in the map-like representation of space across tetrapods, (2) that shared function is associated with considerable variation in cytoarchitectural organization, and (3) that variation defies the identification of any clear, shared subdivisional homology, for example, with the mammalian dentate gyrus (see Bingman & Muzio, 2017), which could explain the observed functional equivalence. The challenge is to ultimately understand how that variation explains differences in the functional profile of the different hippocampi, functional profiles that nonetheless share a common role in the representation of space. What is clear is that if we are ever to have a better understanding of the structural and functional evolution of the hippocampus/medial pallium, what is needed are more data on the neurobiological and functional properties of the nonmam-malian hippocampus in general, and those of the amphibian medial pallium in particular.

ACKNOWLEDGMENTS

The authors are grateful to Andrius Pašukonis for his helpful comments on an earlier draft of the manuscript. The chapter was written while VPB was funded by NSF grant IOS 1457304 and while RNM was funded by Grant PICT 4300 (FONCYT) and by Grant UBACYT P0068BA (Universidad de Buenos Aires), Argentina.

REFERENCES

Adler, K. (1980). Individuality in the use of orientation cues by green frogs. *Animal Behaviour*, 28, 413–425. http://dx.doi.org/10.1016/S0003-3472(80)80050-9

Anderson, J. S., Reisz, R. R., Scott, D., Fröbisch, N. B., & Sumida, S. S. (2008). A stem batrachian from the Early Permian of Texas and the origin of frogs and salamanders. *Nature*, 453, 515–518. http://dx.doi.org/10.1038/nature06865

Bingman, V. P. (1990). Spatial navigation in birds. In D. Olton and R. P. Kesner (Eds.), *Neurobiology of comparative cognition* (pp. 423–447). Erlbaum Press.

Bingman, V. P., Bagnoli, P., Ioalé, P., & Casini, G. (1989). Behavioral and anatomical studies of the avian hippocampus. In V. Chanpalay and C. Kohler (Eds.), *The hippocampus: New vistas* (pp. 379–394). Alan R. Liss.

Bingman, V. P., Jechura, T., & Kahn, M. C. (2006). Behavioral and neural mechanisms of homing and migration in birds. In M. F. Brown and R. G. Cook (Eds.), *Animal spatial cognition: Comparative, neural, and computational approaches* [Online]. www.pigeon.psy .tufts.edu/asc/Bingman

Bingman, V. P., & Muzio, R. N. (2017). Reflections on the structural-functional evolution of the hippocampus: What is the big deal about a dentate gyrus? *Brain, Behavior and Evolution*, 90, 53–61. http://dx.doi.org/10.1159/000475592

Bingman, V. P., Rodríguez, F., & Salas, C. (2017). The hippocampus in nonmammalian vertebrates. In J. Kaas (Ed.), *Evolution of nervous systems* (pp. 479–489). Academic Press.

Bingman, V. P., Salas, C., & Rodriguez, F. (2009). Evolution of the hippocampus. In M. D. Binder, N. Hirokawa and U. Windhorst (Eds.), *Encyclopaedia of neuroscience* (pp. 1356–1360). Springer-Verlag.

Boland, C. R. J. (2004). Introduced cane toads *Bufo marinus* are active nest predators and competitors of rainbow bee-eaters *Merops ornatus*: Observational and experimental evidence. *Biological Conservation, 120,* 53–62. http://dx.doi.org/10.1016/j.biocon.2004 .01.025

Brattstrom, B. H. (1990). Maze learning in the fire-bellied toad, *Bombina orientalis. Journal of Herpetology, 24,* 44–47. http://dx.doi.org/10.2307/1564288

Bruce, L. L., & Neary, T. J. (1995). The limbic system of tetrapods: A comparative analysis of cortical and amygdalar populations. *Brain, Behavior and Evolution, 46,* 224–234. http:// dx.doi.org/10.1159/000113276

Carroll, R. L. (2009). *The rise of amphibians: 365 million years of evolution.* Johns Hopkins University Press.

Cheng, K. (1986). A purely geometric module in the rat's spatial representation. *Cognition, 23,* 149–178. http://dx.doi.org/10.1016/0010-0277(86)90041-7

Chivers, D. P., McCormick, M. I., Mitchell, M. D., Ramasamy, R. A., & Ferrari, M. C. O. (2014). Background level of risk determines how prey categorize predators and non-predators. *Proceedings of the Royal Society B, 281,* 20140355. http://dx.doi.org/10.1098/ rspb.2014.0355

Daneri, M. F., Casanave, E. B., & Muzio, R. N. (2011). Control of spatial orientation in terrestrial toads (*Rhinella arenarum*). *Journal of Comparative Psychology, 125,* 296–307. http://dx.doi.org/10.1037/a0024242

(2015). Use of local visual cues for spatial orientation in toads (*Rhinella arenarum*): The role of distance to a goal. *Journal of Comparative Psychology, 129,* 247–255. http://dx.doi .org/10.1037/a0039461

(In prep.) Blocking, Overshadowing and Latent Inhibition in terrestrial toads (Rhinella arenarum): Use of visual cues for orientation.

Daneri, M. F., & Muzio, R. N. (2013a). El aprendizaje espacial y su relevancia en anfibios [Spatial learning and its relevance in amphibians]. *Revista Argentina de Ciencias del Comportamiento, 5,* 38–49.

(2013b). Fenómenos de Bloqueo y Ensombrecimiento en un grupo filogenéticamente antiguo. Los anfibios [Phenomena of Blocking and Overshadowing in a phylogenetically ancient group. The amphibians]. *Revista Latinoamericana de Psicología, 45,* 185–200.

(In prep.). Medial Pallium lesion affects both turn and cue spatial learning in terrestrial toads (Rhinella arenarum).

Fischer, E. K., Roland, A. B., Moskowitz, N. A., Tapia, E. E., Summers, K., Coloma, L. A., & O'Connell, L. A. (2019). The neural basis of tadpole transport in poison frogs. *Proceedings of the Royal Society B, 286,* 20191084. http://dx.doi.org/10.1098/rspb.2019 .1084

Fischer, J. H., Freake, M. J., Borland, S. C., & Phillips, J. B. (2001). Evidence for the use of magnetic map information by an amphibian. *Animal Behaviour, 62,* 1–10. http://dx.doi .org/10.1006/anbe.2000.1722

Gallistel, C. R. (1990). *The organization of learning.* MIT Press.

González, A., & López, J. M. (2002). A forerunner of septohippocampal cholinergic system is present in amphibians. *Neuroscience Letters, 327,* 111–114. http://dx.doi.org/10.1016/ S0304-3940(02)00397-X

González, A., López, J. M., Morona, R., & Moreno, N. (2017). The organization of the central nervous system of amphibians. In J. Kaas (Ed.), *Evolution of nervous systems* (pp. 141–167). Academic Press.

González, A., López, J. M., Sánchez-Camacho, C., & Marín, O. (2002). Localization of choline acetyltransferase (ChAT) immunoreactivity in the brain of a caecilian amphibian, *Dermophis mexicanus* (Amphibia: Gymnophiona). *Journal of Comparative Neurology, 448,* 249–267. http://dx.doi.org/10.1002/cne.10233

Grant, D., Anderson, O., & Twitty, V. (1968). Homing orientation by olfaction in newts (*Taricha rivularis*). *Science, 160*, 1354–1356. http://dx.doi.org/10.1126/science.160.3834.1354

Greding, E. J. (1971). Comparative rates of learning in frogs (Ranidae) and toads (Bufonidae). *Caribbean Journal of Science, 11*, 203–208.

Grisham, W., & Powers, A. (1990). Effects of dorsal and medial cortex lesions on reversal in turtles. *Physiology and Behavior, 47*, 43–49. http://dx.doi.org/10.1016/0031-9384(90)90040-B

Herold, C., Coppola, V. J., & Bingman, V. P. (2015). The maturation of research into the avian hippocampal formation: Recent discoveries from one of the nature's foremost navigators. *Hippocampus, 25*, 1193–1211. http://dx.doi.org/10.1002/hipo.22463

Hodos, W., & Campbell, C. B. G. (1969). Scala naturae: Why there is no theory in comparative psychology. *Psychological Review, 76*, 337–350. http://dx.doi.org/10.1037/h0027523

Ingle, D., & Sahagian, D. (1973). Solution of a spatial constancy problem by goldfish. *Physiological Psychology, 1*, 83–84. http://dx.doi.org/10.3758/BF03326873

Landler, L., & Gollmann, G. (2011). Magnetic orientation of the Common Toad: Establishing an arena approach for adult anurans. *Frontiers in Zoology, 8*, 6. http://dx.doi.org/10.1186/1742-9994-8-6

Liu, Y., Day, L. B., Summers, K., & Burmeister, S. S. (2019). A cognitive map in a poison frog. *Journal of Experimental Biology, 222*, jeb197467. http://dx.doi.org/10.1242/jeb.197467

Liu, Y., Jones, C. D., Day, L. B., Summers, K., & Burmeister, S. S. (2020). Cognitive phenotype and differential gene expression in a hippocampal homologue in two species of frog. *Integrative and Comparative Biology, 60*(4), 1007–1023. https://doi.org/10.1093/icb/icaa032

López, J. C., Broglio, C., Rodríguez, F., Thinus-Blanc, C., & Salas, C. (1999). Multiple spatial learning strategies in goldfish (*Carassius auratus*). *Animal Cognition, 2*, 109–120. https://doi.org/10.1007/s100710050031

López, J. C., Gómez, Y., Rodríguez, F., Broglio, C., Vargas, J. P., & Salas, C. (2001). Spatial learning in turtles. *Animal Cognition, 4*, 49–59. https://doi.org/10.1007/s100710100091

López, J. C., Vargas, J. P., Gomez, Y., & Salas, C. (2003). Spatial and non-spatial learning in turtles: The role of medial cortex. *Behavioral Brain Research, 143*, 109–120. http://dx.doi.org/10.1016/S0166-4328(03)00030-5

Lüddecke, H. (2003). Space use, cave choice and spatial learning in the dendrobatid frog *Colostethus palmatus*. *Amphibia-Reptilia, 24*, 37–46. http://dx.doi.org/10.1163/15685380376380692O

MacDonald, C. J., Carrow, S., Place, R., & Eichenbaum, H. (2013). Distinct hippocampal time cell sequences represent odor memories in immobilized rats. *Journal of Neuroscience, 33*, 14607–14616. http://dx.doi.org/10.1523/JNEUROSCI.1537-13.2013

Mackintosh, N. J. (2002). Do not ask whether they have a cognitive map, but how they find their way about. *Psicológica, 23*, 165–185.

Marín, O., Smeets, W. J., & González, A. (1997). Distribution of choline acetyltransferase immunoreactivity in the brain of anuran (*Rana perezi, Xenopus laevis*) and urodele (*Pleurodeles waltl*) amphibians. *Journal of Comparative Neurology, 382*, 499–534. http://dx.doi.org/10.1002/(SICI)1096-9861(19970616)382:4%3C499::AID-CNE6%3E3.0.CO;2-Y

Mitchell, M. D., McCormick, M. I., Ferrari, M. C. O., & Chivers, D. P. (2011). Friend or foe? The role of latent inhibition in predator and non-predator labelling by coral reef fishes. *Animal Cognition, 14*, 707–714. http://dx.doi.org/10.1007/s10071-011-0405-6

Muzio, R. N., Segura, E. T., & Papini, M. R. (1993). Effects of lesions in the medial pallium on instrumental learning in the toad (*Bufo arenarum*). *Physiology and Behavior, 54*, 185–188. http://dx.doi.org/10.1016/0031-9384(93)90064-M

(1994). Learning under partial reinforcement in the toad (Bufo arenarum): Effects of lesions in the medial pallium. *Behavioral and Neural Biology, 61*, 36–46.

Nadel, L. (1991). The hippocampus and space revisited. *Hippocampus, 1*, 221–229. http://dx.doi.org/10.1002/hipo.450010302

Nardi, D., & Bingman, V. P. (2007). Asymmetrical participation of the left and right hippocampus for representing environmental geometry in homing pigeons. *Behavioural Brain Research, 178*, 160–171. http://dx.doi.org/10.1016/j.bbr.2006.12.010

Neary, T. J. (1990). The pallium of anuran amphibians. In E. G. Jones and A. Peters (Eds.), *Cerebral cortex. Comparative structure and evolution of cerebral cortex* (part 1, vol. 8A, pp. 107–138). Plenum Press.

Newcombe, N. S., Ratliff, K. R., Shallcross, W. L., & Twyman, A. D. (2010). Young children's use of features to reorient is more than just associative: Further evidence against a modular view of spatial processing. *Developmental Science, 13*, 213–220. http://dx.doi .org/10.1111/j.1467-7687.2009.00877.x

Northcutt, R. G., & Kicliter, E. (1980). Organization of the amphibian telencephalon. In S. O. E. Ebbesson (Ed.), *Comparative neurology of the telencephalon* (pp. 203–225). Plenum.

Northcutt, R. G., & Ronan, M, (1992). Afferent and efferent connections of the bullfrog medial pallium. *Brain Behavior and Evolution, 40*, 1–16. http://dx.doi.org/10.1159/000113898

O'Keefe, J., & Nadel, L. (1978). *The hippocampus as a cognitive map*. Clarendon Press.

Papini, M. R.; Muzio, R. N., & Segura, E. T. (1995). Instrumental learning in toads (*Bufo arenarum*): Reinforcer magnitude and the medial pallium. *Brain, Behavior and Evolution, 46*, 61–71. http://dx.doi.org/10.1159/000113259

Pašukonis, A., Loretto, M. C., & Hödl, W. (2018). Map-like navigation from distances exceeding routine movements in the Three-striped poison frog (*Ameerega trivittata*). *Journal of Experimental Biology, 221*, jeb169714. http://dx.doi.org/10.1242/jeb.169714

Pašukonis, A., Trenkwalder, K., Ringler, M., Ringler, E., Mangione, R., Steininger, J., & Hödl, W. (2016). The significance of spatial memory for water finding in a tadpole-transporting frog. *Animal Behaviour, 116*, 89–98. http://dx.doi.org/10.1016/j.anbehav.2016.02.023

Pašukonis, A., Warrington, I., Ringler, M., & Hödl, W. (2014). Poison frogs rely on experience to find the way home in the rainforest. *Biology letters, 10*, 20140642. http://dx.doi.org/10 .1098/rsbl.2014.0642

Pecchia, T., & Vallortigara, G. (2010). Reorienting strategies in a rectangular array of landmarks by domestic chicks (*Gallus gallus*). *Journal of Comparative Psychology, 124*, 147–158. http://dx.doi.org/10.1037/a0019145

Phillips, J. B. (1987). Laboratory studies of homing orientation in the eastern red-spotted newt, *Notophthalmus viridescens*. *Journal of Experimental Biology, 131*, 215–229.

Phillips, J. B., Adler, K., & Borland, S. C. (1995). True navigation by an amphibian. *Animal Behaviour, 50*, 855–858. http://dx.doi.org/10.1016/0003-3472(95)80146-4

Rodríguez, R., López, J. C., Vargas, J. P., Gómez, Y., Broglio, C., & Salas, C. (2002). Conservation of spatial memory function in the pallial forebrain of reptiles and ray-finned fishes. *Journal of Neuroscience, 22*, 2894–2903. http://dx.doi.org/10.1523/ JNEUROSCI.22-07-02894.2002

Sakimoto, Y., & Sakata, S. (2018). The role of the hippocampal theta rhythm in non-spatial discrimination and associative learning task. *Neuroscience and Biobehavioral Reviews, 110*, 92–99. https://doi.org/10.1016/j.neubiorev.2018.09.016

Salas, C., Rodríguez, F., Vargas, J. P., Durán, E., & Torres, B. (1996). Spatial learning and memory deficits alter telencephalic ablation in goldfish trained in place and turn maze procedures. *Behavioral Neuroscience, 110*, 965–980. http://dx.doi.org/10.1037/0735-7044 .110.5.965

San Mauro, D. (2010). A multilocus timescale for the origin of extant amphibians. *Molecular Phylogenetics and Evolution, 56*, 554–561. http://dx.doi.org/10.1016/j.ympev.2010.04.019

Schoch, R. R. (2014). *Amphibian evolution: The life of early land vertebrates*. John Wiley & Sons.

Sherry, D. F. (2017). Food storing and memory. In C. ten Cate and S. D. Healy (Eds.), *Avian cognition* (pp. 52–74). Cambridge University Press.

Shishimi, A. (1985). Latent inhibition experiments with goldfish (*Carassius auratus*). *Journal of Comparative Psychology, 99*(3), 316–327. https://doi.org/10.1037/0735-7036.99.3.316

Sinsch, U. (1987). Orientation behaviour of toads (*Bufo bufo*) displaced from the breeding site. *Journal of Comparative Physiology A, 161*, 715–727. http://dx.doi.org/10.1007/BF00605013

(1990). Migration and orientation in anuran amphibians. *Ethology Ecology & Evolution, 2*, 65–79. http://dx.doi.org/10.1080/08927014.1990.9525494

(2014). Movement ecology of amphibians: From individual migratory behaviour to spatially structured populations in heterogeneous landscapes. *Canadian Journal of Zoology, 92*, 491–502. http://dx.doi.org/10.1139/cjz-2013-0028

Sinsch, U., & Kirst, C. (2016). Homeward orientation of displaced newts (*Triturus cristatus, Lissotriton vulgaris*) is restricted to the range of routine movements. *Ethology Ecology & Evolution, 28*, 312–328. http://dx.doi.org/10.1080/03949370.2015.1059893

Sotelo, M. I., Alcalá Martín, J. A., Bingman, V. P., & Muzio, R. N. (2020). On the transfer of spatial learning between geometrically different shaped environments in the terrestrial toad, *Rhinella arenarum. Animal Cognition, 23*, 55–70. https://dx.doi.org/10.1007/s10071-019-01315-9

Sotelo, M. I., Bingman, V. P., & Muzio, R. N. (2015). Goal orientation by geometric and feature cues: Spatial learning in the terrestrial toad *Rhinella arenarum. Animal Cognition, 18*, 315–323. http://dx.doi.org/10.1007/s10071-014-0802-8

(2017). Slope-based and geometric encoding of a goal location by the terrestrial toad (*Rhinella arenarum*). *Journal of Comparative Psychology, 131*, 362–369. https://dx.doi.org/10.1037/com0000084

(In prep.). The medial pallium and the spatial encoding of geometric and visual cues in the terrestrial toad, Rhinella arenarum.

Sotelo, M. I., Daneri, M. F., Bingman, V. P., & Muzio, R. N. (2016). Telencephalic neuronal activation associated with spatial memory in the terrestrial toad, *Rhinella arenarum*: Participation of the medial pallium in navigation by geometry. *Brain, Behavior and Evolution, 88*, 149–160. https://dx.doi.org/10.1159/000447441

Sturz, B. R., Gurley, T., & Bodily, K. D. (2011). Orientation in trapezoid-shaped enclosures: Implications for theoretical accounts of geometry learning. *Journal of Experimental Psychology: Animal Behavior Processes, 37*, 246–253. http://dx.doi.org/10.1037/a0021215

Stynoski, J. L. (2009). Discrimination of offspring by indirect recognition in an egg-feeding dendrobatid frog, *Oophaga pumilio. Animal Behaviour, 78*, 1351–1356. http://dx.doi.org/10.1016/j.anbehav.2009.09.002

Summers, K., & Tumulty, J. (2013). Parental care, sexual selection, and mating systems in neotropical poison frogs. In R. H. Macedo and G. Machado (Eds.), *Sexual selection: Perspectives and models from the neotropics* (pp. 289–320). Elsevier Academic Press.

Tennant, W. A., & Bitterman, M. E. (1975). Blocking and overshadowing in two species of fish. *Journal of Experimental Psychology: Animal Behavior Processes, 1*, 22–29. https://doi.org/10.1037/0097-7403.1.1.22

Twitty, V., Grant, D., & Anderson, O. (1964). Long distance homing in the newt *Taricha rivularis. Proceedings of the National Academy of Sciences of the United States of America, 51*, 51–58. http://dx.doi.org/10.1073/pnas.51.1.51

Vargas, J. P., Bingman, V. P., Portavella, M., & López, J. C. (2006). Telencephalon and geometric space in goldfish. *European Journal of Neuroscience, 24*, 2870–2878. http://dx.doi.org/10.1111/j.1460-9568.2006.05174.x

Vargas, J. P., López, J. C., Salas, C., & Thinus-Blanc, C. (2004). Encoding of geometrical and featural spatial information by goldfish (*Carassius auratus*). *Journal of Comparative Psychology, 118*, 206–216. http://dx.doi.org/10.1037/0735-7036.118.2.206

Wang, H. H., Li, L. Y., Wang, L. W., & Liang, C. C. (2007). Morphological and histological studies on the telencephalon of the salamander *Onychodactylus fischeri. Neuroscience Bulletin, 23*, 170–174. http://dx.doi.org/10.1007/s12264-007-0025-y

Westhoff, G., & Roth, G. (2002). Morphology and projection pattern of medial and dorsal pallial neurons in the frog *Discoglossus pictus* and the salamander *Plethodon jordani. Journal of Comparative Neurology, 445*, 97–121. http://dx.doi.org/10.1002/cne.10136

Wolach, A. H., Breuning, S. E., Roccaforte, P., & Solhkhan, N. (1977). Overshadowing and blocking in a Goldfish (*Carassius auratus*) respiratory conditioning situation. *The Psychological Record, 27*(4), 693–702. https://doi.org/10.1007/bf03394492

Yoshida, K., Drew, M. R., Mimura, M., & Tanaka, K. F. (2019). Serotonin-mediated inhibition of ventral hippocampus required for goal-directed behavior. *Nature Neuroscience, 22*, 770–777. http://dx.doi.org/10.1038/s41593-019-0376-5

7

PAVLOVIAN CONDITIONING, SURVIVAL, AND REPRODUCTIVE SUCCESS

Mark A. Krause and Michael Domjan

What factors determine whether an individual organism succeeds at reproducing relative to its competitors? This is the central question in Darwinian evolution. Answers depend on evolutionary, life history, and ecological factors. For example, sexual dimorphism in body size and color influences interactions between conspecifics (e.g., aggression, territoriality), courtship, and mating success, see Andersson & Simmons, 2006. Among social animals, reproductive success may be influenced by dominant-subordinate dynamics or species-specific communication skills that facilitate mating. Learning is another potential factor that influences reproductive success. Learning may contribute to fecundity indirectly, by facilitating survival as an animal learns about the location of food and the location of places that provide safety from predators. Learning may also have a direct effect on reproductive success by facilitating mating interactions and the probability of producing offspring. If learning results in physiological and behavioral changes that increase fertility, then we can add learning to the list of factors that influence relative reproductive success among competing individuals.

A growing body of evidence indicates that learning influences different behavioral and perceptual processes involved in courtship, mating, fertilization, nesting, and other important behaviors related to survival and fitness. Learning is involved in individual recognition and preference (Pandeirada et al., 2017), motor coordination that facilitates increased efficiency of mating (Domjan et al., 2003), instrumental responses that result in sexual reinforcement (Everitt et al., 1987), and Pavlovian conditioned responses to stimuli that are predictive of sexual encounters (Domjan & Gutiérrez, 2019; Zamble et al., 1986). The timing of egg laying, substrate choice, and nest site selection are influenced by learning in insects and birds (Dukas, 2013; Gámez & León, 2018). The animal learning literature is replete with examples of how learning influences survival and mating. In this chapter, we focus on how one form of learning, Pavlovian conditioning, contributes to reproductive success.

7.1 PAVLOVIAN INFLUENCES ON REPRODUCTIVE BEHAVIOR

From a functional perspective, Pavlovian conditioning is an integral component of adaptive behavior because it prepares organisms to interact more effectively with biologically important events, such as food, mates, or predatory danger. A biologically significant event is an unconditioned stimulus (US) that elicits coping responses without prior training. However, interactions with a US can be significantly improved if the organism can learn to predict the US on the basis of a preliminary or antecedent event, the conditioned stimulus or CS (Domjan, 2005). For example, in humans, Pavlovian conditioning facilitates maternal nursing and infant suckling responses. Olfactory and other sensory cues from the infant stimulate oxytocin release in a nursing mother, which in turn stimulates milk letdown (McNeilly et al., 1983). For the infant in the nursing dyad, the orosensory cues of the nipple in the mouth elicit suckling responses unconditionally, and tactile cues that precede this US come to elicit conditioned anticipatory suckling (Blass et al., 1984).

A functional perspective on Pavlovian conditioning views CSs as naturally occurring events that have a close spatiotemporal relationship to a US (Domjan et al., 2004). Food, for example, is not distributed randomly in the environment. Rather, it occurs in connection with various visual, olfactory, or auditory cues. In the natural environment these food-related stimuli serve as CSs that become associated with the food. In a similar fashion, potential mates do not appear at random, but are predicable based on temporal, spatial, visual, or other cues that can serve as potential CSs for sexual conditioning. Functional approaches to studying conditioning contrast with more traditional general-process learning approaches, which ignore the ecological context in which learning normally occurs. General-process approaches have been highly successful in describing various learning phenomena and their underlying mechanisms, but they have fallen short of explaining *why* learning occurs (Domjan & Krause, 2017; Dunlap & Stephens, 2014).

A Pavlovian CS that predicts mating opportunity is functionally important because it prepares the organism to interact more effectively with his or her sexual partner (the US). The features of the cue, whether one or both partners experience its temporal relation to the US (i.e., the CS-US interval) and other factors, provide important information about the US, and in so doing can influence the form of conditioned responding. This has been demonstrated in work on conditioned sexual behavior in Japanese quail (*Coturnix japonica*), laboratory rats (*Rattus norvegicus*), and blue gourami fish (*Trichogaster trichopterus*). A CS consisting of a light, for example, may be associated with presentation of a sexual partner and will come to elicit conditioned approach behavior in both quail and fish (Domjan et al., 1986; Hollis et al., 1997). On the other hand, a contextual CS will elicit conditioned place preference in rats and quail (Akins, 1998; Paredes & Alonso, 1997). A CS that includes conspecific cues elicits both conditioned appetitive and consummatory responses (Domjan & Krause, 2017). How quail interact during an encounter with a sexual partner (US exposure) depends on whether the male, female, or both are signaled (Mahometa & Domjan, 2005). Short CS-US intervals elicit focal search behavior (localized near the CS), whereas long CS-US intervals elicit general searching behavior (Akins, 2000). These results show that overt behavioral mating responses are readily modified by conditioning procedures in many ways. Thus, there is evidence of a strong functional relationship between Pavlovian conditioning and sexual behavior. Pavlovian conditioning also alters reproductive physiology and thereby contributes directly to reproductive success.

7.2 PAVLOVIAN INFLUENCES ON REPRODUCTIVE PHYSIOLOGY

Pavlovian conditioned stimuli can stimulate or augment gonadal hormone responses that regulate sexual arousal and reproductive physiology (Ball & Balthazart, 2010). In experiments demonstrating such effects, CSs are typically paired or unpaired with mating opportunities, the US, and are subsequently presented during test trials in which physiological parameters (e.g., sperm output) are measured. CSs often consist of a discrete signal, such as a light, or a physical context paired with a mating opportunity. Graham and Desjardins (1980) provided an early demonstration of the effects of Pavlovian conditioning on reproductive hormone release in rats. Male rats were exposed to daily pairings of a CS with a sexually receptive female for two weeks. Following this phase of Pavlovian conditioning, the CS alone elicited levels of luteinizing hormone and serum testosterone comparable to what was released in response to a receptive female (luteinizing hormone stimulates testosterone production in Leydig cells).

In a subsequent study with male Japanese quail (*Coturnix japonica*), Domjan et al. (1998) used context cues in a study of the effects of Pavlovian conditioning on sperm output. One group of male quail received exposures to a distinct experimental chamber paired with the opportunity to mate with a female, whereas a control group experienced unpaired access to the chamber and mating opportunity. During test trials, males in the paired and unpaired groups were given access to a probe stimulus in the experimental chamber. The probe stimulus included partial cues of a taxidermic female quail (see Figure 7.1, left panel), but these were so limited that the probe stimulus alone was not sufficient to alter behavior or to prime sperm release. However, after only six conditioning trials, males in the paired group

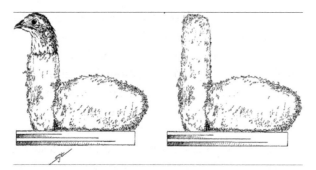

FIGURE 7.1. Conditioned stimuli used in various experiments on conditioned sexual behavior in Japanese quail (*Coturnix japonica*) discussed in the current chapter. Both stimulus objects are made of foam pads with terry cloth covers comprising a "body" and a "neck" region. These stimuli can physically support the full range of copulatory responses shown by male quail, including approaching, grabbing the neck, mounting, and making cloacal contact with the posterior portion of the body region. The object on the left includes the taxidermically prepared head of a female quail affixed to the "neck." This object served as the probe stimulus in Domjan et al. (1998).

From Cusato, B., and Domjan, M. (1998). Special efficacy of sexual conditioned stimuli that include species-typical cues: Tests with a conditioned stimulus preexposure design. *Learning and Motivation, 29,* 152-167.

spent significantly more time in the vicinity of the probe, released greater volumes of semen, and their semen had greater numbers of sperm compared to males in the unpaired group (Figure 7.2).

Higher volumes of sperm at ejaculation are correlated with increased chance of fertilization (Bonde et al., 1998). This is particularly important in species in which sperm competition takes place. Sperm competition occurs when more than one male has reproductive access to a single female, which is a common situation in many vertebrate and invertebrate species. Sperm competition economics predict that sperm quality should vary according to social context, where more resources are allocated to sperm quality when there is increased probability of insemination (Kelly & Jennions, 2011). For example, higher-quality ejaculates should occur in the presence of fecund females. This was demonstrated in horses (*Equus caballus*), where stallions exposed to mares in estrus had higher-quality ejaculates (reduced oxidative stress on cell membranes) than did males exposed to diestrus mares (Jeannerat et al., 2017).

Moatt et al. (2014) reported elevated sperm levels in male fruit flies (*Drosophila melanogaster*) exposed to potential sperm competition. To simulate a context in which sperm competition would be likely, male flies were placed in perforated vials in the vicinity of another male fly that they could detect through visual, auditory, and olfactory cues. Male flies in a noncompetitive group were placed in identically prepared vials but a male was not present in the adjacent vial. Significantly more viable sperm were found in the testes of males kept for seven days in the sperm competition group in comparison to the group isolated from other males.

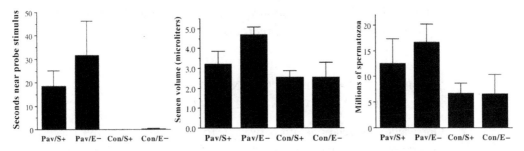

FIGURE 7.2. Mean (+SE) seconds spent near the probe stimulus (left panel) and semen volume (middle panel) and number of spermatozoa (right panel) released upon exposure to distinctive contextual cues in male quail. For the Pavlovian group (Pav), the contextual cues had been previously paired with copulatory opportunity; for the control group (Con), the contextual cues and copulatory opportunity had been unpaired. S+ and E- refer to genetic lines selected for high sociality and low emotionality, respectively.
Redrawn from Domjan, M., Blesbois, E., and Williams, J. (1998). The adaptive significance of sexual conditioning: Pavlovian control of sperm release. *Psychological Science, 9*, 411–415.

Collectively, work on various species demonstrates that Pavlovian conditioning alters reproductive physiology in ways that may influence reproductive success. In male *Coturnix* quail, one of the physiological mechanisms that may facilitate reproduction is the conditioning of rhythmic cloacal sphincter movements (RCSMs). The cloacal gland of the male quail produces a foamy substance that facilitates sperm transport and the fertilization of eggs (Adkins-Regan, 1999). Rhythmic cloacal sphincter movements increase the production and output of this cloacal foam. RCSMs occur as Pavlovian conditioned responses to a sexually conditioned stimulus (Holloway et al., 2005), increasing the availability of cloacal foam during copulation. As other components of copulatory behavior, this conditioned increase in RCSMs is testosterone dependent (Holloway et al., 2005) and requires the aromatization of testosterone. The administration of the aromatase inhibitor Vorozol reduces conditioned RCSMs, as well as mounting and social proximity behavior (Cornil et al., 2004, 2006). Furthermore, these effects probably occurred because of the inhibition of aromatization of testosterone in the preoptic area of the hypothalamus (Cornil et al., 2006).

Research is also starting to uncover the neural mechanisms that mediate Pavlovian conditioning effects on gonadal physiology. Research with male quail indicates that a CS that has been previously paired with copulation increases neural activation of some brain regions and decreases activation of other areas. Exposure to a sexually conditioned CS results in elevated c-fos expression in the medial preoptic area of the hypothalamus and the medial region of the bed nucleus of the stria terminalis (Taziaux et al., 2008). In contrast, exposure to a sexually conditioned stimulus decreases the number of c-fos immunoreactive cells in the nucleus taeniae of the amygdala and in the hippocampus (Taziaux et al., 2007).

As work reviewed here shows, Pavlovian conditioning regulates the underlying physiological processes that are responsible for sexual arousal

and behavior. The next question we address is whether Pavlovian conditioning also has a direct effect on reproductive success.

7.3 PAVLOVIAN EFFECTS ON FERTILITY
AND REPRODUCTIVE INVESTMENT

One way to test relationships between learning and reproductive success is to
directly measure how learning affects fertility rates in animals that copulate
after exposure to a Pavlovian CS that signals access to a mate. Experimental
work in several species has demonstrated that conditioning can enhance
fertility. Hollis et al. (1997) tested whether Pavlovian conditioning influences
mating behavior and reproductive success in the blue gourami (*Trichogaster
trichopterus*). Male gouramis are territorial and direct aggression toward
interloping "intruder" males. Sometimes this can include approaching
females. Therefore, defensive responding can come at a reproductive cost
because it can drive away potentially receptive females. When signaled via a
Pavlovian cue, male gouramis inhibited aggressive responses toward arriving
females. The Pavlovian CS facilitated nest building, reduced the latency to
mate and increased the frequency of mating. Most significantly, males whose
interactions with a female were signaled by a Pavlovian CS produced significantly more offspring than did males that experienced unpaired CS and US
presentations. Similar results were found in a study of poison dart frogs
(*Dendrobates tinctorius*; Gaalema, 2013). This study included three groups of
frogs. In one group, pairs of frogs received a Pavlovian signal prior to mating
opportunities. In a second group, the frogs were not signaled, whereas the
third group was a no-treatment control. The signaled group had shorter
latencies to initiate breeding-related responses and produced more eggs than
did the two control groups.

Pavlovian conditioning also influences reproductive success in Japanese
quail. In the first demonstration of this effect, Adkins-Regan and MacKillop
(2003) reported increased fertilization success in quail that copulated after
exposure to sexually conditioned contextual cues. Subsequent studies replicated these findings and showed that the conditioned fertility effect occurs
not just with contextual cues serving as the CS, but also with conditioned
stimuli that consist of a small light or a terrycloth object, like those shown in
Figure 7.1 (Domjan et al., 2012; Mahometa & Domjan, 2005). Mahometa and
Domjan (2005) systematically explored the role of signaling the male, the
female, or both participants in a copulatory interaction and found that the
conditioned fertility effect occurred if both the male and the female were
signaled, but not if just one or the other received the CS. In fact, if only the
male or only the female were signaled, fertility was no higher than in control
birds that received no signal at all.

In the original demonstration of the conditioned fertility effect in blue gouramis, Hollis et al. (1997) not only measured the number of offspring that were produced but observed that sexual conditioning produced significant changes in how males interacted with females. Furthermore, these behavioral changes (decreased aggression, increased nest building, and more frequent mating) probably contributed to the larger number of offspring that were sired by the Pavlovian males than the control males. Conditioned behavioral changes probably also contribute to the conditioned fertility effect in quail. Sexual conditioning increases the duration of squatting by females in the presence of a male (Gutiérrez & Domjan, 1997). Because the female spends more time squatting, the male is more successful in grabbing and mounting the female, and this leads to an increase in the male's copulatory efficiency (Domjan et al., 2003). The duration of the female squatting and the efficiency of the male's copulatory behavior are both positively correlated with the percentage of fertilized eggs that result from a copulatory interaction (Domjan et al., 2003). Another factor that likely contributes to conditioned fertility effects in quail are the RCSMs that males make in response to a sexually conditioned stimulus (Holloway et al., 2005; Taziaux et al., 2007), since these cloacal sphincter contractions increase cloacal foam that facilitates sperm transport (Adkins-Regan, 1999).

SEXUAL CONDITIONING AND SPERM COMPETITION

For many species, reproductive success is not necessarily guaranteed just because copulation and insemination occur. Sperm competition further complicates reproductive outcomes in species in which females mate with multiple males prior to gestation or egg laying. Sperm competition has been well-documented in birds (Birkhead, 1987), even among species classified as monogamous but which also engage in extra-pair copulations. Numerous physical variables have been considered in analyses of sperm competition, such as overall size, length, and motility of the sperm. Sexual Pavlovian conditioning is also relevant, even though it is a factor not traditionally considered in analyses of sperm competition.

Matthews et al. (2007) tested whether Pavlovian conditioning increases relative reproductive success in a sperm competition situation in Japanese quail. Five sexual conditioning trials were conducted for the male participants. Each male had equal exposure to two distinctively different experimental chambers or contexts. One of these (counterbalanced across subjects) was designated as the "sexual" context whereas the other was designated as the "nonsexual" context. During the conditioning phase, placement in the sexual context was followed by copulatory access to a female, whereas a female was not provided following placement in the nonsexual context. Following five trials in each context, a sperm competition test was conducted.

During this test phase, females were allowed to copulate with two males in succession. One of the males received access to the female in the sexual context whereas the other male copulated with the female in the nonsexual context (in a counterbalanced order). All of these copulations were signaled for the female. Which of the males sired the resultant offspring was determined using a microsatellite DNA analysis. The results indicated that of the 78 fertilized eggs that the females laid in this experiment, 72% were fertilized by the male whose copulation was signaled by exposure to the sexual context. Copulation following exposure to the nonsexual context was responsible for just 28% of the fertilizations.

An important variable in sperm competition is the interval that separates the two sources of sperm the female receives. In this experiment, the two copulatory periods that each female received were separated by 15 minutes. Under these circumstances, if neither male receives a Pavlovian signal, each male ends up fertilizing about the same number of eggs. However, if copulation with the two males is separated by a much longer duration (five hours), the first male's sperm are at a serious disadvantage. Matthews et al. (2007) found that with a five-hour delay between males, if neither of the males receives a Pavlovian signal before the copulations, the first male will be responsible for only 26% of the fertilized eggs and the second male will be responsible for 74% of the fertilizations (reported in Domjan et al., 2012). Matthews et al. (2007) also examined the impact of a Pavlovian signal on sperm competition under these circumstances. In this study, signaling the copulation for the first male raised fertilization rates from 26% to 43%. Thus, Pavlovian signaling helped to overcome the fertility disadvantage suffered by the first male in a sexual competition situation where copulations by the two males are separated by a long period. (For comparable results in a sperm depletion paradigm, see Domjan et al., 2012.)

MATERNAL EFFECTS ON OFFSPRING VIABILITY

Another important consideration is how learning influences reproductive outcomes once fertilization has occurred. Maternal effects on offspring viability are well established across multiple taxa (Langen et al., 2019; Trivers & Willard, 1973). The physical state (e.g., body condition) of females is related to their investment in offspring. Conversely, offspring viability is influenced by maternal characteristics. The fertility advantage of conditioning is therefore constrained by postfertilization maternal effects. In birds, maternal investment in eggs, as well as sex ratio, is influenced by external events such as the quality of mate song, and by internal characteristics such as egg testosterone levels (Ledecka et al., 2019). Rutkowska and Adkins-Regan (2009) examined how learning affects reproductive investment in Japanese quail. The researchers tested whether mating with a familiar male in a context predictive of mating results in increased maternal investment in offspring. This is a departure from other work on conditioned fertility effects utilizing unfamiliar males during test trials. Females that anticipated copulation sired more male offspring and also showed sexual dimorphism in the size of their eggs, producing larger eggs for daughters than for sons. These results indicate that learning influences differential reproductive investment in offspring in ways that enhance fitness.

7.4 PAVLOVIAN CONTRIBUTIONS TO PHENOTYPIC VARIATION IN SEXUAL BEHAVIOR

The findings reviewed thus far provide a wealth of laboratory data showing that conditioning contributes to reproductive success. Further study in natural populations would be of value. In addition, the specific behavioral and physiological mechanisms underlying conditioned fertility advantages require closer examination to establish proximate causation and to better understand how learning relates to natural and sexual selection. As discussed elsewhere in this volume (Dunlap and Dexheimer, Chapter 4; Liefting, Chapter 5; Griffin and Diquelou, Chapter 8), phenotypic variation in mechanisms supporting learning are directly or indirectly influenced by natural selection. Thus, it is necessary to understand these mechanisms, their underlying sources of variation (e.g., allelic, epigenetic effects), and the consequences of this variation in relation to reproductive fitness. Accessing all three measures in a single study species would be a significant contribution. Work with rodents and quail has cast some light into this largely unknown territory.

Males and females differ in their readiness to mate, and strategies employed by either sex influence whether copulation occurs. For example, female rats prefer to control the pacing of copulation and favor contexts in which they are able to exert such control (Pfaus et al., 2001). When receptive, female quail squat and remain still in the presence of a male with which the female is willing to mate. Female quail actively avoid males with which they do not wish to mate. Increased female receptivity, as measured by the duration of squatting behavior, results in efficient copulatory responses in male quail, namely, fewer grab and mount attempts relative to successful cloacal contacts. In turn, the efficiency of male copulatory behavior is positively correlated with fertility in quail (Domjan et al., 2003).

Male rats show "conditioned ejaculatory preferences" (Kippin & Pfaus, 2001). Pairing a neutral odor such as almond or lemon (the CS) with a female rat (the US) results in a preference to ejaculate in female rats scented with that odor during test trials. Conditioned males still mount and intromit unscented females that are presented simultaneously with scented females, but the males selectively ejaculate with scented females (Kippin & Pfaus,

2001). Controlled experiments have demonstrated that it is the pairing of the consummatory act of ejaculation with the odor, rather than other behaviors such as approach or mounting, that results in the ejaculatory preference. Male rats that do not associate the CS odor with ejaculation do not show a preference for scented females in simultaneous choice tests.

Female rats exert control over whether and with whom they mate, and learning plays a role in their mate preference. Experiments examining these phenomena employ an apparatus with two compartments arranged so that the female is free to enter the male's compartment but the male cannot enter the female's compartment. This type of apparatus allows the female to pace its copulations with a male. Female rats can learn that an arbitrary odor cue signals a mating opportunity with a preferred male. Females develop a conditioned place preference for an almond scent if the scent is paired with paced copulation with a male. Preference for the almond odor does not develop if the odor is presented in an unpaired fashion with paced copulation (Coria-Avila et al., 2005). Other studies have shown that female rats have an unconditioned preference to mate with males of their own genetic strain, but this preference can be altered toward males of a different strain if females experience paced copulations with them (Coria-Avila et al., 2006). In summary, it appears that conditioned ejaculatory preference in male rats and conditioned paced mating preferences in females are major behavioral mechanisms for modifying sexual behavior. CS-directed responses to sexual stimuli in male and female rats facilitate reproduction. Although fertility has not been measured directly in the sexual conditioning experiments with rats, the demonstration of an ejaculatory preference and the absence of ejaculation in females unpaired with the almond odor suggest that these conditioning effects probably also produce corresponding advantages in fertility. In sum, results from experiments on conditioned sexual behavior, reproductive physiology, and fertility suggest a critical role for learning in evolutionary processes. What is needed is a coherent framework for integrating these findings.

Domjan and Gutiérrez (2019) used a behavior systems approach (Silva and Silva, Chapter 12; Timberlake, 2001) to summarize the results of numerous studies of sexual conditioning in quail and laboratory rats. A behavior systems approach considers the various types of responses that animals perform in the pursuit of a significant biological goal and the types of stimuli that may be involved in controlling these responses. For the sexual behavior system, the response categories considered follow the classic ethological distinction between appetitive and consummatory responses, but the appetitive behavior category has been expanded to distinguish between general search and focal search behavior. In laboratory studies, general search behavior has been indexed by increased nondirected locomotor behavior. Focal search is approach and search of a specific location, usually the location of a conditioned stimulus or potential sexual partner. Consummatory behavior consists of mounting and other copulatory contact responses. The three categories of stimuli that have been considered in the control of each response mode are contextual cues, arbitrary localized stimuli, and ecological localized stimuli. In studies with quail, the ecological cues that have been studied consist of the visual cues of a female's head and partial neck plumage (left panel of Figure 7.1).

The behavior system for sexual learning in males is summarized in Figure 7.3. In this figure, the background shading in each quadrant represents the strength of control of each behavior category by each of the three stimulus categories unconditionally or prior to any learning manipulations. Contextual cues are assumed to generate general search behavior unconditionally whereas ecological species-typical cues are assumed to stimulate focal search and consummatory responses. Arbitrary localized stimuli have little behavioral effect prior to conditioning.

Changes in the sexual behavior of males produced by Pavlovian conditioning procedures are represented by the stars (quail data) and squares (rat data) that have been added to each quadrant in Figure 7.3. The arrows that connect different quadrants represent conditioned modulatory effects between categories of stimuli. As the figure illustrates, simple Pavlovian conditioning manipulations have been found to alter the sexual behavior profile of males in substantial ways.

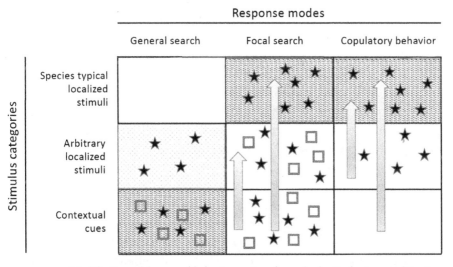

FIGURE 7.3. Modification of the sexual behavior system for males by Pavlovian conditioning. Symbols in each quadrant represent conditioning effects. Stars represent data from studies with quail. Small squares represent data from studies with rats. Arrows indicate how conditioning enables certain cues to modulate responding to other types of stimuli. The origin of each arrow represents the modulating stimulus and the tip of the arrow represents the target of the modulation. The shading of the background represents the strength of control of each response component unconditionally.

From Domjan, M., and Gutiérrez, G. (2019). The behavior system for sexual learning. *Behavioural Processes, 162,* 184–196. https://doi.org/10.1016/j.beproc.2019.01.013

It is common to think about ecological or species-typical cues as being primarily responsible for "instinctive" or unlearned sexual responses. However, as Figure 7.3 illustrates, learning manipulations can substantially enhance how the naturalistic cues provided by a sexual partner influence sexual behavior. Using ecological species-typical cues as Pavlovian CSs enables those naturalistic cues to elicit stronger approach and copulatory responses. Furthermore, as indicated by the arrows that terminate in the top-row quadrants, conditioned contextual cues and conditioned arbitrary cues can substantially increase the effectiveness of ecological species-typical cues in eliciting both approach and copulatory contact responses. These latter effects may be interpreted as representing the learned enhancement of "instinctive" sexual behavior.

The quadrants in the middle row of Figure 7.3 illustrate control of behavior by localized arbitrary cues. This row represents cases in which a localized visual cue (e.g., a light) is used as the CS in sexual conditioning. As the middle row illustrates, arbitrary cues can come to elicit all three categories of sexual responses. Conditioned general search behavior occurs if a long (20 minutes) CS-US interval is used (Akins, 2000). With shorter CS-US intervals (1 minute or less), conditioned approach behavior is the prominent conditioned response. Conditioned copulatory responses may also occur, but only if the CS is a three-dimensional object that allows mounting and copulatory attempts (like the object shown in the right panel of Figure 7.1).

The third row in Figure 7.3 illustrates that Pavlovian conditioning can also increase the effectiveness of contextual cues in controlling sexual behavior. Conditioned contextual cues associated with sexual reinforcement can come to elicit general search and focal search responses. However, the most important consequence of context conditioning is that a context that predicts a sexual encounter enhances the effectiveness of ecological species-typical cues in eliciting and controlling sexual approach and copulatory behavior. These effects are evident in changes in how males and females interact. In a sexually conditioned context, females show greater sexual receptivity to a male, and males show increased efficiency in their copulatory responses to a female.

Evidence of sexual conditioning is not as extensive with females as it is with males. Nevertheless, sufficient progress has been made in studies with rats and quail to permit the characterization of the behavior system for sexual learning in females. The available evidence, as summarized by Domjan and Gutiérrez (2019), is presented in Figure 7.4. The response modes that have been identified and measured in studies with female rats and quail include focal search and squatting (in quail) and lordosis (in rats). Experimenters have not identified or measured responses akin to general search behavior. As with the response profile for male conditioned sexual behavior, the stimulus categories considered involve ecological species-typical cues provided by a sexual partner, localized arbitrary cues, and contextual cues.

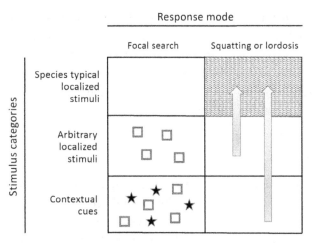

FIGURE 7.4. The response profile for sexual learning in females. Shading represents unconditioned control of behavior. Stars represent conditioning effects with quail. Open squares represent conditioning effects with rats. Arrows represent conditioned modulation of the effectiveness of species-typical cues in eliciting sexual behavior in both quail and rats. From Domjan, M., and Gutiérrez, G. (2019). The behavior system for sexual learning. *Behavioural Processes, 162,* 184–196. https://doi.org/10.1016/j.beproc.2019.01.013

In contrast to male quail, female quail do not approach a conventional CS (an arbitrary localized stimulus) that has been paired with access to a male (Gutiérrez & Domjan, 1997). They do develop a preference for contextual cues paired with exposure to a male (Gutiérrez & Domjan, 2011), and both localized CSs and conditioned contextual cues increase the probability that the female will squat in the presence of a male, thereby facilitating the male's sexual contact responses. These modulatory effects of conditioned localized and contextual cues are represented by the arrows in Figure 7.4.

Female rats will come to approach an arbitrary odor that has been applied to a male (Coria-Avila et al., 2005) and will also show preference for a context in which they have access to a male, but only if the females are permitted to pace their copulations (Paredes & Alonso, 1997). These effects are represented by the squares in Figure 7.4.

The behavioral profile that we have described in some detail here is relevant to the study of how Pavlovian conditioning affects reproductive physiology and fertility. Before fertilization can happen, sexually reproducing organisms must first complete a variety of responses and behavioral sequences. Of course, what these responses look like, and the stimuli that elicit them, vary across species, sex, and may also vary as a function of the mating system of the species. As we have discussed, Pavlovian conditioning plays an important role in modifying the sexual behavior system of quail and rats. Analogous sexual conditioning effects are bound to be discovered with other species for which there is still limited information. Behavioral and physiological responses that enhance fertility are initiated in response to different CS types (contextual, localized, and ecological species-typical). This suggests that conditioned sexual responses, which serve to prepare the organism to interact with a sexual partner (the US), will determine the reproductive outcomes of the sexual encounter. Through these contributions of Pavlovian conditioning to reproductive success, Pavlovian processes are involved in how future generations are shaped by natural selection.

7.5 CONCLUSIONS

Pavlovian conditioning evolved because biologically significant uncondi-tioned stimuli do not occur unannounced in the natural ecology of organ-isms. Significant biological events like food or access to a sexual partner occur in combination with less powerful stimuli that are early components of the causal chain of events that ends in encounter with the US. Learning to predict the US based on those preliminary and early components affords an adaptive advantage because it enables the organism to prepare for the US and respond to it more effectively.

As contributions to this volume show, evolutionary analyses are yielding fascinating insights into the origins and functions of learning and memory. Pavlovian conditioning is phylogenetically widespread, and has spawned numerous empirical and theoretical studies of the evolution of learning (Dunlap et al., 2019). Landmark papers on preparedness, biological con-straints on learning, and adaptive specializations of learning leaned heavily on Pavlovian processes to make the case that learning could be studied from an ecological and evolutionary perspective (Domjan & Galef, 1983; Krause, 2015). Much progress has been made. Advances have come from studies involving phylogenetic analyses (Ginsburg & Jablonka, 2010), experimental evolutionary studies (Dunlap & Stephens, 2014; see Dunlap and Dexheimer, Chapter 4), studies of digital evolution (Pontes et al., 2019), and experiments manipulating the biological relevance of conditioned stimuli (Domjan et al., 2004). A large body of experimental and laboratory-based research with invertebrate and vertebrate species has demonstrated the importance of conditioning in many biological and behavioral systems involved in survival. Conditioned responses prepare organisms to interact with biologically sig-nificant events, such as access to resources, encounters with predators, illness, and mates.

Significant progress in the evolutionary analysis of Pavlovian conditioning has been provided by research that directly ties conditioning to reproductive success. The experiments reviewed in this chapter show that Pavlovian conditioning is involved in altering reproductive behavioral and physio-logical responses that facilitate the transfer of sperm from males to females, and consequently alter rates of fertilization and numbers of offspring that result from sexual encounters. These findings bridge proximate levels of analyses of conditioning, which focus on learning as it benefits the organism on a short timescale, to ultimate levels of analysis that give us insight into the transgenerational and evolutionary consequences of learning (Domjan et al., 2012; Domjan & Gutiérrez, 2019). Behavioral and physical phenotypic traits undergo sexual selection, leading to dimorphic patterns of appearance and responding (Andersson & Simmons, 2006). Pavlovian conditioning may similarly influence the process of sexual selection both within and between males and females. Thus, the relationship between evolution and learning is bidirectional. Evolutionary processes have shaped the mechanisms of Pavlovian learning and how those mechanisms operate. Through conditioned fertility effects, these learning mechanisms can in turn influence genetic transmission and thereby shape the future course of evolution.

REFERENCES

Adkins-Regan, E. (1999). Foam produced by male Coturnix quail: What is its function? *The Auk, 116*(1), 184–193. https://doi.org/10.2307/4089465

Adkins-Regan, E., & MacKillop, E. A. (2003). Japanese quail (*Coturnix japonica*) inseminations are more likely to fertilize eggs in a context predicting mating opportunities. *Proceedings of the Royal Society of London, Series B, 270*, 1685–1689. https://doi.org/10.1098/rspb.2003.2421

Akins, C. K. (1998). Context excitation and modulation of conditioned sexual behavior. *Animal Learning & Behavior, 26*, 416–426. https://doi.org/10.3758/BF03199234

(2000). Effects of species-specific cues and the CS-US interval on the topography of the sexually conditioned response. *Learning and Motivation, 31*, 211–235. https://doi.org/10.1006/lmot.2000.1050

Andersson, M., & Simmons, L. W. (2006). Sexual selection and mate choice. *Trends in Ecology and Evolution, 21*(6), 296–302. https://doi.org/10.1016/j.tree.2006.03.015

Ball, G. F., & Balthazart, J. (2010). Japanese quail as a model system for studying the neuroendocrine control of reproductive and social behaviors. *ILAR Journal, 5*, 310–325. https://doi.org/10.1093/ilar.51.4.310

Birkhead, T. (1987). Sperm competition in birds. *Trends in Ecology & Evolution, 2*(9), 268–272. https://doi.org/10.1016/0169-5347(87)90033-4

Blass, E.M., & Ganchrow, J. R., &, Steiner, J. E. (1984). Classical conditioning in newborn humans 2–48 hours of age. *Infant Behavior and Development, 7*, 223–235. https://doi.org/10.1016/S0163-6383(84)80060-0

Bonde, J. P., Ernst, E., Jensen, T. K., Hjollund, N. H., Kolstad, H., Henriksen, T. B., … Skakkebaek, N. E. (1998). Relation between semen quality and fertility: A population-based study of 430 first-pregnancy planners. *Lancet (London, England), 352*(9135), 1172–1177. https://doi.org/10.1016/S0140-6736(97)10514-1

Coria-Avila, G. A., Jones, S. L., Solomon, C. E., Gavrila, A. M., Jordan, G. J., & Pfaus, J. G. (2006). Conditioned partner preference in female rats for strain of male. *Physiology and Behavior, 88*, 529–537. https://doi.org/10.1016/j.physbeh.2006.05.001

Coria-Avila, G. A., Ouimet, A. J., Pacheco, P., Manzo, J., & Pfaus, J. G. (2005). Olfactory conditioned partner preference in the female rat. *Behavioral Neuroscience, 119*, 716–725. https://doi.org/10.1037/0735-7044.119.3.716

Cornil, C. A., Holloway, K. S., Taziaux, M., & Balthazart, J. (2004). The effects of aromatase inhibition on testosterone-dependent conditioned rhythmic cloacal sphincter movements in male Japanese quail. *Physiology and Behavior, 83*, 99–105. https://doi.org/10.1016/j.physbeh.2004.07.011

Cornil, C. A., Taziaux, M., Baillien, M., Ball, G. F., & Balthazart, J. (2006). Rapid effects of aromatase inhibition on male reproductive behaviors in Japanese quail. *Hormones and Behavior, 49*, 45–67. https://doi.org/10.1016/j.yhbeh.2005.05.003

Cusato, B., & Domjan, M. (1998). Special efficacy of sexual conditioned stimuli that include species-typical cues: Tests with a conditioned stimulus preexposure design. *Learning and Motivation, 29*, 152–167.

Domjan, M. (2005). Pavlovian conditioning: A functional perspective. *Annual Review of Psychology, 56*, 179–206. https://doi.org/10.1146/annurev.psych.55.090902.141409

Domjan, M., Blesbois, E., & Williams, J. (1998). The adaptive significance of sexual conditioning: Pavlovian control of sperm release. *Psychological Science, 9*, 411–415.

Domjan, M., Cusato, B., & Krause, M. (2004). Learning with arbitrary versus ecological conditioned stimuli: Evidence from sexual conditioning. *Psychonomic Bulletin & Review, 11*, 232–246. https://doi.org/10.3758/BF03196565

Domjan, M., & Galef, B. G. Jr. (1983). Biological constraints on instrumental and classical conditioning: Retrospect and prospect. *Animal Learning & Behavior, 11*, 151–161.

Domjan, M., & Gutiérrez, G. (2019). The behavior system for sexual learning. *Behavioural Processes, 162*, 184–196. https://doi.org/10.1016/j.beproc.2019.01.013

Domjan, M., & Krause, M. A. (2017). Adaptive specializations and the generality of the laws of classical and instrumental conditioning. In R. Menzel (Ed.), *Learning theory and behavior: Vol. 1, Learning and memory: A comprehensive reference* (2nd ed., J. H. Byrne (Ed.), pp. 180–201). Academic Press.

Domjan, M., Lyons, R., North, N. C., & Bruell, J. (1986). Sexual Pavlovian conditioned approach behavior in male Japanese quail (*Coturnix coturnix japonica*). *Journal of Comparative Psychology, 100*, 413–421. https://psycnet.apa.org/doi/10.1037/0735-7036.100.4.413

Domjan, M., Mahometa, M. J., & Matthews, R. N. (2012). Learning in intimate connections: Conditioned fertility and its role in sexual competition. *Socioaffective Neuroscience & Psychology, 2*, 1–10. https://doi.org/10.3402/snp.v2i0.17333

Domjan, M., Mahometa, M. J., & Mills, A. D. (2003). Relative contributions of the male and the female to sexual behavior and reproductive success in the Japanese quail (*Coturnix japonica*). *Journal of Comparative Psychology, 117*, 391–399. https://doi.org/10.1037/0735-7036.117.4.391

Dukas, R. (2013). Effects of learning on evolution: Robustness, innovation and speciation. *Animal Behaviour, 85*(5), 1023–1030. https://doi.org/10.1016/j.anbehav.2012.12.030

Dunlap, A. S., Austin, M. W., & Figueiredo, A. (2019). Components of change and the evolution of learning in theory and experiment. *Animal Behaviour, 147*, 157–166. https://doi.org/10.1016/j.anbehav.2018.05.024

Dunlap, A. S., & Stephens, D. W. (2014). Experimental evolution of prepared learning. *Proceedings of the National Academy of Sciences of the United States of America, 111*, 11750–11755. https://doi.org/10.1073/pnas.1404176111

Everitt, B. J., Fray, P., Kostarczyk, E., Taylor, S., & Stacey, P. (1987). Studies of instrumental behavior with sexual reinforcement in male rats (*Rattus norvegicus*): I. Control by brief visual stimuli paired with a receptive female. *Journal of Comparative Psychology, 101*, 395–406. https://doi.org/10.1037/0735-7036.101.4.395

Gaalema, D. E. (2013). Sexual conditioning in the dyeing poison dart frog (*Dendrobates tinctorius*). *International Journal of Comparative Psychology, 26*, 5–18. http://hdl.handle.net/1853/33895

Gámez, A. M., & León, S. P. (2018). The role of learning in the oviposition behavior of the silkworm moth (*Bombyx mori*). *Behavioural Processes, 157*, 286–290. https://doi.org/10.1016/j.beproc.2018.10.023

Ginsburg, S., & Jablonka, E. (2010). The evolution of associative learning: A factor in the Cambrian explosion. *Journal of Theoretical Biology, 266*, 11–20. https://doi.org/10.1016/j.jtbi.2010.06.017

Graham, J. M., & Desjardins, C. (1980). Classical conditioning: Induction of luteinizing hormone and testosterone secretion in anticipation of sexual activity. *Science, 210*(4473), 1039–1041. https://doi.org/10.1126/science.7434016

Gutiérrez, G., & Domjan, M. (1997). Differences in the sexual conditioned behavior of male and female Japanese quail (*Coturnix japonica*). *Journal of Comparative Psychology, 111,* 135–142. https://doi.org/10.1037/0735-7036.111.2.135

(2011). Conditioning of sexual proceptivity in female quail: Measures of conditioned place preference. *Behavioural Processes, 87,* 268–273.

Hollis, K. L., Pharr, V. L., Dumas, M. J., Britton, G. B., & Field, J. (1997). Classical conditioning provides paternity advantage for territorial male blue gouramis (*Trichogaster trichopterus*). *Journal of Comparative Psychology, 111,* 219–225. https://psycnet.apa.org/doi/10.1037/0735-7036.111.3.219

Holloway, K. S., Balthazart, J., & Cornil, C. A. (2005). Androgen mediation of conditioned rhythmic cloacal sphincter movements in Japanese quail (*Coturnix japonica*). *Journal of Comparative Psychology, 119,* 49–57. https://doi.org/10.1037/0735-7036.119.1.49

Jeannerat, E., Janett, F., Sieme, H., Wedekind, C., & Burger, D. (2017). Quality of seminal fluids varies with type of stimulus at ejaculation. *Scientific Reports, 7,* 1–8. https://doi.org/10.1038/srep44339

Kelly, C. D., & Jennions, M. D. (2011). Sexual selection and sperm quantity: Meta-analyses of strategic ejaculation. *Biological Reviews, 86*(4), 863–884. https://doi.org/10.1111/j.1469-185X.2011.00175.x

Kippin, T. E., & Pfaus, J. G. (2001). The nature of the conditioned response mediating olfactory conditioned ejaculatory preference in the male rat. *Behavioural Brain Research, 122*(1), 11–24. https://doi.org/10.1016/S0166-4328(01)00162-0

Krause, M. A. (2015). Evolutionary perspectives on learning: Conceptual and methodological issues in the study of adaptive specializations. *Animal Cognition, 18*(4), 807–820. https://doi.org/10.1007/s10071-015-0854-4

Langen, E. M. A., Goerlich-Jansson, V. C., & von Engelhardt, N. (2019). Effects of the maternal and current social environment on female body mass and reproductive traits in Japanese quail (*Coturnix japonica*). *Journal of Experimental Biology, 222*(5), jeb187005. https://doi.org/10.1242/jeb.187005

Ledecka, D., Zeman, M., & Okuliarova, M. (2019). Genetic variation in maternal yolk testosterone allocation predicts female mating decisions in Japanese quail. *Animal Behaviour, 157,* 35–42. https://doi.org/10.1016/j.anbehav.2019.08.022

Mahometa, M. J., & Domjan, M. (2005). Classical conditioning increases reproductive success in Japanese quail, *Coturnix japonica. Animal Behaviour, 69*(4), 983–989. https://doi.org/10.1016/j.anbehav.2004.06.023

Matthews, R. N., Domjan, M., Ramsey, M., & Crews, D. (2007). Learning effects on sperm competition and reproductive fitness. *Psychological Science, 18*(9), 758–762. https://doi.org/10.1111/j.1467-9280.2007.01974.x

McNeilly, A. S., Robinson, I. C., Houston, M. J., & Howie, H. P. (1983). Release of oxytocin and prolactin in response to suckling. *British Medical Journal, 286,* 257–259. https://doi.org/10.1136/bmj.286.6361.257

Moatt, J. P., Dytham, C., & Thom, M. D. F. (2014). Sperm production responds to perceived sperm competition risk in male *Drosophila melanogaster. Physiology and Behavior, 131,* 111–114. https://doi.org/10.1016/j.physbeh.2014.04.027

Pandeirada, J. N. S., Fernandes, N. L., Vasconcelos, M., & Nairne, J. S. (2017). Adaptive memory: Remembering potential mates. *Evolutionary Psychology, 15,* 1–11. https://doi.org/10.1177/1474704917742807

Paredes, R. G., & Alonso, A. (1997). Sexual behavior regulated (paced) by the female induces conditioned place preference. *Behavioral Neuroscience, 111*(1), 123–128. https://psycnet.apa.org/doi/10.1037/0735-7044.111.1.123

Pfaus, J. G., Kippin, T. E., & Centeno, S. (2001). Conditioning and sexual behavior: A review. *Hormones and Behavior, 40*(2), 291–321. https://doi.org/10.1006/hbeh.2001.1686

Pontes, A., Mobley, R. B., Ofria, C., Adami, C., & Dyer, F. C. (2019). The evolutionary origin of associative learning. *The American Naturalist, 195*(1), E1–E19. https://doi.org/10.1086/706252

Rutkowska, J., & Adkins-Regan, E. (2009). Learning enhances female control over reproductive investment in the Japanese quail. *Proceedings of the Royal Society B: Biological Sciences, 276*(1671), 3327–3334. https://doi.org/10.1098/rspb.2009.0762

Taziaux, M., Kahn, A., Moore, J., Balthazart, J., & Holloway, K. S. (2008). Enhanced neural activation in brain regions mediating sexual responses following exposure to a conditioned stimulus that predicts copulation. *Neuroscience, 151*(3), 644–658. https://doi.org/10.1016/j.neuroscience.2007.10.056

Taziaux, M., Lopez, J., Cornil, C. A., Balthazart, J., & Holloway, K. S. (2007). Differential c-fos expression in the brain of male Japanese quail following exposure to stimuli that predict or do not predict the arrival of a female. *European Journal of Neuroscience, 25,* 2835–2846. https://doi.org/10.1111/j.1460-9568.2007.05542.x

Timberlake, W. (2001). Motivational modes in behavior systems. In R. R. Mowrer & S. J. Klein (Eds.), *Handbook of contemporary learning theories* (pp. 155–209). Erlbaum.

Trivers, R. L., & Willard, D. E. (1973). Natural selection of parental ability to vary the sex ratio of offspring. *Science, 179*(4068), 90–92. https://doi.org/10.1126/science.179.4068.90

Zamble, E., Mitchell, J. B., & Findlay, H. (1986). Pavlovian conditioning of sexual arousal: Parametric and background manipulations. *Journal of Experimental Psychology: Animal Behavior Processes, 12,* 403–411. https://doi.org/10.1037/0097-7403.12.4.403

8

COMPENSATORY RESPONSES TO WILDLIFE CONTROL

Theoretical Considerations and Empirical Findings from the Invasive Common Myna

Andrea S. Griffin and Marie C. Diquelou

Humans have killed nonhuman animals for food, clothes, tools, and entertainment for thousands of years. Anthropogenic mortality associated with animal exploitation has long been acknowledged to cause phenotypic change (Allendorf & Hard, 2009; Burney & Flannery, 2005; Sullivan et al., 2017). In fact, human harvesting, including fishing and hunting, has been recognized to produce more intense and more rapid phenotypic changes than natural selection (Darimont et al., 2009; Hendry et al., 2008; Palumbi, 2001). This has led some to call for the effects of human harvesting to be monitored more closely and knowledge gained to be integrated into the strategic management of resources (Allendorf & Hard, 2009).

Lethal control of alien and pest animals represents an evolutionarily more recent form of anthropogenic predation than animal exploitation. Although many species are currently struggling to adjust to rapidly changing and human-dominated landscapes, some are thriving to a point where their numbers need to be managed (Grarock et al., 2014a; Muñoz & Real, 2006; T. Peacock, 2007). For example, nuisance species (i.e., local species that take advantage of anthropogenic resources) often come into conflict with surrounding human communities (Barrett et al., 2019). Invasive alien species (i.e., nonindigenous species that have been introduced to a novel environment) sometimes come to proliferate (Blackburn et al., 2011). In the USA alone, nuisance and invasive animals cause billions of dollars of ecological and economic damage each year (Pimental et al., 2000; Pimentel et al., 2005). As a consequence, many nuisance and invasive animals are the target of control programs that aim to contain or eradicate their populations (Mack et al., 2000). These lethal control programs typically involve trapping, shooting, and baiting.

Wildlife control is potentially just as likely to cause phenotypic changes in target populations as animal exploitation, but these effects are more difficult to ascertain. Whereas the characteristics of individuals that are hunted and fished are increasingly well documented either because individuals with specific attributes are targeted or because yields are monitored (Hilborn et al., 2020), financial impediments, haphazard implementation, and extensive citizen involvement often mean that control programs proceed in the absence of any attempt to collect information on the phenotypes of shot, trapped, or poisoned individuals (Grarock et al., 2014a). Even abundance information is rarely assessed systematically on a long-term basis (www.wildlife.vic.gov.au/ our-wildlife/kangaroos) (Grarock et al., 2014a; National Pest Control Agencies, 2015). As a result, evidence of phenotypic shifts associated with wildlife control can remain anecdotal (King, 2010).

When considering phenotypical traits that might change in response to wildlife control, it is just as important to consider behavior as it is to consider morphology and life history. This is because behavior constitutes the interface by which an animal interacts with its surroundings, including predators. Therefore, behavior can play a determining role in the effectiveness of a control program (Wong & Candolin, 2015). Behavioral responses to control could take multiple forms. The most obvious is that it reduces the likelihood that individuals can be removed or captured, thereby jeopardizing the long-term sustainability of control. This effect is well documented in the context of wildlife exploitation. For example, the use of passive fishing gear selectively captures behaviorally bold and active individuals, leaving behind more timid individuals and lowering yields (Andersen et al., 2018; Díaz Pauli et al., 2015). Another form of behavioral response has a subtler consequence. Changes in behavior that make a species more cryptic and therefore less likely to be detected during surveys are likely to make an intervention seem more effective than it actually is (Diquelou et al., 2018). Although reduced detectability might be a desirable outcome for a species that is merely a pest to humans, it would be highly detrimental to reduce management pressure based on erroneous abundance trends for a species that poses a threat to an ecosystem. The last form of behavioral response to control is the most undesirable from a manager's perspective. This includes any behavioral change that worsens the impact of the very species for which control is being undertaken. Changes to the temporal and spatial patterning of activity can have just such effects. For example, control by spearfishers has altered the temporal activity patterns of invasive predatory lionfish and increased the probability of encounters between lionfish and native species, which were previously at no predation risk (Côté et al., 2014). Similarly, in Australia, common (Indian) myna(h)s, *Acridotheres tristis*, a member of the starling family and one of the most successful avian invaders globally, undergo heavy trapping pressure in suburban habitats where humans are intolerant of the species (Grarock et al., 2014a). In the long term, this might cause mynas to invade more pristine habitats to escape trapping pressure as suggested by King (2010), which would increase the likelihood of competitive interactions with native secondary cavity-nesting birds and jeopardize control measures

(Grarock et al., 2012, 2014b; Pell & Tidemann, 1997). These considerations highlight the importance of exploring the potential for adaptive behavioral responses in alien and pest populations (Côté et al., 2014).

Here, we begin by providing an overview of the mechanisms by which natural and human predators can cause phenotypic shifts in vertebrate prey populations. Only by understanding how animals change can we reduce the likelihood of an undesirable by-product of a control method. We next explain how a unique series of studies of the invasive common myna has demonstrated that this species learns socially about novel threats and is changing its behavior in response to widespread lethal trapping in Australia.

8.1 PREDATOR-INDUCED PHENOTYPIC CHANGE IN PREY: ROLE OF SELECTION AND PHENOTYPIC PLASTICITY

Both natural and human predators not only reduce prey densities, they also induce profound phenotypic changes in prey populations. A large literature has documented morphological, life history, physiological, behavioral, and neurobiological changes in response to predation (Allendorf & Hard, 2009; Palkovacs et al., 2018; Stamps, 2015). Although the mechanisms underlying these changes are rarely tested systematically, it is useful to think of them in terms how fast they can result in adaptive behavior because this parameter matters for wildlife management. Changes attributable to evolution require several generations while changes attributable to plasticity and cognition occur within an animal's lifetime. We briefly explain what we mean by evolution and plasticity in the next paragraphs and then address cognition much more extensively in the next section because this has been the focus of our own work. In what follows, we acknowledge that no behavioral change is fully caused by one or the other mechanism, and, furthermore, the boundaries between these mechanisms are not always as clear-cut as it might seem (Laland et al., 2020; see Laland, Oudman, and Toyokawa, Chapter 15). Nevertheless, the fact that these mechanisms have a history of study and discussion within the literature on prey responses to natural predators provides a useful model for future research on wildlife control. This is why, in addition to them producing adaptive behavior at differential speeds, we consider it useful to touch on them here.

Evolutionary adaptation to predators arises when individual prey vary in their expression of a highly heritable trait and this variation confers a fitness advantage in the presence of predators. Across generations, selective predation changes the relative frequency of the beneficial trait amongst prey populations. For example, seminal work in Trinidad guppies has demonstrated within-population variation in male color patterns that is highly heritable (Brooks & Endler, 2001; Houde, 1997; Hughes et al., 2005; Reznick, 1982). Although males that are more orange in coloration are preferred by females, they are also at greater risk of predation, causing colorful males to be less common in populations that evolve with predators (Endler, 1982; Farr, 1977; Grether et al., 1999).

Phenotypic plasticity can be defined as the production of multiple phenotypes from a single genotype depending on environmental conditions (Miner et al., 2005; Sultan & Stearns, 2005). Phenotypic plasticity is produced, for example, by hormonally induced epigenetic alterations to the genome (e.g., DNA methylation), which change how genes are expressed in offspring without modifying the genetic code (see Guan, Chapter 25; Badyaev, 2005; Dufty et al., 2002). Such alterations, which are generally thought to be irreversible within the span of a lifetime, can be parentally induced and are known to occur in response to predation (Bell et al., 2016; Dufty et al., 2002; McGhee & Bell, 2014; Roche et al., 2012). For example, female sticklebacks exposed to predators produce embryos that are larger in size than those produced by nonexposed control females, a difference that has been linked to differential transcript expression in biological pathways that have the potential to accelerate embryonic development (Mommer & Bell, 2014).

8.2 PREDATOR-INDUCED PHENOTYPIC CHANGE IN PREY: ROLE OF COGNITION AND LEARNING

Although evolutionary and plastic mechanisms of change can affect the full range of developmental, morphological, life history, and behavioral traits, cognitive mechanisms act primarily on behavior (Brown, 2012; Healy & Jones, 2002). Cognition, including perception, learning, and decision-making processes (Shettleworth, 2010), has the advantage over evolutionary and plastic mechanisms of behavioral change in that it enables dynamic, ongoing, and reversible adjustments in response to spatially and temporally fluctuating levels of predation risk within an animal's lifetime (Ferrari et al., 2005). It is now well established that learning allows animals to adjust their antipredator responses to familiar threats and drives the emergence of antipredator responses to novel threats (Griffin, 2003; Griffin et al., 2000; Lönnstedt et al., 2012).

Learning of predator-related information can be triggered by the prey's own direct interactions with predators (i.e., individual learning), but also by exposure to the interactions of other individuals with predators (i.e., social/ observational learning) (Griffin, 2004). Threat learning in nonhumans is underpinned by an associative process ubiquitous across the animal kingdom known as classical conditioning (Bouton & Bolles, 1979; see Fanselow, Chapter 16; Hollis, 1982; LeDoux, 2014; Mineka & Cook, 1988; Pavlov, 1927). Classical conditioning is a form of prediction learning, in which an initially neutral stimulus indicative of predation (sounds, smells, time of day, location) becomes associated with a threat stimulus to which animals respond with no prior experience (e.g., pain, fear, conspecific alarm calls) (Griffin, 2004; Griffin et al., 2001). Animals learn this cue/threat predictive relationship and as a consequence adjust behavior toward the cue adaptively, that is, in such a way to reduce the likelihood of encountering the threat.

Through individual and social learning, prey learn to recognize visual, chemical and/or auditory cues associated with both known and novel predators (Berger et al., 2001; Ferrari et al., 2005, 2010; Griffin & Evans, 2003; Magrath et al., 2015). For example, an animal might learn to avoid a location in which it previously escaped a predator attack or a location in which it observed predation on a conspecific (Griffin & Boyce, 2009). More generally, learning allows animals to adjust their time budgets adaptively, allocating more or less time to antipredator vigilance depending on the level of perceived predation risk in their environment (Cain et al., 2008).

The taxonomic ubiquity of prediction learning across the animal kingdom makes it highly likely that such learning occurs in a wildlife control context. Based on a vast body of literature on avoidance learning of natural predators, animals are well equipped to learn about cues, including place and time, that predict lethal control via individual learning as long as they survive their encounter with the threat. If they do not interact directly with the threat but witness others interacting with it or come into contact with the by-products of those interactions (e.g., dead bodies, residual alarm odors), then they may also learn predictive cues via social learning. Learning can encompass the flavors and smells associated with poisonous baits; the temporal, spatial and perceptual cues associated with traps; and the people who trap and shoot. The broader implications of prediction learning for control success will depend upon the species' capacity for one further cognitive ability, however, namely, stimulus generalization to which we turn now.

STIMULUS GENERALIZATION

The extent to which prediction learning will jeopardize future control efforts depends not only on individual learning capacity, but also on the extent to which the learner expresses acquired avoidance to other cues that are in some way similar to the original cues (Diquelou & Griffin, 2019). This associative learning mechanism, known as stimulus generalization, is well studied in the context of threat learning (Ferrari et al., 2016). For example, tammar wallabies (*Macropus eugenii*) acquire an antipredator response to a fear-relevant stimulus (fox) and generalize that response to another predator (cat), but not to a nonpredator (goat) (Griffin et al., 2001). This pattern of generalization is thought to be attributable to the presence of frontally placed eyes in both predators, and their absence in the nonpredator (Coss, 1978, 1979, 1999). This example illustrates that prey species show evolutionarily adaptive patterns of generalization without further pairings of learned cues (frontally placed eyes) with indicators of risk (e.g., social alarm signals) or attack (Griffin et al., 2001; Griffin & Evans, 2003). Generalization gradients depend on the level of risk associated with the threat (Ferrari et al., 2008) and its certainty (Ferrari et al., 2016).

Animals' capacities for generalization, and the shape of their generalization gradients, have important implications for wildlife control because they determine whether initial learning will cause behavioral change beyond the initial learning context. For example, one can predict that control effectiveness will be reduced in cases where individuals have learned what one trap looks like and generalize their acquired avoidance response to slightly different-looking traps, that is, traps that share some, but not all, visual attributes. The impact of generalization on control effectiveness will also depend upon what is learned. For example, one can predict that control effectiveness will be reduced more significantly if an animal learns the location of a trap, rather than what a trap looks like. Such place learning might not generalize as easily beyond the original learning context (depending on what learned cues qualify place) so detrimental effects to the control program as a whole might be smaller. This example highlights areas for future research and, in particular, the importance of not only investigating whether learning occurs, but also identifying the content of learning, and patterns of generalization (Diquelou & Griffin, 2019).

8.3 RESPONSE TO CONTROL: THE CASE OF COMMON MYNAS

The common myna (*Acridotheres tristis*) is one of the most successful ecological invaders globally (Lowe et al., 2000; Peacock et al., 2007). Originally from southeast Asia, the species is now established on all continents except Antarctica. Common mynas have undergone multiple introductions into Australia and multiple subsequent transportations and releases along the east coast of Australia over the course of the nineteenth and twentieth centuries, each one of which has generated a population that continues to expand its range (Ewart et al., 2018). Common mynas are now one of most common birds in many urban centers of Australia's east coast (Parsons et al., 2006; Sol et al., 2012). In the state of New South Wales (NSW), the species continues to spread westward from the eastern seaboard (Atlas of Living Australia website www.ala.org.au). In Australia, following evidence that they compete with native secondary cavity-nesting species, mynas have become the target of significant trap-and-cull efforts in some areas of their distribution (Grarock et al., 2012, 2014a, 2014b; Pell & Tidemann, 1997). A highly conservative estimate of the number of birds trapped and killed between 2004 and 2011 amounts to more than 83,500 in the states of NSW and Australian Capital Territory (ACT) (Diquelou, 2017; Diquelou et al., 2018).

8.4 SOCIAL LEARNING OF PREDATORS AND DANGEROUS PLACES: TESTS IN CAPTIVITY

Our initial investigations of the capacity of common mynas to adapt to anthropogenic predation pressure involved examining whether the species was capable of predator recognition learning. In two successive studies, Griffin (2008, 2009) demonstrated that common mynas became warier of a novel stimulus that they experienced together with the sound of conspecific alarm vocalizations. After just one pairing of a taxidermy mount of a pheasant and a two-minute playback of a common myna's distress call – a strident vocalization emitted by mynas when held by a predator, including a human – individually held mynas increased their levels of locomotion, an indicator of wariness, in the presence of the mount (Griffin 2008, 2009).

A further study demonstrated that captive common mynas are capable of learning socially about dangerous places (Griffin & Boyce, 2009). The study used an experimental setup consisting of two 0.6 × 0.6 × 0.6 m cages connected by a pipe. One cage served as a home cage and the other served as a foraging cage. During the pre-training phase, an individually housed myna learned to walk through the pipe from the home cage to the foraging cage to feed on mealworms. The layout of the cages and the action of entering the foraging cage was designed to mimic the experience of entering a walk-in baited trap, the most commonly used method of lethal control for this species, during a phase of free feeding prior to loading the trap (Tidemann, 2005). After learning to enter the foraging cage, each myna underwent two observational conditioning experiences 24 hours apart. During each of the two conditioning trials, the myna was confined to the home cage from which it watched a simulated capture of a conspecific in the foraging cage by a human with a handheld net. The observational experience was designed to emulate managing a trap in the field wherein humans interact with captured birds inside traps. The day after the second observational conditioning trial, the bird was tested once again for its willingness to pass from the home cage into the foraging cage to feed. Results showed that mynas that had watched a human capture a conspecific were significantly warier than mynas in a control group that had watched a human wave a net in an empty foraging cage (Figure 8.1).

Two subsequent studies identified some of the cues triggering learning. It turned out that observers had to see a myna being captured by a human for learning to occur (Griffin & Haythorpe, 2011). Seeing only a human waving a net inside the empty foraging cage, or a myna inside the foraging cage in a fearful state, did not cause birds to become more wary (Griffin et al., 2010;

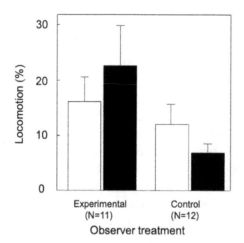

FIGURE 8.1. Locomotion expressed in the feeding cage by experimental observer mynas that viewed the capture of a conspecific by a human during observational training, and control observer mynas that watched a human wave a net with no myna present, both before (pretest, open bars) and after (post-test, black bars) observational training. The mean (±SE) percentage of time allocated to locomotion is indicated for a 90-second period after entering the feeding cage.
(Reproduced under Elsevier copyright permissions from Griffin, A. S., and Boyce, H. M. (2009). Indian mynahs, *Acridotheres tristis*, learn about dangerous places by observing the fate of others. *Animal Behaviour*, *78*, 79–84. https://doi.org/10.1016/j.anbehav.2009.03.012)

Griffin & Haythorpe, 2011). Although more work is needed to identify the content of learning (e.g., whether mynas recognized the foraging cage by its location in space (place learning) or its external appearance (stimulus learning)), this pattern of results implies that observers need to experience the conspecific's alarm behavior as well as its cause (the human predator) for avoidance learning to occur. This is theoretically interesting because it suggests that the social learning process is adaptively shaped to constrain avoidance learning to cases where both social alarm and its cause can be identified. If future research confirms this to be an instance of place learning, this might protect the animal against the risk of learning to avoid every location in which a fearful conspecific is encountered (Griffin & Haythorpe, 2011). Importantly, identifying the stimuli involved in triggering learning was key to recommending how control programs can prevent such learning, namely, that humans should not remove birds from traps during daylight when observers might be present.

8.5 QUANTIFYING BEHAVIORAL CHANGE
AND ITS MECHANISM IN FREE-RANGING MYNAS

Having identified that common mynas had the capacity for social learning of predators and of dangerous places, the focus turned next to determining whether we could find any evidence of behavioral change in response to heavy trapping. This required a large-scale study of myna behavior among areas with different trapping levels. To identify areas of high versus low trapping pressure, Diquelou et al. (2018) undertook a survey of trapping efforts across two Australian states: ACT and NSW. Using survey data from 140 questionnaires to local government and community groups and over 1,000 responses to an online community survey, the authors identified thirty-three 2 × 2 km areas, including 15 where common mynas had undergone heavy trapping pressure and 17 where mynas had undergone low trapping pressure (Diquelou et al., 2018). A comparison of data from 350 transects and point counts alongside 1,000 field observations revealed that mynas were found in smaller groups and closer to cover in areas there they have been heavily trapped (Diquelou et al., 2018). During surveys, they were also observed more often in locomotion, a sign of wariness in mynas (Griffin, 2008), and were less detectable than in areas with less trapping. To the best of our knowledge, these data provide the first systematic evidence of behavioral change in response to a lethal control program in an alien vertebrate species.

The final step in the work involved identifying the mechanism of behavioral change. Diquelou (2017) compared the behavior of mynas captured with a trap and mynas captured using a drop net on a range of personality traits and found no difference, suggesting that trap-friendly mynas are not being selectively captured. Building on earlier captive experiments (see earlier), Diquelou and Griffin (2019) tested the possibility of observational conditioning of trap avoidance learning in free-ranging birds. The study involved setting up 14 experimental foraging sites. Daily feeding of free-ranging mynas at these locations ensured that mynas were waiting at the location at the time of day when the experimenter visited. Once this regularity was established, six days of pre-demonstration feeding began. Each day, an experimenter wearing one of two costumes fed the birds. Each costume was worn on alternate days for three days (six days total). On the seventh day, the experimenter, wearing one of the two costumes (counterbalanced across sites), staged a simulated capture at the feeding site. The experimenter introduced a cage containing two conspecifics at the feeding site and, with free-ranging mynas looking on and expecting to be fed, proceeded to catch the birds inside the cage with a handheld net. A playback of common myna distress calls was broadcast simultaneously. The entire demonstration lasted a few minutes and was conducted once. Across the following six days, and in the absence of any caged birds, feeding by the experimenter clothed on alternate days in each of the costumes was conducted once again. The behavior of birds at the foraging patch was analyzed both before and after the staged capture. Relative to precapture data, mynas landed in smaller numbers at the food patch and took longer to land, suggesting that they had learned the location of the aversive demonstration (Figure 8.2). Furthermore, whereas mynas responded initially equally to the two food-provisioning

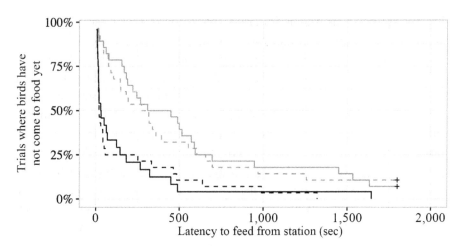

FIGURE 8.2. Kaplan–Meier survival curves of the latency of mynas to feed from the station during each trial. Pre-demonstration trials (black) and post-demonstration trials (gray) are presented, as well as trials with the aversive human identity (solid line) and the neutral human identity (dashed line). Human identity refers to whether the experimenter was wearing the costume involved in the aversive demonstration (aversive) or not (neutral).

(Reproduced from Diquelou, M. C., and Griffin, A. S. (2019). It's a trap! Invasive common mynas learn socially about control-related cues. *Behavioral Ecology, 30*, 1314–1323. https://doi.org/https://doi.org/10 .1093/beheco/arz079 with permission from Oxford University Press.)

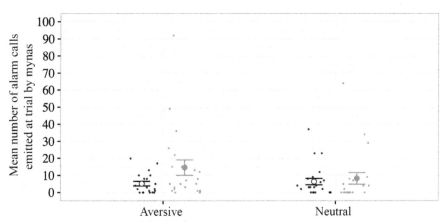

FIGURE 8.3. Mean (±SE) number of alarm calls emitted by common mynas during pre-demonstration trials (large open circle) and during post-demonstration trials (large gray closed circle) as a function of the human identity. Small dots represent the number of calls emitted at each pre-demonstration (black) and post-demonstration (gray) trial.

(Reproduced from Diquelou, M. C., and Griffin, A. S. (2019). It's a trap! Invasive common mynas learn socially about control-related cues. *Behavioral Ecology, 30*, 1314–1323. https://doi.org/https://doi.org/10 .1093/beheco/arz079 with permission from Oxford University Press.)

persons, after the staged trapping demonstration, mynas made more alarm calls when provisioned by the person who had performed the simulated capture than when provisioned by the person who had not (Figure 8.3). Differential alarm calling demonstrated that free-ranging mynas learned quickly the cues associated with the person involved in trapping; that is, they can discriminate them from the cues of a person not involved in trapping. Hence, social learning of place and stimulus discrimination provide mechanisms by which mynas learn about cues associated with control programs.

8.6 CONCLUSIONS

While phenotypic change in response to natural predation is very well established, and attention to phenotypic change in response to wildlife exploitation is increasing, this chapter draws attention to the significant knowledge gap that exists regarding the impact of wildlife control on phenotypes of alien and pest species. After explaining the mechanisms by which animals can change in response to human predation pressure, we have shown how an invasive bird, the common myna, is adjusting behaviorally to heavy trapping pressure in Australia. Future research will need to explore the content of learning more extensively and establish the extent of generalization. This is because the importance of these cognitive abilities for the long-term success of control efforts will vary significantly depending on whether mynas learn about the location of a trap and/or its appearance, whether they generalize from one trap to other similar looking traps, and whether they learn only about one human trapper or generalize to all humans. Despite these knowledge gaps, this research is already being translated into practice, with trapping communities recommending that approaching traps be restricted to nighttime (CIMAG, 2017).

The work described here has focused on demonstrating that learning and generalization likely underpin adaptive responses to trapping in mynas. But it does not exclude that evolution and plasticity might also be inducing behavioral change in mynas. For example, more fearful mynas that avoid novel stimuli more frequently, or less social mynas that avoid joining conspecifics in traps, might evolve via genetic mutation or via DNA alterations to hypothalamic stress pathways (Reeder & Kramer, 2005). Moreover, evolution, plasticity, and learning might interact synergistically (Laland et al., 2020). For example, epigenetic DNA alterations might enhance the effects of associative learning such that a given aversive experience produces a more robust avoidance response (Griffin & Boyce 2009; Griffin et al. 2010; Griffin & Haythorpe 2011). Alternatively, evolution might select for reaction norms that are altered differentially via epigenetic alterations as a function of the environment's predation (trapping) risk (Diquelou & Griffin, 2020). In conclusion, it is clear that over and above its implications for the long-term efficacy of such interventions, lethal control provides an interesting opportunity to investigate how evolution, phenotypic plasticity, and learning allow animals to adjust to novel threats. Research programs of this kind will help us determine how animals adjust to environmental change more generally.

REFERENCES

Allendorf, F. W., & Hard, J. J. (2009). Human-induced evolution caused by unnatural selection through harvest of wild animals. *Proceedings of the National Academy of Sciences of the United States of America, 106*(Suppl.), 9987–9994. https://doi.org/10.1073/pnas.0901069106

Andersen, K. H., Marty, L., & Arlinghaus, R. (2018). Evolution of boldness and life history in response to selective harvesting. *Canadian Journal of Fisheries and Aquatic Sciences, 75,* 271–281. https://doi.org/10.1139/cjfas-2016-0350

Badyaev, A. V. (2005). Stress-induced variation in evolution: From behavioural plasticity to genetic assimilation. *Proceedings of the Royal Society B, 272*(1566), 877–886. https://doi.org/10.1098/rspb.2004.3045

Barrett, L. P., Stanton, L. A., & Benson-Amram, S. (2019). The cognition of "nuisance" species. *Animal Behaviour, 147,* 167–177. https://doi.org/10.1016/j.anbehav.2018.05.005

Bell, A. M., McGhee, K. E., & Stein, L. R. (2016). Effects of mothers' and fathers' experience with predation risk on the behavioral development of their offspring in threespined sticklebacks. *Current Opinion in Behavioral Sciences, 7,* 28–32. https://doi.org/10.1016/j.cobeha.2015.10.011

Berger, J., Swenson, J. E., & Persson, I.-L. (2001). Recolonizing carnivores and naïve prey: Conservation lessons from pleistocene extinctions. *Science, 291,* 1036–1039. https://doi.org/10.1126/science.1056466

Blackburn, T. M., Pyšek, P., Bacher, S., Carlton, J. T., Duncan, R. P., Jarošík, V., Wilson, J. R. U., & Richardson, D. M. (2011). A proposed unified framework for biological invasions. *Trends in Ecology & Evolution, 26,* 333–339. https://doi.org/10.1016/j.tree.2011.03.023

Bouton, M. E., & Bolles, R. C. (1979). Contextual control of the extinction of conditioned fear. *Learning and Motivation, 10*(4), 445–466. https://doi.org/https://doi.org/10.1016/0023-9690(79)90057-2

Brooks, R., & Endler, J. A. (2001). Direct and indirect sexual selection and quantitative genetics of male traits in guppies (*Poecilia reticulata*). *Evolution, 55,* 1002–1015. https://doi.org/10.1554/0014-3820(2001)055[1002:daissa]2.0.co;2

Brown, C. (2012). Experience and learning in changing environments. In U. Candolin & B. B. M. Wong (Eds.), *Behavioural responses to a changing world: Mechanisms and consequences.* Oxford University Press.

Burney, D. A., & Flannery, T. F. (2005). Fifty millennia of catastrophic extinctions after human contact. *Trends in Ecology & Evolution, 20,* 395–401. https://doi.org/10.1016/j.tree.2005.04.022

Cain, S. W., McDonald, R. J., & Ralph, M. R. (2008). Time stamp in conditioned place avoidance can be set to different circadian phases. *Neurobiology of Learning and Memory, 89,* 591–594. https://doi.org/10.1016/j.nlm.2007.07.011

CIMAG (2013). The Canberra Indian Myna Action Group Inc. www.indianmynaaction.org.au (accessed August 30, 2021)

Coss, R. G. (1978). Perceptual determinants of gaze aversion by the Lesser Mouse Lemur (*Microcebus murinus*), the role of two facing eyes. *Behaviour, 64*(3), 248–270. https://doi.org/10.1163/156853978X00053

(1979). Delayed plasticity of an instinct: Recognition and avoidance of 2 facing eyes by the jewel fish. *Developmental Psychobiology, 12*(4), 335–345. https://doi.org/https://doi.org/10.1002/dev.420120408

(1999). Effects of relaxed selection on the evolution of behavior. In S. A. Forster & J. A. Endler (Eds.), *Geographic variation of behavior: An evolutionary perspective* (pp. 180–208). Oxford University Press.

Côté, I. M., Darling, E. S., Malpica-Cruz, L., Smith, N. S., Green, S. J., Curtis-Quick, J., & Layman, C. (2014). What doesn't kill you makes you wary? Effect of repeated culling on the behaviour of an invasive predator. *PLoS ONE, 9*(4), e94248. https://doi.org/10.1371/journal.pone.0094248

Darimont, C. T., Carlson, S. M., Kinnison, M. T., Paquet, P. C., Reimchen, T. E., & Wilmers, C. C. (2009). Human predators outpace other agents of trait change in the wild. *Proceedings of the National Academy of Sciences of the United States of America, 106*, 952–954. https://doi.org/10.1073/pnas.0809235106

Díaz Pauli, B., Wiech, M., Heino, M., & Utne-Palm, A. (2015). Opposite selection on behavioural types by active and passive fishing gears in a simulated guppy fishery. *Journal of Fish Biology, 86*, 1030–1045. https://doi.org/10.1111/jfb.12620

Diquelou, M. C. (2017). *Responses of invasive birds to control: The case of common mynas in Australia.* University of Newcastle.

Diquelou, M. C., & Griffin, A. S. (2019). It's a trap! Invasive common mynas learn socially about control-related cues. *Behavioral Ecology, 30*, 1314–1323. https://doi.org/https://doi.org/10.1093/beheco/arz079

(2020). Behavioral responses of invasive and nuisance vertebrates to harvesting: A mechanistic framework. *Frontiers in Ecology and Evolution, 8*, 1–8. https://doi.org/https://doi.org/10.3389/fevo.2020.00177

Diquelou, M. C., MacFarlane, G. R., & Griffin, A. S. (2018). Investigating responses to control: A comparison of common myna behaviour across areas of high and low trapping pressure. *Biological Invasions, 20*(12), 3591–3604. https://doi.org/10.1007/s10530-018-1798-9

Dufty, A. M., Clobert, J., & Møller, A. P. (2002). Hormones, developmental plasticity and adaptation. *Trends in Ecology & Evolution, 17*, 190–196. https://doi.org/10.1016/S0169-5347(02)02498-9

Endler, J. A. (1982). The impact of predation on life history evolution in trinidadian guppies (*Poecilia reticulata*). *Evolution, 36*, 160–177. https://doi.org/10.2307/2407978

Ewart, K., Griffin, A. S., Johnson, R., Kark, S., Magory Cohen, T., Lo, N., & Major, R. (2018). Two speed invasion: Assisted and intrinsic dispersal of common mynas over 150-years of colonization. *Journal of Biogeography, 46*, 45–57. https://doi.org/10.1111/jbi.13473

Fanselow, M. S., & Sterlace, S. R. (2014). Pavlovian fear conditioning: Function, cause, and treatment. In F. K. McSweeney & E. S. Murphy (Eds.), *The Wiley Blackwell handbook of operant and classical conditioning* (pp. 117–143). Wiley Blackwell. https://doi.org/10.1002/9781118468135.ch6

Farr, J. (1977). Male rarity or novelty, female choice behavior, and sexual selection in the guppy, *Poecilia reticulata* Peters (Pisces: Poeciliidae). *Evolution, 31*(1), 162–168. https://doi.org/10.2307/2407554

Ferrari, M. C. O., Crane, A. L., & Chivers, D. P. (2016). Certainty and the cognitive ecology of generalization of predator recognition. *Animal Behaviour, 111*, 207–211. https://doi.org/10.1016/j.anbehav.2015.10.026

Ferrari, M. C. O., Messier, F., & Chivers, D. P. (2008). Can prey exhibit threat-sensitive generalization of predator recognition? Extending the predator recognition continuum hypothesis. *Proceedings of the Royal Society B, 275*, 1811–1816. https://doi.org/10.1098/rspb.2008.0305

Ferrari, M. C. O., Trowell, J. J., Brown, G. E., & Chivers, D. P. (2005). The role of learning in the development of threat-sensitive predator avoidance by fathead minnows. *Animal Behaviour, 70*, 777–784. https://doi.org/10.1016/j.anbehav.2005.01.009

Ferrari, M. C. O., Wisenden, B. D., & Chivers, D. P. (2010). Chemical ecology of predator-prey interactions in aquatic ecosystems: A review and prospectus. *Canadian Journal of Zoology, 88*, 698–724. https://doi.org/10.1139/Z10-029

Grarock, K., Tidemann, C. R., Wood, J., & Lindenmayer, D. B. (2012). Is it benign or is it a pariah? Empirical evidence for the impact of the common myna (*Acridotheres tristis*) on Australian birds. *PLoS ONE, 7*(7), e40622. https://doi.org/10.1371/journal.pone.0040622

Grarock, K., Tidemann, C. R., Wood, J. T., & Lindenmayer, D. B. (2014a). Understanding basic species population dynamics for effective control: A case study on community-led culling of the common myna (*Acridotheres tristis*). *Biological Invasions, 16*, 1427–1440. https://doi.org/10.1007/s10530-013-0580-2

(2014b). Are invasive species drivers of native species decline or passengers of habitat modification? A case study of the impact of the common myna (*Acridotheres tristis*) on Australian bird species. *Austral Ecology, 39*(1), 106–114. https://doi.org/10.1111/aec.12049

Grether, G. F., Hudon, J., & Millie, D. F. (1999). Carotenoid limitation of sexual coloration along an environmental gradient in guppies. *Proceedings of the Royal Society B, 266* (1426), 1317–1322. https://doi.org/10.1098/rspb.1999.0781

Griffin, A. S. (2003). Training tammar wallabies (*Macropus eugenii*) to respond to predators: A review linking experimental psychology to conservation. *International Journal of Comparative Psychology, 16*, 111–129. http://escholarship.org/uc/item/706146b6

(2004). Social learning about predators: A review and prospectus. *Learning & Behavior, 32*, 131–140. https://doi.org/10.3758/BF03196014

(2008). Social learning in Indian mynahs, *Acridotheres tristis*: The role of distress calls. *Animal Behaviour, 75*(1), 79–89. https://doi.org/10.1016/j.anbehav.2007.04.008

(2009). Temporal limitations on social learning of novel predators by Indian mynahs, *Acridotheres tristis*. *Ethology, 115*(3), 287–295. https://doi.org/10.1111/j.1439-0310.2008.01594.x

Griffin, A. S., Blumstein, D. T., & Evans, C. S. (2000). Training captive-bred or translocated animals to avoid predators. *Conservation Biology, 14*, 1317–1326. https://doi.org/10.1046/j.1523-1739.2000.99326.x

Griffin, A. S., & Boyce, H. M. (2009). Indian mynahs, *Acridotheres tristis*, learn about dangerous places by observing the fate of others. *Animal Behaviour, 78*, 79–84. https://doi.org/10.1016/j.anbehav.2009.03.012

Griffin, A. S., Boyce, H. M., & MacFarlane, G. R. (2010). Social learning about places: Observers may need to detect both social alarm and its cause in order to learn. *Animal Behaviour, 79*, 459–465. https://doi.org/10.1016/j.anbehav.2009.11.029

Griffin, A. S., & Evans, C. S. (2003). Social learning of antipredator behaviour in a marsupial. *Animal Behaviour, 66*, 485–492. https://doi.org/10.1006/anbe.2003.2207

Griffin, A. S., Evans, C. S., & Blumstein, D. T. (2001). Learning specificity in acquired predator recognition. *Animal Behaviour, 62*, 577–589. https://doi.org/10.1006/anbe.2001.1781

Griffin, A. S., & Haythorpe, K. (2011). Learning from watching alarmed demonstrators: Does the cause of alarm matter? *Animal Behaviour, 81*, 1163–1169. www.sciencedirect.com/science/article/pii/S0003347211000753

Healy, S. D., & Jones, C. M. (2002). Animal learning and memory: An integration of cognition and ecology. *Zoology (Jena, Germany), 105*, 321–327. https://doi.org/10.1078/0944-2006-00071

Hendry, A. P., Farrugia, T. J., & Kinnison, M. T. (2008). Human influences on rates of phenotypic change in wild animal populations. *Molecular Ecology, 17*, 20–29. https://doi.org/10.1111/j.1365-294X.2007.03428.x

Hilborn, R., Amoroso, R. O., Anderson, C. M., Baum, J. K., Branch, T. A., Costello, C., De Moor, C. L., Faraj, A., Hively, D., Jensen, O. P., Kurota, H., Little, L. R., Mace, P., McClanahan, T., Melnychuk, M. C., Minto, C., Osio, G. C., Parma, A. M., Pons, M., ... Ye, Y. (2020). Effective fisheries management instrumental in improving fish stock status. *Proceedings of the National Academy of Sciences of the United States of America, 117*, 2218–2224. https://doi.org/10.1073/pnas.1909726116

Hollis, K. L. (1982). Pavlovian conditioning of signal-centered action patterns and autonomic behavior: A biological analysis of function. *Advances in the Study of Behavior, 12*, 1–64. https://doi.org/10.1016/S0065-3454(08)60045-5

Houde, A. E. (1997). Evolutionary mismatch of mating preferences and male colour patterns in guppies. *Animal Behaviour, 53*, 343–351. https://doi.org/10.1006/anbe.1996.0399

Hughes, K. A., Rodd, F. H., & Reznick, D. N. (2005). Genetic and environmental effects on secondary sex traits in guppies (*Poecilia reticulata*). *Journal of Evolutionary Biology, 18*, 35–45. https://doi.org/10.1111/j.1420-9101.2004.00806.x

King, D. H. (2010). The effect of trapping pressure on trap avoidance and the role of foraging strategies in anti-predator beahviour of common mynahs (*Sturnus tristis*). *Canberra Notes, 35*, 85–108.

Laland, K. N., Toyokawa, W., & Oudman, T. (2020). Animal learning as a source of developmental bias. *Evolution and Development, 22*, 126–142. https://doi.org/10.1111/ede.12311

LeDoux, J. E. (2014). Coming to terms with fear. *Proceedings of the National Academy of Sciences of the United States of America, 111*(8), 2871–2878. https://doi.org/10.1073/pnas.1400335111

Lönnstedt, O. M., McCormick, M. I., Meekan, M. G., Ferrari, M. C. O., & Chivers, D. P. (2012). Learn and live: Predator experience and feeding history determines prey behaviour and survival. *Proceedings of the Royal Society B, 279*, 2091–2098. https://doi.org/10.1098/rspb.2011.2516

Lowe, S., Browne, M., Boudjelas, S., De Poorter, M., & World Conservation Union (IUCN). (2000). *100 of the world's worst invasive alien species: A selection from the Global Invasive Species Database*. Invasive Species Specialist Group.

Mack, R. N., Simberloff, D., Lonsdale, W. M., Evans, H., Clout, M., & Bazzaz, F. A. (2000). Causes, epidemiology, global consequences, and control. *Ecological Applications, 10*(3), 689–710. https://doi.org/10.1890/0012-9623(2005)86[249b:IIE]2.0.CO;2

Magrath, R. D., Haff, T. M., Mclachlan, J. R., Igic, B., Magrath, R. D., Haff, T. M., Mclachlan, J. R., & Igic, B. (2015). Wild birds learn to eavesdrop on heterospecific alarm calls. *Current Biology, 25*(15), 2047–2050. https://doi.org/10.1016/j.cub.2015.06.028

McGhee, K. E., & Bell, A. M. (2014). Paternal care in a fish: Epigenetics and fitness enhancing effects on offspring anxiety. *Proceedings of the Royal Society B, 281*, 2–7. https://doi.org/10.1098/rspb.2014.1146

Mineka, S., & Cook, M. (1988). Social learning and the acquisition of snake fear in monkeys. In T. R. Zentall & B. G. J. Galef (Eds.), *Psychological and biological perspectives* (pp. 51–73). Lawrence Erlbaum.

Miner, B. G., Sultan, S. E., Morgan, S. G., Padilla, D. K., & Relyea, R. a. (2005). Ecological consequences of phenotypic plasticity. *Trends in Ecology & Evolution, 20*, 685–692. https://doi.org/10.1016/j.tree.2005.08.002

Mommer, B. C., & Bell, A. M. (2014). Maternal experience with predation risk influences genome-wide embryonic gene expression in threespined sticklebacks (*Gasterosteus aculeatus*). *PloS One, 9*(6), e98564. https://doi.org/10.1371/journal.pone.0098564

Muñoz, A.-R., & Real, R. (2006). Assessing the potential range expansion of the exotic monk parakeet in Spain. *Diversity and Distributions, 12*, 656–665. https://doi.org/10.1111/j.1366-9516.2006.00272.x

National Pest Control Agencies. (2015). Possum population monitoring using the trap-catch, waxtag and chewcard methods. In *National Pest Control Agencies*. www.npca.org.nz

Palkovacs, E. P., Moritsch, M. M., Contolini, G. M., & Pelletier, F. (2018). Ecology of harvest-driven trait changes and implications for ecosystem management. *Frontiers in Ecology and the Environment, 16*(1), 20–28. https://doi.org/10.1002/fee.1743

Palumbi, S. R. (2001). Humans as the world's greatest evolutionary force. *Science, 293*(5536), 1786–1790. http://references.26omb.com/Evolucion/Palumbi2001.pdf

Parsons, H., Major, R. E., & French, K. (2006). Species interactions and habitat associations of birds inhabiting urban areas of Sydney, Australia. *Austral Ecology, 31*(2), 217–227. https://doi.org/10.1111/j.1442-9993.2006.01584.x

Pavlov, I. P. (1927). *Conditioned reflexes: An investigation of the physiological activity of the cerebral cortex*. Oxford University Press.

Peacock, D. S., Rensburg, B. J. Van, & Robertson, M. P. (2007). The distribution and spread of the invasive alien common myna, *Acridotheres tristis* L. (Aves: Sturnidae), in southern Africa. *South African Journal of Science, 103*, 465–473. www.scielo.org.za/scielo.php?script=sci_arttext&pid=S0038-23532007000600008&lng=en&nrm=iso

Peacock, T. (2007). Community on-ground cane toad control in the Kimberley. In *A Review conducted for the Hon. David Templeman MP, Minister for the Environment, Climate Change and Peel.* www.feral.org.au/wp-content/uploads/2010/03/Peacock_Community-toad-control-report_lr.pdf

Pell, A. S., & Tidemann, C. R. (1997). The impact of two exotic hollow-nesting birds on two native parrots in savannah and woodland in the Eastern Australia. *Biological Conservation, 79*(96), 145–153. https://doi.org/10.1016/S0006-3207(96)00112-7

Pimental, D., Lach, L., Zuniga, R., & Morrison, D. (2000). Environmental and economic costs associated with non-indigenous species in the United States. *BioScience, 50*, 53–65. https://doi.org/10.1641/0006-3568(2000)050

Pimentel, D., Zuniga, R., & Morrison, D. (2005). Update on the environmental and economic costs associated with alien-invasive species in the United States. *Ecological Economics, 52* (3 Spec. Iss.), 273–288. https://doi.org/10.1016/j.ecolecon.2004.10.002

Reeder, D. M., & Kramer, K. M. (2005). Stress in free-ranging mammals: Integrating physiology, ecology, and natural history. *Journal of Mammalogy, 86*(2), 225–235. https://doi.org/10.1644/BHE-003.1

Reznick, D. (1982). The impact of predation on life history evolution in trinidadian guppies: Genetic basis of observed life history patterns. *Evolution, 36*, 1236–1250. https://doi.org/10.2307/2408156

Roche, D. P., McGhee, K. E., & Bell, A. M. (2012). Maternal predatorexposure has lifelong consequences for offspring learning in threespined sticklebacks. *Biology Letters, 8*(6), 932–935. https://doi.org/10.1098/rsbl.2012.0685

Shettleworth, S. J. (2010). *Cognition, evolution, and behavior* (2nd ed.). Oxford University Press.

Sol, D., Bartomeus, I., & Griffin, A.S. (2012). The paradox of invasion in birds: Competitive superiority or ecological opportunism? *Oecologia, 169*, 553–564. https://doi.org/10.1007/s00442-011-2203-x

Stamps, J. A. (2015). Individual differences in behavioural plasticities. *Biological Reviews, 7*, 1–37. https://doi.org/10.1111/brv.12186

Sullivan, A. P., Bird, D. W., & Perry, G. H. (2017). Human behaviour as a long-term ecological driver of non-human evolution. *Nature Ecology and Evolution, 1*, 0065. https://doi.org/10.1038/s41559-016-0065

Sultan, S. E., & Stearns, S. C. (2005). Environmentally contingent variation: Phenotypic plasticity and norms of reaction. In B. Hall & B. Hallgrimsson (Eds.), *Variation: A central concept in biology* (pp. 303–332). Academic Press. https://doi.org/10.1016/B978-012088777-4/50016-8

Tidemann, C. (2005). Indian Mynas – Can the problems be controlled? *Urban Animal Management Conference Proceedings 2005.*

Wong, B. B. M., & Candolin, U. (2015). Lessons for a changing world: A response to comments on Wong and Candolin. *Behavioral Ecology, 26*(3), 679–680. https://doi.org/10.1093/beheco/arv040

9

RELATIONAL MEMORY FUNCTIONS OF THE HIPPOCAMPAL PALLIUM IN TELEOST FISH

Antonia Gómez, Francisco M. Ocaña, Tamara del Águila, Fernando Rodríguez, and Cosme Salas

The human hippocampus is a fundamental brain structure for certain forms of memory (Burgess, 2008; Cohen & Eichenbaum, 1993; Eichenbaum, 2004; O'Keefe & Nadel, 1978; Squire et al., 2004). The hippocampus is essential in declarative, semantic, and episodic memory, especially in encoding and recollecting of unique personal past experiences, and in the organization of the experienced events in relational networks that allow for the flexible expression of memory (Aggleton & Brown, 1999; Burgess et al., 2002; Eichenbaum & Cohen, 2001; Ekstrom & Ranganath, 2018).

A region that could be homologous to the human hippocampus has been identified in the telencephalic pallium of other tetrapods. Furthermore, the hippocampus or medial pallium of every tetrapod species studied to date also seems to play a role in memory. We review here the experimental evidence identifying the putative hippocampal homologue in the pallium of teleost fish and revealing its involvement in some kinds of memory.

9.1 THE HIPPOCAMPUS OR MEDIAL PALLIUM OF TETRAPODS PLAYS AN IMPORTANT ROLE IN RELATIONAL MEMORIES

The hippocampus of nonhuman primates and rodents also has an important role in map-like spatial memory and episodic-like memory (Burgess, 2008; Clark & Squire, 2013; Eichenbaum, 2017; O'Keefe & Nadel, 1978). The involvement of the hippocampus is particularly noticeable in the integration of cues separately learned into a representation of space and in the flexible expression of previously acquired spatial knowledge (Bird & Burgess, 2008; Burgess et al., 2002; Hartley et al., 2014). In addition, the mammalian hippocampus is not limited to spatial memories; it also participates in the encoding of nonspatial dimensions of relational memories, including the temporal dimension (Cohen & Eichenbaum, 1993; Eichenbaum, 2014; Ekstrom & Ranganath, 2018; Schiller et al., 2015). In fact, hippocampus-dependent

spatial memories may be just one type of memory in which the hippocampus participates, being the most likely animal equivalent to human
declarative memory (Clayton & Dickinson, 1998; Eichenbaum, 2000;
O'Keefe & Nadel, 1978).

Comparative neuroanatomy shows that the hippocampus originates from
the most distal region of the embryonic prosencephalic alar plate, a structure
that has its equivalent in other vertebrate groups (Striedter & Northcutt,
2020). Thus, a hippocampus homologue can be found in the telencephalic
pallium of birds, reptiles, amphibians, and even fish. As with the mammalian
hippocampus, the hippocampus or medial pallium of birds (Bingman et al.,
1998; Colombo & Broadbent, 2000; Fremouw et al., 1997), reptiles (Holding
et al., 2012; López, Gómez et al., 2003; López, Vargas et al., 2003; Rodríguez
et al., 2002; Salas et al., 2003), and probably amphibians (see Muzio and
Bingman, Chapter 6; Sotelo et al., 2016) is also involved in map-like spatial
memory. From an evolutionary perspective, the similarities in neural mechanisms and functions of the hippocampus through tetrapod taxa could
indicate a long-shared neurobiological ancestry. Interestingly, comparative
evidence indicates that the fish telencephalic pallium also has a homologue to
the mammalian hippocampus and, at least in the fish species studied so far,
spatial and relational memories depend on that pallial region.

9.2 MAP-LIKE, RELATIONAL SPATIAL MEMORIES IN TELEOST FISH

The word "fish" applies to a numerous set of diverse taxa, including lungfish,
ray-finned fish, cartilaginous fish, and agnathans (Nelson et al., 2016).
Neuroanatomical, neurobiological, and behavioral comparative research on
these vertebrate groups is generally scarce. Most of the available information
has focused on actinopterygians, a group of ray-finned fish that include
teleosts such as goldfish (*Carassius auratus*) and zebrafish (*Danio rerio*),
the most intensively studied species.

A considerable amount of experimental evidence shows that teleost fish
possess spatial memory and navigation skills that match those of land
vertebrates. Naturalistic and laboratory studies show that teleost fish rely
on spatial information from multiple sources and different sensory modalities, and that they exhibit sophisticated navigation and spatial orientation
skills involving complex learning and memory mechanisms. Like terrestrial
vertebrates, teleost fish, when navigating, use self-centered orientation strategies as well as strategies based on allocentric (i.e., "external world-
centered"), map-like, relational spatial memory representations of their
environment (Broglio et al., 2003, 2011). Such allocentric representations,
or "cognitive maps," could capture topographic features of the environment
by encoding the spatial relationships between multiple landmarks in a

map-like memory, enabling a representation of the subject's position into a stable, "world-centered" spatial framework (Hartley et al., 2014; Moser et al., 2008; O'Keefe & Nadel, 1978; Tolman, 1948). That hypothetical relational memory representation could be used to navigate accurately and flexibly within that environment, allowing the animal to infer the most direct trajectory to a goal in that environment, even from novel start locations and in the absence of local cues.

Some studies that employ behavioral procedures analogous to those used to investigate mammalian spatial memory have provided evidence on map-like spatial memory in teleost fish. For example, in an experiment using a four-arm maze surrounded by extra-maze visual cues, goldfish were trained in a place task in which they had to navigate to a certain location (Rodríguez et al., 1994). Goldfish readily learned to locate the goal; subsequent probe and transfer tests revealed the strategies that allowed the fish to solve the task (Figure 9.1A). First, in probe tests in which the complete array of visual extra-maze cues was occluded by means of a surrounding curtain, the animals failed to reach the goal site, demonstrating that they relied on those cues for navigation. However, in probe tests with extra-maze cues partially removed, they were still able to accurately find the goal. The results of these probe tests suggest that goldfish navigate using a relational representation of the array of extra-maze cues that provide a stable frame of spatial reference in which none of the individual cues is essential by itself for successful performance (Rodríguez et al., 1994). The fact that goldfish could navigate accurately with a partial loss of spatial information suggests the operation of a pattern-completion mechanism capable of reinstating the complete memory after partial cueing (Rolls, 2013). In mammals, this capacity seems to specifically depend on the autoassociative properties of hippocampal neural networks (Guzowski et al., 2004; Kesner & Rolls, 2015; Leutgeb & Leutgeb, 2007). The same study also involved transfer tests in which animals were required to reach the goal from novel start locations or when the maze was displaced to a new position in the room (Figure 9.1A). These tests revealed that goldfish were able to navigate directly toward the goal by choosing the most direct route (Rodríguez et al., 1994). The fact that goldfish can take shortcuts and detours from novel departure positions choosing the most direct trajectory to the goal without previous training suggests that, like land vertebrates, teleost fish can represent spatial relationships in a map-like, allocentric spatial memory representation. This representational flexibility has been identified as a key property of the map-like hippocampal-dependent memory in mammals.

Convergent results supporting this view have been obtained from goldfish studies using different behavioral procedures. For example, Durán et al. (2008) showed that goldfish relied on the global arrangement of visual landmarks to locate a goal site and used different paths to reach the goal

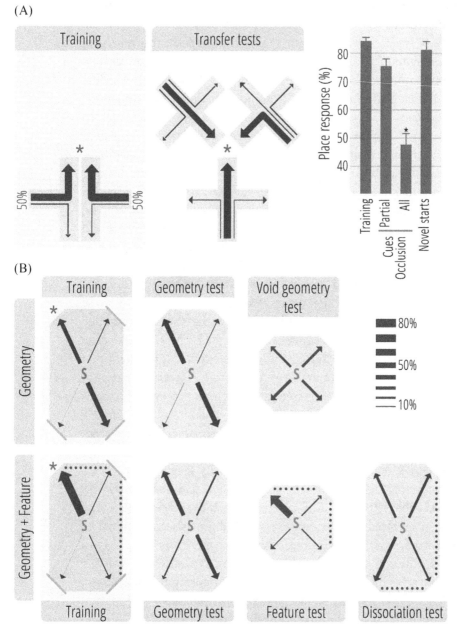

FIGURE 9.1. Map-like spatial memory in teleost fish. (A) Goldfish were trained in an allocentric (place) task to find a reward in a four-arm maze positioned in a room with abundant distal cues. After acquisition, additional sessions were conducted with probe and transfer trials interspersed between training ones. Probe trials consisted of the complete or partial exclusion of the visual cues. In transfer trials, animals started from novel start positions, and the end of one of the arms occupied the same place in the room in which they obtained the reward during training trials. The diagrams show the trajectories chosen by the animals at the end of the training and during transfer trials. The thickness of the arrows denotes the frequency of choice. The asterisks represent the goal location. The histogram shows the percentage of place responses in the probe tests, in which all or one half of the distal cues were occluded, and in the transfer tests in which novel start positions were employed (from Rodríguez et al, 1994; reproduced with permission from Springer Nature). (B) Goldfish trained in a map-like, or relational, procedure encode and use both geometric and feature

when released from different start places. López et al. (1999) showed that the alteration in the topographic features of the environment (modification of the apparatus geometry) disrupted the performance of goldfish trained in a spatial constancy task, even when these modifications left the relationships between the local visual cues and the goal unchanged. Further studies also demonstrated that teleost fish (Sovrano et al., 2003; Vargas et al., 2004), like mammals and birds (Cheng, 1986; Gouteux et al., 2001; Hermer & Spelke, 1994; Tommasi et al., 2012), can use the geometry of the environment's boundaries to orient themselves. Teleost fish can encode information on the geometry of the environment and the shape of the surroundings with non-geometrical, feature information (i.e., the shape or the color of the individual landmarks and surfaces), either using them jointly or one by one alternately depending on the requirements of the task (Vargas et al., 2004; Sovrano et al., 2003; Figure 9.1B). These results are noteworthy because the ability to encode metrical, geometrical, and feature information for allocentric navigation implies knowledge of the spatial relationships between the constituent elements (Cheng, 1994; Cheng & Gallistel, 1984; Hermer & Spelke, 1994; Kamil & Jones, 1997). They also suggest that teleost fish are able to elaborate complex representations of the environment in which the different elements (i.e., landmarks, relevant sites, goals), and properties (i.e., geometry, metrics, featural information) of the environment are encoded and integrated into a single relational, map-like representation (Burgess, 2008; Eichenbaum et al., 1990, 1994; O'Keefe & Nadel, 1978; Thinus-Blanc, 1996). Interestingly, a study by Schluessel and Bleckmann (2005) based on similar behavioral procedures to those used by Rodríguez et al. (1994) suggests that stingrays, an elasmobranch, also use allocentric strategies to navigate. Since elasmobranchs are a sister group of actinopterygians and sarcopterygians, these data suggest the possibility that the capability to form and use a map-like, relational spatial memory for navigation could be a basal feature in vertebrates.

FIGURE 9.1. (*cont.*) information to navigate. In the Geometry task, fish were trained to find the exit door (asterisk) placed in a corner of a rectangular arena that had three additional identical, blocked openings. Note that because of the geometrical characteristics of the apparatus, the correct corner was indistinguishable from the diagonally opposite corner. In the Geometry + Feature task, fish were trained in the same rectangular box but with additional feature information provided by alternate dark gray and white vertical stripes (black dots) on two walls. The diagrams show the trajectories chosen by the animals during training and during postacquisition probe tests. Animals in the Geometry task received two different probe tests. For the Geometry test, the four exits were open. For the void geometry test, the geometric properties of the experimental enclosure were modified. Animals in the Geometry + Feature task received three different probe tests. In the Geometry test, the feature was removed, whereas in the Feature test, a square enclosure with striped panels on adjacent walls was used to make the geometric information irrelevant. In the Dissociation test, the striped walls were rotated to pit the two sources of information against each other. The thickness of the arrows is proportional to the frequency of choice. S: start position (from Vargas, J. P., López, J. C., Salas, C., and Thinus-Blanc, C. (2004). Encoding of geometric and featural spatial information by goldfish (*Carassius auratus*). *Journal of Comparative Psychology, 118,* 206–216. https://doi.org/10.1037/0735-7036.118 .2.206; reproduced with permission from the American Psychological Association).

The data reviewed previously imply close similarities in spatial cognition abilities between teleost fish and other vertebrates, suggesting the possibility of a common evolutionary origin for these map-like spatial memory capabilities. In addition, increasing evidence indicates that, as is the case of land vertebrates, the map-like spatial memory abilities of teleost fish depend critically on the presumed hippocampal homologue.

9.3 MAP-LIKE SPATIAL MEMORY DEPENDS ON THE HIPPOCAMPAL PALLIUM IN TELEOST FISH

The telencephalon of actinopterygian fish presents unique neuroanatomical features among vertebrates caused by a divergent development during early embryogenesis. In actinopterygian fish, the telencephalon is developed in a "folded outward" manner, the so-called eversion process, rather than by an evagination process, or "folded inward," as in the rest of the vertebrates (Nieuwenhuys, 1963, 2011). Due to this process of telencephalic eversion, the topography of the different pallial regions is thought to be reversed compared to the arrangement presented in all other vertebrates. As a consequence, the area considered homologous to the hippocampus of terrestrial vertebrates is found in a lateral position in the telencephalon of actinopterygian fish (Northcutt & Braford, 1980). Neurobiological, neuroanatomical, connectivity, histochemical, and developmental data indicate that the dorsolateral region of the telencephalic pallium (Dl) of teleost fish could be homologous to the hippocampus of land vertebrates (Butler, 2000; Ganz et al., 2014; Northcutt, 2006; Wullimann & Mueller, 2004; Yamamoto et al., 2007). As in the case of the hippocampus, Dl is profusely interconnected with other pallial areas and with contralateral Dl. It receives cholinergic inputs from the ventro-ventral (Vv) area, an area of the subpallium considered homologous to the septal area of terrestrial vertebrates (Butler & Hodos, 2005). Dl also receives inputs from different sensory modalities from the preglomerular complex of the posterior tuberculum of the diencephalon (Ishikawa et al., 2007), and projects to the preoptic area, locus coeruleus, and upper raphe (Northcutt, 2006). This general pattern of connections is reminiscent of that of the hippocampus of terrestrial vertebrates. Embryonic development and gene expression studies also support the hypothesis of the homology of Dl with the hippocampus of other vertebrates (Dirian et al. 2014; Ganz et al., 2014; Harvey-Girard et al., 2012). In addition, growing neurobehavioral evidence indicates that, like the hippocampus of land vertebrates, the hippocampal pallium of teleost fish plays an essential role in map-like spatial memory. Controlled behavioral procedures combined with lesion, neuronal activity recording, and neuromorphofunctional data provide converging evidence for the involvement of the teleost hippocampal pallium in spatial memory.

Hippocampal pallium lesions in goldfish impair behavior in spatial memory tasks requiring the use of allocentric or relational spatial memory strategies, but spare performance in tasks that can be solved by nonspatial discriminations or egocentric strategies (Broglio et al., 2010; Durán et al., 2010; Rodríguez et al., 2002). For example, goldfish with lesions of the hippocampal pallium trained to locate a goal in a plus-maze surrounded by an array of extra-maze visual cues showed selective place memory deficits (Figure 9.2A; Rodríguez et al., 2002). In fact, the spatial memory deficits produced by lesions of the hippocampal pallium were as devastating as those produced by ablation of the entire telencephalon (López et al., 2000; Rodríguez et al., 2002; Salas et al., 1996). After the hippocampal lesion, animals were unable to find a previously learned goal location and navigate to the goal site during transfer tests in which they departed from novel starting places. By contrast, sham operated animals and animals with control lesions in other pallial regions accurately reached the goal, even when forced to use novel routes (Figure 9.2A). Furthermore, these spatial memory deficits seemed to be selective for the use of map-like memory strategies and allo-centric frames of reference for navigation, but did not impair tasks that could be solved using egocentric strategies (López et al., 2000; Rodríguez et al., 2002; Salas et al., 1996).

Convergent results have been obtained in studies using different spatial memory procedures. For example, in an experiment by Durán et al. (2010), goldfish with lesions in the hippocampal pallium, sham operated, or lesioned in other pallial regions, were trained to find a baited feeder in a 5 × 5 feeder matrix surrounded by an array of visual landmarks. Although the performance of all animals improved progressively during training, goldfish with hippocampal lesions failed in probe trials in which the local cues in close proximity to the baited feeder were removed (Figure 9.2B). By contrast, sham operated and control animals accurately navigated to the goal in these trials despite the partial removal of the extra-maze visual landmarks, and their performance only declined when the extra-maze visual cues were massively removed or transposed. Thus, the results of the probe tests closely resembled those reported in mammals with hippocampal lesions tested under similar conditions (O'Keefe & Nadel, 1978; Thinus-Blanc, 1996) and revealed that goldfish with lesions in the hippocampal pallium failed in the use of allo-centric strategies, relying exclusively on a guidance strategy to solve the task: That is, they approached a particular local cue that they associated with the goal. By contrast, the performance of the sham and control fish in these probe tests suggest the use of a map-like, allocentric relational spatial memory representation of the environment that includes the whole arrange-ment of visual cues, and that allows them to flexibly and reliably navigate to the goal even from novel starting locations. As a whole, the pattern of results of the Durán et al. (2010) study indicates that the hippocampal pallium is

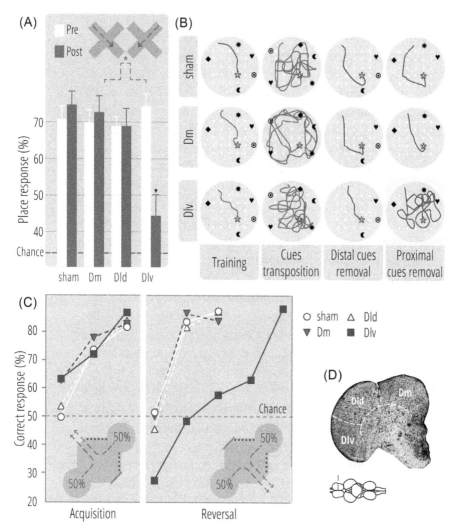

FIGURE 9.2. Hippocampal pallium and map-like memories in teleost fish. (A) Hippocampal pallium (Dlv) lesions produce a spatial memory deficit in goldfish trained in an allocentric task in a plus-maze (see Figure 9.1A for task details). The histogram shows the percentage of place responses for the different groups during pre- and postsurgery transfer trials, in which the maze was displaced and new start sites were employed. The spatial memory deficit was selective for the hippocampal pallium (Dlv) lesion; control lesions in the Dld and Dm pallial regions did not show any impairment relative to sham animals (from Rodríguez, F., López, J. C., Vargas, J. P., Gómez, Y., Broglio, C., and Salas, C. (2002). Conservation of spatial memory function in the pallial forebrain of amniotes and ray-finned fishes. *Journal of Neuroscience, 22,* 2894–2903. https://doi.org/20026211; reproduced with permission from the Society for Neuroscience). (B) Dlv, but not Dm, lesions impair the use of allocentric spatial strategies to locate a goal in a hole-board task. The diagrams show the search trajectories of a representative animal from each group in the last training trials, and in three different probe trials, in which the visual cues were manipulated. Cues transposition tests revealed that animals relied on the visual cues to solve the task, but Dlv animals failed to reach the goal when cues in the proximity of the goal were excluded. The asterisk indicates the baited feeder (goal); the symbols mark the position of the five cues (from Durán, E., Ocaña, F. M., Broglio, C., Rodríguez, F., and Salas, C. (2010). Lateral but not medial telencephalic pallium ablation impairs the use of goldfish spatial allocentric strategies in a "hole-board" task. *Behavioural Brain Research, 214*(2), 480–487. https://doi.org/10.1016/j.bbr.2010.06.010; reproduced with permission from Elsevier). (C) Hippocampal pallium lesions impair reversal learning of a

essential for the goldfish's ability to navigate allocentrically on the basis of a map-like spatial memory. An additional study highlights the relevance of the teleost hippocampal pallium for behavioral flexibility in spatial memory. Goldfish with lesions in the hippocampal pallium were impaired in the reversal learning of a spatial constancy task (Figure 9.2C; Broglio et al., 2010). These animals required a significantly higher number of training trials to learn the new goal location after reversal, compared to sham animals or animals with control lesions in other pallial regions.

Morphofunctional studies also support the involvement of the teleost hippocampus in spatial memory. For example, Vargas et al. (2000) and Broglio et al. (2010) trained goldfish in a spatial constancy task and, once the animals mastered the task, their brains were examined to assess possible spatial-learning-related changes in protein synthesis in different pallial regions. The changes in protein synthesis were evaluated by quantifying the size of nucleolar organizer regions (NORs) of pallial neurons. NORs are cellular organelles associated with the synthesis of ribosomal proteins that increase in size with the rise in the demand for protein synthesis (Derenzini, 2000), indicating that neurons are involved in long-lasting plasticity phenomena associated with learning (García-Moreno et al., 2001). The results showed that NOR's size significantly increased after spatial learning in neurons of the goldfish hippocampal pallium when compared to other pallial areas or in control animals that where either trained in a noncontingent procedure (Vargas et al., 2000) or in a cued version of the same task (Broglio et al., 2010). Costa et al. (2011) reported also positive correlations between the hippocampal pallium size and sex-related increased spatial behavior demands in the rock-pool blenny *Parablennius parvicornis*. In this species, males remain in the nest sites during the breeding season, whereas the females navigate relatively long distances to visit nests and spawn with males. Costa et al. (2011) found that the hippocampal pallium of female blennies is larger than that of males. In line with the results indicating the involvement of the teleost hippocampal pallium in spatial memory, Uceda et al. (2015) and Ocaña et al. (2017) showed selective spatial-memory-related increases in the metabolic activity in the hippocampal pallium of goldfish measured by quantitative histochemistry of cytochrome oxidase, an enzyme involved in

---

FIGURE 9.2. (*cont.*) spatial constancy task requiring the use of allocentric, relational strategies, to locate the exit in a small, stimulus-controlled enclosure. The inserts show the location of the cues (gray dots), the start compartments, the exit door (goal), and the glass barrier that blocked the opposite door (from Broglio, C., Rodríguez, F., Gómez, A., Arias, J. L., and Salas, C. (2010). Selective involvement of the goldfish lateral pallium in spatial memory. *Behavioural Brain Research, 210*(2), 191–201. https://doi.org/10.1016/j.bbr.2010 .02.031; reproduced with permission from Elsevier). (D) Photograph of a transverse section through one telencephalic hemisphere of a goldfish brain showing the location of lesioned pallial areas. Dld and Dlv, dorsal and ventral part of lateral division of area dorsalis telencephalic, respectively; Dm, medial division of area dorsalis telencephalic.

the synthesis of ATP driven by sustained cell metabolic demands (Conejo et al., 2010; Wong-Riley, 1989). Interestingly, unit recording studies described some of the functional characteristics of hippocampal pallium neurons of goldfish in relation to spatial navigation. Fotowat et al. (2019) and Trinh et al. (2019) have described the activity patterns of cells in the hippocampal pallium of electrosensory gymnotiform teleosts that encode some characteristics of the spatial environment, like the presence of borders and landmarks, as well as swimming direction relative to landmarks location, and that are presumably involved in navigation. In addition, single cell activity recordings have identified different cell types in the hippocampal pallium of free-swimming goldfish that encode different features of the space during navigation (Vinepinsky et al., 2020). For example, some cells, called "border cells," become active when the fish is near the boundaries of the environment, and others, called "velocity cells," encode swimming direction and speed. Both types of cells probably represent fish locomotion in allo-centric coordinates. Vinepinsky et al. (2020) suggest that the presence of cells that encode different features of the space in the hippocampal pallium of mammals and teleost fish indicates that hippocampal networks for navigation could have originated from a common ancient circuit.

9.4 NONSPATIAL RELATIONAL MEMORIES AND HIPPOCAMPAL PALLIUM IN TELEOST FISH

The previous review provides evidence that the teleost hippocampal pallium, like the tetrapod hippocampus, is involved in map-like spatial memory, supporting allocentric navigation and the flexible expression of spatial knowledge. However, the role of the mammalian hippocampus in memory is not limited to the spatial domain. Increasing evidence shows that it is also essential for encoding the temporal relationships between events in memory, and to form declarative and episodic memories (see Crystal, Chapter 17) that also include nonspatial associative dimensions (Chersi & Burgess, 2015; Clark & Squire, 1998; Cohen & Eichenbaum, 1993). Because there is no evidence of a nonspatial role of the nonmammalian hippocampus in memory, it has been hypothesized that the hippocampus first evolved in the phylogeny of vertebrates as a dedicated system for spatial navigation. According to this hypothesis, only later during the mammalian transition was the hippocampus co-opted to support a broader role in episodic memory, when time, order of events, and nonspatial contextual information were incorporated into its processing capabilities (Allen & Fortin, 2013; Buzsáki & Moser, 2013; O'Keefe & Nadel, 1978). However, although few studies have addressed the possible nonspatial memory functions of the hippocampus in nonmammalian vertebrates, some evidence from teleost fish casts doubt on this evolutionary scenario, suggesting a more ancient origin of that processing capability. For example, when a temporal gap was introduced between the end of the signal and the onset of the reinforcer in trace avoidance conditioning, lesion of the goldfish hippocampal pallium severely impaired performance (Portavella et al., 2004). This deficit was not observed when signal and reinforcer overlapped in time, as in delay avoidance conditioning (Figure 9.3A). This selective impairment closely parallels that

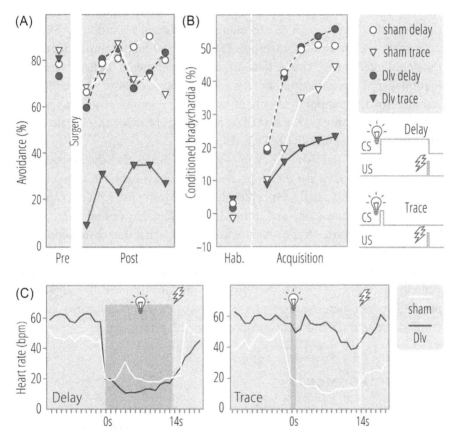

FIGURE 9.3. The goldfish hippocampal pallium is essential for associating temporally discontiguous events. (A) Dlv lesions impair the retention of an avoidance response previously acquired in a trace but not in a delay two-way active avoidance conditioning procedure. The figure shows the mean avoidance percentage in the last acquisition session, and in the six post-surgery retention sessions (from Portavella, M., Torres, B., and Salas, C. (2004). Avoidance response in goldfish: Emotional and temporal involvement of medial and lateral telencephalic pallium. *Journal of Neuroscience, 24,* 2335–2342. https://doi.org/10.1523/JNEUROSCI.4930-03 .2004; reproduced with permission from the Society for Neuroscience). (B) Dlv lesions impair the acquisition of a bradycardia response in classical trace conditioning without producing any deficit in delay conditioning. The figure shows the mean percentage of conditioned bradycardia of animals in the Dlv and Sham groups during habituation and acquisition in both procedures. (C) The curves provide a second-by-second description of the conditioned bradycardia response (in beats per minute) in CS-alone test trials, from a pre-CS baseline period to 5 seconds after the expected US delivery (striped, white bar). The gray region marks the CS duration in both procedures (from Rodríguez-Expósito, B., Gómez, A., Martín-Monzón, I., Reiriz, M., Rodríguez, F., and Salas, C. (2017). Goldfish hippocampal pallium is essential to associate temporally discontiguous events. *Neurobiology of Learning and Memory, 139,* 128–134. https://doi.org/10.1016/j.nlm .2017.01.002; reproduced with permission from Elsevier).

reported in mammals with hippocampal lesions trained in similar tasks (see Fanselow, Chapter 16; Kim & Fanselow, 1992; Maren & Quirk, 2004; Phillips & LeDoux, 1992), suggesting a function of the teleost hippocampus in the temporal dimension of associative memory. Rodríguez-Expósito et al. (2017) have provided additional evidence supporting the involvement of the teleost hippocampal pallium in temporal processing in relational memories. Lesions of the goldfish hippocampal pallium impaired acquisition in a trace classical conditioning procedure, but not in a delay conditioning version of the same task (Figure 9.3B–C). In mammals, classical conditioning has been extensively used to study the temporal dimension of hippocampal-dependent relational memories. The results of such experiments indicate that the mammalian hippocampus, like the hippocampal pallium of goldfish, is essential for the temporal aspects of associative memory required for trace classical conditioning (Kitamura et al., 2015; MacDonald et al., 2011; Meck et al., 1984; Staresina & Davachi, 2009).

In conclusion, a growing body of evidence indicates that the hippocampal pallium of teleost fish, like the hippocampus of land vertebrates, is involved in relational map-like spatial memory, probably endowing fish with the capability for allocentric navigation, and providing considerable flexibility in spatial behavior. In addition, recent evidence also suggests that the teleost hippocampal pallium plays an important role in the processing of the temporal dimensions of relational memory. These functional similarities in the hippocampal pallium of vertebrate groups that diverged millions of years ago suggest the possibility that some features of hippocampal networks appeared early in vertebrate evolution and were conserved through phylogenesis.

ACKNOWLEDGMENTS

We greatly appreciate the English usage review of Diana Badder. This work was supported by grants PSI2017–84970P from the Spanish MINECO and US-1264766 from Junta de Andalucía "US/JUNTA/FEDER, UE". T.A.P. was funded by the grant FPU17/04618.

REFERENCES

Aggleton, J. P., & Brown, M. W. (1999). Episodic memory, amnesia, and the hippocampal-anterior thalamic axis. *Behavioral and Brain Sciences, 22*(03), 425–444. https://doi.org/10.1017/S0140525X99002034

Allen, T. A., & Fortin, N. J. (2013). The evolution of episodic memory. *Proceedings of the National Academy of Sciences, 110*(Supplement 2), 10379–10386. https://doi.org/10.1073/pnas.1301199110

Bingman, V. P., Riters, L. V., Strasser, R., & Gagliardo, A. (1998). Neuroethology of avian navigation. In Balda, R. P., Pepperberg, I. M., & Kamil, A. C. (Eds.), *Animal cognition in nature* (pp. 201–226). Academic Press. https://doi.org/10.1016/b978-012077030-4/50059-3

Bird, C. M., & Burgess, N. (2008). The hippocampus and memory: Insights from spatial processing. *Nature Reviews Neuroscience, 9*(3), 182–194. https://doi.org/10.1038/nrn2335

Broglio, C., Gómez, A., Durán, E., Salas, C., & Rodríguez, F. (2011). Brain and cognition in teleost fish. In Brown, C., Laland, K., & Krause, J. (Eds.), *Fish cognition and behavior* (pp. 325–358). Wiley. https://doi.org/10.1002/9781444342536.ch15

Broglio, C., Rodríguez, F., Gómez, A., Arias, J. L., & Salas, C. (2010). Selective involvement of the goldfish lateral pallium in spatial memory. *Behavioural Brain Research, 210*(2), 191–201. https://doi.org/10.1016/j.bbr.2010.02.031

Broglio, C., Rodríguez, F., & Salas, C. (2003). Spatial cognition and its neural basis in teleost fishes. *Fish and Fisheries, 4*(3), 247–255. https://doi.org/10.1046/j.1467-2979.2003.00128.x

Burgess, N. (2008). Spatial cognition and the brain. *Annals of the New York Academy of Sciences, 1124,* 77–97. https://doi.org/10.1196/annals.1440.002

Burgess, N., Maguire, E., & O'Keefe, J. (2002). The human hippocampus and spatial and episodic memory. *Neuron, 35*(4), 625–641. https://doi.org/10.1016/S0896-6273(02)00830-9

Butler, A. B. (2000). Topography and topology of the teleost telencephalon: A paradox resolved. *Neuroscience Letters, 293*(2), 95–98. https://doi.org/10.1016/S0304-3940(00)01497-X

Butler, A. B., & Hodos, W. (2005). *Comparative vertebrate neuroanatomy.* John Wiley & Sons. https://doi.org/10.1002/0471733849

Buzsáki, G., & Moser, E. I. (2013). Memory, navigation and theta rhythm in the hippocampal-entorhinal system. *Nature Neuroscience, 16*(2), 130–138. https://doi.org/10.1038/nn.3304

Cheng, K. (1986). A purely geometric module in the rat's spatial representation. *Cognition, 23*(2), 149–178. https://doi.org/10.1016/0010-0277(86)90041-7

(1994). The determination of direction in landmark-based spatial search in pigeons: A further test of the vector sum model. *Animal Learning & Behavior, 22,* 291–301. https://doi.org/10.3758/BF03209837

Cheng, K., & Gallistel, C. R. (1984). Testing the geometric power of an animal's spatial representation. In H. L. Roitblat, H.S. Terrace, & T. G. Bever (Eds.), *Animal cognition* (pp. 409–423). Erlbaum. https://doi.org/10.4324/9781315802602

Chersi, F., & Burgess, N. (2015). The cognitive architecture of spatial navigation: Hippocampal and striatal contributions. *Neuron, 88*(1), 64–77. https://doi.org/10.1016/j.neuron.2015.09.021

Clark, R. E., & Squire, L. R. (1998). Classical conditioning and brain systems: The role of awareness. *Science, 280,* 77–81. https://doi.org/10.1126/science.280.5360.77

(2013). Similarity in form and function of the hippocampus in rodents, monkeys, and humans. *Proceedings of the National Academy of Sciences, 110*(Supplement 2), 10365–10370. https://doi.org/10.1073/pnas.1301225110

Clayton, N., & Dickinson, A. (1998). Episodic-like memory during cache recovery by scrub jays. *Nature, 395,* 272–274. https://doi.org/10.1038/26216

Cohen, N. J., & Eichenbaum, H. (1993). *Memory, amnesia, and the hippocampal system.* MIT Press. ISBN: 9780262032032.

Colombo, M., & Broadbent, N. (2000). Is the avian hippocampus a functional homologue of the mammalian hippocampus? *Neuroscience and Biobehavioral Reviews, 24*(4), 465–484. https://doi.org/10.1016/S0149-7634(00)00016-6

Conejo, N. M., González-Pardo, H., Gonzalez-Lima, F., & Arias, J. L. (2010). Spatial learning of the water maze: Progression of brain circuits mapped with cytochrome oxidase histochemistry. *Neurobiology of Learning and Memory, 93*(3), 362–371. https://doi.org/10.1016/j.nlm.2009.12.002

Costa, S. S., Andrade, R., Carneiro, L. A., Gonçalves, E. J., Kotrschal, K., & Oliveira, R. F. (2011). Sex differences in the dorsolateral telencephalon correlate with home range size in blenniid fish. *Brain, Behavior and Evolution, 77*(1), 55–64. https://doi.org/10.1159/000323668

Derenzini, M. (2000). The AgNORs. *Micron, 31*, 117–120. https://doi.org/10.1016/S0968-4328 (99)00067-0

Dirian, L., Galant, S., Coolen, M., Chen, W., Bedu, S., Houart, C., Bally-Cuif, L., & Foucher, I. (2014). Spatial regionalization and heterochrony in the formation of adult pallial neural stem cells. *Developmental Cell, 30*(2), 123–136. https://doi.org/10.1016/j.devcel.2014.05.012

Durán, E., Ocaña, F. M., Broglio, C., Rodríguez, F., & Salas, C. (2010). Lateral but not medial telencephalic pallium ablation impairs the use of goldfish spatial allocentric strategies in a "hole-board" task. *Behavioural Brain Research, 214*(2), 480–487. https://doi.org/10.1016/j .bbr.2010.06.010

Durán, E., Ocaña, F. M., Gómez, A., Jiménez-Moya, F., Broglio, C., Rodríguez, F., & Salas, C. (2008). Telencephalon ablation impairs goldfish allocentric spatial learning in a "hole-board" task. *Acta Neurobiologiae Experimentalis, 68*(4), 519–525. PMID: 19112476.

Eichenbaum, H. (2000). A cortical–hippocampal system for declarative memory. *Nature Reviews Neuroscience, 1*, 41–50. https://doi.org/10.1038/35036213

(2004). Hippocampus: Cognitive processes and neural representations that underlie declarative memory. *Neuron, 44*(1), 109–120. https://doi.org/10.1016/j.neuron.2004.08 .028

(2014). Time cells in the hippocampus: A new dimension for mapping memories. *Nature Reviews Neuroscience, 15*(11), 732–744. https://doi.org/10.1038/nrn3827

(2017). The role of the hippocampus in navigation is memory. *Journal of Neurophysiology, 117*(4), 1785–1796. https://doi.org/10.1152/jn.00005.2017

Eichenbaum, H., & Cohen, N. J. (2001). *From conditioning to conscious recollection: Memory systems of the brain.* Oxford University Press. https://doi.org/10.1093/acprof:oso/ 9780195178043.001.0001

Eichenbaum, H., Otto, T., & Cohen, N. J. (1994). Two functional components of the hippocampal memory system. *Behavioral and Brain Sciences, 17*(3), 449–517. https:// doi.org/10.1017/S0140525X00035391

Eichenbaum, H., Stewart, C., & Morris, R. G. M. (1990). Hippocampal representation in place learning. *Journal of Neuroscience, 10*(11), 3531–3542. https://doi.org/10.1523/jneurosci .10-11-03531.1990

Ekstrom, A. D., & Ranganath, C. (2018). Space, time, and episodic memory: The hippocampus is all over the cognitive map. *Hippocampus, 28*(9), 680–687. https://doi.org/10.1002/hipo .22750

Fotowat, H., Lee, C., Jun, J. J., & Maler, L. (2019). Neural activity in a hippocampus-like region of the teleost pallium is associated with active sensing and navigation. *eLife, 8*, e44119. DOI: https://doi.org/10.7554/eLife.44119

Fremouw, T., Jackson-Smith, P., & Kesner, R. P. (1997). Impaired place learning and unimpaired cue learning in hippocampal- lesioned pigeons. *Behavioral Neuroscience, 111*(5), 963–975. https://doi.org/10.1037/0735-7044.111.5.955

Ganz, J., Kroehne, V., Freudenreich, D., Machate, A., Geffarth, M., Braasch, I., Kaslin, J., & Brand, M. (2014). Subdivisions of the adult zebrafish pallium based on molecular marker analysis. *F1000Research, 3*, 1–20. https://doi.org/10.12688/f1000research.5595.2

García-Moreno, L. M., Conejo, N. M., Pardo, H. G., Gómez, M., Martín, F. R., Alonso, M. J., & Arias, J. L. (2001). Hippocampal AgNOR activity after chronic alcohol consumption and alcohol deprivation in rats. *Physiology and Behavior, 72*, 115–121. https://doi.org/10 .1016/S0031-9384(00)00408-X

Gouteux, S., Thinus-Blanc, C., & Vauclair, J. (2001). Rhesus monkeys use geometric and nongeometric information during a reorientation task. *Journal of Experimental Psychology: General, 130*(3), 505–519. https://doi.org/10.1037/0096-3445.130.3.505

Guzowski, J. F., Knierim, J. J., & Moser, E. I. (2004): Ensemble dynamics of hippocampal regions CA3 and CA1. *Neuron, 44*, 581–584. https://doi.org/10.1016/j.neuron.2004.11 .003

Hartley, T., Lever, C., Burgess, N., & O'Keefe, J. (2014). Space in the brain: How the hippocampal formation supports spatial cognition. *Philosophical Transactions of the*

Royal Society B: Biological Sciences, 369(1635), 20120510. https://doi.org/10.1098/rstb.2012.0510

Harvey-Girard, E., Giassi, A. C., & Maler, L. (2012). The organization of the gymnotiform fish pallium in relation to learning and memory: IV. Expression of conserved transcription factors and implications for the evolution of dorsal telencephalon. *Journal of Comparative Neurology, 520*, 3395–3413. https://doi.org/10.1002/cne.23107

Hermer, L., & Spelke, S. (1994). A geometric process for spatial reorientation in young children. *Nature, 370*, 57–59 https://doi.org/10.1038/370057a0

Holding, M. L., Frazier, J. A., Taylor, E. N., & Strand, C. R. (2012) Experimentally altered navigational demands induce changes in the cortical forebrain of free-ranging Northern Pacific rattlesnakes (*Crotalus o. oreganus*). *Brain, Behavior & Evolution, 79*, 144–154. https://doi.org/10.1159/000335034

Ishikawa, Y., Yamamoto, N., Yoshimoto, M., Yasuda, T., Maruyama, K., Kage, T., Takeda, H., & Ito, H. (2007). Developmental origin of diencephalic sensory relay nuclei in teleosts. *Brain, Behavior and Evolution, 69*, 87–95. https://doi.org/10.1159/000095197

Kamil, A. C., & Jones, J. E. (1997). The seed-storing corvid Clark's nutcracker learns geometric relationships among landmarks. *Nature, 390*, 276–279. https://doi.org/10.1038/36840

Kesner, R. P., & Rolls, E. T. (2015). A computational theory of hippocampal function, and tests of the theory: New developments. *Neuroscience and Biobehavioral Reviews, 48*, 92–147. https://doi.org/10.1016/j.neubiorev.2014.11.009

Kim, J. J., & Fanselow, M. S. (1992). Modality-specific retrograde amnesia of fear. *Science, 256*, 675–677. https://doi.org/10.1126/science.1585183

Kitamura, T., Macdonald, C. J., & Tonegawa, S. (2015). Entorhinal–hippocampal neuronal circuits bridge temporally discontiguous events. *Learning and Memory, 22*, 438–443. https://doi.org/10.1101/lm.038687.115

Leutgeb, S., & Leutgeb, J. K. (2007). Pattern separation, pattern completion, and new neuronal codes within a continuous CA3 map. *Learning and Memory, 14*, 745–757. https://doi.org/10.1101/lm.703907

López, J. C., Bingman, V. P., Rodríguez, F., Gómez, Y., & Salas, C. (2000). Dissociation of place and cue learning by telencephalic ablation in goldfish. *Behavioral Neuroscience, 114*, 687–699. https://doi.org/10.1037/0735-7044.114.4.687

López, J. C., Broglio, C., Rodríguez, F., Thinus-Blanc, C., & Salas, C. (1999). Multiple spatial learning strategies in goldfish (*Carassius auratus*). *Animal Cognition, 2*, 109–120. https://doi.org/10.1007/s100710050031

López, J. C., Gómez, Y., Vargas, J. P., & Salas, C. (2003). Spatial reversal learning deficit after medial cortex lesion in turtles. *Neuroscience Letters, 341*, 197–200. https://doi.org/10.1016/S0304-3940(03)00186-1

López, J. C., Vargas, J. P., Gómez, Y., & Salas, C. (2003). Spatial and non-spatial learning in turtles: The role of medial cortex. *Behavioural Brain Research, 143*, 109–120. https://doi.org/10.1016/S0166-4328(03)00030-5.

MacDonald, C. J., Lepage, K. Q., Eden, U. T., & Eichenbaum, H. (2011). Hippocampal "time cells" bridge the gap in memory for discontiguous events. *Neuron, 71*, 737–749. https://doi.org/10.1016/j.neuron.2011.07.012

Maren, S., & Quirk, G. J. (2004). Neuronal signaling of fear memory. *Nature Reviews Neuroscience, 5*, 844–852. https://doi.org/10.1038/nrn1535

Meck, W. H., Church, R. M., & Olton, D. S. (1984). Hippocampus, time, and memory. *Behavioral Neuroscience, 98*, 3–22. https://doi.org/10.1037/0735-7044.98.1.3

Moser, E. I., Kropff, E., & Moser, M.-B. (2008). Place cells, grid cells, and the brain's spatial representation system. *Annual Review of Neuroscience, 31*, 69–89. https://doi.org/10.1146/annurev.neuro.31.061307.090723

Nelson, J. S., Grande, T. C., & Wilson, M. V. H. (2016). *Fishes of the world.* John Wiley & Sons. https://doi.org/10.1111/jfb.13229

Nieuwenhuys, R. (1963). The comparative anatomy of the actinopterygian forebrain. *Journal für Hirnforschung, 6*, 171–192. PMID: 14121233.

(2011). The development and general morphology of the telencephalon of actinopterygian fishes: Synopsis, documentation and commentary. *Brain Structure and Function, 215,* 141–157. https://doi.org/10.1007/s00429-010-0285-6

Northcutt, R. G. (2006). Connections of the lateral and medial divisions of the goldfish telencephalic pallium. *Journal of Comparative Neurology, 494,* 903–943. https://doi.org/10.1002/cne.20853

Northcutt, R. G., & Braford, M. R. (1980). New observations on the organization and evolution of the telencephalon in actinopterygian fishes. In Ebbesson, S. O. E. (Ed.), *Comparative neurology of the telencephalon* (pp. 41–98). Plenum Press. https://doi.org/10.1007/978-1-4613-2988-6_3

Ocaña, F. M., Uceda, S., Arias, J. L., Salas, C., & Rodríguez, F. (2017). Dynamics of goldfish subregional hippocampal pallium activity throughout spatial memory formation. *Brain, Behavior and Evolution, 90*(2), 154–170. https://doi.org/10.1159/000478843

O'Keefe, J., & Nadel, L. (1978) *The hippocampus as a cognitive map.* Clarendon Press.

Phillips, R. G., & LeDoux, J. E. (1992). Differential contribution of amygdala and hippocampus to cued and contextual fear conditioning. *Behavioral Neuroscience, 106,* 274–285. https://doi.org/10.1037/0735-7044.106.2.274

Portavella, M., Torres, B., & Salas, C. (2004). Avoidance response in goldfish: Emotional and temporal involvement of medial and lateral telencephalic pallium. *Journal of Neuroscience, 24,* 2335–2342. https://doi.org/10.1523/JNEUROSCI.4930-03.2004

Rodríguez, F., Durán, E., Vargas, J., Torres, B., & Salas, C. (1994). Performance of goldfish trained in allocentric and egocentric maze procedures suggests the presence of a cognitive mapping system in fishes. *Animal Learning and Behavior, 22,* 409–420. https://doi.org/10.3758/BF03209160

Rodríguez, F., López, J. C., Vargas, J. P., Gómez, Y., Broglio, C., & Salas, C. (2002). Conservation of spatial memory function in the pallial forebrain of amniotes and ray-finned fishes. *Journal of Neuroscience, 22,* 2894–2903. https://doi.org/20026211

Rodríguez-Expósito, B., Gómez, A., Martín-Monzón, I., Reiriz, M., Rodríguez, F., & Salas, C. (2017). Goldfish hippocampal pallium is essential to associate temporally discontiguous events. *Neurobiology of Learning and Memory, 139,* 128–134. https://doi.org/10.1016/j.nlm.2017.01.002

Rolls, E. T. (2013). The mechanisms for pattern completion and pattern separation in the hippocampus. *Frontiers in Systems Neuroscience, 7,* 74. https://doi.org/10.3389/fnsys.2013.00074

Salas, C., Broglio, C., & Rodríguez, F. (2003). Evolution of forebrain and spatial cognition in vertebrates: Conservation across diversity. *Brain, Behavior and Evolution, 62,* 72–82. https://doi.org/10.1159/000072438

Salas, C., Rodríguez, F., Vargas, J. P., Durán, E., & Torres, B. (1996). Spatial learning and memory deficits after telencephalic ablation in goldfish trained in place and turn maze procedures. *Behavioral Neuroscience, 110,* 965–980. https://doi.org/10.1037/0735-7044.110.5.965

Schiller, D., Eichenbaum, H., Buffalo, E. A., Davachi, L., Foster, D. J., Leutgeb, S., & Ranganath, C. (2015). Memory and space: Towards an understanding of the cognitive map. *Journal of Neuroscience, 35*(41), 13904–13911. https://doi.org/10.1523/JNEUROSCI.2618-15.2015

Schluessel, V., & Bleckmann, H. (2005). Spatial memory and orientation strategies in the elasmobranch *Potamotrygon motoro. Journal of Comparative Physiology, A191,* 695–706. https://doi.org/10.1007/s00359-005-0625-9

Sotelo, M. I., Daneri, M. F., Bingman, V. P., & Muzio, R. N. (2016). Telencephalic neuronal activation associated with spatial memory in the terrestrial toad *Rhinella arenarum*: Participation of the medial pallium during navigation by geometry. *Brain, Behavior and Evolution, 88,* 149–160. https://doi.org/10.1159/000447441

Sovrano, V. A., Bisazza, A., & Vallortigara, G. (2003). Modularity as a fish (*Xenotoca eiseni*) views it: Conjoining geometric and nongeometric information for spatial reorientation.

Journal of Experimental Psychology: Animal Behavior Processes, 29, 199–210. https://doi
.org/10.1037/0097-7403.29.3.199

Squire, L. R., Stark, C. E., & Clark, R. E. (2004) The medial temporal lobe. *Annual Review of
Neuroscience, 27*, 279–306. http://dx.doi.org/10.1146/annurev.neuro.27.070203.144130.

Staresina, B. P., & Davachi, L. (2009). Mind the gap: Binding experiences across space and
time in the human hippocampus. *Neuron, 63*, 267–276. https://doi.org/10.1016/j.neuron
.2009.06.024.Mind

Striedter, G. F., & Northcutt, R. G. (2020). *Brains through time: A natural history of vertebrates.* Oxford University Press. https://doi.org/10.1093/oso/9780195125689.001.0001

Thinus-Blanc, C. (1996). *Animal spatial cognition: Behavioral and neural approaches.* World
Scientific Publishing. https://doi.org/10.1142/3246

Tolman, E. C. (1948). Cognitive maps in rats and men. *Psychological Review, 55*, 189–208.
https://doi.org/10.1037/h0061626

Tommasi, L., Chiandetti, C., Pecchia, T., Sovrano, V. A., & Vallortigara, G. (2012). From
natural geometry to spatial cognition. *Neuroscience and Biobehavioral Reviews, 36*,
799–824. https://doi.org/10.1016/j.neubiorev.2011.12.007

Trinh, A. T., Clarke, S. E., Harvey-Girard, E., & Maler, L. (2019). Cellular and network
mechanisms may generate sparse coding of sequential object encounters in
hippocampal-like circuits. *eNeuro, 6*(4), 1–21. https://doi.org/10.1523/ENEURO.0108-
19.2019.

Uceda, S., Ocaña, F. M., Martín-Monzón, I., Rodríguez-Expósito, B., Durán, E., & Rodríguez,
F. (2015). Spatial learning-related changes in metabolic brain activity contribute to the
delimitation of the hippocampal pallium in goldfish. *Behavioural Brain Research, 292*,
403–408. https://doi.org/10.1016/j.bbr.2015.06.018

Vargas, J. P., López, J. C., Salas, C., & Thinus-Blanc, C. (2004). Encoding of geometric and
featural spatial information by goldfish (*Carassius auratus*). *Journal of Comparative
Psychology, 118*, 206–216. https://doi.org/10.1037/0735-7036.118.2.206

Vargas, J. P., Rodríguez, F., López, J. C., Arias, J. L., & Salas, C. (2000). Spatial learning-
induced increase in the argyrophilic nucleolar organizer region of dorsolateral telencephalic neurons in goldfish. *Brain Research, 865*, 77–84. https://doi.org/10.1016/S0006-
8993(00)02220-4

Vinepinsky, E., Cohen, L., Perchik, S., Ben-Shahar, O., Donchin, O., & Segev, R. (2020).
Representation of edges, head direction, and swimming kinematics in the brain of
freely-navigating fish. *Scientific Reports, 10*, 14762. https://doi.org/10.1038/s41598-020-
71217-1

Wong-Riley, M. T. (1989). Cytochrome oxidase: An endogenous metabolic marker for
neuronal activity. *Trends in Neuroscience, 12*, 94–101. https://doi.org/10.1016/0166-
2236(89)90165-3

Wullimann, M. F., & Mueller, T. (2004). Teleostean and mammalian forebrains contrasted:
Evidence from genes to behavior. *Journal of Comparative Neurology, 75*, 143–162. https://
doi.org/10.1002/cne.20183

Yamamoto, N., Ishikawa, Y., Yoshimoto, M., Xue, H. G., Bahaxar, N., Sawai, N., Yang, C. Y.,
Ozawa, H., & Ito, H. (2007). A new interpretation on the homology of the teleostean
telencephalon based on hodology and a new eversion model. *Brain, Behavior and
Evolution, 69*, 96–104. https://doi.org/10.1159/000095198

10

MECHANISMS UNDERLYING ABSOLUTE AND RELATIVE REWARD VALUE IN VERTEBRATES

Mauricio R. Papini

...yet the Absolute, or Substance, is prior in nature to the Relative, which seems to be an offshoot or "accident" of Substance; so that there cannot be a common Idea corresponding to the absolutely good and the relatively good.

Aristotle (2003, Nichomachean ethics, I, 6:2).

Aristotle's epigraph resonates with the topic of this chapter, although he surely had problems other than the nature of incentive valuation in mind when this passage was written. Moreover, for all his genius and however close he came to the idea, Aristotle never explicitly developed the notion of biological evolution. Still, his works are inspiring to those interested in natural phenomena.

Putting Aristotle's epigraph in contemporary perspective, I argue that the learning mechanisms responsible for assigning absolute incentive value to a resource have evolved prior to those that control relative incentive value. This chapter centers on vertebrates as a monophyletic group with a significant degree of homology in the organization and functions of the central nervous system (e.g., Schneider, 2014; Striedter, 2005) and on ingestive behaviors. When a vertebrate comes in contact with resources such as foods or fluids, it automatically evaluates their quality and quantity, two dimensions that contribute to assigning value to the incentive. The anticipation of reward with a given incentive value tends to promote changes in approach responses – behaviors related to search and procurement of the resource (see Silva and Silva, Chapter 12). As one might suppose, the strength of an approach response to reward location after some accumulated experience with the situation tends to reflect the value of the reward, at least up to a point. Several theorists have formalized this simple statement in terms of a discrepancy between obtained and expected rewards, suggesting that the value of a reward signal grows in direct proportion to the size of this discrepancy (e.g., Rescorla & Wagner, 1972). If the parameter coding for the obtained reward is allowed variation as a function of its size or quality, then the size of the discrepancy will be directly proportional to the magnitude of the reward. In this view, "discrepancy" is another term for surprising or unexpected (Kamin, 1969). When the obtained reward is larger than the expected reward, the discrepancy between the two is positive and the procedure can be labeled surprising reward. When, however, the obtained reward is smaller than expected, the discrepancy is negative and the procedure is called surprising nonreward. An obtained-vs.-expected discrepancy, whether positive or negative, implies that the obtained reward was not predicted on the basis of prevailing signals and approach behavior should adjust to this reality. In these views, surprising reward leads to the acquisition of incentive value (i.e., an increase in response strength), whereas surprising nonreward leads to the extinction of incentive value (i.e., a decrease in response strength). This can be called the *strengthening–weakening (S/W) principle* of learning. The origin of the S/W principle is found in Thorndike's (1911) law of effect, according to which reinforcement and nonreinforcement affect the strength of a stimulus–response association. Here, however, the S/W principle will be used in a descriptive fashion irrespective of its underlying mechanism.

10.1 DEFINITIONS

Absolute reward value would appear to be simple to assess, but a closer look suggests otherwise. Ideally, absolute value requires that no other incentives are available for comparison, whether simultaneously or because of prior experience. Even if an animal had been raised with access to only a single reward, it is difficult to imagine that there would be no generalization to other rewards. Perhaps the closest one can come to an absolute reward assessment occurs in between-subject designs that measure the behavior of different groups of animals each trained with a single reward magnitude or quality. Even in such a case, comparisons with rewards available outside the training situation are impossible to prevent completely. Whether such comparisons affect behavior, however, is an empirical question. In experiments involving food restriction and postsession feeding in the colony room, consumption of saccharin and sucrose during a training session was reduced by the opportunity to feed in the cage 5 minutes after the end of the session, but not 90 minutes after the session ended (Lucas et al., 1988).

Whereas acquisition rate is generally accepted to be directly related to reward magnitude, this outcome is not always the case. Different reward magnitudes can support similar behavioral levels during acquisition training, especially in the asymptotic stage. McCain et al. (1971) trained rats in a runway procedure and varied the number of acquisition trials reinforced with large (500 g) or small (45 mg) amounts of food. They concluded that, although differences were observed early in training, they disappeared in asymptotic performance. Interestingly, a shift to extinction usually allowed differences to reemerge: Groups trained with large rewards extinguished faster than groups reinforced with small rewards. Notice two points for debate: (1) extinction potentially involves a successive comparison between current (obtained) and previous (expected) reward conditions and (2) the S/W principle would have predicted that extinction should be slower after acquisition with a large reward than with a small reward because these magnitudes would generate differential response strengths.

The inverse relationship between reward magnitude and extinction rate (i.e., a larger reward leads to faster extinction) violates the S/W principle and suggests that animals compare the current reward and the expected reward based on prior experience. Moreover, this inverse relationship suggests that current conditions have a relative impact on behavior. In the absence of such comparisons, the rate of extinction should be directly related to the value of the incentive experienced during acquisition. Two generalizations follow from these results:

* *Adherence to the S/W principle suggests that behavior is controlled by absolute reward value.*
* *Violations of the S/W principle suggest that behavior is controlled by relative reward value.*

The interplay between control by absolute vs. relative reward value can be appreciated in situations that compare two types of choice tests. In *forced choice*, a single response and a single reward are available in any given trial, and the choice is between responding vs. not responding. In some sessions, a second type of test involving a second response and a second reward are presented in different trials. In *free choice*, at least two responses related to two rewards are available simultaneously in any particular trial. Choices include responding to one option, to the other option, to both options, or not responding. This interplay is illustrated in an autoshaping (Pavlovian) experiment in which rats faced two levers (Right, Left) paired with two reward magnitudes (2 pellets, 12 pellets; Conrad & Papini, 2018). During training, R ➜ 2 and L ➜ 12 forced-choice trials produced similar levels of lever pressing, suggesting no control of lever pressing by reward magnitude. However, in nonreinforced free-choice trials with both levers presented simultaneously, within the same session, rats exhibited preference for the lever associated with the larger of the two rewards (i.e., R < L), thus exhibiting control by reward magnitude.

Comparisons involving different reward magnitudes would generally yield either no differences (as in the forced-choice tests mentioned before) or a bias in favor of the large-reward option (as in free-choice tests). This is hardly surprising. All else equal, at any given time, it would be generally favorable in an evolutionary sense to choose the largest possible reward or to be indifferent (e.g., under satiety). It is difficult to picture a scenario in which natural selection would favor choosing the lowest or smallest reward.

Up to this point, I have considered changes in the quantitative value of rewards, but estimating reward value is a less obvious task if the rewards are qualitatively different. One approach consists of training independent groups of animals in a task reinforced with qualitatively different rewards and then comparing the acquisition rate – a forced-choice task. Of the two rewards, the one supporting the faster acquisition rate is assumed to have the higher value. In an early experiment, Elliott (1928) reported that rats acquired a spatial orientation task faster when reinforced with a mixture of wet bran cereal than with sunflower seeds.

Elliott (1928) did not report conducting free-choice tests to assess the relative incentive value of these rewards, but instead estimated their relative value using a successive procedure. After acquisition, the group rewarded with the bran cereal mix was shifted to sunflower seeds. In the following trials, the performance of these shifted animals deteriorated relative to that of the group always rewarded with sunflower seeds. Figure 10.1 shows a similar successive task together with a free-choice test involving 2% sucrose and food pellets. In this case, free-choice tests show that rats prefer standard food pellets to 2% sucrose, but prefer 30% sucrose over food pellets. In agreement with these results, a two-phase successive test showed faster acquisition of lever pressing for food pellets in a Pavlovian autoshaping task (Phase 2) preceded by exposure to unsignaled delivery of 2% sucrose compared to 30% sucrose (Phase 1; Papini et al., 2001). Thus, the reward value of the pellets depended on concurrent or previous experience with sucrose of different concentrations – low sucrose promoted lever pressing while high sucrose suppressed this behavior. From Elliott's results previously described, one would predict that rats given a free-choice test would prefer the wet cereal to the sunflower seeds. This outcome would support the assumption that the absolute values of two rewards should map onto preference for the reward that supports the highest acquisition rate in a free-choice test. Thus, if reward

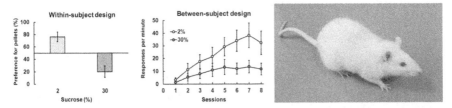

FIGURE 10.1. Free choice between food pellets when the other option is either 2% or 30% sucrose (left panel). Lever pressing for pellets in an autoshaping situation when animals were previously exposed to free delivery of either 2% or 30% sucrose (right panel).

(Data from Papini et al., 2001; reproduced with permission from Elsevier. Photo courtesy of Sara Guarino.)

A leads to faster acquisition than reward B in independent groups, then A should also be preferred to B in free-choice, within-subject tests.

When a successive shift in reward magnitude or quality (A-to-B) results in differential postshift performance relative to an unshifted control (B-to-B), it can be persuasively argued that the difference in response strength is caused by prior experience (with A vs. B), rather than current reward conditions (B for both groups). Results violating the S/W principle require a mechanism for assessing relative reward value.

10.2 REWARD RELATIVITY IN MAMMALS

Reward relativity occurs when behavior in a situation involving a particular reward depends on other rewards previously experienced (successive comparison), currently present (simultaneous comparison), or forthcoming (anticipatory comparison), in the same or similar context (Flaherty, 1996; Torres & Papini, 2017). A variety of contrast procedures have been developed to study reward relativity, but this chapter centers on the successive case because a more extensive comparative database is available (see Anselme, Chapter 11). Moreover, I will concentrate on negative contrast effects involving worse-than-expected rewards because they tend to be more reliable than positive contrast effects (e.g., Annicchiarico et al., 2016). I assume that the S/W principle is the basal condition in vertebrate learning and the key question is whether there is evidence for violations of this principle in some vertebrate groups.

SUCCESSIVE CONTRAST

Successive contrasts can be studied in two basic situations: appetitive extinction (hereafter extinction), involving a downshift from some reward to no reward, and successive negative contrast (SNC), involving a downshift from a large reward to a small reward.

MAMMALS Extensive research on extinction and SNC in mammals shows that reward downshift has negative hedonic value. In one experiment (Norris et al., 2009), rats had access to 32% sucrose in a box during 10 sessions. In session 11, animals encountered water rather than sucrose (reward downshift) and, after 30 seconds in contact with the water, a door facing a previously unavailable compartment was open. Downshifted rats learned to jump over a barrier and move into the new compartment faster than control animals that had always received water. In instrumental SNC situations, a downshift also leads to the rapid acquisition of a jumping response that allows the animal to move away from the compartment (Daly, 1974). These could be interpreted as escape responses, although following Elliott (1928,

p. 29), one could argue that rats are "searching for the accustomed (and more desirable) food." However, additional results suggest that the emotional response plays an important role in these situations. Pigs (*Sus scrofa*) trained to press a panel with their snout to receive food and then shifted to extinction exhibited increased plasma levels of corticosteroid hormones (markers of emotional stress) and displayed increased aggressive behavior (pushing, biting, and fighting; Dantzer et al., 1980). Primates and rodent exhibit similar aggressive behaviors during extinction (see Papini & Dudley, 1997). Tinklepaugh (1928) noted aggressive displays directed at the experimenter in an earlier study with rhesus monkeys in which the animal found a piece of lettuce (less preferred) in place of the expected piece of banana (more preferred). However, reward omission can also reduce aggressive behavior (Mustaca et al., 2000).

Additional aftereffects have been reported in the seconds-to-minutes range after reward downshifts. For example, release of stress hormones (Pecoraro et al., 2009), increased body temperature (Pecoraro et al., 2007), hypoalgesia (Mustaca & Papini, 2005; ~~Jiméez-Garcia~~Jiménez-García et al., 2016), distress vocalizations (Binkley et al., 2014), release of species-typical odorants (Ludvigson, 1999), changes in facial expression related to palatability (Cuenya et al., 2018), deficits in male sexual behavior (Freidín & Mustaca, 2004), and increased consumption of anxiolytic solutions (Manzo et al., 2015) have been observed in rats. Surprising nonreward tends to invigorate subsequent behaviors (Dudley & Papini, 1995; Stout et al., 2003), an effect that is eliminated by the removal of the adrenal glands, a source of stress hormones (Thomas & Papini, 2001). In turn, coping with reward downshift is influenced by stress, including exposure to open spaces (Justel et al., 2014) and physical restraint (Ortega et al., 2013), and by peripheral pain (Ortega et al., 2011), suggesting that sources of negative valence (stress, pain, surprising nonreward) summate to influence behavior.

Given the negative valence of events involving reward downshifts, it is not surprising that they induce long-term memories. The instrumental SNC effect described earlier (e.g., Elliott, 1928) requires the reactivation of memories formed during exposure to the large reward, before the downshift. Typically, the memory of a downshift event tends to inhibit anticipatory approach behavior, that is, the suppression of actions that previously led to a large reward (Papini, 2003). Unlike aftereffects of surprising nonreward, these anticipatory effects are not restricted to the seconds-to-minutes time range because they rely on long-term memory.

In addition to rats, SNC has been reported in human babies, monkeys, mice, dogs, and opossums trained in situations involving instrumental responses such as running or lever pressing and consummatory responses such as fluid consumption (Papini, 2014). Figure 10.2 shows an example of consummatory SNC in two species of marsupials, white-eared opossums

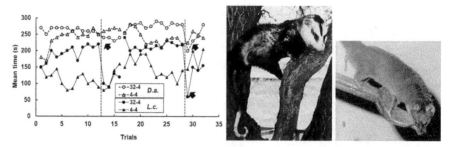

FIGURE 10.2. Consummatory behavior (time licking at a tube delivering sucrose) in two species of didelphid marsupials, *Didelphis albiventris* (*D.a.*, left picture) and *Lutreolina crassicaudata* (*L.c.*, right picture). The dashed vertical lines mark the transition from preshift to postshift and the arrows point to a suppression of behavior following the reward downshift. In both cases, animals received five minutes of access to 32% or 4% sucrose for 12 daily trials followed for all animals by 4 equal sessions of access to 4% sucrose.
(Data from Papini et al., 1988; reproduced with permission from Springer; *D.a.* picture by the author; *L.c.* picture courtesy of Omar Iodice.)

(*Didelphis albiventris, D.a.*) and red opossums (*Lutreolina crassicaudata, L. c.*), exposed to successive downshifts from 32% to 4% sucrose versus unshifted controls always exposed to 4% sucrose (Papini et al., 1988). Both species exhibited significant suppression of sucrose intake after the downshift relative to unshifted controls. Notice, however, that *D.a.* drank for a longer time than *L.c.* during 300-seconds-long sessions and that *L.c.* did not show contrast during the first downshift event, but it did during the second downshift event. The first point is likely related to the difference in body size; for adult individuals, *D.a.* tends to be about twice the size of *L.c.* Thus, the focus of comparative research on learning and memory is more product- ively placed on functional relationships between independent and dependent variables across species, rather than on absolute scores on some behavioral task (Bitterman, 1975). The second point suggests that occasional failures to exhibit a learning phenomenon (e.g., the SNC effect) need to be understood in a broader context. In this case, two additional sucrose downshifts (not shown in Figure 10.2) provided further evidence of contrast in *L.c.* Opossums are widely considered a basal group among marsupials and, except for the egg-laying mammals of Australia, are among the most conservative species of living mammals in terms of fossil and molecular evidence (Nilsson et al., 2010). Based on these results, it can be hypothesized that *the brain mechan- isms underlying reward relativity are common to at least all mammals* (Papini, 2002).

MECHANISMS Many vertebrate species can be trained for a few weeks and under conditions requiring daily consumption of rewards, which are two prerequisites to test for SNC under widely spaced training (i.e., one trial per day). Spaced training minimizes the chances that short-term memory or

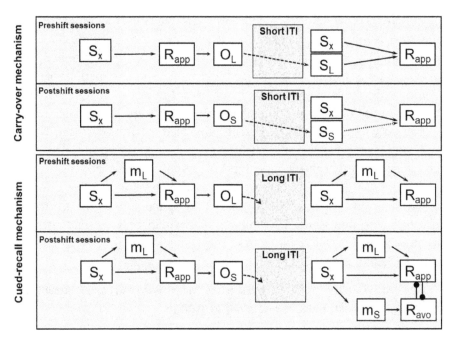

FIGURE 10.3. A representation of the carry-over mechanism (top) and the cued-recall mechanism (bottom). In the presence of contextual cues (S_X), the animal develops an approach response (R_{app}) leading to a large reward (O_L). With a short intertrial interval (ITI), stimuli related to the outcome (dashed arrow) persist long enough to control the approach response in the following trial. A downshift to a small reward (O_S) modifies carry-over stimuli such that the approach response is weakened. This mechanism explains SNC as an instance of stimulus generalization decrement. With long intertrial intervals, carry-over stimuli decay (dashed arrows) before the next trial. The spaced-trial SNC effect depends on retrieval of long-term memories of the large (m_L) and the small rewards (m_S), which tend to control competing responses, such as approach (R_{app}) and avoidance (R_{avo}). The memory of the small reward may be conceptualized as an emotional memory anticipating a hedonically negative outcome – frustration.

even the remains of rewards (e.g., food particles) from one trial would acquire control over behavior on the next trial. As represented in Figure 10.3, top panel, such carry-over stimuli can lead to a SNC effect by generalization decrement and without requiring the retrieval of a long-term memory encoding the preshift reward magnitude. Other effects related to SNC (such as increased persistence in extinction after partial reinforcement training) have been reported in nonmammalian vertebrates when the inter-trial interval is in the order of seconds to minutes (e.g., in turtles: Murillo et al., 1961; in toads: Muzio et al., 1992). The carry-over mechanism provides a parsimonious explanation for SNC requiring no retrieval of the long-term memory of previous outcomes. Basically, the compound stimulus controlling preshift behavior includes contextual and carry-over stimuli; when the latter are modified after a downshift from a large to a small reward, behavior changes because of generalization decrement – to the animal, the postshift situation is different from preshift training.

For effects observed after extended intertrial intervals (e.g., 24 hours), as in the experiments shown in Figure 10.2, it is not plausible to assume that carryover stimuli would remain available, without decay or interference, after extensive time without access to food and water, and after periods of sleep. A mechanism involving the retrieval of reward information stored in long-term memory offers a possible alternative explanation of the SNC effect. Figure 10.3, bottom panel, represents this cued-recall mechanism. In this case, SNC is attributed to the retrieval of conflicting memories of the large and small rewards controlling competing response tendencies to approach and avoid the goal. The memory of the small reward acquired after the downshift could be described as an emotional memory of the frustrating effects of the downshift, a hypothesis that would be consistent with the negative hedonic value resulting from surprising nonreward events described earlier (Papini, 2003). A final tentative conclusion suggests that:

* *Reward relativity can be detected when the disparity between current and previous rewards induces emotional activation.*

OTHER VERTEBRATES Experiments with several nonmammalian vertebrates reveal a different adjustment to reward downshift from that shown in Figure 10.2. In goldfish (*Carassius auratus*; Couvillon & Bitterman, 1985; Lowes & Bitterman, 1967), toads (*Rhinella arenarum*; Muzio et al., 2011; Papini et al., 1995), turtles (*Chrysemys picta*; Pert & Bitterman, 1970), and pigeons (*Columba livia*; Papini, 1997) there is evidence that different reward magnitudes control instrumental behavior during preshift trials, but a reward downshift leads to a gradual adjustment of behavior. This pattern can be described as a *reversed SNC* effect. Figure 10.4 illustrates this adjustment mode with data from spaced-trial experiments with toads and pigeons.

Consider the reversed SNC effect involving pigeons trained to peck at a key light to obtain either 15 pigeon pellets in one group (L) or 1 pellet in the other (S; Papini, 1997). Response latencies decreased faster for the large-reward group than for the small-reward group, suggesting that the magnitude difference had an impact on behavior. Subsequently, a downshift from 15 pellets to 1 pellet per trial (L-S) yielded a gradual adjustment to the new reward without any evidence of overshooting of latencies during the postshift period. These results with pigeons were similar to those obtained with toads (Figure 10.4) and with other nonmammalian vertebrates (see Muzio and Bingman, Chapter 6; Gómez et al., Chapter 9).

Do these results suggest that the evolution of mechanisms underlying spaced-trial SNC effects can be understood exclusively in terms of phylogenetic history? This hypothesis suggests that what determines whether a particular species will produce evidence of SNC is its "mammalian status," rather than some local adaptive process tuning these mechanisms to specific

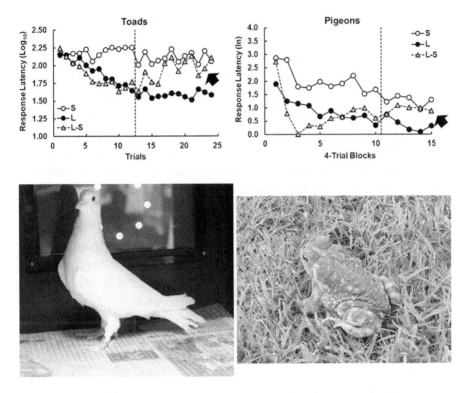

FIGURE 10.4. The effects of reward downshift in toads (*Rhinella arenarum*) and pigeons (*Columba livia*). The dashed vertical lines mark the transition from a large to a small reward in the group labeled L-S. The other two groups are unshifted controls always trained with either large (L) or small rewards (S). The arrows point to the adjustment of behavior following the downshift. This gradual adjustment combined with evidence of control of behavior by reward magnitude defines a reversed SNC effect. Toads were moving along a runway and found different amounts of water at the goal. Pigeons were pecking at a key for different number of food pellets. In both cases, animals received one trial per day.
(Toad data from Muzio et al., 2011; reproduced with permission from *PLOS One*; photo courtesy of Rubén Muzio. Pigeon data from Papini, 1997; reproduced with permission from the American Psychological Association; photo courtesy of Aaron Blaisdell.)

ecological conditions. Three sources of evidence suggest that the phylogenetic history hypothesis is premature (Papini, 2014). First, under some conditions, rats produce no evidence of a SNC effect. For example, rats trained in a runway to lick at sucrose solutions in the goal do not exhibit instrumental SNC in terms of the running response (Sastre et al., 2005). Similarly, in an autoshaping situation, rats downshifted from a large to a small pellet reward showed either no change, or even an increase in lever pressing (Conrad & Papini, 2018). Interestingly, reward relativity effects can be detected in both scenarios. In the runway, a sucrose downshift in the goal produces a consummatory SNC, whereas in autoshaping, free-choice trials with both options available lead to a rejection of the downshifted option. Moreover, whereas free-choice trials are sensitive to reward downshift in anticipatory behavior (e.g., autoshaping; Conrad & Papini, 2018), a similar series of experiments involving free choice in consummatory behavior provided only evidence of control by absolute reward value (Guarino et al., 2020a). These results suggest that situations involving forced-choice consummatory responses and free-choice anticipatory responses might be more sensitive to detect reward relativity effects in nonmammalian vertebrates, as shown below. Still, the reasons for the absence of SNC effects in rats exposed to these situations remain elusive.

Second, an experiment with starlings (*Sturnus vulgaris*) provides support for consummatory situations being more sensitive than instrumental situations. Freidín et al. (2009) trained two groups of starlings to feed on either meal worms (preferred food) or turkey crumbs in preshift trials. Mealworm-fed animals consumed more food than turkey-crumb-fed animals, thus showing control of consummatory behavior by these rewards. When mealworm-fed animals were downshifted to turkey crumbs, they consumed less than unshifted controls always receiving turkey crumbs, thus showing evidence of consummatory SNC. In addition, probing the target (i.e., inserting the beak into the bowl that used to contain mealworms in preshift trials) produced no evidence of SNC. If such probing behavior was instrumentally reinforced by access to mealworms, then these results would be consistent with consummatory behavior being more sensitive to reward downshift than instrumental behavior in forced-choice situations. Nonetheless, at least in goldfish, whether the reward downshift was measured in terms of consummatory or instrumental behavior, these animals yielded no evidence of reward relativity (Couvillon & Bitterman, 1985; Lowes & Bitterman, 1967).

Third, isolated effects in a particular species reveal little about the underlying mechanisms of any learning phenomenon. Dissociations of related learning effects within the same experiment are more revealing. In pigeons, for example, a downshift from a large reward to extinction, a procedure analogous to SNC, yields slower extinction than a downshift from a small to no reward (the opposite of rats, see earlier; McCain et al., 1971). In the same spaced-trial experiment, partial reinforcement training with the large reward revealed a strong persistence of runway performance during extinction relative to continuous reinforcement training (Thomas & Papini, 2003). In other vertebrates, these extinction effects tend to co-vary: they are either both present or both absent (Papini, 2014). Clearly, the effects of spaced-trial partial reinforcement training on extinction in pigeons could reflect the operation of different mechanisms from those present under analogous conditions in rats (Stout et al., 2002; Thomas & Papini, 2003). Consistent with this possibility, pharmacological manipulations in pigeons produce different results from those reported in rats (Thomas & Papini, 2003). For example, the benzodiazepine anxiolytic chlordiazepoxide eliminates the extinction effects of partial reinforcement in rats, but it only delays the emergence of persistence in pigeons. Similar species differences in the effects of partial reinforcement on extinction occur with nicotine (a cholinergic stimulant) and haloperidol (a dopamine antagonist). Pigeons also exhibit conflicting results in aftereffects experiments. In agreement with mammalian results, pigeons exposed to extinction display aggressive behavior to a stuffed bird, a live pigeon, or a mirror reflection (see Papini et al., 2019). But unlike in mammalian experiments, pigeons fail to exhibit response invigoration after surprising nonreward in instrumental tasks (Dudley & Papini, 1995; Stout et al., 2002, 2003). For these three reasons, a phylogenetic history hypothesis seems premature at this point.

10.3 FRUSTRATION AND FEAR

Effects involving surprising nonreward suggest a distinction between (1) *Memory update*, which refers to tracking and adjusting reward value as conditions change in the environment, and (2) *Emotional activation*, which involves tagging such changes in reward as emotionally significant (Papini, 2003). In the SNC situation, L-S transitions followed by decrements in behavior reflect memory update. Acquiring information of such changes is a key function of conditioning mechanisms and can be described in terms of the S/W principle, suggested to be common to all vertebrates and responsible for processing absolute reward value. Memory update is a cognitive process encoding knowledge of the relationship between behavior and environmental events. In the SNC effect, there is also a difference in the rate of behavioral change. Behavior can change abruptly after a reward downshift, an effect related to emotional activation (Papini et al., 2015). Emotion is recruited when the degree of disparity between the expected and obtained rewards surpasses a threshold. Increasing reward disparity leads to greater behavioral suppression following reward downshift (Papini & Pellegrini, 2006).

The distinction between memory update and emotional activation contributes to organizing the results of comparative experiments. Species that exhibit reversed SNC effects discriminate reward magnitudes, as demonstrated by preshift performance, and track changes in reward magnitude, as demonstrated by the adjustment of behavior after incentive downshift (see Figure 10.4). These results provide evidence of memory update, but no evidence of emotional activation since changes in behavior are gradual. Interestingly, animals that show no evidence of anticipatory emotional activation in surprising nonreward situations readily provide evidence of fear conditioning, a type of anticipatory emotional activation that allows for adjustment to impending painful events and coordinate defensive responses, such as avoidance (see Fanselow, Chapter 16). Experiments with goldfish and pigeons have produced evidence of the acquisition of fear. Goldfish trained under spaced-trial conditions exhibit avoidance learning

(Portavella et al., 2003) dependent on the medial pallium, an area homologous to the mammalian amygdala (Portavella et al., 2004). Likewise, pigeons trained to peck at a key for food show suppression of key-pecking performance when pecking is punished with electric shock (Azrin, 1959). Such suppression is alleviated by treatment with benzodiazepine anxiolytics that enhance GABAergic transmission (Mansbach et al., 1988). Thus, both goldfish and pigeons, neither one exhibiting SNC, share with mammals some of the components of the brain circuit (amygdala) and psychopharmacology (GABAergic transmission) of avoidance learning and conflict (Korn et al., 2017). Importantly, as stated, the amygdala and benzodiazepine anxiolytics play similar roles in surprising nonreward effects. What do these results suggest about the evolutionary relationship between the conditioning of fear and frustration?

An intriguing possibility is that the anticipatory emotional activation responsible for effects such as SNC is based on a set of brain mechanisms that evolved in early mammals from the circuit responsible for fear conditioning (Papini, 2003). Knowledge about patterns of gene expression during emotional activation in frustration (e.g., SNC) and fear situations (e.g., avoidance learning) should provide a basis to test this hypothesis (Sabariego et al., 2013). Extensive genetic similarities would suggest a process of gene duplication and functional cooption analogous to those postulated to explain the evolution of a quadruplicate set of Hox genes in vertebrates, feathers in birds, and the lenses of the vertebrate eye among others (Hoke et al., 2019; Raff, 1996; True & Carroll, 2002).

10.4 CONCLUSIONS

Two generalizations were suggested in this chapter. First, absolute reward effects can be detected when behavior follows the S/W principle. This is perhaps most clearly observed in situations in which animals are reinforced with a single reward magnitude or quality. Second, relative reward effects are suggested by outcomes contradicting the S/W principle. In the case of the SNC, the cued recall of emotional memories may be needed to demonstrate reward relativity when short-term factors are minimized or excluded (i.e., widely spaced training).

Future research could tackle any of a number of questions in a comparative framework. SNC can be viewed as a biased response to a reward downshift induced by the emotional content of the event, but are there purely cognitive mechanisms that would yield reward relativity? Or is it the role of higher cognitive processes to overcome such biases in behavior? Is SNC an exclusively mammalian phenomenon? Are the different effects of reward downshift observed in mammalian and nonmammalian vertebrates a matter of degree (e.g., larger memory capacity, enhanced response inhibition) or of new mechanisms present in only some groups of vertebrates (e.g., anticipatory frustration)? Research on the SNC effect has barely touched on factors at lower levels of analysis. The fact that highly conserved brain areas are critical for the SNC effect in mammals, such as the amygdala (Guarino et al., 2020b), suggests the possibility that a neurobiological approach could finally answer some of these questions. A useful guide into a comparative neurobiological approach to SNC would require a more detailed model of the brain circuitry underlying this effect in a mammal (Ortega et al., 2017). A validated mammalian circuit could be a heuristic guide for understanding reward relativity in an evolutionary context.

Aristotle proposed a priority: absolute before relative. Comparative research shows that, indeed, control of behavior by absolute reward value is a widespread factor in vertebrate learning. However, reward relativity in the successive comparison case requires the ability to reinstate emotional memories from past frustrating events, a capacity that may be unique to mammals.

REFERENCES

Annicchiarico, I., Glueck, A. C., Cuenya, L., Kawasaki, K., Conrad, S. E., & Papini, M. R. (2016). Complex effects of reward upshift on consummatory behavior. *Behavioural Processes, 129*, 54–67 (https://doi.org/10.1016/j.beproc.2016.06.006).

Aristotle (2003). *Nichomachean ethics.* Translated by H. Rackham. Cambridge, MA: Harvard University Press.

Azrin, N. H. (1959). A technique for delivering shock to pigeons. *Journal of the Experimental Analysis of Behavior, 2*, 161–163 (https://doi.org/10.1901/jeab.1959.2-161).

Binkley, K. A., Webber, E. S., Powers, D. D., & Cromwell, H. C. (2014). Emotion and relative reward processing: An investigation on instrumental successive negative contrast and ultrasonic vocalizations in the rat. *Behavioural Processes, 107*, 167–174 (https://doi.org/10.1016/j.beproc.2014.07.011).

Bitterman, M. E. (1975). The comparative analysis of learning. *Science, 188*, 699–709 (https://doi.org/10.1126/science.188.4189.699).

Conrad, S. E., & Papini, M. R. (2018). Reward shifts in forced-choice and free-choice autoshaping with rats. *Journal of Experimental Psychology: Animal Learning and Cognition, 44*, 422–440 (https://doi.org/10.1037/xan0000187).

Couvillon, P. A., & Bitterman, M. E. (1985). Effect of experience with a preferred food on consummatory responding for a less preferred food in goldfish. *Animal Learning & Behavior, 13*, 433–438 (https://doi.org/10.3758/BF03208020).

Cuenya, L., Bura, S., Serafini, M., & López, M. (2018). Consummatory successive negative contrast in rats: Assessment through orofacial taste reactivity responses. *Learning & otivation, 63*, 98–104 (https://doi.org/10.1016/j.lmot.2018.04.001).

Daly, H. B. (1974). Reinforcing properties of escape from frustration. In G. H. Bower (Ed.), *Psychology of learning and motivation* (pp. 187–232). New York: Academic Press.

Dantzer, R., Arnone, M., & Mormede, P. (1980). Effects of frustration on behaviour and plasma corticosteroid levels in pigs. *Physiology & Behavior, 24*, 1–4 (https://doi.org/10.1016/0031-9384(80)90005-0).

Dudley, R. T., & Papini, M. R. (1995). Pavlovian performance of rats following unexpected reward omissions. *Learning & Motivation, 26*, 63–82 (https://doi.org/10.1016/0023-9690(95)90011-X).

Elliott, M. H. (1928). The effect of change of reward on the maze performance of rats. *University of California Publications in Psychology, 4*, 19–30.

Flaherty, C. F. (1996). *Incentive relativity*. Cambridge: Cambridge University Press.

Freidín, E., Cuello, M. I., & Kacelnik, A. (2009). Successive negative contrast in a bird: Starlings' behavior after unpredictable negative changes in food quality. *Animal Behaviour, 77*, 857–865 (https://doi.org/10.1016/j.anbehav.2008.12.010).

Freidín, E., & Mustaca, A. E. (2004). Frustration and sexual behavior in male rats. *Learning & Behavior, 32*, 311–320 (https://doi.org/10.3758/bf03196030).

Guarino, S., Conrad, S. E., & Papini, M. R. (2020a). Control of free-choice consummatory behavior by absolute reward value. *Learning & Motivation, 72*, 101682 (https://doi.org/10.1016/j.lmot.2020.101682).

(2020b). Frustrative nonreward: Chemogenetic inactivation of the central amygdala abolishes the effect of reward downshift without affecting alcohol intake. *Neurobiology of Learning & Memory, 169*, 107173 (https://doi.org/10.1016/j.nlm.2020.107173).

Hoke, K. L., Adkins-Regan, E., Bass, A. H., McCune, A. R., & Wolfner, M. F. (2019). Co-opting evo-devo concepts for new insights into mechanisms of behavioural diversity. *Journal of Experimental Biology, 222*, jeb190058 (https://doi.org/10.1242/jeb.190058).

Jiménez-García, A. M., Ruíz-Leyva, L., Cendán, C. M., Torres, C., Papini, M. R., & Morón, I. (2016). Hypoalgesia induced by reward devaluation in rats. *PLOS ONE, 11*, e0164331 (https://doi.org/10.1371/journal.pone.0164331).

Justel, N., Pautassi, R., & Mustaca, A. E. (2014). Proactive interference of open field on consummatory successive negative contrast. *Learning & Behavior, 42*, 58–68 (https://doi.org/10.3758/s13420-013-0124-8).

Kamin, L. J. (1969). Predictability, surprise, attention and conditioning. In B. A. Campbell & R. M. Church (Eds.), *Punishment and aversive behavior* (pp. 279–296). New York: Appleton-Century-Crofts.

Korn, C. W., Vunder, J., Miró, J., Fuentemilla, L., Hurlemann, R., & Bach, D. R. (2017). Amygdala lesions reduce anxiety-like behavior in a human benzodiazepine-sensitive approach-avoidance conflict test. *Biological Psychiatry, 82*, 522–531. (https://doi.org/10.1016/j.biopsych.2017.01.018).

Lowes, G., & Bitterman, M. E. (1967). Reward and learning in the goldfish. *Science, 157*, 455–457 (https://doi.org/10.1126/science.157.3787.455).

Lucas, G. A., Gawley, D. J., & Timberlake, W. (1988). Anticipatory contrast as a measure of time horizons in the rat: Some methodological determinants. *Animal Learning & Behavior, 16*, 377–382 (https://doi.org/10.3758/BF03209375).

Ludvigson, H. W. (1999) (Ed.). Odorous episodes and episodic odors. Special Issue. *Psychological Record, 49*, No. 3.

Mansbach, R. S., Harrod, C., Hoffmann, S. M., Nader, M. A., Lei, Z., Witkin, J. M., & Barrett, J. E. (1988). Behavioral studies with anxiolytic drugs. V. Behavioral and in vivo neurochemical analyses in pigeons of drugs that increase punished responding. *Journal of Pharmacology & Experimental Therapeutics, 246*, 114–120.

Manzo, L., Donaire, R., Sabariego, M., Papini, M. R., & Torres, C. (2015). Anti-anxiety self-medication in rats: Oral consumption of chlordiazepoxide and ethanol after reward devaluation. *Behavioural Brain Research, 278*, 90–97 (https://doi.org/10.1016/j.bbr.2014.09.017).

McCain, G., Dyleski, K., & McElvain, G. (1971). Reward magnitude and instrumental responses: Consistent reward. *Psychonomic Monograph Supplements, 3*, No. 48.

Murillo, N. R., Diercks, J. K., & Capaldi, E. J. (1961). Performance of the turtle, *Pseudemys scripta troostii*, in a partial-reinforcement situation. *Journal of Comparative & Physiological Psychology, 54*, 204–206 (https://doi.org/10.1037/h0040813).

Mustaca, A. E., Martínez, C., & Papini, M. R. (2000). Surprising nonreward reduces aggressive behavior in rats. *International Journal of Comparative Psychology, 13*, 91–100.

Mustaca, A. E., & Papini, M. R. (2005). Consummatory successive negative contrast induces hypoalgesia. *International Journal of Comparative Psychology, 18*, 333–339.

Muzio, R. N., Pistone-Creydt, V., Iurman, M., Rinaldi, M. A., Sirani, B., & Papini, M. R. (2011). Incentive or habit learning in amphibians? *PLoS One, 6*, 1–12 (https://doi.org/10.1371/journal.pone.0025798).

Muzio, R. N., Segura, E. T., & Papini, M. R. (1992). Effect of schedule and magnitude of reinforcement on instrumental learning in the toad (*Bufo arenarum*). *Learning & Motivation, 23*, 406–429 (https://doi.org/10.1016/0023-9690(92)90004-6).

Nilsson, M. A., Churakov, G., Sommer, M., Tran, N. V., Zemann, A., Brosius, J., & Schmitz, J. (2010). Tracking marsupial evolution using archaic genomic retroposon insertions. *PLOS Biology, 8*, e1000436 (https://doi.org/10.1371/journal.pbio.1000436).

Norris, J. N., Pérez-Acosta, A. M., Ortega, L. A., & Papini, M. R. (2009). Naloxone facilitates appetitive extinction and eliminates escape from frustration. *Pharmacology, Biochemistry & Behavior, 94*, 81–87 (https://doi.org/10.1016/j.pbb.2009.07.012).

Ortega, L. A., Daniel, A. M., Davis, J. B., Fuchs, P. N., & Papini, M. R. (2011). Peripheral pain enhances the effects of incentive downshifts. *Learning & Motivation, 42*, 203–209 (https://doi.org/10.1016/j.lmot.2011.03.003).

Ortega, L. A., Prado-Rivera, M. A., Cárdenas-Poveda, D. C., McLinden. K. A., Glueck, A. C., Gutiérrez, G., Lamprea, M. R., & Papini, M. R. (2013). Tests of the aversive summation hypothesis in rats: Effects of restraint stress on consummatory successive negative contrast and extinction in the Barnes maze. *Learning & Motivation, 44*, 159–173 (https://doi.org/10.1016/j.lmot.2013.02.001).

Ortega, L. A., Solano, J. L., Torres, C., & Papini, M. R. (2017). Reward loss and addiction: Opportunities for cross-pollination. *Pharmacology, Biochemistry, & Behavior, 154*, 39–52 (http://dx.doi.org/10.1016/j.pbb.2017.02.001).

Papini, M. R. (1997). Role of reinforcement in spaced-trial operant learning in pigeons (*Columba livia*). *Journal of Comparative Psychology, 111*, 275–285 (https://doi.org/10.1037/0735-7036.111.3.275).

(2002). Pattern and process in the evolution of learning. *Psychological Review, 109*, 186–201 (https://doi.org/10.1037/0033-295x.109.1.186).

(2003). Comparative psychology of surprising nonreward. *Brain, Behavior and Evolution, 62*, 83–95 (https://doi.org/10.1159/000072439).

(2014). Diversity of adjustments to reward downshifts in vertebrates. *International Journal of Comparative Psychology, 27*, 420–445.

Papini, M. R., & Dudley, R. T. (1997). Consequences of surprising reward omissions. *Review of General Psychology, 1*, 175–197 (https://doi.org/10.1037/1089-2680.1.2.175).

Papini, M. R., Fuchs, P. N., & Torres, C. (2015). Behavioral neuroscience of psychological pain. *Neuroscience & Biobehavioral Reviews, 48*, 53–69 (https://doi.org/10.1016/j.neubiorev.2014.11.012).

Papini, M. R., Ludvigson, H. W., Huneycutt, D., & Boughner, R. L. (2001). Apparent incentive contrast effects in autoshaping with rats. *Learning & Motivation, 32*, 434–456 (https://doi.org/10.1006/lmot.2001.1088).

Papini, M. R., Mustaca, A. E., & Bitterman, M. E. (1988). Successive negative contrast in the consummatory responding of didelphid marsupials. *Animal Learning & Behavior, 16*, 53–57 (https://doi.org/10.3758/BF03209043).

Papini, M. R., Muzio, R. N., & Segura, E. T. (1995). Instrumental learning in toads (*Bufo arenarum*): Reinforcer magnitude and the medial pallium. *Brain, Behavior, & Evolution, 46*, 61–71 (https://doi.org/10.1159/000113259).

Papini, M. R., & Pellegrini, S. (2006). Scaling relative incentive value in consummatory behavior. *Learning & Motivation, 37*, 357–378 (https://doi.org/10.1016/j.lmot.2006.01.001).

Papini, M. R., Penagos-Corzo, J. C., & Pérez-Acosta, A. M. (2019). Avian emotions: Comparative perspectives on fear and frustration. *Frontiers in Psychology, 9*, 2707 (https://doi.org/10.3389/fpsyg.2018.02707).

Pecoraro, N., Ginsberg, A. B., Akana, S. F., & Dallman, M. F. (2007). Temperature and activity responses to sucrose concentration reductions occur on the 1st but not the 2nd day of concentration shifts, and are blocked by low, constant glucocorticoids. *Behavioral Neuroscience, 121,* 764–778 (https://doi.org/10.1037/0735-7044.121.4.764).

Pecoraro, N., de Jong, H., & Dallman, M. F. (2009). An unexpected reduction in sucrose concentration activates the HPA axis on successive post shift days without attenuation by discriminative contextual stimuli. *Physiology & Behavior, 96,* 651–661 (https://doi.org/10.1016/j.physbeh.2008.12.018).

Pert, A., & Bitterman, M. R. (1970). Reward and learning in the turtle. *Learning & Motivation, 1,* 121–128 (https://doi.org/10.1037/0735-7036.111.3.275).

Portavella, M., Salas, C., Vargas, J. P., & Papini, M. R. (2003). Involvement of the telencephalon in spaced-trial avoidance learning in the goldfish (*Carassius auratus*). *Physiology & Behavior, 80,* 49–56 (https://doi.org/10.1016/S0031-9384(03)00208-7).

Portavella, M., Torres, B., Salas, C., & Papini, M. R. (2004). Lesions of the medial pallium, but not of the lateral pallium, disrupt spaced-trial avoidance learning in goldfish (*Carassius auratus*). *Neuroscience Letters, 362,* 75–78 (https://doi.org/10.1016/j.neulet.2004.01.083).

Raff, R. A. (1996). *The shape of life.* Chicago: University of Chicago Press.

Rescorla, R. A., & Wagner, A. R. (1972). A theory of Pavlovian conditioning: Variations in the effectiveness of reinforcement and nonreinforcement. In A. H. Black & W. F. Prokasy (Eds.), *Classical conditioning II* (pp. 64–99). New York: Appleton-Century-Crofts.

Sabariego, M., Morón, I., Gómez, M. R., Donaire, R., Tobeña, A., Fernández-Teruel, A., Martínez-Conejero, J. A., Esteban, F. J., & Torres, C. (2013). Incentive loss and hippocampal gene expression in inbred Roman high- (RHA-I) and Roman low- (RLA-I) avoidance rats. *Behavioural Brain Research, 257,* 62–70 (https://doi.org/10.1016/j.bbr.2013.09.025).

Sastre, A., Lin, J.-Y., & Reilly, S. (2005). Failure to obtain instrumental successive negative contrast in tasks that support consummatory successive negative contrast. *International Journal of Comparative Psychology, 18,* 307–319.

Schneider, G. E. (2014). *Brain structure and its origins.* Cambridge, MA: MIT Press.

Stout, S. C., Boughner, R. L., & Papini, M. R. (2003). Reexamining the frustration effect in rats: Aftereffects of surprising reinforcement and nonreinforcement. *Learning & Motivation, 34,* 437–456 (https://doi.org/10.1016/S0023-9690(03)00038-9).

Stout, S. C., Muzio, R. N., Boughner, R. L., & Papini, M. R. (2002). Aftereffects of the surprising presentation and omission of appetitive reinforcers on key pecking performance in pigeons. *Journal of Experimental Psychology: Animal Behavior Processes, 28,* 242–256 (https://doi.org/10.1037/0097-7403.28.3.242).

Striedter, G. F. (2005). *Principles of brain evolution.* Sunderland, MA: Sinauer.

Thomas, B. L., & Papini, M. R. (2001). Adrenalectomy eliminates the extinction spike in autoshaping with rats. *Physiology & Behavior, 72,* 543–547 (https://doi.org/10.1016/S0031-9384(00)00448-0).

(2003). Mechanisms of spaced-trial runway extinction in pigeons. *Learning & Motivation, 34,* 104–126 (https://doi.org/10.1016/S0023-9690(02)00506-4).

Thorndike, E. L. (1911). *Animal intelligence: Experimental studies.* New York: Macmillan.

Tinklepaugh, O. L. (1928). An experimental study of representative factors in monkeys. *Journal of Comparative Psychology, 8,* 197–236 (https://doi.org/10.1037/h0075798).

Torres, C., & Papini, M. R. (2017). Incentive relativity. In J. Vonk & T. K. Shackelford (Eds.), *Encyclopedia of animal cognition and behavior.* New York: Springer (https://doi.org/10.1007/978-3-319-47829-6_1079-1).

True, J. R., & Carroll, S. B. (2002). Gene co-option in physiological and morphological evolution. *Annual Review of Cellular and Developmental Biology, 18,* 53–80 (https://doi.org/10.1146/annurev.cellbio.18.020402.140619).

11

THE OPTIMALITY OF "SUBOPTIMAL" CHOICE

A Psycho-evolutionary Perspective

Patrick Anselme

Environmental resources are often uncertain and/or scarce, inducing constraints that may force organisms to make survival-related choices – eating or not eating this food item, exploring or not exploring that location, etc. Thus, organisms should have brain mechanisms, shaped by natural selection, that increase the probability of making good rather than bad choices. They should therefore attempt to maximize benefits – in the form of rewards – when possible (Stephens & Krebs, 1986). Accordingly, a body of evidence provides support for the view that organisms develop strong motivational attraction for conditioned stimuli (CSs) predictive of reward procurement (Bindra, 1978; Berridge, 2007). Also, in a simple free-choice task, organisms from various species exposed to two distinct CSs – one associated with a 50% and the other with a 100% chance of reward – do *not* typically prefer the uncertain option and, often enough, clearly prefer certainty (bees: Anselme, 2018; pigs: de Jonge et al., 2008; macaques: Eisenreich et al., 2019; humans: Kahneman & Tversky, 1979). In addition, the energy budget rule, which postulates that food deprivation should favor "risky" choice (uncertainty), finds only poor empirical support in the literature (Kacelnik & Mouden, 2013).

Despite the obvious effect of rewards in motivating behavior and promoting survival, some experimental findings indicate that a free choice may sometimes lead to a consistent propensity to choose the alternative with the *lowest* profitability (Kendall, 1974; Spetch et al., 1990; Zentall, 2016). This form of choice behavior is therefore labeled suboptimal. In pigeons, suboptimal choice (SOC) occurs even when the amount of food in the optimal option is 35-fold higher (Fortes et al., 2016). And starlings persevere in that preference despite a probability of reward reduced to 5% in the suboptimal option (Vasconcelos et al., 2015). In a similar vein, people value an uncertain, random prospect (e.g., €50 or €100) less than its worst possible certain outcome (€50), even though they know that the uncertain alternative is more profitable on average (Gneezy et al., 2006; Simonsohn, 2009). These findings contradict the principle of reward maximization, and recall older studies showing that animals are not necessarily trying to maximize the total number of calories per se, but, rather, depending on the species, to maximize rare nutrients (Belovsky, 1978), the execution of innate behavioral programs (Breland & Breland, 1961), or the exploration of a wider environment despite abundant food in the local environment (Inglis et al., 1997). Are these findings mere exceptions or do they mean that something more potent determines choice behavior?

This chapter reports evidence that SOC is not a strange phenomenon and can be reconciled with optimal foraging under the assumption that optimality denotes sensitivity to reward-associated environmental properties rather than the ability to obtain more rewards in itself. Psychologically, I suggest that SOC is partly under the control of incentive salience (or "wanting"), the modern theory of incentive motivation for CSs and rewards (Blaiss & Janak, 2009; Flagel et al., 2011; Robinson & Berridge, 2013; Saunders et al., 2018). But more is required to explain the absence of reward maximization. After all, a CS is assumed to get its incentive value from that of the associated reinforcer (Bindra, 1978; Rescorla & Wagner, 1972). So, the higher the reward amount or quality, the higher should be the motivation for its predictive CS – and the more rewarded CSs should be preferred under any circumstances. By contrast, I suggest that SOC occurs because organisms track the *reliability* of the reward signal more than the reward itself – a view that derives from the incentive hope hypothesis, which posits that reward uncertainty often invigorates responding to a CS because organisms "hope" that the CS will be associated reliably with food in the ongoing trial (Anselme, 2015; Anselme & Güntürkün, 2019). The special arrangement of stimuli in the SOC procedure indicates that the incentive hope hypothesis might be relevant to explain some aspects of choice behavior in a motivational perspective where reward is not the only factor to consider.

11.1 WHAT MOTIVATES SOC?

Although organisms may appear optimal in their choices, because they favor the more rewarding option (Cabanac, 1992), the use of a sophisticated design such as the SOC procedure indicates that their preference is motivated by something else. In this task, pigeons – the most studied animal species in this respect – are exposed to two white response keys (Figure 11.1). Responding to either of the two white keys has the immediate effect of changing its color, revealing the probability of being rewarded. (The principle remains the same with rats, although nose-poke holes and levers rather than illuminated keys are used.) For example, if pigeons select the left option, the initial-link (white) stimulus can immediately turn red with a 20% probability and is always followed by food after a fixed delay or can immediately turn green with an 80% probability and is never followed by food after the same delay.

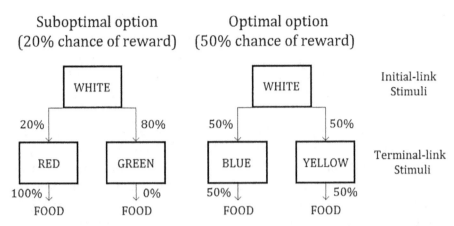

FIGURE 11.1. Representative illustration of a free choice in the SOC procedure with pigeons. After choosing one of the two white initial-link stimuli, it turns a different color with a fixed probability. This terminal-link stimulus is then followed by food or no food in a response-independent manner with a probability that depends on reward contingency (i.e., independently of responding). The transition from the initial to the terminal link consists of an immediate color change following an operant peck. The duration of the terminal link consists of a fixed-time schedule. (Modified after Smith and Zentall, 2016.)

Here, the terminal-link CSs (red and green) are reliable or discriminative. By contrast, if pigeons select the right option, the initial-link (white) stimulus can immediately turn blue or yellow on a random basis and food is delivered with a 50% probability after the same fixed delay in each case. Here, the terminal-link CSs (blue and yellow) are unreliable or nondiscriminative. Despite the fact that the left – suboptimal – option guarantees lower amounts of food than the right – optimal – option (2.5 times less; 20% vs. 50%), the pigeons strongly prefer the former to the latter, suggesting that their choice is suboptimal (for reviews, see McDevitt et al., 2016; Zentall, 2016). A number of other probabilities and training conditions have been tested but pigeons mostly prefer the reliable over the unreliable configuration. (Note that, in the text, "reliability" refers to the ability of the CS to predict reward delivery, while "uncertainty" refers to the status of the reward to be delivered – an uncertain reward is the consequence of an unreliable CS.)

 Several interpretations of SOC have been proposed. One of them, the Signal for Good News (SiGN) hypothesis (McDevitt et al., 2016), suggests that an event is reinforcing provided that it decreases the waiting time to food (Fantino, 1969). The SiGN hypothesis suggests that the terminal-link CS not associated with food in the suboptimal option creates a context of uncertainty about the delay for food: In the example, if the red CS occurs, it is good news that food is to be delivered soon relative to the green CS. Delay is therefore assumed to act as a conditioned reinforcer. On the contrary, in the optimal option, both terminal-link CSs (blue and yellow) are associated with the same expectation of food delivery; neither represents good or bad news.

So, delay does not act as a conditioned reinforcer, and the optimal option is less often preferred over the suboptimal one. Another hypothesis, called within-trial contrast or positive contrast (Stagner & Zentall, 2010), posits that animals are aroused by the discrepancy between what is expected in the initial link (in the example, 20% chance of reward) and what occurs in the terminal link of the suboptimal option when successful (100% chance of reward). No contrast exists in the optimal option, as the animals receive what they expect (50% chance of food), which is therefore not preferred. Both theories are difficult to distinguish in terms of the predictions they make. However, although the SiGN hypothesis provides an explanation related to reward timing that is reasonable both psychologically and evolutionarily, the positive contrast hypothesis fails to explain how any contrast generates suboptimal preference or any advantage in terms of survival (see Pisklak et al., 2019 for discussion; see González et al., 2020 for a recent model that also insists on probabilistic contrasts).

All studies converge toward this evidence that pigeons are insensitive to the probability and to the amount of reward per se in the SOC task. Instead, as the previous hypotheses suggest, temporal and perhaps probabilistic contrasts determine preference. However, these views align poorly with the fact that preference varies as a function of the placement of the reliable CSs. Smith and Zentall (2016) could reverse preference after placing the reliable CSs in the optimal option only, despite the absence of any temporal/probabilistic contrast in that option (Figure 11.2A). They could also produce indifference in choice after placing reliable CSs in both options, despite the presence of a temporal/probabilistic contrast in the suboptimal option only (Figure 11.2B). Thus, a deeper explanation of SOC may be required. Pigeons seem to track the presence of CSs that reliably predict food vs. no food. More specifically, these results suggest that SOC occurs because of the presence of a reliable food-predictive CS (red in the example), as the reliable no-food predictive CS (green) is almost – if not totally – ignored (Fortes et al., 2016; McDevitt et al., 1997; Laude et al., 2014). Such results may demonstrate the powerful attractiveness of CSs, which is sometimes so high that it is able to generate "irrational" behaviors (Domjan et al., 1988; Hearst & Jenkins, 1974) and addictive pathologies (Robinson & Berridge 1993; Rosse et al., 1993). But they may also demonstrate something more fundamental: the conditioned reinforcer is not itself reward or delay; rather, it is the reliability of the CS-Food association. Furthermore, this view encompasses the preference for short delays (Fantino, 1969; Mazur, 1987; McDevitt et al., 2016), given that short delays make a reward more likely, and hence motivationally more salient.

Rats and starlings also track reliable CSs despite strong decreases in reward rates (Chow et al., 2017; Vasconcelos et al., 2015), although rats might be much more sensitive to signals of food omission than are pigeons

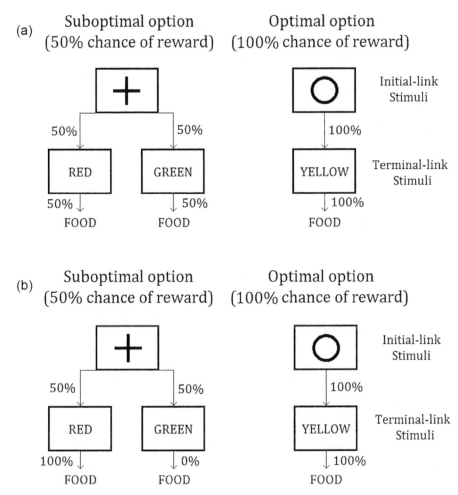

FIGURE 11.2. Evidence that pigeons choose the initial link depending on the reliability of the CS in the terminal link (modified from Smith and Zentall, 2016). (A) Pigeons prefer the optimal option despite the absence of a contrast. (B) Pigeons show indifference between both options despite the presence of a contrast in the suboptimal option. The transition from the initial to the terminal link consists of an immediate color change following an operant peck. The duration of the terminal link consists of a fixed-time schedule.
(Modified after Smith and Zentall, 2016.)

(Trujano & Orduña, 2015; Martinez et al., 2017). Indeed, contrary to pigeons and starlings, rats choose optimally when a lever rather than mere blackout (in place of the green CS) reliably predicts no food. However, the designs used with birds and rats are not totally comparable. In birds, the CSs have distinct colors that depend on the reward contingency in the terminal link (see Figure 11.1). In rats, however, the four contingencies are signaled by identical levers that can be distinguished only by their location in the Skinner box. Despite having learned the different contingencies, rats might therefore find the levers similarly salient and decide to focus only on the incentive value of food – which is higher in the optimal option. This hypothesis could be tested using levers with distinct tactile properties or perhaps illuminated with distinct colors for each reward contingency.

If organisms track reliable CSs in the SOC procedure, this CS reliability could also be what motivates their choice in simpler free-choice tasks. Evidence shows that an unreliable CS predictive of a 50% chance of food is unlikely to be preferred to a reliable CS predictive of a 100% chance of food in any free-choice task. If my hypothesis regarding reliability is correct, the 100% option is preferred because of the predictive reliability of its CS, not because of the higher amount of food per unit time provided. The motivational attraction for reliable CSs is consistent with the incentive salience hypothesis (Berridge, 2007), which posits that CSs and rewards are "wanted" due to the release of mesolimbic dopamine in the nucleus accumbens and other reward-related brain areas. But, as discussed in more detail later, the incentive salience hypothesis does not explain why the predictive reliability of a CS is sought more avidly than the reward from which the CS's incentive value derives. Before reconsidering the psychological mechanisms possibly responsible for SOC, I focus on the so-called suboptimality of SOC from an evolutionary viewpoint.

11.2 IS SOC SUBOPTIMAL?

Hinnenkamp et al. (2017) conducted three ingenious experiments that demonstrate that SOC is not the consequence of a lower unit price associated with food in the suboptimal alternative or of a misattribution of the suboptimal losses to the optimal alternative. They argued that pigeons actually choose suboptimally. Vasconcelos et al. (2018) argued from an evolutionary perspective that SOC may exist without being a violation of optimal foraging theory. Natural selection cannot design organisms to act optimally in all situations; structural and functional constraints may restrict the landscape of evolutionary possibilities and organisms may have to act in an environment that is very different from the one in which they evolved. SOC would be the side effect of an inappropriate environment: "the so-called 'suboptimal' choice is essentially a consequence of using a mechanism that is advantageous in the wild but suboptimal in a controlled, artificial environment like the operant box" (Fortes et al., 2016, p. 344).

However, this conclusion that pigeons' choice is suboptimal is only correct under the original definition of optimality as net energy gain per unit time (see Stephens & Krebs, 1986, for a review of early optimality models), where ingesting more food is necessarily more optimal – more advantageous – in terms of survival. One problem with this restrictive, early definition is that it hides the nonadaptive consequences that optimal decisions may have for survival. In a food-rich environment, individuals may eat more than immediately needed – and become overweight – in preparation for hibernation and migration, for example. This strategy is necessary to stay alive over long periods of food scarcity or of prolonged effort. However, fattening increases a number of overweight-related risks, from predation to injury and reproductive costs (Witter & Cuthill, 1993). So, when possible, animals restrain their food consumption despite abundant food, notably to remain fast and agile when a predator appears (Brodin, 2007; Lima, 1986). During the summer period, when food densities are high, small passerine birds – such as chickadees and titmice – are leaner than they could be because they reject opportunities to eat. This behavior is hardly compatible with the principle of reward maximization but nevertheless depends on an *optimal* rule that consists of trying to satisfy various constraints (risks of starvation, predation, injury, etc.) instead of ingesting food at all costs.

The special arrangement of stimuli in the SOC procedure may certainly produce unexpected behavioral outcomes in animals. Nevertheless, I argue that SOC does not reveal suboptimal decision but rather the highly optimal decision – for survival – that consists of tracking reliable CSs in nature, regardless of the probability and the amount of food to be obtained (Anselme & Güntürkün, 2019). The high motivation for stimulus reliability beyond that for reward itself *is the astonishing fact* revealed by the SOC procedure. In terms of evolution, tracking reliable CSs might be more optimal than reward maximization per se, because identifying stable food sources is always advantageous in the long term in comparison with the mere consumption of food items found accidentally. The high adaptive value of reliable CSs has also been shown with other experimental methods, such as delay and ratio schedules: Animals invariably prefer to obtain food following a variable delay or a variable number of responses over a fixed delay or a fixed number of responses corresponding to the mean of the variable option (Kacelnik & Bateson, 1996). The reason for this preference might be that variability is half of the time associated with quicker food delivery than the constant alternative – a preference that can be amplified using a dopamine agonist such as pramipexole in rats (Johnson et al., 2011). A CS that predicts quicker food delivery is so attractive that it largely compensates for sometimes having to wait longer durations – a well-confirmed prediction of the temporal discounting model (Mazur, 1987). Similarly, starlings prefer a random mixture of intervals of 3 and 18 seconds instead of a predictable alternation of these two intervals (Bateson & Kacelnik, 1997). Here again, the random option may potentially offer quicker food delivery on any next trial, while alternation guarantees a long delay every two trials. The same argument can be used with respect to probabilistic schedules: Macaques prefer a random delivery of small or large juice drops instead of their alternation (Hayden et al., 2008) because the random option may potentially offer a large drop on any next trial, while alternation guarantees a small drop every two trials.

In nature, the longer the delay before obtaining a reward, the less likely is the reward – for example, a lion that smells the presence of a dead prey must rush to find it before other lions or a group of hyenas gain possession of the carcass. The propensity to track a CS should therefore increase in inverse proportion to the signal's duration. How, then, might we explain the finding that SOC increases with short initial-link stimuli and decreases with short terminal-link stimuli (Cunningham & Shahan, 2019; Dunn & Spetch, 1990; Spetch et al., 1990, 1994)? In fact, these decisions are optimal. The initial link leaves the outcome uncertain and should be as short as possible to quickly resolve the ambiguity. As for the terminal link, if the CSs are of short duration, probabilistic reliability is hardly significant because food is quickly delivered in both options (SOC is not preferred). By contrast, if the terminal-link CSs are of longer duration, it is better to wait for a guaranteed reward (SOC is preferred). These results suggest that delay does not relate linearly to choice. Delay-related choice is dependent on the organism's capacity to quickly resolve uncertainty and find reliable CS-Food associations.

11.3 PARTIAL REINFORCEMENT AND THE SEARCH FOR RELIABLE CSs

How can CS reliability in the terminal link be preferred to the reward itself, which is available in a higher amount via the so-called optimal option? According to the traditional view, the reward transfers its incentive salience to the CS (Bindra, 1978), which should therefore be higher for a CS (whether in the initial or the terminal link) associated with a higher amount of food irrespective of its reliability in predicting food delivery. On account of this, I argue that incentive salience theory does not fully capture what happens in the SOC situation, because it is focused on CS approach while remaining silent about the role of CS reliability. Let's see why dissociating both components is important.

The process of incentive salience (Berridge, 2007) accounts for the dopamine-dependent motivational "appetite" for (operationalized as approach behavior to) CSs and rewards in Pavlovian tasks. Indeed, CS appetite has extensively been shown to control responding in rats exposed to a reliable lever CS – predictive of food on each trial – inserted a few seconds before food delivery (autoshaping). Reducing CS reliability should therefore reduce the transfer of incentive salience from the reward, and hence reduce CS appetite. On the contrary, an unreliable lever CS – predictive of food or no food on a random basis on each trial – increases mesolimbic dopamine release in comparison with a reliable one (Fiorillo et al., 2003; Hart et al., 2015). The unreliable CS also generates more responses – in the form of lever pressing and nibbling – than the reliable one (e.g., Anselme et al., 2013; Glueck et al., 2018). Are these effects a product of incentive salience?

If so, why an unreliable CS is generally not preferred over a reliable CS in any choice task is hard to understand. With respect to SOC, the optimal option (where the terminal-link CSs are unreliable, randomly associated with food or no food) should also be preferred to the suboptimal option (where the terminal-link CSs are reliable, consistently associated with food or no food). Given that the two initial-link CSs are associated with uncertainty in the SOC procedure, could it be that the uncertainty resulting from unreliable terminal-link CSs is motivationally less potent than that induced by reliable terminal-link CSs? This hypothesis is plausible because, at the moment of choice (initial link), the uncertainty in the suboptimal option (red or green) has more distinctive consequences and might therefore be preferred over the optimal option (blue or yellow), but the incentive salience hypothesis is silent in this respect. However, a recent autoshaping study might reveal the non-zero attractiveness of the unreliable CSs in the terminal link.

Robinson et al. (2019) designed an autoshaping task for rats in which a trial consisted of a presentation of two successive lever CSs (4 seconds each), the first one being retracted just before the second one is presented, followed by a food outcome. They reasoned that two CSs presented sequentially should not share the same predictive and incentive values (see also Tindell et al., 2005). The first CS in the sequence (such as the initial link in the SOC procedure) has a high predictive value because it starts the trial, but its incentive value remains low due to the lack of temporal proximity to reward delivery. By contrast, the second CS (such as the terminal link in the SOC procedure) carries no more predictive value than the first one but is associated with greater incentive value because of its temporal proximity to reward delivery. The retraction of the second lever CS was consistently followed by the delivery of one food pellet in Group Certainty (reliable) and by nothing (50% of the time) or one, two, or three pellets on a random basis (16.7% of the time each) in Group Uncertainty (unreliable). They found that rats in the group that experienced certainty pressed the first lever CS when it was presented but developed little attraction for the second lever CS. However, rats in the group that experienced uncertainty pressed both levers equally, and significantly more the second lever than the rats under certainty. This result suggests that an unreliable terminal-link CS should be attractive in the SOC procedure. But the fact that it is not preferred to the reliable terminal-link CS in the suboptimal option might indicate that unreliability is not attractive in the same sense as the incentive salience hypothesis would predict. As already pointed out, unreliability has unpredictable consequences that are less present in the terminal link in the suboptimal option, which allows the animals to potentially find out what they seek when exposed to the initial-link stimuli: a reliable CS-Reward association.

I have argued that animals that experienced uncertainty in autoshaping are neither focused on the appetitive reward nor on aversive uncertainty per se but rather on the *reliability* of the CS-Reward association. They are assumed to behave on the basis of a psychological state that I have called *incentive hope* (e.g., Anselme, 2015; Anselme & Güntürkün, 2019; but see Torres et al., 2016). Animals do not directly "hope" for reward procurement or for uncertainty dissipation but simply "hope" that the ongoing or the next CS-Reward association will be reliable. They are motivated to seek reliable associations because of uncertainty, which explains why they respond more vigorously to an unreliable rather than a reliable CS lever in autoshaping – no need to "hope" for CS reliability in the absence of uncertainty since the reward is guaranteed. Applied to a free-choice task, where response rate does not matter and uncertainty can sometimes be avoided, this view may appear useless. However, its focus on CS reliability helps explain the evidence that organisms, including humans, prefer a 100% over a 50% predictive option, even when the former is less profitable – in terms of reward magnitude – than the latter (e.g., Gneezy et al., 2006; Simonsohn, 2009; Zentall, 2016). This aspect is relevant to SOC. Between the two forms of uncertainty present before choice in the initial links, pigeons prefer the one where uncertainty resolution is the quickest, irrespective of the food probability or amount, like in the case of simpler free-choice tasks. In other words, organisms "hope" for CS reliability when reward uncertainty is unavoidable but try to avoid it when possible (Anselme & Güntürkün, 2019). Importantly, there is no anthropomorphic presupposition that a rat or a pigeon can subjectively hope for anything when the word "hope" is used in this context; "hope" (between quotation marks, similarly to "wanting") simply means that animals behave *as if* they had a subjective experience of hope. Incentive hope denotes a brain process responsible for the increase in an individual's motivation and effort to seek a reliable CS-Reward association when it is unpredictable.

11.4 POSSIBLE UNCERTAINTY-INDUCED BEHAVIORAL SENSITIZATION IN SOC

Despite the high motivation of animals for reliable reward signals, recent evidence suggests that SOC is also promoted by positive contrast (Case & Zentall, 2018; Zentall et al., 2019). One group of pigeons was trained in a SOC procedure in which both options contained reliable CSs that signaled 50% (suboptimal) vs. 100% (optimal) chance of food. Another group of pigeons was also trained with reliable CSs in both options, one providing 75% (suboptimal) and the other 100% (optimal) chance of food. After comparing the responses in the two suboptimal conditions (50% vs. 75%), the pigeons from group 50% appeared to prefer the suboptimal option more than the pigeons from group 75% (Zentall et al., 2019). A greater contrast between what is expected in the initial link and what occurs in the terminal link of the suboptimal option when successful would reveal the importance of positive contrast for SOC. Positive contrast would also explain why more responses are given to a terminal-link CS reliably predictive of reward when the initial expectation is 50% rather than 100% (Case & Zentall, 2018).

Such results can also be explained by the SiGN hypothesis (McDevitt et al., 2016): the context of uncertainty that makes delay reinforcing is simply more pronounced in the 50% than in the 75% condition. At first glance, however, they sound inconsistent with the incentive hope hypothesis: the two options should have been chosen similarly because they both contained reliable CSs. But a closer look at the findings by Zentall et al. (2019) indicates that the incentive hope hypothesis is perhaps not wrong in its prediction. They trained their pigeons for 100 training sessions, namely, 20 blocks of 5 sessions. The means remained near the indifference point for dozens of sessions, and they found a significant effect only in the last block of 5 sessions – that is, sessions 96–100. The number of sessions used here largely exceeds the training conditions in most experimental protocols, suggesting that contrast may play a relatively marginal role in SOC. A convincing demonstration that contrast is also a potent process in SOC would be to show that the difference in preference and the speed at which it is established increase in proportion to the difference in probabilities in the suboptimal options with reliable CSs – for example, 20% vs. 75% should produce a greater, quicker difference in preference than 50% vs. 75%.

Incentive hope does not favor preference for CS unreliability, contrary to what has been reported (Chow et al., 2017). But explaining why some reliable CSs could be preferred to other reliable CSs is beyond the explanatory limits of that concept. Nevertheless, incentive hope can have implications that could help account for the findings by Zentall et al. (2019). Given that the 50% vs. 75% contrast emerges very slowly, this finding could be compatible with current direct and indirect evidence that repeated exposure to uncertain rewards is able to sensitize responding to a CS or to an operant schedule (Fuentes-Verdugo et al., 2020; Mascia et al., 2019; Robinson et al., 2014; Zeeb et al., 2017). So, overtraining may have had the effect of sensitizing the propensity of pigeons to preferentially select the 50% option (more uncertain) than the 75% option (less uncertain) relative to the 100% optimal option. In this context, behavioral sensitization is a dopamine-dependent process also observed in various addictions (Berridge, 2007), which causes a similar bias in preference following the injection of a dopaminergic agonist in simpler free-choice tasks (e.g., Johnson et al., 2011; Oinio et al., 2018; Tremblay et al., 2017). At this stage, further investigation is needed to determine how overtraining can influence dopamine release in the SOC procedure.

11.5 DOES POSITIVE CONTRAST EXPLAIN CHOICE BEHAVIOR?

The study of contrast has a long tradition in psychology (see Papini, Chapter 10). Rewarding one monkey's action with a piece of banana (very attractive) and another monkey, which has observed the rewarded behavior, with a piece of lettuce (less attractive) for exactly the same action, makes this second monkey angry (Tinklepaugh, 1928). The negative contrast between what the second monkey expected (banana) and what it received (lettuce) produces negative emotion; however, the piece of lettuce is accepted in the absence of negative contrast with another individual. Similarly, if rats repeatedly trained to expect a 32% sucrose solution receive a 4% sucrose solution (less than expected), they drastically reduce licking behavior during the first downshifted session – a behavior traditionally interpreted in terms of frustration or anxiety (e.g., Flaherty, 1996; Papini, 2014). Positive contrast denotes the reverse situation, where initial training is with the low-quality reward and the (up)shift with the higher-quality reward.

In most behavioral studies, whether positive or negative, contrast "has been seen as a pattern of behavior and not an explanation of it" (Pisklak et al., 2019, p. 35). In particular, successive contrast effects result from a comparison between a *learned* expectation and an actual outcome. Positive contrast can be the consequence of a positive prediction error signal and negative contrast of a negative prediction error signal in the brain (Schultz, 1998). However, a learning mechanism does not carry any motivational value on its own (Berridge, 2012). As such, contrast does not explain what an animal is doing; a motivational/emotional interpretation is required. Two distinct, complementary components account for the behavior of animals exposed to negative contrast. First, a learning process such as a negative prediction error signal in the brain allows the animal to compare its expectation (32% sucrose) to what occurs (4% sucrose). Second, a negative emotion (frustration, anxiety) relies on this comparison and leads the animal transiently away from the low-quality reward (Flaherty, 1996; Gray & McNaughton, 2000; Kawasaki et al., 2017). The negative emotion rather than the comparison itself is *at the origin* of the observed behavior.

If positive contrast plays a role in the responses to reward uncertainty, the same reasoning must apply. Explaining uncertainty-induced behavior – whether under partial reinforcement in autoshaping or in the SOC procedure – in terms of positive contrast is to disregard the motivational process relying on the learning of a mere comparison without intrinsic motivational value. In Pavlovian autoshaping with rats, there is a total absence of contrast in the number of responses to a CS that follows rewarded or nonrewarded trials following a 45-second intertrial interval (Anselme & Robinson, 2019), although a contrast effect has been shown with intertrial interval durations shorter than 8 seconds (Stout et al., 2003). But here again, this contrast is not part of the explanation: frustration or anxiety after a short CS-Food interval is just more likely than after a longer one. In the SOC procedure, this interval is typically nil, because the transition between the initial-link CS (uncertain outcome) and the terminal-link CS (uncertainty resolution) is immediate. So, pigeons might be in a situation of high sensitivity to contrast, even higher than rats in the Stout et al. study. But the motivational/emotional effect of this immediate contrast should explain choice behavior. The exact relation between motivation, emotion, and prediction error is not yet well understood. Studying this question by means of the SOC procedure is worth being investigated in the future.

11.6 CONCLUSION

SOC in the kind of experiments described here has essentially been studied with pigeons and only a few other species (starlings and rats), so many questions remain open with respect to the generality of the conditions of its occurrence. However, the body of evidence accumulated during the recent decades may suggest that SOC is not suboptimal and relates to the search for reliable reward signals in the environment. From an animal's perspective, how many food items can be obtained now is possibly less important than knowing where the reliable signals that lead to food items can be found. This interpretation agrees with optimal foraging theory and may help understand the common evolutionary reasons behind various forms of "suboptimality." One of them is contrafreeloading, the propensity to make an effort to obtain uncertain food when the same food is available galore. Although contra-freeloading is a biological adaptation that consists of exploring the environment to exploit its resources more efficiently in the future (Inglis et al., 1997), what motivates organisms to behave this way remains unclear. The suggestion that they seek security (through CS reliability) more than immediate gratification could be an explanation. Understanding this requires to elaborate performance models of CS-Reward associations that go beyond motivational and learning models in the strict sense.

ACKNOWLEDGMENT

This work was supported by the Deutsche Forschungsgemeinschaft (DFG) through An1067/3-1.

REFERENCES

Anselme, P. (2015). Incentive salience attribution under reward uncertainty: A Pavlovian model. *Behavioural Processes, 111*, 6–18. https://doi.org/10.1016/j.beproc.2014.10.016

(2018). Uncertainty processing in bees exposed to free choices: Lessons from vertebrates. *Psychonomic Bulletin & Review, 25*, 2024–2036. https://doi.org/10.3758/s13423-018-1441-x

Anselme, P., & Güntürkün, O. (2019). How foraging works: Uncertainty magnifies food-seeking motivation. *Behavioral and Brain Sciences, 42*(e35), 1–59. https://doi.org/10.1017/S0140525X18000948

Anselme, P., & Robinson, M. J. F. (2019). Evidence for motivational enhancement of sign-tracking behavior under reward uncertainty. *Journal of Experimental Psychology: Animal Learning and Cognition, 45,* 350–355. https://doi.org/10.1037/xan0000213

Anselme, P., Robinson, M. J. F., & Berridge, K. C. (2013). Reward uncertainty enhances incentive salience attribution as sign-tracking. *Behavioural Brain Research, 238,* 53–61. https://doi.org/10.1016/j.bbr.2012.10.006

Bateson, M., & Kacelnik, A. (1997). Starlings' preference for predictable and unpredictable delays to food. *Animal Behaviour, 53,* 1129–1142. https://doi.org/10.1006/anbe.1996 .0388

Belovsky, G. E. (1978). Diet optimization in a generalist herbivore: The moose. *Theoretical Population Biology, 14,* 105–134. https://doi.org/10.1016/0040-5809(78)90007-2

Berridge, K. C. (2007). The debate over dopamine's role in reward: The case for incentive salience. *Psychopharmacology, 191,* 391–431. https://doi.org/10.1007/s00213-006-0578-x
  (2012). From prediction error to incentive salience: Mesolimbic computation of reward motivation. *European Journal of Neuroscience, 35,* 1124–1143. https://doi.org/10.1111/j .1460-9568.2012.07990.x

Bindra, D. (1978). How adaptive behavior is produced: A perceptual-motivational alternative to response-reinforcement. *Behavioural and Brain Sciences, 1,* 41–91.

Blaiss, C. A., & Janak, P. H. (2009). The nucleus accumbens core and shell are critical for the expression, but not the consolidation, of Pavlovian conditioned approach. *Behavioural Brain Research, 200,* 22–32. https://doi.org/10.1016/j.bbr.2008.12.024

Breland, K., & Breland, M. (1961). The misbehavior of organisms. *American Psychologist, 16,* 681–684. https://psycnet.apa.org/doi/10.1037/h0040090

Brodin, A. (2007). Theoretical models of adaptive energy management in small wintering birds. *Philosophical Transactions of the Royal Society B: Biological Sciences, 362,* 1857–1871. https://doi.org/10.1098/rstb.2006.1812

Cabanac, M. (1992). Pleasure: The common currency. *Journal of Theoretical Biology, 155,* 173–200. https://doi.org/10.1016/S0022-5193(05)80594-6

Case, J. P., & Zentall, T. R. (2018). Suboptimal choice in pigeons: Does the predictive value of the conditioned reinforcer alone determine choice? *Behavioural Processes, 157,* 320–326. https://doi.org/10.1016/j.beproc.2018.07.018

Chow, J. J., Smith, A. P., Wilson, A. G., Zentall, T. R., & Beckmann, J. S. (2017). Suboptimal choice in rats: Incentive salience attribution promotes maladative decision-making. *Behavioural Brain Research, 320,* 244–254. https://doi.org/10.1016/j.bbr.2016.12.013

Cunningham, P. J., & Shahan, T. A. (2019). Rats engage in suboptimal choice when the delay to food is sufficiently long. *Journal of Experimental Psychology: Animal Learning and Cognition, 45,* 301–310. https://doi.org/10.1037/xan0000211

Domjan, M., O'Vary, D., & Greene, P. (1988). Conditioning of appetitive and consummatory sexual behavior in male Japanese quail. *Journal of the Experimental Analysis of Behavior, 50,* 505–519. https://doi.org/10.1901/jeab.1988.50-505

Dunn, R., & Spetch, M. L. (1990). Choice with uncertain outcomes: Conditioned reinforcement effects. *Journal of the Experimental Analysis of Behavior, 53,* 201–218. https://doi .org/10.1901/jeab.1990.53-201

Eisenreich, B. R., Hayden, B. Y., & Zimmermann, J. (2019). Macaques are risk-averse in a freely moving foraging task. *Scientific Reports, 9,* 15091. https://doi.org/10.1038/s41598-019-51442-z

Fantino, E. (1969). Choice and rate of reinforcement. *Journal of the Experimental Analysis of Behavior, 12,* 723–730. https://doi.org/10.1901/jeab.1969.12-723

Fiorillo, C. D., Tobler, P. N., & Schultz, W. (2003). Discrete coding of reward probability and uncertainty by dopamine neurons. *Science, 299,* 1898–1902. https://doi.org/10.1126/ science.1077349

Flagel, S. B., Clark, J. J., Robinson, T. E., Mayo, L., Czuj, A., Willuhn, I., Akers, C. A., Clinton, S. M., Phillips, P. E. M., & Akil, H. (2011). A selective role for dopamine in stimulus-reward learning. *Nature, 469,* 53–57. https://doi.org/10.1038/nature09588

Flaherty, C. F. (1996). *Incentive relativity*. Cambridge University Press.

Fortes, I., Vasconcelos, M., & Machado, A. (2016). Testing the boundaries of "paradoxical" predictions: Pigeons do disregard bad news. *Journal of Experimental Psychology: Animal Learning and Cognition, 42*, 336–346. https://doi.org/10.1037/xan0000114

Fuentes-Verdugo, E., Pellón, R., Papini, M. R., Torres, C., Fernández-Teruel, A., & Anselme, P. (2020). Effects of partial reinforcement on autoshaping in inbred Roman high- and low-avoidance rats. *Physiology and Behavior, 225*, 113111. https://doi.org/10.1016/j.physbeh.2020.113111

Glueck, A. C., Torres, C., & Papini, M. R. (2018). Transfer between anticipatory and consummatory tasks involving reward loss. *Learning and Motivation, 63*, 105–125. https://doi.org/10.1016/j.lmot.2018.05.001

Gneezy, U., List, J. A., & Wu, G. (2006). The uncertainty effect: When a risky prospect is valued less than its worst possible outcome. *Quarterly Journal of Economics, 121*, 1283–1309. https://doi.org/10.1093/qje/121.4.1283

González, V.V., Macías, A., Machado, A., & Vasconcelos, M. (2020). The Δ-Σ hypothesis: How contrast and reinforcement rate combine to generate suboptimal choice. *Journal of the Experimental Analysis of Behavior, 113*, 591–608. https://doi.org/10.1002/jeab.595

Gray, J. A., & McNaughton, N. (2000). *The neuropsychology of anxiety* (2nd ed.). Oxford University Press.

Hart, A. S., Clark, J. J., & Phillips, P. E. M. (2015). Dynamic shaping of dopamine signals during probabilistic Pavlovian conditioning. *Neurobiology of Learning and Memory, 117*, 84–92. https://doi.org/10.1016/j.nlm.2014.07.010

Hayden, B. Y., Heilbronner, S. R., Nair, A. C., & Platt, M. L. (2008). Cognitive influences on risk-seeking by rhesus macaques. *Judgment and Decision Making, 3*, 389–395.

Hearst, E., & Jenkins, H. M. (1974). *Sign-tracking: The stimulus-reinforcer relation and directed action*. Austin: Psychonomic Society.

Hinnenkamp, J. E., Shahan, T. A., & Madden, G. J. (2017). How suboptimal is suboptimal choice? *Journal of the Experimental Analysis of Behavior, 107*, 136–150. https://doi.org/10.1002/jeab.239

Inglis, I. R., Forkman, B., & Lazarus, J. (1997). Free food or earned food? A review and fuzzy model of contrafreeloading. *Animal Behaviour, 53*, 1171–1191. https://doi.org/10.1006/anbe.1996.0320

Johnson, P. S., Madden, G. J., Brewer, A. T., Pinkston, J. W., & Fowler, S. C. (2011). Effects of acute pramipexole on preference for gambling-like schedules of reinforcement in rats. *Psychopharmacology, 213*, 11–18. https://doi.org/10.1007/s00213-010-2006-5

de Jonge, F. H., Ooms, M., Kuurman, W. W., Maes, J. H. R., & Spruijt, B. M. (2008). Are pigs sensitive to variability in food rewards? *Applied Animal Behaviour Science, 114*, 93–104. https://doi.org/10.1016/j.applanim.2008.01.004

Kacelnik, A., & Bateson, M. (1996). Risky theories: The effects of variance on foraging decisions. *American Zoologist, 36*, 402–434. https://doi.org/10.1093/icb/36.4.402

Kacelnik, A., & Mouden, C. E. (2013). Triumphs and trials of the risk paradigm. *Animal Behaviour, 86*, 1117–1129. https://doi.org/10.1016/j.anbehav.2013.09.034

Kahneman, D., & Tversky, A. (1979). Prospect theory: An analysis of decision under risk. *Econometrica, 47*, 263–292. https://doi.org/10.1142/9789814417358_0006

Kawasaki, K., Annicchiarico, I., Glueck, A. C., Morón, I., & Papini, M. R. (2017). Reward loss and the basolateral amygdala: A function in reward comparisons. *Behavioural Brain Research, 331*, 205–213. https://doi.org/10.1016/j.bbr.2017.05.036

Kendall, S. B. (1974). Preference for intermittent reinforcement. *Journal of the Experimental Analysis of Behavior, 21*, 463–473. https://doi.org/10.1901/jeab.1974.21-463

Laude, J. R., Stagner, J. P., & Zentall, T. R. (2014). Suboptimal choice by pigeons may result from the diminishing effect of nonreinforcement. *Journal of Experimental Psychology: Animal Learning and Cognition, 40*, 12–21. https://doi.org/10.1037/xan0000010

Lima, S. L. (1986). Predation risk and unpredictable feeding conditions: Determinants of body mass in birds. *Ecology, 67*, 377–385. https://doi.org/10.2307/1938580

Martinez, M., Alba, R., Rodriguez, W., & Orduña, V. (2017). Incentive salience attribution is not the sole determinant of suboptimal choice in rats: Conditioned inhibition matters. *Behavioural Processes, 142*, 99–105. https://doi.org/10.1016/j.beproc.2017.06.012

Mascia, P., Neugebauer, N. M., Brown, J., Bubula, N., Nesbitt, K. M., Kennedy, R. T., & Vezina, P. (2019). Exposure to conditions of uncertainty promotes the pursuit of amphetamine. *Neuropsychopharmacology 44*, 274–280. https://doi.org/10.1038/s41386-018-0099-4

Mazur, J. E. (1987). An adjusting procedure for studying delayed reinforcement. In: M. L. Commons, J. E. Mazur, J. A. Nevin, & H. Rachlin (Eds.), *Quantitative analyses of behavior (Vol. 5). The effect of delay and of intervening events on reinforcement value* (pp. 55–73). Erlbaum Associates.

McDevitt, M. A., Dunn, R. M., Spetch, M. L., & Ludvig, E. A. (2016). When good news leads to bad choices. *Journal of the Experimental Analysis of Behavior, 105*, 23–40. https://doi.org/10.1002/jeab.192

McDevitt, M. A., Spetch, M. L., & Dunn, R. (1997). Contiguity and conditioned reinforcement in probabilistic choice. *Journal of the Experimental Analysis of Behavior, 68*, 317–327. https://doi.org/10.1901/jeab.1997.68-317

Oinio, V., Sundström, M., Bäckström, P., Uhari-Väänänen, J., Kiianmaa, K., Raasmaja, A., & Piepponen, P. (2018). Amphetamine primes enhanced motivation toward uncertain choices in rats with genetic alcohol preference. *Psychopharmacology, 235*, 1361–1370. https://doi.org/10.1007/s00213-018-4847-2

Papini, M. R. (2014). Diversity of adjustments to reward downshifts in vertebrates. *International Journal of Comparative Psychology, 27*, 420–445.

Pisklak, J. M., McDevitt, M. A., & Dunn, R. M. (2019). Clarifying contrast, acknowledging the past, and expanding the focus. *Comparative Cognition and Behavior Reviews, 14*, 33–38. https://doi.org/10.3819/CCBR.2019.140004

Rescorla, R. A., & Wagner, A. R. (1972). A theory of Pavlovian conditioning: Variations in the effectiveness of reinforcement and nonreinforcement. In: Black, A. H. & Prokasy, W. F. (Eds.), *Classical conditioning II: Current theory and research* (pp. 64–99). Appleton-Century-Crofts.

Robinson, M. J. F., Anselme, P., Fischer, A. M., & Berridge, K. C. (2014). Initial uncertainty in Pavlovian reward prediction persistently elevates incentive salience and extends sign-tracking to normally unattractive cues. *Behavioural Brain Research, 266*, 119–130. https://doi.org/10.1016/j.bbr.2014.03.004

Robinson, M. J. F., & Berridge, K. C. (2013). Instant transformation of learned repulsion into motivational "wanting." *Current Biology, 23*, 282–289. https://doi.org/10.1016/j.cub.2013.01.016

Robinson, M. J. F., Clibanoff, C., Freeland, C. M., Knes, A. S., Cote, J. R., & Russell, T. I. (2019). Distinguishing between predictive and incentive value of uncertain gambling-like cues in a Pavlovian autoshaping task. *Behavioural Brain Research, 371*, 111971. https://doi.org/10.1016/j.bbr.2019.111971

Robinson, T. E., & Berridge, K. C. (1993). The neural basis of drug craving: An incentive-sensitization theory of addiction. *Brain Research Review, 18*, 247–291. https://doi.org/10.1016/0165-0173(93)90013-P

Rosse, R. B., Fay-McCarthy, M., Collins, J. P., Jr., Risher-Flowers, D., Alim, T. N., & Deutsch, S. I. (1993). Transient compulsive foraging behavior associated with crack cocaine use. *American Journal of Psychiatry, 150*, 155–156. http://dx.doi.org/10.1176/ajp.150.1.155

Saunders, B. T., Richard, J. M., Margolis, E. B., & Janak, P. H. (2018). Dopamine neurons create Pavlovian conditioned stimuli with circuit-defined motivational properties. *Nature Neuroscience, 21*, 1072–1083. https://doi.org/10.1038/s41593-018-0191-4

Schultz, W. (1998). Predictive reward signal of dopamine neurons. *Journal of Neurophysiology, 80*, 1–27. https://doi.org/10.1152/jn.1998.80.1.1

Simonsohn, U. (2009). Direct risk aversion: Evidence from risky prospects valued below their worst outcome. *Psychological Science, 20*, 686–692. https://doi.org/10.1111/j.1467-9280.2009.02349.x

Smith, A. P., & Zentall, T. R. (2016). Suboptimal choice in pigeons: Choice is primarily based on the value of the conditioned reinforcers rather than overall reinforcement rate. *Journal of Experimental Psychology: Animal Learning and Cognition, 42,* 212–220. https://doi.org/10.1037/xan0000092

Spetch, M., Belke, T., Barnet, R., Dunn, R., & Pierce, W. (1990). Suboptimal choice in a percentage reinforcement procedure: Effects of signal condition and terminal-link length. *Journal of the Experimental Analysis of Behavior, 53,* 219–234. https://doi.org/https://doi.org/10.1901/jeab.1990.53-219

Spetch, M., Mondloch, M., Belke, T., & Dunn, R. (1994). Determinants of pigeons' choice between certain and probabilistic outcomes. *Animal Learning & Behavior, 22,* 239–251. https://doi.org/10.3758/BF03209832

Stagner, J. P., & Zentall, T. R. (2010). Suboptimal choice behavior by pigeons. *Psychonomic Bulletin & Review, 17,* 412–416. http://dx.doi.org/10.3758/PBR.17.3.412

Stephens, D. W., & Krebs, J. R. (1986). *Foraging theory.* Princeton University Press.

Stout, S. C., Boughner, R. L., & Papini, M. R. (2003). Reexamining the frustration effect in rats: Aftereffects of surprising reinforcement and nonreinforcement. *Learning and Motivation, 34,* 437–456. https://doi.org/10.1016/S0023-9690(03)00038-9

Tindell, A. J., Berridge, K. C., Zhang, J., Peciña, S., & Aldridge, J. W. (2005). Ventral pallidal neurons code incentive motivation: Amplification by mesolimbic sensitization and amphetamine. *European Journal of Neuroscience, 22,* 2617–2634. https://doi.org/10.1111/j.1460-9568.2005.04411.x

Tinklepaugh, O. L. (1928). An experimental study of representative factors in monkeys. *Journal of Comparative Psychology, 8,* 197–236. https://psycnet.apa.org/doi/10.1037/h0075798

Torres, C., Glueck, A. C., Conrad, S. E., Morón, I., & Papini, M. R. (2016). Dorsomedial striatum lesions affect adjustment to reward uncertainty, but not to reward devaluation or omission. *Neuroscience, 332,* 13–25. http://dx.doi.org/10.1016/j.neuroscience.2016.06.041

Tremblay, M., Silveira, M. M., Kaur, S., Hosking, J. G., Adams, W. K., Baunez, C., & Winstanley, C. A. (2017). Chronic D2/3 agonist ropinirole treatment increases preference for uncertainty in rats regardless of baseline choice patterns. *European Journal of Neuroscience, 45,* 159–166. https://doi.org/10.1111/ejn.13332

Trujano, R. E., & Orduña, V. (2015). Rats are optimal in a choice task in which pigeons are not. *Behavioural Processes, 119,* 22–27. https://doi.org/10.1016/j.beproc.2015.07.010

Vasconcelos, M., Machado, A., & Pandeirada, J. N. S. (2018). Ultimate explanations and suboptimal choice. *Behavioural Processes, 152,* 63–72. https://doi.org/10.1016/j.beproc.2018.03.023

Vasconcelos, M., Monteiro, T., & Kacelnik, A. (2015). Irrational choice and the value of information. *Scientific Reports, 5,* 13874. https://doi.org/10.1038/srep13874

Witter, M. S., & Cuthill, I. C. (1993). The ecological costs of avian fat storage. *Philosophical Transactions of the Royal Society B: Biological Sciences, 340,* 73–92. https://doi.org/10.1098/rstb.1993.0050

Zeeb, D. F., Li, Z., Fisher, D. C., Zack, M. H., & Fletcher, P. J. (2017). Uncertainty exposure causes behavioural sensitization and increases risky decision-making in male rats: Toward modelling gambling disorder. *Journal of Psychiatry Neuroscience, 42,* 404–413. https://doi.org/10.1503%2Fjpn.170003

Zentall, T. R. (2016). Resolving the paradox of suboptimal choice. *Journal of Experimental Psychology: Animal Learning and Cognition, 42,* 1–14. https://doi.org/10.1037/xan0000085

Zentall, T. R., Andrews, D. M., & Case, J. (2019). Contrast between what is expected and what occurs increases pigeon's suboptimal choice. *Animal Cognition, 22,* 81–87. https://doi.org/10.1007/s10071-018-1223-x

12

A BEHAVIOR SYSTEMS FRAMEWORK

What It Is and How to Use It

Kathleen M. Silva and Francisco J. Silva

Outside the world of academia and laboratories, hunters and anglers are aware that understanding an animal's behavior requires taking into account environmental conditions and the animal's physiology and motivational state. Anglers know that an artificial lure has to be sensed before a fish can track, chase, and strike it. Whether a fish can see, smell, and feel a lure depends on the clarity of the water, whether the lure has been sprayed with scent, and how much a lure rattles and vibrates. The effectiveness of different lures depends on a fish's motivational state, which is affected by when the fish last ate, the water temperature, the amount of oxygen in the water, the season, and whether the fish is pre-spawn, spawning, or post-spawn. The effectiveness of a lure also depends on a fish's search image, which is affected by the distributions of different prey at different times of the year. Likely through trial-and-error learning and cultural transmission, anglers came to know that many variables affect a fish's behavior and thus consider these variables before deciding what lure to use and how to use it. Under one set of conditions, rapidly retrieving a spinning lure just below the surface of the water is best for triggering a fish to strike. Under other conditions, slowly bouncing and dragging an artificial critter off the bottom of a lake might be best. In the world of angling, a fish's response to a lure cannot be isolated from its sensory and perceptual-motor responses, its motivational state, and its past and present environments.

12.1 BEHAVIOR SYSTEMS AND LEARNING

Inside the world of academia and laboratories, Timberlake and Lucas's (1989) behavior systems framework formalizes and adds to what hunters and anglers know. Their framework consists of a conceptual foundation and a set of pragmatic considerations, rooted in the naturalistic study of animal behavior, that can be used in the study of learning and behavior analysis. According to this framework, learning cannot be isolated from the conditions under which it is studied or the species under investigation. Because learning and behavior are the result of integrated physiological structures and processes that include sensory, perceptual, cognitive, and response components, the study of learning should explicitly consider the influence of these components in the design of its studies and the interpretation of results.

Timberlake and Lucas's (1989) behavior systems approach assumes that an animal's sensory, perceptual, cognitive, and response components are hierarchically organized. The top level of behavioral control consists of a *system* that serves an important biological function (e.g., feeding). Systems consist of *subsystems* that share common features (e.g., predation vs. browsing), *modes* that are collections of stimulus sensitivities and responses related to important events and to cues that announce them (e.g., general search, focal search, handling/consuming food), *perceptual-motor modules* that respond to particular stimuli with particular actions (e.g., capturing or securing food is a stimulus event that may trigger biting), and specific *actions* themselves (e.g., biting, chewing, swallowing).

Figure 12.1 illustrates a sequence of search modes for a rat's predation subsystem. Encountering predictors of food at different spatiotemporal distances from food evokes repertoires of stimulus sensitivities and responses: general search, focal search, and handle/consume. Once food is found and eaten, the animal re-enters a focal search mode. If more food is found quickly, the animal re-enters the handling/consuming mode. If food is not found quickly, the animal returns to a general search mode and repeats the cycle or stops foraging.

Learning evolved to improve functions such as procuring food, finding water, attracting mates, caring for offspring, and escaping and avoiding predators in a changing environment. In other words, learning is a mechanism that tunes behavior systems to variations in the environment. When different biological functions (e.g., procuring food vs. obtaining water) share common response classes (e.g., searching) and consequences (e.g., the rapidity with which food or water are found), learning looks similar. When biological functions share fewer response classes and consequences, learning looks different. Thus, hungry rats need multiple tone-food pairings before they reliably approach the food site during the tone, but only a single flavor-toxin pairing before they start avoiding that flavor. Whether this difference in the number of pairings reflects different learning processes and mechanisms is unclear. As Innis and Staddon (1989) noted, "Different performance patterns cannot be taken as evidence for different underlying mechanisms. And, symmetrically, similar performance cannot be taken as evidence for similar mechanisms" (p. 155). In addition, mechanisms can be analyzed at different levels (e.g., psychological, physiological, neurological, molecular), which adds to the difficulty of identifying and understanding mechanisms. Learning itself is a mechanism (Beecher, 1988).

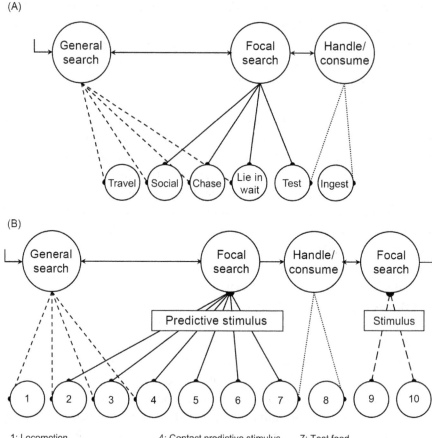

(A)

(B)

1: Locomotion
2: Attend to predictive stimulus
3: Approach predictive stimulus
4: Contact predictive stimulus
5: Attend to food location
6: Approach food location
7: Test food
8: Eat
9: Scan area where food eaten
10: Attend to moving stimuli

FIGURE 12.1. (A) Representation of the sequence of search modes related to a rat's predation subsystem (Timberlake & Lucas, 1989) and (B) how those modes may be expressed in a laboratory study of Pavlovian conditioning. Each mode is a repertoire of stimulus sensitivities (not illustrated) and responses. In the lab, the responses depend on the physical characteristics of stimuli associated with food and the spatial and temporal distance of these stimuli from food. Panel (B) shows how a stimulus presented before or after food could come to control different search modes and their responses. In the natural environment, these responses consist of traveling, socializing, investigating, chasing, etc. In the lab, these responses might consist of locomotion around the conditioning chamber, responses directed at a conditioned stimulus (CS), responses directed at the location of the unconditioned stimulus (US), etc. When different CSs, USs, and species are used, different actions with a different organization may be evident.

A BEHAVIOR SYSTEMS FRAMEWORK: WHAT'S NOT TO LIKE?

We would guess that most people who study animal learning agree with the general features of Timberlake and Lucas's (1989) behavior systems framework – that behavior is organized, that learning depends on a set of starting conditions that consist of the past and present state of an animal (including its evolutionary history), and that learning is influenced by the physical characteristics of the environments in which it is studied. And yet there are two broad traditions within the study of animal learning and behavior analysis that differ in terms of how much importance they attach to those general features. In one tradition, the importance of the starting conditions is acknowledged but otherwise ignored. In this tradition, an animal serves as a model system for discovering and studying general laws of learning and behavior. Apparatus, stimuli, and procedures are engineered to a particular species. Thus, pigeons peck keys, rats press levers, and rabbits blink in response to different stimulus-stimulus or response-consequence arrangements. The learning processes that are studied are similar across animals. This is the *general process* view of the study of learning. In another tradition, considerations of the initial conditions that an animal brings to an experiment – conditions that are rooted in an animal's ecological environment – and the physical features of stimuli, reinforcers, and other aspects of environments used to study learning are incorporated into hypotheses, theories, methods, and interpretations of the results. This is the *ecological* view of learning.

INCOMPATIBLE GOALS

Although the ecological view "threatened to shake the foundations of learning theory ... the threat to general process theory turned out to be short lived" (Domjan, 2000, p. 103). This raises the question: If few animal learning researchers would disagree that behavior is organized, that learning depends on initial conditions, and that learning is influenced by the physical characteristics of the environments where it occurs, then why have investigators "returned to characterizing mechanisms of conditioned behavior in terms of generic models in which responses and stimuli are presumed to be interchangeable with one another" (Domjan, 2000, p. 104)? One reason is that animal learning researchers and behavior analysts are primarily interested in discovering and understanding general mechanisms and rules of learning. The ecological view seems to trade simple generalities for complex idiosyncratic explanations and thus seems at odds with the goals of the general process view (Davey, 1989; Timberlake, 1994; see Blaisdell and Seitz, Chapter 26).

UNCONVINCING ARGUMENTS

Additionally, although behavior analysts and animal learning researchers may agree with some aspects of the ecological view, they may not agree with the implications of this view. For example, animal learning researchers may not agree that it is necessary to incorporate the physical features of the conditioning environment into hypotheses or interpretations of results. Why? Because tuning environments to a species' perceptual-motor tendencies standardizes apparatus and stimuli so that these can be ignored (Timberlake, 1990, 2004) – at least until an anomalous result is observed (e.g., Fortes et al., 2017). More broadly, animal learning researchers may disagree with the implication that "the very *laws* of learning might vary with the preparedness of the organism from one class of situations to another" (Seligman, 1970, p. 408).

UNCONVINCING DATA

A third reason why researchers continue to characterize conditioned behavior from a general process view is that what appears to be an anomalous result that requires consideration of adaptive specializations is really a result that is consistent with a general process view of learning (see Bitterman, 1976; LoLordo, 1979). Inferential oversights resulting from inadequate control conditions are the source for much that has been characterized as specialized learning (Overmier & Meyers-Manor, 2015). Revusky (1977) expressed a similar view when he concluded that, with the exception of parametric differences, nothing about learned flavor aversion was at odds with what was known about learning produced by Pavlovian conditioning.

UNCERTAINTY OF USE

Many researchers have written about general process versus ecological views' seemingly incompatible goals, the clarity and merits of their arguments, and the interpretation of data (e.g., Beecher, 1988; Davey, 1989; Domjan, 2005; Hollis, 1997; Krause & Domjan, 2017; Papini, 2002; Shettleworth, 2010; Timberlake, 2001; see Blaisdell and Seitz, Chapter 26). In this chapter, we consider a fourth reason why animal learning researchers and behavior analysts have not widely incorporated ecological views into their research: the uncertainty of how to use this view to study general principles of learning and behavior. It is in the pursuit of this goal that Timberlake and Lucas's (1989) behavior systems framework, which provides a bridge between ecological and general process views (Lucas, 2019; Timberlake, 2001), may be helpful. In what follows, we illustrate how their behavior systems approach has been used to situate variables, constructs, and actions within a functional context in studies that use Pavlovian conditioning. In doing so, we will show how this approach provides theoretical scaffolding and pragmatic guidance for studying the generality of results, constructs, and mechanisms in animal learning.

12.2 BEHAVIOR SYSTEMS AND ANOMALIES

Historically, the behavior systems framework has been used to explain anomalies – results at odds with the field's basic conceptions or theories of behavior and learning – such as misbehavior, constraints on learning, and why different CSs paired with the same US produce different conditioned responses (CRs). Using a behavior systems framework to explain anomalies is so central to its purpose that Timberlake and Lucas (1989) entitled their chapter "Behavior Systems and Learning: From Misbehavior to General Principles," and Killeen (2019) entitled his article about the behavior systems approach "Timberlake's Theories Dissolve Anomalies."

The use of the behavior systems framework to explain anomalies is exemplified by Timberlake and Lucas's (1989) analysis of why a CS that consists of a rat that predicts a food-US evokes CRs that consist of social behaviors directed toward the rat-CS. Because rats are social feeders, they orient toward, approach, sniff, paw, groom, and contact the rat-CS that predicts food (Timberlake & Grant, 1975). Rats do not bite or attack the rat-CS like they do an insertable lever or a rolling ball-bearing that predicts food. Nor do rats attack a rat-sized block of wood that predicts food. In this case, rats usually only orient toward the wooden block. What seems like a puzzle – that is, why the form of the CR varies with the type of CS when all other aspects of the conditioning situation are held constant – is less so in the context of a behavior systems framework, which claims that the CR is related to the supporting characteristics of a CS and the organization of a species' behavior system related to the US.

Misbehavior of the sort reported by Breland and Breland (1961) is another anomaly whose explanation is "straight-forward from a behavior systems view" (Timberlake & Lucas, 1989, p. 254). The Brelands described examples of conditioning in which the experimenters' response-consequence contingency failed to produce the desired result. In one of these now-famous examples, raccoons were trained to pick up, carry, and deposit a coin into a container to obtain a food reward. Training progressed uneventfully until the raccoons had to perform the task with more coins, at which time the animals preferred to rub the coins together rather than deposit them into the container. The raccoons misbehaved in the sense that they stopped doing what they needed to do to obtain the reward. Timberlake and Lucas explained that the food activated the racoon's feeding system. The training resulted in repeated pairings of the coins and food. The instrumental requirement of carrying more coins caused the coin-food interval to increase. In the context of an active feeding system and longer coin-food intervals, the physical features of the coin supported responses appropriate to more delayed food (e.g., food washing), the emergence of which interfered with the instrumental contingencies.

Flavor aversion learning is an example of a result that was once considered so anomalous that researchers questioned its authenticity (see Bitterman, 1976; Garcia, 1981). Today, Garcia and Koelling's (1966) bright-noisy-water experiment is considered a landmark in the study of biological constraints on learning (Domjan, 2015), and conditioned flavor aversion is explained by appealing to adaptive specializations related to the ingestion of noxious substances (Davidson & Riley, 2015). When a behavior systems framework has been discussed alongside conditioned flavor aversion, the framework and the phenomenon benefit mutually but circularly: the relative uniqueness of conditioned flavor aversion suggests that the organization of an animal's feeding system influences learning, and vice versa (see Domjan, 2015). But a behavior systems framework also explains why poisoning more readily suppresses ingestion than predation in several carnivorous and omnivorous mammals (e.g., Gustavson et al., 1976; Holland & Straub, 1979). From a behavior systems perspective, poisoned food should affect the handling/consuming mode and its responses (e.g., eating) more than it should affect an earlier search mode (e.g., focal search) and its responses (e.g., tracking). Why? Because although eating is tied to the feeding system in mammals, the general and focal search responses that lead to eating are also part of the search modes of other behavior systems (e.g., mating).

12.3 BEHAVIOR SYSTEMS AND GENERALIZABILITY

Although Timberlake and Lucas's (1989) behavior systems framework can explain anomalies, its executive function may be to prompt behavioral scientists to think about the generality of their findings, constructs, and theories. And it does this while providing guidance for where behavioral scientists can look to assess generality and ways to test for it. One place to look for generalizability is across species, a subject that has long been of interest to behavioral scientists (e.g., Beach, 1950; Davey, 1989; Papini, 2008; Shettleworth, 2010; Sidman, 1960). In addition to generality across species, a behavior systems framework can guide research on the generality *of* variables, methods, constructs, mechanisms, phenomena, and processes *across* subjects, settings, and responses (see Cook & Campbell, 1979; Johnston & Pennypacker, 1980).

Importantly, a behavior systems framework brings to the forefront aspects of generalizability that might not be readily apparent. For instance, determining generality across responses means more than assessing whether an effect depended on pigeons pecking a key or pressing a treadle. Because of the spatiotemporal continuity of behavior, generality across responses also means assessing how multiple responses measured simultaneously are affected by an independent variable. This emphasis contrasts with the typical laboratory study of animal learning in which a single response such as key pecking, lever pressing, eye blinking, and approach-avoidance is measured (Domjan, 2000). Of course, there have been exceptions. Eldridge and Pear (1987) measured pigeons' key pecking and spatial movements in a study of autoshaping and omission training. Silva and Timberlake (2005) measured rats' nosing in the feeder, time spent at different locations within the conditioning chamber, and contact with rolling ball-bearings during an interfood clock that predicted food. The asymptotes of these actions depended on the time during the interfood clock and whether every presentation of the clock was followed by food (100% clock-food pairings) or not (50% clock-food pairings).

Measuring just one response limits generalizability because "if only one behavior is measured, one cannot determine how the rules of conditioned behavior depend on the response itself" (Domjan, 2000, p. 104). Why take this risk? The first reason is methodological. It is simpler and more convenient to measure one behavior instead of several. This is especially true given researchers' reliance on automated measures (Timberlake & Silva, 1994). The second reason is theoretical. There are few theories of behavior or associative learning that provide guidance on what to measure. But there are exceptions. Konorski (1967) distinguished between preparatory and consummatory responses. Preparatory CRs are more diffuse and general than consummatory CRs, which are more focused and reflexive. Wagner and Brandon's (1989) AESOP model of Pavlovian conditioning assumes that different CS-US intervals and orders (forward vs. backward) can produce CSs that are more or less likely to control the sensory or affective qualities of a US. The third reason is conceptual. Associative constructs are difficult to use when more than one response is measured.

To illustrate this last point, consider the phenomena of blocking. Blocking can be produced as follows. In the first phase of training, a group of rats (Group Blocking) is presented with pairings of a light that is followed by shock (i.e., Light → Shock). In the second phase, Group Blocking and a new group of rats (Group Control) are presented with a compound stimulus consisting of the light and a tone, which is then followed by shock (i.e., Light + Tone → Shock). During the third (test) phase, both groups are given several presentations of the tone by itself. The typical result is that, during the test phase, the tone evokes a CR for the rats in Group Control but not Group Blocking (see Kamin, 1969). One explanation for these results is that, because the US was fully predicted by the light in Group Blocking, the rats did not form an association between the tone and the US (see Rescorla & Wagner, 1972). Another explanation is that the rats in Group Blocking did not attend to the tone during compound conditioning because the tone was not a better predictor of shock than the light was (see Mackintosh, 1975).

Regardless of which account is correct, neither can be easily applied if more than one behavior is measured. Consider the following situation. In the first phase of training, a group of rats (Group Blocking) are presented with several pairings of a light followed by food (i.e., Light → Food). In the second phase, these rats and a new group of rats (Group Control) receive several presentations of the light compounded with the insertion of a lever, which is then followed by food (i.e., Light + Lever → Food). During the test phase, both groups are given presentations of the lever by itself.

Before continuing, let us ask: "What would evidence of blocking look like?" If we measure only a single behavior such as nosing in the feeder, blocking would be evident if presentations of the lever during the test phase evoked nosing in the feeder for Group Control but not Group Blocking. But if we measure two responses, such as nosing in the feeder and contacting the lever, it is unclear what evidence of blocking would look like. During the test phase, the lever could evoke nosing in feeder and/or contacting the lever. If the lever evokes only nosing in the feeder, then the light did not block learning about the lever. But what if the lever exclusively evokes lever contact? Since nosing in the feeder never occurred, should we conclude that the light blocked learning about the lever? (No.) Additional control groups during the two conditioning phases and the test phase will not make it easier to answer the question of what counts as evidence of blocking when multiple responses are measured. If the reason is not yet clear, imagine a situation where an animal's movements are recorded in real time and the data also consist of the animal's distance from any experimenter-specified location (e.g., Silva et al., 1992). Did the light block learning about the lever if the rats in Group Blocking reliably retreat to the back of the chamber during presentations of the lever but the rats in Group Control approach the lever?

CONDITIONED INHIBITION AND BACKWARD CONDITIONING

A behavior systems perspective and the measurement of multiple responses can help animal learning researchers identify conceptual and pragmatic difficulties of associative constructs. To illustrate how, let us consider a study about the concurrent development of excitatory and inhibitory associations during backward conditioning. Tait and Saladin (1986) presented rabbits with backward pairings of a paraorbital shock and a tone. The response that was measured was the rabbits' nictitating membrane response (NMR). Tait and Saladin then used a retardation of learning test to assess whether these US-CS pairings produced an inhibitory CS. Based on this test, the previously backward-paired tone was a conditioned inhibitor. However, when the researchers used a conditioned emotional response (CER) paradigm and measured whether the tone could suppress the operant response of licking for water, they found that it could. Thus, when the NMR was measured during a retardation of learning test, the tone was inhibitory. When licking was measured, the tone was excitatory. It seems that conditioned associative inhibition is response specific and test dependent.

A theory such as AESOP can explain these results by assuming that a CS has both affective and sensory associations with the US (McNish et al., 1997). A short US-CS interval results in a CS that evokes fear (the affective connection) and inhibits eye blinking (the sensory connection). When this sort of CS is used in a retardation of learning test and eye blinking is measured, the sensory connection inhibits eye blinking. When this CS is presented during appetitive responding such as licking for water, the affective connection evokes fear and suppresses responding.

A behavior systems framework provides another way of looking at Tait and Saladin's (1986) results, conditioned inhibition, and backward conditioning. Using this framework begins by reframing Tait and Saladin's experiment as a study of rabbits' antipredator defense (cf., Fanselow et al., 2019). In their natural environment, rabbits have a repertoire of responses that they use to avoid and defend themselves against predators. For example, rabbits become increasingly vigilant (immobile with head up and ears erect) as predation risk increases (Blanchard et al., 2018). They also freeze, flee, or hide at the sight or sound of a predator. If there is tactile contact with a predator, rabbits will fight (e.g., bite and kick) or become immobile (e.g., Ewell et al., 1981). In short, rabbits possess several responses for avoiding and defending themselves against predators. If a paraorbital shock engages a rabbit's antipredator system, then US-CS pairings could result in a CS that evokes stimulus sensitivities and responses related to a *post*-US encounter that interferes with a behavioral baseline related to an appetitive goal. If this happens, the backward-paired CS is excitatory. But a backward-paired CS could also come to evoke a post-US encounter response or response tendency that interferes with learning a *pre*-US preparatory or avoidance response. If this happens, the backward-paired CS appears to be inhibitory. In reality, the CS could be excitatory in both cases, and the result dependent on the response that was measured and how the CS was tested (see also Boughner & Papini, 2003).

From a behavior systems perspective, conditioned inhibition is related to the conditioning of different motivational modes to a CS+ and a CS−. When food is the US, a small localizable CS+ is more likely to control features of focal search related to proximal food; a CS− is more likely to control aspects of a general search mode. Rather than being opposing associative dimensions (excitatory vs. inhibitory), search modes consist of different perceptual-motor repertoires related to the same US (Timberlake, 1994, 2001; Timberlake & Lucas, 1989). Thus, for example, the avoidance of a CS− by pigeons could be the result of their engaging in locomotion as part of searching for better predictors of food (cf., Hearst & Franklin, 1977). A behavior systems perspective tries to explain the form of the CR: Why do pigeons avoid the CS− rather than simply not approach it? Or why does a pigeon approach a CS+ rather than the site of the US? A behavior systems framework helps with the translation of learning into performance.

To test a behavior systems view of conditioned inhibition, Tinsley et al. (2002) presented rats with two types of counterbalanced trials: a tone that was followed by food (Tone → Food) and white noise that was not followed by food (White Noise → No Food). The CR was nosing in the feeder. Tinsley et al. then used a novel auditory stimulus in retardation of learning and summation tests to determine if the white noise was a conditioned inhibitor. Based on the results of both tests, the white noise was a conditioned inhibitor. However, if the white noise was compounded with a novel stimulus that consisted of a rolling ball-bearing, the white noise facilitated contact with the ball-bearing. Like Tait and Saladin's (1986) results, whether a stimulus was a conditioned inhibitor or excitor depended on the response that was measured to test the CS−. Although the white noise inhibited nosing in the feeder, it facilitated contact with a moving ball-bearing.

Tinsley et al.'s (2002) results illustrate the value of measuring more than a single behavior, having a theory that can accommodate the dynamics of multiple responses, and the difficulties of using associative constructs when multiple responses are measured. With regard to this last point, although the CS− may have facilitated contact with the moving ball-bearing as the result of superconditioning, why this superconditioning should be expressed as contact with the ball-bearing instead of nosing in the feeder (or any other response) is unclear. By contrast, a behavior systems framework provides guidance about which responses to measure and how to explain their inter-relations. For appetitive stimuli (e.g., food, water, warmth in a cold environment), animals are motivated to search for increasingly better predictors of a desired stimulus, where better means more spatially and temporally contiguous with the desired stimulus. After finding food and having eaten, an animal is likely to search the area where it just consumed food. If the animal does not find food in the vicinity where it just ate, it begins searching increasingly larger areas for food or predictors of food.

It was from this perspective that a behavior systems framework was used to examine another aspect of Tait and Saladin's (1986) experiment: backward conditioning. A contingency-based analysis suggests that backward conditioning is likely to result in an inhibitory CS because this stimulus predicts the absence of the US. From a behavior systems perspective, though, an animal's behavior consists of interrelated responses whose form and timing are related to the spatiotemporal characteristics of important environmental events. A brief stimulus that follows an appetitive US such as food should come to control stimulus sensitivities and responses appropriate to having just eaten. Some of these responses include scanning the area where food was consumed for bits of carelessly chewed food or additional prey. Some of the stimulus sensitivities might include a reactivity to stimuli related to food, such as certain smells, sights, or sounds. When detected, these stimuli evoke behavior directed toward them. Situated in a broader context of a foraging rat, the behavior systems perspective predicts that a backward-paired CS that is compounded with a small localizable moving object, such as the insertion of a lever, should facilitate contact with the object relative to various control conditions. From a behavior systems perspective, because a backward-paired CS controls a mode related to a *post*-US encounter, activation of this mode during a retardation of learning or summation test may interfere with a *pre*-encounter response such as approaching the food site. But if a response appropriate to a post-US encounter is measured, then the CS should facilitate responding (Silva & Timberlake, 2000). The behavior systems framework thus provides a means to understanding the divergence of responses and asymmetrical effects of conditioning.

It may be tempting to dismiss the preceding analysis as a story rather than a theoretical basis for an experiment. But theories come in many flavors (cf., a detective's theory of a crime vs. Einstein's theory of relativity). A behavior systems view of rats' feeding behavior is based on the observation and study of rats in the wild and in laboratories (e.g., Barnett, 1975; Ewer, 1971; Silva & Timberlake, 2005; Timberlake et al., 1982). In addition, a behavior systems framework incorporates mechanisms such as contingency (Timberlake, 1994) and contiguity (e.g., Silva & Timberlake, 2000) into its analyses and predictions. For those and other reasons, a behavior systems framework is not an alternative to associative theories; it is an add-on that tries to situate variables, constructs, actions, and results within a functional context (see also Davey, 1989; Hollis, 1997; Krause & Domjan, 2017).

BEHAVIORAL SEQUENCES AND EXTINCTION

A key feature of a behavior systems framework is its emphasis on functional behavioral sequences. It was this emphasis that provided the theoretical foundation for Hilliard et al.'s (1998) study of the effects of extinction on the sexual behavior of Japanese quail. In their study, male quail were presented with a 2-minute CS that consisted of a facsimile of a female quail (see Krause and Domjan, Chapter 7). The US was access to a real female quail. The CRs consisted of approaching and mounting the CS. Once the CRs occurred reliably, extinction was started.

Similar to the reason why poisoning more readily suppresses ingestion than predation in some mammals, a behavior systems framework predicts that extinction is more likely to disrupt a mode that is temporally proximal to an appetitive US (e.g., focal search) than a mode that is more temporally distal (e.g., general search). Thus, late focal search responses such as mounting the CS should extinguish before early focal search or late general search responses do. Consistent with this interpretation, extinction disrupted mounting and other copulatory actions more than it disrupted approaching the CS. Hilliard et al. (1998) concluded that conditioned approach and sexual contact with a CS are differentially sensitive to extinction. More importantly, the functional properties of the CRs depended on the behaviors that were measured.

Because biological constraints on learning accounts can be loose and speculative (Papini, 2002), it is worth considering what a general process view predicts. The answer depends on how the male quail's behavior is conceptualized. If the bird's behavior is a chain of responses maintained by reinforcement, then the bird may stop engaging in the terminal behavior but continue engaging in actions that precede the terminal response (e.g., Fantino, 1965). If the male quail's behavior is a heterogeneous chain consisting of procurement and consumption responses, then extinction should reduce both responses (e.g., Thrailkill & Bouton, 2016). Other analyses and predictions are possible – and possibly depend on how a researcher uses mechanisms, processes, and constructs such as differential associations to different stimulus features (e.g., Holland & Ross, 1981), excitatory and inhibitory associations (e.g., Holland & Sherwood, 2008), stimulus generalization (see Inman et al., 2016; Pearce, 1987), evaluation of the CS relative to comparator stimuli during extinction (Miller & Matzel, 1988), evocation of memory representations that may be in different states (see Wagner, 1981), and various modulatory mechanisms (see Swartzentruber, 1995). Predicting an outcome is doubly difficult if we consider any of the preceding factors alongside the fact that different stimuli of different durations can produce different results (e.g., tones vs. lights in an autoshaping preparation with rats). Predicting behavioral outcomes, especially in novel circumstances, is difficult regardless of the starting point (Killeen, 2018).

12.4 CONCLUSION

According to an evolutionary account of learning, the ability to learn about stimuli associated with important events provides the learner with an adaptive advantage when it comes to dealing with future occurrences of the important event or related ones. This advantage can be immediate, such as when male blue gouramis defend their territories more efficiently when rivals are signaled than when they are not (Hollis, 1984), or delayed, such as when males of this same species produce more offspring when rivals are signaled rather than unsignaled (Hollis et al., 1997). A behavior systems view of Pavlovian conditioning (see also Krause and Domjan, Chapter 7) adds to evolutionary accounts of learning by emphasizing that an animal comes to an experiment with a physiology and encoded experiences that affect how it can or will interact with stimuli associated with important events. The physical features of environmental stimuli combine with the experimental procedures to activate organized behavior systems whose subsystems and modes vary and cycle in accordance with important spatiotemporal events.

This focus on the organization of behavior provides the basis for predicting and understanding the form of conditioned behavior. Different CS-US intervals, including backward-paired CSs and CSs that are never paired with a US, should come to control distributions of responses appropriate to the supporting features of the apparatus and the conditioning procedure. Thus, for a hungry rat, a long-duration tone that predicts food is more likely to evoke chasing and contacting a moving stimulus than a short-duration tone that predicts food, which is more likely to evoke behavior directed toward the location of the food. In a context where food is predicted by a CS+ but not a CS−, this latter stimulus should acquire the capacity to evoke stimulus sensitivities and responses appropriate to searching for other sources of food.

It is important to state again that a behavior framework does not exist in opposition to traditional associative views of learning or behavior analysis (Timberlake, 1994, 2004). Rather, it is a means for how to think about mechanisms of learning and the interrelation of multiple responses in a functional context. In doing so, Timberlake and Lucas's (1989) behavior systems framework helps behavioral scientists to identify the generalizability of their results, mechanisms, constructs, and theories.

REFERENCES

Barnett, S. A. (1975). *The rat: A study in behavior*. University of Chicago Press.
Beach, F. A. (1950). The Snark was a boojum. *American Psychologist, 5*, 115–124. https://doi .org/10.1037/h0056510
Beecher, M. D. (1988). An adaptationist approach to learning. In R. C. Bolles & M. D. Beecher (Eds.), *Evolution and learning* (pp. 239–248). Erlbaum.
Bitterman, M. E. (1976). Flavor aversion studies. *Science, 192*, 266–267. https://doi.org/10 .1126/science.1257768
Blanchard, P., Lauzeral, C., Chamaillé-Jammes, S., Brunet, C., Lec'hvien, A., Péron, G., & Pontier, D. (2018). Coping with change in predation risk across space and time through complementary behavioral responses. *BMC Ecology, 18*(1), 60. https://doi.org/10.1186/ s12898-018-0215-7
Boughner, R. L., & Papini, M. R. (2003). Appetitive latent inhibition in rats: Now you see it (sign tracking), now you don't (goal tracking). *Learning & Behavior, 31*, 387–392. https:// doi.org/10.3758/BF03195999
Breland, K., & Breland, M. (1961). The misbehavior of organisms. *American Psychologist, 16*, 681–684. https://doi.org/10.1037/h0040090
Cook, T. D., & Campbell, D. T. (1979). *Quasi-Experimentation: Design and analysis issues for field settings*. Houghton Mifflin.
Davey, G. (1989). *Ecological learning theory*. Routledge.
Davidson, T. L., & Riley, A. L. (2015). Taste, sickness, and learning: Understanding how we form aversions to particular flavors has led to new ideas about learning – and could have implications for treating obesity and drug use. *American Scientist, 103*(3). www .americanscientist.org/article/taste-sickness-and-learning

Domjan, M. (2000). General process learning theory: Challenges from response and stimulus factors. *International Journal of Comparative Psychology*, *13*, 101–118. https://escholarship.org/uc/item/0b69j9v1

(2005). Pavlovian conditioning: A functional perspective. *Annual Review of Psychology*, *56*, 179–206. https://doi.org/10.1146/annurev.psych.55.090902.141409

(2015). The Garcia–Koelling selective association effect: A historical and personal perspective. *International Journal of Comparative Psychology*, *28*, 25645. https://escholarship.org/uc/item/5sx993rm

Eldridge, G. D., & Pear, J. J. (1987). Topographical variations in behavior during autoshaping, automaintenance, and omission training. *Journal of the Experimental Analysis of Behavior*, *47*, 319–333. https://doi.org/10.1901/jeab.1987.47-319

Ewell, A. H., Jr., Cullen, J. M., & Woodruff, M. L. (1981). Tonic immobility as a predator-defense in the rabbit (*Oryctolagus cuniculus*). *Behavioral Neural Biology*, *31*, 483–489. https://doi.org/10.1016/S0163-1047(81) 91585-5

Ewer, R. F. (1971). The biology and behavior of a free-living population of black rats (*Rattus rattus*). *Animal Behavior Monographs*, *4*(3), 127–174.

Fanselow, M. S., Hoffman, A. N., & Zhuravka, I. (2019). Timing and the transition between modes in the defensive behavior system. *Behavioural Processes*, *166*, 103890. https://doi.org/10.1016/j.beproc.2019.103890

Fantino, E. (1965). Some data on the discriminative stimulus hypothesis of conditioned reinforcement. *The Psychological Record*, *15*, 409–415. https://doi.org/10.1007/BF03393607

Fortes, I., Machado, A., & Vasconcelos, M. (2017). Do pigeons (*Columba livia*) use information about the absence of food appropriately? A further look into suboptimal choice. *Journal of Comparative Psychology*, *131*, 277–289. https://doi.org/10.1037/com0000079

Garcia, J. (1981). Tilting at the paper mills of academe. *American Psychologist*, *36*, 149–158. https://doi.org/10.1037/0003-066X.36.2.149

Garcia, J., & Koelling, R. A. (1966). Relation of cue to consequence in aversion learning. *Psychonomic Science*, *4*, 123–124. https://doi.org/10.3758/BF03342209

Gustavson, C. R., Kelly, D. J., Sweeney, M., & Garcia, J. (1976). Prey-lithium aversions: I. Coyotes and wolves. *Behavioral Biology*, *17*, 61–72. https://doi.org/10.1016/S0091-6773(76)90272-8

Hearst, E., & Franklin, S. R. (1977). Positive and negative relations between a signal and food: Approach-withdrawal behavior to the signal. *Journal of Experimental Psychology: Animal Behavior Processes*, *3*, 37–52. https://doi.org/10.1037/0097-7403.3.1.37

Hilliard, S., Domjan, M., Nguyen, M., & Cusato, B. (1998). Dissociation of conditioned appetitive and consummatory sexual behavior: Satiation and extinction tests. *Animal Learning & Behavior*, *26*, 20–33. https://doi.org/10.3758/BF03199159

Holland, P. C., & Ross, R. T. (1981). Within-compound associations in serial compound conditioning. *Journal of Experimental Psychology: Animal Behavior Processes*, *7*, 228–241. https://doi.org/10.1037/0097-7403.7.3.228

Holland, P. C., & Sherwood, A. (2008). Formation of excitatory and inhibitory associations between absent events. *Journal of Experimental Psychology: Animal Behavior Processes*, *34*, 324–335. https://doi.org/10.1037/0097-7403.34.3.324

Holland, P. C., & Straub, J. J. (1979). Differential effects of two ways of devaluing the unconditioned stimulus after Pavlovian appetitive conditioning. *Journal of Experimental Psychology: Animal Behavior Processes*, *5*, 65–78. https://doi.org/10.1037/0097-7403.5.1.65

Hollis, K. L. (1984). The biological function of Pavlovian conditioning: The best defense is a good offense. *Journal of Experimental Psychology: Animal Behavior Processes*, *10*, 413–425. https://doi.org/10.1037/0097-7403.10.4.413

(1997). Contemporary research on Pavlovian conditioning: A "new" functional analysis. *American Psychologist*, *52*, 956–965. https://doi.org/10.1037/0003-066X.52.9.956

Hollis, K. L., Pharr, V. L., Dumas, M. J., Britton, G. B., & Field, J. (1997). Classical conditioning provides paternity advantage for territorial male blue gouramis (*Trichogaster trichopterus*). *Journal of Comparative Psychology, 111*, 219–225. https://doi.org/10.1037/0735-7036.111.3.219

Inman, R. A., Honey, R. C., Eccles, G. L., & Pearce, J. M. (2016). Asymmetry in the discrimination of quantity by rats: The role of the intertrial interval. *Learning & Behavior, 44*, 67–77. https://doi.org/10.3758/s13420-015-0191-0

Innis, N. K., & Staddon, J. E. R. (1989). What should comparative psychology compare? *International Journal of Comparative Psychology, 2*, 145–156.

Johnston, J. J., & Pennypacker, H. S. (1980). *Strategies and tactics of human behavioral research*. Erlbaum.

Kamin, L. J. (1969). Predictability, surprise, attention, and conditioning. In B. A. Campbell & R. M. Church (Eds.), *Punishment and aversive behavior* (pp. 276–296). Appleton-Century-Crofts.

Killeen, P. R. (2018). The futures of experimental analysis of behavior. *Behavior Analysis: Research and Practice, 18*, 124–133. https://doi.org/10.1037/bar0000100

(2019). Timberlake's theories dissolve anomalies. *Behavioural Processes, 166*, 103894. https://doi.org/10.1016/j.beproc.2019.103894

Konorski, J. (1967). *Integrative activity of the brain*. University of Chicago Press.

Krause, M. A., & Domjan, M. (2017). Ethological and evolutionary perspectives on Pavlovian conditioning. In J. Call (Ed.), *Handbook of comparative psychology: Vol 2: Perception, learning and cognition* (pp. 247–266). American Psychological Association.

LoLordo, V. W. (1979). Constraints on learning. In Bitterman, M. E., LoLordo, V. M., Overmier, J. B., & Rashotte, M. E. (Eds.), *Animal learning. Survey and analysis* (pp. 473–504). Springer. http://doi.org/10.1007/978-1-4684-3387-6_15

Lucas, G. A. (2019). Adaptive systems influence both learning and conscious attention. *Behavioural Processes, 168*, 103871. https://doi.org/10.1016/j.beproc.2019.05.018

Mackintosh, N. J. (1975). A theory of attention: Variations in the associability of stimuli with reinforcement. *Psychological Review, 82*, 276–298. https://doi.org/10.1037/h0076778

McNish, K. A., Betts, S. L., Brandon, S. E., & Wagner, A. R. (1997). Divergence of conditioned eyeblink and conditioned fear in backward Pavlovian training. *Animal Learning & Behavior, 25*, 43–52. https://doi.org/10.3758/BF03199023

Miller, R. R., & Matzel, L.D. (1988). The comparator hypothesis: A response rule for the expression of associations. *Psychology of Learning and Motivation, 22*, 51–92. https://doi.org/10.1016/S0079-7421(08)60038-9

Overmier, J. B., & Meyers-Manor, J. (2015). Alerts for assessing "biological constraints" on learning. *International Journal of Comparative Psychology, 28*, 1–12. https://escholarship.org/uc/item/8tk8h8c4

Papini, M. R. (2002). Pattern and process in the evolution of learning. *Psychological Review, 109*, 186–220. https://doi.org/10.1037//0033-295X.109.1.186

(2008). *Comparative psychology: Evolution and development of behavior* (2nd ed.). Psychology Press.

Pearce, J. M. (1987). A model for stimulus generalization in Pavlovian conditioning. *Psychological Review, 94*, 61–73. https://doi.org/10.1037/0033-295X.94.1.61

Rescorla, R. A., & Wagner, A. R. (1972). A theory of Pavlovian conditioning: Variations in the effectiveness of reinforcement and nonreinforcement. In A. H. Black & W. F. Prokasy (Eds.), *Classical conditioning II: Current research and theory* (pp. 64–99). Appleton-Century-Crofts.

Revusky, S. (1977). Learning as a general process with an emphasis on data from feeding experiments. In N. W. Milgram, L. Krames, & T. M. Alloway (Eds.), *Food aversion learning* (pp. 1–71). Plenum Press.

Seligman, M. E. P. (1970). On the generality of the laws of learning. *Psychological Review, 77*, 406–418. https://doi.org/10.1037/h0029790

Shettleworth, S. J. (2010). *Cognition, evolution, and behavior* (2nd ed.). Oxford University Press.

Sidman, M. (1960). *Tactics of scientific research: Evaluating experimental data in psychology*. Basic Books.

Silva, F. J., Silva, K. M., & Pear, J. J. (1992). Sign- versus goal-tracking: Effects of conditioned-stimulus-to-unconditioned-stimulus distance. *Journal of the Experimental Analysis of Behavior, 57*, 17–31. https://doi.org/10.1901/jeab.1992.57-17

Silva, F. J., & Timberlake, W. (2000). A clarification of the nature of backward excitatory conditioning. *Learning and Motivation, 31*, 67–80. https://doi.org/10.1006/lmot.1999.1042

Silva, K. M., & Timberlake, W. (2005). A behavior systems view of the organization of multiple responses during a partially or continuously reinforced interfood clock. *Animal Learning & Behavior, 33*, 99–110. https://doi.org/10.3758/BF03196054

Swartzentruber, D. (1995). Modulatory mechanisms in Pavlovian conditioning. *Animal Learning & Behavior, 23*, 123–143. https://doi.org/10.3758/BF03199928

Tait, R. W., & Saladin, M. E. (1986). Concurrent development of excitatory and inhibitory associations during backward conditioning. *Animal Learning & Behavior, 14*, 133–137. https://doi.org/10.3758/BF03200047

Thrailkill, E. A., & Bouton, M. E. (2016). Extinction of chained instrumental behaviors: Effects of consumption extinction on procurement responding. *Learning & Behavior, 44*, 85–96. https://dx.doi.org/10.3758/s13420-015-0193-y

Timberlake, W. (1990). Natural learning in laboratory paradigms. In D. A. Dewsbury (Ed.), *Contemporary issues in comparative psychology* (pp. 31–54). Sinauer Associates.

(1994). Behavior systems, associationism, and Pavlovian conditioning. *Psychonomic Bulletin & Review, 1*, 405–420. https://doi.org/10.3758/BF03210945

(2001). Integrating niche-related and general process approaches in the study of learning. *Behavioural Processes, 54*, 79–94. http://10.1016/S0376-6357(01)00151-6

(2004). Trends in the study of Pavlovian conditioning. *International Journal of Comparative Psychology, 17*, 119–130.

Timberlake, W., & Grant, D. L. (1975). Auto-shaping in rats to the presentation of another rat predicting food. *Science, 190*, 690–692. https://doi.org/10.1126/science.190.4215.690

Timberlake, W., & Lucas, G. A. (1989). Behavior systems and learning: From misbehavior to general principles. In S. B. Klein & R. R. Mowrer (Eds.), *Contemporary learning theories: Instrumental conditioning theory and the impact of biological constraints on learning* (pp. 237–275). Erlbaum.

Timberlake, W., & Silva, F. J. (1994). Observation of behavior, inference of function, and the study of learning. *Psychonomic Bulletin & Review, 1*, 73–88. https://doi.org/10.3758/BF03200762

Timberlake, W., Wahl, G., & King, D. (1982). Stimulus and response contingencies in the misbehavior of rats. *Journal of Experimental Psychology: Animal Behavior Processes, 8*, 62–85. https://doi.org/10.1037/0097-7403.8.4.328

Tinsley, M. R., Timberlake, W., Sitomer, M., & Widman, D. R. (2002). Conditioned inhibitory effects of discriminated Pavlovian training with food in rats depend on interactions of search modes, related repertoires, and response measures. *Animal Learning & Behavior, 30*, 217–227. https://doi.org/10.3758/BF03192831

Wagner, A. R. (1981). SOP: A model of automatic memory processing in animal behavior. In N. E. Spear & R. R. Miller (Eds.), *Information processing in animals: Memory mechanisms* (pp. 5–47). Erlbaum.

Wagner, A. R., & Brandon, S. E. (1989). Evolution of a structured connectionist model of Pavlovian conditioning (AESOP). In S. B. Klein & R. R. Mowrer (Eds.), *Contemporary learning theories: Pavlovian conditioning and the status of traditional learning theory* (pp. 149–189). Erlbaum.

13

DISSOCIABLE LEARNING PROCESSES

A Comparative Perspective

Barbara A. Church, Brooke N. Jackson, and J. David Smith

Theories in comparative and cognitive psychology are sometimes dissonant. Comparative psychologists often take associative learning as animals' dominant learning mechanism. By doing so, they instantiate Morgan's (1906) interpretative conservatism and honor the simplicity and parsimony aesthetic in science. By contrast, cognitive psychologists accept that humans have more than one kind of learning and memory (e.g., Ashby & Maddox, 2011; Knowlton et al., 1996; Yonelinas, 2002). In particular, they accept humans' explicit-declarative cognition as a complement to their associative learning. Humans transcend associative learning. Their cognition is often conscious, grounded in working memory and executive attention. They deliberately test hypotheses and formulate verbalizable rules.

We believe the theoretical divide is not optimal. It minimizes the demonstrable continuities between human and animal cognition – in category learning (Smith et al., 2016), in memory (e.g. Basile et al., 2015), and in metacognition (Zakrzewski et al., 2017). It is wasteful of the potential synergy that could arise from cognitive and comparative psychologists interacting. It impedes the development of animal models of human cognition and the neuroscientific research on the neural and chemical bases of human cognition.

The divide also blocks the consideration of important comparative issues. When did forms of explicit cognition emerge evolutionarily? Why? What is the species breadth of explicit cognition? Does explicit cognition exist only in vertebrate lines evolving toward a prefrontal locus of higher cognition? Or do brains organized differently (avian brains) produce isomorphic processes? Has this convergent evolution occurred? What mental-representational formats ground an animal's explicit cognition? What role does language play in this grounding? How is explicit cognition limited absent language? Accordingly, this chapter considers the possibility of complementary implicit-associative and explicit-declarative systems of learning in human and nonhuman animals.

13.1 DISSOCIABLE SYSTEMS OF LEARNING

Neuroscientists generally accept that humans have dissociable systems of learning as we describe in this section (see Hampton, Chapter 22). Other species may, too.

IMPLICIT-PROCEDURAL LEARNING

We will focus on a form of implicit learning that is energized by reinforcement learning. This is a crucially important learning system for human and nonhuman animals – this is why comparative psychology justifiably weights it heavily. This system is proposed to underlie skill and habit learning and performance in some perceptual-categorization tasks (Waldschmidt & Ashby, 2011). It is allied to the learning that researchers observe in many tasks of instrumental conditioning and discrimination learning (Ashby et al., 1998; Yin et al., 2005). During this type of implicit-procedural learning, learning occurs associatively through processes akin to conditioning. This learning is gradual, reliant on immediate reinforcement, and its contents are generally nonverbalizable (Ashby et al., 1998; Ashby & Ell, 2001).

This implicit system may be linked to specific parts of the basal ganglia (discussion in Smith & Church, 2018). In primates, the extrastriate visual cortex projects to the tail of the caudate nucleus – with visual cells converging to caudate cells that project onto the premotor cortex. The caudate nucleus is thus well positioned to participate in building percept-action associations, and this may be one of its main functions. Lesion studies confirm that the tail of the caudate nucleus is important for learning discriminations that map multiple stimuli to multiple responses.

EXPLICIT-DECLARATIVE LEARNING

We will focus on a form of explicit learning that uses executive attention (Posner & Petersen, 1990) and working memory (Fuster, 1989). These cognitive utilities support rule learning (Robinson et al., 1980). A rule is a diagnostic criterion (usually quite low dimensional) that can be used to systematically differentiate the member of contrasting categories (e.g., Category A members are Red; Category B members are Blue). The explicit system learns by testing hypotheses – that is, by evaluating the performance success achieved by alternative rules. In essence, participants provisionally self-construe the task, develop/discover their own performance rule, and maintain that rule consciously as performance continues. This self-construal process can occur successfully even when immediate reinforcement is not given (Smith et al., 2014; 2018). Rule discovery is often through a sudden realization—an insight (Smith et al., 2014; Smith & Ell, 2015). Humans can then generally verbalize their rules. This explicit-declarative learning is linked to the prefrontal cortex, the anterior cingulate gyrus, the head of the caudate nucleus, and the hippocampus (Ashby et al., 1998; Elliott & Dolan, 1998). Patients with basal ganglia or frontal dysfunction are impaired in rule tasks (Robinson et al., 1980). Rao et al. (1997) found activation during a rule task in the dorsolateral prefrontal cortex, the anterior cingulate, and the head of the caudate nucleus. From the foregoing description, one sees that explicit rule learning can be diagnosed in diverse ways, including sudden perform-ance improvements, verbalizations (in humans!), neuroimaging studies, and other techniques described here.

Readers will understand that the verbal grounding and the conscious availability of these self-construal, rule-formation, and hypothesis-testing processes might vary across species. In fact, this is an important possibility for it might open windows to researchers seeking to study different forms of explicit learning during infancy, after stroke, and during the evolutionary emergence of explicit cognition. It might also present to comparative researchers the tools for exploring phenomena relating to animals' working task consciousness.

13.2 A METHOD FOR STUDYING DISSOCIABLE SYSTEMS OF LEARNING

Implicit and explicit learning systems can be dissociated using the information-integration (II) and rule-based (RB) categorization tasks (Figure 13.1A and B). These are typical discrimination tasks. Exemplars are defined by their values on two perceptual dimensions. For example, as one perceptual dimension one might vary along the X axis the width or spatial frequency of a striping pattern. As the other perceptual dimension, one might vary along the Y axis the tilt/orientation of that striping pattern within the circle. These stimuli can then be grouped into elliptical Category A and B stimulus distributions. Of course, participants are not shown these whole distributions. They must learn the categories on their own through the feedback that occurs trial by trial.

In an II task, the Category A and B distributions are partitioned diagonally across the stimulus space. Both dimensions present valid but insufficient category information. To perform well, participants must integrate the dimensional information into an overall category decision. The cognitive system accomplishes this integration implicitly, essentially as a behavioral – not verbal – procedure. In particular, the correct rule – Category A exemplars are more Y than they are X; Category B exemplars are more X than they are Y – cannot be discovered or learned explicitly, given the extensive range of X and Y variation, the overlapping of X and Y values across categories, the XY covariation, the incommensurability of the two perceptual dimensions,

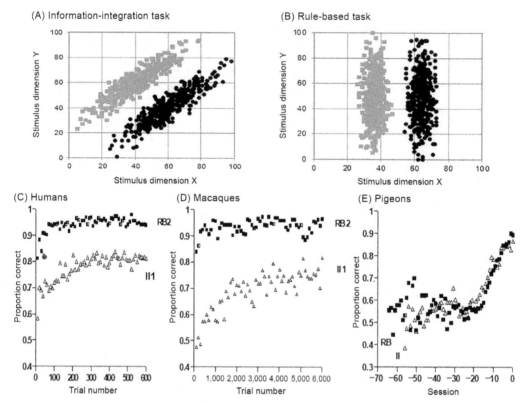

FIGURE 13.1. Top. Information-integration (A) and rule-based (B) category structures, depicted within an abstract 100 × 100 stimulus space. The gray squares and black circles, respectively, indicate Category A and B stimuli. Bottom: Proportion of correct responses by block for humans learning RB (filled squares) and II (open triangles) categories (C). Performance by block for macaques learning RB and II tasks, depicted in the same way (D). Pigeons' learning curves in RB and II tasks, depicted in the same way. The pigeon data were plotted from the criterial block backward (E).

From "Implicit and explicit categorization: A tale of four species" by J. D. Smith, M. E. Berg, R. G. Cook, J. Boomer, M. J. Crossley, M. S. Murphy, B. Spiering, M. J. Beran, B. A. Church, F. G. Ashby, and R. C. Grace, 2012, *Neuroscience and Biobehavioral Reviews, 36*, pp. 2359, 2360, 2364. Copyright 2012 by Elsevier. Reprinted with permission.

and the task's trial-by-trial format. Evidence from cognitive studies, patient data, and neuroimaging provide converging evidence that the II task is learned through the implicit-procedural learning described earlier (Ashby et al., 2002; Maddox & Ashby, 2004; Maddox & Ing, 2005; Waldron & Ashby, 2001).

In an RB task, the Category A and B distributions are partitioned vertically or horizontally across the stimulus space. Only one dimension presents useful category information, and a unidimensional rule captures the category-separation principle. Such rules can be held in working memory and verbalized.

The II and RB category tasks are matched for category size, elliptical category shape, within-category exemplar similarity, between-category exemplar separation, and many metrics of category discriminability (Ashby et al., 2020). Indeed, the RB category structure is exactly the II category structure rotated 45 degrees. These tasks are strong mutual controls that are equated in their *a priori* perceptual difficulty.

This fact is crucial to understanding cross-species research in this area. If the X and Y dimensions were integral (not separately attendable, Garner, 1974), the tasks would be identical for learners, because there would be no privileged dimensional axes or category rules. But with separable dimensions, the tasks differ exactly and only in the value of selective attention and rule formation in one task but not the other. Therefore, by rotating the task axis, from II to RB, one can ask whether the cognitive systems of different species are integrally or separably organized in Garner's sense of those terms. If the former, II and RB tasks will be learned equally well because the task's dimensions will not be sources of selective attention or rule formation. If the latter, the RB task may support faster learning grounded in rules. This integral-separable species evaluation can be made regarding any species able to participate in discrimination-learning tasks, making the RB-II framework a valuable comparative assay.

13.3 EVOLUTIONARY PATH TO DIMENSIONAL CATEGORIZATION

HUMANS

Ongoing research is exploring the phylogenetic map of an emerging explicit system (acknowledging, of course, that species widely share a robust capacity for implicit-associative learning). Figure 13.1C illustrates a typical result from humans given RB and II tasks (Smith et al., 2010). The stimuli were circles varying in the width and tilt of a striping pattern. Humans learned the RB task quickly to a high level. There was a strong RB performance advantage over the II task, which showed the gradual learning curve typical of associative learning. Other RB-II dissociations have been published (Ashby & Valentin, 2017; Smith et al., 2020). Humans in RB tasks test hypotheses and discover rules to produce this learning advantage. They have a powerful form of rule learning. It can sometimes even be intrusive, controlling cognitive performance inappropriately. But which species share these rule processes with humans? How crucial is humans' language capacity; which rule processes are possible without language, and which are not? Intriguing evolutionary questions attend rule-based categorization.

MONKEYS

Smith et al. (2010) tested rhesus macaques (*Macaca mulatta*) – an Old World primate – in the tasks just described. Macaques have smaller frontal cortices than humans (Semendeferi et al., 2002), producing performance difficulties when response competition or the need for response inhibition arises (Roberts, 1996; Washburn, 1994). They might substantially lack a rule-based system. Then they might learn RB and II tasks equivalently because the tasks are matched in inherent difficulty unless the organism brings dimensional attention selectively to the RB task.

Figure 13.1D shows the result. Macaques also showed a strong RB-II advantage, though they learned more slowly. Their category-learning system clearly included some useable dimensional-attention process. Despite lesser frontal-cortical development and lacking language, macaques showed RB-II similarities to humans. Smith, Crossley et al. (2012) found similar results with capuchin monkeys (*Cebus apella*), a New World primate. Thus, some dimensional-attention processes transcend language. Dimensional categorization had an earlier evolutionary origin. But when? And why?

PIGEONS

Smith et al. (2011) evaluated pigeons' RB-II performance but found strikingly different results. Figure 13.1E shows learning curves for pigeons backward from the criterion block, so that the birds' arrivals at the criterion were aligned and one could see their path toward it. There is no RB advantage. The learning curves are identical. Seemingly, pigeons learned two category tasks of the same psychological character and difficulty, with no preference for the task allowing dimensional focusing or rule learning. *Perhaps they did not even attend to the informative dimension selectively!* The indication of an integral pattern of perception and classification resonates with findings by Pearce et al. (2008), who also demonstrated a striking failure of selective attention by pigeons and who also wondered whether pigeons have central processes of selective attention. The RB-II results with pigeons have been replicated by Qadri et al. (2019). Broschard et al. (2019) showed equivalent RB and II performance by rats. It is remarkable that two of the most studied cognitive systems in comparative psychology, those of pigeons and rats, show the integral pattern of classification and not the dimensional focusing shown by diverse primates. In these results, we could be seeing the character of the stem vertebrate category-learning system before dimensional analysis and category rules augmented it.

13.4 EVOLUTIONARY PATH TO EXPLICIT CATEGORY RULES

However, even monkeys must be viewed as a transitional form in the development of explicit category rules. That is, monkeys may show dimensional categorization, but they may not go further to the point of learning abstract rules that generalize flexibly.

Zakrzewski et al. (2018) explored these constraints as follows. II category learning should be welded to the original (training) stimulus contexts. This is true because II learning is essentially stimulus-response (SR) learning – immediate reinforcement links correct responses to training stimuli. Therefore, generalization to novel stimuli should be constrained by the training-transfer dissimilarity stretch involved in the generalization. In addition, II learning is behavioral. There need be no separate category knowledge held in working memory to afford generalization in another way. However, RB categorization is ideally based on an explicit rule. That rule should be abstract and applicable to new stimuli. For example, a shape rule would apply even as stimulus sizes or colors changed. RB learning should generalize gracefully. Casale et al. (2012) confirmed this for humans.

Figure 13.2 depicts Zakrzewski et al.'s (2018) situation for testing this transfer in macaques. They divided the typical II and RB category structures in two (Figure 13.2), trained macaques in the lower part of the stimulus space and then transferred them to the upper part. In this way, they could evaluate the transferability of category knowledge to novel stimuli. A generalizeable rule would extend to the new region of the stimulus space. Conditioned responses to training stimuli might not.

This experiment has been done in two different ways (Smith et al., 2015; Zakrzewski et al., 2018). We summarize the overall empirical situation. Humans and monkeys dramatically fail to extend their II category knowledge to a novel region of the stimulus space. II category knowledge is stimulus circumscribed as theory predicts. Humans show complete analogical extension of their RB category knowledge to novel stimuli. Their category rule is abstract and transferable to new stimuli. Macaques overall do not show this

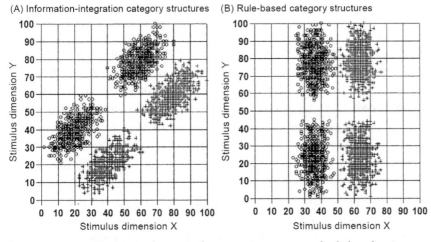

FIGURE 13.2. Training-generalization information-integration and rule-based category structures, depicted in the same way as Figure 13.1A and B. The bottom and top pair of stimulus ellipses, respectively, are the defined categories during training and generalization.

analogical extension. Their RB category knowledge is circumscribed compared to humans'. This result highlights the abstractness and stimulus independence of humans' category rules. It demonstrates that though macaques show strong performance advantages from selective attention in the RB task, they are still not learning fully abstract and transferable category representations as humans do. The difference could be macaques' smaller working memory capacity, language deficit, or other factors. Our work continues to try to foster more abstract category rules in macaques. We will give macaques symbol training that amounts to providing abstract "names" for categories like shape and color. These labels could let their category knowledge become more abstract. Nonetheless, macaques are a transitional form, "between" pigeons and humans, along the evolutionary path to explicit, abstract, rule-based categorization.

13.5 IMPLICIT AND EXPLICIT LEARNING: ADAPTATION AND FITNESS CONSIDERATIONS

A multiple-systems perspective toward learning raises intriguing questions about the fitness of different learning processes in animals' natural ecology. What value does a second, explicit-declarative learning system bring to the organism? What costs does the organism pay by committing solely to one system, or by needing to switch among multiple systems? Possibly, the forms of implicit and explicit learning that we are discussing in this chapter allow for an elegant division of labor.

The implicit system described here creates the bonds between perceptual stimuli and actions that can ground a form of associative learning and adaptive responding. Reinforcement is the binding force in forging these associations. This learning dynamic has strengths. It produces durable performance "memory" and stable behavior. It commits to behavioral solutions slowly as consequences accrue. It lets go behavioral solutions slowly under extinction. Because this form of implicit learning can occur non-attentionally, it can learn about a broad range of complex stimuli and about categories that are not linearly separable. Because it needs no conscious awareness, it is potentially available to many or all vertebrate lines. So, there is adaptive power in an implicit system that simply associates responses to stimuli, without requiring dimensions and rules to layer onto the processing unnecessarily. This power could explain why associative learning is so important in the discriminative capacity broadly distributed across vertebrates.

However, this system for implicit learning has weaknesses. It depends on immediate reinforcement, time-critical event sequences (stimulus-response-reinforcement), and persistent event repetition. This form of learning cannot occur offline or with displacement in time or space from the task's trials. That is, the organism can never think in the burrow at night what might have been better to do as the fox approached and might be better to do next time. Implicit learning cannot take instruction, instantly drop a bad habit, or instantly choose a new approach. Knowledge accrues through trial-repetition sedimentation. And knowledge is limited to the concrete and perceptual – the organism is denied cognition about the abstract and conceptual.

These constraints may explain why some vertebrate lines complementarily emphasize dimensional analysis and rules. These explicit processes have their own strengths. They are not rigidly time-locked. They do not depend on immediate reinforcement or arduous trial repetition. The organism ideally can say: the world changed, act anew. Learning can occur offline and with displacement, through reflecting on events after the fact. Learning can even occur by deliberate hypothesis testing. Learning and unlearning can be instantaneous. Rules are analogically extendable. They can also be abstract and conceptual. For these reasons, explicit learning is a good complement to implicit learning. Moreover, the psychological salience that accrued to dimensional analysis and category rules may have been an important pre-adaptation that set the stage for cognitive evolution in the primate-hominid lineage.

13.6 DISABLING IMPLICIT-PROCEDURAL LEARNING TO STUDY EXPLICIT-DECLARATIVE LEARNING

We are currently exploring additional dissociative paradigms that may let researchers study animals' explicit cognition *with other learning processes held at bay.* These paradigms intend to isolate the reinforcement-learning system already described that controls learning in many discrimination tasks, and then to disable it. Then, animals' explicit cognitive capabilities will be freed from the shaping force of reinforcement-based associative learning. Indeed, those explicit processes may be required to guide the learning process – if they can! These paradigms grant subjects alternative kinds of feedback that instruct about the task solution and sustain task engagement, but they ensure that feedback is not entraining associative responding.

This research plan understandably meets sharp resistance. In essence, it requires treating immediate reinforcement as an interpretative confound. But this clashes with the venerable idea within learning theory that immediate reinforcement is the necessary binding force creating SR associations. To cast immediate reinforcement aside as a confound can be troubling. Therefore, we stress that we agree that associative learning plays an important role in animals' learning, and that the associative-learning construct will and should remain a central aspect of theory. The paradigms discussed now do not criticize the associative perspective at all. They only (possibly) illuminate a complementary facet of animal minds. We begin by describing the reinforcement-learning system that is important to discrimination learning and that we believe can be disabled using a suitable dissociative paradigm.

13.7 REINFORCEMENT IN IMPLICIT-PROCEDURAL LEARNING

Task reinforcements cause dopamine release into the tail of the caudate nucleus. This reinforcement signal can strengthen synapses that were just active (Arbuthnott et al., 2000; Hollerman & Schultz, 1998; Schultz, 1992; Smith & Church, 2018). These likely were participatory in producing the correct response, so learning results. However, this learning mechanism is time-limited (e.g., Yagishita et al., 2014). These synapses soon return to baseline. The brain retains no activation "memory." Then, there is no means to selectively assign "credit" for the reinforcement. So, after a delay, the reinforcement mechanism that underlies an important form of associative learning is no longer effective. That form of implicit learning – the time-locked sequence of stimulus, response, reward – should collapse if this timing is disrupted.

Yagishita et al. (2014) imaged this collapse at the cellular level. They controlled the temporal asynchrony between sensory (stimulus) input and dopamine (reward) inputs by optically stimulating glutamatergic and dopaminergic inputs separately. They found that dopamine promoted spine enlargement (i.e., synaptic strengthening, learning) only during a narrow time window (two seconds) after the glutamatergic stimulation. This time window is confirmed when humans learn categories at reinforcement delays (Maddox & Ing, 2005). This frequently observed temporal restriction has long been known to learning theorists (Pavlov, 1927).

Therefore, we concluded that the alternative feedback methodologies described next might eliminate this reinforcement-learning mechanism and require an alternative learning process that might be more explicit and rule-based. This system would still function well under these alternative methods. Explicit cognition can access memory for stimuli, responses, and consequences in interpreting feedback and in choosing performance strategies. It probably can hold onto information for several trials, pending feedback. So even summary feedback after a trial block might not derail explicit learning. When the memory of a conscious hypothesis that was used during a block of trials received its summary success report, that combination would be fully sufficient for learning: "In that block I used the rule: BIG-Small is Cat. A-B; I was mainly right; the rule works!" Of course, animals' hypotheses/rules would not be verbalizable. This does not matter – it is a serious theoretical mistake to conflate the explicit and the verbal. Hypotheses could be represented and evaluated nonverbally within awareness. In fact, the ancestral explicit-learning system may well have been nonverbal.

13.8 TWO DISSOCIATIVE PARADIGMS

We have developed two paradigms that demonstrate in humans a transition from implicit to explicit learning under the conditions just described. Both were designed so that comparative researchers might adopt them with multiple species.

ONE-BACK REINFORCEMENT

Smith et al. (2018) taught humans RB and II categories as shown in Figure 13.1. On each trial, a stimulus appeared at the screen's far right. Toward the left of the screen were the letters "A" (on the left) and "B" (on the right), with a cursor between them. Moving the cursor let the participant choose a Category A or B response. In the zero-back reinforcement condition, trials ran off as usual in discrimination tasks. Stimulus, response, then immediate feedback occurred in that time-locked sequence. In the one-back reinforcement condition, subjects received feedback delayed by one trial, breaking the stimulus-response-reinforcement sequence needed for the type of striatal learning considered here. This lagged feedback operated as follows: When a subject made their categorization response on Trial N, they received no feedback cues regarding that trial yet. Instead, they received feedback cues about Trial N-1. To help participants bookkeep this deferred-feedback situation, trials alternated between presentation at the top or bottom of the screen. Feedback was placed in the top-bottom location at which the trial originally appeared, to help participants keep track of which trial the feedback referenced. In Smith et al. (2018), the feedback comprised a representation of the original N-1 stimulus, and information about whether they had been correct or not and their point totals.

The objective was to delay the reinforcement signal outside the tolerance of the striatal learning being considered. Our hypothesis was that one-back reinforcement would undermine the associative-learning system temporally and associatively (the reinforcement did NOT pertain to the most recent response made). If so, then (1) participants should no longer learn the correct II diagonal decision bound, (2) but they should still learn the correct RB explicit rule because displaced reinforcement would not disrupt hypothesis testing and rule learning. (3) Also, one-back II participants, unable to learn associatively, might instead adopt explicit superstitious rules and hypotheses because that was all they still could do. Were these predictions confirmed, it would provide a strong confirmation that displaced reinforcement disables associative, reinforcement-based learning, while leaving other types of learning intact.

Figure 13.3 shows the experiment's results. We used strategy modeling to summarize each participant's performance as a decision bound that best segregates their Category A and B responses. These bounds are shown as drawn through Figure 13.3's two-dimensional stimulus space.

Panels A and B in Figure 13.3 show clearly that RB performance was completely unaffected by the one-back manipulation. Theory predicts this

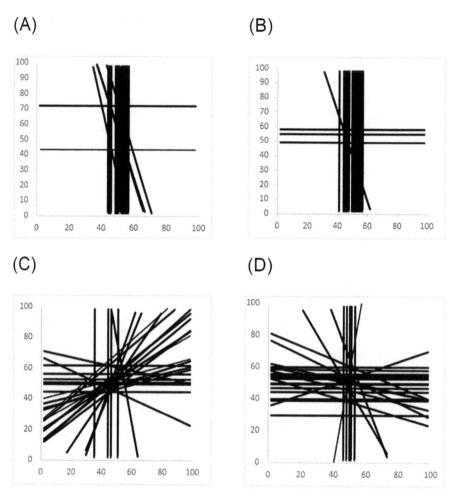

FIGURE 13.3. The decision bounds that provided the best fits to the last 100 responses of participants in the (A) zero-back – rule-based, (B) one-back – rule-based, (C) zero-back information-integration, and (D) one-back – information-integration conditions. The X axis denotes the level of the Size dimension. The Y axis denotes the level of the Density dimension. From "One-back reinforcement dissociates implicit and explicit category learning" by J. D. Smith, S. Jamani, J. Boomer, and B. A. Church, 2018, *Memory & Cognition, 46*, p. 262. Copyright 2018 by Springer. Reprinted with permission.

result as just indicated. The explicit learning process, with hypotheses held in memory to be evaluated by summary feedback later, is immune to reinforcement's delay.

Panels C and D present a different picture. In the zero-back condition (C), many of the decision bounds had the correct II diagonal orientation – running from bottom-left to top-right – that correctly partitions the II categories. Thus, many zero-back participants appreciated the task's actual (diagonal) category structure and responded to the task's true reinforcement contingencies. But the one-back participants (D) did not. Only 1 of 30 participants was modeled by a major-diagonal decision bound. This is very strong evidence that one-back reinforcement was not able to condition the correct diagonal partition between the categories. In this sense, the effective reinforcement signal was blocked. Instead, most participants produced vertical or horizontal bounds. Confirming this, they performed poorly (averaging 65% correct). Instead, their decision bounds suggest they chose a one-dimensional, rule-based (wrong) performance strategy. They did the best they could in the circumstances, trying to solve the task explicitly because they could not learn to solve it associatively.

DEFERRED-BLOCKED REINFORCEMENT

Smith et al. (2014) also taught humans RB and II categories. In their immediate-reinforcement condition, trials again unfolded in the time-locked sequence – stimulus, response, immediate feedback. In their deferred-reinforcement condition, though, participants made category decisions in six-trial blocks without any feedback cues until the block's end. Then, participants received feedback about their positive outcomes grouped together and then their negative outcomes grouped together. The next trial block followed. Associative learning was thoroughly disrupted in this condition because the feedback signal was displaced in time and scrambled out of trial-by-trial presentation order. The implicit-procedural system could not track which SR pairs were correct or which SR bonds should strengthen.

Figure 13.4 shows the decision bounds from this study that fit very closely those in Smith et al. (2018). Once again, performance in the RB task, presumed to be explicit and to be immune to displaced reinforcement, was immune as predicted. Once again, though, implicit-procedural learning was disabled, because reinforcement could not exert its binding force. Many participants receiving immediate reinforcement produced the appropriate diagonal decision bounds – indicating sensitivity to the task's true reinforcement structure. No participants receiving deferred reinforcement did so. Instead, they resorted to explicit strategies – that is, to adventitious and inappropriate rules that resulted in vertical or horizontal decision bounds. These participants even showed the common pattern of discovering their "rule" suddenly (Figure 13.3, Smith et al., 2014). When associative learning is prevented, the explicit mind tries to fill the void. The explicit mind of animals might do the same and observing this self-directed rule learning would have important theoretical implications.

The dissociations just described are quite strong, nearly qualitative. We describe our methods conservatively, as only disabling the striatal, SR mapping function powered by immediate reinforcement. But these methods disable more broadly than that. If participants could map the task associatively in any way whatsoever – mapping stimuli to outcomes, responses to outcomes, stimuli to responses in some way untied from reinforcement –

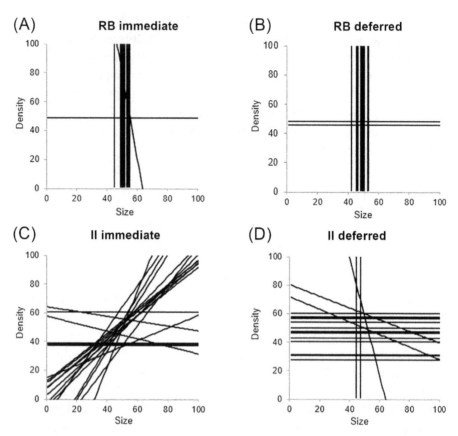

FIGURE 13.4. The decision bounds that provided the best fits to the last 100 responses of the four conditions (A–D) of Smith et al. (2014).

From "Deferred feedback sharply dissociates implicit and explicit category learning," by J. D. Smith, J. Boomer, A. C. Zakrzewski, J. Roeder, B. A. Church, and F. G. Ashby, *Psychological Science, 25*, p. 453. Copyright 2013 by Sage Publishing. Reprinted with permission.

then they would learn showing appropriate diagonal decision bounds in the task. They do not. And moreover, they exhibit the signs of performing explicitly using simple conscious rules, even when those rules are super- stitious. Thus, we urge associative theorists to take seriously the overarching idea suggested here that one may be able to disable animals' crucial associative-learning processes, and see whether they can step in with more explicit learning processes.

13.9 A PRELIMINARY STUDY OF MONKEYS' LEARNING UNDER DISPLACED REINFORCEMENT

We are exploring this possibility presently. In Smith et al. (2020), macaques completed two-choice discrimination tasks (they saw two dissimilar objects and had to move to the A for one and B for the other). Reinforcement lagged by one trial as already described. The displacement of the reinforcement should prevent SR associative learning in monkeys as it was shown to do in humans. Then, if monkeys have no alternative learning system to swap in, they would fail to learn. But if they can construe the task and its feedback in some fashion not dependent on time-locked reinforcement, they should still learn.

Monkeys do learn under one-back reinforcement. Three macaques reached a learning criterion in multiple tasks – sometimes fairly quickly. One monkey was not engaged by the lagged reinforcement and was less successful. Possibly, interpreting displaced reinforcement is cognitively effortful and dis-preferred for that reason. The results indicate that monkeys do have backstopping learning mechanisms they can rely on when immediate-reinforcement learning is blocked. Existing neuroscience suggests that a strong candidate for this backstopping mechanism would be category rules held in working memory. However, we emphasize that this preliminary demonstration is not as strong and qualitative as our human dissociations have been. In continuing studies, we will evaluate how far monkeys can travel toward explicit cognition when their associative-learning system is disabled. In the end, this line of research could be very constructive within comparative research. For paradigms like ours could bring comparative psychologists to the brink of being able to study animals' self-instructing and possibly conscious minds as they develop their own task strategies when the processes of association are eliminated.

13.10 EXTENSIONS OF THE DISSOCIATIVE FRAMEWORK TO OTHER COGNITIVE CAPACITIES

The dissociative framework described here might explain comparative phenomena beyond the domain of categorization. We consider two extensions briefly.

First, strong evidence suggests that explicit-declarative cognition powers humans' performance in relational-cognition tasks, including in the well-known relational-matching-to-sample (RMTS) task. For example, in Smith, Flemming et al. (2013), humans performed at the high levels consistent with rule-based, not implicit-procedural, cognition (Smith et al., 2010). They discovered their RMTS task solution suddenly, diagnostic of explicit learning (Smith & Ell, 2015). Moreover, Smith et al. (2019) showed that humans' RMTS performance was undermined by a concurrent working-memory load. Thus, explicit, working-memory processes are likely crucial to humans' RMTS conceptualization. This might be true for other species, too.

Chimpanzee research supports this idea. Language-trained apes succeed more robustly in RMTS tasks than those inexperienced. Language would offer a representational assist toward explicit relational cognition. Based on this article's section on the evolutionary path of explicit category rules, monkeys should falter in RMTS tasks. They do. Smith, Flemming et al. (2013) used a weaning procedure to slowly remove a perceptual cue from macaques, leaving them (hopefully) with pure RMTS performance. However, performance collapsed as weaning progressed. Yet, in Fagot and Thompson (2011), baboons (macaque relatives) demonstrated a rudimentary capacity to perform RMTS tasks if given extensive training and trial repetition. Moreover, in Maugard et al. (2013), a working-memory load compromised baboons' RMTS performance as was found in humans. Here, too, as we saw in the sections on the evolutionary path of dimensional categorization and explicit category rules, monkeys seem to be a transitional form.

Finally, the present dissociative framework would grant pigeons the least capacity for RMTS conceptualization, and this appears correct. Pigeons only succeed on RMTS-like tasks if the task makes available a concrete, first-order perceptual cue like visual entropy (Young et al., 1997). That is, pigeons might detect Sameness not as an abstract conceptual relation between objects, but as an overall perceptual calmness and order, and Differentness also not as an abstract relation between objects, but as visual disorder.

Second, our framework also illuminates the animal metacognition literature, which long attempted to explain associatively metacognitive phenomena in animals (Smith, Couchman et al., 2012). However, the strong consensus now is that some species share with humans a basic metacognitive capacity, including the capacities for uncertainty monitoring and information seeking. Apes and macaques clearly show forms of metacognition (Beran et al., 2013; Smith, Coutinho et al., 2013). Moreover, working-memory resources may underlie these phenomena. For example, Smith, Coutinho et al. (2013) found that monkeys' capacity to make adaptive uncertainty responses was impaired when they were given a concurrent working-memory load. The use of the perceptual discrimination responses was not affected by the load. The implication is that the metacognitive response alone reflected some higher-level uncertainty process that is working-memory intensive. In this area, too, the comparative map completes as expected. As the section on the evolutionary path of dimensional categorization here would suggest, pigeons have persistently not shown clear signs of uncertainty monitoring or metacognition (Sutton & Shettleworth, 2008).

Thus, we believe the implicit-explicit dissociative perspective has substantial utility for comparative psychology considered broadly. It suggests the same theoretical lessons for the literatures on categorization, relational conceptualization, and metacognition. It sketches the same phylogenetic map of competence in all three domains. Thus, it explains many empirical phenomena parsimoniously.

13.11 CONCLUSION

We hope the perspective of dissociative learning systems will continue to productively contribute to, and benefit from, crosstalk among cognitive psychologists, neuroscientists, and comparative psychologists. Cognitive psychologists know best the sophisticated dissociative methodologies that have been developed in their fields, and comparative psychologists have much to learn from them on that front. Neuroscientists understand the detailed dynamics of associative-response binding, and they have much to offer comparative psychology in the possible methods that can liberate learning from association and reinforcement to the extent that is possible. They have much to teach us as well.

In return, comparative psychology stands to make extraordinary contributions. A systems approach to animal minds may let us provide to cognitive psychology animal models of high-level human cognitive capacities. Comparative psychologists might also illuminate the earliest developmental stages that children pass through on their path to mature explicit-declarative cognition. They could illuminate the psychological character of explicit cognition when – as in nonverbal animals – it is shorn of its language and symbolic basis. This would set the stage for understanding the unique affordance that language offers to humans' explicit cognition. Finally, they could participate in broadening the present understanding about humans' cognitive emergence, by determining when and how the initial forms of important cognitive capacities arose.

ACKNOWLEDGMENTS

The preparation of this publication was supported by the NICHD, R01HD093690. The content is solely the responsibility of the authors and does not necessarily represent the official views of the National Institutes of Health. The authors declare no financial interest and no conflicts of interest.

REFERENCES

Arbuthnott, G. W., Ingham, C. A., & Wickens, J. R. (2000). Dopamine and synaptic plasticity in the neostriatum. *Journal of Anatomy, 196,* 587–596. https://doi.org/10.1046/j.1469-7580.2000.19640587.x

Ashby, F. G., Alfonso-Reese, L. A., Turken, A. U., & Waldron, E. M. (1998). A neuropsychological theory of multiple systems in category learning. *Psychological Review, 105,* 442–481. https://doi.org/10.1037/0033-295X.105.3.442

Ashby, F. G., & Ell, S. W. (2001). The neurobiology of human category learning. *Trends in Cognitive Sciences, 5,* 204–210. https://doi.org/10.1016/S1364-6613(00)01624-7

Ashby, F. G., & Maddox, W. T. (2011). Human category learning 2.0. *Annals of the New York Academy of Sciences, 1224,* 147–161. https://doi.org/10.1111/j.1749-6632.2010.05874.x

Ashby, F. G., Maddox, W. T., & Bohil, C. J. (2002). Observational versus feedback training in rule-based and information-integration category learning. *Memory & Cognition, 30,* 666–677. https://doi.org/10.3758/BF03196423

Ashby, F. G., Smith, J. D., & Rosedahl, L. (2020). Dissociations between rule-based and information-integration categorization are not caused by differences in task difficulty. *Memory & Cognition, 48,* 541–552. https://doi.org/10.3758/s13421-019-00988-4

Ashby, F. G., & Valentin, V. V. (2017). Multiple systems of perceptual category learning: Theory and cognitive tests. In H. Cohen & C. Lefebvre (Eds.), *Handbook of Categorization in Cognitive Science* (2nd ed., pp. 157–188). Elsevier. https://doi.org/10.1016/B978-0-08-101107-2.00007-5

Basile, B. M., Schroeder, G. R., Brown, E. K., Templer, V. L., & Hampton, R. R. (2015). Evaluation of seven hypotheses for metamemory performance in rhesus monkeys. *Journal of Experimental Psychology: General, 144,* 85–102. https://doi.org/10.1037/xge0000031

Beran, M. J., Smith J. D., & Perdue, B. M. (2013). Language-trained chimpanzees name what they have seen but look first at what they have not seen. *Psychological Science, 24,* 660–666. https://doi.org/10.1177/0956797612458936

Broschard, M. B., Kim, J., Love, B. C., Wasserman, E. A., & Freeman, J. H. (2019). Selective attention in rat visual category learning. *Learning & Memory, 26,* 84–92. https://doi.org/10.1101/lm.048942.118

Casale, M. B, Roeder, J. L., & Ashby, F. G. (2012). Analogical transfer in perceptual categorization. *Memory & Cognition, 40,* 434–449. https://doi.org/10.3758/s13421-011-0154-4

Elliott, R., & Dolan, R. J. (1998). Activation of different anterior cingulate foci in association with hypothesis testing and response selection. *Neuroimage, 8,* 17–29. https://doi.org/10.1006/nimg.1998.0344

Fagot, J., & Thompson, R. K. R. (2011). Generalized relational matching by guinea baboons (*Papio papio*) in two-by-two-item analogy problems. *Psychological Science, 22,* 1304–1309. https://doi.org/10.1177/0956797611422916

Fuster, J. M. (1989). *The Prefrontal Cortex* (2nd ed.). Raven Press.

Garner, W. (1974). *The Processing of Information and Structure.* Wiley.

Hollerman, J. R., & Schultz, W. (1998). Dopamine neurons report an error in the temporal prediction of reward during learning. *Nature Neuroscience, 1,* 304–309. https://doi.org/10.1038/1124

Knowlton, B. J., Mangels, J. A., & Squire, L. R. (1996). A neostriatal habit learning system in humans. *Science, 273*(5280), 1399–1402. https://doi.org/10.1126/science.273.5280.1399

Maddox, W. T., & Ashby, F. G. (2004). Dissociating explicit and procedural-learning based systems of perceptual category learning. *Behavioural Processes, 66,* 309–332. https://doi.org/10.1016/j.beproc.2004.03.011

Maddox, W. T., & Ing, A. D. (2005). Delayed feedback disrupts the procedural-learning system but not the hypothesis-testing system in perceptual category learning. *Journal of Experimental Psychology: Learning, Memory, and Cognition, 31,* 100–107. https://doi.org/10.1037/0278-7393.31.1.100

Maugard, A., Marzouki, Y., & Fagot, J. (2013). Contribution of working memory processes to relational matching-to-sample performance in baboons (*Papio papio*). *Journal of Comparative Psychology, 127,* 370–379. http://doi.org/10.1037/a0032336

Morgan, C. L. (1906). *An introduction to comparative psychology.* W. Scott.

Pavlov, I. P. (1927). *Conditioned reflexes: An investigation of the physiological activity of the cerebral cortex.* Oxford University Press. https://doi.org/10.5214/ans.0972-7531.1017309

Pearce, J. M., Esber, G. R., George, D. N., & Haselgrove, M. (2008). The nature of discrimination learning in pigeons. *Learning & Behavior, 36,* 188–199. https://doi.org/10.3758/LB.36.3.188

Posner, M. I., & Petersen, S. E. (1990). The attention system of the human brain. *Annual Review of Neuroscience, 13,* 25–42. https://doi.org/10.1146/annurev.ne.13.030190.000325

Qadri, M. A.-J., Ashby, F. G., Smith, J. D., & Cook, R. G. (2019). Testing analogical rule transfer in pigeons (*Columba livia*). *Cognition, 183,* 256–268. https://doi.org/10.1016/j.cognition.2018.11.011

Rao, S. M., Bobholz, J. A., Hammeke, T. A., Rosen, A. C., Woodley, S. J., Cunningham, J. M., & Binder, J. R. (1997). Functional MRI evidence for subcortical participation in conceptual reasoning skills. *Neuroreport, 8,* 1987–1993. https://doi.org/10.1097/00001756-199705260-00038

Roberts, A. C. (1996). Comparison of cognitive function in human and non-human primates. *Cognitive Brain Research, 3,* 319–327. https://doi.org/10.1016/0926-6410(96)00017-1

Robinson, A. L., Heaton, R. K., Lehman, R. A., & Stilson, D. W. (1980). The utility of the Wisconsin Card Sorting Test in detecting and localizing frontal lobe lesions. *Journal of Consulting and Clinical Psychology, 48,* 605–614. https://doi.org/10.1037/0022-006X.48.5.605

Schultz, W. (1992). Activity of dopamine neurons in the behaving primate. *Seminars in Neuroscience, 4,* 129–138. https://doi.org/10.1016/1044-5765(92)90011-P

Semendeferi, K., Lu, A., Schenker, N., & Damásio, H. (2002). Humans and great apes share a large frontal cortex. *Nature Neuroscience, 5,* 272–276. https://doi.org/10.1038/nn814

Smith, J. D., Ashby, F. G., Berg, M. E., Murphy, M. S., Spiering, B., Cook, R. G., & Grace, R. C. (2011). Pigeons' categorization may be exclusively nonanalytic. *Psychonomic Bulletin & Review, 18,* 414–421. http://doi.org/10.3758/s13423-010-0047-8

Smith, J. D., Beran, M. J., Crossley, M. J., Boomer, J., & Ashby, F. G. (2010). Implicit and explicit category learning by macaques (*Macaca mulatta*) and humans (*Homo sapiens*). *Journal of Experimental Psychology: Animal Behavior Processes, 36,* 54–65. https://doi.org/10.1037/a0015892

Smith, J. D., Berg, M. E., Cook, R. G., Boomer, J., Crossley, M. J., Murphy, M. S., Spiering, B., Beran, M. J., Church, B. A., Ashby, F. G., & Grace. R. C. (2012). Implicit and explicit categorization: A tale of four species. *Neuroscience and Biobehavioral Reviews, 36,* 2355–2369. https://doi.org/10.1016/j.neubiorev.2012.09.003

Smith, J. D., Boomer, J., Zakrzewski, A. C., Roeder, J. L., Church, B. A., & Ashby, F. G. (2014). Deferred feedback sharply dissociates implicit and explicit category learning. *Psychological Science, 25,* 447–457. https://doi.org/10.1177/0956797613509112

Smith, J. D. & Church, B. A. (2018). Dissociable learning processes in comparative psychology. *Psychonomic Bulletin & Review, 25,* 1565–1584. http://doi.org/10.3758/s13423-017-1353-1

Smith, J. D., Couchman, J. J., & Beran, M. J. (2012). The highs and lows of theoretical interpretation in animal metacognition research. *Philosophical Transactions of the Royal Society of London B: Biological Sciences, 367,* 1297–1309. https://doi.org/10.1098/rstb.2011.0366

Smith, J. D., Coutinho, M. V. C., Church, B. A., & Beran, M. J. (2013). Executive-attentional uncertainty responses by rhesus macaques (*Macaca mulatta*). *Journal of Experimental Psychology: General, 142,* 458–475. https://doi.org/10.1037/a0029601

Smith, J. D., Crossley, M. J., Boomer, J., Church, B. A., Beran, M. J., & Ashby, F. G. (2012). Implicit and explicit category learning by capuchin monkeys (*Cebus apella*). *Journal of Comparative Psychology, 126,* 294–304. https://doi.org/10.1037/a0026031

Smith, J. D., & Ell, S. W. (2015). One giant leap for categorizers: One small step for categorization theory. *PLoS ONE, 10*(9), e0137334. https://doi.org/10.1371/journal.pone.0137334

Smith, J. D., Flemming, T. M., Boomer, J., Beran, M. J., & Church B. A. (2013). Fading perceptual resemblance: A path for rhesus macaques (*Macaca mulatta*) to conceptual matching? *Cognition, 129,* 1598–1614. https://doi.org/10.1016/j.cognition.2013.08.001

Smith, J. D., Jackson, B. N., & Church, B. A. (2019). Breaking the perceptual-conceptual barrier: Relational matching and working memory. *Memory & Cognition, 47,* 544–560. https://doi.org/10.3758/s13421-018-0890-9

(2020). Monkeys (*Macaca mulatta*) learn two-choice discriminations under displaced reinforcement. *Journal of Comparative Psychology, 134,* 423–434. https://doi.org/10.1037/com0000227

Smith, J. D., Jamani, S., Boomer, J., & Church, B. A. (2018). One-back reinforcement dissociates implicit-procedural and explicit-declarative category learning. *Memory & Cognition, 46,* 261–273. https://doi.org/10.3758/s13421-017-0762-8

Smith, J. D., Zakrzewski, A. C., Johnston, J. J. R., Roeder, J. L., Boomer, J., Ashby, F. G., & Church, B. A. (2015). Generalization of category knowledge and dimensional categorization in humans (*Homo sapiens*) and nonhuman primates (*Macaca mulatta*). *Journal of Experimental Psychology: Animal Learning and Cognition, 41*, 322–335. https://doi.org/10.1037/xan0000071

Smith, J. D., Zakrzewski, A. C., Johnson, J. M., Valleau, J. C., & Church, B. A. (2016). Categorization: The view from animal cognition. *Behavioural Science, 6*, 12. https://doi.org/10.3390/bs6020012

Sutton, J. E., & Shettleworth, S. J. (2008). Memory without awareness: Pigeons do not show metamemory in delayed matching to sample. *Journal of Experimental Psychology: Animal Behavior Processes, 34*, 266–282. https://doi.org/10.1037/0097-7403.34.2.266

Waldron, E. M., & Ashby, F. G. (2001). The effects of concurrent task interference on category learning: Evidence for multiple category learning systems. *Psychonomic Bulletin & Review, 8*, 168–176. https://doi.org/10.3758/BF03196154

Waldschmidt, J. G., & Ashby, F. G. (2011). Cortical and striatal contributions to automaticity in information-integration categorization. *NeuroImage, 56*, 1791–1802. https://doi.org/10.1016/j.neuroimage.2011.02.011

Washburn, D. A. (1994). Stroop-like effects for monkeys and humans: Processing speed or strength of association? *Psychological Science, 5*, 375–379. https://doi.org/10.1111/j.1467-9280.1994.tb00288.x

Yagishita, S., Hayashi-Takagi, A., Ellis-Davies, G. C. R., Urakubo, H., Ishii, S., & Kasai, H. (2014). A critical time window for dopamine actions on the structural plasticity of dendritic spines. *Science, 345*(6204), 1616–1620. https://doi.org/10.1126/science.1255514

Yin, H. H., Ostlund, S. B., Knowlton, B. J., & Balleine, B. W. (2005). The role of the dorsomedial striatum in instrumental conditioning. *European Journal of Neuroscience, 22*(2), 513–523. https://doi.org/10.1111/j.1460-9568.2005.04218.x

Yonelinas, A. P. (2002). The nature of recollection and familiarity: A review of 30 years of research. *Journal of Memory and Language, 46*, 441–517. https://doi.org/10.1006/jmla.2002.2864

Young, M. E., Wasserman, E. A., & Garner, K. L. (1997). Effects of number of items on the pigeon's discrimination of same from different visual displays. *Journal of Experimental Psychology: Behavior Processes, 23*, 491–501. https://doi.org/10.1037/0097-7403.23.4.491

Zakrzewski, A. C., Church, B. A., & Smith, J. D. (2018). The transfer of category knowledge by macaques (*Macaca mulatta*) and humans (*Homo sapiens*). *Journal of Comparative Psychology, 132*, 58–74. https://doi.org/10.1037/com0000095

Zakrzewski, A. C., Johnson, J. M., & Smith, J. D. (2017). The comparative psychology of metacognition. In J. Call, G. M. Burghardt, I. M. Pepperberg, C. T. Snowdon, & T. Zentall (Eds.), *APA handbook of comparative psychology: Perception, learning, and cognition* (pp. 703–721). American Psychological Association. https://doi.org/10.1037/0000012-031

14

SOCIAL LEARNING STRATEGIES

Rachel L. Kendal

Social learning, defined as "learning that is facilitated by observation of, or interaction with, another individual (or its products)" (Heyes et al., 1994, p. 207), is often characterized as relatively cheap and risk free when compared to individual learning (Hoppitt & Laland, 2013). Accordingly, social learning is an adaptive way to gain information about the environment, explaining why it is taxonomically widespread, having been found in mammals, birds and insects, and across a variety of behavioral domains, including skills, calls, predation, mate choice, and resource use (Hoppitt & Laland, 2013). Different types of social learning have been described in terms of what information an individual attends to and processes when learning from others. (e.g., Galef, 1988; Heyes et al., 1994; Hoppitt & Laland, 2013; Whiten & Ham, 1992). There is consensus on their basic categorization, which vary from an inadvertent process, such as when an individual's attention is drawn to a new resource by another individual "going about its business" after which it learns for itself (asocially), to active teaching of skills by experienced individuals to naïve ones.

Social learning is often contrasted with asocial (or individual) learning and arguments abound as to whether there is anything different or special about social, compared with asocial learning, and whether social learning can be adequately explained in conditioning terms (see Kendal et al., 2018). Social learning abilities have been found in solitary species such as the common octopus and red-footed tortoise (Fiorito & Scotto, 1992; Wilkinson et al., 2010), which might not be expected if social learning evolved independently of asocial learning and in response to the selection pressures of social living. However, it is unrealistic to assume that solitary species never interact with conspecifics or heterospecifics, thus social learning remains useful to them (Kendal et al., 2018). Moreover, one popular argument (Heyes, 2012) is that, at the cognitive level, all that is "social about social learning" is the biasing or tuning of input mechanisms (perception, attention, and motivation) toward other agents, as the actual long-term encoding of information is mediated by general learning mechanisms. In Section 14.2, I provide an alternative, and more in-depth, discussion of the biological basis of social learning.

Where social information transmission is sufficient to propagate the diffusion of novel behavior patterns through populations, it may result in distinct behavioral traditions between different populations of the same species. Such traditions, whether in humans or nonhuman species, can be described as "culture" (Laland & Janik, 2006; see Laland, Oudman, and Toyokawa, Chapter 15). In this context, the use of the term "culture" indicates that the behavior concerned has been socially learned. Whether the species has a repertoire of behavioral traditions (Whiten & van Schaik, 2007) and cultural norms or indeed exceptional linguistic or cognitive capabilities (Tylor, 1871) are further features on which some may insist in their definitions of culture. Moreover, social learning is regarded as pivotal to a number of social intelligence hypotheses, which maintain that the evolution of high intelligence or large brains was driven by a capacity for social learning and culture. Explaining the extent of continuity of culture between humans and nonhumans is a key aim of many researchers. Species differences in the types of social learning processes and presence of biases in social learning often feature in these explanations. I will now consider key social learning processes before discussing cultural transmission biases (i.e., social learning strategies, or SLSs) in more depth.

14.1 SOCIAL LEARNING PROCESSES

Although social learning, as an umbrella term, may include active teaching (see Hoppitt & Laland, 2008) or explicit communication, researchers of nonhumans mean no more by the term than the acquisition of information by "observers" from other individuals, called "demonstrators," who inadvertently emit information when going about their business. The simplest social learning processes do not affect the form of a learned behavior, influencing only *when* animals perform it. *Social facilitation* occurs when a conspecific's presence increases the likelihood that an individual performs an action (e.g., bird song: Jesse & Riebel, 2012), whether or not the conspecific is performing that action (Hoppitt & Laland, 2013). Similarly, we see *response facilitation* when a conspecific's behavior (e.g., placing a blade of grass in the ear in chimpanzees: van Leeuwen et al., 2014) triggers performance of the behavior in others that already had the behavior in their repertoire (Byrne, 1994).

Animals may also learn the form of a behavior asocially after their attention is drawn to a particular location (*local enhancement*, Spence, 1937) or stimulus (*stimulus enhancement*, Thorpe, 1956) by another individual's behavior. Wild British blue tits and great tits (*Paridae*) learned to peck open milk bottles to drink the cream (Hinde & Fisher, 1951) because the by-products (open tops) of feeding birds' behavior attracted their attention to milk bottles (Sherry & Galef, 1990). Likewise, due to a shoaling tendency in fish, knowledgeable guppies may lead naïve individuals to novel resource locations (Laland & Williams, 1997). "Observational conditioning" occurs when the observer learns under what circumstances a specific behavioral response should occur. For example, infant rhesus macaques learn to fear and avoid snakes through observations of adults behaving fearfully when exposed to snakes (Mineka & Cook, 1988).

Observational learning occurs when an observer learns a relationship between a behavior and its outcome. *Imitation* is within this class of social learning processes and occurs when "B learns from A some part of the form of a behavior" (Whiten & Ham, 1992, p. 247). Actions are not learned by trial-and-error (asocial) learning but by recreating them after observing a demonstrator perform the behavior. The "two-action method" (Dawson & Foss, 1965) is widely used to infer imitation. For example, a puzzle box that can be solved in two ways (e.g., "lift" or "poke," Whiten et al., 2005) to gain a food reward, is given to two groups of animals (e.g., chimpanzees), each seeded with a demonstrator trained to use only one method. Imitation may be claimed when naïve individuals within the group are more likely to adopt the method they had witnessed than the alternative. Imitation is, however, the most contentious of all of the social learning processes with researchers calling for various additional delineations to the definition (see Hoppitt & Laland, 2008, 2013, for details). Likewise, there are various forms of *emulation* (Byrne, 2002), whereby individuals copy the results of a demonstrator's behavior rather than the actions themselves (see Hoppitt & Laland, 2008). Famously, chimpanzees (unlike children) parse out causally irrelevant actions produced by a demonstrator to retrieve a reward when given an opportunity to attempt a puzzle box themselves (Horner & Whiten, 2005).

Key in the many delineations for both imitation and emulation is the question of the observer's intentionality. Although the role of intentional action is disputed, social learning is inextricably linked to other factors believed pivotal in the evolution of humanity's sociocognitive niche (Whiten & Erdal, 2012). In the cultural niche theory of human evolution (Boyd et al., 2011), imitation and teaching are vital in promoting the high-fidelity transmission deemed necessary for cumulative culture. Note that *teaching* is the only non-inadvertent social learning process, whereby the demonstrator intentionally conveys information to the observer to hasten its learning (Hoppitt & Laland, 2008). The cumulative cultural ability to generate complex traits by building upon existing behavior patterns, generation after generation, is widely thought to enable the extraordinary achievements of humans (Boyd & Richerson, 1985; Galef, 1992; Tomasello, 1994). Accordingly, a major unanswered question in the social learning field is why nonhumans do not have, or have impoverished forms of, cumulative culture (Dean et al., 2014). One of many explanations (see Dean et al., 2012) is differential prevalence of social learning strategies across species, a topic I turn to next.

14.2 SOCIAL LEARNING STRATEGIES

Although social learning is intuitively useful, researchers from several fields have, over the last 30 years, increasingly recognized that it is not inherently adaptive. Individuals certainly can gain fitness benefits by learning from others as they may acquire adaptive information, yet avoid costs associated with the acquisition of asocial information, such as time or energy loss, opportunity costs, and predation. However, theoretical (Boyd & Richerson, 1985; Rendell et al., 2011) and empirical (Avarguès-Weber et al., 2018; Rieucau & Giraldeau, 2011) research indicates that social information use does not guarantee success. Theoretical models predict that social learning will not be employed in an indiscriminate manner (Boyd & Richerson, 1985; Laland, 2004). Instead, heuristics, or *social learning strategies* (also termed "transmission biases") should bias individuals to copy particular behaviors ("what" strategies), performed by specific others ("who" strategies), under suitable circumstances ("when" strategies). However, individuals need not be consciously aware of following a strategy, and the underlying neural mechanisms are, as yet, unknown (Kendal et al., 2018). Moreover, an understanding of the extent to which social learning strategies are products of evolution and/or learning requires detailed experimentation (Heyes & Pearce, 2015; Morgan et al., 2011) and increased interdisciplinary work capable of integrating mechanism and function (see Kendal et al., 2018).

Theoretical analyses have explored the circumstances under which natural selection will favor reliance on social learning, as opposed to asocial learning (see Dunlap and Dexheimer, Chapter 4) or evolved nonlearned behavior (see Laland et al., 1996, for an overview). A consensus has been reached that the issue hangs, in part, on patterns of variability in the environment. In an environment that is changing comparatively slowly or that exhibits relatively little spatial heterogeneity in resources, populations are able to evolve appropriate behavior patterns through natural selection, and learning is of little adaptive value. By contrast, in rapidly changing or highly variable environments asocial learning pays. Here, natural selection cannot track environmental fluctuations quickly enough, while social learning is unreliable because it may lead individuals to acquire outdated or locally inappropriate behaviors. Intermediate rates of change and patterns of spatial heterogeneity favor social learning, and within this window vertical transmission of information (social learning by offspring from parents) is thought to be an adaptation to slower rates of change than horizontal transmission (social learning among unrelated individuals of the same age cohort).

EVIDENCE FOR SOCIAL LEARNING STRATEGIES

There is now evidence for various social learning strategies that shape when, what, and whom to copy (Table 14.1). What follows is a brief, nonexhaustive, review.

TABLE 14.1. *The classification scheme of cognitive heuristics or "rules of thumb" known variously as social learning strategies or transmission biases in the social learning field*

The examples given all have empirical support as either discussed in this chapter or cited in Rendell et al. (2011) and Kendal et al. (2018). The shaded portions of the table indicate the social learning strategies that I focus upon in this chapter.

Transmission bias	Unbiased (random)	Context dependent (indirect)			Content dependent (direct)	Guided variation
		"When" State based	*"Who"* Frequency dependent	*"Who"* Model based	*"What"* (most accurate)	
Strategy type						
Examples	"copy friends"	"copy if uncertain"	"copy the majority"	"copy males"	"copy if better" (payoff bias)	Trial-and-error learning combined with unbiased transmission
	"copy kin"	"copy if hungry"	"copy rare behavior"	"copy dominants"	Bias for social information	
		"copy if low-ranking"	"copy variants increasing in frequency"	"copy adults"	Bias for emotional information	
		"copy if pregnant"		"copy prestigious"		

"WHEN" STRATEGIES (STATE-BASED BIASES)

Individuals should use social information when uncertain, because they possess no relevant prior information or because their personal information is outdated or unreliable (Boyd & Richerson, 1985) or because the accumulated knowledge of conspecifics is more reliable (Rieucau & Giraldeau, 2011). Across multiple taxa, a lack of personal information increases reliance on social learning (e.g., fish: Kendal et al., 2004; chimpanzees: Kendal et al., 2015; ants: Stroeymert et al., 2017; humans: Wood et al., 2013). Stickleback fish are more likely to use social information pertaining to foraging when their personal information is outdated or unreliable (van Bergen et al., 2004). Likewise, adult humans use social information when lacking reliable personal knowledge (Toelch et al., 2014) or confidence, and this is an adaptive strategy in enhancing task success (Morgan et al., 2011). The reverse can also be the case of course; individuals may innovate more when social demonstrations are unreliable (e.g., children: Carr et al., 2015).

Reliance on cheap, but less accurate, social information should increase as the costs associated with asocially acquiring accurate information increase (Boyd & Richerson, 1985; Feldman et al., 1996). Indeed, evidence from multiple taxa indicates that individuals use social information more as task difficulty (and associated energetic or opportunity costs of solving the task asocially) increases (e.g., humans: Morgan et al., 2011; bees: Baracchi et al., 2017; fish: Laland et al., 2011; monkeys: Kendal et al., 2009a). Likewise, individuals are more likely to collect social information whenever learning for themselves exposes them to predation risk (e.g., minnows: Webster & Laland, 2008; guppies: Kendal et al., 2004; but see Galef & Yarkovsky, 2009).

Other state-based biases of the learner, such as age, social rank, and reproductive state (Webster & Laland, 2011), also influence the use of social information. For example, juvenile primates pay more attention to others' foraging behavior than do adults (Coelho et al., 2015; Matsuzawa, 1994), and in humans and birds, juveniles socially learn vocalizations (Bolhuis et al., 2010). Likewise, children use social information more than adults (Carr et al., 2015; Flynn et al., 2016), perhaps because it is mostly during childhood that task-relevant knowledge is accumulated. Moreover, lower-ranking blue tits (Aplin et al., 2013) and chimpanzees (Kendal et al., 2015) are more likely to use social information than high-ranking individuals. Early-life stress can also shape social learning strategies in later life (Boogert et al., 2013; Farine et al., 2015). Finally, bumblebees (Jones et al., 2015), bats (Jones et al., 2013), and chimpanzees (Vale et al., 2017) use social information when the payoff of their own current behavior is poor (Schlag, 1998), known as a "copy if dissatisfied" strategy (Laland, 2004).

FREQUENCY-DEPENDENT STRATEGIES (CONTEXT-DEPENDENT BIASES) A "copy the majority" strategy, where the most common behavioral variant in a population is disproportionately adopted, harnesses the collective wisdom of others. There is much theoretical work regarding the circumstances under which individuals are expected to display this conformist bias (Boyd & Richerson, 1985; Efferson et al., 2008; Eriksson et al., 2007), but the evidence is mixed (Efferson et al., 2008; Henrich & Boyd, 1998; Morgan et al., 2011). Conformity has been observed in fruit flies choosing mates (Danchin et al., 2018) and implicated in foraging choices of wild great tits (Aplin et al., 2015, 2017), immigrant chimpanzees (Luncz et al., 2012), and vervet monkeys (van de Waal et al., 2013; but see van Leeuwen et al., 2015, 2016).

A key question of evolutionary relevance is whether the behavior copied is the one actually exhibited by the majority of individuals, or just the behavior observed most frequently by the individual (Aplin et al., 2015; van Leeuwen et al., 2015, 2016). In support of an emphasis on individuals as representing collective wisdom, children and chimpanzees copy the behavior demonstrated by three different individuals over the behavior demonstrated, three times, by one individual (Haun et al., 2012). Yet the likelihood of conforming is culture- (Clegg & Legare, 2016), context- (Toyokawa et al., 2019), and individual-dependent (Efferson et al., 2008). Moreover, conforming is sensitive to whether the demonstrators have obtained their information from independent sources or from each other (Whalen et al., 2017), as well as to the apparent efficacy of the behavior demonstrated by the majority (Evans et al., 2018).

"WHO" STRATEGIES (CONTEXT-DEPENDENT BIASES)

Social learning may be *indirectly* biased, whereby individuals copy any trait displayed by an individual who is, for example, high status, whether or not that trait helped the individual attain high status (Boyd & Richerson, 1985). We see such *model-based biases* in many taxa. Capuchin monkeys preferentially learn from older/higher-ranking over younger/lower-ranking individuals (Coelho et al., 2015), and chimpanzees preferentially observe and copy dominants (Horner & Whiten, 2005; Kendal et al., 2015; but see Watson et al., 2017) as well as apparent task experts (Horner & Whiten, 2005; Wood, 2013). In the wild, vervet monkeys learn from dominant philopatric females, who likely possess more ecologically relevant information, rather than dominant immigrant males (Canteloup et al., 2020; van de Waal et al., 2010); long-tailed macaques preferentially attend to closer, older, and better tool users (Tan et al., 2018); meerkats learn foraging preferences from older individuals (Thornton & Malapert, 2009); and orca preferentially learn from older females (Brent et al., 2015).

In humans, children tend to copy high-status (older, popular, socially dominant) individuals (Flynn & Whiten, 2012), and copy the most "prestigious" (or most attended to) individual of two unfamiliar adults (Chudek et al., 2012). Moreover, they copy adults over their same-age peers, even when the peer professes greater task-relevant knowledge than the adult (Wood et al., 2012). Adults also display prestige bias: Fijian villagers trust the advice of a successful yam grower with regard to use of medicinal plants, as success at the latter is difficult to determine (Henrich & Broesch, 2011). The use of celebrities in marketing campaigns clearly taps into our prestige bias. Although model-based biases may be prone to error, such heuristics generally lead to the copying of successful individuals (those reaching older ages, higher dominance rank, or, in humans, higher social status), who presumably display behavioral traits worth adopting.

"WHAT" STRATEGIES (CONTENT-DEPENDENT BIASES)

These strategies are considered "direct" as *what* is learned is influenced by the observer's direct assessment of a displayed trait's value. This assessment can be based on the nature of the information itself, or its relative/perceived effectiveness. In the former case, humans express a preference for social content (e.g., gossip), emotional content (e.g., disgust), threat or survival content, and minimally counterintuitive content (e.g., ghosts) when transmitting stories, urban legends, or "fake news" (Acerbi, 2019; Mesoudi et al., 2006, Stubbersfield et al., 2015; Vosoughi et al., 2018). Such preferences are sometimes referred to as "cognitive attractors" particularly in the field of cultural attraction (Sperber & Hirschfeld, 2004). There is comparatively little evidence of these types of attractor biases in nonhumans, although we know that socially learned antipredator behavior is more likely when fear-relevant rather than fear-irrelevant stimuli are paired with the observation of conspecific fear responses (Griffin, 2004).

Another type of "what" social learning strategy or content bias constitutes an assessment of payoffs associated with a behavioral trait (Schlag, 1998), for example, the richness of a food resource acquired with a foraging strategy, and has been observed to influence transmission in both humans and nonhumans. Payoff biases are arguably the most accurate, yet most cognitively difficult, social learning strategies an individual can implement. Accordingly, studies have reported that payoff bias is adaptive and used in preference to other social learning strategies in humans (McElreath et al., 2008; Mesoudi, 2011; Watson et al., 2021) and chimpanzees (van Leeuwen et al., 2013). An ability to copy the highest payoff foraging behavior has also been reported recently in wild capuchin monkeys (Barrett et al., 2017) and male vervet monkeys (Bono et al., 2018), in the latter case overriding the previously mentioned bias to copy the dominant (philopatric) female. There is also empirical evidence of a "copy if better"-type strategy where the behavioral payoffs of others are compared to your own; this strategy could be important for cumulative cultural evolution. A version of this strategy has been reported in captive sticklebacks (Kendal et al., 2009b) and young children (Vale et al., 2017). It has also been investigated in chimpanzees (van Leeuwen & Call, 2017; Vale et al., 2017), where it seems individuals do not compare their behavior to that of others, but rely on an assessment of their own behavioral payoff only (a "when" strategy of "copy if dissatisfied").

INSIGHTS REGARDING THE EVOLUTION AND USE OF SLSS

Several key insights have resulted from the increasing body of research regarding SLSs (Kendal et al., 2018). Two of these insights are of particular importance. First is the finding of individual- and population-level flexibility in the use of SLSs. Several recent studies have shown that individuals from the same population can adopt different strategies depending on subtle differences in context (Wood et al., 2013), developmental experience (Farine et al., 2015; Leris & Reader, 2016), or other individual-level variation (reviewed by Mesoudi et al., 2016). Although flexible use of SLSs is not evidence that a SLS has not evolved (Call, 2017), they are best regarded as biases shaping behavior, not rigid rules blindly applied by all individuals or in all contexts (Kendal et al., 2018).

Second, multiple social learning strategies may be deployed simultaneously in any one learning event (e.g., chimpanzees: Kendal et al., 2015; vervet monkeys: Bono et al., 2018; sticklebacks: Laland et al., 2011; humans: Morgan et al., 2011). As is the case for social learning processes, SLSs are likely to operate in concert to bias learning, rather than merging into fine-grained decision rules (Hoppitt & Laland, 2013). More systematic research is required to identify any phylogenetic patterns in the use of SLSs that may explain, for example, the taxonomic distribution of cumulative culture (Vale et al., 2017). In this endeavor, we should note that multiple SLSs can generate the same population-level pattern of behavior, and a particular SLS can generate different population-level outcomes (van Leeuwen et al., 2015; Morgan et al., 2011). Thus, population-level patterns do not provide a robust signature of particular cognitive heuristics or SLSs. Moreover, consideration of the temporal phase of a tradition's establishment is key, as the utility of different SLSs will change over time. Soon after the first innovation, individuals will use more accurate but costly SLSs (e.g., payoff bias) as skilled practitioners of the establishing tradition will be few. Once the innovation has become an established tradition, individuals may use less accurate but easily implemented SLSs (e.g., model-based biases) as the behavior is more prevalent, for example, being displayed by all adults (Coelho et al., 2015).

INSIGHTS REGARDING THE MECHANISMS UNDERLYING SLSS

The research reviewed here assumes that the underlying mechanisms do not greatly constrain the adaptive SLSs that evolve (Fawcett et al., 2013). This assumption has enabled theoretical work (e.g., Enquist et al., 2007; Kendal et al., 2009c; Rendell et al., 2010; Schlag, 1998) to stimulate and guide empirical research (e.g., Mesoudi, 2011; Rendell et al., 2011; Vale et al., 2017). This "blackboxing" (Heyes, 2016a) has, however, led to much debate regarding whether social learning strategies are domain-specific or domain-general mechanisms, and whether they are an alternative to associative learning mechanisms (Heyes & Pearce, 2015; see Kendal et al., 2018, for a review).

The SLSs field has been explicit since its inception in its lack of commitment to mechanism and to conscious decision-making (Laland, 2004). Accordingly, the use of the term strategy (as indicated in this chapter) does not imply domain specificity, or that strategies are unlearned or under tight genetic-control. Researchers of social learning strategies view them as products of cultural and/or biological evolution. Nevertheless, recent research may provide evidence of evolved aspects of SLSs. For example, children, chimpanzees, and gorillas showed enhanced learning from animate (versus inanimate) models, which is not merely due to changes in input mechanisms such as reduced attention (Heyes, 2012), but to deeper encoding and enhanced memory of socially mediated events (Howard et al., 2017). The authors have suggested relatability of goal-directed actions between observer and model as an explanation, and such may mediate evolved enhancements in memory for, and thus replication of, the actions of specific models, represented in specific social learning strategies.

Although domain-general associative learning processes can often explain the findings of many social learning experiments (Heyes, 2012; Heyes & Pearce, 2015), it is worth noting that social learning strategies and associative learning theories are not alternatives (Kendal et al., 2018). This is because SLSs are explicitly a functional account of behavior and agnostic regarding mechanism, although researchers of SLSs do routinely employ asocial learning controls and consider associative learning explanations (Coolen et al., 2003; Jones et al., 2013; Kendal et al., 2004). However, we ought to consider that the extensive evidence for neurological and genetic differences between chimpanzees and humans (e.g., Boyd et al., 2015; Laland, 2017) make it unlikely that attentional or motivational variation, aligned with general associative learning processes, could fully explain the differences in social learning between chimpanzees and humans (Kendal et al., 2018). Further research is also required to determine whether such species differences in social learning represent the effect of differing computational power aligned with general underlying learning mechanisms.

In fact, neuroscience research is revealing that social interactions are heavily embedded in human and nonhuman brains. For instance, a brain region known as the ACCg, a subregion of the anterior cingulate cortex lying in the gyrus, appears to be specialized for the processing of social information in humans and nonhumans, as evidenced by neurophysiology, neuroimaging, lesion studies, and studies of autistic individuals (Apps et al., 2016; Hill et al., 2016).

In combination with other brain regions that signal in a more egocentric frame, this allocentrically signaling brain region (ACCg) may enable integration of information regarding the actions of oneself and those of others (Apps & Sallet, 2017), which could potentially enable the payoff bias of "copy if better." Moreover, there is indicative evidence that frequency-dependent biases may be facilitated by specific brain regions (anterior insula, rostral cingulate zone, and ventral striatum) whose activity increases in response to consensus or lack of consensus between demonstrators which predicts changes in behavior (Morgan & Laland, 2012). Such studies and others in the area of evolutionary neuroscience (reviewed in Kendal et al., 2018) highlight the possibility for some social learning processes and SLSs to derive from domain-specific capacities.

SLSs provide an exciting avenue for investigation of the complementarity between functional and mechanistic perspectives. Such studies will be fruitful in perhaps identifying distinctive patterns of neural connectivity associated with different SLSs. Moreover, such studies may assist developmental and comparative psychologists as well as cognitive neuroscientists in understanding population- or individual-level differences in cognitive development or neural connectivity in terms of alternative SLS deployment. Likewise, the detailed functional questions brains have evolved to deal with, as exemplified by SLSs, may explain differences in brain architecture between species. Although consideration that any apparent domain-specific capacities necessarily involve brain regions that participate in a variety of other functions will be required.

14.3 CONCLUSION

SLSs influence when individuals learn from others, as opposed to innovating, as well as what they socially learn and whom they learn from. Such strategies, though not necessarily consciously applied, enable individuals to acquire useful skills, or information, with minimal opportunity or predation costs. The many different SLSs can be classified into those that are dependent upon the context in which individuals find themselves – including their own state, the frequency of traits they observe around them, and the characteristics of models, or demonstrators, displaying those traits – and the content of the trait in question. The strategies differ in the ease with which they may be applied and their likely accuracy in enabling the observer to acquire the "best" information. Recent research has highlighted that (i) SLS use is widespread in the animal kingdom; (ii) SLSs are often used in combination; and (iii) a SLS does not have a particular population-level signal. These considerations will influence research regarding the role of SLSs in the evolution of social intelligence or cumulative culture, for example. Finally, although the precise mechanisms underlying SLSs remain unknown, recent findings highlight that SLSs may involve both domain-general and domain-specific capacities. Accordingly, the SLSs field is ripe for a combined functional and mechanistic investigation of social learning. Such may be particularly interesting regarding the utility of metacognitive SLSs in cumulative cultural evolution (Dunstone & Caldwell, 2018; Heyes, 2016b).

REFERENCES

Acerbi, A. (2019). Cognitive attraction and online misinformation. *Palgrave Communications, 5*, 15. https://doi.org/10.1057/s41599-019-0224-y

Aplin, L. M., Farine, D. R., Moran-Ferron, J., Cockburn, A., Thornton, A., & Sheldon, B. (2015). Experimentally induced innovations lead to persistent culture via conformity in wild birds. *Nature, 518*, 538–541. https://doi.org/10.1038/nature13998

Aplin, L. M. Sheldon, B. C., & McElreath, R. (2017). Conformity does not perpetuate suboptimal traditions in a wild population of songbirds. *Proceedings of the National Academy of Sciences, 114*, 7830–7837. https://doi.org/10.1073/pnas.1621067114

Aplin, L.M., Sheldon, B., & Morand-Ferron, J. (2013). Milk-bottles revisited: Social learning and individual variation in the blue tit, *Cyanistes caeruleus. Animal Behaviour, 85*, 1225–1232. https://doi.org/10.1016/j.anbehav.2013.03.009

Apps, M. A. J., Rushworth, M. F. S., & Chang, S. W. C. (2016). The anterior cingulate gyrus and social cognition: Tracking the motivation of others. *Neuron, 90*, 692–707. https://doi.org/10.1016/j.neuron.2016.04.018

Apps, M. A. J., & Sallet, J. (2017). Social learning in the medial prefrontal cortex. *Trends in Cognitive Sciences, 21*, 151–152. https://doi.org/10.1016/j.tics.2017.01.008

Avarguès-Weber, A., Lachlan, R., & Chittka, L., (2018). Bumblebee social learning can lead to suboptimal foraging choices. *Animal Behaviour, 135*, 209–214. https://doi.org/10.1016/j.anbehav.2017.11.022

Baracchi, D., Vasas, V., Iqbal, S. J., & Alem, S. (2017). Foraging bumblebees use social cues more when the task is difficult. *Behavioural Ecology, 29*, 186–192. https://doi.org/10.1093/beheco/arx143

Barrett, B. J., McElreath, R. L., & Perry, S. (2017). Payoff-biased social learning underlies the diffusion of novel extractive foraging traditions in a wild primate. *Proceedings of the Royal Society B, Biological Sciences, 284*, 20170358. https://doi.org/10.1098/rspb.2017.0358

van Bergen, Y., Coolen, I., & Laland, K.N. (2004). Nine-spined sticklebacks exploit the most reliable source when public and private information conflict. *Proceedings of the Royal Society B, Biological Sciences, 271*, 957–962. https://doi.org/10.1098/rspb.2004.2684

Bolhuis, J. J., Okanoya, K., & Scharff, C. (2010). Twitter evolution: converging mechanisms in bird song and human speech. *Nature Reviews Neuroscience, 11*, 747–759. https://doi.org/10.1038/nrn2931

Bono, A. E. J., Whiten, A., van Schaik, C., Krützen, M., Eichenberger, F., Schnider, A., & van de Waal, E. (2018). Payoff- and sex-biased social learning interact in a wild primate population. *Current Biology, 2*, 2800–2805. https://doi.org/10.1016/j.cub.2018.06.015

Boogert, N. J., Zimmer, C., & Spencer, K. A. (2013). Pre- and post-natal stress have opposing effects on social information use. *Biology Letters, 9*, 20121088. https://doi.org/10.1098/rsbl.2012.1088

Boyd, J. L., Skove, S. L., Rouanet, J. P., Pilaz, L.-J., Bepler, T., Gordân, R., Wray, G. A., & Silver, D. L. (2015) Human-chimpanzee differences in a FZD8 enhancer alter cell-cycle dynamics in the developing neocortex. *Current Biology, 25*, 772–779. https://doi.org/10.1016/j.cub.2015.01.041

Boyd, R., & Richerson, P. J. (1985). *Culture and the evolutionary process*. University of Chicago Press.

Boyd, R., Richerson, P. J., & Henrich, J. (2011). The cultural niche: Why social learning is essential for human adaptation. *Proceedings of the National Academy of Sciences, 108,* 10918–10925. https://doi.org/10.1073/pnas.1100290108

Brent, L. J. N., Franks, D. W., Foster, E. A., Balcomb, K. C., Cant, M. A., & Croft, D. P. (2015). Ecological knowledge, leadership, and the evolution of menopause in killer whales. *Current Biology, 25,* 746–750. https://doi.org/10.1016/j.cub.2015.01.037

Byrne, R. (1994). The evolution of intelligence. In P. J. B. Slater & T. R. Halliday (Eds.), *Behaviour and evolution* (pp. 223–265). Cambridge University Press.

Byrne, R. W. (2002). Imitation of novel complex actions: What does the evidence from animals mean? *Advances in the Study of Behavior, 31,* 77–105. https://doi.org/10.1016/S0065-3454(02)80006-7

Call, J. (2017). *APA handbook of comparative psychology.* The American Psychological Association.

Canteloup, C., Hoppitt, W., & van de Waal, E. (2020). Wild primates copy higher ranked individuals in a social transmission experiment. *Nature Communications, 11,* 459. https://doi.org/10.1038/s41467-019-14209-8

Carr, K., Kendal, R. L., & Flynn, E. G. (2015). Imitate or innovate? Children's innovation is influenced by the efficacy of observed behaviour. *Cognition, 142,* 322–332. https://doi.org/10.1016/j.cognition.2015.05.005

Chudek, M., Heller, S., Birch, S., & Henrich, J. (2012). Prestige-biased cultural learning: Bystander's differential attention to potential models influences children's learning. *Evolution & Human Behavior, 33,* 46–56. https://doi.org/10.1016/j.evolhumbehav.2011.05.005

Clegg, J. M., & Legare, C. H. (2016). A cross-cultural comparison of children's imitative flexibility. *Developmental Psychology, 52,* 1435–1444. https://psycnet.apa.org/doi/10.1037/dev0000131

Coelho, C. G., Falotico, T., Izar, P., Mannu, M., Resende, B. D., Siqueira, J. O., & Ottoni, E. B. (2015). Social learning strategies for nut-cracking by tufted capuchin monkeys (*Sapajus* spp.). *Animal Cognition, 18,* 911–919. https://doi.org/10.1007/s10071-015-0861-5

Coolen, I., van Bergen, Y., Day, R. L., & Laland, K. N. (2003). Species differences in adaptive use of public information in sticklebacks. *Proceedings of the Royal Society B, Biological Sciences, 270,* 2413–2419. https://doi.org/10.1098/rspb.2003.2525

Danchin, E., Nobel, S., Pocheville, A., Dagaeff, A.-C., Demay, L., Alphand, M., Ranty-Roby, S., van Renssen, L., Monier, M., Gazagne, E., Allain, M., & Isabel, G. (2018). Cultural flies: Conformist social learning in fruitflies predicts long-lasting mate-choice traditions. *Science, 362,* 1025–1030. https://doi.org/10.1126/science.aat1590

Dawson, B. V., & Foss, B. M. (1965). Observational learning in budgerigars. *Animal Behavior, 13*(4), 470–474. https://psycnet.apa.org/doi/10.1016/0003-3472(65)90108-9

Dean, L., Kendal, R. L., Schapiro, S., Lambeth, S., Thierry, B., & Laland, K. N. (2012). Identification of the social and cognitive processes underlying human cumulative culture. *Science, 335,* 1114–118. https://doi/doi/10.1126/science.1213969

Dean, L. G., Vale, G. L., Laland, K. N., Flynn, E., & Kendal, R. L. (2014). Human cumulative culture: A comparative perspective. *Biological Reviews, 89*(2), 284–301. https://doi.org/10.1111/brv.12053

Dunstone, J., & Caldwell, C. A. (2018). Cumulative culture and explicit metacognition: A review of theories, evidence and key predictions. *Palgrave Communications, 4*(1), 1–11. https://doi.org/10.1057/s41599-018-0200-y

Efferson, C., Lalive, R., Richerson, P. J., McElreath, R., & Lubell, M. (2008). Conformists and mavericks: The empirics of frequency-dependent cultural transmission. *Evolution & Human Behavior 29,* 56–64. https://doi.org/10.1016/j.evolhumbehav.2007.08.003

Enquist, M., Eriksson, K., & Ghirlanda, S. (2007). Critical social learning: A solution to Roger's paradox of non-adaptive culture. *American Anthropologist, 109,* 727–734. https://doi.org/10.1525/aa.2007.109.4.727

Eriksson, K., Enquist, M., & Ghirlanda, S. (2007). Critical points in current theory of conformist social learning. *Journal of Evolutionary Psychology*, 5, 67–87. https://doi .org/10.1556/jep.2007.1009

Evans, C., Laland, K. N., Carpenter, M., & Kendal, R. L. (2018). Selective copying of the majority suggests children are broadly "optimal-" rather than "over-" imitators. *Developmental Science*, 21, e12637. https://doi.org/10.1111/desc.12637

Farine, D. R., Spencer, K. A., & Boogert, N. J. (2015). Early-life stress triggers juvenile zebra finches to switch social learning strategies. *Current Biology*, 25, 2184–2188. https://doi .org/10.1016/j.cub.2015.06.071

Fawcett, T. W., Hamblin, S., & Giraldeau, L.-A. (2013). Exposing the behavioral gambit: The evolution of learning and decision rules. *Behavioral Ecology*, 24, 2–11. https://doi.org/10 .1093/beheco/ars085

Feldman, M. W., Aoki, K., & Kumm, J. (1996). Individual versus social learning: Evolutionary analysis in a fluctuating environment. *Anthropological Science*, 104, 209–231. https://doi .org/10.1537/ase.104.209

Fiorito, G., & Scotto, P. (1992). Observational learning in *Octopus vulgaris*. *Science*, 256, 545–547. https://doi.org/10.1126/science.256.5056.545

Flynn, E. G., Turner, C., & Giraldeau, L.-A. (2016). Selectivity in social and asocial learning: Investigating the prevalence, effect and development of young children's learning preferences. *Philosophical Transactions of the Royal Society B*, 371, 20150189. https://doi.org/10 .1098/rstb.2015.0189

Flynn, E., & Whiten, A. (2012). Experimental "microcultures" in young children: Identifying biographic, cognitive, and social predictors of information transmission. *Child Development*, 83, 911–925. https://doi.org/10.1111/j.1467-8624.2012.01747.x

Galef, B. G. (1988). Imitation in animals: History, definition, and interpretation of the data from the laboratory. In T. R. Zentall & B. G. Galef (Eds.), *Social learning: Psychological and biological perspectives* (pp. 3–27). Lawrence Elbaum Associates.

(1992). The question of animal culture. *Human Nature*, 3, 157–178. https://doi.org/10 .1007/BF02692251

Galef, B. G. & Yarkovsky, N. (2009). Further studies of reliance on socially acquired information when foraging in potentially risky situations. *Animal Behaviour*, 77, 1329–1335. https://doi.org/10.1016/j.anbehav.2009.01.038

Griffin, A. (2004). Social learning about predators: a review and prospectus. *Learning & Behavior*, 32, 131–140. https://doi.org/10.3758/BF03196014

Haun, D. B. M., Rekers, Y., & Tomasello, M. (2012). Majority-biased transmission in chimpanzees and human children, but not orangutans. *Current Biology*, 22, 727–731. https:// doi.org/10.1016/j.cub.2012.03.006

Henrich, J., & Boyd, R. (1998). The evolution of conformist transmission and the emergence of between-group differences. *Evolution & Human Behavior*, 19(4), 215–241. https://doi .org/10.1016/S1090-5138(98)00018-X

Henrich, J., & Broesch, J. (2011). On the nature of cultural transmission networks: Evidence from Fijian villages for adaptive learning biases. *Philosophical Transactions of the Royal Society, B*, 366, 1139–1148. https://doi.org/10.1098/rstb.2010.0323

Heyes, C. M. (2012). What's social about social learning? *Journal of Comparative Psychology*, 126, 193–202. https://psycnet.apa.org/doi/10.1037/a0025180

(2016a). Blackboxing: Social learning strategies and cultural evolution. *Philosophical Transactions of the Royal Society, B*, 371, 20150369. https://doi.org/10.1098/rstb.2015.0369

(2016b). Who knows? Metacognitive social learning strategies. *Trends in Cognitive Sciences*, 20(3), 204–213. https://doi.org/10.1016/j.tics.2015.12.007

Heyes, C. M., Jaldow, E., & Dawson, G. R. (1994). Imitation in rats: Conditions of occurrence in a bidirectional control procedure. *Learning & Motivation* 25, 276–287. https://doi.org/ 10.1016/0376-6357(94)90074-4

Heyes, C. M., & Pearce, J. M. (2015). Not-so-social learning strategies. *Proceedings of the Royal Society B, Biological Sciences*, 282, 20141709. https://doi.org/10.1098/rspb.2014.1709

Hill, M. R., Boorman, E. D., & Itzhak, F. (2016). Observational learning computations in neurons of the human anterior cingulate cortex. *Nature Communications, 7,* 12722. https://doi.org/10.1038/ncomms12722

Hinde, R. A., & Fisher, J. (1951). Further observations on the opening of milk bottles by birds. *British Birds, 44,* 393–396.

Hoppitt, W., & Laland, K. N. (2008). Social processes influencing learning in animals: A review of the evidence. *Advances in the Study of Behavior, 38,* 105–166. https://doi.org/10.1016/S0065-3454(08)00003-X

(2013). *Social learning mechanisms: An introduction to mechanisms, methods and models.* Princeton University Press.

Horner, V., & Whiten, A. (2005). Causal knowledge and imitation/emulation switching in chimpanzees (*Pan troglodytes*) and children (*Homo sapiens*). *Animal Cognition, 8,* 164–181. https://doi.org/10.1007/s10071-004-0239-6

Howard, L. H., Wagner, K. E., Woodward, A. L., Ross, S. R., & Hopper, L. M. (2017). Social models enhance apes' memory for novel events. *Scientific Reports, 7,* 40926. https://doi.org/10.1038/srep40926

Jesse, F., & Riebel, K. (2012). Social facilitation of male song by male and female conspecifics in the zebra finch, *Taeniopygia guttata. Behavioural Processes 91*(3), 262–266. https://doi.org/10.1016/j.beproc.2012.09.006

Jones, P. L., Ryan, M. J., & Chittka, L. (2015). The influence of past experience with flower reward quality on social learning in bumblebees. *Animal Behaviour, 101,* 11–18. https://doi.org/10.1016/j.anbehav.2014.12.016

Jones, P. L., Ryan, M. J., Flores, V., & Page, R. A. (2013). When to approach novel prey cues? Social learning strategies in frog-eating bats. *Proceedings of the Royal Society B, Biological Sciences, 280,* 20132330. https://doi.org/10.1098/rspb.2013.2330

Kendal, R. L., Coolen, I., & Laland, K. N. (2004). The role of conformity in foraging when personal and social information conflict. *Behavioral Ecology, 15,* 269–277. https://doi.org/10.1093/beheco/arh008

Kendal, R. L., Kendal, J. R., Hoppitt, W., & Laland, K. N. (2009a). Identifying social learning in animal populations: A new 'option-bias' method. *PLoS ONE, 4,* e6541. https://doi.org/10.1371/journal.pone.0006541

Kendal, J. R., Rendell, L., Pike, T. W., & Laland, K. N. (2009b). Nine-spined sticklebacks deploy a hill-climbing social learning strategy. *Behavioral Ecology, 20*(2), 238–244. https://doi.org/10.1093/beheco/arp016

Kendal, J. R., Giraldeau, L.-A., & Laland, K. N. (2009c). The evolution of social learning rules: Payoff-biased and frequency-dependent biased transmission. *Journal of Theoretical Biology, 260,* 210–219. https://doi.org/10.1016/j.jtbi.2009.05.029

Kendal, R. L., Hopper, L. M., Whiten, A., Brosnan, S. F., Lambeth, S. P., Schapiro, S. J., & Hoppitt, W. (2015). Chimpanzees copy dominant and knowledgeable individuals: Implications for cultural diversity. *Evolution & Human Behavior, 36,* 65–72. https://doi.org/10.1016/j.evolhumbehav.2014.09.002

Kendal, R. L., Boogert, N., Rendell, L., Laland, K. N., Webster, M. & Jones, P. L. (2018). Social learning strategies: Bridge-building between fields. *Trends in Cognitive Sciences, 22*(7), 651–665. https://doi.org/10.1016/j.tics.2018.04.003

Laland, K. N. (2004). Social learning strategies. *Learning & Behavior, 32,* 4–14. https://doi.org/10.3758/BF03196002

(2017). *Darwin's unfinished symphony: How culture made the human mind.* Princeton University Press.

Laland, K. N., Richerson, P. J., and Boyd, R. (1996). Developing a theory of animal social learning. In C. M. Heyes and B. G. Galef, Jr. (Eds.), *Social learning in animals: The roots of culture.* San Diego, CA: Academic Press. https://psycnet.apa.org/doi/10.1016/B978-012273965-1/50008-X

Laland, K. N., & Williams, K. (1997). Shoaling generates social learning of foraging information in guppies. *Animal Behaviour, 53,* 1161–1169. https://doi.org/10.1006/anbe.1996.0318

Laland, K. N., & Janik, V. M. (2006). The animal cultures debate. *Trends in Ecology & Evolution, 21*(10), 542–547. https://doi.org/10.1016/j.tree.2006.06.005

Laland, K. N., Atton, N., & Webster, M. M. (2011). From fish to fashion: Experimental and theoretical insights into the evolution of culture. *Philosophical Transactions of the Royal Society B., 366*, 958–968. https://doi.org/10.1098/rstb.2010.0328

van Leeuwen, E. J. C., Acerbi, A., Kendal, R. L., Tennie, C., & Haun, D. B. M. (2016). A reappreciation of "conformity." *Animal Behaviour, 122*, e5–e10. https://doi.org/10.1016/j.anbehav.2016.09.010

van Leeuwen, E. J. C., and Call, J. (2017). Conservatism and "copy-if-better" in chimpanzees (*Pan troglodytes*). *Animal Cognition, 20*(3), 575–579. https://doi.org/10.1007/s10071-016-1061-7

van Leeuwen, E. J. C., Cronin, K. A., Schütte, S., Call, J., & Haun, D. B. M. (2013). Chimpanzees (*Pan troglodytes*) flexibly adjust their behaviour in order to maximize payoffs, not to conform to majorities. *PLoS ONE, 8*, e80945. https://doi.org/10.1371/journal.pone.0080945

van Leeuwen, E. J. C., Cronin, K. A., & Haun, D. B. (2014). A group-specific arbitrary tradition in chimpanzees (*Pan troglodytes*). *Animal Cognition 17*(6), 1421–1425. https://doi.org/10.1007/s10071-014-0766-8

van Leeuwen, E. J. C., Kendal, R. L., Tennie, C., & Haun, D. B. M. (2015). Conformity and its look-a-likes. *Animal Behaviour, 110*, e1–e4.

Leris, I., & Reader, S. M. (2016). Age and early social environment influence guppy social learning propensities. *Animal Behaviour, 120*, 11–19. https://doi.org/10.1016/j.anbehav.2016.07.012

Luncz, L., Mundry, R., & Boesch, C. (2012). Evidence for cultural differences between neighboring chimpanzee communities. *Current Biology, 22*(10), 922–926. https://doi.org/10.1016/j.cub.2012.03.031

Mesoudi, A. (2011). An experimental comparison of human social learning strategies: Payoff-biased social learning is adaptive but underused. *Evolution & Human Behavior, 32*(5), 334–342. https://doi.org/10.1016/j.evolhumbehav.2010.12.001

Mesoudi, A., Chang, L., Dall, S. R. X., & Thornton, A. (2016). The evolution of individual and cultural variation in social learning. *Trends in Ecology and Evolution, 31*(3), 215–225. https://doi.org/10.1016/j.tree.2015.12.012

Mesoudi, A., Whiten, A., & Dunbar, R. (2006). A bias for social information in human cultural transmission. *British Journal of Psychology, 97*, 405–423. https://doi.org/10.1348/000712605X85871

Matsuzawa, T. (1994). Field experiments on use of stone tools by chimpanzees in the wild. In R. W. Wrangham, W. C. McGrew, F. B. M. de Waal, & P. Heltne (Eds.), *Chimpanzee cultures* (pp. 351–370). Harvard University Press.

McElreath, R., Bell, A. V., Efferson, C., Lubell, M., Richerson, P. J., & Waring, T. M. (2008). Beyond existence and aiming outside the laboratory: Estimating frequency-dependent and pay-off-biased social learning strategies. *Philosophical Transactions of the Royal Society B, 363*, 3515–3528. https://doi.org/10.1098/rstb.2008.0131

Mineka, S., & Cook, M. (1988). Social learning and the acquisition of snake fear in monkeys. In B. G. Galef & T. R. Zentall (Eds.), *Social learning: Psychological and biological perspectives* (pp. 51–73). Lawrence Erlbaum.

Morgan, T. J. H., Rendell, L. E., Ehn, M., Hoppitt, W., & Laland, K. N. (2011). The evolutionary basis of human social learning. *Proceedings of the Royal Society B, Biological Sciences, 279*, 653–662. https://doi.org/10.1098/rspb.2011.1172

Morgan, T. J. H., & Laland, K. N. (2012). The biological bases of conformity. *Frontiers in Neuroscience, 6*, 87. https://doi.org/10.3389/fnins.2012.00087

Rieucau, G., & Giraldeau, L.-A. (2011). Exploring the costs and benefits of social information use: An appraisal of current experimental evidence. *Philosophical Transactions of the Royal Society, B, 366*, 949–957. https://doi.org/10.1098/rstb.2010.0325

Rendell, L., Fogarty, L., & Laland, K. N. (2010). Roger's paradox recast and resolved: Population structure and the evolution of social learning strategies. *Evolution, 64*, 534–548. https://doi.org/10.1111/j.1558-5646.2009.00817.x

Rendell, L., Fogarty, L., Hoppitt, W. J. E., Morgan, T. J. H., Webster, M. M., & Laland, K. N. (2011). Cognitive culture: Theoretical and empirical insights into social learning strategies. *Trends in Cognitive Science, 15*, 68–76. https://doi.org/10.1016/j.tics.2010.12.002

Schlag, K. H. (1998). Why imitate, and if so, how? A bounded rationality approach to multi-armed bandits. *Journal of Economic Theory, 78*, 130–156. https://doi.org/10.1006/jeth.1997.2347

Sherry, D. F., & Galef, B. G. (1990). Social learning without imitation. *Animal Behaviour, 40*, 987–989. https://psycnet.apa.org/doi/10.1016/S0003-3472(05)81004-8

Spence, K. W. (1937). Experimental studies of learning and the higher mental processes in infra-human primates. *Psychological Bulletin, 34*(10), 806. https://psycnet.apa.org/doi/10.1037/h0061498

Sperber, D., & Hirschfeld, L. A. (2004). The cognitive foundations of cultural stability and diversity. *Trends in Cognitive Science 8*(1), 40–46. https://doi.org/10.1016/j.tics.2003.11.002

Stroeymert, N., Giurfa, M., & Franks, N. R. (2017). Information certainty determines social and private information use in ants. *Scientific Reports, 7*, 43607. https://doi.org/10.1038/srep43607

Stubbersfield, J. M., Tehrani, J. J., Flynn, E. G. (2015). Serial killers, spiders and cybersex: Social and survival information bias in the transmission of urban legends. *British Journal of Psychology, 106*, 288–307. https://doi.org/10.1111/bjop.12073

Tan, A. W. Y., Hemelrijk, C. K., Malaivijitnond, S., & Gumert, M. D. (2018). Young macaques (*Macaca fascicularis*) preferentially bias attention towards closer, older, and better tool users. *Animal Cognition, 21*, 551–563. https://doi.org/10.1007/s10071-018-1188-9

Thornton, A., & Malapert, A. (2009). Experimental evidence for social transmission of food acquisition techniques in wild meerkats. *Animal Behaviour, 78*(2), 255–264. https://doi.org/10.1016/j.anbehav.2009.04.021

Thorpe, W. H. (1956). *Learning and instinct in animals*. Methuen & Co., Ltd.

Toelch, U., Bruce, M. J., Newson, L., Richerson, P. J., & Reader, S. M. (2014). Individual consistency and flexibility in human social information use. *Proceedings of the Royal Society B, Biological Sciences, 281*, 20132864. https://doi.org/10.1098/rspb.2013.2864

Tomasello, M. (1994). The question of chimpanzee culture. In R. W. Wrangham, W. C. McGrew, F. B. M. de Waal, & P. Heltne (Eds.), *Chimpanzee cultures* (pp. 301–317). Harvard University Press.

Toyokawa, W., Whalen, A., & Laland, K. N. (2019). Social learning strategies regulate the wisdom and madness of interactive crowds. *Nature Human Behaviour, 3*, 183–193. https://doi.org/10.1038/s41562-018-0518-x

Tylor, E. B. (1871). *Primitive culture: Researches into the development of mythology, philosophy, religion, art and custom*. Murray.

Vale, G. L., Flynn, E. G., Kendal, J. R., Rawlings, B., Hopper, L. M., Schapiro, S. J., Lambeth, S. P., & Kendal, R. L. (2017). Testing differential use of payoff-biased social learning strategies in children and chimpanzees. *Proceedings of the Royal Society B, Biological Sciences, 284*, 1751. https://doi.org/10.1098/rspb.2017.1751

Vosoughi, S., Roy, D., & Aral, S. (2018). The spread of true and false news online. *Science, 359*, 1146–1151. https://doi.org/10.1126/science.aap9559

van de Waal, E., Renevey, N., Favre, C. M., & Bshary, R. (2010). Selective attention to philopatric models causes directed social learning in wild vervet monkeys. *Proceedings of the Royal Society B, Biological Sciences, 277*, 2105–2111. https://doi.org/10.1098/rspb.2009.2260

van de Waal, E., Borgeaud, C., & Whiten, A. (2013). Potent social learning and conformity shape a wild primate's foraging decisions. *Science, 340* (6131), 483–485. https://doi.org/10.1126/science.1232769

Watson, R., Morgan, T., Kendal, R.L., van de Vyver, J., Kendal, J.R. (2021). Social learning strategies and cooperative behaviour: Evidence of payoff bias, but not prestige or conformity, in a social dilemma game. Games, 12, 89. https://doi.org/10.3390/g12040089

Watson, S. K., Reamer, L. A., Mareno, M. C., Vale, G., Harrison, R. A., Lambeth, S. P., & Schapiro, S. J. (2017). Socially transmitted diffusion of a novel behavior from subordinate chimpanzees. *American Journal of Primatology*, 79, e22642. https://doi.org/10.1002/ajp.22642

Webster, M. M., & Laland, K. N. (2008). Social learning strategies and predation risk: minnows copy only when using private information would be costly. *Proceedings of the Royal Society B. Biological Sciences*, 275, 2869–2876. https://doi.org/10.1098/rspb.2008.0817

    (2011). Reproductive state affects reliance on public information in sticklebacks. *Proceedings of the Royal Society B, Biological Sciences*, 278, 619–627. https://doi.org/10.1098/rspb.2010.1562

Whalen, A., Griffiths, T. L., & Buchsbaum, D. (2017). Sensitivity to shared information in social learning. *Cognitive Science*, 42, 168–187. https://doi.org/10.1111/cogs.12485

Whiten, A., & Ham, R. (1992). On the nature and evolution of imitation in the animal kingdom: Reappraisal of a century of research. *Advances in the Study of Behavior*, 21, 239–283.

Whiten, A., & van Schaik, C. P. (2007). The evolution of animal "cultures" and social intelligence. *Philosophical Transactions of the Royal Society B*, 362(1480), 603–620. https://doi.org/10.1098/rstb.2006.1998

Whiten, A., & Erdal, D. (2012). The human sociocognitive niche and its evolutionary origins. *Philosophical Transactions of the Royal Society B.*, 367, 2119–2129. https://doi.org/10.1098/rstb.2012.0114

Whiten, A., Horner, V., & de Waal, F. B. M. (2005). Conformity to cultural norms of tool use in chimpanzees. *Nature*, 437(7059), 737–740. https://doi.org/10.1038/nature04047

Wilkinson, A., Kuenstner, K., Mueller, J., & Huber, L. (2010). Social learning in a non-social reptile (*Geochelone carbonaria*). *Biology Letters*, 6, 614–616. https://doi.org/10.1098/rsbl.2010.0092

Wood, L. A., Kendal, R. L., & Flynn, E. G. (2012). Context-dependent model-based biases in cultural transmission: Children's imitation is affected by model age over model knowledge state. *Evolution & Human Behavior*, 33, 387–394. https://doi.org/10.1016/j.evolhumbehav.2011.11.010

    (2013). Copy me or copy you? The effect of prior experience on social learning. *Cognition*, 127, 203–213. https://doi.org/10.1016/j.cognition.2013.01.002

Wood, L. A. (2013). Chimpanzee tool-use is biased by the prior proficiency of known conspecifics. In *The influence of model-based biases and observer prior experience on social learning mechanisms and strategies*. Durham theses, Durham University. http://etheses.dur.ac.uk/7274/

15

HOW LEARNING AFFECTS EVOLUTION

Kevin Laland, Thomas Oudman, and Wataru Toyokawa

Since the early twentieth century, biological research has focused on genetic transmission as the primary form of inheritance. However, there are other processes that cause organisms to resemble their relatives, and these include learning. Here we embrace this broader conception of inheritance (Bondurianský & Day, 2018; Danchin et al., 2011). Biologists dating back to Darwin, in *The Descent of Man* – notably also Alfred Wallace, George Romanes, and Conwy Lloyd Morgan – have argued that animals, and humans in particular, inherit behaviors through "imitation" or social learning (Hoppitt & Laland, 2013). However, while it has long been recognized that inheritance mediated by social learning (i.e., "cultural inheritance") differs in important respects from genetic inheritance, the development of a formal theoretical framework that makes these differences explicit only began to emerge in the 1970s (Boyd & Richerson, 1985, Cavalli-Sforza & Feldman, 1973, 1981). Historically, most researchers, be they biologists, psychologists, or anthropologists, regarded social learning as rare among animals, and assumed cultural inheritance to be of marginal significance to organisms other than humans (Hoppitt & Laland, 2013). Yet, in the last 50 years, vast evidence for social learning has emerged through scientific investigations of a broad array of animals, both in the field and laboratory. Social learning and culture is not the sole province of humans, apes, or large-brained mammals, but is widespread across animals, including invertebrates (see Yu and Rankin; Wright; Kriete and Hollis; Dunlap and Dexheimer; Liefting, Chapters 1–5; Aplin, 2019; Danchin et al., 2010; Hoppitt & Laland, 2013; Leadbeater & Dawson, 2017; Whiten, 2017). In this section, we briefly summarize the current evidence for inheritance mediated by social learning, and then discuss how this can change the direction and speed of genetic evolution.

15.1 INHERITANCE THROUGH SOCIAL LEARNING ACROSS ANIMALS

Outside of humans, much social learning research has focused on other primates. Historically, that is because "imitation" was regarded by nineteenth-century evolutionists as a bridge between "instinctual animals" and human "reason," with species most closely related to humans assumed to be most likely to exhibit "intelligent" behavior. Subsequently, evidence began to emerge of the social learning of foraging techniques, from potato-washing by macaques in Japan (Kawai, 1965) to termite-fishing with sticks and nut-cracking with stones by chimpanzees in Africa (Goodall, 1986; Whiten et al., 1999). Early evidence that a variety of garden birds learned foraging habits socially, such as how to open milk bottles (Fisher & Hinde, 1949), acquired calls and songs from conspecifics (e.g., Marler & Tamura, 1964), and anti-predator behavior (Curio, 1988), broadened horizons concerning the breadth of animal culture. Examples of cultural inheritance began to accumulate in other mammalian species, and social learning is now known to be responsible for the development of foraging strategies by dolphins as well as song types in male humpback whales (Rendell & Whitehead, 2001; Whitehead & Rendell, 2014) and migratory routes by southern right whales (Carroll et al., 2015), and by moose and bighorn sheep (Jesmer et al., 2018). Among birds, too, several large migratory species such as geese, storks, and cranes have long been known to learn migratory behavior by following others (Sutherland, 1998), and there is extensive evidence that foraging behavior, song type, nest building, courtship, and predator recognition are influenced by social learning in many bird species (Aplin, 2019; Slagswold & Wiebe, 2007). For fish, there is evidence that social learning plays a crucial role in movement decisions concerning foraging and migration (Brown & Laland, 2001), as well as in mating preferences (Jones & DuVal, 2019). Evidence for socially learned mating preferences is most extensive in invertebrates (Jones & DuVal, 2019; see Kriete and Hollis; Dunlap and Dexheimer; Liefting, Chapters 3–5). Also, foraging and colony location choices in social insects can be socially learned (Leadbeater & Dawson, 2017). Much work remains to be done to determine the extent of social learning across the vast range of other invertebrates (Danchin et al., 2010), but that social learning is widespread among animals for an array of behavioral traits is beyond doubt.

15.2 CONSEQUENCES OF CULTURAL INHERITANCE FOR THE EVOLUTIONARY PROCESS

Social learning of mate choice and of other behavioral traits involved in mating decisions, such as song, have the potential to affect the occurrence of speciation and hybridization (Verzijden & ten Cate, 2007; Verzijden et al.,

2012). Theoretical studies find that learning can both enhance and reduce sexual selection (Beltman et al., 2004; Laland, 1994a,b; Varela et al., 2018). Mate-choice copying has been shown to affect mating decisions in a wide variety of species, by generating skews in male mating success, potentially leading to divergent selection and speciation (Beltman et al., 2004; Laland, 1994a,b; Verzijden & ten Cate, 2007; Verzijden et al., 2012). Extensive evidence implicates learning in mate choice, sexual selection, and reproductive isolation, where experimental studies show that learning imposes biases on signal evolution (ten Cate & Rowe, 2007; Verzijden et al., 2012). A role for learning in sexual selection is supported by a growing number of studies.

Evidence is accumulating that social learning was pivotal to the evolution of the large human brain and intelligence, and that culture is an important driver of brain evolution (Henrich, 2016; Laland, 2017; Muthukrishna & Henrich, 2016). The key observation supporting this "cultural intelligence hypothesis" is that large brains are energetically costly, and social learning is vital to animals that need to gather the resources necessary to grow and maintain a large brain efficiently. Comparative analyses (e.g., Dunbar & Shultz, 2017; Kaplan et al., 2000; Navarrete et al., 2016; Reader et al., 2011; Street et al., 2017) report associations between cultural and behavioral complexity, longevity and extended developmental period, general intelligence, and brain size in primates. Many animals solve problems through devising a new or modified learned behavior, or "innovation" (Reader & Laland, 2003; Reader et al., 2016). Innovation in general (Lefebvre et al., 1997; Reader & Laland, 2002), and "technical innovation" (i.e., novel tool-using and extractive foraging behavior) in particular (Navarrete et al., 2016; Overington et al., 2009), correlate with brain size measures in both birds and primates.

Collectively this work implies that complex cognition, large brains, and longer lives coevolved in hominins because our ancestors' intellectual (and particularly cultural) capabilities allowed them to exploit high-quality, but otherwise difficult-to-access, food resources, with the nutrients gleaned "paying" for brain growth, and with increased longevity favored because it allowed more time to cash in on complex, difficult-to-master, foraging skills with fitness benefits that pay off only later in life (Dunbar & Shultz, 2017; Kaplan et al., 2000; Laland, 2017; Street et al., 2017). Experiments with humans and other primates have provided circumstantial evidence for this hypothesis. For example, human children differ from other infant primates not so much in their physical cognition, but for their social/cultural intelligence, including the tendency to imitate the actions of others (Herrmann et al., 2007), teaching (including, donating information to other children and adults), and language (Dean et al., 2012).

For humans, it is obvious that cultural practices such as building shelter, growing food, and taking medicine have decreased mortality (Henrich, 2016). For other animals, the adaptive value of social learning has been more difficult to establish, although circumstantial evidence is found in the behavior of some social migrants. For example, the loss of cultural knowledge of foraging grounds during migration is thought to have prevented further recovery of southern right whale populations after their decimation by whaling in previous centuries (Carroll et al., 2015). Evidence is also accumulating that social learning allows social migrants to adjust their migration strategies to environmental changes (Sutherland, 1998). For example, through social learning over a few generations, barnacle geese have changed their stopover locations during spring migration in response to recent climate change (Oudman et al., 2020; Tombre et al., 2019). Reintroduced bighorn sheep and moose in a number of wild parks in the United States follow grass phenology more closely with each generation, presumably by social learning (Jesmer et al., 2018). Hence, depending on the particular circumstances, cultural inheritance can help (as in barnacle geese) or hinder (as in right whales) behavioral adaptation.

Cultural evolution is thought to work particularly well with "needle-in-a-haystack" problems: when the optimal behavior is among many possible actions or comprises a long sequence of actions that must be performed in the correct order (Hoppitt & Laland, 2013; Rendell et al., 2010; Whalen et al., 2015). Whale migration typically is such a problem: it is about finding resources that occur only at particular locations during particular times of the year, in a vast and otherwise empty ocean (Abrahms et al., 2019).

While animal cultures can be sustained for long periods (Mercader et al., 2007), it would be a mistake to assume that culture must exhibit gene-like stability to be evolutionarily important. We have already discussed mate-choice copying, which propagates mating preferences over short time periods, such as a single season. Yet population-genetic models have shown that mate-choice copying can strongly affect the strength of sexual selection. Another illustration comes from studies of bird song, for which mathematical models have shown that song learning can affect the frequency of alleles that influence song acquisition and preference (Lachlan & Slater, 1999), promote the evolution of brood parasitism (Beltman et al., 2003), and facilitate speciation (Beltman et al., 2004). A third case is the socially transmitted mobbing of cuckoos by reed warblers, which affects the balance of costs to benefits in the evolution of brood parasitism (Thorogood & Davies, 2012). There are other candidates, with a recent review concluding: "animal culture plays an important evolutionary role, and we encourage explicit analyses of gene–culture coevolution in nature" (Whitehead et al., 2019, p. 1).

15.3 LEARNING CAN INSTIGATE PLASTICITY-FIRST EVOLUTION

Plasticity-first evolution occurs when organisms adjust to environmental change through phenotypic plasticity, followed by refinement or stabilization of the trait through selection of genetic variation (Levis & Pfennig, 2016; West-Eberhard, 2003), a process also known as "genetic accommodation" (West-Eberhard, 2003). A special case of plasticity-first evolution occurs when an originally environmentally induced character (such as a learned trait) through natural selection of relevant genetic variation becomes fixed (or "canalized") and is produced even in the absence of the environmental cue that originally induced it, known as "genetic assimilation" (Waddington, 1953), or the "Baldwin effect" (Baldwin, 1896). Social learning can buffer selection of genetic variation that would otherwise lead to genetic change and adaptation (Griffiths, 2002). However, this buffering is rarely perfect, and hence does not preclude selection of alleles that increase the probability of producing, or the performance of, the learned phenotype (West-Eberhard, 2003).

There is growing empirical evidence that learning can generate plasticity-first evolution (Whitehead et al., 2019). For instance, killer whale (*Orcinus orca*) populations exhibit culturally transmitted specializations on particular prey resources (e.g., fish, dolphins, pinnipeds). These dietary traditions have favored population-specific genes influencing morphology and digestion, giving rise to distinct "ecotypes" (Foote et al., 2016; Hoelzel & Moura, 2016). Population-genomic studies confirm that these lineages have diverged genetically, and that functional genes associated with digestion differ between ecotypes. Seemingly, the ecotypes arose through culturally mediated specialization in matrilineal groups, which later developed reproductive barriers, potentially leading to speciation (Riesch et al., 2012). Culturally transmitted dietary traditions have caused the natural selection of genes for morphologies and physiologies that match the whales' learned habits.

Another example may be observational fear conditioning of snake stimuli in rhesus monkeys (aka "vicarious instigation"). Early studies, in which rhesus monkeys were conditioned to acquire a fear of snakes, but not flowers, through observing fearful companions (Mineka & Cook, 1988), appeared to suggest tight genetic constraints on learning. Subsequent research has established that observational fear learning is extremely widespread in animals (Olsson & Phelps, 2007), an ancient mechanism through which animals acquire novel fears. For instance, blackbirds learn to recognize and mob predators through social transmission but will also acquire a fear of arbitrary objects such as plastic bottles in this manner (Curio, 1988). Moreover, studies have established that rhesus monkeys can be socially conditioned to acquire a fear of novel arbitrary objects, including kitchen utensils (Stephenson, 1967). Although monkeys can connect arbitrary stimuli to fear in a social setting, there is evidence for the partial canalization of perceptual systems in this context. For example, neuroscientific experiments have established the primate brain contains neurons that respond rapidly and selectively to visual images of snakes (Le et al., 2013). Such experiments combine with comparative evidence to imply that, because snakes were a regularly present threat in ancestral environments, natural selection has fine-tuned the perceptual systems of these animals, leaving snake-shaped objects particularly salient to rhesus monkeys, but without constraining their general learning capabilities.

In the killer whale example, learning is not just codirecting the outcome but also changing the rate of evolution. As the aforementioned discussion of mate-choice copying illustrates, theoretical work has established that learning can both speed up and slow down genetic evolution (Ancel, 2000; Borenstein et al., 2006), and that phenotypic plasticity can both drive and inhibit genetic evolution (e.g., Edelaar et al., 2017; Price et al., 2003). Theoretical models have established that learning has a beneficial effect on adaptation in relatively quickly changing environments, allowing individuals to acclimate to changes that occur too quickly to be tracked by the natural selection of genetic variation (Aoki & Feldman, 2014; Boyd & Richerson, 1985; Cavalli-Sforza & Feldman, 1981). In unchanging, or slowly changing, environments the benefits of learning are more complex. Hinton and Nowlan (1987) suggested that learning could accelerate evolution in a static environment by helping genotypes to locate otherwise difficult-to-find fitness peaks. However, learning can also weaken selection by reducing phenotypic differences between genotypes (Ancel, 2000; Frank, 2011). These seemingly conflicting results follow from different theoretical assumptions (Borenstein et al., 2006; Frank, 2011; Paenke et al., 2007). The emerging consensus is that individual learning typically slows evolution in static unimodal fitness landscapes, but will accelerate evolution in dynamic or static multimodal fitness landscapes. The existence of multiple optima usually slows down evolution as populations get trapped on suboptimal fitness peaks but, by generating adaptive variation and thereby smoothing the fitness landscape, learning increases the likelihood of a directly increasing path of fitness to the global optimum (Borenstein et al., 2006; Frank, 2011; Mills & Watson, 2006).

15.4 LEARNING CAN INFLUENCE NICHE CONSTRUCTION

Organisms, through their metabolism, activities, and choices, modify environments, thereby changing their own and other species' ecological niches. For instance, animals dig burrows, build nests, construct webs, migrate, disperse, and select habitats (Laland et al., 2016; Lewontin, 1983; Odling-Smee et al., 2003). When such organism-induced environmental modifications alter, or regulate, natural selection pressures in nonrandom ways, niche construction can impose a systematic bias on the selection they generate, allowing organisms to exert some influence over their own evolution (Clark et al., 2019; Odling-Smee et al., 2013).

CULTURAL NICHE CONSTRUCTION

Mathematical analyses suggest that culturally transmitted behavior that modifies environmental conditions can trigger evolutionary episodes (e.g., Laland et al., 2001; Laland & O'Brien, 2011; Rendell et al., 2011). Learned niche-constructing traits can drive themselves to fixation by generating nonrandom statistical associations between niche-constructing alleles and alleles with higher fitness in organism-modified environments (Rendell et al., 2011).

Thus far, research into cultural niche construction has focused on humans. It is readily apparent that contemporary humans are born into a massively constructed world, with an ecological inheritance that includes houses, hospitals, farms, factories, computers, satellites, and the World Wide Web. One of the best-researched examples is the agriculture-induced evolution of the hemoglobin S allele (HbS) that provides protection against malaria in the heterozygote form. In the Kwa-speaking, yam-cultivating region of West Africa, an agricultural practice of tree removal had the effect of inadvertently increasing the amount of standing water when it rained, which provided richer breeding grounds for malaria-carrying mosquitoes, thereby intensifying natural selection on HbS (Durham, 1991). This example demonstrates that learned and culturally transmitted activities can create selection on human genes (Laland et al., 2001; O'Brien & Laland, 2012; Rendell et al., 2011).

Humans have modified natural selection through their learning and culture, for instance, by dispersing into new environments with different climatic regimes, by devising agricultural practices, domesticating livestock, and by causing extinctions and dramatic shifts in community structure (Boivin et al., 2016). It is now well established that dairy farming created the selection pressure that led to the spread of alleles for human adult lactase persistence (Gerbault et al., 2011). Such examples illustrate how learning can affect evolutionary outcomes, and not just rates. Producing and consuming milk and alcohol has selected for alleles for adult lactose absorption and alcohol dehydrogenase, respectively, while agricultural practices that led to greater consumption of starch, protein, lipids, and phosphate have each selected for alleles that metabolize these foods (Laland et al., 2010).

With the recognition that both culture and niche construction are widespread in animals, it is timely to consider whether cultural niche construction might also be playing important roles in animal evolution more generally. In fact, a closer look reveals numerous examples of animals engaging in cultural niche construction in the social learning literature. For instance, when leaving a feeding site, adult rats deposit scent trails that direct young rats seeking food to locations where food was ingested (Galef & Buckley, 1996), whilst feeding adults deposit residual urine marks and feces, both in the vicinity of a food source and on foods they are eating, via which young rats acquire dietary preferences (Galef & Beck, 1985; Galef & Heiber, 1976; Laland & Plotkin, 1991). Similarly, fish secrete food cues in their mucus, as well as in their urine, to which other fish attend (Atton, 2013). If a recently fed fish emits chemical cues of stress at the same time as these food cues, other fish seemingly learn that the new food is one to be avoided. Conversely, when there are no such stress chemicals in the water, the mucus cues are acted upon and observing fish rapidly develop a preference for the newly consumed diet (Atton, 2013). Many fish can also learn to recognize a novel predator through associating predator cues with an alarm substance that other fearful fish have released into the water (Brown & Laland, 2003; Suboski et al., 1990). Likewise, amongst bumblebees, when successful foragers bring home nectar to the nest, they deposit the scented solution in honeypots, where other colony members sample it and thereby acquire a preference for the oral scent (Dornhaus & Chittka, 1999; Leadbeater & Chittka, 2007).

In many animals, enduring physical traces that accompany foraging or tool-using activities have been found to scaffold the learning experience of the novice (Fragaszy, 2011). Gunst and colleagues (2008, 2010) describe how young wild brown capuchins (*Sapajus apella*) learn to find and retrieve beetle larvae hidden inside bamboo stalks. Young monkeys are attracted to canes already opened by adults, and at these sites they practice behaviors that contribute to finding and obtaining larvae. Here, the physical traces left by skilled foragers stimulate youngsters to perform the activities most likely to lead them to acquire the foraging skill, perpetuating the dietary tradition. Similarly, black rats (*Rattus rattus*) learn to strip pine cones for their seeds through the (tolerated) theft by pups of partially opened pine cones from their mothers, which gives them the opportunity to learn the task (Zohar & Terkel, 1996). Without the scaffolding provided by maternally modified cones, rats cannot learn to access the seeds efficiently. Young chimpanzees (*Pan troglodytes*) learn appropriate wand selection for termite fishing through utilizing the discarded or donated wands of their mothers (Musgrave et al., 2016). Black-capped chickadees (*Parus atricapillus*) learned to open the foil tops of milk bottles through exposure to the milk bottles opened by other birds (Sherry & Galef, 1984). Many animals, particularly mammals, exhibit traditional use of their environment mediated by their utilizing the tracks, trails, and pathways created by conspecifics (Hoppitt & Laland, 2013).

COLLECTIVE BEHAVIOR AND SOCIAL NICHE CONSTRUCTION

Humans, and other animals, can also modify their social environment by changing their social network, creating new behavioral roles, sharing norms, and adopting institutions. These activities construct a new form of social interaction in collective behavior, a process called "social niche construction" (Flack et al., 2006; Yamagishi & Hashimoto, 2016). For instance, Flack et al. (2006) demonstrated that policing behavior by dominant pigtail macaques (*Macaca nemestrina*) mitigates conflicts among individuals, thereby facilitating contagion and cooperation, making group-living advantageous. In game-theoretic terms, the social niche is the game being played (Ryan et al., 2016), with social-niche-constructing behavior being a modifier of the incentive structure and payoff matrix of the game. Although changes in social institution and their effects on human behavior have been studied in economics (e.g., Aoki, 2001), how cultural evolutionary processes might affect social niche construction remains underexplored. Yet there is little doubt that systematic biases imposed by the recursive process of cultural transmission and learning could plausibly affect patterns of emerging institutions and norms (e.g., Currie et al., 2010; Richerson & Henrich, 2012). Marrying the biases imposed by learning and decision-making with a niche-construction perspective potentially provides a synthetic overarching framework for the evolutionary human sciences (Kendal et al., 2011; O'Brien & Laland, 2012).

15.5 LEARNING CAN GENERATE DEVELOPMENTAL BIAS

The term "developmental bias" refers to a "bias imposed on the distribution of phenotypic variation, arising from the structure, character, composition, or dynamics of the developmental system" (Uller et al., 2018, p. 949). Such biases can arise in behavior, and they are of interest to the evolutionary biology community because (1) learning allows animals to tune their behavior to environments, including novel environments, by selectively generating adaptive (i.e. fitness-enhancing) behaviors more readily than nonadaptive behaviors, and (2) adaptive behaviors can be propagated to other individuals, including nonrelatives, and across generations, through social learning, again in an adaptively biased manner (Laland et al., 2019).

Here we focus primarily on "operant" (aka "instrumental") conditioning, which is thought to be the primary means by which animals acquire behavior (Staddon, 2016). Learned behavior is often the result of an exploratory search conducted over multiple trials, through which individuals hone their behavior to exploit their environment. This generates behavioral flexibility and variability, allowing animals potentially to form a large number of operant associations. An episode of learning often begins with exploration or sampling, and initial trials may not be biased toward adaptive decisions (e.g., random choice of which food patch to try first); however, after multiple trials, the animal's behavior will adjust to the reinforcement encountered, and the final behavior will be generally highly adaptive (i.e., feeding at the richest food patch) (Staddon, 2016). When animals learn socially, this exploratory search is expanded to encompass the learning trials of multiple individuals, allowing for more rapid and more effective homing in on the optimal solution (Rendell et al., 2010). The shift toward adaptive or optimal behavior as a consequence of reinforcement learning constitutes an "adaptive bias" (Laland et al., 2019).

The ability to generate diverse behavioral patterns is strongly associated with problem-solving capabilities in animals. In a survey spanning diverse vertebrate species, Griffin and Guez (2014) report a relationship between motor diversity and problem solving, with those animals that express a greater range of motor actions more likely, or faster, to solve a problem. This pattern is a general feature of many complex developmental systems, known as "exploratory mechanisms" (Gerhart & Kirschner, 1997), which operate by generating variation (i.e., exploring possibilities), testing variants' functionality, and selecting the best solutions, in an iterative developmental process that resembles adaptation by natural selection. Theoretical work has shown that a highly variable and random component to the generation of variation is critical for effective search (Deneubourg et al., 1983; Stickland et al., 1995). The association between motor diversity and problem-solving thus can be viewed as one manifestation of a general pattern in which ontogenetic exploration and selection provides a mechanism for finding effective solutions in changing, variable, or unpredictable contexts.

Through learning, for instance, how to discover and exploit new foods, or devising novel means to escape or avoid a threat, animals can introduce new behavior into the population's repertoire. Such instances are labeled behavioral innovations (Reader & Laland, 2003) – novel functional solutions tailored to new challenges or hitherto unexploited opportunities. Behavioral innovation is now extensively documented in animals (Lefebvre et al., 1997; Reader & Laland, 2003; Reader et al., 2016). While analogous to genetic mutation in the respect that they introduce novel variation, behavioral innovations are usually not random but exhibit an adaptive bias (Laland et al., 2019; Snell-Rood et al., 2018). Animals vary in how readily they generate behavioral innovations, and innovative species of birds have been found to be more likely to survive when introduced into novel habitats (Sol & Lefebvre, 2000), implying that innovation could aid survival. Consistent with this, migratory species of birds are reported to be less innovative than nonmigrants, who deploy innovation to help them survive the harsh winter months (Sol et al., 2005). Moreover, innovative bird lineages have been found to be more speciose (i.e., more likely to give rise to new species), which would make sense if innovation allows animals to open up new niches for themselves (Nicolakakis et al., 2003), in line with the "flexible stem" hypothesis (West-Eberhard, 2003).

Through learning (particularly operant learning, social learning, and innovation) animals can learn about entirely novel stimuli or events, and devise appropriate responses to them (e.g., birds learn to evade a novel predator, Davies & Welbergen, 2009). As a consequence, animals can generate adaptive responses to conditions without prior evolution of dedicated traits with suitable reaction norms. Learning can also generate adaptive phenotypic change in the absence of any immediate environmental change or stressor (e.g., when orangutans, *Pongo pygmaeus*, proactively devise new food-processing techniques, such as eating palm heart, Russon, 2003). Amongst the most-celebrated examples of animal innovation are the invention by primates and cetaceans of new food-processing methods (Goodall, 1986; Sargeant & Mann, 2009).

Social learning is also typically nonrandom and strategic, with evidence that individuals often disproportionately copy successful individuals and high-payoff behavior (Laland, 2004; Rendell et al., 2011). Fitness-enhancing learned behavior is far more likely to be propagated than bad information. There are well-documented tendencies of animals to copy successful individuals and high-payoff behavior preferentially, to conform to the majority behavior (known to be adaptive in spatially variable environments; Boyd & Richerson, 1985), and also to copy more when uncertain or when learning asocially would be costly or difficult (Kendal et al., 2018; Laland, 2004; Rendell et al., 2011). For instance, red-winged blackbirds (*Agelaius phoeniceus*) copy feeding conspecifics except when they exhibit an aversive reaction to the food (Mason & Reidinger, 1982). Nine-spined sticklebacks (*Pungitius pungitius*) monitor the foraging success of other fish through observation and subsequently select the richer of the alternative food patches (Coolen et al., 2003). Bats that are unsuccessful at locating food alone follow previously successful bats to feeding sites (Wilkinson, 1992). Insects and birds, too, are known to copy the nest-site decisions of successful conspecifics and heterospecifics (Forsman & Seppänen, 2011; Sarin & Dukas, 2009; Seppänen et al., 2011). As a result of these transmission biases, learned information does not spread randomly, but along specified (i.e., biased) pathways. Biased cultural transmission is a general property of animal social learning, with random copying a special case (Hoppitt & Laland, 2013).

15.6 CONCLUSIONS

For many biologists, "biological evolution" equates to genetic evolution, and "inheritance" to genetic inheritance. The research discussed in this chapter shows that social learning is widespread across the animal kingdom. The reviewed investigations, each of them the result of careful experiments in the laboratory and/or detailed observations in the wild, strongly imply that social learning is an influential form of behavioral inheritance in animals. Moreover, processes of learning – particularly operant conditioning, behavioral innovation, and social learning – can affect evolution in important ways, including generating adaptive biases in phenotypic variation, eliciting plasticity-first evolution, and triggering genetic responses to selection through cultural niche construction. The evidence suggests that learning should be regarded as an integral aspect of the evolution of many animals, in constant interplay with the selection of genetic variation.

REFERENCES

Abrahms, B., Hazen, E. L., Aikens, E. O., Savoca, M. S., Goldbogen, J. A., Bograd, S. J., Jacox, M. G., Irvine, L. M., Palacios, D. M., & Mate, B. R. (2019). Memory and resource tracking drive blue whale migrations. *Proceedings of the National Academy of Sciences*, *116*, 5582–5587. https://doi.org/10.1073/pnas.1819031116

Ancel, L. W. (2000). Undermining the Baldwin expediting effect: Does phenotypic plasticity accelerate evolution? *Theoretical Population Biology*, *58*, 307–319. https://doi.org/10.1006/tpbi.2000.1484

Aoki, K., & Feldman, M. W. (2014). Evolution of learning strategies in temporally and spatially variable environments: A review of theory. *Theoretical Population Biology*, *91*, 3–19. https://doi.org/10.1016/j.tpb.2013.10.004

Aoki, M. (2001). *Toward a comparative institutional analysis*. MIT Press.

Aplin, L. M. (2019). Culture and cultural evolution in birds: A review of the evidence. *Animal Behaviour*, *147*, 179–187. https://doi.org/10.1016/j.anbehav.2018.05.001

Atton, N. (2013). *Investigations into Stickleback Social Learning* [PhD dissertation, University of St Andrews].

Baldwin, J. M. (1896). A new factor in evolution. *The American Naturalist*, *30*(354), 441–451.

Beltman, J. B., Haccou, P., & ten Cate, C. (2003). The impact of learning foster species' song on the evolution of specialist avian brood parasitism. *Behavioral Ecology*, *14*(6), 917–923. https://doi.org/10.1093/beheco/arg082

Beltman, J., Haccou, P., & ten Cate, C. (2004). Learning and colonization of new niches: A first step toward speciation. *Evolution*, *58*, 35–46. https://doi.org/10.1554/03-339

Boivin, N. L., Zeder, M. A., Fuller, D. Q., Crowther, A., Larson, G., Erlandson, J. M., Denham, T., & Petraglia, M. D. (2016). Ecological consequences of human niche construction: Examining long-term anthropogenic shaping of global species distributions. *Proceedings of the National Academy of Sciences*, *113*(23), 6388–6396. https://doi.org/10.1073/pnas.1525200113

Bondurianasky, R. & Day, T. (2018). *Extended heredity*. Princeton University Press.

Borenstein, E., Meilijson, I., & Ruppin, E. (2006). The effect of phenotypic plasticity on evolution in multipeaked fitness landscapes. *Journal of Evolutionary Biology*, *19*(5), 1555–1570. https://doi.org/10.1111/j.1420-9101.2006.01125.x

Boyd, R., & Richerson, P. J. (1985). *Culture and the evolutionary process*. University of Chicago Press.

Brown, C., & Laland, K. N. (2001). Social learning and life skills training for hatchery reared fish. *Journal of Fish Biology*, *59*(3), 471–493. https://doi.org/10.1111/j.1095-8649.2001.tb02354.x

(2003). Social learning in fishes: A review. *Fish and Fisheries*, *4*(3), 280–288. https://doi.org/10.1046/j.1467-2979.2003.00122.x

Carroll, E. L., Baker, C. S., Watson, M., Alderman, R., Bannister, J., Gaggiotti, O. E., Gröcke, D. R., Patenaude, N., & Harcourt, R. (2015). Cultural traditions across a migratory network shape the genetic structure of southern right whales around Australia and New Zealand. *Scientific Reports*, *5*(1), 16182. https://doi.org/10.1038/srep16182

ten Cate, C., & Rowe, C. (2007). Biases in signal evolution: learning makes a difference. *Trends in Ecology and Evolution*, *22*, 380–387. https://doi.org/10.1016/j.tree.2007.03.006

Cavalli-Sforza, L. L., & Feldman, M. W. (1973). Models for cultural inheritance I. Group mean and within group variation. *Theoretical Population Biology, 4*(1), 42–55. https://doi.org/10.1016/0040-5809(73)90005-1

(1981). *Cultural transmission and evolution: A quantitative approach.* Princeton University Press.

Clark, A. D., Deffner, D., Laland, K. N., Odling-Smee, J., & Endler, J. (2019). Niche construction affects the variability and strength of natural selection. *The American Naturalist, 195* (1), 16–30. https://doi.org/10.5061/dryad.g66n3h5

Coolen, I., Bergen, Y. V., Day, R. L., & Laland, K. N. (2003). Species difference in adaptive use of public information in sticklebacks. *Proceedings of the Royal Society B: Biological Sciences, 270,* 2413–2419. https://doi.org/10.1098/rspb.2003.2525

Curio, E. (1988). Cultural transmission of enemy recognition by birds. In T. R. Zentall & B. G. Galef (Eds.), *Social learning: Psychological and biological perspectives* (pp. 75–97). Lawrence Erlbaum Associates, Inc.

Currie, T. E., Greenhill, S. J., Gray, R. D., Hasegawa, T., & Mace, R. (2010). Rise and fall of political complexity in island South-East Asia and the Pacific. *Nature, 467*(7317), 801–804. https://doi.org/10.1038/nature09461

Danchin, É. G. J., Blanchet, S., Mery, F., & Wagner, R. H. (2010). Do invertebrates have culture? *Communicative & Integrative Biology, 3*(4), 303–305. https://doi.org/10.4161/cib.3.4.11970

Danchin, É. G. J., Charmantier, A., Champagne, F. A., Mesoudi, A., Pujol, B., & Blanchet, S. (2011). Beyond DNA: Integrating inclusive inheritance into an extended theory of evolution. *Nature Reviews Genetics, 12,* 475–486. https://doi.org/10.1038/nrg3028

Davies, N. B., & Welbergen, J. A. (2009). Social transmission of a host defense against cuckoo parasitism. *Science, 324*(5932), 1318–1320. https://doi.org/10.1126/science.1172227

Dean, L. G., Kendal, R. L., Schapiro, S. J., Thierry, B., & Laland, K. N. (2012). Identification of the social and cognitive processes underlying human cumulative culture. *Science, 335,* 1114–1118. https://doi.org/10.1126/science.1213969

Deneubourg, J. L., Pasteels, J. M., & Verhaeghe, J. C. (1983). Probabilistic behaviour in ants: A strategy of errors? *Journal of Theoretical Biology, 105*(2), 259–271. https://doi.org/10.1016/S0022-5193(83)80007-1

Dornhaus, A., & Chittka, L. (1999). Evolutionary origins of bee dances. *Nature, 401*(6748), 38. https://doi.org/10.1038/43372

Dunbar, R. I. M., & Shultz, S. (2017). Why are there so many explanations for primate brain evolution? *Philosophical Transactions of the Royal Society B: Biological Sciences, 372* (1727), 20160244. https://doi.org/10.1098/rstb.2016.0244

Durham, W. H. (1991). *Coevolution: Genes, culture, and human diversity.* Stanford University Press.

Edelaar, P., Jovani, R., & Gomez-Mestre, I. (2017). Should I change or should I go? Phenotypic plasticity and matching habitat choice in the adaptation to environmental heterogeneity. *The American Naturalist, 190*(4), 506–520. https://doi.org/10.1086/693345

Fisher, J. B., & Hinde, R. A. (1949). Opening of milk bottles by birds. *British Birds, XLII,* 347–357.

Flack, J. C., Girvan, M., de Waal, F. B. M., & Krakauer, D. C. (2006). Policing stabilizes construction of social niches in primates. *Nature, 439,* 426–429. https://doi.org/10.1038/nature04326

Foote, A. D., Vijay, N., Ávila-Arcos, M. C., Baird, R. W., Durban, J. W., Fumagalli, M., Gibbs, R. A., Hanson, M. B., Korneliussen, T. S., Martin, M. D., Robertson, K. M., Sousa, V. C., Vieira, F. G., Vinař, T., Wade, P., Worley, K. C., Excoffier, L., Morin, P. A., Gilbert, M. T. P., & Wolf, J. B. W. (2016). Genome-culture coevolution promotes rapid divergence of killer whale ecotypes. *Nature Communications, 7,* 11693. https://doi.org/10.1038/ncomms11693

Forsman, J. T., & Seppänen, J.-T. (2011). Learning what (not) to do: Testing rejection and copying of simulated heterospecific behavioural traits. *Animal Behaviour, 81*(4), 879–883. https://doi.org/10.1016/j.anbehav.2011.01.029

Fragaszy, D. M. (2011). Community resources for learning: How capuchin monkeys construct technical traditions. *Biological Theory*, *6*(3), 231–240. https://doi.org/10.1007/s13752-012-0032-8

Frank, S. A. (2011). Natural selection. II. Developmental variability and evolutionary rate. *Journal of Evolutionary Biology*, *24*(11), 2310–2320. https://doi.org/10.1111/j.1420-9101.2011.02373.x

Galef, B. G., & Beck, M. (1985). Aversive and attractive marking of toxic and safe foods by Norway rats. *Behavioral and Neural Biology*, *43*(3), 298–310. https://doi.org/10.1016/s0163-1047(85)91645-0

Galef, B. G., & Buckley, L. L. (1996). Use of foraging trails by Norway rats. *Animal Behaviour*, *51*, 765–771. https://doi.org/10.1006/anbe.1996.0081

Galef, B. G., & Heiber, L. (1976). Role of residual olfactory cues in the determination of feeding site selection and exploration patterns of domestic rats. *Journal of Comparative and Physiological Psychology*, *90*, 727–739. https://doi.org/10.1037/h0077243

Gerbault, P., Liebert, A., Itan, Y., Powell, A., Currat, M., Burger, J., Swallow, D. M., & Thomas, M. G. (2011). Evolution of lactase persistence: An example of human niche construction. *Philosophical Transactions of the Royal Society B: Biological sciences*, *366*, 863–877. https://doi.org/10.1098/rstb.2010.0268

Gerhart, J., & Kirschner, M. (1997). *Cells, embryos & evolution*. Wiley.

Goodall, J. (1986). *The chimpanzees of Gombe: patterns of behavior*. Harvard University Press.

Griffiths, P. E. (2002). What is innateness? *The Monist*, *85*, 70–85. https://doi.org/10.5840/monist20028518

Griffin, A. S., & Guez, D. (2014). Innovation and problem solving: A review of common mechanisms. *Behavioural Processes*, *109*, 121–134. https://doi.org/10.1016/j.beproc.2014.08.027

Gunst, N., Boinski, S., & Fragaszy, D. (2008). Acquisition of foraging competence in wild brown capuchins (*Cebus apella*), with special reference to conspecifics' foraging artefacts as an indirect social influence. *Behaviour*, *145*, 195–229. https://doi.org/10.1163/156853907783244701

    (2010). Development of skilled detection and extraction of embedded prey by wild brown capuchin monkeys (*Cebus apella apella*). *Journal of Comparative Psychology*, *124*, 194–204. https://doi.org/10.1037/a0017723

Henrich, J. (2016). *The secret of our success: How culture is driving human evolution, domesticating our species, and making us smarter*. Princeton University Press.

Herrmann, E., Call, J., Hernàndez-Lloreda, M. V., Hare, B., & Tomasello, M. (2007). Humans have evolved specialized skills of social cognition: the cultural intelligence hypothesis. *Science*, *317*(5843), 1360–1366. https://doi.org/10.1126/science.1146282

Hinton, G. E., & Nowlan, S. J. (1987). How learning can guide evolution. *Complex systems*, *1*, 495–502.

Hoelzel, A. R., & Moura, A. E. (2016). Killer whales differentiating in geographic sympatry facilitated by divergent behavioural traditions. *Heredity*, *117*, 481–482. https://doi.org/10.1038/hdy.2016.112

Hoppitt, W., & Laland, K. N. (2013). *Social learning: An introduction to mechanisms, methods, and models*. Princeton University Press.

Jesmer, B. R., Merkle, J. A., Goheen, J. R., Aikens, E. O., Beck, J. L., Courtemanch, A. B., Hurley, M. A., McWhirter, D. E., Miyasaki, H. M., Monteith, K. L., & Kauffman, M. J. (2018). Is ungulate migration culturally transmitted? Evidence of social learning from translocated animals. *Science*, *361*, 1023–1025. https://doi.org/10.1126/science.aat0985

Jones, B. C., & DuVal, E. H. (2019). Mechanisms of social influence: A meta-analysis of the effects of social information on female mate choice decisions [Systematic Review]. *Frontiers in Ecology and Evolution*, *7*, 390. https://doi.org/10.3389/fevo.2019.00390

Kaplan, H., Hill, K., Lancaster, J., & Hurtado, A. M. (2000). A theory of human life history evolution: Diet, intelligence, and longevity. *Evolutionary Anthropology: Issues, News, and Reviews*, *9*, 156–185. https://doi.org/10.1002/1520-6505(2000)9:4<156::AID-EVAN5>3.0.CO;2-7

Kawai, M. (1965). Newly-acquired pre-cultural behavior of the natural troop of Japanese monkeys on Koshima islet. *Primates*, 6, 1–30. https://doi.org/10.1007/BF01794457

Kendal, J., Tehrani, J. J., & Odling-Smee, J. (2011). Human niche construction in interdisciplinary focus. *Philosophical Transactions of the Royal Society B: Biological Sciences*, 366, 785–792. https://doi.org/10.1098/rstb.2010.0306

Kendal, R. L., Boogert, N. J., Rendell, L., Laland, K. N., Webster, M., & Jones, P. L. (2018). Social learning strategies: Bridge-building between fields. *Trends in Cognitive Sciences*, 22, 651–665. https://doi.org/10.1016/j.tics.2018.04.003

Lachlan, R. F., & Slater, P. J. B. (1999). The maintenance of vocal learning by gene-culture interaction: The cultural trap hypothesis. *Proceedings of the Royal Society B: Biological Sciences*, 266, 701–706. https://doi.org/10.1098/rspb.1999.0692

Laland, K. N. (1994a). Sexual selection with a culturally transmitted mating preference. *Theoretical Population Biology*, 45, 1–15. https://doi.org/10.1006/tpbi.1994.1001

(1994b). On the evolutionary consequences of sexual imprinting. *Evolution*, 48, 477–489. https://doi.org/10.1111/j.1558-5646.1994.tb01325.x.

(2004). Social learning strategies. *Animal Learning & Behavior*, 32, 4–14. https://doi.org/10.3758/BF03196002

(2017). *Darwin's Unfinished Symphony: How culture made the human mind*. Princeton University Press.

Laland, K. N., Matthews, B., & Feldman, M. W. (2016). An introduction to niche construction theory. *Evolutionary Ecology*, 30, 191–202. https://doi.org/10.1007/s10682-016-9821-z

Laland, K. N., & O'Brien, M. J. (2011). Cultural niche construction: An introduction. *Biological Theory*, 6, 191–202. https://doi.org/10.1007/s13752-012-0026-6

Laland, K. N., Odling-Smee, J., & Feldman, M. W. (2001). Cultural niche construction and human evolution. *Journal of Evolutionary Biology*, 14, 22–33. https://doi.org/10.1073/pnas.96.18.10242

Laland, K. N., Odling-Smee, J., & Myles, S. (2010). How culture shaped the human genome: Bringing genetics and the human sciences together. *Nature Reviews Genetics*, 11, 137–148. https://doi.org/10.1038/nrg2734

Laland, K. N., & Plotkin, H. C. (1991). Excretory deposits surrounding food sites facilitate social learning of food preferences in Norway rats. *Animal Behaviour*, 41, 997–1005. https://doi.org/10.1016/S0003-3472(05)80638-4

Laland, K. N., Toyokawa, W., & Oudman, T. (2019). Animal learning as a source of developmental bias. *Evolution & Development*, 22, 126–142. https://doi.org/10.1111/ede.12311

Le, Q. V., Isbell, L. A., Matsumoto, J., Nguyen, M., Hori, E., Maior, R. S., Tomaz, C., Tran, A. H., Ono, T., & Nishijo, H. (2013). Pulvinar neurons reveal neurobiological evidence of past selection for rapid detection of snakes. *Proceedings of the National Academy of Sciences*, 110, 19000. https://doi.org/10.1073/pnas.1312648110

Leadbeater, E., & Chittka, L. (2007). Social learning in insects – From miniature brains to consensus building. *Current Biology*, 17, R703–R713. https://doi.org/10.1016/j.cub.2007.06.012

Leadbeater, E., & Dawson, E. H. (2017). A social insect perspective on the evolution of social learning mechanisms. *Proceedings of the National Academy of Sciences*, 114, 7838. https://doi.org/10.1073/pnas.1620744114

Lefebvre, L., Whittle, P., Lascaris, E., & Finkelstein, A. (1997). Feeding innovations and forebrain size in birds. *Animal Behaviour*, 53, 549–560. https://doi.org/10.1006/anbe.1996.0330

Levis, N. A., & Pfennig, D. W. (2016). Evaluating 'plasticity-first' evolution in nature: Key criteria and empirical approaches. *Trends in Ecology and Evolution*, 31, 563–574. https://doi.org/10.1016/j.tree.2016.03.012

Lewontin, R. C. (1983). Gene, organism, and environment. In D. S. Bendall (Ed.), *Evolution from molecules to men* (pp. 273–285). Cambridge University Press.

Marler, P., & Tamura, M. (1964). Culturally transmitted patterns of vocal behavior in sparrows. *Science*, 146(3650), 1483–1486. https://doi.org/10.1126/science.146.3650.1483

Mason, J. R., & Reidinger, R. F. (1982). Observational learning of food aversions in red-winged blackbirds (*Agelaius phoeniceus*). *The Auk*, 99, 548–554. https://doi.org/10.1093/auk/99.3.548

Mercader, J., Barton, H., Gillespie, J., Harris, J., Kuhn, S., Tyler, R., & Boesch, C. (2007). 4,300-Year-old chimpanzee sites and the origins of percussive stone technology. *Proceedings of the National Academy of Sciences*, 104, 3043. https://doi.org/10.1073/pnas.0607909104

Mills, R., & Watson, R. A. (2006). On crossing fitness valleys with the Baldwin effect. In L. M. Rocha, M. Bedau, D. Floreano, R. Goldstone, A. Vespignani, & L. Yaeger (Eds.), *Proceedings of the tenth international conference on the simulation and synthesis of living systems* (pp. 493–499). MIT Press.

Mineka, S., & Cook, M. (1988). Social learning and the acquisition of snake fear in monkeys. In B. G. Galef & T. R. Zentall (Eds.), *Social learning: Psychological and biological perspectives* (pp. 51–73). Lawrence Erlbaum.

Musgrave, S., Morgan, D., Lonsdorf, E., Mundry, R., & Sanz, C. (2016). Tool transfers are a form of teaching among chimpanzees. *Scientific Reports*, 6, 34783. https://doi.org/10.1038/srep34783

Muthukrishna, M., & Henrich, J. (2016). Innovation in the collective brain. *Philosophical Transactions of the Royal Society B: Biological Sciences*, 371(1690), 20150192. https://doi.org/10.1098/rstb.2015.0192

Navarrete, A. F., Reader, S. M., Street, S. E., Whalen, A., & Laland, K. N. (2016). The coevolution of innovation and technical intelligence in primates. *Philosophical Transactions of the Royal Society B: Biological Sciences*, 371(1690), 20150186. https://doi.org/10.1098/rstb.2015.0186

Nicolakakis, N., Sol, D., & Lefebvre, L. (2003). Behavioural flexibility predicts species richness in birds, but not extinction risk. *Animal Behaviour*, 65, 445–452. https://doi.org/10.1006/anbe.2003.2085

O'Brien, M. J., & Laland, K. N. (2012). Genes, culture, and agriculture: An example of human niche construction. *Current Anthropology*, 53, 434–470. https://doi.org/10.1086/666585

Odling-Smee, F., Laland, K., & Feldman, M. (2003). *Niche construction: The neglected process in evolution*. Princeton University Press.

Odling-Smee, J., Erwin, D. H., Palkovacs, E. P., Feldman, M. W., & Laland, K. N. (2013). Niche construction theory: A practical guide for ecologists. *The Quarterly Review of Biology*, 88, 3–28. https://doi.org/10.1086/669266

Olsson, A., & Phelps, E. A. (2007). Social learning of fear. *Nature Neuroscience*, 10, 1095–1102. https://doi.org/10.1038/nn1968

Oudman, T., Laland, K., Ruxton, G., Tombre, I., Shimmings, P., & Prop, J. (2020). Young birds switch but old birds lead: how barnacle geese adjust migratory habits to environmental change. *Frontiers in Ecology and Evolution*, 7, 502). https://doi.org/10.3389/fevo.2019.00502

Overington, S. E., Morand-Ferron, J., Boogert, N. J., & Lefebvre, L. (2009). Technical innovations drive the relationship between innovativeness and residual brain size in birds. *Animal Behaviour*, 78, 1001–1010. https://doi.org/10.1016/j.anbehav.2009.06.033

Paenke, I., Sendhoff, B., & Kawecki, Tadeusz J. (2007). Influence of plasticity and learning on evolution under directional selection. *The American Naturalist*, 170, E47–E58. https://doi.org/10.1086/518952

Price, T. D., Qvarnström, A., & Irwin, D. E. (2003). The role of phenotypic plasticity in driving genetic evolution. *Proceedings of the Royal Society B: Biological Sciences*, 270, 1433–1440. https://doi.org/10.1098/rspb.2003.2372

Reader, S. M., Hager, Y., & Laland, K. N. (2011). The evolution of primate general and cultural intelligence. *Philosophical Transactions of the Royal Society B*, 366, 1017–1027. https://doi.org/10.1098/rstb.2010.0342

Reader, S. M., & Laland, K. N. (2002). Social intelligence, innovation, and enhanced brain size in primates. *Proceedings of the National Academy of Sciences*, 99, 4436. https://doi.org/10.1073/pnas.062041299

(2003). Animal innovation: An introduction. In S. M. Reader & K. N. Laland (Eds.), *Animal innovation* (pp. 3–35). Oxford University Press. https://doi.org/10.1093/acprof:oso/9780198526223.003.0001

Reader, S. M., Morand-Ferron, J., & Flynn, E. (2016). Animal and human innovation: Novel problems and novel solutions. *Philosophical Transactions of the Royal Society B: Biological Sciences, 371*, 20150182. https://doi.org/10.1098/rstb.2015.0182

Rendell, L., Boyd, R., Cownden, D., Enquist, M., Eriksson, K., Feldman, M. W., Fogarty, L., Ghirlanda, S., Lillicrap, T., & Laland, K. N. (2010). Why copy others? Insights from the social learning strategies tournament. *Science, 328*, 208–213. https://doi.org/10.1126/science.1184719

Rendell, L., Fogarty, L., & Laland, K. N. (2011). Runaway cultural niche construction. *Philosophical Transactions of the Royal Society B: Biological Sciences, 366*, 823–835. https://doi.org/10.1098/rstb.2010.0256

Rendell, L., & Whitehead, H. (2001). Culture in whales and dolphins. *Behavioral and Brain Sciences, 24*, 309–324; discussion 324–382. https://doi.org/10.1017/s0140525x0100396x

Richerson, P., & Henrich, J. (2012). Tribal social instincts and the cultural evolution of institutions to solve collective action problems. *Cliodynamics: The Journal of Theoretical and Mathematical History, 3*, 38–80. http://dx.doi.org/10.2139/ssrn.1368756

Riesch, R., Barrett-Lennard, L., Ellis, G., Ford, J., & Deecke, V. (2012). Cultural traditions and the evolution of reproductive isolation: Ecological speciation in killer whales? *Biological Journal of the Linnean Society, 106*, 1–17. https://doi.org/10.1111/j.1095-8312.2012.01872.x

Russon, A. E. (2003). Innovation and creativity in forest-living rehabilitant orangutans. In S. M. Reader & K. N. Laland (Eds.), *Animal innovation* (pp. 279–306). Oxford University Press. https://doi.org/10.1093/acprof:oso/9780198526223.003.0013

Ryan, P. A., Powers, S. T., & Watson, R. A. (2016). Social niche construction and evolutionary transitions in individuality. *Biology & Philosophy, 31*, 59–79. https://doi.org/10.1007/s10539-015-9505-z

Sargeant, B. L., & Mann, J. (2009). Developmental evidence for foraging traditions in wild bottlenose dolphins. *Animal Behaviour, 78*, 715–721. https://doi.org/10.1016/j.anbehav.2009.05.037

Sarin, S., & Dukas, R. (2009). Social learning about egg-laying substrates in fruitflies. *Proceedings of the Royal Society B: Biological Sciences, 276*, 4323–4328. https://doi.org/10.1098/rspb.2009.1294

Seppänen, J.-T., Forsman, J. T., Mönkkönen, M., Krams, I., & Salmi, T. (2011). New behavioural trait adopted or rejected by observing heterospecific tutor fitness. *Proceedings of the Royal Society B: Biological sciences, 278*, 1736–1741. https://doi.org/10.1098/rspb.2010.1610

Sherry, D., & Galef, B. (1984). Cultural transmission without imitation: Milk bottle opening by birds. *Animal Behaviour, 32*, 937–938. https://doi.org/10.1016/S0003-3472(84)80185-2

Slagsvold, T., & Wiebe, K. (2007). Learning the ecological niche. *Proceedings of the Royal Society B: Biological Sciences, 274*, 19–23. https://doi.org/10.1098/rspb.2006.3663

Snell-Rood, E. C., Kobiela, M. E., Sikkink, K. L., & Shephard, A. M. (2018). Mechanisms of plastic rescue in novel environments. *Annual Review of Ecology, Evolution, and Systematics, 49*, 331–354. https://doi.org/10.1146/annurev-ecolsys-110617-062622

Sol, D., & Lefebvre, L. (2000). Behavioural flexibility predicts invasion success in birds introduced to New Zealand. *Oikos, 90*, 599–605. https://doi.org/10.1034/j.1600-0706.2000.900317.x

Sol, D., Stirling, D. G., & Lefebvre, L. (2005). Behavioral drive or behavioral inhibition in evolution: Subspecific diversification in Holarctic passerines. *Evolution, 59*, 2669–2677. https://doi.org/10.1111/j.0014-3820.2005.tb00978.x

Staddon, J. E. R. (2016). *Adaptive behavior and learning* (2nd ed.). Cambridge University Press.

Stephenson, G. (1967). Cultural acquisition of a specific learned response among rhesus monkeys. In D. Starek, R. Schneider, & H.J. Kuhn (Eds.), *Progress in Primatology* (pp. 279–288). Gustav Fisher Verlag.

Stickland, T. R., Britton, N. F., & Franks, N. R. (1995). Complex trails and simple algorithms in ant foraging. *Proceedings of the Royal Society B: Biological Sciences*, *260*, 53–58. https://doi.org/10.1098/rspb.1995.0058

Street, S. E., Navarrete, A. F., Reader, S. M., & Laland, K. N. (2017). Coevolution of cultural intelligence, extended life history, sociality, and brain size in primates. *Proceedings of the National Academy of Sciences*, *114*, 7908. https://doi.org/10.1073/pnas.1620734114

Suboski, M. D., Bain, S., Carty, A. E., McQuoid, L. M., Seelen, M. I., & Seifert, M. (1990). Alarm reaction in acquisition and social transmission of simulated-predator recognition by zebra danio fish (*Brachydanio rerio*). *Journal of Comparative Psychology*, *104*, 101–112. https://doi.org/10.1037/0735-7036.104.1.101

Sutherland, W. J. (1998). Evidence for flexibility and constraint in migration systems. *Journal of Avian Biology*, *29*, 441–446. https://doi.org/10.2307/3677163

Thorogood, R., & Davies, N. B. (2012). Cuckoos combat socially transmitted defenses of reed warbler hosts with a plumage polymorphism. *Science*, *337*(6094), 578–580. https://doi.org/10.1126/science.1220759

Tombre, I. M., Oudman, T., Shimmings, P., Griffin, L., & Prop, J. (2019). Northward range expansion in spring-staging barnacle geese is a response to climate change and population growth, mediated by individual experience. *Global Change Biology*, *25*, 3680–3693. https://doi.org/10.1111/gcb.14793

Uller, T., Moczek, A. P., Watson, R. A., Brakefield, P. M., & Laland, K. N. (2018). Developmental bias and evolution: A regulatory network perspective. *Genetics*, *209*, 949. https://doi.org/10.1534/genetics.118.300

Varela, S. A. M., Matos, M., & Schlupp, I. (2018). The role of mate-choice copying in speciation and hybridization. *Biological Reviews*, *93*, 1304–1322. https://doi.org/10.1111/brv.12397

Verzijden, M. N., & ten Cate, C. (2007). Early learning influences species assortative mating preferences in Lake Victoria cichlid fish. *Biology Letters*, *3*, 134–136. https://doi.org/10.1098/rsbl.2006.0601

Verzijden, M. N., ten Cate, C., Servedio, M. R., Kozak, G. M., Boughman, J. W., & Svensson, E. I. (2012). The impact of learning on sexual selection and speciation. *Trends in Ecology and Evolution*, *27*, 511–519. https://doi.org/10.1016/j.tree.2012.05.007

Waddington, C. H. (1953). Genetic assimilation of an acquired character. *Evolution*, *7*, 118–126. https://doi.org/10.1111/j.1558-5646.1953.tb00070.x

West-Eberhard, M. J. (2003). *Developmental plasticity and evolution*. Oxford University Press.

Whalen, A., Cownden, D., & Laland, K. (2015). The learning of action sequences through social transmission. *Animal Cognition*, *18*, 1093–1103. https://doi.org/10.1007/s10071-015-0877-x

Whitehead, H., Laland, K. N., Rendell, L., Thorogood, R., & Whiten, A. (2019). The reach of gene–culture coevolution in animals. *Nature Communications*, *10*(1), 1–10. https://doi.org/10.1038/s41467-019-10293-y

Whitehead, H., and Rendell, L. (2014). *The cultural lives of whales and dolphins*. University of Chicago Press.

Whiten, A. (2017). A second inheritance system: The extension of biology through culture. *Interface Focus*, *7*, 20160142. https://doi.org/10.1098/rsfs.2016.0142

Whiten, A., Goodall, J., McGrew, W. C., Nishida, T., Reynolds, V., Sugiyama, Y., Tutin, C. E., Wrangham, R. W., & Boesch, C. (1999). Cultures in chimpanzees. *Nature*, *399*, 682–685. https://doi.org/10.1038/21415

Wilkinson, G. S. (1992). Information transfer at evening bat colonies. *Animal Behaviour*, *44*, 501–518. https://doi.org/10.1016/0003-3472(92)90059-I

Yamagishi, T., & Hashimoto, H. (2016). Social niche construction. *Current Opinion in Psychology*, *8*, 119–124. https://doi.org/10.1016/j.copsyc.2015.10.003

Zohar, O., & Terkel, J. (1996). Social and environmental factors modulate the learning of pine-cone stripping techniques by black rats, *Rattus rattus*. *Animal Behaviour*, *51*(3), 611–618. https://doi.org/10.1006/anbe.1996.0065

PART II

EVOLUTION OF MEMORY PROCESSES

16

THE EVOLUTION OF MEMORY AS AN IMMEDIATE PERCEPTUAL IDENTIFICATION MECHANISM

Michael S. Fanselow

In this chapter I want to speculate about the initial selection pressures that led to the evolution of memory. The answer to the question of why did anything evolve typically starts with some supposition about function and benefit. For memory, both scientist and layperson likely think the answer is obvious and simple. It goes something like, we remember so we do not make the mistakes of the past. Wikipedia states, "memory is the ... retention of information over time for the purpose of influencing future action." The psychologist Alan Baddeley, a well-regarded memory researcher, similarly proclaims, "one function that these (memory) systems have in common is that of storing information for future use" (Baddeley, 1982, p1). Clearly, this ability to profit from previous experience must confer an adaptive benefit. However, the question I am raising is about the *origin* of memory, what was the original problem that applied the selection pressure that forced memory to evolve? I think there are both logical and empirical grounds that cast doubt on the notion that improving the future was the original selective force. Additionally, I do not think that improving the future is currently the primary benefit of memory. First, I will describe some of my logical objections to this notion with respect to selection pressure. Next, I will describe empirical evidence that provides a basis for an alternative, proposing that what we call memory actually evolved as a mechanism of immediate perceptual identification. I recognize that there are multiple forms of memory that likely evolved from somewhat unique selection pressures (Sherry & Schacter, 1987). To support my arguments, I will rely primarily on fear conditioning, but I will also use Pavlov's conditional salivation to make a case for generality of these ideas.

16.1 THE BENEFITS AND COSTS OF MEMORY

Certainly, once formed, memories can last a long time. In rats a conditional fear memory, once established, lasts the animal's lifespan (Gale et al., 2004).

This capacity suggests potential for a memory to provide some future benefit. However, it seems that these benefits would not provide much selection pressure when the advantage is so temporally removed from the mechanism being selected for. If prey see and smell a predator just before being attacked, learning these associations for future use does nothing if the animal does not survive the encounter. Many of the details of the encounter are likely to change if a second attack occurs at a later time. Therefore, the value of encoding those details will diminish over time because the situation will become progressively less likely to be repeated. It should also be recognized that many memories do not provide future benefit; some have a negative impact on fitness. Posttraumatic Stress Disorder (PTSD) is a powerful example. When faced with a major traumatic threat, immediate engagement of overwhelming fear and powerful defensive responses are a must, but the memories formed during such episodes cause a future characterized by severe debilitation, not benefit.

On the other hand, a much more powerful selective driving force would occur if the operation of the mechanism was immediately followed by a benefit. If forming a memory somehow helped the prey survive the current attack, the selective advantage would be both obvious and powerful. So, the first part of my argument is that benefits that do not manifest until well into the future will apply a lower, albeit not zero, increase in fitness compared to something that fosters immediate success on a problem that an animal is currently facing.

Of course, a benefit is only part of the equation; it has to be balanced against costs. Memory is an incredibly costly process. The brain is one of the most energetically demanding organs (Herculano-Houzel, 2011) and the mechanisms of memory formation are extremely expensive (Mery & Kawecki, 2005; Plaçais et al., 2017). Long-term potentiation, the physiological process responsible for association formation, requires neurons to fire at very high rates. Neurons must engage mechanisms to clear the calcium and sodium that enters the cell with this activity and this process is energetically costly (Voet et al., 2016). To make memories, gene expression and protein synthesis have to occur rapidly and these processes also impart an energy demand (Bier, 1999; Plaçais & Preat, 2013). Such costly processes would need to be balanced against very high benefits. Sufficient benefit is not likely to come from something that only matters well into the future. The benefit/cost ratio does not seem to favor the common view of the function of memory.

If we reject the notion that memory evolved to provide future benefits, the idea must be replaced by something that does provide sufficient benefits. I will describe two types of Pavlovian conditioning that suggest what this benefit is. Before I do so, I need to clarify some common fallacies about Pavlovian conditioning.

16.2 MISPERCEPTION OF PAVLOVIAN CONDITIONING

Pavlov's work had a major impact during the formative years of American psychology. In particular, Watson's views of behavior were profoundly influenced by Pavlov (Bolles, 1993; Watson, 1913). This is a bit ironic because during the period that Watson formulated his behavioristic approach, translations of Pavlov were not available. Given the lack of translation there had to be a bit of guesswork and filling in of details of Pavlov's findings. Furthermore, initial translations from Russian to English were highly inaccurate (Todes, 2014). These inaccuracies led to some important misrepresentations of both Pavlov's theories and empirical work. Terminology and definitions were adopted that diverged from Pavlov's appreciation of conditioning phenomena, and these have become etched into the dogma of conditioning theory.

Rescorla (1988) laid out how the current understanding of conditioning is very different from what is commonly described in both psychology and neuroscience texts. Central to this modern understanding is that Pavlovian conditioning is not simply a way of getting a reflexive response to a new stimulus; it is the way we learn relationships between stimuli, a view that emerged from research during the late 1960s and early 1970s (Rescorla, 1967, 1973, 1974). However, in Pavlov's writings toward his later years, which have been translated only recently into English (Yokoyama, in press, chapter 60), he concluded that associations form between the sensory elements of stimuli that co-occur and that these associations are bidirectional. With this understanding that Pavlovian conditioning is the learning of relationships between stimuli, I want to focus on two common but inaccurate beliefs about conditioning because they are particularly relevant to my argument. First is the need for repeated pairings of the Conditional Stimulus (CS) and Unconditional Stimulus (US). Second concerns the nature of a CS.

REPETITION

If you search definitions of conditioning, you will find that most definitions say something about repeated pairings of the CS and US. The necessity of repetition was so dogmatic in conditioning theory that the field was astounded when Garcia and Koelling (1966) reported that rats formed an aversion to a taste after a single pairing with a nausea-inducing stimulus. Later, researchers appreciated that fear conditioning also occurs with a single pairing (e.g., Fanselow, 1990). However, the idea that one can observe a conditional response (CR) after a single trial was recognized to be the case by Pavlov in his work on conditional salivation (Yokoyama, in press). Throughout his papers he often reported that a single pairing was sufficient for a salivatory CR. Repetition was necessary to maintain the CR. The primary reason Pavlov chose the term conditional (not conditioned, that was a mistranslation) was because he was struck by the temporary nature of the CR (Yokoyama, in press). Although a CR would occur after a single pairing, the CR would be lost through extinction if pairing was not maintained. Because several procedures caused the extinguished CR to return, expression of a CR could wax and wane in a manner that was dependent, or conditional, on experience. One critical assumption in the theory I am outlining is that one-trial conditioning is common.

NATURE OF THE CS

The second misconception concerns what a CS is. Laboratory experiments often use a CS that bears no relationship whatsoever to the US, such as a buzzer and food. This segregation of CS and US is used in the laboratory to allow greater control of stimuli. However, when Pavlov described the function of conditioning and how it most commonly occurred both in the lab and the real world, CSs were most often elements of the stimulus used as a US (Yokoyama, in press). Food is a US because it drives salivation without prior experience. However, food also has an appearance, a taste, a smell, and a texture, which will not produce a response until the animal has experienced food in its entirety. These components of food are CSs. After experiencing them together, the dog recognizes the food, and salivates, just from its smell or look. Domjan (2005) has also made the point that for conditional reproductive behavior, quail associate the coloration and feather pattern with sexual activity, binding these elements together to form the sex object. After such object learning, the male quail's reproductive behavior becomes directed at females that have these features and not toward other quail even if they have more natural coloration and feathers. The general point here is that normally CSs are not some arbitrary stimuli; they can be stimuli that are part of, or have a physical relationship with, the US (Domjan, 2005).

Although in nature most CSs and USs are part of the same object, this arrangement is not particularly convenient for laboratory manipulation. Pavlov wanted to manipulate how often a CS was presented with and without a US. He was interested in studying how the timing of the CS with respect to the US influenced conditioning. It would be extremely difficult to do these experiments with the taste, texture, or smell of food. It is much easier with a more arbitrary and discrete stimulus such as a buzzer or light. The emphasis on the use of discrete CSs in the laboratory left the impression that the CS must have no relationship with the US, even though Pavlov recognized that such stimuli are not what most often functioned as a CSs in the real world.

CONTEXTS AS CSs

Contextual fear conditioning exemplifies many of these characteristics of conditioning. The basic procedure is quite simple: A rat or mouse is placed into a novel chamber (context) that serves as a CS and shortly thereafter it receives an aversive electric foot shock US. Substantial fear conditioning occurs after a single context-shock pairing (Fanselow, 1990).

The simplicity of the procedure and the rapidity of learning belies the complexity of the underlying process. Contexts are inherently multimodal CSs because they are made up of a myriad of independent features. Before a context can serve as a stimulus, before it can be recognized, these features must be integrated into a unified representation (Fanselow, 2000; Krasne et al., 2015). This is illustrated by the immediate shock deficit (Fanselow, 1986). In the typical procedure the subject is given a few minutes to explore the context before the shock is delivered. If the time prior to shock is greatly reduced or eliminated, when the shock is administered immediately upon placement in the chamber, no conditioning occurs. A minimum of 20 seconds seems to be necessary to obtain detectable conditioning, and the amount of conditioning increases with additional time (Fanselow, 1986, 1990; Landeira-Fernandez et al., 2006). However, when the intervals are just long enough to allow substantial conditioning, the animals are very poor at accurately recognizing the context and overgeneralize the fear CR to other contexts (Zinn et al., 2020). Longer preshock periods, 3 min or more, are needed for the animal to later differentiate the shocked context from a somewhat different novel one. The left side of Figure 16.1 shows that when rats are tested in the same context in which they were shocked, the CR (freezing) monotonically increases as exploration time is increased from 15 to 720 seconds. However, the right-hand side shows that when tested in a different context that shares just some of the features of the conditioning context, the generalized freezing CR first increases and then decreases with exploration time.

Such data suggest that, as the animal explores the chamber, progressively more features are incorporated into its representation of context. With short intervals, the representation is too underdeveloped to support conditioning. With some exploration, the representation is effective at supporting conditioning but is still too impoverished to allow differentiation, which only emerges with the substantial exploration needed to form a detailed representation (Krasne et al., 2021). The fundamental point I wish to make is that animals do not simply or instantly recognize a context or place; that recognition involves a learning process whereby sensory elements become connected to each other. In the case of contextual fear, Pavlovian conditioning serves as a place identification mechanism.

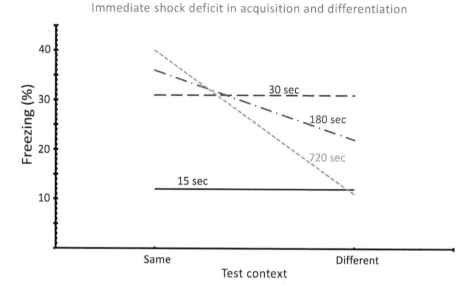

FIGURE 16.1. Rats received shock in a one context at different intervals between placement in the context and shock. The next day rats were placed in either the same context as they received shock or a different context. Percentage of time freezing in the two test contexts is presented.
The figure is based on data provided by Zinn et al. (2020).

Unlike the traditional discrete CS, contexts are continuously available. They appear as soon as the session starts and remain until the animal is removed from the conditioning chamber. In a one-trial conditioning experiment, the subject is not removed until sometime after US delivery. Although discrete CSs terminate prior to, or coincident with, US termination, context CSs persist beyond US termination. This means that any behavior that occurs after the US may be a CR because conditioning happens in one trial and the CS is still present after the US. Indeed, substantial research indicates that the freezing that occurs after a shock is fully a CR and not an unconditional response (UR) to the shock. Removing an animal from the training context immediately after shock and placing it in a different chamber eliminates freezing in the second chamber, but freezing is present if the animal is returned to the training context, indicating that even post-shock freezing is a CR and not a UR (Fanselow, 1980). I will label this sort of CS, one that precedes the US by enough time to allow conditioning and that still remains after US termination, a *Persistent CS*. The defining characteristics of a Persistent CS is one that begins sufficiently prior to the US to support one trial conditioning and remains present after the US terminates. Later I will describe some other examples of Persistent CSs.

The point that the postshock freezing as well as other fear responses, such as postshock defecation, are CRs and not URs is most dramatically made by the immediate shock deficit (Fanselow, 1986). When animals are given a shock immediately upon placement in a novel chamber they do not freeze, defecate, become analgesic, or show potentiated startle after the shock (Fanselow, 1986; Fanselow et al., 1994, Kiernan et al., 1995). They even readily reenter a chamber where they received an immediate shock (Kiernan et al., 1995). Certainly, rats will show reflexive activity to the shock as a UR, but they show none of the classic indicators of conditional fear. In other words, they do not recognize the shock as an aversive or threatening stimulus by itself. Fear responses occur only if shock is integrated, or associated, with other cues that are present. In this experimental example those cues are the features of the context that must also become associated with one another. It is Pavlovian context-shock conditioning that causes the sensory integration, which in turn allows the animal to recognize shock as a threat. Because that threatening CS persists after shock the animal engages in conditional defensive behavior commencing with shock termination. This example is one in which Pavlovian conditioning acts as a mechanism of immediate perceptual identification. This learning occurs instantly when conditions are favorable and is expressed immediately after the US because of the presence of a Persistent CS; however, without the context-shock association, the shock does not produce a fear response.

16.3 ROBOTS AS SUBJECTS AND STIMULI

I am going to use a fictional example to illustrate that the concept of association as a perceptual recognition mechanism is embodied in our common way of thinking. Our subject is a robot, WALL·E, from the Disney Pixar film of the same name. At about 15 minutes into the film, WALL·E has left his home to forage, and encounters EVE for the first time. EVE is also a robot but of a very different design than our subject. Perhaps because she is novel, or maybe because she is moving, she is a salient stimulus that draws WALL·E's attention. Shortly after he begins observing, EVE shoots and vaporizes a nearby object with a laser. WALL·E immediately shows a fear CR to EVE, quivering uncontrollably. At this point EVE has become a threat. WALL·E's reaction required the integration of EVE's sensory features and the laser blast. EVE is a persistent CS; she remains after the laser fired. EVE might well be dangerous and the immediate learning that occurred helps protect WALL·E during this potentially deadly encounter. Notice that this associative learning is serving an immediate, not a future, function. I chose the robot example because it is less inclined to be interpreted via a common biological speculation. If WALL·E were a mouse and EVE a cat, we might have been inclined to speculate that cat EVE was an innately recognized predator. With robots we are free of this interpretational bias and it becomes easier to see that what we have in this scene is a mechanism for immediate perceptual identification through associative learning. Another point here is that WALL·E is not afraid of the context or environment here; rather, the fear is specifically of EVE. This lack of contextual fear likely occurred because EVE was more salient than the context, but she still meets the requirements of a Persistent CS.

A brilliant laboratory embodiment of this type of scenario was conducted by Kim and colleagues (Choi & Kim, 2010; Kim et al., 2016). We still have a robot analog of EVE, but the robot is an automated Lego alligator-like construction named robogator. The experiment replaces WALL·E with a lab rat. The rat leaves a home area to forage for food, which it has done many times previously. In this instance, for the first time the rat encounters robogator, which surges toward the rat as it is about to retrieve a piece of food. Immediately the rat frantically scurries back to its home area, where it freezes before emerging again. Robogator is a novel complex stimulus, a composite of visual and auditory elements that include a surging movement. That movement seems to be a critical feature (Kim et al., 2016). However, movement is not a stimulus; it is a feature of a stimulus. The stimulus and its movement must become associated with each other. Experiencing all these features together turns robogator into a threatening CS and because this CS persists after the surge, the rat defends itself by running away and freezing. It is pretty unlikely that countless generations of attack by Lego robots resulted in rats evolving an innate ability to recognize robogators. What we again have is associative learning providing a mechanism for immediate perceptual identification that aids the rodent in instantly defending against this potential threat.

If a cat or snake had been the stimulus, we may have been inclined to interpret what happened as an instance of innate recognition. Using a robot disabuses us of a hasty and inaccurate interpretation, an interpretation that is often made but rarely tested. Experiments on innately recognized predators often rely totally on the argument that a defensive response was observed the first time the stimulus was encountered. This argument is based on the assumption that learning only emerges with repeated trials, but we have already rejected that assumption. Elsewhere, I have called this erroneous assumption the *myth of the first time* (Fanselow, 2018). We have just seen that rats react with conditional defensive behaviors the first time they encounter shock or robots. These are not innately recognized danger stimuli; they require perceptual learning to produce their reactions. Observing a response the first time a stimulus is presented cannot be taken as evidence of innate recognition. Yet, there is little other evidence that can be used to support the innate recognition hypothesis.

16.4 OF CATS AND RATS

The two robot examples are good vehicles for making the point that Pavlovian conditioning can provide a mechanism to identify threats. Does this mechanism apply to more natural threats that we might have thought were innately recognized? One aspect of the model being developed here is that it suggests that a brief but requisite time is needed to integrate features of the stimulus together before the US (shock, laser blast, or movement) is delivered. This requirement is most clear in the immediate shock experiments in which time before shock was manipulated (e.g., Figure 16.1). The robogator and EVE were also present for a period before the US was administered to enable the learning to occur.

For a rat to react to a cat, it also needs this time to integrate the cat stimulus; there is an *immediate cat deficit*. Blanchard et al. (1976) reported that rats will not freeze to a cat if the cat and rat are placed into the chamber at the same time. Freezing is observed only if the rat is in the chamber for a period of time prior to the presentation of the cat. Figure 16.2 shows that during the first minute after cat exposure, rats that were placed into the chamber two minutes prior to the cat froze more and moved less than rats that had an immediate presentation of the cat. Indeed, there was no freezing in the Immediate Cat Group. If the cat remains in the chamber with the rat, after about three minutes the rat will begin to freeze, but again this period affords the opportunity for perceptual integration of the cat's features. Figure 16.3 shows rats' initial reaction to the cat. In the Immediate Cat condition, rats were equally likely to move toward as away from the cat. These initial movements were suppressed in the Delayed Cat Group probably

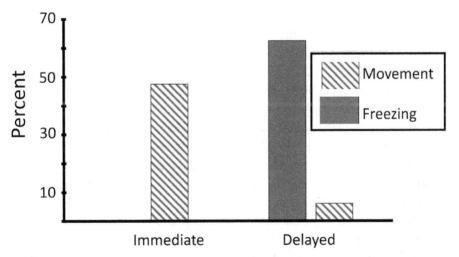

FIGURE 16.2. The percentage of time rats spent either freezing or moving during the first minute of exposure to a cat. The cat was placed in the chamber at the same time (immediate) or two minutes after (delayed) the rat.

The graph is based on data presented in Blanchard et al. (1976).

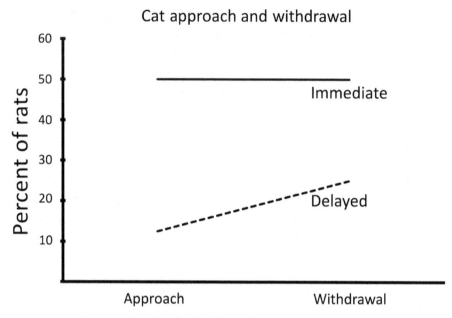

FIGURE 16.3. A cat was placed in the chamber at the same time (Immediate Group) or two minutes after (Delayed Group) the rat. The figure shows the percentage of the two groups of rats whose first movement in response to the cat was approach versus withdrawal.
The graph is based on data presented in Blanchard et al. (1976).

because they were freezing, but any movement that occurred was more likely to be retreat from the cat. The presence of an immediate cat deficit suggests that rats must associate the cat's features with each other to recognize the cat as a threat. Figures 16.2 and 16.3 concentrate on the first reactions to the predator because it provides evidence that the process is fast enough to dictate the animal's first reactions to this potential threat.

Interestingly, as with the robogator, movement seems to be a critical feature to produce rat's freezing to a cat (Blanchard et al., 1975; Bronstein & Hirsch, 1976). Indeed, Blanchard et al. reported that cat sounds and odor do not produce freezing. Even a dead cat will not produce freezing. The cat needs to move, but similar freezing is produced by a suddenly moving Masonite card. All of this suggests that when a cat's odor, appearance, sound, and movement are experienced together the rat integrates these features and this perceptual learning is how they come to fear cats. Because the learning and performance of the CR is immediate and the cat as CS persists during the episode, it fulfills the purpose that innate recognition would.

The presence of both an immediate shock and an immediate cat deficit suggests that similar sensory integration mechanisms play a critical role in the ability for these stimuli to drive defensive behaviors. There are other similarities. The developmental onset of rat's freezing to cats and shock occurs at the same age (Bronstein & Hirsch, 1976). It is well established that for contextual fear conditioning this integration requires the hippocampus, the quintessential memory structure (e.g., Kim & Fanselow, 1992; Squire & Zola, 1996). Interestingly, hippocampal lesions prevent freezing to cats (Blanchard & Blanchard, 1972). Both development and anatomy suggest similar learning mechanisms serve the two.

16.5 WHY SHOULD RECOGNITION OF BIOLOGICALLY IMPORTANT STIMULI REQUIRE LEARNING?

Obviously, predation poses a massive cost on prey because a failure to defend will likely preclude future reproduction. If defense is so urgent, why should it depend on learning and why would selection have favored learning over innate recognition of these threats? I think the answer is that genetic encoding of predators is too burdensome on the genome and too unreliable. Feral rats in my neighborhood need to worry about cats, a variety of canines, owls, hawks, people, raccoons, an occasional coyote, cars, trucks, and probably several other things I have not imagined. The genetic load of innately encoding all of these threats in all their permutations would be staggering. Even if many of these threats were encoded, new unencoded threats would likely be encountered, making innate recognition too unreliable for such an important function. If a fast and reliable learning mechanism, as described here and outlined in Table 16.1, were available, it would solve the problems of genetic burden and unreliability. Our rat is ready to deal with the sudden entry of a robogator into its territory. If it relied on innate recognition mechanisms it would have little chance of success.

16.6 GENERALITY

Although the evidence I have marshalled is based on defensive behavior and fear conditioning, there is every reason to think that the rules described here would apply to other functional/motivational systems. Pavlov recognized similar limitations to relying on innate signals when it comes to feeding:

> First, countless, variable and distant external agents act as if they are signals for food substances; they direct the higher animals to seize them, move them

TABLE 16.1. *Assumptions that allow Pavlovian conditioning to serve as a mechanism of immediate perceptual identification (MIPI)*

Pavlovian conditioning is the learning of relations or connections between stimuli.
Significant conditioning often occurs in a single trial.
CSs and USs are often features of the same object.
Real-world objects are a collection of multiple features, from multiple modalities.
CS aspects of these objects are often present after US delivery (Persistent CSs).
Post-US reactions often depend on the presence of these Persistent CSs; they are CRs not URs.

to establish the food connection with the external world. … second, given their huge number, they would not fit, if they were permanent, even in the most capacious apparatuses.

(Yokoyama, in press, chapter 11).

Pavlov's first point seems to suggest the problem of unreliability of depending exclusively on innate signals and the second to the genetic burden for innate encoding of all potentially relevant items.

The feeding and the defense system serve very different functions. The demands on each are quite different. They are served by different memory systems and anatomies. If conditioning provides a mechanism for immediate perceptual identification in both of these systems, it suggests that this process is very general. This generality may have come about through convergent evolution. Another possibility is that once the mechanism evolved in one system, other systems co-opted that machinery for their own use. One caveat is that I am not arguing that innate recognition does not exist but it may be limited to species that experience little variance in the biologically relevant object and especially if that object has a single salient identifiable feature. For example, if animals of a particular species eat only one type of food and that food has a reliably present unidimensional feature, such as an odor, there may be little advantage to using this learning mechanism for food identification. However, such simplicity is likely to be rare in animals that exploit varied environments.

16.7 MULTIPLE MEMORY SYSTEMS

The brain does not encode memory in one place and in one way (Squire, 2004). Researchers have identified several different types of memory and they are served by different anatomical substrates. A reasonable question is whether immediate perceptual identification is performed by a specific memory system or if it is a function of several of these memory systems. In rats, hippocampal damage severely impairs both contextual fear conditioning and reactions to a cat; and, the hippocampus is closely associated with episodic memory (Eldridge et al., 2000). This form of memory is a memory of a single event, experienced by an individual and includes the time, place, and what happened during the experience (Tulving, 2002). Episodic memory requires an integration of all these features (see Crystal, Chapter 17). Rudy and Teyler (2010) have argued that the hippocampus is required for contextual fear conditioning because the hippocampus is needed to form conjunctions of multiple features just as formation of an episodic memory does (see Gómez et al., Chapter 9). I have just argued that a similar process happens for predator recognition; it is a conjunction of several features and once these features are amalgamated into a single object the predator can be identified. Because episodic memory is by its nature a single event it fits well with something that is learned in a single trial or experience. Episodic memory is what allows us to reminisce about past events and imagine future events (Ingvar, 1985; Schacter et al., 2012). However, although episodic memory may allow reminiscence and imagination, these are probably not what initially drove the evolution of episodic memory. Rather, I argue that it evolved to deal with the current episode. Episodic memory immediately grabs the current events, allows them to be instantly integrated, and allows us to deal appropriately with the situation currently at hand.

Although immediate perceptual identification may be a function of episodic memory, this function does not preclude that identification of novel objects was the force behind the evolution of other types of memory. Pavlov's observation about salivation to foods suggests that immediate perceptual identification may be a function of many memory systems. Despite conditional salivation being the oldest model system for Pavlovian conditioning, surprisingly we know little about its precise anatomy. It may be that the initial identification of a novel food requires episodic memory, but once that memory is formed it is handed off to other memory systems. This process would be similar to how instrumental memories initially encode the specific food object but later, with repetition, food rewarded behavior is handed off to habitual systems (Dezfouli & Balleine, 2012). But it may be the case that the evolution in other memory systems was also driven by a need to identify novel stimuli and objects. This possibility remains an open question.

Pavlovian conditioning is a sensory integration that allows preprogramed behavior patterns such as freezing to be directed at relevant stimuli. It is not a system of motor learning, although Pavlov's later works did provide a framework whereby acquired sensory associations might mediate voluntary behavior (Yokoyama, in press). However, learning novel motor actions requires considerable tuning and adjustment of action. Learning systems that mediate fine motor movements seem to be quite different than the identification of sensory objects. Consistent with this observation is that systems primarily concerned with such actions tend to be very slow at learning, requiring many trials (e.g., Thompson & Steinmetz, 2009). Repetition would be necessary to appropriately tune complex motor activity.

16.8 EVOLUTION OF A MECHANISM FOR IMMEDIATE PERCEPTUAL IDENTIFICATION

Immediately recognizing and immediately reacting to a biologically significant stimulus would be a significant benefit that would be worthy of the costs associated with learning and plasticity. Although such a mechanism takes appreciable genetic space, it is likely to be far less than that required to encode all possible biologically relevant stimuli. Additionally, unlike innate recognition, the mechanism for immediate perceptual identification (MIPI) is prepared to deal immediately with novel items. I argue that these forces led to the initial selection pressure to evolve a memory mechanism. These benefits are sufficient to overcome the costs.

Certainly, many memories can last a very long time (e.g., Gale et al., 2004). I would argue that longevity is an elaboration of MIPI that followed its initial evolution. A predatory encounter will last until the prey has managed to fully evade the predator or is consumed by it. The memory cannot fade with momentary evasion, it must last the entire episode. Similarly, if a predator has just learned of a new type of food in a particular local, it should maintain that representation at least until the patch is optimally exploited. Certainly, salivation should not stop after the first bite of food but continue throughout the meal. To be effective the memory must have some degree of longevity, at least long enough to last the current episode or encounter. The mechanism responsible for that bit of longevity then provides a substrate for selection to operate on and produce even greater longevity. That longevity would have a great benefit when the biologically significant event was again encountered, but it is not the ability to deal with the future that initially drove the evolution of memory. In this way, the longevity of memory, and its ability to influence more distal future behavior, is an *exaptation*, similar to the way a bird's feathers evolved to support thermoregulation but were shaped by subsequent selection pressure to facilitate flight (Gould & Vrba, 1982; Williams, 1966). However, unlike feathers, whose major function is an adaptation for flight, I would argue that immediate perceptual identification is still the primary benefit provided by memory.

Maintaining, and further strengthening, such object memories would be of value when the object was again encountered. The argument here is not that dealing with the future is unimportant, just that it was not what initially led to the emergence of memory mechanisms. It is important to accurately recognize the original reasons that drove the evolution of memory because our failure to do so has been misleading. When we think of memory as something that is only there to direct future action, we need additional mechanisms to deal with situations that immediately confront an organism. The idea that memory requires repetition and is there for the distal future makes innate recognition an attractive explanatory idea. The evolution and elaboration of MIPI is more parsimonious in that it explains both immediate and future actions. By providing both immediate and future advantage the benefits are high. Costs are lowered by having a single mechanism accomplish both benefits. The reduction in information that must be genetically encoded also provides cost saving.

16.9 CONCLUSIONS

I present evidence that conditioning occurs the first time a complex multi-featured object is encountered, and it results in the immediate binding of these sensory features. This process allows a novel object to be recognized. Some of the features of an object have special significance. For example, sudden movement promotes recognizing the object as a threat. Such recognition allows the object to engage prewired motor programs such as freezing in the rodent. Because the conditional stimuli that compose the object persist throughout the encounter, conditional responding persists until the object is dealt with. Either the predator has left or the food object is consumed. Thus, a critical concept for this model is the idea of persistent CSs. These CSs start somewhat before the significant feature and persist for the duration of the encounter. Pavlovian conditioning is recast as a mechanism that allows organisms to immediately recognize and deal with biologically significant objects. I suggest that this immediate perceptual identification process, and not innate recognition, is the principal mechanism that allows animals to deal with significant objects the first time they are confronted. The biological importance of doing so provided the initial selection pressure that drove the evolution of memory. I further argue that this mechanism for immediate perceptual identification remains the primary function of memory.

REFERENCES

Baddeley, A. D. (1982) *Your memory: A user's guide.* McGraw Hill.

Bier, D. M. (1999). Institute of Medicine (US) Committee on Military Nutrition Research. The Role of Protein and Amino Acids in Sustaining and Enhancing Performance. Washington, D): National Academies Press (US). The Energy Costs of Protein Metabolism: Lean and Mean on Uncle Sam's Team. www.ncbi.nlm.nih.gov/books/NBK224633/

Blanchard, R. J., & Blanchard, D. C. (1972). Effects of hippocampal lesions on the rat's reaction to a cat. *Journal of Comparative and Physiological Psychology, 78,* 77–82. https://doi.org/10.1037/h0032176

Blanchard, R. J., Fukunaga, K. K., & Blanchard, D. C. (1976). Environmental control of defensive reactions to a cat. *Bulletin of the Psychonomic Society, 8,* 179–181. https://doi.org/10.3758/BF03335118

Blanchard, R. J., Mast, M., & Blanchard, D. C. (1975). Stimulus control of defensive reactions in the albino rat. *Journal of Comparative and Physiological Psychology, 88,* 81–88. https://doi.org/10.1037/h0076213

Bolles, R. C. (1993). *The Story of psychology: A thematic history.* Brooks/Cole Publishing.

Bronstein, P. M., & Hirsch, S. M. (1976). Ontogeny of defensive reactions in Norway rats. *Journal of Comparative and Physiological Psychology, 90,* 620–629. http://dx.doi.org/10.1037/h0077224

Choi, J.-S., & Kim, J. J. (2010). Amygdala regulates risk of predation in rats foraging in a dynamic fear environment. *Proceedings of the National Academy of Sciences, 107,* 21773–21777. https://doi.org/10.1073/pnas.1010079108

Dezfouli, A., & Balleine, B. W. (2012). Habits, action sequences and reinforcement learning. *European Journal of Neuroscience, 35*, 1036–1051. https://doi.org/10.1111/j.1460-9568 .2012.08050.x

Domjan, M. (2005). Pavlovian conditioning: A functional perspective. *Annual Review of Psychology, 56*, 179–206. https://doi.org/10.1146/annurev.psych.55.090902.141409

Eldridge, L. L., Knowlton, B. J., Furmanski, C. S., Bookheimer, S. Y., & Engel, S. A. (2000). Remembering episodes: A selective role for the hippocampus during retrieval. *Nature Neuroscience, 3*, 1149–1152. https://doi.org/10.1038/80671

Fanselow, M. S. (1980). Conditional and unconditional components of post-shock freezing in rats. *Pavlovian Journal of Biological Sciences, 15*, 177–182. https://doi.org/10.1007/ BF03001163

(1986). Associative vs. topographical accounts of the immediate shock freezing deficit in rats: Implications for the response selection rules governing species specific defensive reactions. *Learning & Motivation, 17*, 16–39. https://doi.org/10.1016/0023-9690(86)90018-4

(1990). Factors governing one trial contextual conditioning. *Animal Learning & Behavior, 18*, 264–270. https://doi.org/10.3758/BF03205285

(2000). Contextual fear, gestalt memories, and the hippocampus. *Behavioural Brain Research, 110*, 73–81. https://doi.org/10.1016/s0166-4328(99)00186-2

(2018). The role of learning in threat imminence and defensive behaviors. *Current Opinion in Behavioral Sciences, 24*, 44–49. https://doi.org/10.1016/j.cobeha.2018.03.003

Fanselow, M. S., Landeira-Fernandez, J., DeCola, J. P., & Kim, J. J. (1994). The immediate shock deficit and postshock analgesia: Implications for the relationship between the analgesic CR and UR. *Animal Learning & Behavior, 22*, 72–76. https://doi.org/10.3758/ BF03199957

Gale, G. D., Anagnostaras, S. G., Godsil, B. P., Mitchell, S., Nozawa, T., Sage, J. R., Wiltgen, B., & Fanselow, M. S. (2004). Role of the basolateral amygdala in the storage of fear memories across the adult lifetime of rats. *Journal of Neuroscience, 24*, 3810–3815. https://doi.org/10.1523/JNEUROSCI.4100-03.2004

Garcia, J., & Koelling, R. A. (1966). Relation of cue to consequence in avoidance learning. *Psychonomic Science, 4*, 123–124. https://doi.org/10.3758/BF03342209

Gould, S. J., & Vrba, E. S. (1982). Exaptation – A missing term in the science of form. *Paleobiology,8*, 4–15. https://doi.org/10.1017/S0094837300004310

Herculano-Houzel, S. (2011). Scaling of brain metabolism with a fixed energy budget per neuron: Implications for neuronal activity, plasticity and evolution. *PLoS ONE, 6*, e17514. https://doi.org/10.1371/journal.pone.0017514

Ingvar, D. H. (1985). Memory of the future: An essay on the temporal organization of conscious awareness. *Human Neurobiology, 4*, 127–136.

Kiernan, M. J., Westbrook, R. F., & Cranney, J. (1995). Immediate shock, passive avoidance, and potentiated startle: Implications for the unconditioned response to shock. *Animal Learning & Behavior, 23*, 22–30. https://doi.org/10.3758/BF03198012

Kim, J. J., Choi, J.-S., & Lee, H. J. (2016). Foraging in the face of fear: Novel strategies for evaluating amygdala functions in rats. In D. G. Amaral & R. Adolphs (Eds.), *Living without an amygdala* (pp. 129–148). The Guilford Press.

Kim, J. J., & Fanselow, M. S. (1992). Modality-specific retrograde amnesia of fear following hippocampal lesions. *Science, 256*, 675–677. https://doi.org/10.1126/science.1585183

Krasne, F. B., Cushman, J. D., & Fanselow, M. S. (2015). A Bayesian context fear learning algorithm/automaton. *Frontiers in Behavioral Neuroscience, 9*, 1–22. https://doi.org/10 .3389/fnbeh.2015.00112

Krasne, F. B., Zinn, R., Vissel, B., & Fanselow, M. S. (2021). Extinction and discrimination in a Bayesian model of context fear conditioning (BaconX). *Hippocampus, 31*, 790–814. https://doi.org/10.1002/hipo.23298

Landeira-Fernandez, J., Decola, J. P., Kim, J. J., & Fanselow, M. S. (2006). Immediate shock deficit in fear conditioning: Effects of shock manipulations. *Behavioral Neuroscience, 120*, 873–879. https://doi.org/10.1037/0735-7044.120.4.873

Mery, F., & Kawecki, T. J. (2005). A cost of long-term memory in *Drosophila*. *Science, 308,* 1148. https://doi.org/10.1126/science.1111331

Plaçais, P.-Y., & Preat, T. (2013). To favor survival under food shortage, the brain disables costly memory. *Science, 339,* 440–442. https://doi.org/10.1126/science.1226018

Plaçais, P.-Y., de Tredern, É., Scheunemann, L., Trannoy, S., Goguel, V., Han, K.-A., Isabel, G., & Prea, T. (2017). Upregulated energy metabolism in the *Drosophila* mushroom body is the trigger for long-term memory. *Nature Communications, 8,* 11510. https://doi.org/10 .1038/ncomms15510

Rescorla, R. A. (1988). Pavlovian conditioning: It's not what you think it is. *American Psychologist, 43,* 151–160. https://doi.org/10.1037/0003-066X.43.3.151

Rudy, J. W., & Teyler, T .J. (2010). Episodic memory and the hippocampus. In I. B. Weiner & W. E. Craighead (Eds.), *Corsini encyclopedia of psychology*. John Wiley & Sons. https:// doi.org/10.1002/9780470479216.corpsy0316

Schacter, D. L., Addis, D. R., Hassabis, D., Martin, V. C., Spreng, R. N., & Szpunar, K. K. (2012). The future of memory: Remembering, imagining, and the brain. *Neuron, 76,* 677–694. https://doi.org/10.1016/j.neuron.2012.11.001

Sherry, D. F., & Schacter, D. L. (1987). The evolution of multiple memory systems. *Psychological Review, 94,* 439–454. https://dx.doi.org/10.1037/0033-295X.94.4.439

Squire, L. R. (2004). Memory systems of the brain: A brief history and current perspective. *Neurobiology of Learning and Memory, 82,* 171–177. https://doi.org/10.1016/j.nlm.2004 .06.005

Squire, L. R., & Zola, S. M. (1996). Structure and function of declarative and nondeclarative memory systems. *Proceedings of the National Academy of Sciences, 93,* 13515–13522. https://doi.org/10.1073/pnas.93.24.13515

Thompson, R. F., & Steinmetz, J. E. (2009). The role of the cerebellum in classical conditioning of discrete behavioral responses. *Neuroscience, 162,* 732–755. https://doi.org/10.1016/j .neuroscience.2009.01.041

Todes, D. P. (2014). *Ivan Pavlov: A Russian life in science*. Oxford University Press.

Tulving, E. (2002). Episodic memory: From mind to brain. *Annual Review of Psychology, 53,* 1–25. https://doi.org/10.1146/annurev.psych.53.100901.135114

Voet, D., Voet, V. G., & Pratt, C. W. (2016). *Fundamentals of biochemistry: Life at the molecular level*. John Wiley & Sons.

Watson, J. B. (1913). Psychology as the behaviorist views it. *Psychological Review, 20,* 158–177. https://dx.doi.org/10.1037/h0074428

Williams, G. C. (1966). *Adaptation and natural selection*. Princeton University Press.

Yokoyama, O. T. (in press). *Pavlov on the conditional reflex: Papers, 1903–1936*. Oxford University Press.

Zinn, R., Leake, J., Krasne, F. B., Corbit, L. H., Fanselow, M. F. & Vissel, B. (2020) Maladaptive properties of context-impoverished memories. *Current Biology, 30,* 1–12. https://doi.org/ 10.1016/j.cub.2020.04.040

17

EPISODIC MEMORY IN ANIMALS

Jonathon D. Crystal

A fundamental problem concerning the evolution of cognition is to identify the extent to which cognitive processes are uniquely human. Historically, episodic memory was considered to be unique to humans, although more than 20 years of research established that nonhuman animals have several elements of episodic memory (see Schnell and Clayton, Chapter 18; Clayton & Dickinson, 1998; Crystal, 2018, 2021). Episodic memory consists of representations of an individual's past experiences (Tulving, 1972, 1983). Almost all of the research focused on episodic memory in animals may be characterized as demonstrating that nonhumans remember a single episode; an episode may be multidimensional, but we refer to such an episode as a single event. One potential interpretation is that nonhumans have a quite limited capacity for episodic memory, which would suggest a critical limitation of episodic memory in animals. I propose that rats represent multiple events in episodic memory and engage in memory replay, a process by which the rat searches its representational space in episodic memory to find events at specific points in the sequence. This approach focuses on the content of episodic memories, rather than the subjective experiences that may accompany episodic memory in humans (Crystal & Suddendorf, 2019).

Tulving (1972) proposed a distinction between semantic and episodic memory. *Semantic memory* consists of factual knowledge about the world, whereas *episodic memory* consists of memories of specific events. A major step to validate an animal model of episodic memory involves ruling out nonepisodic hypotheses (Roberts et al., 2008). Critically, episodic memory involves memory of a unique episode or event. Notably, episodic memory is distinct from judgments of familiarity. Episodic memory involves remembering an episode and the contextual details of the event, whereas familiarity is the somewhat vague judgment that an item is known (Eichenbaum, 2007; Eichenbaum et al., 2007, 2012; Yonelinas, 2001; Yonelinas & Levy, 2002). My colleagues and I developed a model of episodic memory in rats that uses multiple, diverse techniques, each of which rules out familiarity (Crystal, 2021;

Crystal & Alford, 2014; Crystal et al., 2013; Crystal & Smith, 2014; Panoz-Brown et al., 2016, 2018; Zhou & Crystal, 2009, 2011; Zhou et al., 2012).

I have argued that the *central hypothesis* of an animal model of episodic memory proposes that, at the moment of a memory assessment, the animal remembers back in time and retrieves a memory of the earlier event or episode (Crystal, 2013b, 2016a, 2016b, 2018, 2021). An alternative hypothesis (which I refer to as the *familiarity* hypothesis) proposes that the animal solves the memory test without remembering back to the specific earlier event. The presentation of a stimulus gives rise to a memory trace that decays over time. Because the age of memories can be inferred from a comparison of memory trace strengths, an animal may solve a memory test by following a relatively simple rule, such as choose the item that currently produces the lowest level of familiarity (which is reliably the new item). Critically, an animal that uses judgments of relative familiarity generates the correct answer but does not need to retrieve an episodic memory of the earlier event.

Early research on episodic memory in nonhumans focused on establishing that the animal indeed remembered a single event using episodic memory (Babb & Crystal, 2005, 2006a, 2006b; Clayton & Dickinson, 1998; Crystal & Alford, 2014; Crystal et al., 2013; Crystal & Smith, 2014; Eacott et al., 2005; Ergorul & Eichenbaum, 2004; Naqshbandi et al., 2007; Roberts et al., 2008; Zhou & Crystal, 2009, 2011; Zhou et al., 2012). This is a pragmatic place to begin by asking if animals can remember an event. Recently, we have explored the possibility that rats remember multiple events using episodic memory. Once we established that rats remember many events using episodic memory (Panoz-Brown et al., 2016), we were in a position to ask if rats remember the sequential order of multiple events (Panoz-Brown et al., 2018). We call evidence of this type the *replay of episodic memories*. People, in natural situations, recount their memories of ordered events (Dede et al., 2016; Kurth-Nelson et al., 2016; Paz et al., 2010; Staresina et al., 2013). Of course, memory is riddled with errors (e.g., failure to retrieve memories, retrieval of false memories, etc.). Nonetheless, in everyday situations we frequently remember the order of events. Indeed, we use this natural form of recall to solve frequently occurring problems. For example, we mnemonically retrace our steps in an effort to discover where we left a sought after (and now apparently missing) item (e.g., keys, phones, eyeglasses, remote controls). Moreover, some scenarios are not coherent without an ordered representation of events. For example, in assessing fault in a car crash, the observer needs to remember the location of vehicles before, during, and after the incident.

In the sections that follow, I describe evidence that rats remember multiple episodic memories and the order of such memories. I propose that rats form a representation of multiple items in episodic memory and search this representational space to find items that occurred in specific ordinal positions. Next, I explore connections between episodic memory replay in animals with a growing body of research that suggests that the hippocampus replays sequential memories of spatial locations. Finally, I outline some open questions for future research, with a focus on implications for the evolution of cognition.

17.1 MEMORY OF MULTIPLE ITEMS IN CONTEXT

In this section I develop the case that rats remember many items in context using episodic memory. The need to provide many trial-unique events in memory led us to develop an approach using odors because rats have excellent olfaction (Lancet, 1986; Mori et al., 1999; Rubin & Katz, 2001; Uchida & Mainen, 2003). In this work, we have a large pool of odors available so that rats are not required to choose an odor more than once per day. We use household spices and oils to infuse odors on plastic lids that can be placed on top of plastic containers where food may be presented.

Because presentation of a stimulus always gives rise to a familiarity signal, ruling out the use of familiarity is a pervasive problem. Thus, we sought to develop a technique to dissociate familiarity and episodic memory solutions to a memory problem. We recently developed such a dissociation (Panoz-Brown et al., 2016). In our approach (reviewed in Wright, 2018), we rewarded novel odors, whereas old (i.e., familiar) odors were not rewarded. We presented odors in each of two distinctive contexts, using arenas that differed in a number of features (e.g., size, pattern, extra-arena cues, etc.) in succession (Context A → B). In the first context, the first odor of the day (e.g., cinnamon) is presented alone and is rewarded. Next, pairs of odors are presented, one of which is new (e.g., cardamom) and is rewarded, and the other odor is old (e.g., cinnamon) and not rewarded. After 16 new odors have been presented in the first context, the same set of new odors are presented in the second context (in a new random order). Items that are new to the second context are rewarded, despite the fact that they have previously been presented in the first context; old odors are not rewarded. This is a challenging memory problem because all items have been presented earlier in the day, but they are *new* to the second context.

Initially, we presented all of the odors in each of two distinctive contexts in succession (Context A → B). According to the episodic memory hypothesis, the rats used episodic memory to remember the presentation of each item and the context in which it had been previously presented (Eichenbaum, 2007). Alternatively, according to a nonepisodic familiarity hypothesis, the rats chose new odors by avoiding the familiar items (or equivalently by choosing odors based on memory trace strength or based on the age of memories).

To dissociate episodic memory from judgments of relative familiarity, we unexpectedly transitioned between the contexts (e.g., context A → B → A). Critically, we identified sequences of odor presentations across the unexpected context transitions that predict *above chance* performance for item-in-context (i.e., episodic) memory and *below chance* performance for selecting the least familiar item.

In most naturally occurring situations, familiarity cues and episodic memories are confounded. Thus, we identified sequences of odors that put familiarity cues and episodic memory in conflict. Consider a particular pair of odors such as strawberry and blueberry (depicted as light gray and dark gray, respectively, in Figure 17.1A). Each odor is rewarded when the animal selects it upon *first* presentation in a given context (i.e., rewarded in the first context and rewarded in the second context). Initially, we presented one item (strawberry) but not the other (blueberry) in the first context. Next, both items were presented in the second context, importantly with strawberry followed by blueberry. Finally, the memory assessment occurred upon return to the first context. In the memory assessment, the rats were given a choice between strawberry and blueberry. Blueberry is the correct choice based on item-in-context because it has not yet been presented in the first context; thus, blueberry is rewarded when chosen in this test, and our measure of accuracy is the proportion of choices of the rewarded item. Note that, prior to the memory assessment, blueberry was presented *more recently* than strawberry (see Figure 17.1A). Because blueberry would be more familiar relative to strawberry in the memory assessment, an animal that relied on judgments of relative familiarity (i.e., follow the rule "avoid familiar items") would choose the strawberry item. Choice of strawberry would result in accuracy *below chance* by our measure of accuracy (because strawberry has already been rewarded in this initial context). By contrast, an animal that relied on item-in-context memory would choose blueberry in the memory assessment, resulting in *above chance* accuracy. Notably, this memory assessment dissociates item-in-context memory (above chance) from judgments of relative familiarity (below chance). We restricted our analysis to items that dissociated familiarity and episodic memory using the pattern described but with random odors that varied across trials.

To test whether the rats were relying on item-in-context episodic memory or nonepisodic judgments of familiarity, we examined the rats' accuracy in the initial memory assessments. The initial data were collected before the rats had the opportunity to learn from feedback provided by rewards in the novel condition. When the identity of items in context was put in conflict with familiarity cues (Figure 17.1B), initial performance was above chance (80% ± 6%; mean ± SEM; chance = 50%) using 32 odors and context transitions that ranged from 2 (shown in Figure 17.1A) to 15. We recreated novel conditions with each new number of context transitions because it was not possible for

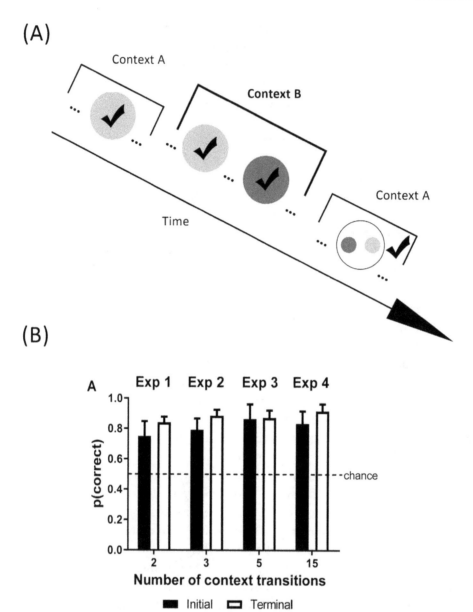

FIGURE 17.1. Dissociating episodic item-in-context memory from familiarity cues. (A) Light gray and dark gray, respectively, are used to depict strawberry and blueberry odors. Strawberry (light gray) is initially presented in Context A, and both strawberry (light gray) and blueberry (dark gray) are presented in Context B. Note that blueberry (dark gray) was *not* presented in Context A, and strawberry (light gray) occurred before blueberry (dark gray) in Context B. Finally, the memory assessment is conducted in Context A, and the rats are confronted with a choice between strawberry (light gray) and blueberry (dark gray). The correct choice, based on item-in-context, is blueberry (dark gray) because it has not yet been presented in Context A. Blueberry (dark gray) is rewarded when chosen in this test, and the proportion of choices of the rewarded item is the measure of accuracy. Importantly, prior to the memory assessment, blueberry (dark gray) was presented more recently than strawberry (light gray). Consequently, in the memory assessment, strawberry (light gray) is less familiar relative to blueberry (dark gray). Thus, an animal that relies on judgments of relative familiarity would choose the strawberry (light gray) item in the memory assessment. By our measure of accuracy, this choice produces *below chance* accuracy. By contrast, an animal that relied on item-in-context

the rat to anticipate a new transition between contexts. High accuracy in the novel conditions (Figure 17.1B) provides evidence that rats relied on episodic item-in-context memory rather than judgments of familiarity. Item-in-context episodic memories are also intact after a long retention interval (45 minutes), which is consistent with the hypothesis that episodic memory is an aspect of long-term memory (Panoz-Brown et al., 2016).

The data from Panoz-Brown et al. (2016) suggest that rats remember many unique events using episodic memory. The rats remember at least 30 item-in-context events using episodic memory based on the number of items in context in this work. Longer sequences of odors can be used to investigate limits on episodic memory in future research.

17.2 REPLAY OF EPISODIC MEMORIES

In the previous section I developed the case that rats remember at least 30 item-in-context events using episodic memory. In this section, I develop the case that rats remember the sequential order of episodic memories, an ability that would enable a rat to *replay* its episodic memories. Panoz-Brown et al. (2018) proposed that rats represent multiple items in episodic memory and engage in memory replay, a process by which the rat searches its representational space in episodic memory to find items at particular points in the sequence. Episodic memories in people have been characterized as the replay of the flow of past events in sequential order (Dede et al., 2016; Eichenbaum, 2000; Eichenbaum et al., 2007; Kurth-Nelson et al., 2016; Staresina et al., 2013; Tulving, 2002). Electrophysiological studies in animals suggest that rats *replay* the sequence of hippocampal place cells (Carr et al., 2011, 2012; Ego-Stengel & Wilson, 2010; Jadhav et al., 2012). However, these studies primarily use relatively inactive rats (e.g., sleeping, walking along a track without any behavioral choice points). These studies have not used behavioral tasks such as those described above to document episodic memory. Yet, episodic memory replay is likely to be found (Buzsáki, 2015) because the

---

FIGURE 17.1. (*cont.*) memory would choose blueberry (dark gray) in the memory assessment, which produces *above chance* accuracy. Notably, this memory assessment dissociates item-in-context memory (above chance) from judgments of relative familiarity (below chance). The presence of additional odors (not shown) is identified by "..." in the schematic. The schematic focuses on rewarded items (denoted by "√") by omitting comparison nonrewarded items prior to the memory assessment. Note that on other occasions (not shown) dark gray precedes light gray in Context B, accuracy is high (91%), but item-in-context episodic memory and familiarity judgments are not dissociated on these occasions. (B) Accuracy in episodic memory assessment depicted in (A) is above chance, documenting episodic memory for multiple items in context (~30 items). Accuracy was equivalent (not shown) if an item was rewarded once or twice (JZS Bayes factor = 4.0). Error bars represent 1 SEM.

Reproduced with permission from Panoz-Brown, D. E., Corbin, H. E., Dalecki, S. J., Gentry, M., Brotheridge, S., Sluka, C. M., Wu, J.-E., and Crystal, J. D. (2016). Rats remember items in context using episodic memory. *Current Biology*, 26(20), 2821–2826. ©2016.

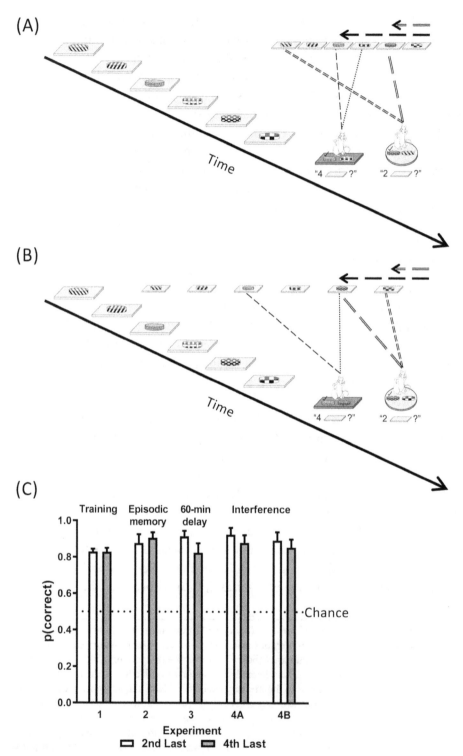

FIGURE 17.2. Rats replay a stream of multiple episodic memories. (A) A list of odors (, , , etc.) is presented in a distinctive context (). When the list ends, the rat is moved to one of two different contexts (, ; randomly selected). In one context (), the second from

hippocampus is a critical processing center for episodic memory in humans (Tulving & Markowitsch, 1998) and rats (Crystal et al., 2013; Eacott et al., 2005; Fortin et al., 2004; Zhou et al., 2012). Therefore, we provided rats with opportunities to report about a stream of events in sequential order using episodic memory.

In our approach (reviewed in Wright, 2018), rats were presented with a list of odors (Figure 17.2A). The length of the list ranged from 5 to 12 items that were randomly selected on each trial. Therefore, the rat *could not predict* the length of the list until it ended; this critical feature made it impossible for the rat to identify the correct choices before the list ended. When a list ended, the rat was placed in one of two distinctive contexts, where two items from the list were presented as an assessment of memory (locations of odors were randomly selected and provided no information about the correct choice). The correct item was rewarded. In one context, the second to the last item from the list was the correct choice. In the other context, the fourth from the last item was the correct choice. Our strategy was to ask: What could a rat with episodic replay do via its behavior? If the rat could replay the sequence of episodic memories, it would select the correct item in second and fourth last contexts. The rats passed a number of tests for episodic memory replay (Figure 17.2C) with accuracy above chance in both second and fourth last memory assessments. In one test (Figure 17.2B), we dissociated episodic memory replay from nonepisodic memory alternatives. As noted before, familiarity cues are pervasive; thus, we again developed a technique to dissociate familiarity and episodic memory solutions to the memory problem. According to the episodic memory replay hypothesis, rats represent multiple items in episodic memory and engage in memory replay, a process by which the rat searches its representational space in episodic memory to

FIGURE 17.2. (*cont.*) the last item from the list is the correct choice (depicted by "√"); the foil is another item from the list. In the other context (⊂⊃), the fourth from the last item is correct. The correct item is not known until the list ends because the list length is randomly selected on each trial. (B) The presentation of an item gives rise to a memory trace that decays with the passage of time (delays depicted by arrows at top of (A) and (B)). Thus, the correct choice in (A) could be based on judgments of relative familiarity (memory trace strength) of second and fourth last items (the time between second last item and memory assessment is shorter than between fourth last item and memory assessment). Familiarity and sequential information are dissociated in (B) by doubling the amount of time between list items. The foils in (B) were selected to pit the "correct" familiarity item vs. the "correct" sequential item. (C) Rats chose the correct sequential item when familiarity and sequential information were dissociated (Exp 2). Similarly, high accuracy was observed in training (Exp 1, depicted in (A)) and other conditions (Exp 3: long retention interval (60 minutes)); replay was intact when other items were remembered after list encoding (Exp 4A: foils from list; Exp 4B: foils from interference task). Our approach provides an animal model of episodic memory replay, a process by which the rat searches its representations in episodic memory in sequential order to find information. Error bars represent 1 SEM.

find information. Alternatively, we outline a nonepisodic memory solution. As noted, when an item is presented, it gives rise to a memory trace that decays over time. Therefore, it is possible that the rats were judging the relative familiarity of memory traces to successfully choose the second last (relatively large trace) and the fourth last (smaller trace) items in the appropriate context. Notably, such a solution would *not* require the replay of episodic memories to search the representational space in episodic memory for the second and fourth last items. To dissociate familiarity and sequence information, we *doubled the time between list items*, which impacts relative familiarity of items without impacting the sequential order of items. The dissociation is shown in Figure 17.2B. Importantly, in the fourth last context, the foil (i.e., incorrect choice) was an attractive choice because it had occurred in the list at the delay typical of a fourth last item; thus, an animal that is relying on familiarity would choose the wrong item (*below* chance). By contrast, an animal that uses episodic memory replay would choose the fourth last item correctly (*above* chance) despite the unusually long delay since this particular fourth last item's appearance in the list. Similarly, in the second last context, the foil was an attractive choice because it had occurred in the list at the delay typical of a second last item. In both dissociation tests, we observed above chance accuracy (Figure 17.2C), which rules out judgments of familiarly (or equivalently memory trace strengths, the age of memories, and timing intervals from each event to the memory assessment) and supports the hypothesis that rats replay episodic memory. In other experiments, we showed that episodic replay is intact after at least a one-hour retention interval and survives interference provided by memory of other odors; these data are also consistent with the hypothesis that episodic memory is an aspect of long-term memory. High accuracy provides strong evidence that rats relied on episodic replay (Figure 17.2C). Finally, we used DREADDs (Designer Receptor Exclusively Activated by Designer Drug) to document that temporary inhibition of hippocampal neurons impaired replay of episodic memories while sparing measures of hippocampal-independent memory (new-old recognition memory and an associative discrimination) (Panoz-Brown et al., 2018).

17.3 HIPPOCAMPAL REPLAY

Substantial evidence suggests that the hippocampus replays the sequence of recently visited spatial locations. Place cells exhibit stable, spatially constrained firing fields, referred to as place fields (typically pyramidal neurons from areas CA1 and CA3 of the hippocampus). Place fields provide a representation of self-location while an animal moves through the environment (Moser et al., 2015). Place cells are also coordinated with other neural representations of the environment, namely, head direction cells (which signal the direction the animal is facing), grid cells (which provide a metric representation of the environment), and border cells (which represent boundary features of the environment) (Moser et al., 2015; Ólafsdóttir et al., 2018).

Spatial representations in the brain are activated not only when an animal navigates through space, but also under circumstances in which past experiences are replayed. Brief bursts of place cell activity occur within high-frequency fluctuations in the hippocampal local field potential of CA1, a phenomenon referred to as sharp-wave ripples. The sequence of place cells is activated in a time-compressed cascade during sharp-wave ripples. Place cells that were active during recent exploration are reactivated during subsequent periods of sleep (Pavlides & Winson, 1989) with relative timing in sharp-wave ripples that matches the sequence of place cells from earlier awake experience (Skaggs & McNaughton, 1996). Because the reactivations during sharp wave ripples recapitulate the relative timing of place cells from awake behavior, this phenomenon is known as hippocampal replay (Ólafsdóttir et al., 2018).

Hippocampal replay not only occurs during sleep and quiet rest, but also when animals are awake and engaging in relatively simple tasks. As an animal runs down a track, place cells are sequentially activated, and subsequently these place cells are reactivated in the same sequence (forward replay) and in the opposite sequence (reverse replay). Interestingly, hippocampal replay occurs during pauses at the time of decision-making in behavioral tasks. Reverse replay has been observed when animals receive reward at the end of a track, which suggests that reverse replay may be important for learning from recent experience (Diba & Buzsáki, 2007). Forward replay follows the direction animals are about to travel (Ólafsdóttir et al., 2017; Pfeiffer & Foster, 2013). Moreover, hippocampal replay has been observed for trajectories of a path through the environment that the animal had seen but has not yet experienced (Pfeiffer & Foster, 2013). This raises the intriguing possibility that hippocampal replay may be involved in constructing future scenarios (Cheng et al., 2016; Corballis, 2013a, 2013b). Although hippocampal replay is typically restricted to a very short temporal scale (e.g., 50–120 ms), it has also been observed over an extended scale (~1 minute) (Davidson et al., 2009).

17.4 THE EVOLUTION OF COGNITION

There is a long-standing tradition of primate-centered studies to explore comparative cognition. The *traditional approach* assumes that evidence of cognitive complexity is most profitably pursued in nonhuman primates (Premack & Woodruff, 1978). A more recent approach focuses on corvids (Emery & Clayton, 2004; Powell et al., 2017). The *recent approach* assumes the convergent evolution of cognition in corvids and apes. Convergence is plausible in this case because primates and corvids both have relatively large brains (encephalization) and no other species in their shared lineage displays a high degree of encephazliation. Thus, according to the traditional and recent approaches, advances in animal cognition will come from research using nonhuman primates or corvids, respectively. By contrast, the perspective from either approach suggests that species outside of primates and corvids are unlikely to lead to advances in our understanding of the evolution of cognition. However, cognitive complexity may be more broadly distributed across species. Thus, the strategy for our empirical work is to *not* follow existing trends noted earlier. Instead, our efforts focus on exploring the elements (including limits) of cognitive complexity in rats. At a minimum, evaluating cognitive complexity in animals distantly related to humans is needed to test the hypothesis that cognitive complexity in animals distantly related to humans is primarily developed in nonhuman primates (the traditional approach) or in corvids (the more recent approach; see Schnell and Clayton, Chapter 18; Vonk, Chapter 20). One view about this effort notes that animals may not have the same level of these capacities as do humans, but it is likely that they have important evolutionary precursors. The exact degree of similarity or dissimilarity remains to be empirically established.

I outline four questions that may shed some light on the limits of episodic memory in rats: Can rats search forward and backward in time when replaying episodic memory? Can rats search for a target when the target's identity was not known before encoding the sequence? Can rats search for a target when the importance of the sequence was not known when it was encoded (incidental encoding) and when unexpectedly asked to report the information (an unexpected question)? Can rats form a representation of a target, store it in memory, and then retrieve it while replaying the sequence (using prospective memory; Crystal, 2013a; Wilson & Crystal, 2012; Wilson et al., 2013)?

Answers to these questions may identify the range and limits of the rat's ability to replay episodic memories. Evidence of this type will inform our understanding about the uniqueness of human cognition and cognitive complexity. Although the capacity for cognitive processes is likely pervasively distributed, the exact distribution remains to be established.

Another question focuses on developing evidence of hippocampal replay of episodic memories. This effort would combine approaches to episodic memory replay with high-density electrophysiological recordings in animals performing episodic memory replay tasks.

17.5 CONCLUSIONS

We have provided evidence for episodic memory when judgments of familiarity cannot produce accurate choices in memory assessments. We have provided such documentation by dissociating episodic memory and familiarity (in item-in-context memory and in episodic memory replay). In other work, we have equated familiarity cues across conditions to prevent the use of familiarity (Crystal et al., 2013; Crystal & Smith, 2014; Dalecki et al., 2017; Smith, Dalecki, et al., 2017; Smith, Slivicki, et al., 2017; Zhou & Crystal, 2009, 2011). These approaches may be used to explore the evolution of cognition in other species.

Evidence that rats replay episodic memories suggests that they remember the order of multiple episodic memories, an ability that would enable a rat to *replay* its episodic memories. We propose that rats represent multiple items in episodic memory and engage in memory replay, a process by which the rat searches its representational space in episodic memory to find items at particular points in the sequence (Panoz-Brown et al., 2018). Evidence that rats replay episodic memories opens new opportunities to understand the mechanisms of episodic memory, to identify limits in rats' cognitive processes, and to identify similarities and differences in memory across species. Future research may identify rich representations of the flow of past events, forward and/or backward replay of episodic memories, potentially advanced memory searching abilities that use episodic memories to plan for the future, and electrophysiological correlates of replaying episodic memories.

ACKNOWLEDGMENTS

This work was supported by National Institute on Aging grant AG051753 and National Science Foundation grant NSF/BCS-1946039.

REFERENCES

Babb, S. J., & Crystal, J. D. (2005). Discrimination of what, when, and where: Implications for episodic-like memory in rats. *Learning & Motivation, 36*, 177–189. https://doi.org/https://doi.org/10.1016/j.lmot.2005.02.009

(2006a). Discrimination of what, when, and where is not based on time of day. *Learning & Behavior, 34*, 124–130. https://doi.org/10.3758/bf03193188

(2006b). Episodic-like memory in the rat. *Current Biology, 16*, 1317–1321. https://doi.org/https://doi.org/10.1016/j.cub.2006.05.025

Buzsáki, G. (2015). Hippocampal sharp wave-ripple: A cognitive biomarker for episodic memory and planning. *Hippocampus, 25*, 1073–1188. https://doi.org/10.1002/hipo.22488

Carr, M. F., Jadhav, S. P., & Frank, L. M. (2011). Hippocampal replay in the awake state: A potential substrate for memory consolidation and retrieval. *Nature Neuroscience, 14*, 147–153. https://doi.org/https://doi.org/10.1038/nn.2732

Carr, M. F., Karlsson, M. P., & Frank, L. M. (2012). Transient slow gamma synchrony underlies hippocampal memory replay. *Neuron, 75*, 700–713. https://doi.org/https://doi.org/10.1016/j.neuron.2012.06.014

Cheng, S., Werning, M., & Suddendorf, T. (2016). Dissociating memory traces and scenario construction in mental time travel. *Neuroscience and Biobehavioral Reviews, 60*, 82–89. https://doi.org/https://doi.org/10.1016/j.neubiorev.2015.11.011

Clayton, N. S., & Dickinson, A. (1998). Episodic-like memory during cache recovery by scrub jays. *Nature, 395,* 272–274. https://doi.org/10.1038/26216

Corballis, M. C. (2013a). Mental time travel: A case for evolutionary continuity. *Trends in Cognitive Sciences, 17,* 5–6. http://linkinghub.elsevier.com/retrieve/pii/S1364661312002458

(2013b). The wandering rat: Response to Suddendorf. *Trends in Cognitive Sciences, 17,* 152. https://doi.org/https://doi.org/10.1016/j.tics.2013.01.012

Crystal, J. D. (2013a). Prospective memory. *Current Biology, 23,* R750–R51. https://doi.org/https://doi.org/10.1016/j.cub.2013.07.081

(2013b). Remembering the past and planning for the future in rats. *Behavioural Processes, 93,* 39–49. https://doi.org/http://dx.doi.org/10.1016/j.beproc.2012.11.014

(2016a). Animal models of source memory. *Journal of the Experimental Analysis of Behavior, 105,* 56–67. https://doi.org/10.1002/jeab.173

(2016b). Comparative cognition: Action imitation using episodic memory. *Current Biology, 26,* R1226–R1228. https://doi.org/10.1016/j.cub.2016.10.010

(2018). Animal models of episodic memory. *Comparative Cognition & Behavior Reviews, 13,* 105–122. https://doi.org/10.3819/ccbr.2018.130012

(2021). Event memory in rats. In A. Kaufman, J. Call, & J. Kaufman (Eds.), *Cambridge handbook of animal cognition* (pp. 190–209). Cambridge University Press.

Crystal, J. D., & Alford, W. T. (2014). Validation of a rodent model of source memory. *Biology Letters, 10,* 20140064. https://doi.org/10.1098/rsbl.2014.0064

Crystal, J. D., Alford, W. T., Zhou, W., & Hohmann, A. G. (2013). Source memory in the rat. *Current Biology, 23,* 387–391. https://doi.org/http://dx.doi.org/10.1016/j.cub.2013.01.023

Crystal, J. D., & Smith, A. E. (2014). Binding of episodic memories in the rat. *Current Biology, 24,* 2957–2961. https://doi.org/10.1016/j.cub.2014.10.074

Crystal, J. D., & Suddendorf, T. (2019). Episodic memory in nonhuman animals? *Current Biology, 29,* R1291–R1295. https://doi.org/https://doi.org/10.1016/j.cub.2019.10.045

Dalecki, S. J., Panoz-Brown, D. E., & Crystal, J. D. (2017). A test of the reward-contrast hypothesis. *Behavioural Processes, 145,* 15–17. https://doi.org/https://doi.org/10.1016/j.beproc.2017.09.018

Davidson, T. J., Kloosterman, F., & Wilson, M. A. (2009). Hippocampal replay of extended experience. *Neuron, 63,* 497–507. https://doi.org/https://doi.org/10.1016/j.neuron.2009.07.027

Dede, A. J. O., Frascino, J. C., Wixted, J. T., & Squire, L. R. (2016). Learning and remembering real-world events after medial temporal lobe damage. *Proceedings of the National Academy of Sciences, 113,* 13480–13485. https://doi.org/10.1073/pnas.1617025113

Diba, K., & Buzsáki, G. (2007). Forward and reverse hippocampal place-cell sequences during ripples. *Nature Neuroscience, 10,* 1241. https://doi.org/10.1038/nn1961

Eacott, M. J., Easton, A., & Zinkivskay, A. (2005). Recollection in an episodic-like memory task in the rat. *Learning and Memory, 12*(3), 221–223. https://doi.org/http://www.learnmem.org/cgi/doi/10.1101/lm.92505

Ego-Stengel, V., & Wilson, M. A. (2010). Disruption of ripple-associated hippocampal activity during rest impairs spatial learning in the rat. *Hippocampus, 20,* 1–10. https://doi.org/10.1002/hipo.20707

Eichenbaum, H. (2000). A cortical-hippocampal system for declarative memory. *Nature Reviews Neuroscience, 1,* 41–50. https://doi.org/10.1038/35036213

(2007). Comparative cognition, hippocampal function, and recollection. *Comparative Cognition & Behavior Reviews, 2,* 47–66. https://doi.org/doi:10.3819/ccbr.2008.20003

Eichenbaum, H., Sauvage, M., Fortin, N., Komorowski, R., & Lipton, P. (2012). Towards a functional organization of episodic memory in the medial temporal lobe. *Neuroscience and Biobehavioral Reviews, 36,* 1597–1608. https://doi.org/https://doi.org/10.1016/j.neubiorev.2011.07.006

Eichenbaum, H., Yonelinas, A. P., & Ranganath, C. (2007). The medial temporal lobe and recognition memory. *Annual Review of Neuroscience, 30,* 123–152. https://doi.org/doi:10.1146/annurev.neuro.30.051606.094328

Emery, N. J., & Clayton, N. S. (2004). The mentality of crows: Convergent evolution of intelligence in corvids and apes. *Science, 306,* 1903-1907. https://doi.org/10.1126/science.1098410

Ergorul, C., & Eichenbaum, H. (2004). The hippocampus and memory for "what," "where," and "when." *Learning and Memory, 11*(4), 397-405. https://doi.org/doi.org/10.1101/lm.73304

Fortin, N. J., Wright, S. P., & Eichenbaum, H. (2004). Recollection-like memory retrieval in rats is dependent on the hippocampus. *Nature, 431,* 188-191. https://doi.org/10.1038/nature02853

Jadhav, S. P., Kemere, C., German, P. W., & Frank, L. M. (2012). Awake hippocampal sharp-wave ripples support spatial memory. *Science, 336,* 1454-1458. https://doi.org/10.1126/science.1217230

Kurth-Nelson, Z., Economides, M., Dolan, R. J., & Dayan, P. (2016). Fast sequences of non-spatial state representations in humans. *Neuron, 91*(1), 194-204. https://doi.org/https://doi.org/10.1016/j.neuron.2016.05.028

Lancet, D. (1986). Vertebrate olfactory reception. *Annual Review of Neuroscience, 9,* 329-355. https://doi.org/10.1146/annurev.ne.09.030186.001553

Mori, K., Nagao, H., & Yoshihara, Y. (1999). The olfactory bulb: Coding and processing of odor molecule information. *Science, 286,* 711-715. https://doi.org/10.1126/science.286.5440.711

Moser, M.-B., Rowland, D. C., & Moser, E. I. (2015). Place cells, grid cells, and memory. *Cold Spring Harbor Perspectives in Biology, 7*(2), 1-15. https://doi.org/10.1101/cshperspect.a021808

Naqshbandi, M., Feeney, M. C., McKenzie, T. L. B., & Roberts, W. A. (2007). Testing for episodic-like memory in rats in the absence of time of day cues: Replication of Babb and Crystal. *Behavioural Processes, 74,* 217-225. https://doi.org/10.1016/j.beproc.2006.10.010

Ólafsdóttir, H. F., Bush, D., & Barry, C. (2018). The role of hippocampal replay in memory and planning. *Current Biology, 28,* R37-R50. https://doi.org/10.1016/j.cub.2017.10.073

Ólafsdóttir, H. F., Carpenter, F., & Barry, C. (2017). Task demands predict a dynamic switch in the content of awake hippocampal replay. *Neuron, 96,* 925-935.e926. https://doi.org/https://doi.org/10.1016/j.neuron.2017.09.035

Panoz-Brown, D., Iyer, V., Carey, L. M., Sluka, C. M., Rajic, G., Kestenman, J., Gentry, M., Brotheridge, S., Somekh, I., Corbin, H. E., Tucker, K. G., Almeida, B., Hex, S. B., Garcia, K. D., Hohmann, A. G., & Crystal, J. D. (2018). Replay of episodic memories in the rat. *Current Biology, 28,* 1628-1634.e1627. https://doi.org/https://doi.org/10.1016/j.cub.2018.04.006

Panoz-Brown, D. E., Corbin, H. E., Dalecki, S. J., Gentry, M., Brotheridge, S., Sluka, C. M., Wu, J.-E., & Crystal, J. D. (2016). Rats remember items in context using episodic memory. *Current Biology, 26,* 2821-2826. https://doi.org/http://dx.doi.org/10.1016/j.cub.2016.08.023

Pavlides, C., & Winson, J. (1989). Influences of hippocampal place cell firing in the awake state on the activity of these cells during subsequent sleep episodes. *The Journal of Neuroscience, 9,* 2907-2918. https://doi.org/10.1523/jneurosci.09-08-02907.1989

Paz, R., Gelbard-Sagiv, H., Mukamel, R., Harel, M., Malach, R., & Fried, I. (2010). A neural substrate in the human hippocampus for linking successive events. *Proceedings of the National Academy of Sciences, 107,* 6046-6051. https://doi.org/10.1073/pnas.0910834107

Pfeiffer, B. E., & Foster, D. J. (2013). Hippocampal place-cell sequences depict future paths to remembered goals. *Nature, 497,* 74-79. https://doi.org/https://doi.org/10.1038/nature12112

Powell, R., Mikhalevich, I., Logan, C., & Clayton, N. S. (2017). Convergent minds: The evolution of cognitive complexity in nature. *Interface Focus, 7*(3), 1-5. https://doi.org/10.1098/rsfs.2017.0029

Premack, D., & Woodruff, G. (1978). Does the chimpanzee have a theory of mind? *Behavioral and Brain Sciences, 1,* 515-526. https://doi.org/https://doi.org/10.1017/S0140525X00076512

Roberts, W. A., Feeney, M. C., MacPherson, K., Petter, M., McMillan, N., & Musolino, E. (2008). Episodic-like memory in rats: Is it based on when or how long ago? *Science, 320,* 113-115. https://doi.org/10.1126/science.1152709

Rubin, B. D., & Katz, L. C. (2001). Spatial coding of enantiomers in the rat olfactory bulb. *Nature Neuroscience, 4,* 355. https://doi.org/10.1038/85997

Skaggs, W. E., & McNaughton, B. L. (1996). Replay of neuronal firing sequences in rat hippocampus during sleep following spatial experience. *Science, 271,* 1870–1873. https://doi.org/10.1126/science.271.5257.1870

Smith, A. E., Dalecki, S. J., & Crystal, J. D. (2017). A test of the reward-value hypothesis. *Animal Cognition, 20,* 215–220. https://doi.org/10.1007/s10071-016-1040-z

Smith, A. E., Slivicki, R. A., Hohmann, A. G., & Crystal, J. D. (2017). The chemotherapeutic agent paclitaxel selectively impairs learning while sparing source memory and spatial memory. *Behavioural Brain Research, 320,* 48–57. https://doi.org/http://dx.doi.org/10.1016/j.bbr.2016.11.042

Staresina, B. P., Alink, A., Kriegeskorte, N., & Henson, R. N. (2013). Awake reactivation predicts memory in humans. *Proceedings of the National Academy of Sciences, 110,* 21159–21164. https://doi.org/10.1073/pnas.1311989110

Tulving, E. (1972). Episodic and semantic memory. In E. Tulving & W. Donaldson (Eds.), *Organization of Memory* (pp. 381–403). Academic Press.

(1983). *Elements of Episodic Memory*. Oxford University Press.

(2002). Episodic memory: From mind to brain. *Annual Review of Psychology, 53,* 1–25. https://doi.org/10.1146/annurev.psych.53.100901.135114

Tulving, E., & Markowitsch, H. J. (1998). Episodic and declarative memory: Role of the hippocampus. *Hippocampus, 8*(3), 198–204. https://doi.org/10.1002/(SICI)1098-1063(1998)8:3%3C198::AID-HIPO2%3E3.0.CO;2-G

Uchida, N., & Mainen, Z. F. (2003). Speed and accuracy of olfactory discrimination in the rat. *Nature Neuroscience, 6,* 1224. https://dx.doi.org/10.1038/nn1142

Wilson, A. G., & Crystal, J. D. (2012). Prospective memory in the rat. *Animal Cognition, 15,* 349–358. https://doi.org/10.1007/s10071-011-0459-5

Wilson, A. G., Pizzo, M. J., & Crystal, J. D. (2013). Event-based prospective memory in the rat. *Current Biology, 23,* 1089–1093. https://doi.org/http://dx.doi.org/10.1016/j.cub.2013.04.067

Wright, A. A. (2018). Episodic memory: Manipulation and replay of episodic memories by rats. *Current Biology, 28,* R667–R669. https://doi.org/https://doi.org/10.1016/j.cub.2018.04.060

Yonelinas, A. P. (2001). Components of episodic memory: The contribution of recollection and familiarity. *Philosophical Transactions of the Royal Society of London. Series B: Biological Sciences, 356,* 1363–1374. https://doi.org/10.1098/rstb.2001.0939

Yonelinas, A. P., & Levy, B. J. (2002). Dissociating familiarity from recollection in human recognition memory: Different rates of forgetting over short retention intervals. *Psychonomic Bulletin & Review, 9,* 575–582. https://doi.org/10.3758/BF03196315

Zhou, W., & Crystal, J. D. (2009). Evidence for remembering when events occurred in a rodent model of episodic memory. *Proceedings of the National Academy of Sciences of the United States of America, 106,* 9525–9529. https://doi.org/10.1073/pnas.0904360106

(2011). Validation of a rodent model of episodic memory. *Animal Cognition, 14*(3), 325–340. https://doi.org/10.1007/s10071-010-0367-0

Zhou, W., Hohmann, A. G., & Crystal, J. D. (2012). Rats answer an unexpected question after incidental encoding. *Current Biology, 22,* 1149–1153. https://doi.org/10.1016/j.cub.2012.04.040

18

EVOLUTIONARY ORIGINS OF COMPLEX COGNITION

Alexandra K. Schnell and Nicola S. Clayton

Primates were once considered to be the pinnacle of cognitive complexity. They have large brains and extended life spans, two characteristics that have been linked to complex cognition (Street et al., 2017). Primates, particularly nonhuman great apes (henceforth apes), perform a range of behaviors (e.g., tool-use, cooperative problem-solving, and tactical deception) that appear to be governed by complex cognitive abilities, including flexible learning and memory (Bobrowicz et al., 2020; Martin-Ordas et al., 2010), causal reasoning (i.e., understanding cause and effect; Hanus & Call, 2008; Mulcahy & Call, 2006), foresight (i.e., planning for future scenarios; Mulcahy & Call, 2006; Osvath & Osvath, 2008), and perspective taking (i.e., attributing a mental state or desire to others; Hare et al., 2000, 2001; Premack & Woodruff, 1978). However, increasing evidence has revealed that several other large-brained mammals, such as cetaceans and elephants (Jaakola et al., 2018; Marino, 2002; Plotnik et al., 2006, 2011) are capable of cognitive feats comparable to those of primates. But, perhaps a more striking discovery is that some groups of birds, including corvids and parrots, have cognitive abilities that match or exceed those of large-brained mammals (Clayton & Dickinson, 1998; Emery & Clayton, 2001; Gruber et al., 2019; Kabadayi & Osvath, 2017; Pepperberg et al., 2013; Raby et al., 2007; Taylor et al., 2009).

Corvids have large brains relative to their size (Olkowicz et al., 2016) and are also long-lived. Corvids and primates are separated by approximately 300 million years of evolution and exhibit significant divergences in both morphology and brain anatomy (Clayton & Emery, 2015; Emery & Clayton, 2004, 2005; Güntürkün & Bugnyar, 2016) (Figure 18.1). Despite this divergence, corvids and primates share similar cognitive traits, suggesting that complex cognition evolved multiple times independently in response to similar evolutionary pressures (Emery & Clayton, 2004; Osvath et al., 2014).

One group of invertebrates, the coleoid cephalopods (henceforth cephalopods), have also garnered the attention of scientists because of their cognitive abilities. Cephalopods, including octopus, cuttlefish, and squid, are

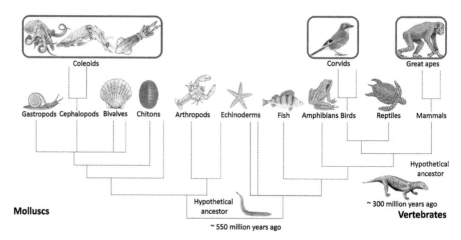

FIGURE 18.1. Phylogenetic tree depicting the evolutionary divergence between apes, corvids, and cephalopods (© CCBY-SA: gastropod, echinoderm, chiton, reptile ancestor; © CCBY-NC-ND: cuttlefish; © CCBYSA-NC: worm ancestor; © jenesesimre, stock.adobe.com: octopus, squid, arthropod, bivalve; © artbalitskiy, stock.adobe.com: ape, fish, amphibian, reptile; © ericisselée, stock.adobe.com: corvid).

(Reprinted with permission of Schnell, A. K., Amodio, P., Boeckle, M., and Clayton, N. S. (2021). How intelligent is a cephalopod? Lessons from comparative cognition. *Biological Reviews*, 96(1), 162–178. https://doi.org/doi:10.1111/brv.12651).

soft-bodied mollusks with the largest brain-to-body size ratio of all invertebrates (Nixon & Young, 2003; Packard, 1972). Despite diverging from the vertebrate lineage more than 550 million years ago (Figure 18.1), cephalopods possess a range of impressive cognitive capacities such as highly developed perception (Abbott et al., 1995; Budelmann, 1995), learning (Agin et al., 2006a; Boal, 1996; Cole & Adamo, 2005; Darmaillacq et al., 2014), and memory abilities (Agin et al., 2006b; Boal, 1991; Sanders & Young, 1940; Wells, 1978; Zepeda et al., 2017). Increasing evidence suggests that they also exhibit attributes of complex cognition (Jozet-Alves et al., 2013; Billard et al., 2020a, 2020b; Schnell, Boeckle et al., 2021; Schnell, Clayton et al., 2021). The prospect that complex cognition emerged in cephalopods challenges fundamental aspects of our understanding of the evolution of intelligence because cephalopods are short-lived (~two years) and evolved under partially different evolutionary pressures than those experienced by large-brained vertebrates (Amodio et al., 2018; Schnell & Clayton, 2019; Schnell, Amodio et al., 2021).

This chapter will discuss the evolutionary origins of complex cognition. First, we outline the evolutionary pressures that are thought to favor the emergence of complex cognition. Second, to emphasize how similar pressures might result in the convergent evolution of similar cognitive traits, we describe the ecological and social challenges that are thought to have driven intelligence in apes and corvids. Finally, we describe the evolutionary challenges that have been proposed as key drivers of cephalopod intelligence.

18.1 EVOLUTIONARY PRESSURES

Complex cognition is thought to have evolved to help animals produce flexible adaptive behaviors in response to socio-ecological complexity. Thus, in large-brained vertebrates several current hypotheses place emphasis on either social or ecological challenges as key factors for driving cognitive evolution.

The *social intelligence hypothesis* predicts that living in a group can result in significant challenges (Humphrey, 1976). Group-living individuals require the need to coordinate and maintain multiple relationships, establish and maintain dominance hierarchies, and recognize suitable cooperative partners. Such challenges may be a driving force for elevated cognitive abilities in social species (Byrne & Whiten, 1988; Dunbar, 1998). Indeed, previous research on various species have demonstrated a link between social group structure and cognitive performance (Amici et al., 2008; Bond et al., 2003). For example, wild Australian magpies, *Cracticus tibicen dorsalis*, living in larger groups show increased cognitive performance across four cognitive tasks that quantify inhibitory control, learning, and spatial memory (Ashton et al., 2018) compared to members of the same species living in smaller groups. It has also been proposed that some animal societies exhibit "Machiavellian" intelligence, in which individuals have evolved the enhanced ability to outwit others during competitive interactions through manipulation or tactical deception (Byrne & Whiten, 1988; Hopper et al., 2018; Whiten & Byrne, 1997).

The *ecological intelligence hypothesis* predicts that complex cognition emerged due to the physical demands of the environment, such as the necessity to memorize food availability, where it is located, and when it would be optimal to eat (Rosati, 2017). If the availability of the resource is difficult to forecast, then selection may favor the evolution of advanced learning and memory abilities to optimize foraging behavior. There is evidence to suggest that unpredictable resource availability selects for innovative foraging techniques, facilitating the exploitation of new food resources (Lefebvre et al., 2004). It has also been suggested that seasonality selects for enhanced cognitive abilities (Sol et al., 2005; van Woerden et al., 2012). Species respond to seasonal changes differently: Some species withstand harsher environmental conditions, while others migrate to warmer climates. Both scenarios may generate circumstances that select for increased cognitive performance (Cristol et al., 2003; Pravosudov et al., 2001).

Another ecological theory predicts that challenges within predator-prey interactions might also be a driving factor (Byrne & Bates, 2007; Kotrschal et al., 2017; Skelhorn & Rowe, 2016; Zuberbühler & Jenny, 2002). Some researchers suggest that the challenges involved in predatory-prey interactions are equivalent to those involved in social competition with group members since both circumstances require individuals to "outwit" other individuals in pursuit of personal gains (Byrne & Bates, 2007). This idea has been supported by studies on primates, demonstrating that strong predatory pressures have played a key role in the emergence of sophisticated communication systems (Zuberbühler & Jenny, 2002). For instance, various species of monkeys can produce distinct vocalizations that contain semantic information about the presence of specific predators, including snakes, eagles, and leopards (Seyfarth et al., 1980; Zuberbühler, 2000, 2001).

Notice that these hypotheses are not seen as mutually exclusive. Several studies suggest that ecological pressures alone cannot adequately explain interspecific differences in cognitive ability (Emery et al., 2007; Shultz & Dunbar, 2006; Silk, 2007). It is thus likely that more than one of these evolutionary pressures has driven the emergence of complex cognition.

18.2 APES AND CORVIDS: A CASE OF CONVERGENT COGNITIVE EVOLUTION

ECOLOGICAL PRESSURES

APES The ecological conditions that prevailed during the late period in the evolution of apes are thought to have had significant consequences on their cognitive evolution. Amid the Late Miocene to the Pliocene (5–10 million years ago), a reduced number of species of great apes were confined to the forest and woodland areas in the tropics of Africa and Southeast Asia (Potts, 2004). In the period that followed, the Pleistocene, these equatorial habitats experienced significant climatic instabilities leading to unpredictable variations in the ecosystem (Potts, 2004). Despite these changes, apes continued to rely heavily on ripe fruit. This sustained dependence on a spatiotemporally dispersed resource in an unpredictable environment is likely to have triggered the evolution of complex spatial learning and memory abilities in apes (Clutton-Brock & Harvey, 1980; Milton, 1981; Potts, 2004). Such unstable ecological conditions also would have favored the emergence of complex cognitive abilities such as episodic-like memory and foresight. Episodic-like memory (see Crystal, Chapter 17) involves the binding of information from specific situations and experiences, based on *what* happened, *where*, and *when*, allowing the individual to recall subjective past memories to guide both current and future behavior. Both episodic memory and foresight are commonly referred to as the retrospective and prospective components of mental time travel, a capacity that allows an individual to mentally travel both backward and forward in time. This capacity was once thought to be uniquely human because it involves a form of consciousness that allows individuals to think about the subjective time in which they live (Clayton et al., 2003; Suddendorf & Corballis, 1997; Tulving, 1972, 1985). Without language it is difficult to investigate such capacities in nonverbal animals; however, research has shown that apes exhibit behavioral indicators that suggests that they possess attributes of mental time travel (Martin-Ordas et al., 2010; Osvath & Osvath, 2008). Despite robust experiments that specifically test for alternative associative learning mechanisms (Clayton & Dickinson, 1999a, Clayton et al., 2001), there will always be critics, and evidence for animal mental time travel remains contested (Suddendorf & Corballis, 2010; Suddendorf et al., 2017). This debate is fueled by some studies showing mixed results (Redshaw & Suddendorf, 2016; Tecwyn et al., 2013) and others failing to control for alternative explanations for the observed behaviors such as the possibility that future actions might be guided by learned reward associations (Kabadayi & Osvath, 2017; Redshaw et al., 2017). On the other hand, emerging evidence from neuroscience indicates that mental time travel may not be unique to humans (see Corballis, 2013).

The ecological variability in the paleoenvironment is also predicted to have led to the emergence of new adaptive foraging behaviors in apes. Thus, rather than solely relying on fruit, apes developed an omnivorous and generalist diet, supplemented by leaves, honey, nuts, small insects and meat as a high source of energy. Many of these resources required substantial periods of exploration; and processing such foods required some form of extraction through the use of tools (Brewer & McGrew, 1990; Matsuzawa, 1994; Matsuzawa et al., 2011; Musgrave et al., 2016; Sanz et al., 2004) (Figure 18.2A). Consequently, it has been argued that adapting an omnivorous, generalist diet has driven the emergence of complex sensorimotor coordination and innovation, both of which are thought to underpin sophisticated tool-use (Brewer & McGrew, 1990; Byrne, 2004; Goodall, 1964; Parker & Gibson, 1977). More recent research has demonstrated that sophisticated tool-use amongst apes is also a result of social factors such as teaching and learning. Specifically, wild chimpanzees have been shown to teach tool skills to other group members by providing them with termite fishing probes, which ultimately leads to improved termite fishing behavior in the learner (Musgrave et al., 2016). These findings support the idea that ecological and social pressures are not mutually exclusive; rather, it is likely that both pressures have driven the emergence of various intelligent behaviors.

CORVIDS Emery (2006) suggests that a similar scenario is likely to have unfolded for corvids and potentially parrots. The climatic instability in the paleoenvironment of these large-brained birds means that they might have had to adapt foraging strategies to support their omnivorous and generalist diets and their reliance on spatiotemporally dispersed food. Although many corvids include fruit in their diet, unlike apes they do not rely heavily on ripe fruit. However, a prominent aspect of their foraging behavior does involve

FIGURE 18.2. Examples of tool-use in diverse taxa. (A) Chimpanzee, *Pan troglodytes*, using a stone tool to crack open a Panda nut (*Panda oleosa*) (photo by Cedric Girard-Buttoz/Taï Chimpanzee Project); (B) New Caledonian crow, *Corvus moneduloides*, using a stick to extract a piece of meat from inside a trap tube (photograph courtesy of Romana Gruber); (C) Veined octopus, *Amphioctopus marginatus*, encased in two halves of a coconut shell in Lembeh Strait, Indonesia
(photograph courtesy of Massimo Capodicasa, flickr.com).

locating food dispersed in space and time. Many species of corvids can cache between 5,000–11,000 food items in different locations and retrieve them at a later date (Chettleburgh, 1952; de Kort & Clayton, 2006). Studies have shown that California scrub-jays, *Aphelocoma californica*, not only can remember what they have cached but also are capable of discriminately retrieving food depending on the perishability of the cached item and the time that has lapsed since caching (Clayton & Dickinson, 1998, 1999b). Remembering the location of thousands of caches that vary in perishability is likely to be a similar spatiotemporal challenge to finding ripe fruit. Moreover, such conditions are also thought to have triggered well-developed future planning abilities in corvids. Indeed, some corvid species parallel apes in future planning tasks (Boeckle et al., 2020; Cheke & Clayton, 2012; Correia et al., 2007; Kabadayi & Osvath, 2017; Raby et al., 2007).

Similar to apes, some species of corvids rely on extractive foraging to supplement a large percentage of their dietary requirements. The majority of their diet is composed of food that needs to be extracted from the soil such as earthworms, roots, and tubers. Other forms of extractive foraging include hammering or prying open the hard encasings of nuts, acorns, and shelled mollusks with their beaks. Many species also drop these foods from high altitudes until the shells break (Seed et al., 2009). While most corvids use both beak and feet to process foods, there are some species that have been observed using tools (Lefebvre et al., 2002). For example, New Caledonian crows, *Corvus moneduloides*, are known to manufacture and use tools to extract insect larvae from otherwise inaccessible locations (Hunt, 2000). Moreover, they manufacture different types of tools (e.g., stepped-cut tools and hook tools) to optimize their extraction behavior (Hunt & Gray, 2004a; 2004b). Manufacturing behaviors in crows is thought to be governed by causal reasoning and foresight (Emery & Clayton, 2004; Seed et al., 2009).

SOCIAL PRESSURES

Living socially is also likely to have had significant consequences on the cognitive evolution of large-brained vertebrates. The challenges and opportunities presented by the social environment is typically divided into three categories: cooperation, social learning, and competition.

APES Apes live in individualized societies where battles for dominance can be fierce. Nevertheless, adaptations that improve social cohesion are likely to be favored. Consequently, group living is predicted to have led to the emergence of behaviors that minimize the likelihood of conflict occurring, lessen the costs of conflict after an encounter has taken place, and repair affected relationships (e.g., third-party affiliation, reconciliation) (de Waal & van Roosmalen, 1979). Evidence suggests that these forms of conflict management are important characteristics of primate societies (Tomasello & Call, 1994; de Waal, 1986). For example, chimpanzees (*Pan troglodytes*), bonobos (*Pan paniscus*), and gorillas (*Gorilla gorilla* and *Gorilla beringei*) all have been observed to reconcile with group members after a dispute (de Waal & van Roosmalen, 1979). Interestingly, conflict resolution has not been observed in other closely related primates such as orangutans, *Pongo abelii*, and Old-World monkeys. One explanation as to why some primates evolved this type of behavior and not others is that conflict management might be a pre-adaptation, namely a preexisting trait that was coopted to a different function. Current evidence does not settle this explanation; our aim is only to raise this as a possibility.

Group living also provides opportunities for individuals to increase their fitness by combining their efforts for activities such as group hunting or group defense. Smaller groups of animals may also participate in cooperative behaviors such as social grooming, pro-social helping, and acquisition of resources. All ape species form cooperative bonds with group members for defense against rivals, rank acquisition, and maintenance (Tomasello & Call, 1994). When animals cooperate in this way, it is beneficial for individuals to select the most effective and/or reciprocal cooperative partners (Seed et al., 2009).

The formation of strong cooperative bonds requires individuals to recognize one another, maintain long-term relationships, and keep track of the social relationships of others. Such behaviors might be underpinned by complex cognitive abilities including perspective taking – the ability to attribute mental states to others, recognizing others as individuals with their own thoughts, knowledge, and desires different from their own. Several studies on apes suggest that maintaining cooperative bonds and social status is governed by perspective taking (Call & Tomasello, 2008; Krupenye et al., 2016; Krupenye & Call, 2019); however, this remains a contentious idea and is still highly debated (Heyes, 2014, 2015; Penn & Povinelli, 2007). At the center of the debate is the issue that it is often challenging to control for behavior reading – an alternative mechanism to perspective taking. The crucial difference between these two mechanisms is that perspective taking involves mental attribution, whereas in behavior reading the focal subject cues on the conspecific's behavior using stimulus-response associations without attributing a mental state to the individual (Call & Tomasello, 2008; Krebs & Dawkins, 1984; Povinelli & Vonk, 2003). Behavior reading is typically assumed to be a simpler mechanism (Heyes, 2014, 2015) but a study in pre-verbal children found that predicting a parent's actions based on their "simple" behaviors can be nonetheless difficult (see Teufel et al., 2013).

Living in social groups also provides opportunities for individuals to learn from others (see Kendal, Chapter 14), which can be advantageous because asocial learning might be costly in terms of time and risk (e.g., eating poisonous food). Furthermore, innovation is likely to occur at a higher frequency when observing and learning from other individuals (Seed et al., 2009). Many large-brained vertebrates, including apes, are known to take advantage of the opportunity to learn socially (Seed et al., 2009). Moreover, positive correlations have been found between the frequency of social learning, innovation, and tool-use, and the relative size of the executive brain (i.e., neocortex and striatum) (Reader & Laland, 2002).

The pressure of competition is also predicted to have played a key role in the cognitive evolution of apes. Individuals living in a group are likely to benefit from intelligent social strategies such as tactical deception, whereby individuals convey misinformation to alter another animal's behavior with the aim of misleading the other individual. For example, in various primate species, subordinate individuals evade giving away cues about the location of a desirable resource (e.g., food) by averting their eye gaze in the presence of a dominant individual, retrieving the object only once the dominant individual is no longer in view (Whiten & Byrne, 1988). Evidence of intentional deceit in apes suggests that they possess some aspects of perspective taking (Kirkpatrick, 2011). However, there is no more consensus as to the cognitive mechanisms that underpin these behaviors than there is for the mechanisms that underpin cooperative behaviors in apes.

CORVIDS The details of corvid sociality vary across species and even across populations of the same species. Corvids display a variety of social structures, ranging from pair-living territorial species (e.g., Eurasian jay, *Garrulus glandarius*) to cooperative breeders living in group-defended territories (e.g., Florida scrub-jays, *Aphelocoma coerulescens*) to gatherings of young fledglings in groups called crèches (e.g., pinyon jays, *Gymnorhinus cyanocephalus*) to communal-living species comprised of tens to hundreds of individuals (e.g., rooks, *Corvus frugilegus*). Despite these social variations, most corvids form long-term monogamous pairs and typically mate for life. However, the success of the relationship depends on both coordination and cooperation. If pairs exhibit poor-quality coordination and cooperation "divorce" can ensue (Mock & Fujioka, 1990). Studies on rooks suggest that long-term partners coordinate their behaviors across multiple contexts and these alliances are maintained through the use of reconciliation and affiliative behaviors (Emery et al., 2007). However, there are no reports of reconciliation occurring between nonpaired group members. This is perhaps unsurprising, given that rooks do not form strong relationships with group members outside of their partnership (Seed et al., 2009). Although the pressure to increase the cooperative quality of social relationships appears to apply to both apes and corvids, the pressure to keep track of a number of collaborative partners in a group may be less relevant for corvids.

Cases of social learning (see Kendal, Chapter 14) in corvids are relatively rarer than those reported in apes (Lefebvre & Bouchard, 2003; Reader & Laland, 2002; Seed et al., 2009). Nevertheless, studies have demonstrated that foraging strategies in corvids are subject to social influence. For example, Florida scrub-jays are able to learn novel foraging techniques through social learning (Midford et al., 2000). In New Caledonian crows, tool selection and manufactruing is optimized through social learning, as well as asocial learning, innovation, and foresight (Gruber et al., 2019; Hunt & Gray, 2002).

Competition pressure within corvid societies is thought to be an important driver of intelligent social strategies, particularly in the context of caching. Many corvid species not only need to remember the location of their own caches but they also sometimes memorize the location of caches that belong to conspecifics (Clayton et al., 2007). Consequently, there is often a need for individuals to protect their caches from the possibility of theft. Some species have developed various cache-protection tactics to deprive competitors of information (Clayton et al., 2007; Grodzinski & Clayton, 2010). For example, if observed by competitors, Californian scrub-jays will often retrieve food from old sites and re-cache in new sites once the competitor has departed (Emery & Clayton, 2001). Scrub-jays also conceal auditory information about caching events when competitors can hear but cannot see them, preferentially caching in substrates that make little detectable noise (i.e., soil) rather than caching in "noisy" substrates (i.e., pebbles) (Stulp et al., 2009). Accumulating evidence demonstrates that corvids flexibly adjust their cache-protection tactics by incorporating the knowledge state of their observers (Dally et al., 2006; Emery & Clayton, 2001).

18.3 CEPHALOPOD COGNITION: A CASE OF CONVERGENT EVOLUTION OR NOT?

ECOLOGICAL PRESSURES

Despite living in significantly different ecosystems, cephalopods are thought to have faced ecological challenges that are comparable to those faced by large-brained vertebrates (Amodio et al., 2018). The immediate ancestors of soft-bodied cephalopods relied on their external shell for protection as well as for movement. The loss of this structure was followed by a wide colonization of diverse ecosystems ranging from tropical to polar environments (Amodio et al., 2018). This wide dispersal exposed cephalopods to a novel range of ecological pressures, which are thought to have driven the emergence of complex foraging strategies.

Although cephalopods are carnivorous, they possess highly generalist diets. For example, the diet of common octopuses, *Octopus vulgaris*, is extremely diverse, composed of approximately 35 prey species, including fish, crustaceans, and gastropods (Smith, 2003). Moreover, many cephalopod species predate on transitory resources that demand substantial periods of exploration to be located, seized, and processed (Amodio et al., 2018). These demands are likely to have triggered advanced navigational, learning, and memory abilities. For example, in the wild, common octopuses avoid visiting the same foraging areas that were recently depleted of resources from previous visits (Mather, 1991), which suggests that they flexibly update their memory to optimize their foraging behaviors. In the laboratory, common cuttlefish, *Sepia officinalis*, use episodic-like memory to discriminately forage for food based on their prey preferences, the learned location of different prey items, and the learned availability of each prey item (Jozet-Alves et al.,

2013; Schnell, Clayton et al., 2021). Episodic-like memory is considered to be a precursor for foresight, as it functions as a database to predict future scenarios (Clayton et al., 2003; Schacter et al., 2012). Interestingly, apes and corvids that possess the capacity for episodic-like memory also demonstrate future planning abilities (Clayton & Dickinson, 1998; Correia et al., 2007; Martin-Ordas et al., 2010; Osvath & Osvath, 2008; Raby et al., 2007), but the capacity for future planning is yet to be tested in cephalopods. Nevertheless, recent research suggests that cuttlefish are suitable candidates for this line of inquiry because they can flexibly adjust their foraging behavior in response to changing prey conditions, that they have learnt across time, as well as proximate-future expectations (Billard et al., 2020b). Future research might be able to determine whether this future-oriented foraging behavior is also governed by foresight. Another recent study has found that cuttlefish can exert self-control to wait for better but delayed future possibilities (Schnell, Boeckle et al., 2021). Self-control is considered to be an important pre-cursor of future planning because an individual must overcome immediate gratification in the present moment to receive better rewards in the proximate future.

Similar to some species of cetaceans, both octopuses and cuttlefish use water as a tool – squirting water jets from their siphons to uncover prey and aid in foraging (Mann & Patterson, 2013; Mather, 1995). Octopuses rely heavily on extractive foraging to exploit their preferred prey – crustaceans and bivalves, which are encased in hard shells. For soft-bodied octopuses, extracting food from a hard encasing may represent a significant challenge but octopuses are able to pry open and pull apart bivalves using their suckered arms (Amodio et al., 2018; Schnell & Clayton, 2019). If this strategy is not successful, they can drill through the bivalve shells using salivary enzymes and a band of tiny teeth known as a radula (Fiorito & Gherardi, 1999). While extractive foraging appears to be confined to octopuses, cuttlefish have developed alternative strategies to supplement their generalist diets and optimize their foraging behavior. For example, pharaoh cuttlefish, *Sepia pharaonis*, have been observed using mimicry to disguise themselves as nonthreatening hermit crabs while hunting to allegedly catch more prey (Okamoto et al., 2017).

The loss of the external shell, in combination with colonizing new habitats, is likely to have dramatically increased predation pressures on cephalopods. This increase in predation pressure is predicted to have triggered the emergence of sophisticated antipredatory behaviors (Amodio et al., 2018; Schnell & Clayton, 2019). Like many animals, cephalopods use camouflage to conceal themselves from predators. However, their camouflage is dynamic and unique in that cephalopods can change the pattern of their skin within milliseconds. The patterns in their skin, and the speed with which they change, are due to chromatophore organs, which are under neuromuscular control (Hanlon & Messenger, 2018). In addition to using camouflage to blend in with their surroundings, cephalopods use masquerade to resemble inanimate objects to conceal themselves from both predators and prey (Hanlon & Messenger, 2018). For example, some species can modify both body posture and skin texture to masquerade as a rock (Huffard, 2006; Panetta et al., 2017). Other species (e.g., *Thaumoctopus* sp. and *Macrotritopus defilippi*) mimic different animals to potentially evade predation and optimize foraging behavior, disguising themselves as small sponges, flounder, banded sea snakes, and venomous lionfish (Hanlon et al., 2008, 2010; Norman et al., 2001). Other sophisticated antipredatory strategies observed in cephalopods include defensive tool-use. A range of octopus species have been observed transporting various objects (e.g., coconut shells, conch shells, glass bottles) and using them as mobile dens (Finn et al., 2009; Mather, 1994) (Figure 18.2C). These observations have led to claims of foresight, suggesting that octopuses can perceive that the objects will provide protection from predators that they may face in the future (Mather & Dickel, 2017). However, whether such behaviors are governed by foresight or are driven by simpler learning mechanisms remains to be tested.

SOCIAL PRESSURES

The social environments of cephalopods differ substantially across groups. Octopuses live mostly solitary lives and rarely interact with conspecifics but there are some minor exceptions. Some species can live in moderate densities where a single site (3.5 × 2.5 m) can be occupied by 10–15 individuals (Huffard, 2006; Scheel et al., 2014). Cuttlefish are also thought to live mostly solitary lives but some species form aggregations for breeding. These aggregations differ substantially in size from species to species, and even from population to population, ranging in size from an assembly of a few (~7 individuals) to hundreds of thousands of individuals (~250,000; Hall & Hanlon, 2002; Hanlon & Messenger, 2018). Squid are the most gregarious of the cephalopods and begin schooling several weeks after hatching. Schooling behavior continues throughout their adult lives and most squid species aggregate for breeding, forming groups from hundreds to hundreds of thousands (Hanlon & Messenger, 2018).

Across all cephalopod groups, social interactions, particularly the cooperative kind, are limited. Indeed, there have been no reports of long-term relationships or cooperative behaviors among conspecifics. Consequently, it is unsurprising that the social recognition abilities of cephalopods are rather primitive (Boal, 2006). To date, strong evidence of cephalopods exhibiting the capacity for self-recognition is lacking, or even the capacity to recognize specific individuals (Boal, 2006; Morse & Huffrard, 2019; Schnell & Clayton, 2019). Instead, social recognition appears to be rudimentary. For some species such as giant Australian cuttlefish, *Sepia apama*, individuals are capable of binary recognition, distinguishing between familiar and unfamiliar mates (Schnell et al., 2015). Moreover, males use a simple signal-advertisement system, whereby they display a visual signal to communicate their "maleness" to conspecifics (e.g., passing cloud, which involves dynamic dark and light bands that move across the body of the animal). For other species, sexual recognition appears to be completely absent. For instance, blue-ringed octopuses, *Hapalochlaena lunulata*, attempt to copulate with either sex, suggesting that they are unable to visually distinguish between male and female conspecifics (Cheng & Caldwell, 2000).

The life history and social structure of cephalopods negates any opportunity for social interactions between kin. For most species of octopus, females delay death long enough to care for their eggs and perish after the hatching of their young, whereas cuttlefish and squid typically die shortly after laying eggs (Hanlon & Messenger, 2018). Consequently, there is no overlap of generations, restricting opportunities for social behavior between parents and offspring. Furthermore, cephalopods tend to disperse after hatching, denying any opportunity to learn socially from others. Intriguingly, one study on octopuses, typically a solitary animal, suggested that they are able to learn by first observing a conspecific demonstrator (Fiorito & Scotto, 1992). This finding is thought provoking given that such mechanisms were once thought to be a by-product of social living. However, it has since been suggested that alternative mechanisms such as highly developed perception, attention, and motivation might underpin the capacity for observational learning (Lefebvre & Giraldeau, 1996; Heyes, 2012). Worth noting is that the original finding in octopuses has not been replicated, and studies on cuttlefish report conflicting results (Biederman & Davey, 1993; Boal et al., 2000; Huang & Chiao, 2013; Schnell, Amodio et al., 2021).

Although the social organization of cephalopods does not foster cooperation, individuals are still exposed to strong competition pressure, particularly in the context of mating. Most species of cephalopods have a single breeding period within their short life spans (Hanlon & Messenger, 2018). Limited breeding periods combined with highly skewed operational sex ratios experienced by various species result in intense mating competition (Hanlon et al., 2005; Moynihan & Rodaniche, 1982). In response to these pressures, some species use deceptive resemblance during mating. That is, both cuttlefish and squid species change their body patterning to mimic members of the opposite sex (DeMartini et al., 2013; Hanlon et al., 2005; Norman et al., 1999). Sexual mimicry in cephalopods is a dynamic behavior that is usually performed under specific social conditions and has been described as a form of tactical deception (Brown et al., 2012). However, further investigation is required to determine if this form of deception is underpinned by complex cognition such as perspective taking.

18.4 CONCLUDING REMARKS

Compelling evidence suggests that complex cognition emerged multiple times, independently. The independent evolution of intelligence in large-brained vertebrates such as apes and corvids are likely to have evolved in response to similar socio-ecological pressures such as dealing with the challenge of living in a complex social group or finding unpredictable food resources distributed in space and time. Increasing evidence suggests that cephalopods also exhibit attributes of complex cognition despite living in relatively simple social environments. These findings suggest that sociality may not be a prerequisite for intelligence to emerge. However, many behavioral phenomena in cephalopods await detailed analysis of underlying mechanisms, making it difficult to gauge the extent to which their behaviors are governed by complex cognition or simpler learning mechanisms. Future research should aim to test whether cephalopods exhibit comparable cognitive sophistication to large-brained vertebrates or whether their cognitive complexity plateaued in the absence of having to deal with social challenges that require recognition and cooperation. By investigating the capacity for complex cognition beyond the realm of large-brained vertebrates, we can gain a better understanding of the different socio-ecological pressures and the role that they play in cognitive evolution. This in turn will facilitate a more comprehensive reconstruction of the evolution of intelligence.

REFERENCES

Abbott, N. J., Williamson, R., & Maddock, L. (1995). *Cephalopod neurobiology*. Oxford University Press.

Agin, V., Chichery, R., Chichery, M. P., Dickel, L., Darmaillacq, A. S., & Bellanger, C. (2006a). Behavioural plasticity and neural correlates in adult cuttlefish. *Vie Milieu*, *56*, 81–87.

Agin, V., Chichery, R., Dickel, L., & Chichery, M. P. (2006b). The "prawn-in-the-tube" procedure in the cuttlefish: Habitation or passive avoidance learning? *Learning and Memory*, *13*, 97–101. https://doi.org/10.1101/lm.90106

Amici, F., Aureli, F., & Call, J. (2008). Fission-fusion dynamics, behavioral flexibility, and inhibitory control in primates. *Current Biology*, *18*, 1415–1419. https://doi.org/10.1016/j.cub.2008.08.020

Amodio, P., Boeckle, M., Schnell, A. K., Ostojić, L., Fiorito, G., & Clayton, N. S. (2018). Grow smart and die young: Why did cephalopods evolve intelligence? *Trends in Ecology and Evolution*, *34*, 45–56. https://doi.org/10.1016/j.tree.2018.10.010

Ashton, B. J., Ridley, A. R., Edwards, E. K., & Thornton, A. (2018). Cognitive performance is linked to group size and affects fitness in Australian magpies. *Nature*, *554*, 364–367. https://doi.org/10.1038/nature25503

Biederman, G. B., & Davey, V. A. (1993). Social learning in invertebrates. *Science*, *259*, 2413–2419. https://doi.org/10.1126/science.259.5101.1627

Billard, P., Clayton, N. S., & Jozet-Alves, C. (2020a). Cuttlefish retrieve whether they smelt or saw a previously encountered item. *Scientific Reports*, *10*, 5413. https://doi.org/10.1038/s41598-020-62335-x

Billard, P., Schnell, A. K., Clayton, N. S., & Jozet-Alves, C. (2020b). Cuttlefish show flexible and future-dependent foraging cognition. *Biology Letters, 16*, 20190743. https://doi.org/10.1098/rsbl.2019.0743

Boal, J. G. (1991). Complex learning in *Octopus bimaculoides. American Malacological Bulletin, 9*, 75–80.

(1996). A review of simultaneous visual discrimination as a method of training octopuses. *Biological Reviews, 71*, 157–190. https://doi.org/10.1111/j.1469-185x.1996.tb00746.x

(2006). Social recognition: A top down view of cephalopod behavior. *Vie Millieu, 56*, 69–79.

Boal, J. G., Wittenberg, K. M., & Hanlon, R. T. (2000). Observational learning does not explain improvement in predation tactics by cuttlefish (Mollusca: Cephalopoda). *Behavioural Processes, 52*, 141–153. https://doi.org/10.1016/S0376-6357(00)00137-6

Bobrowicz, K., Johansson, M., & Osvath, M. (2020). Great apes selectively retrieve relevant memories to guide action. *Scientific Reports, 10*, 12603. https://doi.org/10.1038/s41598-020-69607-6

Boeckle, M., Schiestl, M., Frohnwieser, A., Gruber, R., Miller, R., Suddendorf, T., Gray, R. D., Taylor, A. H., & Clayton, N. S. (2020). New Caledonian crows plan for specific future tool use. *Proceedings of the Royal Society B, 287*, 20201490. https://doi.org/10.1098/rspb.2020.1490

Bond, A. B., Kamil, A. C., & Balda, R. P. (2003). Social complexity and transitive inference in corvids. *Animal Behaviour, 65*, 479–487. https://doi.org/10.1006/anbe.2003.2101

Brewer, S. M., & McGrew, W. C. (1990). Chimpanzee use of a tool-set to get honey. *Folia Primatology, 54*, 100–104. https://doi.org/10.1159/000156429

Brown, C., Garwood, M. P., & Williamson, J. E. (2012). It pays to cheat: Tactical deception in a cephalopod social signalling system. *Biology Letters, 8*, 729–732. https://doi.org/10.1098/rsbl.2012.0435

Budelmann, B. U. (1995). The cephalopod nervous system: What evolution has made of the molluscan design. In O. Breidbach, & W. Kutsch (Eds.), *The nervous systems of invertebrates: An evolutionary and comparative approach* (pp. 115–138). Birkhauser Verlag.

Byrne, R. W. (2004). The manual skills and cognition that lie behind hominid tool use. In A. E. Russon, & D. R. Begun (Eds.), *The evolution of thought: Evolutionary origins of great ape intelligence* (pp. 31–44). Cambridge University Press.

Byrne, R. W., & Bates, L. A. (2007). Sociality, evolution and cognition. *Current Biology, 17*, R714–R723. https://doi.org/10.1016/j.cub.2007.05.069.

Byrne, R. W., & Whiten, A. (1988). *Machiavellian intelligence: Social expertise and the evolution of intellect in monkeys, apes and humans.* Oxford University Press.

Call, J., & Tomasello, M. (2008). Does the chimpanzee have a theory of mind? 30 years later. *Trends in Cognitive Sciences, 12*, 187–192. https://doi.org/10.1016/j.tics.2008.02.010

Cheke, L. C., & Clayton, N. S. (2012). Eurasian jays (*Garrulus glandarius*) overcome their current desires to anticipate two distinct future needs and plan for them appropriately. *Biology Letters, 8*, 71–175. https://doi.org/10.1098/rsbl.2011.0909

Cheng, M. A., & Caldwell, R. (2000). Sex identification and mating in the blue-ringed octopus, *Hapalochlaena lunulata. Animal Behaviour, 60*, 27–33. https://doi.org/10.1006/anbe.2000.1447

Chettleburgh, M. (1952). Observations on the collection and burial of acorns by jays in Hainault Forest. *British Birds, 45*, 359–364.

Clayton, N. S., Bussey, T. J., & Dickinson, A. (2003). Can animals recall the past and plan for the future? *Nature Reviews Neuroscience, 4*, 685–691. https://doi.org/10.1038/nrn1180

Clayton, N. S., Dally, J. M., & Emery, N. J. (2007). Social cognition by food-caching corvids. The western scrub-jay as a natural psychologist. *Philosophical Transactions of the Royal Society B, 362*, 507–522. https://doi.org/10.1098/rstb.2006.1992

Clayton, N. S., & Dickinson, A. (1998). Episodic-like memory during cache recovery by scrub jays. *Nature, 395*, 272–274. https://doi.org/10.1038/26216

(1999b). Memory for the content of caches by scrub jays. *Journal of Experimental Psychology: Animal Behavior Processes, 25*, 82–91. http://dx.doi.org/10.1037//0097-7403.25.1.82

(1999a). Scrub jays (*Aphelocoma coerulescens*) remember the relative time of caching as well as the location and content of their caches. *Journal of Comparative Psychology, 113*, 403–416. https://doi.org/10.1037/0735-7036.113.4.403

Clayton, N. S., & Emery, N. J. (2015). Avian models of human cognitive neuroscience: A proposal. *Neuron, 86,* 1330–1342. https://doi.org/10.1016/j.neuron.2015.04.024

Clayton, N. S., Yu, K. S., Dickinson, A. (2001). Scrub jays (*Aphelocoma coerulescens*) form integrated memories of the multiple features of caching episodes. *Journal of Experimental Psychology Animal Behavior Processes, 27,* 17–29.

Clutton-Brock, T. H., & Harvey, P. H. (1980). Primates, brain and ecology. *Journal of Zoology, 190*, 309–323. https://doi.org/10.1111/j.1469-7998.1980.tb01430.x

Cole, P. D., & Adamo, S. A. (2005). Cuttlefish (*Sepia officinalis:* Cephalopoda) hunting behavior and associative learning. *Animal Cognition, 8,* 27–30. https://doi.org/10.1007/s10071-004-0228-9

Corballis, M. C. (2013). Mental time travel: A case for evolutionary continuity. *Trends in Cognitive Sciences, 17,* 5–6. https://doi.org/10.1016/j.tics.2012.10.009

Correia, S. P. C., Dickinson, A., & Clayton, N. S. (2007). Western scrub-jays anticipate future needs independently of their current motivational state. *Current Biology, 17,* 856–861. https://doi.org/10.1016/j.cub.2007.03.063

Cristol, D. A., Reynolds, E. B., Leclerc, J. E., Donner, A. H., Farabaugh, C. S., & Ziegenfus, C. W. S. (2003). Migratory dark-eyed juncos, *Junco hyemalis,* have better spatial memory and denser hippocampal neurons than nonmigratory conspecifics. *Animal Behaviour, 66,* 317–328. https://doi.org/10.1006/anbe.2003.2194

Dally, J. M., Emery, N. J., & Clayton, N. S. (2006). Food-caching western scrub-jays keep track of who was watching when. *Science, 312,* 1662–1665. https://doi.org/10.1126/science.1126539

Darmaillacq, A. S., Dickel, L., & Mather, J. A. (2014). *Cephalopod cognition.* Cambridge University Press.

DeMartini, D. G., Ghoshal, A., Pandolfi, E., Weaver, A. T., Baum, M., & Morse, D. E. (2013). Dynamic biophotonics: Female squid exhibit sexually dimorphic tunable leucophores and iridocytes. *Journal of Experimental Biology, 216,* 3733–3741. https://doi.org/10.1242/jeb.090415

Dunbar, R. I. M. (1998). The social brain hypothesis. *Evolutionary Anthropology, 9,* 178–190. https://doi.org/10.1002/(SICI)1520-6505(1998)6:5<178::AID-EVAN5>3.0.CO;2-8

Emery, N. J. (2006). Cognitive ornithology: The evolution of avian intelligence. *Philosophical Transactions of the Royal Society B, 361,* 23–43. https://doi.org/10.1098/rstb.2005.1736

Emery, N. J., & Clayton, N. S. (2001). Effects of experience and social context on prospective caching strategies by scrub jays. *Nature, 414,* 443–-446. https://doi.org/10.1038/35106560

    (2004). The mentality of crows: Convergent evolution of intelligence in corvids and apes. *Science, 306,* 1903–1907. https://doi.org/10.1126/science.1098410

    (2005). Evolution of avian brain and intelligence. *Current Biology, 15,* R946–R950. https://doi.org/10.1016/j.cub.2005.11.029

Emery, N. J., Seed, A. M., von Bayern, A. M. P., & Clayton, N. S. (2007). Cognitive adaptations of social bonding in birds. *Philosophical Transactions of the Royal Society B, 362,* 489–505. https://doi.org/10.1098/rstb.2006.1991

Finn, J. K., Tregenza, T., & Norman, M.D. (2009). Defensive tool use in a coconut-carrying octopus. *Current Biology, 19,* R1069–R1070. https://doi.org/10.1016/j.cub.2009.10.052

Fiorito, G., & Gherardi, F. (1999). Prey-handling behaviour of *Octopus vulgaris* (Mollusca, Cephalopoda) on bivalve preys. *Behavioural Processes, 46,* 75–88. https://doi.org/10.1016/S0376-6357(99)00020-0

Fiorito, G., & Scotto, P. (1992). Observational learning in *Octopus vulgaris. Science, 256,* 545–547. https://doi.org/10.1126/science.256.5056.545

Goodall, J. (1964). Tool-using and aimed throwing in a community of free-living chimpanzees. *Nature, 201,* 1264–1266. https://doi.org/10.1038/2011264a0

Grodzinski, U., & Clayton, N. S. (2010). Problems faced by food-caching corvids and the evolution of cognitive solutions. *Philosophical Transactions of the Royal Society B*, *365*, 977–987. https://doi.org/10.1098/rstb.2009.0210

Gruber, R., Schiestl, M., Boeckle, M., Frohnwieser, A., Miller, R., Gray, R. D., Clayton, N. S., & Taylor, A. H. (2019). New Caledonian crows use mental representations to solve meta-tool problems. *Current Biology*, *29*, 686–692. https://doi.org/10.1016/j.cub.2019.01.008

Güntürkün, O., & Bugnyar, T. (2016). Cognition without cortex. *Trends in Cognitive Sciences*, *20*, 291–303. https://doi.org/10.1016/j.tics.2016.02.001

Hall, K. C., & Hanlon, R. T. (2002). Principal features of the mating system of a large spawning aggregation of the giant Australian cuttlefish *Sepia apama* (Mollusca: Cephalopoda). *Marine Biology*, *140*, 533–545. https://doi.org/10.1007/s00227-001-0718-0

Hanlon, R. T., Conroy, L. A., & Forsythe, J. W. (2008). Mimicry and foraging behaviour of two tropical sand-flat octopus species off North Sulawesi, Indonesia. *Biological Journal of Linnean Society*, *93*, 23–38. https://doi.org/10.1111/j.1095-8312.2007.00948.x

Hanlon, R. T., & Messenger, J. B. (2018). *Cephalopod behaviour*, 2nd ed. Cambridge University Press. https://doi.org/10.1017/9780511843600

Hanlon, R. T., Naud, M. J., Shaw, P. W., & Havenhand, J. N. (2005). Transient sexual mimicry leads to fertilization. *Nature*, *433*, 212. https://doi.org/10.1038/433212a

Hanlon, R. T., Watson, A. C., & Barbosa, A. (2010). A "mimic octopus," in the Atlantic: Flatfish mimicry and camouflage by *Macrotritopus defilippi*. *Biological Bulletin*, *218*, 15–24. https://doi.org/10.1086/BBLv218n1p15

Hanus, D., & Call, J. (2008). Chimpanzees infer the location of a reward on the basis of the effect of its weight. *Current Biology*, *18*, R370–R372. https://doi.org/10.1016/j.cub.2008.02.039

Hare, B., Call, J., Agnetta, B., & Tomasello, M. (2000). Chimpanzees know what conspecifics do and do not see. *Animal Behaviour*, *59*, 771–785.

Hare, B., Call, J., & Tomasello, M. (2001). Do chimpanzees know what conspecifics know? *Animal Behaviour*, *61*, 139–151.

Heyes, C. (2012). What's social about social learning? *Journal of Comparative Psychology*, *126*, 193–202. https://doi.org/10.1037/a0025180

(2014). Submentalizing: I am not really reading your mind. *Perspectives on Psychological Sciences*, *9*, 131–143. https://doi.org/10.1177/1745691613518076

(2015). Animal mindreading: What's the problem? *Psychonomic Bulletin Review*, *22*, 313–327. https://doi.org/10.3758/s13423-014-0704-4

Hopper, L. M., van de Waal, E., & Caldwell, C. A. (2018). Celebrating the continued importance of "Machiavellian Intelligence" 30 years on. *Journal of Comparative Psychology*, *132*, 427–431. https://doi.org/10.1037/com0000157

Huang, K. L., & Chiao, C. C. (2013). Can cuttlefish learn by observing others? *Animal Cognition*, *16*, 313–320. https://doi.org/10.1007/s10071-012-0573-z

Huffard, C. L. (2006). Locomotion by *Abdopus aculeatus* (Cephalopod: Octopodidae): Walking the line between primary and secondary defenses. *Journal of Experimental Biology*, *209*, 3697–3707. https://doi.org/10.1242/jeb.02435

Humphrey, N. K. (1976). The social function of intellect. In P. P. G. Bateson & R. A. Hinde (Eds.), *Growing points in ethology* (pp. 303–317). Cambridge University Press.

Hunt, G. R. (2000). Tool use by the New Caledonian crow *Corvus moneduloides* to obtain cerambycidae from dead wood. *Emu*, *100*, 109–114. https://doi.org/10.1071/MU9852

Hunt, G. R., & Gray, R. D. (2002). Species-wide manufacture of stick-type tools by New Caledonian crows. *Emu*, *102*, 349–353. https://doi.org/10.1071/MU01056

(2004a). Direct observations of pandanus-tool manufacture and use by a New Caledonian crow (*Corvus moneduloides*). *Animal Cognition*, *7*, 114–120. https://doi.org/10.1007/s10071-003-0200-0

(2004b). The crafting of hook tools by wild New Caledonian crows. *Biology Letters*, *271*, 88–90. *https://doi.org/10.1098/rsbl.2003.0085*

Jaakola, K., Guarino, E., Donegan, K., & King, S. L. (2018). Bottlenose dolphins can understand their partner's role in a cooperative task. *Proceedings of the Royal Society B, 285,* 20180948. https://doi.org/10.1098/rspb.2018.0948

Jozet-Alves, C., Bertin, M., & Clayton, N. S. (2013). Evidence of episodic-like memory in cuttlefish. *Current Biology, 23,* R1033–R1035. https://doi.org/10.1016/j.cub.2013.10.021

Kabadayi, C., & Osvath, M. (2017). Ravens parallel great apes in flexible planning for tool-use and bartering. *Science, 375,* 202–204. https://doi.org/10.1126/science.aam8138

Kirkpatrick, C. (2011). Tactical deception and the great apes: Insight into the question of Theory of Mind. *Totem: The University of Western Ontario Journal of Anthropology, 1,* 31–37.

de Kort, S. R., & Clayton, N. S. (2006). An evolutional perspective on caching by corvids. *Proceedings of the Royal Society B, 273,* 417–423. https://doi.org/10.1098/rspb.2005.3350

Kotrschal, A., Deacon, A. E., Magurran, A. E., & Kolm, N. (2017). Predation pressure shapes brain anatomy in the wild. *Evolutionary Ecology, 31,* 619–633. https://doi.org/10.1007/s10682-017-9901-8

Krebs, J. R., & Dawkins, R. (1984). Animal signals: Mind-reading and manipulation. In J. Krebs & N. Davies (Eds.), *Behavioural ecology: An evolutionary approach* (pp. 380–402). Blackwell Scientific Publications.

Krupenye, C., & Call, J. (2019). Theory of Mind in animals: Current and future directions. *WIREs Cognitive Sciences,* e1503. https://doi.org/10.1002/wcs.1503

Krupenye, C., Kano, F., Hirata, S., Call, J., & Tomasello, M. (2016). Great apes anticipate that other individuals will act according to false beliefs. *Science, 354,* 110–114. https://doi.org/10.1126/science.aaf8110

Lefebvre, L., & Bouchard, J. (2003), Social learning about food in birds. In D. M. Fragaszy & S. Perry (Eds.), *The biology of traditions: Models and evidence* (pp. 94–126). Cambridge University Press.

Lefebvre, L., & Giraldeau, L.-A. (1996). Is social learning an adaptive specialization? In C. M. Heyes & B. G. Galef, Jr. (Eds.), *Social learning in animals: The roots of culture* (pp. 107–128). Academic Press.

Lefebvre, L., Nicolakakis, N., & Boire, D. (2002). Tools and brains in birds. *Behaviour, 139,* 939–973. https://doi.org/10.1163/156853902320387918

Lefebvre, L., Reader, S. M., & Sol, D. (2004). Brains, innovations and evolution in birds and primates. *Brain, Behavior and Evolution, 63,* 233–246. https://doi.org/10.1159/000076784

Mann, J., & Patterson, E. M. (2013). Tool use by aquatic animals. *Proceedings of the Royal Society B, 368,* 20120424. https://doi.org/10.1098/rstb.2012.0424

Marino, L. (2002). Convergence of complex cognitive abilities in cetaceans and primates. *Brain, Behavior and Evolution, 59,* 21–32. https://doi.org/10.1159/000063731

Martin-Ordas, G., Haun, D., Colmenares, F., & Call, J. (2010). Keeping track of time: Evidence for episodic-like memory in great apes. *Animal Cognition, 13,* 331–340. https://doi.org/10.1007/s10071-009-0282-4

Mather, J. A. (1991). Navigation by spatial memory and use of visual landmarks in octopuses. *Journal of Comparative Physiology A, 168,* 491–497. https://doi.org/10.1007/BF00199609

(1994). "Home" choice and modification by juvenile *Octopus vulgaris* (Mollusca: Cephalopoda): Specialized intelligence and tool use? *Journal of Zoology, 233,* 359–368. https://doi.org/10.1111/j.1469-7998.1994.tb05270.x

(1995). Cognition in cephalopods. *Advances in the Study of Behavior, 24,* 317–353.

Mather, J. A., & Dickel, L. (2017). Cephalopod complex cognition. *Current Opinion in Behavioral Sciences, 16,* 131–137. https://doi.org/10.1016/j.cobeha.2017.06.008

Matsuzawa, T. (1994). Field experiments on use of stone tools by chimpanzees in the wild. In R. W. Wrangham, W. C. McGrew, F. B. M. de Waal FBM, & P. G. Heltone (Eds.), *Chimpanzee cultures* (pp. 351–370). Harvard University Press.

Matsuzawa, T., Humle, T., & Sugiyama, Y. (2011). *The chimpanzees of Bossou and Nimba.* Springer.

Midford, P. E., Hailman, J. P., & Woolfenden, G. E. (2000). Social learning of a novel foraging patch in families of free-living Florida scrub-jays. *Animal Behaviour, 59,* 1199–1207. https://doi.org/10.1006/anbe.1999.1419

Milton, K. (1981). Distribution patterns of tropical plant foods as an evolutionary stimulus to primate mental development. *American Anthropologist, 83,* 543–548. https://doi.org/10.1525/aa.1981.83.3.02a00020

Mock, D. W., & Fujioka, M. (1990). Monogamy and long-term pair bonding in vertebrates. *Trends in Ecology and Evolution, 5,* 39–43. https://doi.org/10.1016/0169-5347(90)90045-F

Morse, P., & Huffrard, C. L. (2019). Tactical tentacles: New insights on the proves of sexual selection among the Cephalopoda. *Frontiers in Physiology, 10,* 1035. https://doi.org/10.3389/fphys.2019.01035

Moynihan, M. H., & Rodaniche, A. F. (1982). The behavior and natural history of the Caribbean reef squid *Sepioteuthis sepioidea* with a consideration of social, signal, and defensive patterns for difficult and dangerous environments. *Fortschritte der Verhaltensforschung, 25,* 9–150 [*Advanced Ethology, 125,* 1–150].

Mulcahy, N. J., & Call, J. (2006). Apes save tools for future use. *Science, 312,* 1038–1040. https://doi.org/10.1126/science.1125456

Musgrave, S., Morgan, D., Lonsdorf, E., Mundry, R., & Sanz, C. (2016). Tool transfers are a form of teaching among chimpanzees. *Scientific Reports, 6,* 34783. https://doi.org/10.1038/srep34783

Nixon, M., & Young, J. Z. (2003). *The brains and lives of cephalopods.* Oxford University Press.

Norman, M. D., Finn, J., & Tregenza, T. (1999). Female impersonation as an alternative reproductive strategy in giant cuttlefish. *Proceedings of the Royal Society B, 266,* 1347–1349. https://doi.org/10.1098/rspb.1999.0786

(2001). Dynamic mimicry in an indo-Malayan octopus. *Proceedings of the Royal Society B, 268,* 1755–1758. https://doi.org/10.1098/rspb.2001.1708

Okamoto, K., Yasumuro, H., Mori, A., & Ikeda, Y. (2017). Unique arm-flapping behavior of the pharaoh cuttlefish, *Sepia pharaonis:* Putative mimicry of a hermit crab. *Journal of Ethology, 35,* 307–311. https://doi.org/10.1007/s10164-017-0519-7

Olkowicz, S., Kocourek, M., Lučan, R. K., Porteš, M., Fitch, W. T., Herculano-Houzel, S., & Němec, P. (2016). Birds have primate-like numbers of neurons in the forebrain. *Proceedings of the National Academy of the United States of America, 113,* 7255–7260. https://doi.org/10.1073/pnas.1517131113

Osvath, M., Kabadayi, C., & Jacobs, I. (2014). Independent evolution of similar complex cognitive skills: The importance of embodied degrees of freedom. *Animal Behaviour and Cognition, 1,* 249–264. https://doi.org/10.12966/abc.08.03.2014

Osvath, M., & Osvath, H. (2008). Chimpanzee (*Pan troglodytes*) and orangutan (*Pongo abelii*) forethought: Self-control and pre-experience in the face of future tool use. *Animal Cognition, 11,* 661–674. https://doi.org/10.1007/s10071-008-0157-0

Packard, A. (1972). Cephalopods and fish: The limits of convergence. *Biological Reviews, 47,* 241–301. https://doi.org/10.1111/j.1469-185X.1972.tb00975.x

Panetta, D., Buresch, K., & Hanlon, R. T. (2017). Dynamic masquerade with morphing three-dimensional skin in cuttlefish. *Biology Letters, 13,* 20170070. https://doi.org/10.1098/rsbl.2017.0070

Parker, S. T., & Gibson, B. M. (1977). Object manipulation, tool use and sensorimotor intelligence as feeding adaptations in cebus monkeys and great apes. *Journal of Human Evolution, 6,* 623–641. https://doi.org/10.1016/S0047-2484(77)80135-8

Penn, D. C., & Povinelli, D. J. (2007). On the lack of evidence that non-human animals possess anything remotely resembling a "Theory of Mind". *Philosophical Transactions of the Royal Society B, 362,* 731–744. https://doi.org/10.1098/rstb.2006.2023

Pepperberg, I. M., Koepke, A., Livingston, P., Girard, M., & Hartsfield, L. A. (2013). Reasoning by inference: Further studies on exclusion in grey parrots (*Psittacus erithacus*). *Journal of Comparative Psychology, 127,* 272–281. https://doi.org/10.1037/a0031641

Plotnik, J. M., Lair, R., Suphachoksahakun, W., & de Waal, F. B. M. (2011). Elephants know when they need a helping trunk in a cooperative task. *Proceedings of the National Academy of Sciences of the United States of America, 108*, 5116–5121. https://doi.org/10.1073/pnas.1101765108

Plotnik, J. M., de Waal, F. B. M., & Reiss, D. (2006). Self-recognition in an Asian elephant. *Proceedings of the National Academy of Sciences of the United States of America, 103*, 17053–17057. https://doi.org/10.1073/pnas.0608062103

Potts, R. (2004). Paleo-environmental basis of cognitive evolution in great apes. *American Journal of Primatology, 62*, 209–228. https://doi.org/10.1002/ajp.20016

Povinelli, D. J., & Vonk, J. (2003). Chimpanzee minds: Suspiciously human? *Trends in Cognitive Sciences, 7*, 157–160. https://doi.org/10.1016/S1364-6613(03)00053-6

Pravosudov, V. V., Kitaysky, A. S., Wingfield, J. C., & Clayton, N. S. (2001). Long-term unpredictable foraging conditions and physiological stress response in mountain chickadees (*Poecile gambeli*). *General and Comparative Endocrinology, 123*, 324–331. https://doi.org/10.1006/gcen.2001.7684

Premack, D., & Woodruff, G. (1978). Does the chimpanzee have a theory of mind? *Behavioral and Brain Sciences, 1*, 515–526.

Raby, C. R., Alexis, D. M., Dickinson, A., & Clayton, N. S. (2007). Planning for the future by western scrub-jays. *Nature, 445*, 919–921. https://doi.org/10.1038/nature05575

Reader, S. M., & Laland, K. N. (2002). Social intelligence, innovation and enhanced brain size in primates. *Proceedings of the National Academy of Sciences of the United States of America, 99*, 4436–4441. https://doi.org/10.1073/pnas.062041299

Redshaw, J. & Suddendorf, T. (2016). Children's and Apes' preparatory responses to two mutally exclusive possibilities. *Current Biology, 26*, 1758–1762.

Redshaw, J., Taylor, A. H., & Suddendorf, T. (2017). Flexible planning in ravens? *Trends on Cognitive Sciences, 21*, 821–822.

Rosati, A. G. (2017). Foraging cognition: Reviving the ecological intelligence hypothesis. *Trends in Cognitive Sciences, 21*, 691–702. https://doi.org/10.1016/j.tics.2017.05.011

Sanders, F. K., & Young, J. Z. (1940). Learning and other functions of the higher nervous centers of *Sepia*. *Journal of Neurophysiology, 3*, 501–526.

Sanz, C., Morgan, D., & Gulick, S. (2004). New insights into chimpanzees, tools, and termites from the Congo Basin. *American Naturalist, 164*, 567–581. https://doi.org/10.1086/424803

Schacter, D. L., Addis, D. R., Hassabis, D., Martin, V. C., Spreng, R. N., & Szpunar, K. K. (2012). The future of memory: Remembering, imagining, and the brain. *Neuron, 76*, 677–694. https://doi.org/10.1016/j.neuron.2012.11.001

Scheel, D., Godfrey-Smith, P., & Lawrence, M. (2014). *Octopus tetricus* (Mollusca: Cephalopoda) as an ecosystem engineer. *Scientia Marina, 78*, 521–528. https://doi.org/10.1080/19420889.2017.1395994

Schnell, A. K., Amodio, P., Boeckle, M., & Clayton, N. S. (2021a). How intelligent is a cephalopod? Lessons from comparative cognition. *Biological Reviews, 96*(1), 162–178. https://doi.org/doi:10.1111/brv.12651

Schnell, A. K., Boeckle, M., Rivera, M., Clayton, N. S., & Hanlon, R. T. (2021b). Cuttlefish exert self-control in a delay of gratification task. *Proceedings of the Royal Society B, 288*, 20203161. https://doi.org/10.6084/m9.figshare.c.5309888

Schnell, A. K., Clayton, N. S., Hanlon, R. R. T., & Jozet-Alves, C. (2021c). Episodic-like memory is preserved with age in cuttlefish. *Proceedings of the Royal Society B, 288*, 20211052. https://doi.org/10.1098/rspb.2021.1052

Schnell, A. K., & Clayton, N. S. (2019). Cephalopod cognition. *Current Biology, 29*, R726–R732. https://doi.org/10.1016/j.cub.2019.06.049

Schnell, A. K., Smith, C. L., Hanlon, R. T., & Harcourt, R. (2015). Giant Australian cuttlefish use mutual assessment to resolve male-male contests. *Animal Behaviour, 107*, 31–40.

Seed, A. M., Emery, N. J., & Clayton, N. S. (2009). Intelligence in corvids and apes: A case of convergent evolution? *Ethology, 115*, 401–420. https://doi.org/10.1111/j.1439-0310.2009.01644.x

Seyfarth, R. M., Cheney, D. L., & Marler, P. (1980). Vervet monkey alarm calls: Semantic communication in a free-ranging primate. *Animal Behaviour, 28,* 1070–1094. https://doi .org/10.1016/S0003-3472(80)80097-2

Shultz, S., & Dunbar, R. I. (2006). Both social and ecological factors predict ungulate brain size. *Proceedings of the Royal Society B, 273,* 207–215. https://doi.org/10.1098/rspb.2005 .3283

Silk, J. B. (2007). Social components of fitness in primate groups. *Science, 317,* 1347–1351. https://doi.org/10.1126/science.1140734

Skelhorn, J., & Rowe, C. (2016). Cognition and the evolution of camouflage. *Proceedings of the Royal Society B, 283,* 20152890. https://doi.org/10.1098/rspb.2015.2890

Smith, C. D. (2003). Diet of *Octopus vulgaris* in False Bay, South Africa. *Marine Biology, 143,* 1127–1133.

Sol, D., Duncan, R. P., Blackburn, T. M., Cassey, P., & Lefebvre, L. (2005). Big brains, enhanced cognition, and response of birds to novel environments. *Proceedings of the National Academy of Sciences of the United States of America, 102,* 5460–5465. https://doi .org/10.1073/pnas.0408145102

Street, S. E., Navarrete, A. F., Reader, S. M., & Laland, K. N. (2017). Coevolution of cultural intelligence, extended life history, sociality, and brain size in primates. *Proceedings of the National Academy of Sciences of the United States of America, 114,* 7908–7914. https://doi .org/10.1073/pnas.1620734114

Stulp, G., Emery, N. J., Verhulst, S., & Clayton, N. S. (2009). Western scrub-jays conceal auditory information when competitors can hear but cannot see. *Biology Letters, 5,* 20090330. https://doi.org/10.1098/rsbl.2009.0330

Suddendorf, T., & Corballis, M. C. (1997). Mental time travel and the evolution of the human mind. *Genetic, Social, and General Psychology Monographs, 123,* 133–167.

   (2010). Behavioural evidence for mental time travel in nonhuman animals. *Behavioural Brain Research, 215,* 292–298.

Suddendorf, T., Crimston, J., & Redshaw, J. (2017). Preparatory responses to socially deter-mined, mutually exclusive possibilities in chimpanzees and children. *Biology Letters, 13,* 20170170.

Taylor, A. H., Hunt, G. R., Medina, F. S., & Gray, R. D. (2009). Do new Caledonian crows solve physical problems through causal reasoning? *Proceedings of the Royal Society B, 276,* 247–254. https://doi.org/10.1098/rspb.2008.1107

Tecwyn, E. C., Thorpe, S. K. S., & Chappell, J. (2013). A novel test of planning ability: Great apes can pla step-by-step, but not in advance of action. *Behavioural Processes, 100,* 174–184.

Teufel, C. R., Clayton, N. S., & Russell, J. R. (2013). Two-year-old children's understanding of visual perception and knowledge formation in others. *Journal of Cognition and Development, 14,* 203–228. https://doi.org/10.1080/15248372.2012.664591

Tomasello, M., & Call, J. (1994). Social cognition of monkeys and apes. *American Journal of Physical Anthropology, 37,* 273–305. https://doi.org/10.1002/ajpa.1330370610

Tulving, E. (1972). Episodic and semantic memory. In E. Tulving and W. Donaldson (Eds.), *Organization of memory* (pp. 381–402). Academic Press.

   (1985). Memory and consciousness. *Canadian Psychology, 26,* 1–12.

de Waal, F. B. M. (1986) Conflict resolution in monkeys and apes. In K. Benirschke (Ed.), *Primates. Proceedings in life sciences* (pp. 341–350). Springer. https://doi.org/10.1007/ 978-1-4612-4918-4_26

de Waal, F. B. M., & van Roosmalen, A. (1979). Reconciliation and consolation among chimpanzees. *Behavioral Ecology and Sociobiology, 5,* 55–66. https://doi.org/10.1007/ BF00302695

Wells, M. J. (1978). *Octopus: Physiology and behaviour of an advanced invertebrate.* Chapman & Hall.

Whiten, A., & Byrne, R. W. (1988). Tactical deception in primates. *Behavioral and Brain Sciences, 11,* 233–273. https://doi.org/10.1017/S0140525X00049682

(1997). *Machiavellian intelligence II: Extension and evaluations.* Cambridge University Press.

van Woerden, J. T. Willems, E. P., van Schaik, C. P., & Isler, K. (2012). Large brains buffer energetic effects of seasonal habitats in catarrhine primates. *Evolution, 66,* 191–199. https://doi.org/10.1111/j.1558-5646.2011.01434.x

Zepeda, E. A., Veline, R. J., & Crook, R. J. (2017). Rapid associative learning and stable long-term memory in the squid *Euprymna scolopes. Biological Bulletin, 232,* 212–218. https://doi.org/10.1086/693461

Zuberbühler, K. (2000). Referential labelling in Diana monkeys. *Animal Behaviour, 59,* 917–927. https://doi.org/10.1006/anbe.1999.1317

(2001). Predator-specific alarm calls in Campbell's monkeys, *Cercopithecus campbelli. Behavioral Ecology and Sociobiology, 50,* 414–422. https://doi.org/10.1007/s002650100383

Zuberbühler, K., & Jenny, D. (2002). Leopard predation and primate evolution. *Journal of Human Evolution, 43,* 873–886. https://doi.org/10.1006/jhev.2002.0605

19

EVOLUTION OF MEMORY SYSTEMS IN ANIMALS

Johan Lind, Stefano Ghirlanda, and Magnus Enquist

Memory lies at the heart of animal behavior because it provides information necessary for adaptive decision-making. Thus, understanding what animals can remember is informative about what they can and cannot do. In this review we categorize memory systems in animals in terms of their generality and their temporal characteristics. We will introduce below a simple taxonomy of memory systems looking at both general and specialized memories that can store information for either a short duration (seconds to minutes) or for much longer (months to years). Our goal is also to review memory systems from an evolutionary point of view. We therefore explore how evolution has tailored memory systems, taking into account their costs and benefits.

19.1 BENEFITS AND COSTS OF REMEMBERING

When exploring the evolution of memory, we must consider both the benefits of having access to information and the costs that arise from acquiring and remembering information. Here we focus on combinatorial costs and the need for efficient decision-making.

The combinatorial costs of remembering arise as follows. Consider an animal that can perceive n different stimuli. If the animal decides what to do based only on the current stimulus, then n memory variables are in principle sufficient, each one storing the best response to one of the n stimuli (if the decision strategy assigns a probability to each of m behaviors, then $n \times m$ memory variables are required, and in what follows, n can be replaced with $n \times m$ to analyze probabilistic decision strategies). The current stimulus, however, may not be fully informative. For example, a predator should continue its chase even if the prey disappears behind a bush and is no longer perceived. In this case, it appears beneficial to remember the previous stimulus. This, however, means that the animal must be prepared to learn up to n^2 events (all possible combinations of two stimuli), requiring added memory storage and – importantly – more time, because the significance of n^2 rather than n events must be discovered. In general, remembering the last l stimuli means having to learn up to n^l events. While not all combinations of events may occur, remembering many events can lead to rapidly increasing learning costs. If, for example, only 100 stimuli can be perceived, remembering just the last three results in $n^l = 100^3 = 1$ million potential sequences. Learning about sequences of events is favored by natural selection only if these are truly informative.

Another constraint arises from the necessity of fast decision-making, requiring information to be readily accessible. Consider an animal that remembers every single experience. Although information is preserved perfectly, extracting it would be time consuming and computationally demanding. For example, when deciding whether to eat a berry, a bird would need to search its memory for all experiences of similar berries, and decide how each one weighs in favor or against the current berry.

19.2 A SIMPLE TAXONOMY OF MEMORY SYSTEMS

We describe memory systems based on their generality and temporal characteristics. A general system handles information from many domains, whereas a specialized system stores only specific information used for specific purposes. As a rule, information stored in a specialized memory, and how it is used, are under strong genetic control. We further distinguish between short- and long-term memories. The former refers to memories that last up to a few minutes and decay once a stimulus is removed, while the latter refers to memories that are stable over long time periods and that, typically, change only because of experience with relevant stimuli. This two-way categorization of memory systems is helpful, but not perfect, as both distinctions may represent continua rather than dichotomies.

19.3 GENERAL-PURPOSE LONG-TERM MEMORY

Our understanding of general-purpose long-term memory derives mainly from studies of associative learning, either instrumental or Pavlovian. This literature provides information about several general aspects of memory, and here we will look at how long such memories last, how much information can be stored, what kind of memories can be formed, and, finally, what can be remembered. Before we look into this literature we start by introducing a way to analyze learning experiments.

The elementary learning experience in instrumental learning has the form:

$$S \rightarrow B \rightarrow S' \tag{19.1}$$

where S and S' are stimuli and B is a behavior. A typical example is:

$$light \rightarrow leverpress \rightarrow food \tag{19.2}$$

Such experiences readily produce changes in behavior when S' is a stimulus with positive or negative value. In the example, lever pressing in the presence of the light would increase. In a typical experiment, food is experienced only if the lever is pressed when the light is on, but not if it is off or if other behavior is used. S is called the discriminative stimulus, B the operant or instrumental response, and S' the reinforcer.

Pavlovian experiments can also be described in terms of $S \rightarrow B \rightarrow S'$ experiences, but S and S' follow each other irrespective of the intervening behavior. An example is:

$$tone \rightarrow B \rightarrow shock \tag{19.3}$$

where B signifies any behavior. Over repeated experiences, however, a typical behavior B emerges. In Example 3, the animal would display fear-motivated behavior, for example, avoidance behavior or freezing. In Pavlov's paradigmatic experiments, dogs learned to salivate to auditory or visual stimuli that were followed by food. In customary terminology, S is the conditioned stimulus (CS), the learned behavior B is the conditioned response (CR), and S' is the unconditioned stimulus (US).

In both instrumental and Pavlovian conditioning, stimuli experienced before S are sometimes important, which we consider further below. We refer to the literature for further details on associative learning (Mackintosh, 1983; Bouton, 2016). Here we are concerned with what such learning tells us about animal memory and its evolution.

DURABILITY: HOW LONG DO MEMORIES LAST?

Vaughan and Greene (1984) trained pigeons to earn food by pecking at images from a "positive" set, while pecks at images from a "negative" set earned no food. The arbitrary nature of the images makes it unlikely that the animals could use specialized memories. For example, one negative set was obtained by mirroring images from the positive set. The pigeons learned the tasks almost perfectly, and showed barely any decline in performance after 1.3–2 years without training.

In Table 19.1 we summarize similar results. Decreases in performance with time have been observed by Gleitman (1971), but typically after much shorter training. Moreover, the studies in Table 19.1 typically featured choices between different stimuli, which appears to yield longer-lasting performance than go/no-go decisions (Gleitman, 1971). In conclusion, although performance can decrease over time, many animals can retain accurate memories of hundreds of stimuli over a period of years.

TABLE 19.1. *Some studies of animal general-purpose long-term memory in which performance showed little or no decline after a prolonged interval without training*

Study	Task	Species	N	Stimuli	Test interval (year)
Johnson and Davis (1973)	Oddity	Rhesus monkey	8	9–189	7
Patterson and Tzeng (1979)	Discrimination reversal	Gorilla	4	200	2.5
Vaughan and Greene (1984)	Image recognition	Pigeon	13	80–320	1.3–2
Burdyn et al. (1984)	Oddity, conditional discrimination, numerosity discrimination	Squirrel monkey	4	Up to 240	1.3–5
Kastak and Schusterman (2002)	Categorization, sameness	Sea lion	1	20–300[a]	1–10
Hanggi and Ingersoll (2009)	Discrimination, categorization, relative size	Horse	3	16–36[a]	6–7

See the original studies for detailed task descriptions. N: number of subjects.
[a] Estimated based on methods descriptions.

CAPACITY: HOW MANY MEMORIES CAN BE STORED?

The capacity of general-purpose long-term memory in animals is as impressive as its durability. The dog Chaser remembered 1,022 toys (Pilley & Reid, 2011), and some of the pigeons trained by Vaughan and Greene (1984) remembered the correct response to 320 images for more than one year. Cook et al. (2005) showed that pigeons could remember the correct response to more than 800 images for at least six months. Lastly, Fagot and Cook (2006) showed memory of 800–1,200 images in pigeons and 3,500–5,000 in baboons using a procedure in which all images were periodically trained. As brain tissue used to store memories is expensive, these results suggest that many species learn many associations in their natural environment, and that such learning is important for adaptive behavior.

GENERALITY: WHAT MEMORIES CAN BE FORMED?

In a completely general-purpose memory, S, B, and S' would be arbitrary. However, constraints on learning are especially common in Pavlovian learning, where S and S' determine strictly what behavior B emerges during learning. For example, rats develop freezing (*B*) to a tone (*S*) that signals shock (*S'*), but they try to bury an object (*S*) introduced in the cage just before the shock (Pinel & Treit, 1978). Instrumental learning is more flexible in that different behaviors can be learned given the same *S* and *S'*, but it also has restrictions. Already Thorndike (1898) noted that cats learned readily to pull and push objects in order to escape from a box, but would not learn reliably to lick or scratch themselves. Restrictions in both Pavlovian and instrumental learning are today well known (Domjan, 1993, Domjan & Krause, 2017, but see Bevins, 1992), and probably speed up learning by focusing it on relevant stimuli.

CONTENT: WHAT IS REMEMBERED?

Given the experience $S \rightarrow B \rightarrow S'$, what information is memorized? This is a difficult question. An early idea is that a valuable S' strengthens an $S \rightarrow B$ association, but that no information about S' is retained (Thorndike, 1911; Guthrie, 1935; Hull, 1943). Thus, when a rat learns to press a lever, it would neither remember past food deliveries, nor expect any food after pressing (Pearce, 2008). This stimulus-response account is traditionally contrasted with a "cognitive" account, in which whole $S \rightarrow B \rightarrow S'$ experiences are memorized and can later be searched and used for decision-making (Tolman, 1932; Griffiths et al., 1999). The cognitive rat would expect food after lever pressing, and it would also infer that it should press only if it wants the food. Early latent learning experiments supported this cognitive view (Tolman & Honzik, 1930), but later work could not replicate these findings (Thistlethwaite, 1951; Jensen, 2006). However, a lively debate continues to this date concerning what aspects of $S \rightarrow B \rightarrow S'$ experiences are memorized (Hall, 2002; Holland, 2008; Bouton, 2016; Ghirlanda et al., 2020). Here we look at the question from an evolutionary perspective.

Consider a frugivorous bird like a warbler learning about an unknown berry. The sequence to learn may be:

$$berry \rightarrow peck \rightarrow openberry \rightarrow eat \rightarrow sweet \qquad (19.4)$$

If whole $S \rightarrow B \rightarrow S'$ experiences are remembered, the warbler could search its memory upon experiencing *sweet*, and it could infer that pecking the unopened berry is beneficial. This strategy, however, incurs the combinatorial costs discussed in our Introduction, resulting in slower learning and decision-making. Using $S \rightarrow B$ associations minimizes these costs, but it also limits what can be learned. For example, $S \rightarrow B$ associations alone would not be able to learn the sequence in (19.4) because the stimulus *openberry* has no value (the berry is unknown) and thus it cannot strengthen the *berry* → *peck* association.

It seems necessary to store more than just $S \to B$ associations, but less than all $S \to B \to S'$ experiences. In the last few years, we have investigated the idea that stimulus values can be learned, which is related to conditioned reinforcement and second-order conditioning (Skinner, 1936; Pierce & Cheney, 2008). According to this idea, an $S \to B \to S'$ experience has two effects. First, it updates the $S \to B$ association. Second, it updates the value of S. Thus, in example (19.4), the experience *openberry* $\to$ *eat* $\to$ *sweet* would increase the value of *openberry*. On successive experiences, the warbler would then perceive that *berry* $\to$ *peck* has a valuable outcome, and could eventually learn the complete sequence. This is consistent with how animals learn sequences of actions (Pierce & Cheney, 2008). We refer to Enquist et al. (2016), Lind (2018), Ghirlanda et al. (2020), and Lind et al. (2019) for detailed analyses of this idea. This long-term storage of information about both the world and own behaviors makes evolutionary sense as it greatly expands the domain of what can be learned without introducing combinatorial costs. In addition, general decision-making and associative learning mechanisms can be unified with instinctual aspects of behavior and fine-tuned to balance costs and benefits of memory, learning, and behavioral flexibility.

19.4 GENERAL-PURPOSE SHORT-TERM MEMORY

In contrast with long-term memories that are updated after learning experiences, here we examine general short-term memories of perceived arbitrary stimuli. We first look into memories of perceived single stimuli, before we explore how animals recognize and remember sequences of stimuli.

MEMORY FOR SINGLE STIMULI

Delayed match-to-sample (DMTS) experiments provide a wealth of data on general-purpose short-term memory for single stimuli. A DMTS trial starts with a sample stimulus. After a few seconds, the sample is removed and the delay starts. At the end of the delay, two comparison stimuli are presented, one matching the sample. If the matching stimulus is chosen, the animal is rewarded. By varying the delay, one can measure how long an animal remembers the sample stimulus.

In a review, we found that memory performance deteriorates to chance levels within a few seconds or minutes (Lind et al., 2015). To compare species, we estimated performance half-life (Figure 19.1a, b). No clear patterns related to taxonomic or ecological similarity emerged (Figure 19.1c). For example, the performance of primates is inter-mixed with both birds and other mammals. In addition, caching corvids (nutcrackers and scrub jays),

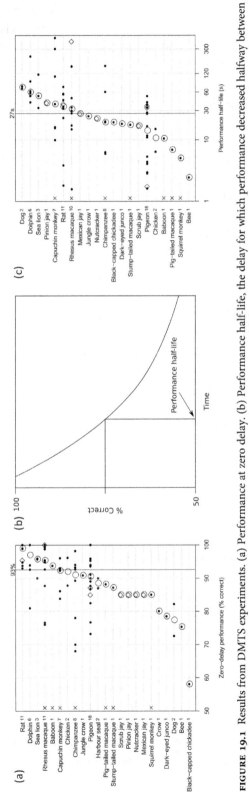

FIGURE 19.1 Results from DMTS experiments. (a) Performance at zero delay. (b) Performance half-life, the delay for which performance decreased halfway between zero-delay performance and chance performance. (c) Performance half-life estimates. Black vertical line is the median of all data, species medians are shown as open circles, and crosses highlight primates. Number of data sets is given next to the species name. Species are arranged by median value. A review of delayed matching-to-sample data, Copyright 2015, with permission from Elsevier.

Reprinted from *Behavioural Processes*, *117*, 52–58, Lind, J., Enquist, M., and Ghirlanda, S., Animal memory: from Elsevier.

which have exceptional long-term memory for food locations (see the section on specialized memories), performed similarly to nonspecialists (Mexican jays, *Aphelocoma wollweberi*, and pinion jays *Gymnorhinus cyanocephalus*). Indeed, pigeons have the longest half-life estimate among birds, including caching corvids. More generally, species differences could not be evaluated reliably because experimental procedures varied substantially between species, making comparisons uncertain at best (Lind et al., 2015). For example, pigeons appear to have shorter memory span than dolphins, but pigeon data come mainly from naïve subjects while dolphin data come from individuals trained over many years.

In conclusion, DMTS studies reveal that information about generic stimuli, such as lights, pictures, or sounds, starts to decay within seconds after stimulus removal, and is lost within a few minutes.

MEMORY FOR STIMULUS SEQUENCES

A swimmer's optimal response to the warning "killer whale!" is different from the optimal response to "whale killer!" Making decisions based on the order of stimuli requires order to be recognized and remembered. To gauge animals' memory for stimulus sequences, we surveyed sequence discrimination studies in mammals and birds (Ghirlanda et al., 2017). For example, Weisman et al. (1980) rewarded pigeons for responding to an *AB* sequence (a green light followed by a red light), but not for responding to *BA*, *AA*, or *BB*. We found that stimulus sequences are much harder to recognize and remember than single stimuli (Figure 19.2). To perform above chance, animals need many hundreds or thousands of trials, while a discrimination between single stimuli can be acquired within tens of trials. Additionally, certain errors are remarkably persistent. In a striking example with pigeons, Weisman et al. (1985) reported no progress in a discrimination between a *BAB* and an *AAB* sequence for more than 2,000 trials.

Statistically, we found no species variation in learning speed of sequence discriminations, except for humans (Ghirlanda et al., 2017, p. 3). We found, however, significant effects offering clues to how animals memorize sequences. Namely, we found that sequence discriminations were more difficult between sequences sharing the last stimulus. That is, discriminating *AB* from *BB* is more difficult than discriminating *AB* from *AA* (Figure 19.2b). These results suggest that sequence memory depends on memory traces just like memory of single stimuli (MacDonald, 1993, and Figure 19.1b). According to this idea, the memory trace for a stimulus builds up as long as the stimulus is present, while removal of the stimulus results in a progressively fading memory. We formalized this idea mathematically

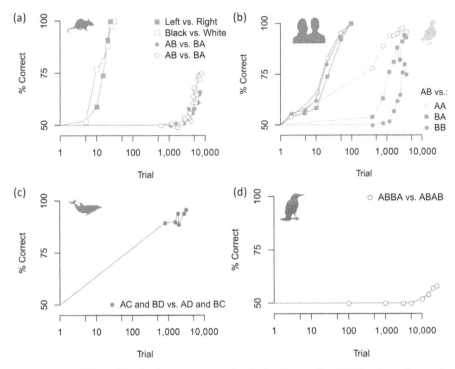

FIGURE 19.2. Selected results from sequence discrimination studies (Ghirlanda et al., 2017). Examples of acquisition curves for different species. Panel (a) shows a comparison between single stimulus discriminations and sequence discriminations in rats. Panel (b), (c) and (d), respectively, show data on sequence discriminations from humans and pigeons, dolphins, and starlings.

Reprinted from *Royal Society Open Science, 161011*, 1–12, Ghirlanda, S., Lind, J., and Enquist, M., Memory for stimulus sequences: A divide between humans and other animals?

(Ghirlanda et al., 2017), and assumed that the discriminability between two sequences depends on their distance in memory space (Figure 19.3a). This model fits the data remarkably well, with a mean correlation of 0.88 and a mean absolute error for each data point of 5.9% across 68 data sets. The model also replicated crucial qualitative results, such as the recency effects mentioned earlier.

The trace model suggests that animals do not represent sequences of stimuli faithfully, as one cannot in general recover the structure of a sequence from its trace. For example, if *A* is long and *B* is short, the sequence *AB* may result in a stronger memory trace for *A* than for *B*, which under most circumstances would result from a *BA* sequence (MacDonald, 1993). Based on the excellent fit of the trace model and on the presence of systematic errors compatible with the model, we find it hard to escape the conclusion that animals represent stimulus sequences only approximately.

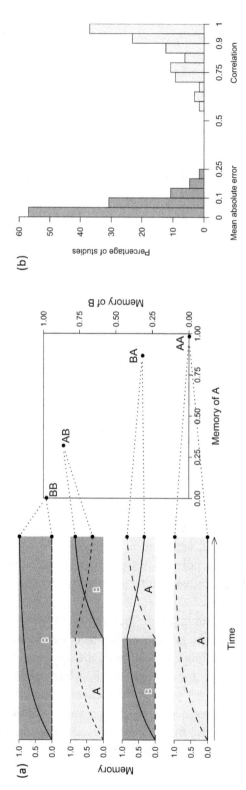

FIGURE 19.3. Illustration of the memory trace model for sequence discrimination (Ghirlanda et al., 2017). (a) At the onset of a stimulus (*A* or *B*) a memory is activated, and upon removal of the stimulus the memory fades progressively. The discriminability between a pair of two sequences (e.g., *AB* vs. *BA*) is given by the level of activation of the memories in the stimulus sequences, which can be plotted in a two-dimensional memory space. The difficulty of a discrimination is inversely proportional to distance in this space, so that it is more difficult to tell *BB* and *AB* apart than to discriminate between *BB* and *BA*. (b) Summary plot of test of model predictions and observed performance across 68 fitted datasets (distribution of mean absolute errors and Pearson's correlations are in light grey). Reprinted from *Royal Society Open Science, 161011*, 1–12, Ghirlanda, S., Lind, J., and Enquist, M., Memory for stimulus sequences: A divide between humans and other animals?

19.5 SPECIALIZED LONG-TERM MEMORIES

SPECIALIZED MEMORIES OF SINGLE STIMULI

Animals often remember locations and landmarks better than other stimulus features (Gallistel, 1990). Caching birds provide a striking example as they can remember food locations for months but colors for less than a minute (Bossema, 1979). Similar results have been obtained in several species (e.g., chimpanzees: Yerkes & Yerkes, 1928; rats: Ormerod & Beninger, 2002). Zeldin and Olton (1986) offer a direct comparison of location and visual cues in rats, which could not solve a task (within 1,000 trials) using visual cues, but learned within 50 trials using spatial cues. Specialized memories have been found in many domains (Gould & Marler, 1984), including filial and sexual imprinting (Lorenz, 1935; Immelmann, 1972; Bischof, 1994), and migratory orientation based on celestial cues (Emlen, 1970).

SPECIALIZED MEMORIES OF STIMULUS SEQUENCES

A well-studied example of specialized long-term memory for stimulus sequences is song learning in birds, in which juveniles store information about songs heard from adults, and later use this information to develop their own song (Soha, 2016). These specialized memories can encode temporal information about songs and are often prepared to learn about natural song elements rather than arbitrary sounds (Hultsch & Todt, 1989; Mets & Brainard, 2019). Other examples of specialized sequence memories may exist, such as vocal learning in cetaceans (e.g., Janik & Slater, 1997). However, specialized sequence memories appear more rare than specialized memories for single events.

19.6 SPECIALIZED SHORT-TERM MEMORIES

The idea of specialized short-term memories is somewhat unorthodox, but it may cover various mechanisms that track specific kinds of short-lived information – internal or external – for which general-purpose memory would not suffice. Examples may include memories dedicated to monitor currently active food sources or nearby predators, or memories maintaining information about an animal's current activity, such as feeding. Such memories may cut learning costs, but exhibit low flexibility.

As mentioned in our Introduction, it is hard to draw a sharp line between specialized short- and long-term memories, but the idea is that short-term memories hold information that diminishes in value quickly, for example, about renewable food sources like nectar. To be useful, these memories must be updated quickly, and may decay at a rate reflecting the rapidly decreasing value of information (McFarland, 1971; Hogan, 1997; Staddon, 2001). We discuss two kinds of mechanisms with these properties: motivational systems and associative learning with fast updating.

MOTIVATION AS SHORT-TERM MEMORY

From a functional point of view, changes in motivational states such as hunger and thirst can provide information for behavior and decision-making in a similar way as memories. First, they are used in decision-making to regulate activities such as feeding and drinking, so that an animal can focus on one activity at a time (McFarland, 1985; Hogan, 1997). Second, motivational states can effectively store information about internal and external events (Hogan, 2017, pp. 66–68). For example, an animal that senses a predator can enter a state of fear that engages defensive behaviors and inhibits other activities. Fear states persist even after triggering stimuli disappear, and thus can be said to maintain a memory of such stimuli. The spontaneous decay of fear with time allows animals to resume other activities when the danger has, presumably, decreased (birds: Kullberg & Lind, 2002; fish: Barham et al., 1985; see Gross & Canteras, 2012 for a review of the fear system in rats).

FAST ASSOCIATIVE LEARNING

Specialized memories may arise as modifications of general-purpose memory. Consider, for example, associative learning. A simple learning equation for an associative memory v is:

$$\Delta v = \alpha(u - v) \tag{19.5}$$

where Δv is the change in associative strength when an outcome with reinforcement value u is experienced, and α is the learning rate (see Pearce, 2008; Bouton, 2016, for more detailed models). Most often, α is rather small, such that it takes many experiences to form a strong association. This is optimal for general-purpose learning in a complex environment, when the potential predictors of meaningful outcomes are unknown (see Stephens, 1987, for the analogous concept of "low tracking"). However, if α is close to one, the memory will update quickly and mainly reflect the last experience. Such a memory can be useful to track short-lived information, for example, about currently active food sources. To avoid encoding spurious information, however, a quickly updated memory needs to be focused on a limited set of stimulus features.

Animals may also use several associative memories that track information from the same context with different learning rates (different α) (Staddon, 2001; McLaren & Mackintosh, 2000, 2002). For example, hummingbirds exploit flowers efficiently by both remembering their location and avoiding returning to recently emptied ones (Cole et al., 1982; Healy & Hurly, 2003). To achieve this, a fast memory (high α) could be hardwired to decay spontaneously, and to inhibit visits to locations recently exploited, while a slower memory (low or medium α) would work as a regular associative memory to remember the location of food patches. Arrangements of several associative memories with different learning rates could also explain phenomena such as spontaneous recovery of responding and reversal learning (Pavlov, 1927; Holmes & Bitterman, 1966).

19.7 CONSEQUENCES AND CONCLUSIONS

The apparent limits of general-purpose memory discussed here may originate from the fact that remembering only single stimuli, or very short sequences, is in fact adaptive because it minimizes storage and learning costs. It would be prohibitive to remember more information in a general-purpose memory, because more time is needed to learn the significance of more information (see our Introduction). Specialized memories, on the other hand, limit learning costs by storing only a few, relevant stimulus features, or by storing them for longer than it would be adaptive in a general-purpose memory. We also note that limitations in general-purpose short-term memory likely carry over to general-purpose long-term memory, because information cannot be committed to long-term memory if it is not initially represented faithfully. The flexibility of decision-making, however, can be increased by combining more memory systems with different degrees of specialization and duration, creating the opportunity for natural selection to tune memory systems to a species' niche.

Although human memory is not without constraints (Simons & Chabris, 1999; Lieberman, 2011), humans can remember briefly experienced stimuli for days and months (Overman Jr & Doty, 1980; Kristo et al., 2009). Differences in general-purpose short-term memory for sequences appear even more pronounced, as faithful representations of ordered sequences are necessary for most human activities, such as remembering the order of events, understanding instructions about how to perform a behavioral sequence, or imitating a sequence of notes while learning to play a musical instrument (Ghirlanda et al., 2017).

ANIMAL MEMORY FOR SEQUENCES

As summarized, animal general-purpose short-term memory for stimulus sequences appears well described by a memory trace model. That animals may not be able to represent or remember sequences of stimuli faithfully has implications for many lines of research in animal cognition.

CAUSAL LEARNING IN APES

We concluded that animal memory for order is poor, but data from nonhuman apes are lacking (Ghirlanda et al., 2017). Suggestions that nonhuman apes learn causal relationships between neutral stimuli, such that stimulus *A* would always cause stimulus *B*, would indicate a good memory for order (Völter & Call, 2014; Tennie et al., 2019). However, the poor performance observed in these studies, after extended training, appears more compatible with results from sequence discrimination experiments with other species than with the idea that apes have an accurate memory for order. At present, we cannot adjudicate whether the observed performance is superior to what would be expected from a simple trace memory.

LANGUAGE AND RULES

Many have attempted to teach animals grammatical rules, or to detect such rules in natural vocalizations (Gentner et al., 2006; Herbranson & Shimp, 2008; Murphy et al., 2008; Chen et al., 2015; Suzuki et al., 2016). Intriguingly, many such studies amount to training discriminations between sets of stimulus sequences, and their results are reproduced very accurately by the trace model of sequence memory (Ghirlanda et al., 2017). Because a trace memory makes it possible to discriminate between stimulus sequences at least to some extent, that animals can solve sequence discriminations is not sufficient evidence that they do so based on a rudimentary language competence, especially when systematic errors are found that are readily predicted by a trace memory model (discussed in general-purpose short-term memory earlier, and Ghirlanda, 2017; Bolhuis et al., 2018, for further concerns). Future studies would be strengthened by explicitly ruling out the memory trace model.

IMITATION

Imitating a behavioral sequence requires remembering stimulus sequences faithfully. Imitation of single behaviors can develop through associative learning (Lind et al., 2019), which can also support simple traditions of the kind often seen in animals (Helfman & Schultz, 1984; Perry & Manson, 2003; van de Waal et al., 2013). It is likely, however, that accurate imitation of behavioral sequences ("production" or "true" imitation; Byrne, 2002) requires additional memory and learning processes (Lind et al., 2019). One possibility is to have a specialized memory, such as for song in songbirds, that enables the imitation of specific types of behavior. General-purpose imitation, on the other hand, may require an accurate general-purpose memory for ordered sequences similar to human memory.

EPISODIC MEMORY

Episodic memory is often called what-where-when memory or episodic-like memory to leave room for differences with human episodic memory (Clayton & Dickinson, 1998, reviewed in Crystal, 2010; see Crystal, Chapter 17). Findings of episodic-like memory in animals do not necessarily indicate human-like episodic abilities because some general purpose episodic-like memory may emerge from associative learning. Associative memories can readily encode stimulus features (what) and locations (where), and may encode temporal cues (when) by leveraging either external stimuli such as the night-day cycle, or internal ones such as circadian clocks. In addition, specialized memories may result in episodic-like abilities in specific domains (Clayton & Dickinson, 1998, 1999). Indeed, reports of episodic memories across many taxa are primarily about the temporal and spatial coordinates of food in, for example, insects (Pahl et al., 2007), cephalopods (Jozet-Alves et al., 2013), birds (Zentall et al., 2001), and mammals (Babb & Crystal, 2006; but see Roberts et al., 2008).

Two features of human episodic memory may be absent in animal episodic-like memory. First, human episodic memory is general purpose, capable of encoding almost any episode without immediate reference to biologically salient stimuli. Second, human episodic memory enables a recollection of sequences of events in order of occurrence (not necessarily perfectly), rather than of single events (Baddeley, 2001). We have no evidence of the latter capacity in animals, and the limitations of animal sequence memory (as discussed earlier under general-purpose short-term memory) suggest that an accurate episodic memory for sequences may not exist in nonhuman animals.

19.8 CONCLUSIONS

Evolution has tailored memory systems both in temporal characteristics and degree of generality. Can the same learning and memory machinery account for both general and specialized memory systems? Similarities between general and specialized systems are often put forward as an argument in favor of the view that memory processes share great similarities across species (Macphail & Bolhuis, 2001). Phenomena like one-trial learning can still be described as associative learning, and phenomena like overshadowing and blocking are evident in specialized memory systems like filial imprinting (van Kampen & de Vos, 1995). But then, what makes a specialized memory? It is possible that natural selection changes memory mainly by changing learning parameters, such as what events are reinforcing, what behaviors should be selected in given contexts, and what are optimal learning rates for different associations. Specialized memories may arise from tuning general-purpose memories and perceptual systems, and do not necessarily require new mechanisms, although highly specialized cases exist (e.g., Emlen, 1970; Wehner, 2003). Importantly, any hypothesis about the evolution of memory systems needs to consider the massive learning costs associated with memories that are open to more information, including encoding more features of stimuli and longer stimulus sequences.

ACKNOWLEDGMENTS

This research was supported by the Knut and Alice Wallenberg Foundation, grant 2015-0005, and by a fellowship leave from Brooklyn College to SG.

REFERENCES

Babb, S. J., & Crystal, J. D. (2006). Episodic-like memory in the rat. *Current Biology, 16*(13), 1317–1321. https://doi.org/10.1016/j.cub.2006.05.025

Baddeley, A. (2001). The concept of episodic memory. *Philosophical Transactions of the Royal Society of London, Series B: Biological Sciences, 356*(1413), 1345–1350. https://doi.org/10.1098/rstb.2001.0957

Barham, W., Visser, J., Schoonbee, H., & Evans, L. (1985). Some observations on the influence of stress on ECG patterns in *Oreochromis mossambicus* and *Cyprinus carpio*. *Comparative Biochemistry and Physiology. A, Comparative Physiology, 82*(3), 549–552. https://doi.org/10.1016/0300-9629(85)90431-1

Bevins, R. A. (1992). Selective associations: A methodological critique. *The Psychological Record, 42*(1), 57–73. https://doi.org/10.1007/BF03399587

Bischof, H. J. (1994). Sexual imprinting as a two-stage process. In J. A. Hogan and J. J. Bolhuis (Eds.), *Causal mechanisms of behavioural development* (pp. 82–97). Cambridge University Press.

Bolhuis, J. J., Beckers, G. J., Huybregts, M. A., Berwick, R. C., & Everaert, M. B. (2018). Meaningful syntactic structure in songbird vocalizations? *PLoS Biology, 16*(6), e2005157. https://doi.org/10.1371/journal.pbio.2005157

Bossema, I. (1979). Jays and oaks: an eco-ethological study of a symbiosis. *Behaviour, 70*, 1–116. https://doi.org/10.1163/156853979X00016

Bouton, M. E. (2016). *Learning and behavior: A contemporary synthesis*, 2nd ed. Sinauer.

Burdyn, L. E., Noble, L. M., Shreves, L. E., & Thomas, R. K. (1984). Long-term memory for concepts by squirrel monkeys. *Physiological Psychology, 12*(2), 97–102. https://doi.org/10.3758/BF03332174

Byrne, R. W. (2002). Imitation of novel complex actions: What does the evidence from animals mean? *Advances in the Study of Behavior, 31*, 77–105. https://doi.org/10.1016/S0065-3454(02)80006-7

Chen, J., Van Rossum, D., & Ten Cate, C. (2015). Artificial grammar learning in zebra finches and human adults: XYX versus XXY. *Animal Cognition, 18*(1), 151–164. https://doi.org/10.1007/s10071-014-0786-4

Clayton, N. S., & Dickinson, A. (1998). Episodic-like memory during cache recovery by scrub jays. *Nature, 395*(6699), 272–274. https://doi.org/10.1038/26216

(1999). Scrub jays (*Aphelocoma coerulescens*) remember the relative time of caching as well as the location and content of their caches. *Journal of Comparative Psychology, 113*(4), 403–416. https://doi.org/10.1037/0735-7036.113.4.403

Cole, S., Hainsworth, F. R., Kamil, A. C., Mercier, T., & Wolf, L. L. (1982). Spatial learning as an adaptation in hummingbirds. *Science, 217*(4560), 655–657. https://doi.org/10.1126/science.217.4560.655

Cook, R. G., Levison, D. G., Gillett, S. R., & Blaisdell, A. P. (2005). Capacity and limits of associative memory in pigeons. *Psychonomic Bulletin & Review, 12*(2), 350–358. https://doi.org/10.3758/BF03196384

Crystal, J. D. (2010). Episodic-like memory in animals. *Behavioural Brain Research, 215*(2), 235–243. https://doi.org/10.1016/j.bbr.2010.03.005

Domjan, M. (1993). Biological constraints on instrumental and classical conditioning: Implications for general process theory. In G. H. Bower (Ed.), *The psychology of learning and motivation* (vol. 17, pp. 215–277). Academic Press. https://doi.org/10.1016/S0079-7421(08)60100-0

Domjan, M., & Krause, M. (2017). Generality of the laws of learning: from biological constraints to ecological perspectives. In R. Menzel (Ed.), *Learning theory and behavior, Vol. 1, Learning and memory: A comprehensive reference* (2nd ed., pp. 189–201). Academic Press. https://doi.org/10.1016/B978-0-12-809324-5.21012-2

Emlen, S. T. (1970). Celestial rotation: Its importance in the development of migratory orientation. *Science, 170*(3963), 1198–1201. https://doi.org/10.1126/science.170.3963.1198

Enquist, M., Lind, J., & Ghirlanda, S. (2016). The power of associative learning and the ontogeny of optimal behaviour. *Royal Society Open Science, 3*(11), 160734. https://doi.org/10.1098/rsos.160734

Fagot, J., & Cook, R. G. (2006). Evidence for large long-term memory capacities in baboons and pigeons and its implications for learning and the evolution of cognition. *Proceedings of the National Academy of Sciences, 103*(46), 17564–17567. https://doi.org/10.1073/pnas.0605184103

Gallistel, C. R. (1990). *The organization of learning*. MIT Press.

Gentner, T. Q., Fenn, K. M., Margoliash, D., & Nusbaum, H. C. (2006). Recursive syntactic pattern learning by songbirds. *Nature, 440*(7088), 1204–1207. https://doi.org/10.1038/nature04675

Ghirlanda, S. (2017). Can squirrel monkeys learn an ABnA grammar? A re-evaluation of Ravignani et al. (2013). *PeerJ, 5*, e3806. https://doi.org/10.7717/peerj.3806

Ghirlanda, S., Lind, J., & Enquist, M. (2017). Memory for stimulus sequences: A divide between humans and other animals? *Royal Society Open Science, 4*(6), 161011. https://doi.org/10.1098/rsos.161011

(2020). A-learning: A new formulation of associative learning theory. *Psychonomic Bulletin & Review, 27*, 1166–1194. https://doi.org/10.3758/s13423-020-01749-0

Gleitman, H. (1971). *Forgetting of long-term memories in animals*. In W. K. Honig & P. H. R. James (Eds.), *Animal memory* (pp. 1–44). Academic Press.

Gould, J. L., & Marler, P. (1984). Ethology and the natural history of learning. In P. Marler & H. S. Terrrace (Eds.), *The biology of learning* (pp. 47–74). Springer. https://doi.org/10.1007/978-3-642-70094-1_3

Griffiths, D., Dickinson, A., & Clayton, N. (1999). Episodic memory: What can animals remember about their past? *Trends in Cognitive Sciences, 3*(2), 74–80. https://doi.org/10.1016/S1364-6613(98)01272-8

Gross, C. T., & Canteras, N. S. (2012). The many paths to fear. *Nature Reviews Neuroscience, 13*(9), 651. https://doi.org/10.1038/nrn3301

Guthrie, E. R. (1935). *The psychology of learning*. Harper.

Hall, G. (2002). Associative structures in Pavlovian and instrumental conditioning. In R. Gallistel (Ed.), *Stevens' handbook of experimental psychology* (3rd ed., pp. 1–45). Wiley Online Library. https://doi.org/10.1002/0471214426.pas0301

Hanggi, E. B., & Ingersoll, J. F. (2009). Long-term memory for categories and concepts in horses (*Equus caballus*). *Animal Cognition, 12*(3), 451–462. https://doi.org/10.1007/s10071-008-0205-9

Healy, S. D., & Hurly, T. A. (2003). Cognitive ecology: Foraging in hummingbirds as a model system. *Advances in the Study of Behavior, 32*, 325–359. https://doi.org/10.1016/S0065-3454(03)01007-6

Helfman, G. S., & Schultz, E. T. (1984). Social transmission of behavioural traditions in a coral reef fish. *Animal Behaviour, 32*, 379–384. https://doi.org/10.1016/S0003-3472(84)80272-9

Herbranson, W. T., & Shimp, C. P. (2008). Artificial grammar learning in pigeons. *Learning & Behavior, 36*(2), 116–137. https://doi.org/10.3758/LB.36.2.116

Hogan, J. A. (1997). Energy models of motivation: A reconsideration. *Applied Animal Behaviour Science, 53*, 89–105. https://doi.org/10.1016/S0168-1591(96)01153-7

(2017). *The study of behavior: Organization, methods, and principles.* Cambridge University Press. https://doi.org/10.1017/9781108123792

Holland, P. C. (2008). Cognitive versus stimulus-response theories of learning. *Learning & Behavior, 36*(3), 227–241. https://doi.org/10.3758/LB.36.3.227

Holmes, P. A., & Bitterman, M. (1966). Spatial and visual habit reversal in the turtle. *Journal of Comparative and Physiological Psychology, 62*(2), 328–331. https://doi.org/10.1037/h0023675

Hull, C. L. (1943). *Principles of behaviour.* Appleton-Century-Crofts.

Hultsch, H., & Todt, D. (1989). Memorization and reproduction of songs in nightingales (*Luscinia megarhynchos*): Evidence for package formation. *Journal of Comparative Physiology A, 165*(2), 197–203. https://doi.org/10.1007/BF00619194

Immelmann, K. (1972). The influence of early experience upon the development of social behaviour in estrildine finches. *Proceedings XVth Ornithological Congress*, Den Haag 1970, pp. 316–338.

Janik, V. M., & Slater, P. J. (1997). Vocal learning in mammals. *Advances in the Study of Behaviour, 26*, 59–100. https://doi.org/10.1016/S0065-3454(08)60377-0

Jensen, R. (2006). Behaviorism, latent learning, and cognitive maps: Needed revisions in introductory psychology textbooks. *The Behavior Analyst, 29*(2), 187–209. https://doi.org/10.1007/BF03392130

Johnson, C. K., & Davis, R. T. (1973). Seven-year retention of oddity learning set in monkeys. *Perceptual and Motor Skills, 37*(3), 920–922. https://doi.org/10.2466/pms.1973.37.3.920

Jozet-Alves, C., Bertin, M., & Clayton, N. S. (2013). Evidence of episodic-like memory in cuttlefish. *Current Biology, 23*(23), R1033–R1035. https://doi.org/10.1016/j.cub.2013.10.021

van Kampen, H. S., & de Vos, G. J. (1995). A study of blocking and overshadowing in filial imprinting. *Quarterly Journal of Experimental Psychology, 49B*, 346–356. https://doi.org/10.1080/14640749508401457

Kastak, C. R., & Schusterman, R. J. (2002). Long-term memory for concepts in a California sea lion (*Zalophus californianus*). *Animal Cognition, 5*(4), 225–232. https://doi.org/10.1007/s10071-002-0153-8

Kristo, G., Janssen, S. M., & Murre, J. M. (2009). Retention of autobiographical memories: An internet-based diary study. *Memory, 17*(8), 816–829. https://doi.org/10.1080/09658210903143841

Kullberg, C., & Lind, J. (2002). An experimental study of predator recognition in great tit fledglings. *Ethology, 108*, 429–441. https://doi.org/10.1046/j.1439-0310.2002.00786.x

Lieberman, D. A. (2011). *Human learning and memory.* Cambridge University Press.

Lind, J. (2018). What can associative learning do for planning? *Royal Society Open Science, 5*(11), 180778. https://doi.org/10.1098/rsos.180778

Lind, J., Enquist, M., & Ghirlanda, S. (2015). Animal memory: A review of delayed matching-to-sample data. *Behavioural Processes, 117*, 52–58. https://doi.org/10.1016/j.beproc.2014.11.019

Lind, J., Ghirlanda, S., & Enquist, M. (2019). Social learning through associative processes: A computational theory. *Royal Society Open Science, 6*, 181777. https://doi.org/10.1098/rsos.181777

Lorenz, K. (1935). Der Kumpan in der Umwelt des Vogel. *Journal of Ornithology, 83*, 137–413. https://doi.org/10.1007/BF01905355

MacDonald, S. E. (1993). Delayed matching-to-successive-samples in pigeons: Short-term memory for item and order information. *Animal Learning & Behavior, 21*(1), 59–67. https://doi.org/10.3758/BF03197977

Mackintosh, N. J. (1983). *Conditioning and associative learning.* Oxford University Press. https://doi.org/ 10.2307/1422540

Macphail, E. M., & Bolhuis, J. J. (2001). The evolution of intelligence: Adaptive specializations versus general process. *Biological Reviews, 76*(3), 341–364. https://doi.org/10.1017/s146479310100570x

McFarland, D. (1985). *Animal behaviour,* vol. 1. Pitman.

McFarland, D. J. (1971). *Feedback mechanisms in animal behaviour.* Academic Press.

McLaren, I. P. L., & Mackintosh, N. J. (2000). An elemental model of associative learning: I. Latent inhibition and perceptual learning. *Animal Learning & Behavior, 28*(3), 211–246. https://doi.org/10.3758/BF03200258

(2002). Associative learning and elemental representation: II. Generalization and discrimination. *Animal Learning & Behavior, 30*, 177–200. https://doi.org/10.3758/BF03192828

Mets, D. G., & Brainard, M. S. (2019). Learning is enhanced by tailoring instruction to individual genetic differences. *eLife, 8*, e47216 https://doi.org/10.7554/eLife.47216

Murphy, R. A., Mondragón, E., & Murphy, V. A. (2008). Rule learning by rats. *Science, 319* (5871), 1849–1851. https://doi.org/10.1126/science.1151564

Ormerod, B. K., & Beninger, R. J. (2002). Water maze versus radial maze: Differential performance of rats in a spatial delayed match-to-position task and response to scopolamine. *Behavioural Brain Research, 128*(2), 139–152. https://doi.org/10.1016/S0166-4328 (01)00316-3

Overman Jr., W., & Doty, R. (1980). Prolonged visual memory in macaques and man. *Neuroscience, 5*(11), 1825–1831. https://doi.org/10.1016/0306-4522(80)90032-9

Pahl, M., Zhu, H., Pix, W., Tautz, J., & Zhang, S. (2007). Circadian timed episodic-like memory – A bee knows what to do when, and also where. *The Journal of Experimental Biology, 210*(20), 3559–3567. https://doi.org/10.1242/jeb.005488

Patterson, T. L., & Tzeng, O. J. (1979). Long-term memory for abstract concepts in the lowland gorilla (*Gorilla g. gorilla*). *Bulletin of the Psychonomic Society, 13*(5), 279–282. https://doi.org/10.3758/BF03336870

Pavlov, I. P. (1927). *Conditioned reflexes.* Oxford University Press.

Pearce, J. M. (2008). *Animal learning and cognition,* 3rd ed. Psychology Press. https://doi.org/ 10.4324/9781315782911

Perry, S. E., & Manson, J. H. (2003). Traditions in monkeys. *Evolutionary Anthropology, 12*, 71–81. https://doi.org/10.1002/evan.10105

Pierce, W. D., & Cheney, Carl D. (2008). *Behavior analysis and learning.* Psychology Press. https://doi.org/10.4324/9780203441817

Pilley, J. W., & Reid, A. K. (2011). Border collie comprehends object names as verbal referents. *Behavioural Processes, 86*(2), 184–195. https://doi.org/10.1016/j.beproc.2010.11.007

Pinel, J. P., & Treit, D. (1978). Burying as a defensive response in rats. *Journal of Comparative and Physiological Psychology, 92*(4), 708–712. https://doi.org/10.1037/h0077494

Roberts, W. A., Feeney, M. C., MacPherson, K., Petter, M., McMillan, N., & Musolino, E. (2008). Episodic-like memory in rats: Is it based on when or how long ago? *Science, 320* (5872), 113–115. https://doi.org/ 10.1126/science.1152709

Simons, D. J., & Chabris, C. F. (1999). Gorillas in our midst: Sustained inattentional blindness for dynamic events. *Perception, 28*(9), 1059–1074. https://doi.org/10.1068/p281059

Skinner, B. (1936). Conditioning and extinction and their relation to drive. *The Journal of General Psychology, 14*(2), 296–317. https://doi.org/10.1080/00221309.1936.9713156

Soha, J. (2016). The auditory template hypothesis: A review and comparative perspective. *Animal Behaviour, 124*, 247–254. https://doi.org/10.1016/j.anbehav.2016.09.016

Staddon, J. E. R. (2001). *The new behaviorism: Mind, mechanism and society.* Taylor & Francis.

Stephens, D. W. (1987). On economically tracking a variable environment. *Theoretical Population Biology, 32*(1), 15–25. https://doi.org/10.1016/0040-5809(87)90036-0

Suzuki, T. N., Wheatcroft, D., & Griesser, M. (2016). Experimental evidence for compositional syntax in bird calls. *Nature Communications, 7,* 10986. https://doi.org/10.1038/ncomms10986

Tennie, C., Völter, C. J., Vonau, V., Hanus, D., Call, J., & Tomasello, M. (2019). Chimpanzees use observed temporal directionality to learn novel causal relations. *Primates, 60*(6), 517–524. https://doi.org/10.1007/s10329-019-00754-9

Thistlethwaite, D. (1951). A critical review of latent learning and related experiments. *Psychological Bulletin, 48*(2), 97–129. https://doi.org/10.1037/h0055171

Thorndike, E. L. (1898). *Animal intelligence, an experimental study of the associative processes in animals.* Macmillan. https://doi.org/10.1037/h0092987

    (1911). *Animal intelligence. Experimental studies.* Macmillan. https://doi.org/10.5962/bhl.title.55072

Tolman, E. C. (1932). *Purposive behavior in animals and men.* University of California Press.

Tolman, E. C., & Honzik, C. H. (1930). Introduction and removal of reward, and maze performance in rats. *University of California Publications in Psychology, 4,* 257–275.

Vaughan, W., & Greene, S. L. (1984). Pigeon visual memory capacity. *Journal of Experimental Psychology: Animal Behavior Processes, 10*(2), 256–271. https://doi.org/10.1037/0097-7403.10.2.256

Völter, C. J., & Call, J. (2014). Great apes (*Pan paniscus, Pan troglodytes, Gorilla gorilla, Pongo abelii*) follow visual trails to locate hidden food. *Journal of Comparative Psychology, 128*(2), 199–208. https://doi.org/10.1037/a0035434

van de Waal, E., Borgeaud, C., & Whiten, A. (2013). Potent social learning and conformity shape a wild primate's foraging decisions. *Science, 340*(6131), 483–485. https://doi.org/10.1126/science.1232769

Wehner, R. (2003). Desert ant navigation: How miniature brains solve complex tasks. *Journal of Comparative Physiology A, 189*(8), 579–588. https://doi.org/10.1007/s00359-003-0431-1

Weisman, R. G., Duder, C., & von Konigslow, R. (1985). Representation and retention of three-event sequences in pigeons. *Learning and Motivation, 16*(3), 239–258. https://doi.org/10.1016/0023-9690(85)90014-1

Weisman, R. G., Wasserman, E., Dodd, P., & Larew, M. B. (1980). Representation and retention of two-event sequences in pigeons. *Journal of Experimental Psychology: Animal Behavior Processes, 6*(4), 312–325. https://doi.org/10.1037/0097-7403.6.4.312

Yerkes, R. M., & Yerkes, D. N. (1928). Concerning memory in the chimpanzee. *Journal of Comparative Psychology, 8*(3), 237–271. https://doi.org/10.1037/h0073804

Zeldin, R. K., & Olton, D. S. (1986). Rats acquire spatial learning sets. *Journal of Experimental Psychology: Animal Behavior Processes, 12*(4), 412–419. https://doi.org/10.1037/0097-7403.12.4.412

Zentall, T. R., Clement, T. S., Bhatt, R. S., & Allen, J. (2001). Episodic-like memory in pigeons. *Psychonomic Bulletin & Review, 8*(4), 685–690. https://doi.org/10.3758/BF03196204

20

WHAT LABORATORY AND FIELD APPROACHES BRING TO BEAR FOR UNDERSTANDING THE EVOLUTION OF URSID COGNITION

Jennifer Vonk

A broad aim of comparative psychology is to produce a framework for understanding the selective pressures shaping cognition across diverse species, with a particular interest in the evolution of abilities thought to be uniquely human. If elements of these capacities are found in other species, the ecological pressures facing these species might provide clues as to which pressures are necessary or sufficient for their emergence. Exploring phylogenetic relatedness among species that show varying degrees of these capacities would help to establish the timeline for their emergence and provide evidence of convergent evolution. However, establishing human-like abilities as the starting point for comparative explorations, a top-down strategy, may diminish the likelihood of finding and appreciating traits that are unique to other species. This anthropocentric focus may also hinder progress in understanding distinct underlying mechanisms for behavior that may, on the surface, appear similar. An exclusive focus on outcomes versus processes masks diversity in cognitive mechanisms across species. Whereas top-down approaches aim to provide evidence for preconceived models of cognition, bottom-up approaches start with observations specific to the model species and use these to derive a species-specific model of cognition (de Waal & Ferrari, 2010). An integration of laboratory and field studies will promote a bottom-up understanding of the unique traits of various species and the selective pressures driving these traits (Eaton et al., 2018; Vonk et al., 2020). This approach should paint a clearer portrait of cognition across and within phylogenetic lineages. Applying this approach to the study of ursid cognition may be particularly revealing of the selective pressures underlying learning and memory.

20.1 WHY BEARS?

Studies of the evolution of cognition have been dominated by a focus on the Social Intelligence Hypothesis, proposed by Jolly (1965), Humphrey (1976), and Dunbar (1998, 2009) with more recent competition from the Technical Intelligence Hypothesis (Byrne, 1997). The Technical Intelligence Hypothesis, like Milton's (1981) proposal, focuses on the role of foraging, rather than social, complexity. More recently, Sol (2009) has emphasized the role of environmental complexity in shaping larger brain size, which, in turn, led to more advanced cognition. Although presented as competing hypotheses, social and foraging challenges are not mutually exclusive and both could drive the evolution of larger brains and cognitive complexity (Vonk et al., 2020). Comparing species within the order Carnivora allows for an assessment of the relative roles of foraging complexity, social complexity, and environmental variation in predicting cognitive complexity because this order is composed of species that exhibit sufficient variation in both foraging and social strategies to allow for useful comparisons (Vonk & Leete, 2017). For example, carnivora includes highly social species such as canids, pinnipeds, lions, most hyena species, and relatively less social species, such as striped hyenas, ursids, and almost all felids. Furthermore, domesticated canids and felids interact closely with humans, allowing researchers to disentangle the role of domestication versus evolutionary adaptations to social lifestyles in these genera. Moreover, carnivores include generalist feeders (e.g., brown bears, black bears, canids), obligate carnivores (felids, polar bears) and obligate herbivores (giant pandas). Bears, in particular, exhibit a wide range of foraging strategies, allowing for exploration of how various aspects of foraging complexity (e.g., extractive foraging, patchy food distribution, and a generalist diet) might predict cognitive capacities (Byrne, 1997). Bears, however, show less variability in sociality (e.g., group size, group composition, group complexity), and thus, the effects of foraging complexity can be studied independently of variation in social structure. Bears, therefore, allow for the important yet neglected "control group" for studies aiming to show the importance of sociality in predicting complex cognition (Humphrey, 1976; Jolly, 1965). The recent extension of comparative laboratories to zoological settings allows for cognitive studies of species like bears, which will better position researchers to understand the associations between sociality, foraging strategies, and cognitive capacities like learning and memory.

20.2 INTEGRATING FIELD AND LABORATORY APPROACHES

Within comparative psychology, a tension exists between laboratory-based studies and field studies. Laboratory studies tend to use the top-down strategy of searching for evidence of a particular ability (typically based on what is known about human cognition), whereas field studies are more likely to describe traits and behaviors observed in a species' natural behavioral repertoire with an attempt to explain why and how that behavior might emerge. For example, laboratory studies have focused on identifying evidence for prosocial preferences in nonhumans using a food delivery paradigm (the prosocial choice task, or PCT: Silk et al., 2005), even though food sharing among nonkin is relatively rare in nonhuman primates (Stevens & Gilby, 2004) and may be induced by harassment (Stevens & Stephens, 2002). Although primates are the closest relatives to humans, other, more distantly related species might be better candidates with which to explore the pressures supporting cooperation and altruism. Observations of cooperative hunting in solitary species, like brown bears foraging for salmon, may reveal how tolerance of agonistic-like predatory actions and the ability to read intentions – something that has yet to be studied in these species (Stringham, 2012) – contribute to the emergence of full-blown cooperation. Although such cooperative acts are rare in natural settings, bears are frequently housed together in zoological settings, and well-used cooperation paradigms like the loose string problem (Marshall-Pescini et al., 2017) could be adapted to examine how their attempts differ from those of more social carnivores.

Existing studies provide a clear demonstration of the utility of blending field and laboratory approaches. For example, vampire bats exhibit a unique strategy of feeding exclusively on blood (hematophagy) and can expire after missing a single night's meal. Thus, vampire bats may depend upon conspecifics to provide them with a blood meal, requiring the donor to give up their own meal at personal cost (Wilkinson, 1988). Researchers have examined the factors underlying food sharing in vampire bats in both laboratory and field settings with the goal of understanding its emergence in this species, rather than using vampire bats as a species with which to understand the evolution of pro-sociality in humans. In this example, researchers identified a behavior that is specific to a single subfamily (*Desmodontinae*) and examined it in detail to better understand the role of various factors, such as kin selection, affiliation, and reciprocity in maintaining the behavior (e.g., Carter et al., 2019; Carter & Wilkinson, 2013). The same research team (Ripperger et al., 2019) recently demonstrated that vampire bats that cooperate in laboratory settings maintain their social networks after being released into the wild, beautifully blending laboratory and field approaches to study animal behavior.

Such studies demonstrate how work can be initiated in captive environments where better control can be exerted over subject history, stimuli, and environmental confounds, and extended to improve our understanding of wild animals. In another representative study, Ripperger et al. (2020) captured wild female vampire bats, allowed them to breed in captivity, and then released them with their offspring. Using proximity sensors and tracking social encounters, they found that captive-born individuals preferred to associate with unfamiliar kin compared to nonkin. Thus, kin preferences could not be attributed to familiarity or learned behavior. Only through combining laboratory and field approaches could such natural preferences be determined. A recent study of social tolerance in a solitary species, the puma, revealed that tracking social interactions may be more important for these species than previously believed (Elbroch et al., 2017), opening the door for further study of other species generally considered to be asocial (Vonk, 2018). Release and tracking of rehabilitated bears could similarly reveal preferences in habitat overlap that might suggest the ability to track social relationships over long periods without contact. Støen et al. (2005) found that overlap in home range in wild brown bears was predicted by relatedness, suggesting the possibility of kin recognition as a mechanism. Further study of how bears might recognize kin would benefit from a laboratory approach where genetic relatedness is known and bears could be presented with information in multiple modalities to elucidate what cues are used to determine relatedness (e.g., chemical, olfactory, visual). For example, researchers have shown that domestic dogs respond differently to scents of kin and unrelated conspecifics even in the absence of any exposure to kin early in life (Hamilton & Vonk, 2015; Hepper, 1994). Therefore, differential responding to kin and nonkin may not rely on learning.

Questions about interspecies interactions, such as whether prey species innately detect predator scents, or learn to do so through experience, can also be explored through integrating field and lab work. For example, Samuel et al. (2020) collected fecal samples of bear, lynx, and beaver from the wild and presented these scents to domestic dogs in a captive setting. Using domestic dogs allowed the researchers to control prior exposure to such scents and to present the scents in a controlled manner along with a neutral scent. They found that dogs spent less time in the vicinity of bear scat compared to beaver or control scents even in the absence of any prior experience with the predators. Bears may also attend to vocal cues of competing predators. Suraci et al. (2017) used a classic vocal playback approach to show that both black bear mothers with cubs and solitary bears responded to the calls of cougars by advancing and vocalizing. These authors suggest that bears can eavesdrop on other predators both to avoid conflict and to scavenge cougar kills. Cross-species interactions like these are difficult to study in captive settings where mixed species exhibits are rare.

20.3 HUMAN-WILDLIFE INTERACTIONS

Humans interact with animals in natural settings, sometimes to the detriment of both parties. Studies of wild bears have shown that black bears detect risk from human disturbance and adjust their spatial movements accordingly (Stillfried et al., 2015). Brown bears are also sensitive to the density of human road traffic (Ordiz et al., 2014). Thus, increasing cues of risk in areas of human-bear conflict could reduce unwanted interactions. While studies of natural behavior are helpful to inform our approach to dealing with human-wildlife interactions (see Griffin and Diquelou, Chapter 8), basic principles obtained through the tradition of laboratory approaches can be generalized to help mitigate problem behavior of both humans and wildlife as well. For example, basic research on conditioning has successfully been applied to the problem of livestock depredation by wild carnivores. Emetic chemical compounds have been paired with baited items to reduce black bear consumption of beehives (Colvin, 1975; Polson, 1983) and the raiding of human campgrounds (Ternent & Garshelis, 1999), although this approach is not always successful (Smith et al., 2000). Classical conditioning has also been used with mixed results to pair pain from bear-deterrent flash bullets and rubber bullets with recordings associated with human-developed areas (Gillin et al., 1994). The construct of behavioral syndrome from traditional personality research, commonly applied to captive populations, has also been shown to predict the spatial movements of wild bears (Hertel et al., 2019). Such studies demonstrate that laboratory research can help to promote more positive human-wildlife interactions or at least reduce the frequency of potentially negative interactions.

20.4 STUDYING COGNITION IN BEARS

The study of cognition poses particular challenges in that cognitive processes are difficult to uncover with observational studies alone. Studies of cognition typically require manipulation and extended training to reveal internal knowledge states and thought processes, making it more difficult to dissociate natural abilities from trained responses. In addition, laboratory studies have suffered from the criticism that they test subjects in artificial, sometimes sterile environments, that do not capture important elements of animals' natural habitats (e.g., Boesch, 2020). For example, captive bears may be particularly motivated to participate in experimental studies because of a lack of external stimulation. They do not face the same challenges of wild bears in having to find dens, mates, or food sources. For wild bears that face starvation, particularly as they prepare for hibernation, finding food is critical to their survival. Captive bears are well fed and protected from the elements, as well as human predation, and, thus, may either be less motivated to forage effectively or more motivated to explore all novel sites in a foraging study, regardless of distance or likelihood of baiting (e.g., Vonk et al., 2015; Zamisch & Vonk, 2012). Motivation to perform a particular behavior depends upon perceived necessity, interest, and comfort in the testing situation. Although recently receiving greater attention (Schubiger et al., 2020), motivation is often neglected in studies of cognitive abilities. Factors such as neophobia and personality characteristics, such as boldness versus shyness, and how these might impact comparative studies in particular, given typically small sample sizes, has received significant attention only within the last decade (e.g., Beran & Highfill, 2011).

The issue of external validity is critical when laboratory studies are used to determine the ceiling of a species' capacity for a given cognitive trait. For example, Zamisch and Vonk (2012) tested spatial memory in captive black bears and grizzly bears (Vonk et al., 2015) and found little evidence that the bears made use of spatial memory to visit baited sites when foraging. These data contradict conventional wisdom that bears remember sites where they have found food, locate dens within large home ranges, and return to territories after relocation (Gittleman, 1986; Hertel et al., 2016; Mazur & Seher, 2008; Mitchell & Powell, 2007; Noyce & Garshelis, 2011). Consequently, Zamisch and I did not conclude that bears were lacking spatial abilities; rather, that much smaller habitats in captivity were not conducive for testing spatial memory abilities given that there was no significant loss of energy in exploring all sites, nor was there any risk of predation from travelling between sites. Although tasks may have to be implemented in somewhat unnatural ways in captivity, attending to the natural foraging strategy of a species in the wild should help inform the design of the task in captive settings. Spatial memory tasks requiring animals to use a win-stay strategy in which they would benefit from revisiting sites that had been baited earlier in the day (Zamisch & Vonk, 2012) do not mirror natural environments where foods such as fruits and berries do not replenish quickly and in which animals might be better served by using a win-shift strategy. Because these types of foods may replenish in the same location but on a longer temporal schedule, it might not make sense to change the location of baited foods at every test session. Zamisch and Vonk (2012) found better evidence of spatial memory in black bears when baited locations were stable across test days and both win-stay and win-shift strategies were examined (Zamisch & Vonk, 2012). Similarly, Tarou (2004) contrasted the use of win-stay and win-shift strategies in two species of bears from different ecologies: giant pandas and spectacled bears. Testing zoo-housed bears allows other aspects of the environment to be matched or explicitly compared, which may be more complicated in natural settings. Spectacled bears outperformed giant pandas in a win-shift task, whereas the opposite was true in a win-stay task. Although these strategies are likely to have evolved based on species' natural diets, preferences are likely maintained in captive populations, despite the lack of a need to exhibit the same strategies. Interestingly, an early study of captive black bears' food preferences suggests stability in preferences for foods high in protein and carbohydrates across seasons (Bacon & Burghardt, 1983).

Because the regular feeding schedule in captivity does not approximate the temporal availability of natural foods, such as shrubs and berries, an appropriate exploration of spatial memory in captive bears would need to mimic the costs of exploring multiple sites, whether attempting to mimic the distance between food sites in wild bear habitats or imposing a comparable cost. Imposing costs comparable to those faced in the wild would raise ethical concerns due to the risks to the animals' welfare, thus limiting the ecological validity of studies in captive settings (see also Boesch, 2020). Creating analogous challenges across wild and captive environments may result in implementing a task in drastically different, sometimes unnatural ways. For example, it is unlikely that a captive situation can replicate the large home range of a wild brown bear. Similarly, the possibilities for denning and mating are much more constrained in captivity. Fortunately, threats, such as those posed by hunters, and lack of nourishment are also reduced or eliminated in captivity. Therefore, the goal should not be to attempt to replicate natural environments in lab studies, but to replicate the essential elements of the task that would best allow the natural ability to be exhibited. For example, if use of spatial memory is advantageous only when there is a cost to visiting all possible sites, costs can be implemented in both wild and captive settings that differ from each other but impose the same motivation to recall the location of previously baited sites. A cost to visit unbaited food sites might not result in considerable energy loss in captivity, but introducing competitors imposes another cost that should result in bears travelling immediately to baited sites, bypassing unbaited sites, if they remember which sites are baited (Zamisch & Vonk, 2012). This approach of course works only if animals are socially housed, a situation that, in itself, is unnatural for many solitary species.

With this in mind, it is unsurprising that social cognition is poorly examined in solitary species, despite the importance of doing so for evaluating hypotheses about the role of sociality in shaping cognition (Vonk, 2018; Vonk et al., 2020). As Udell (2018, p. 330) pointed out, "identical rearing or testing conditions may not guarantee equivalent task performance, even if both species or populations share the capacity for a specific behavior or cognitive ability." She stressed the importance of considering the rearing and testing environments of subjects, and whether these environments facilitate other important equivalences. For example, a surprising finding that wolves outperformed domestic dogs in a cooperative task (Marshall-Pescini et al., 2017) contradicted a longstanding notion that domestication had better equipped domestic dogs to cooperate, compared to their wild counterparts (see Range & Virányi, 2015; Virányi, & Range, 2014). However, these more recent results and a more careful consideration of socioecological factors suggest that what was once attributed to species differences could be better explained by the strength of the social relationship between participants. Domestic dogs tend to perform better in cooperative tasks if they, too, have been raised together in the same household (Ostojić & Clayton, 2014). When comparing more distantly related species, it is also important to note that rearing and testing with human experimenters may be more natural for some species (e.g., domestic dogs) than for others (e.g., chimpanzees). Although animals may be group-housed in captivity, the groupings are likely to be unnatural, for example, consisting entirely of related individuals that would have dispersed in the wild. Thus, tests of social cognition in captive populations should be interpreted with skepticism, particularly when involving species that would not exist in close proximity in the wild. This limitation makes it challenging to compare social cognition between social and solitary species.

This challenge notwithstanding, investigators took an innovative approach to exploring the contribution of genetics versus social learning to problem behavior in brown bears by genotyping and tracking grizzly bear activity at sites where problem behavior was reported (Morehouse et al., 2016). The researchers collected hair samples at locations where bears had destroyed human property, pets, or livestock, or gained access to anthropogenic food. Their research revealed that offspring of problem mothers, but not fathers, were more likely than offspring of nonproblem mothers to cause problems themselves. Therefore, they concluded that social learning superseded genetic contributions to problem behavior. Similarly, Mazur, and Seher (2008) found that black bears learned to forage using the same food sources as their mothers (either wild or anthropogenic food sources). Not only do these results suggest an important role of social learning in problem behavior, they have implications for prevention of proliferation of problem behavior learned early from problem mother bears. Studies of social learning in the laboratory were less successful when sloth bears observed human demonstrators in a task where they had to move a bucket and climb on it to access honey (Amici et al., 2019). Unlike these sloth bears, brown bears learned to position objects under suspended food rewards to retrieve the rewards but they did so independently (Waroff et al., 2017). Taking the field and laboratory results together suggests that social learning may be limited to mother/offspring relationships in bears, but further work is necessary to test this hypothesis.

Given the challenges of testing social cognition in less social species, it is somewhat unsurprising that, within Carnivora, tests of social cognition are primarily limited to canids and pinnipeds, with the exception of studies of human/feline interactions. Studies of carnivore cognition have more typically involved tests of physical cognition, such as olfactory discrimination, vision, memory, and spatial ability. For example, one of the earliest studies of bear cognition examined color discrimination and learning (Bacon & Burghardt, 1976). More recently, Amici et al. (2017) investigated short-term memory and object permanence in sloth bears by presenting the bears with food rewards hidden in holes of a tree trunk. This procedure mimicked the natural foraging of the bears that feed on termites and honeybees. The authors examined the bears' use of acoustic and olfactory cues to find the food, taking note of modalities used by the bears naturally. The authors aimed to test object permanence, but the test also served to establish short-term memory for the location of hidden food. The bears were expected to exhibit short-term memory after delays of 30 seconds, 60 seconds, or 120 seconds given that their diet is highly reliant on insects that are not always visible during hunting, thus seeming to require that bears remember they exist in their absence. However, surprisingly, the bears performed at chance levels unless there was virtually no delay. In contrast, they performed well when auditory, but not olfactory cues were provided, suggesting that they rely heavily on auditory cues when hunting live insects.

Furthermore, wild black bears failed to recognize snakes by sight or smell alone, but appeared to respond to the movements of snakes (Rogers et al., 2014), corroborating the importance of the modality in which cues are presented or experienced. Spatial memory may not play a crucial role for species that subsist primarily on live prey, such as insects, or on readily available foods such as grasses. However, for frugivores, it would be essential to track the location and timing of ripe fruits that replenish at particular intervals and do not change locations. Milton's (1981) classic work showed that frugivorous primates outperformed folivorous primates on tests of spatial memory. Sloth bears are omnivores that also feed on fruit, so it is surprising that they did not perform better in Amici et al.'s laboratory test. Hartmann et al. (2017) also tested sloth bears, along with sun bears – another omnivorous species – on visible displacement and transposition tasks, which also tap into spatial memory. Somewhat in contrast to Amici et al.' s results, these authors found that both sun and sloth bears tracked invisible objects, even in the absence of olfactory and auditory cues. Notably, Hartmann and colleagues use their data, in conjunction with other studies also discussed here, to argue that bears rely more heavily on vision than previously supposed.

Tarou (2004) also tested reliance on color as a cue to the location of hidden food, which spectacled bears, but not pandas, learned to do. Like most other studies of its kind, the sample size prohibited firm conclusions about species or sex differences, although female spectacled bears outperformed males. Perdue et al. (2011) found sex differences in spatial memory in giant pandas – a species in which males have a larger home range than females – but not in monogamous Asian small-clawed otters that share their habitat, supporting the range size hypothesis. Similar arguments have been made for human sex differences in spatial ability based on evolutionarily distinct roles in foraging in hunter/gatherer societies (Silverman et al., 2007). Studying other species can help determine whether division of labor is likely to lead to cognitive differences between the sexes, as such divisions may be more apparent in nonhumans compared to humans today. Perdue et al.'s (2011) study is an excellent example of a study conducted in captivity but motivated by questions about species' unique natural environments rather than by an explicit, sometimes arbitrary, comparison to human behaviors and abilities.

Other laboratory studies may impose less natural tasks to test memory in animals like bears, such as using a light board (Perdue et al., 2009) or a touchscreen (Vonk & Jett, 2018). Although bears would not encounter such apparatuses in the wild, they allow for carefully controlled presentation of stimuli in which different elements (such as location or perceptual cues) can be balanced. For example, tests of quantity discrimination often involve the presentation of arrays of black dots on computer screens, where the size, area, density, and movement of the dots can be controlled to contrast animals' use of continuous features, such as area versus numerosity (e.g., Vonk & Beran, 2012). Whereas such studies are useful for demonstrating that black bears, like most other animals tested, show ratio effects whereby discrimination is better at larger differences between the numerosity of stimulus arrays, they also raise questions about why abilities such as numerosity might exist in certain species. For example, Vonk and Beran (2012) found that bears could use number in addition to area to discriminate arrays, even with chaotically moving stimuli, but it is unclear why non-group-living bears would need to count – as opposed to estimating quantity – in the wild. This ability might be under selection pressure in highly social species that must keep track of group members, or potentially detect the size of rival groups to assess threat (e.g., McComb et al., 1994), but is more difficult to reconcile in solitary species. Thus, lab studies can sometimes reveal traits for which the evolutionary history is undetermined, leaving open further questions to be addressed in both captive and natural settings. Studies of the foraging patterns of wild brown bears suggest that probability of occurrence, rather than abundance of resources (in this case, berries), might predict bears' choice of foraging sites (Hertel et al., 2016). Scientists have not yet examined how bears might calculate probabilities, but this ability could be explored further in captive environments.

Black bears (Vonk et al., 2012; Vonk & Johnson-Ulrich, 2014) and giant pandas (Dungl et al., 2008) exhibit impressive long-term memory capacity in tasks that rely heavily on the presentation of visual stimuli, which is not bears' primary sensory modality. Black bears were able to reach impressive levels of discrimination of abstract concepts such as "animal" (Vonk et al., 2012) and "mother offspring," but control tests suggested that bears were likely remembering associations of particular images or features with reward rather than forming abstract overarching concepts, at least for social categories (Vonk & Johnson-Ulrich, 2014). The fact that bears can learn to associate visual cues with reward, and retain memory of these associations for long periods of time, is more consistent with their natural ecology than the notion that they represented constructs of social relationships, which was the impetus for the research. Indeed, a task designed to assess memory for categorically related items was not successful (Vonk & Jett, 2018). Future studies should aim to explore the cognitive processes underlying natural behaviors of bears rather than setting out to test whether bears can reason about constructs that are highly relevant for humans. Although bears might perceive two-dimensional stimuli presented via a touchscreen as representative of real-life objects (Johnson-Ulrich et al., 2016), questions remain whether these somewhat artificial tasks allow bears to fully demonstrate their capacity to learn and remember given that the stimuli are absent of a salient cue used by bears – scent.

20.5 CONCLUSIONS

This chapter has focused almost entirely on research with bears, an interesting group within which to study the selective pressures driving learning and memory. Bears, like canids and felids, belong to the order Carnivora and are distinguished from their counterparts in important ways. Bears are not group-living like canids, corvids, cetaceans, or primates – all species that have evidenced complex cognition. However, in comparison to other carnivores, they have relatively large brains, large home ranges, and vary significantly in diet with most species being omnivorous (Benson-Amram et al., 2016; Gittleman, 1986). Polar bears and giant pandas are notable exceptions, being obligate carnivores and herbivores, respectively. Thus, they contrast with the sociality of canids and the strictly carnivorous diet of felids. There is a steadily increasing volume of work on canine cognition with a focus on the potential impact of domestication in shaping dog cognition, allowing for fruitful comparisons of domestic dog to wild canid cognition (Arden et al., 2016; Lea & Osthaus, 2018; Wynne, 2016). There is a growing literature on cat cognition as well, although the bulk of the work has focused on domestic cats with little known about cognition in wild felids (Udell & Vitale Shreve, 2017; although see Borrego, 2017). Despite these significant gaps in the study of carnivore cognition, it can contribute to understanding the evolution of cognition (Vonk & Leete, 2017). Similarly, Holekamp et al. (2015; Sakai et al., 2011) have discussed the evolution of intelligence by examining brain size, sociality, and dietary complexity in hyenas.

Thus far, few ursid species have been tested in the same tasks, limiting our ability to draw conclusions at this juncture. Because bears are more commonly studied in the wild, researchers studying learning and memory in bears can use such studies as a blueprint for how to examine the mechanisms underlying bear behavior in more detail in captive settings. In a rare large-scale comparative study, Benson-Amram et al. (2016) tested 39 species of carnivore from 9 different families in a simple, extractive foraging task and concluded that brain size, rather than sociality, predicted success. Bears were among the most successful species. Not surprisingly, our own analysis (Johnson-Ulrich, 2017) revealed that a generalist diet was the best predictor of success in this task. The task, however, did not involve a social component, nor was it complex. Subjects simply had to open a latched box to retrieve the food inside, and some subjects opened the box through aggressive maneuvering rather than intentional problem solving per se (Vonk, 2016).

Further studies that include social and non-social components in comparable tasks and test diverse species will be needed to explore the selective pressures for cognition. Many canid species exhibit distinct social structures and have not been extensively compared; e.g., coyotes, dingoes, African painted dogs, and various fox species. There is little data on cognition in many bear species, for example, polar bears, spectacled bears, and Asian black bears. There are also many members of the order Carnivora of which almost nothing is known. Additionally, studies will need to better equate testing situations – not necessarily creating identical tasks, but creating analogous tasks that build on an understanding of species' natural, spontaneously exhibited abilities. Only with this jumping off point can we further investigate the conditions under which typical cognition emerges and then test the limits of such abilities under ideal circumstances. For now, it is clear that ursids are a promising family within which to explore the evolution of learning and memory mechanisms.

REFERENCES

Amici, F., Cacchione, T., & Bueno-Guerra, N. (2017). Understanding of object properties by sloth bears. *melursus ursinusursinus*. *Animal Behaviour, 134*, 217–222. http://dx.doi.org/10.1016/j.anbehav.2017.10.028

Amici, F., Holland, R., & Cacchione, T. (2019). Sloth bears (*Melursus ursinus*) fail to spontaneously solve a novel problem even if social cues and relevant experience are provided. *Journal of Comparative Psychology, 133*, 373–379. http://dx.doi.org/10.1037/com0000167

Arden, R., Bensky, M. K., & Adams, M. J. (2016). A review of cognitive abilities in dogs, 1911 through 2016: More individual differences, please! *Current Directions in Psychological Science, 25*, 307–312. http://dx.doi.org/10.1177/0963721416667718

Bacon, E. S., & Burghardt, G. M. (1976). Learning and color discrimination in the American black bear. *Ursus, 3*, 27–36.

(1983). Food preferences in the American black bear: An experimental approach. *Ursus, 5*, 102–105. https://doi.org/10.2307/3872525

Benson-Amram, S., Dantzer, B., Stricker, G., Swanson, E. M., & Holekamp, K. E. (2016). Brain size predicts problem-solving ability in mammalian carnivores. *PNAS Proceedings of the National Academy of Sciences of the United States of America, 113*, 2532–2537. http://dx.doi.org/10.1073/pnas.1505913113

Beran, M. J., & Highfill, L. E. (2011). Paying more attention to what (some) nonhuman animals and (some) humans can do: An introduction to the special issue on individual differences in comparative psychology. *International Journal of Comparative Psychology*, *24*, 1–3.

Boesch, C. (2020). Listening to the appeal from the wild. *Animal Behavior and Cognition, 7*, 257–263. https://doi.org/10.26451/abc.07.02.15.2020

Borrego, N. (2017). Big cats as a model system for the study of the evolution of intelligence. *Behavioural Processes, 141*, 261–266. http://dx.doi.org/10.1016/j.beproc.2017.03.010

Byrne, R. (1997). The technical intelligence hypothesis: An additional evolutionary stimulus to intelligence? In A. Whiten & R. Byrne (Eds.), *Machiavellian intelligence II: Extensions and evaluations* (pp. 289–311). Cambridge University Press. http://dx.doi.org/10.1017/CBO9780511525636.012

Carter, G. G., Schino, G., & Farine, D. (2019). Challenges in assessing the roles of nepotism and reciprocity in cooperation networks. *Animal Behaviour, 150*, 255–271. http://dx.doi.org/10.1016/j.anbehav.2019.01.006

Carter, G. G., & Wilkinson, G. S. (2013). Food sharing in vampire bats: Reciprocal help predicts donations more than relatedness or harassment. *Proceedings of the Royal Society, B, 280*, 20122573. https://doi.org/10.1098/rspb.2012.2573

Colvin, T. R. (1975). Aversive conditioning black bear to honey utilizing lithium chloride. *Proceedings of the Annual Conference of the Southeastern Association of Game and Fish Commissions, 29*, 450–453.

Dunbar, R. I. M. (1998). The social brain hypothesis. *Evolutionary Anthropology, 6*, 178–189. https://doi.org/10.1002/(SICI)1520-6505(1998)6:5%3C178::AID-EVAN5%3E3.0.CO;2-8
  (2009). The social brain hypothesis and its implications for social evolution. *Annals of Human Biology, 36*, 562–572. https://doi.org/10.1080/03014460902960289

Dungl, E., Schratter, D., & Huber, L. (2008). Discrimination of face-like patterns in the giant panda (*Ailuropoda melanoleuca*). *Journal of Comparative Psychology, 122*, 335e343. https://doi.org/10.1037/0735-7036.122.4.335

Eaton, T., Hutton, R., Leete, J., Lieb, J., Robeson, A., & Vonk, J. (2018). Bottoms-up: Rejecting top-down human-centered approaches in comparative psychology. *International Journal of Comparative Psychology, 31*. https://escholarship.org/uc/item/11t5q9wt

Elbroch, M. L., Levy, M., Lubell, M., Quigley, H., & Caragiulo, A. (2017). Adaptive social strategies in a solitary carnivore. *Science Advances, 3*, e1701218. https://doi.org/10.1126/sciadv.1701218

Gillin, C. M., Hammond, F. M., & Peterson, C. M. (1994). Evaluation of an aversive conditioning technique used on female grizzly bears in the Yellowstone Ecosystem. *International Conference on Bear Restoration and Management, 9*, 503–512.

Gittleman, J. L. (1986). Carnivore brain size, behavioral ecology, and phylogeny. *Journal of Mammalogy, 67*, 23–36. https://doi.org/10.2307/1380998

Hamilton, J., & Vonk, J. (2015). Do dogs (*Canis lupus familiaris*) recognize kin? *Behavioural Processes, 119*, 123–134. https://doi.org/10.1016/j.beproc.2015.08.004

Hartmann, D., Davila-Ross, M., Wong, S. T., Call, J., & Scheumann, M. (2017). Spatial transposition tasks in Indian sloth bears (*melursus ursinus*) and Bornean sun bears (*helarctos malayanus euryspilus*). *Journal of Comparative Psychology, 131*, 290–303. http://dx.doi.org/10.1037/com0000077

Hepper, P. G. (1994). Long-term retention of kinship recognition established during infancy in the domestic dog. *Behavioural Processes, 33*, 3–14. http://dx.doi.org/10.1016/0376-6357(94)90056-6

Hertel, A. G., Leclerc, M., Warren, D., Pelletier, F., Zedrosser, A., & Mueller, T. (2019). Don't poke the bear: Using tracking data to quantify behavioural syndromes in elusive wildlife. *Animal Behaviour, 147*, 91–104. http://dx.doi.org/10.1016/j.anbehav.2018.11.008

Hertel, A. G., Steyaert, S. M. J. G., Zedrosser, A., Mysterud, A., Lodberg-Holm, H., Gelink, H. W., Kindberg, J., & Swenson, J. E. (2016). Bears and berries: Species-specific selective foraging on a patchily distributed food resource in a human-altered landscape. *Behavioral Ecology and Sociobiology, 70*, 831–842. http://dx.doi.org/10.1007/s00265-016-2106-2

Holekamp, K. E., Dantzer, B., Stricker, G., Shaw Yoshida, K. C., & Benson-Amram, S. (2015). Brains, brawn and sociality: A hyaena's tale. *Animal Behaviour, 103*, 237–248. http://dx .doi.org/10.1016/j.anbehav.2015.01.023

Humphrey, N. K. (1976). The social function of intellect. In P. P. G. Bateson & R. A. Hinde (Eds.), *Growing points in ethology* (pp. 303–317). Cambridge University Press.

Johnson-Ulrich, Z. (2017). *Predictors of behavioral flexibility and problem-solving in carnivora* (Order No. 10615355). Available from Dissertations & Theses @ Oakland University. (1980794459).

Johnson-Ulrich, Z., Vonk, J., Humbyrd, M., Crowley, M., Wojtkowski, E., Yates, F., & Allard, S. (2016). Picture object recognition in an American black bear (*Ursus americanus*). *Animal Cognition, 19*, 1237–1242. https://doi.org/10.1007/s10071-016-1011-4

Jolly, A. (1965). Lemur social behavior and primate intelligence. *Science, 153*, 501–506. https:// doi.org/10.1126/science.153.3735.501

Lea, S. E. G., & Osthaus, B. (2018). In what sense are dogs special? Canine cognition in comparative context. *Learning & Behavior, 46*, 335–363. http://dx.doi.org/10.3758/ s13420-018-0349-7

Marshall-Pescini, S., Schwarz, J. F. L., Kostelnik, I., Virányi, Z., & Range, F. (2017). Importance of a species' socioecology: Wolves outperform dogs in a conspecific cooperation task. *Proceedings of the National Academy of Sciences, 114*, 11793–11798. https://doi .org/10.1073/pnas.1709027114

Mazur, R., & Seher, V. (2008). Socially learned foraging behaviour in wild black bears, *Ursus americanus. Animal Behaviour, 75*, 1503–1508. https://doi.org/10.1016/j.anbehav.2007.10.027

McComb, K., Packer, C., & Pusey, A. (1994). Roaring and numerical assessment in contests between groups of female lions *Panthera leo. Animal Behaviour, 47*, 379–387. http://dx .doi.org/10.1006/anbe.1994.1052

Milton, K. (1981). Distribution patterns of tropical plant foods as an evolutionary stimulus to primate mental development. *American Anthropologist, 83*, 534–548. https://doi.org/10 .1525/aa.1981.83.3.02a00020

Mitchell, M. S., & Powell, R. A. (2007). Optimal use of resources structures home ranges and spatial distribution of black bears. *Animal Behaviour, 74*, 219–230. http://dx.doi.org/10 .1016/j.anbehav.2006.11.017

Morehouse, A. T., Graves, T. A., Mikle, N., & Boyce, M. S. (2016). Nature vs. nurture: Evidence for social learning of conflict behaviour in grizzly bears. *PLoS ONE, 11*, 15. https://doi.org/10.1371/journal.pone.0165425

Noyce, K. V., & Garshelis, D. L. (2011). Seasonal migrations of black bears (*Ursus americanus*): Causes and consequences. *Behavioral Ecology and Sociobiology, 65*, 823–835. http://dx.doi.org/10.1007/s00265-010-1086-x

Ordiz, A., Kindberg, J., Saebo, S., Swenson, J., & Stoen, O. (2014). Brown bear circadian behavior reveals human environmental encroachment, *Biological Conservation, 173*, 1–9. https://doi.org/10.1016/j.biocon.2014.03.006

Ostojić, L., & Clayton, N. S. (2014). Behavioural coordination of dogs in a cooperative problem-solving task with a conspecific and a human partner. *Animal Cognition, 17*, 445–459. https://doi.org/10.1007/s10071-013-0676-1

Perdue, B. M., Snyder, R. J., Pratte, J., Marr, M. J., & Maple, T. L. (2009). Spatial memory recall in the giant panda (*Ailuropoda melanoleuca*). *Journal of Comparative Psychology, 123*, 275–279. https://doi.org/10.1037/a0016220

Perdue, B. M., Snyder, R., Zhihe, Z., Marr, J., & Maple, T. (2011) Sex differences in spatial ability: A test of the range size hypothesis in order carnivore. *Animal Behaviour, 7*, 380–383. https://doi.org/10.1098/rsbl.2010.1116

Polson, J. E. (1983). *Application of aversion techniques for the reduction of losses to beehives by black bears in Northeastern Saskatchewan*, SRC Publication No. C-805-13-E-83.

Range, F., & Virányi, Z. (2015). Tracking the evolutionary origins of dog-human cooperation: The "canine cooperation hypothesis". *Frontiers in Psychology, 5*, 2. https://doi.org/10 .3389/fpsyg.2014.01582

Ripperger, S. P., Carter, G. G., Duda, N., Koelpin, A., Cassens, B., Kapitza, R., Josic, D., Berrío-Martínez, J., Page, R. A., & Mayer, F. (2019). Vampire bats that cooperate in the lab maintain their social networks in the wild. *Current Biology, 23*, 4139–4144. https://doi.org/10.1016/j.cub.2019.10.024

Ripperger, S. P., Page, R. A., Mayer, F., & Carter, G. G. (2020). Evidence for unfamiliar kin recognition in vampire bats. *BioRxiv.* https://doi.org/10.1101/2019.12.16.874057

Rogers, L. L., Mansfield, S. A., Hornby, K., Hornby, S., Debruyn, T. D., Mize, M., Clark, R., & Burghardt, G. M. (2014). Black bear reactions to venomous and non-venomous snakes in eastern North America. *Ethology, 120*, 641–651. http://dx.doi.org/10.1111/eth.12236

Sakai, S. T., Arsznov, B. M., Lundrigan, B. L., & Holekamp, K. E. (2011). Brain size and social complexity: A computed tomography study in hyaenidae. *Brain, Behavior and Evolution, 77*, 91–104. http://dx.doi.org/10.1159/000323849

Samuel, L., Arnesen, C., Zedrosser, A., & Rosell, F. (2020). Fears from the past? The innate ability of dogs to detect predator scents. *Animal Cognition, 23*, 721–729. http://dx.doi.org/10.1007/s10071-020-01379-y

Schubiger, M. N., Fichtel, C., & Burkart, J. M. (2020). Validity of cognitive tests for non-human animals: Pitfalls and prospects. *Frontiers in Psychology, 11*, 1835. https://doi.org/10.3389/fpsyg.2020.01835

Silk, J., Brosnan, S. F., Vonk, J., Henrich, J., Povinelli, D. J., Shapiro, S., Richardson, A., Lambeth, S. P., & Mascaro, J. (2005). Chimpanzees are indifferent to the welfare of unrelated group members. *Nature, 437*, 1357–1359. https://doi.org/10.1038/nature04243

Silverman, I., Choi, J., & Peters, M. (2007). The hunter-gatherer theory of sex differences in spatial abilities: Data from 40 countries. *Archives of Sexual Behavior, 36*, 261–268. http://dx.doi.org/10.1007/s10508-006-9168-6

Smith, M. E., Linnell, J. D., Odden, J., & Swenson, J. E. (2000). Review of methods to reduce livestock depradation: I. Guardian animals. *Acta Agriculturae Scandinavica, Section A-Animal Science, 50*, 279–290. https://doi.org/10.1080/090647000750069476

Sol, D. (2009). The cognitive-buffer hypothesis for the evolution of large brains. In R. Dukas & J. M. Ratcliffe (Eds.), *Cognitive ecology II* (pp. 111–136). University of Chicago Press.

Stevens, J. R., & Gilby, I. C. (2004). A conceptual framework for nonkin food sharing: Timing and currency of benefits. *Animal Behaviour, 67*, 603–614. http://dx.doi.org/10.1016/j.anbehav.2003.04.012

Stevens, J. R., & Stephens, D. W. (2002). Food sharing: A model of manipulation by harassment. *Behavioral Ecology, 13*, 393–400. http://dx.doi.org/10.1093/beheco/13.3.393

Stillfried, M., Belant, J. L., Svoboda, N. J., Beyer, D. E., & Kramer-Schadt, S. (2015). When top predators become prey: Black bears alter movement behaviour in response to hunting pressure. *Behavioural Processes, 120*, 30–39. http://dx.doi.org/10.1016/j.beproc.2015.08.003

Støen, O., Bellemain, E., Sæbø, S., & Swenson, J. E. (2005). Kin-related spatial structure in brown bears *Ursus arctos. Behavioral Ecology and Sociobiology, 59*, 191–197. http://dx.doi.org/10.1007/s00265-005-0024-9

Stringham, S. F. (2012). Salmon fishing by bears and the dawn of cooperative predation. *Journal of Comparative Psychology, 126*, 329–338. http://dx.doi.org/10.1037/a0028238

Suraci, J. P., Clinchy, M., Roberts, D. J., & Zanette, L. Y. (2017). Eavesdropping in solitary large carnivores: Black bears advance and vocalize toward cougar playbacks. *Ethology, 123*, 593–599. http://dx.doi.org/10.1111/eth.12631

Tarou, L. R. (2004). An examination of the role of associative learning and spatial memory in foraging of two species of bear (family: Ursidae) (*Ailuropoda melanoleuca, Tremarctos ornatus*). *Dissertation Abstracts International: Section B: The Sciences and Engineering, 64*, 5260.

Ternent, M. A., & Garshelis, D. L. (1999). Taste-aversion conditioning to reduce nuisance activity by black bears in a Minnesota military reservation. *Wildlife Society Bulletin*, 720–728.

Udell, M. A. R. (2018). A new approach to understanding canine social cognition. *Learning & Behavior, 46*, 329–330. http://dx.doi.org/10.3758/s13420-018-0334-1

Udell, M. A. R., & Vitale Shreve, K. R. (2017). Editorial: Feline behavior and cognition. *Behavioural Processes*, *141*, 259–260. http://dx.doi.org/10.1016/j.beproc.2017.04.005

Virányi, Z., & Range, F. (2014). On the way to a better understanding of dog domestication: Aggression and cooperativeness in dogs and wolves. In J. Kaminski & S. Marshall-Pescini (Eds.), *The social dog: Behaviour and cognition* (pp. 35–62). Academic Press.

Vonk, J. (2016). Bigger brains may make better problem-solving carnivores. *Learning and Behavior*, *44*, 99–100. https://doi.org/10.3758/s13420-016-0222-5

(2018). Social strategies in a not-so-social pumas. *Learning and Behavior*, *46*, 105–106. https://doi.org/10.3758/s13420-017-0312-z

Vonk, J., Allard, S., Torgerson-White, L., Bennett, C., Galvan, M., McGuire, M. M., Hamilton, J., Johnson-Ulrich, Z., & Lieb, J. (2015). Manipulating spatial and visual cues in a win-stay foraging task in captive grizzly bears (*Ursus arctos horribilus*). In E. A. Thayer (Ed.), *Spatial, long-and short-term memory: Functions, differences and effects of injury* (pp. 47–60). Nova Publishers.

Vonk, J., & Beran, M. J. (2012). Bears "count" too: Quantity estimation and comparison in black bears (*Ursus americanus*). *Animal Behaviour*, *84*, 231–238. https://doi.org/10.1016/j.anbehav.2012.05.001

Vonk, J., Edge, J., Pappas, J., Robeson, A., & Jordan, A. (2020). Cross species comparisons: When comparing apples to oranges is fruitful. In T. K. Shackelford (Ed.), *The Sage handbook of evolutionary psychology* (pp. 285–310). Sage.

Vonk, J., & Jett, S. E. (2018). "Bear-ly" learning: Limits of abstraction in black bear cognition. *Animal Behavior and Cognition*, *5*, 68–78. https://doi.org/10.26451/abc.05.01.06.2018

Vonk, J., Jett, S. E., & Mosteller, K. W. (2012). Concept formation in American black bears (*Ursus americanus*). *Animal Behaviour*, *84*, 953–964. https://doi.org/10.1016/j.anbehav.2012.07.020

Vonk, J. & Johnson-Ulrich, Z. (2014). Social and non-social category discriminations in a chimpanzee (*Pan troglodytes*) and American black bears (*Ursus americanus*). *Learning and Behavior*, *42*, 231–245. https://doi.org/10.3758/s13420-014-0141-2

Vonk, J., & Leete, J. (2017). Carnivore concepts: Categorization in carnivores "bears" further study. *International Journal of Comparative Psychology*, *30*. http://escholarship.org/uc/item/61363164

de Waal, F. B., & Ferrari, P. F. (2010). Towards a bottom-up perspective on animal and human cognition. *Trends in Cognitive Sciences*, *14*, 201–207. https://doi.org/10.1016/j.tics.2010.03.003

Waroff, A. J., Fanucchi, L., Robbins, C. T., & Nelson, O. L. (2017). Tool use, problem-solving, and the display of stereotypic behaviors in the brown bear (*Ursus arctos*). *Journal of Veterinary Behavior: Clinical Applications and Research*, *17*, 62–68. https://doi.org/10.1016/j.jveb.2016.11.003

Wynne, C. D. L. (2016). What is special about dog cognition? *Current Directions in Psychological Science*, *25*, 345–350. http://dx.doi.org/10.1177/0963721416657540

Wilkinson, G. S. (1988). Reciprocal altruism in bats and other mammals. *Ethology & Sociobiology*, *9*, 85–100. https://doi.org/10.1016/0162-3095(88)90015-5

Zamisch, V., & Vonk, J. (2012). Spatial memory in captive American black bears (*Ursus americanus*). *Journal of Comparative Psychology*, *126*, 372–387. https://doi.org/10.1037/a0028081

21

DISTINGUISHING MECHANISMS OF BEHAVIORAL INHIBITION AND SELF-CONTROL

Michael J. Beran and Audrey E. Parrish

What does the term *self-control* mean to you? Almost certainly, your definition likely does not align with that of many other people or with how "pop psychology" books and websites define the term. In fact, within the scientific literature, there has been a long-running debate about what self-control is (see Beran, 2015, 2018; Inzlicht et al., 2014). Add to this debate the many educational and clinical questionnaire ratings of "self-control" which often contain items such as "Child bullies, is cruel, or mean," "Child is impulsive or acts without thinking," "Child is restless, overly active, or cannot sit still," "Child cheats or tells lies," and similar items. The term self-control loses value when it can be applied to so many behaviors, motivational states, or motor actions. This creates a disconnect among developmental, cognitive, and comparative researchers who cannot be faulted for being unable to see cross-connections in their efforts to understand different kinds of intertemporal choice behavior or delayed gratification or inhibitory control.

The goal of this chapter is to present a framework for defining self-control and other, sometimes erroneously interchangeable terms that we argue should not be confused with self-control. These include other forms of behavioral inhibition, cognitive control, and even motivational influences on behavior. The framework presented here borrows heavily from that originally presented by Beran (2018) when considering comparative and developmental studies that often were all subsumed under the name *self-control*, and the reader is directed there for a much longer description of the ideas presented here. Our expertise is largely in the behavior of nonhuman primates, but we believe this framework applies across cognitive, comparative, and developmental psychology, and in solitary and social settings where choices are made by individuals or groups.

Studies of self-control (including assessments of intertemporal choices and assessments of the ability to delay gratification) and behavioral inhibition are relevant and integral to understanding how mechanisms of perception, learning, and memory pertain to choice behavior. Self-control is often required when individuals are making choices, and choices have consequences that engage learning mechanisms and shape subsequent choices. Not responding (behavioral inhibition) also has consequences, and those consequences can shape subsequent choices. Cognitive processes also play a role in self-control and inhibition, including executive functions and memory. The relative contributions of perception, learning, and cognition are not always easy to distinguish, and it is likely that all three play a role in choice situations for which self-control is relevant.

Comparative and developmental assessments of self-control and behavioral inhibition can help distinguish mechanisms of learning and cognitive processes that underlie behavior when faced with these choices. Consistent performance across species (and across development in children) likely reflects shared perceptual and learning mechanisms whereas differences may reflect cognitive processes that are less widespread across species and emerge later in development. As one example, delay discounting (i.e., more steeply discounting the value of reward the farther in time it is displaced from the present) likely relies on timing mechanisms that are evolutionarily conserved, as evidenced by such discounting in a wide range of species (Madden & Bickel, 2010; Takahashi, 2005; Vanderveldt et al., 2016). However, differences in delay of gratification likely reflect, in part, differences in metacognitive control and monitoring, and aspects of working and episodic memory across species.

At the same time, choices are not predictable solely on the basis of learning mechanisms or memory for past outcomes. It is also essential to understand the context in which each choice is made. It has been reported that relations among tasks that are called self-control tasks or tests of impulsivity (which is often defined as the lack of self-control) are sometimes weak (e.g., Duckworth & Kern, 2011). This suggests that these constructs are not unitary (and, some would argue, not valuable at all: Strickland & Johnson, 2020). However, it is also possible that learning mechanisms and cognitive processes often generate different responses based on the environmental context in which options present themselves. For example, one might exercise self-control amongst others due to real or perceived social pressures yet fail to exert such self-control when alone (e.g., sticking to a diet when out with friends and picking up dessert on the way home). Another possibility, and one that we focus on in this chapter, is that self-control is defined too broadly, and behavioral inhibition is not distinguished from self-control in ways that would allow for clearer assessments of each of these phenomena. As a result, understanding the underlying learning and memory mechanisms of self-control can be impaired if the behavioral tests are not measuring what they are claimed to measure. We propose a framework for classifying tasks based on underlying mechanisms including perception, learning, and cognitive control mechanisms. This framework lends itself to generating comparative studies that can document homologous mechanisms of self-control if those exist.

21.1 DEFINING SELF-CONTROL

We define self-control *as the ability or capacity to obtain a subjectively more valuable outcome rather than a subjectively less valuable outcome through choosing and then tolerating a longer delay or a greater effort requirement for obtaining that more valuable outcome* (Beran, 2018). In this definition, it is important to note that self-control must be a choice, rather than being simply the requirement of waiting through a delay to get a reward. For example, having to wait to renew a driver's license does not require self-control because otherwise one cannot drive. But, giving up free time to take a safe-driving class does, because one loses free time now for the chance to save money (and avoid injury) later. In the second case, both options have tangible benefits, but on different time scales (having fun now, saving money later). The second essential aspect is in defining these outcomes in choice situations as being *subjectively* valued by the chooser. Each choice between something now or something better later can be different from all past similar circumstances even if the options are the same (e.g., you might exercise self-control in foregoing dessert today but not tomorrow). The context of the choice interacts with the motivations of the chooser at the time of the choice (see Lempert & Phelps, 2016; Paglieri, 2013; Paglieri et al., 2015). From this perspective, choices to delay gratification and other inter-temporal choices are like many other decisions in terms of being subjective and contextual as shown in behavioral economics (e.g., Kahneman & Tversky, 1984; Tversky & Kahneman, 1981). And, this point is true also for other animals (e.g., Stevens & Stephens, 2010).

From this definition, one can then begin to describe essential features of any test of self-control (see Beran, 2018, for a longer discussion of these features). There must be at least two known options available. Each of these outcomes must be available to the subject at the moment of choice, and they must be differentially preferred by the subject (see Paglieri et al., 2015). There also must be some temporal delay or cost in terms of effort for obtaining the more preferred outcome and the choice options must be known in terms of when their delivery will occur. This last point is really about probability estimates, because if any choice option is not well-defined in terms of its probability of occurring, then it is difficult or impossible to define a self-control choice.

21.2 SITUATING SELF-CONTROL AND INHIBITION WITHIN A BROADER BEHAVIORAL FRAMEWORK

It is important to distinguish between *self-control* and *behavioral inhibition*. Inhibition occurs whenever a natural tendency to perform a behavior is suppressed. These natural tendencies reflect that the behavior in question is either pleasurable or it is prepotent (i.e., easier to do or habitual). Self-control *is one form of behavioral inhibition*, but not all forms of behavioral inhibition require self-control (e.g., successfully performing a Stroop, 1935, task in which one must ignore the written word and respond to font color). And, there are other constructs related to behavioral inhibition, to self-control, and to each other that are sometimes used interchangeably, *but this usage is in error.* Our goal now is to attempt to sort through some of these constructs, define and classify tasks that we believe measure these things uniquely or, in some cases, measure two or more of these constructs at the same time, and thereby provide a framework to allow cross-talk among people working in any of these areas. This framework is outlined graphically in Figure 21.1.

Human and nonhuman animals (hereafter, animals) have perceptual experiences that constrain their estimations of time and space in meaningful ways for understanding choice behavior. They are also subject to some control of their behavior by well-known mechanisms of associative learning (called Perception & Learning in Figure 21.1). In addition, cognitive mechanisms are at work in numerous species that manipulate information, engage in memory storage and retrieval and do things such as engage in planning to guide subsequent responding (called Cognitive Control in Figure 21.1).

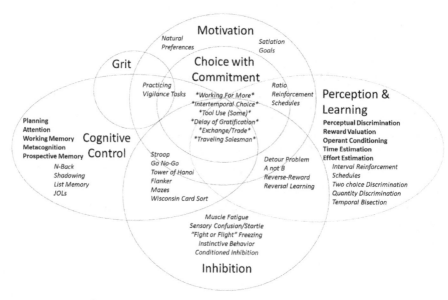

FIGURE 21.1. Mechanisms and tasks relevant to studying self-control. Each module in the model represents a system in large bolded letters (Motivation, Cognitive Control, Perception & Learning, Grit, Inhibition, and Choice with Commitment) as well as subsystems (small bolded letters) in some cases. Points of overlap reflect areas in which different behavioral tests (in italics) may be relevant. Those highlighted with an asterisk (*) are self-control tasks. See text and Beran (2018) for more details.

From M. J. Beran, *Self-control in animals and people,* copyright 2018. Reprinted with permission of Elsevier.

Motivational components also are included, and these directly affect many choices (called Motivation in Figure 21.1). This framework attempts to integrate the idea of grit, which has been defined as passion and perseverance toward goals, and especially longer-term goals (Duckworth et al., 2007). Choice with Commitment (Figure 21.1) refers to the mechanism of engaging a behavioral response and then sustaining that response in the face of competing response tendencies (i.e., to do something else, or to simply stop that response commitment). This can occur in situations only partially related to self-control, as when we feel compelled to complete a project such as building a table even though we have other things we could be doing because we need the table to be finished by end of the day. And, finally, there is a general capacity for inhibitory control of responding (called Inhibition in Figure 21.1). It is important to note that self-control does not have to be motivated simultaneously by all of these factors, but instead may emerge from one or a combination of these factors. From this view of different factors that influence choice behavior, we can then move to the level of describing how empirical tasks tap into motivation, perceptual processes, inhibition, grit, choice commitment, associative learning, and cognitive processing. And, we can classify tasks within this framework, then, as being tests of self-control or not. Importantly, this is true across the life span for humans, and across species for those taking a comparative approach to understanding self-control and its evolutionary emergence.

21.3 SELF-CONTROL TASKS

In the center of Figure 21.1 are what we define as examples of self-control tasks, based on the definition offered earlier. For these tasks, motivation, perception and learning, cognition, and behavioral inhibition systems overlap. *Working for more* tasks include any tasks for which the reward or goal of a behavior improves quantitatively or qualitatively as one puts in more effort. In perhaps the most famous example of this, a particular porcine gave up the leisure time enjoyed by his two conspecifics so that he might construct a dwelling made of bricks, while they instead chose immediate leisure at the later cost of having only houses of straw and sticks to hide in when a hungry wolf appeared at their door. They played now, and ended up as dinner later, whereas our self-controlled main character gave up immediate pleasure for long-term safety.

Intertemporal choice tasks involve options that vary in their delay to reward (or difficulty to gain reward) as well as their relative value of reward (Rachlin, 2000). These often are called smaller-sooner, larger-later choices (Logue, 1988). Self-control is shown in these tasks when one chooses the larger or better reward that is more delayed or harder to obtain. This type of task has been used with many species, including pigeons (Ainslie, 1974;

Rachlin & Green, 1972; Tobin & Logue, 1994), rats (Galtress et al., 2012; Kirkpatrick et al., 2015; Tobin & Logue, 1994; Tobin et al., 1993), macaque monkeys (Freeman et al., 2012; Hayden & Platt, 2007; Tobin et al., 1996), capuchin monkeys (De Petrillo et al., 2015), lemurs (Stevens & Mühlhoff, 2012), honeybees (Cheng et al., 2002), and humans (Tobin & Logue, 1994), including in tests with all manner of reward types (and magnitudes) and all manner of delays.

Delay of gratification involves foregoing the immediate consumption or enjoyment of a presently available reward so that one might get something bigger or better at a later time, but then having to maintain the commitment to the delay. It is this requirement for delay maintenance, in the face of repeated or continual temptation to instead take the more immediate reward, that distinguishes delay of gratification tasks from the intertemporal-choice tests that require only a choice between smaller-sooner, larger-later option with no chance to change that response if the delayed option is selected. The most famous delay of gratification test is the marshmallow test (Mischel, 2014) in which one marshmallow (or other treat) was the temptation, and if a child (or nonhuman animal) waited without taking that temptation, two marshmallows (or other treats) could be obtained. A number of species have been presented with tests that are analogous to the marshmallow test (e.g., chimpanzees: Beran et al., 1999; dogs: Brucks et al., 2017; pigeons: Grosch & Neuringer, 1981). Sometimes, this includes variations in which the immediate reward must be moved past (tamarins and marmosets: Stevens, Rosati et al., 2005) or allowed to move past the subject (capuchin monkeys: Bramlett et al., 2012; Perdue et al., 2015) so that the later-better reward can come to the subject. Other tests of delayed gratification also exist. In the accumulation test, the preferred reward items accumulate in their amount through a delay, as long as none are taken by the subject. Self-control is demonstrated through waiting for accumulation to occur (this is a measure of delay maintenance). The accumulation test has been used with children (Toner et al., 1979; Toner & Smith, 1977) and other species (chimpanzees: Beran, 2002; Beran & Evans, 2006; Evans & Beran, 2007a, 2007b; parrots: Koepke et al., 2015; Vick et al., 2010; orangutans: Parrish et al., 2014; bonobos: Stevens et al., 2011). There are wide variations across species (and individuals within species) using this task as well as some of the other tasks described, but these performances provide insights into relative degrees of self-control as evidenced through delay maintenance (e.g., Beran, Perdue et al., 2016; Stevens, Hallinan et al., 2005).

Another popular test that we include among the assessments of self-control is the *exchange task*. One could argue that the exchange task is better conceptualized as another form of delayed gratification task, but with an even more difficult response requirement than the inhibitory control needed in the marshmallow task or the accumulation task. In the exchange task, the reward (which, for animals, is usually an edible item) is possessed and must be held so that it can be given back to an experimenter for something else. This requires inhibiting the consumption of the possessed food items, which is the prepotent, natural response. And yet, numerous species show some ability (and sometimes, they show great ability) in exchanging food back for better food, even when there are long delays between each chance to exchange (Goffin cockatoos: Auersperg et al., 2013; corvids: Dufour et al., 2012; dogs: Leonardi et al., 2012; capuchin monkeys: Drapier et al., 2005; Parrish et al., 2018; macaque monkeys: Pelé et al., 2010; chimpanzees: Beran, Rossettie et al., 2016; Dufour et al., 2007).

An interesting class of behaviors for considering what does or does not require self-control is the use and making of tools. We would argue that such behaviors may require self-control, at least in some contexts. The essential feature of these cases is that the tool user must have an alternative choice that leads to a faster or easier outcome. In most cases of tool use by animals, the goal is food acquisition. In these cases, the alternative would be a lower preference food item that does not require the manufacture, transport, or use of a tool to acquire. But only the acquisition and use of the tool, and the time and expertise that is required to use the tool, can lead to the best outcome. For example, one could eat a kiwi with the skin still on it, and do that right away, or instead use a knife or peeler to remove the skin first, take longer to do that, and then enjoy the kiwi more without the skin as part of the gustatory experience. Here, again, we see evidence that nonhuman animals engage in tool-using scenarios that might qualify as requiring self-control (e.g., Beck, 1980; Seed & Byrne, 2010; Shumaker et al., 2011). For example, chimpanzees will crack nuts that they first have to gather, take to an object that acts as an anvil, and then retrieve a hammer (Boesch-Achermann & Boesch, 1993). Without this effort, the high-value nuts cannot be opened and consumed, whereas leaves or other lower-preference items are readily and more immediately available. In some cases, apes will collect tools ahead of time for later use (e.g., Mulcahy & Call, 2006; Osvath & Osvath, 2008), or otherwise form plans for how tools will be used (e.g., Byrne et al., 2013). They do this at a time cost and effort cost relative to simply browsing on immediately available plant material or other more accessible food items, or engaging in other behaviors that are more immediately beneficial than is the collection of tools for later use (see Evans & Westergaard, 2006 for an experimental approach to this idea).

Of course, the reader may argue that some of these tasks framed here as being qualitatively different are not that different from each other. And, the reader may disagree that all these tasks are tests of self-control, or that other tasks we placed elsewhere in our framework should be included here. But, we have attempted to remain faithful to the definition of self-control presented in outlining why these tasks fit (and, see Beran, 2018, for a more exhaustive discussion of the many tasks that are used to assess the various constructs shown in Figure 21.1). We now turn to tasks that do not fit because they do not require self-control so much as they reflect other aspects of behavioral inhibition. This is not to suggest they are less important behavioral capacities – to the contrary, we see many of these as just as essential to adaptive responding to changing environments and likely more phylogenetically widespread. But, for our framework, they are not tasks that necessitate or justify being called tests of self-control.

21.4 BEHAVIORAL INHIBITION WITHOUT SELF-REGULATION

Some inhibitory behaviors are generated by physiological states or reflexive/instinctive responding. As a simple example, when muscles fatigue, behavior decreases or stops. Some forms of unconditioned responding are elicited by unconditioned stimuli in the environment, such as when the perception of a predator leads a prey animal to freeze. There are other examples of classical conditioning (such as conditioned inhibition) that one should not ascribe to self-control but rather to associative or cognitive processes that make up part of the framework in Figure 21.1.

SELF-REGULATORY INHIBITION TASKS

An important mechanism to contrast with self-control is self-regulatory inhibition. Here, we are discussing a mechanism assessed through tasks that can also overlap with perceptual processes, learning mechanisms, or cognitive processes that also influence self-control behavior. We suggest these should be called tasks of *self-regulatory inhibition*, because these are situations in which individuals are faced with competing response options from which to choose, but only one outcome is of any benefit to the chooser. That outcome also is the one that is less prepotent (easier, faster), and so the only way to succeed is to inhibit more natural (prepotent) behavior in favor of less natural (i.e., slower, more difficult) behavior that can produce the desired goal. Put simply, these are tasks in which one has to do the opposite of what would normally be the response. The normal response leads to an outcome that is not desired.

One of the best examples of a task that is sometimes called a self-control task but is instead an inhibitory control task is the detour task (see Kabadayi et al., 2018). In the detour problem, a direct approach to an item actually blocks your ability to retrieve it. For example, think about a ball on the other side of a fence. Walking directly toward the ball (the usual response under most conditions) does not let you get it. Instead, you have to walk around the fence, moving away from the ball to eventually get close enough to retrieve it.

One of the first descriptions of the task came from Hobhouse (1901), who wrote about dogs running toward a door after seeing an owner through a window, rather than running to the window. Thorndike (1911) used the detour problem extensively as a tool for comparative assessment of learning and inhibition. He studied species as diverse as chickens and fish, and he stated that success in the test would demonstrate responding that was not the result of an innate approach mechanism to move toward appetitive stimuli. Köhler (1925) tested dogs, chickens, and chimpanzees. He suggested that success on the task reflected insight or even future-oriented prospection because successful animals had to evaluate and "think through" the problem. The detour task is used frequently (e.g., Kabadayi et al., 2016, 2017; Vernouillet et al., 2016; Vlamings et al., 2010; Zucca et al., 2005), and it was the central task in one of the largest studies ever conducted that purported to be about self-control. In that study (MacLean et al., 2014), 36 species (29 mammals and 7 birds) were tested on a version of the detour task called the cylinder task. They titled their paper "The evolution of self-control" and argued that their detour task measured self-control. Beran (2015) argued that it did not, for the reasons we have outlined here. We believe this is an interesting and informative test regarding inhibitory control, but it is not a test of self-control because it lacks some of the essential features in our definition, including a decision process between two viable choices, and the need to tolerate the cost for choosing the larger/later reward.

Another widely used test of inhibitory control is the reverse-reward contingency task (RRCT). This test was first presented to chimpanzees to determine how well they could point to *what they did not want* to receive the unselected set. The idea behind the RRCT is to have subjects examine two options and indicate the nonpreferred option. They then would receive the unselected set and the selected set would be given to a partner animal. Typically, nonhuman animals struggle to do this as it requires inhibition of the prepotent response (i.e., selection of the desired food set), and this is true for primates and nonprimate species (for a review, see Shifferman, 2009). The first animals tested were chimpanzees, in a long series of experiments to determine what would allow those chimpanzees to show success (Boysen & Berntson, 1995; Boysen et al., 1996, 1999). Other species that have been tested include lemurs (Genty et al., 2004, 2011), squirrel monkeys (Anderson et al., 2000), mangabeys (Albiach-Serrano et al., 2007), tamarins (Kralik, 2005), capuchin monkeys (Addessi & Rossi, 2010; Anderson et al., 2008), macaque monkeys (Murray et al., 2005; Silberberg & Fujita, 1996), all four species of great apes (Uher & Call, 2008; Vlamings et al., 2006), and sea lions (Genty & Roeder, 2006). In most cases, animals struggle to select the non-preferred set, instead showing perseverative responding by pointing to the larger or better rewards across trials. This is a failure of inhibitory control. We argue that this is not a test of self-control, as we define it, because in these cases there is no way to know that animals are making choices, rather than failing to inhibit prepotent responses. Delay maintenance is not required either, making this test less ideal as an assessment of self-control, although we would argue that it is a closer approximation than the detour task outlined earlier.

We conducted an experiment that helps illustrate why the RRCT may not be assessing self-control in the way that other tests, such as the accumulation task, do (Beran, James et al., 2016). We asked what it was about the RRCT task that made it so difficult for animals, and whether the ability to engage in delay of gratification could be shown to be present while performance also still showed that this inhibitory task was too difficult for chimpanzees. First, we confirmed that our chimpanzees would not (or could not) point to a smaller pile of food rewards to gain a larger pile. Then, we presented them with a single food item and an empty bowl, and as one would expect, they pointed to the food item. Here, we changed the nature of the task by transferring the food item into the bowl. Then, we presented the bowl and another single item as choice options. If the bowl was chosen, the chimpanzee got all items in it, but if the single item was chosen, it was added to the bowl. In this way, a successful chimpanzee would be *pointing at one item rather than a larger number of items* and would continue to do so in order to keep the accumulation going. We found that all chimpanzees could accumulate rewards by pointing to a single item, and they could do so easily. The reason we think this was easy was because this task leads to the chimpanzees accumulating their own pile of rewards, which they could receive whenever they wanted. Their success showed that in such cases as choosing to accumulate rewards, and deciding when to collect that accumulation, pointing was optimal. In other words, when they engaged a self-control mechanism that involved choice and delay maintenance, the inhibitory demand to point away from their accumulation set and toward a single item was easy. But, when the contingencies were again set to require pointing to a low-quality reward to immediately get a high-quality reward, performance again dropped to very low levels for the chimpanzees in our study. We concluded that the chimpanzees engaged different mechanisms for the same kind of basic task when it was either presented as a test of what would be lost (in the RRCT, this is what they pointed to), or whether it was presented as what they could accumulate.

As Beran (2018) noted, the RRCT task may be difficult for animals to perform because they are faced with a choice of what they want (the greater number of items) but when they point to it, they get something else that was not their focus, and they get that immediately. So, there is no option to delay reward, or get something better, except at the initial point of choosing. However, if the task requires choosing a less appealing item so that it gets added to a more appealing, accumulating set, this may "reframe" the choice in a way that then engages self-control and behavior reflective of longer-term positive outcomes. Careful consideration of how tasks are framed shows us that self-control decisions are dissociable from inhibitory control responses even within virtually identical kinds of stimulus comparisons with identical response demands (here, points to food items). This behavioral difference in what option is chosen also indicates potential differences in the mechanisms underlying choice behavior in these kinds of closely related tasks, in support of our idea that some definitions of self-control are too broad and include too many unrelated tasks.

COGNITIVE CONTROL TASKS

Tasks of executive function that reflect control mechanisms also often involve inhibition, but these are not tests of self-control exclusively. Some examples of these tests include the Stroop test (Stroop, 1935), flanker tests (e.g., Eriksen & Eriksen, 1974), and the Tower of Hanoi task (Simon, 1975). These tasks require degrees of self-regulation and inhibition. For example, the famous Stroop test requires subjects to report the font color of printed words while ignoring the name of the word itself. This scenario creates instances of interference, such that sometimes the font color is consistent with the color word (e.g., the word blue is printed in blue font) or inconsistent with the color word (e.g., the word blue is printed in red font). The latter condition requires inhibition of the prepotent response to read the color word under speeded judgments for human subjects, typically resulting in slower response times or incorrect responding (Zhang et al., 1999). These tasks may tap into basic mechanisms that are relevant to self-control choices, even if they are not self-control tasks themselves.

As one example of the extension of cognitive control tasks to animals, Stroop-like tests have been presented to macaque monkeys and chimpanzees to assess performance when conflicting information is presented. Washburn (1994) presented rhesus macaques and human adults with a numeric task that required monkeys to select the larger of two sets of Arabic numerals, in which the number of items within the set was either congruent or incongruent with their numeral value. Interference effects in the form of increased response time were seen for incongruent trials (e.g., a set of two 3s versus a set of five 2s, the latter of which was the correct response) relative to congruent trials (e.g., a set of two 3s versus a set of five 5s, the latter of which was the correct response). Recently, chimpanzees have shown varying degrees of success in the face of interference using a task that pitted the learned value of different containers (associated with higher and lower valued foods) with food quantity (Parrish et al., 2017). Incongruent trials presented higher-valued containers on top of smaller food quantities and lower-valued containers on top of larger food quantities. These trials created conflict for the chimpanzees, although they displayed varying degrees of success, inhibiting responses based exclusively on the associated value of the container. Thus, cognitive control tasks can be adapted to use with animal species whose response patterns reflect a variety of executive function mechanisms, including attentional control, inhibition, and memory.

21.5 SUMMARY

When examining the framework offered in Figure 21.1, the self-control tasks presented herein fit our criteria noted earlier. These tasks all present two or more viable and beneficial outcomes. This means that either outcome is acceptable, it is just that one outcome would always be preferred to the other if all else were equal (the delay, effort, etc.). This is in contrast to self-regulatory inhibition tasks, where a failure to inhibit leads to a negative outcome, usually in the form of no reward at all. Bumping into a fence and not being able to reach the ball on the other side is not immediately rewarding. Reaching toward a bigger or better food item only to have it be lost is not a good thing. Taking the shortest immediate route that seems to lead to the goal of a maze even though it will dead-end is not a good thing.

In self-control tasks, the available options are all valuable. They would all be acceptable if given freely. Being handed one marshmallow to eat is a positive experience. Keeping the first item you are handed is still better than having nothing. Saving a little bit of money in the bank or working for a short while to build a straw house is better than no house at all. But, in each of those cases, it is still possible to get something better (two marshmallows, a better item obtained through exchange, more money in the bank, a brick house). That these better outcomes require an active choice for more waiting (or more work) is the cost of engaging in self-control, and such engagement is decisional and reflects aspects of cognitive control, learning, and perhaps also certain traits as might be defined as "grit" or other motivational factors. The framework outlined here is offered as a way to organize tasks around overlapping constructs that sometimes are used interchangeably but should not be. We hope to have provided a starting point for a more careful analysis of this issue, and a means of thinking about self-control in a more focused way that can then allow researchers in diverse areas to relate that construct to others of importance in human and nonhuman animal behavior.

REFERENCES

Addessi, E., & Rossi, S. (2010). Tokens improve capuchin performance in the reverse–reward contingency task. *Proceedings of the Royal Society of London B: Biological Sciences*, rspb20101602. https://doi.org/10.1098/rspb.2010.1602

Ainslie, G. W. (1974). Impulse control in pigeons. *Journal of the Experimental Analysis of Behavior*, 21, 485–489. https://doi.org/10.1901/jeab.1974.21-485

Albiach-Serrano, A., Guillén-Salazar, F., & Call, J. (2007). Mangabeys (*Cercocebus torquatus lunulatus*) solve the reverse contingency task without a modified procedure. *Animal Cognition, 10*, 387–396. https://doi.org/10.1007/s10071-007-0076-5

Anderson, J. R., Awazu, S., & Fujita, K. (2000). Can squirrel monkeys (*Saimiri sciureus*) learn self-control: A study using food array selection tests and reverse-reward contingency. *Journal of Experimental Psychology: Animal Behavior Processes, 26*, 87–97. https://doi.org/10.1037//0097-7403.26.1.87

Anderson, J. R., Hattori, Y., & Fujita, K. (2008). Quality before quantity: Rapid learning of reverse-reward contingency by capuchin monkeys (*Cebus apella*). *Journal of Comparative Psychology, 122*, 445–448. https://doi.org/10.1037/a0012624

Auersperg, A. M. I., Laumer, I. B., & Bugnyar, T. (2013). Goffin cockatoos wait for qualitative and quantitative gains but prefer "better" to "more". *Biology Letters, 9*, Article 20121092. https://doi.org/10.1098/rsbl.2012.1092

Beck, B. B. (1980). *Animal tool behavior: The use and manufacture of tools by animals.* Garland STPM Press.

Beran, M. J. (2002). Maintenance of self-imposed delay of gratification by four chimpanzees (*Pan troglodytes*) and an orangutan (*Pongo pygmaeus*). *Journal of General Psychology, 129*, 49–66. https://doi.org/10.1080/00221300209602032

(2015). The comparative science of "self-control": What are we talking about? *Frontiers in Psychology, 6*, Article 51. https://doi.org/10.3389/fpsyg.2015.00051

(2018). *Self-control in animals and people.* Academic Press. https://doi.org/10.1016/C2016-0-03559-3

Beran, M. J., & Evans, T. A. (2006). Maintenance of delay of gratification by four chimpanzees (*Pan troglodytes*): The effects of delayed reward visibility, experimenter presence, and extended delay intervals. *Behavioural Processes, 73*, 315–324. https://doi.org/10.1016/j.beproc.2006.07.005

Beran, M. J., James, B. T., Whitham, W., & Parrish, A. E. (2016). Chimpanzees can point to smaller amounts of food to accumulate larger amounts but they still fail the reverse-reward contingency task. *Journal of Experimental Psychology: Animal Learning and Cognition, 42*, 347–358. https://doi.org/10.1037/xan0000115

Beran, M. J., Perdue, B. M., Rossettie, M. S., James, B. T., Whitham, W., Walker, B., Futch, S. E., & Parrish, A. E. (2016). Self-control assessments of capuchin monkeys with the rotating tray task and the accumulation task. *Behavioural Processes, 129*, 68–79. https://doi.org/10.1016/j.beproc.2016.06.007

Beran, M. J., Rossettie, M. S., & Parrish, A. E. (2016). Trading up: Chimpanzees (*Pan troglodytes*) show self-control through their exchange behavior. *Animal Cognition, 19*, 109–121. https://doi.org/10.1007/s10071-015-0916-7

Beran, M. J., Savage-Rumbaugh, E. S., Pate, J. L., & Rumbaugh, D. M. (1999). Delay of gratification in chimpanzees (*Pan troglodytes*). *Developmental Psychobiology, 34*, 119–127. https://doi.org/10.1002/(sici)1098-2302(199903)34:2<119::aid-dev5>3.0.co;2-p

Boesch-Achermann, H., & Boesch, C. (1993). Tool use in wild chimpanzees: New light from dark forests. *Current Directions in Psychological Science, 2*, 18–21. https://doi.org/10.1111/1467-8721.ep10770551

Boysen, S. T., & Berntson, G. G. (1995). Responses to quantity: Perceptual versus cognitive mechanisms in chimpanzees (*Pan troglodytes*). *Journal of Experimental Psychology: Animal Behavior Processes, 21*, 82–86. https://doi.org/10.1037//0097-7403.21.1.82

Boysen, S. T., Berntson, G. G., Hannan, M. B., & Cacioppo, J. T. (1996). Quantity-based interference and symbolic representations in chimpanzees (*Pan troglodytes*). *Journal of Experimental Psychology: Animal Behavior Processes, 22*, 76–86. https://doi.org/10.1037/0097-7403.22.1.76

Boysen, S. T., Mukobi, K. L., & Berntson, G. G. (1999). Overcoming response bias using symbolic representations of number by chimpanzees (*Pan troglodytes*). *Animal Learning and Behavior, 27*, 229–235. https://doi.org/10.3758/BF03199679

Bramlett, J. L., Perdue, B. M., Evans, T. A., & Beran, M. J. (2012). Capuchin monkeys (*Cebus apella*) let lesser rewards pass them by to get better rewards. *Animal Cognition, 15,* 963–969. https://doi.org/10.1007/s10071-012-0522-x

Brucks, D., Soliani, M., Range, F., & Marshall-Pescini, S. (2017). Reward type and behavioural patterns predict dogs' success in a delay of gratification paradigm. *Scientific Reports, 7,* 42459. https://doi.org/10.1038/srep42459

Byrne, R. W., Sanz, C. M., & Morgan, D. B. (2013). Chimpanzees plan their tool use. In C. M. Sanz, J. Call, & C. Boesch (Eds.), *Tool use in animals. Cognition and ecology* (pp. 48–64). Cambridge University Press. https://doi.org/10.1017/CBO9780511894800.004

Cheng, K. E. N., Peña, J., Porter, M. A., & Irwin, J. D. (2002). Self-control in honeybees. *Psychonomic Bulletin & Review, 9,* 259–263. https://doi.org/10.3758/BF03196280

De Petrillo, F., Gori, E., Micucci, A., Ponsi, G., Paglieri, F., & Addessi, E. (2015). When is it worth waiting for? Food quantity, but not food quality, affects delay tolerance in tufted capuchin monkeys. *Animal Cognition, 18,* 1019–1029. https://doi.org/10.1007/s10071-015-0869-x

Drapier, M., Chauvin, C., Dufour, V., Uhlrich, P., & Thierry, B. (2005). Food-exchange with humans in brown capuchin monkeys. *Primates, 46,* 241–248. https://doi.org/10.1007/s10329-005-0132-1

Duckworth, A. L., & Kern, M. L. (2011). A meta-analysis of the convergent validity of self-control measures. *Journal of Research in Personality, 45,* 259–268. https://doi.org/10.1016/j.jrp.2011.02.004

Duckworth, A. L., Peterson, C., Matthews, M. D., & Kelly, D. R. (2007). Grit: Perseverance and passion for long-term goals. *Journal of Personality and Social Psychology, 92,* 1087–1101. https://doi.org/10.1037/0022-3514.92.6.1087

Dufour, V., Pelé, M., Sterck, E. H. M., & Thierry, B. (2007). Chimpanzee (*Pan troglodytes*) anticipation of food return: Coping with waiting time in an exchange task. *Journal of Comparative Psychology, 121,* 145–155. https://doi.org/10.1037/0735-7036.121.2.145

Dufour, V., Wascher, C. A. F., Braun, A., Miller, R., & Bugnyar, T. (2012). Corvids can decide if a future exchange is worth waiting for. *Biology Letters, 8,* 201–204. https://doi.org/10.1098/rsbl.2011.0726

Eriksen, B. A., & Eriksen, C. W. (1974). Effects of noise letters upon the identification of a target letter in a nonsearch task. *Perception & Psychophysics, 16*(1), 143–149. https://doi.org/10.3758/BF03203267Evans, T. A., & Beran, M. J. (2007a). Delay of gratification and delay maintenance by rhesus macaques (*Macaca mulatta*). *Journal of General Psychology, 134,* 199–216. https://doi.org/10.3200/GENP.134.2.199-216

Evans, T. A., & Beran, M. J. (2007b). Chimpanzees use self-distraction to cope with impulsivity. *Biology Letters, 3,* 599–602. https://doi.org/10.1098/rsbl.2007.0399

Evans, T. A., & Westergaard, G. C. (2006). Self-control and tool use in tufted capuchin monkeys (*Cebus apella*). *Journal of Comparative Psychology, 120,* 163–166. https://doi.org/10.1037/0735-7036.120.2.163

Freeman, K. B., Nonnemacher, J. E., Green, L., Myerson, J., & Woolverton, W. L. (2012). Delay discounting in rhesus monkeys: Equivalent discounting of more and less preferred sucrose concentrations. *Learning & Behavior, 40,* 54–60. https://doi.org/10.3758/s13420-011-0045-3

Galtress, T., Garcia, A., & Kirkpatrick, K. (2012). Individual differences in impulsive choice and timing in rats. *Journal of the Experimental Analysis of Behavior, 98,* 65–87. https://doi.org/10.1901/jeab.2012.98-65

Genty, E., Chung, P. C., & Roeder, J. J. (2011). Testing brown lemurs (*Eulemur fulvus*) on the reverse-reward contingency task without a modified procedure. *Behavioural Processes, 86,* 133–137. https://doi.org/10.1016/j.beproc.2010.10.006

Genty, E., Palmier, C., & Roeder, J. J. (2004). Learning to suppress responses to the larger of two rewards in two species of lemurs, *Eulemur fulvus* and *E. macaco. Animal Behaviour, 67,* 925–932. https://doi.org/10.1016/j.anbehav.2003.09.007

Genty, E., & Roeder, J. J. (2006). Self-control: Why should sea lions, *Zalophus californianus,* perform better than primates? *Animal Behaviour, 72,* 1241–1247. https://doi.org/10.1016/j.anbehav.2006.02.023

Grosch, J., & Neuringer, A. (1981). Self-control in pigeons under the Mischel paradigm. *Journal of the Experimental Analysis of Behavior, 35*, 3–21. https://doi.org/10.1901/jeab .1981.35-3

Hayden, B. Y., & Platt, M. L. (2007). Temporal discounting predicts risk sensitivity in rhesus macaques. *Current Biology, 17*, 49–53. https://doi.org/10.1016/j.cub.2006.10.055

Hobhouse, L. T. (1901). *Mind in evolution*. The Macmillan Company.

Inzlicht, M., Schmeichel, B. J., & Macrae, C. N. (2014). Why self-control seems (but may not be) limited. *Trends in Cognitive Sciences, 18*, 127–133. https://doi.org/10.1016/j.tics.2013.12.009

Kabadayi, C., Bobrowicz, K., & Osvath, M. (2018). The detour paradigm in animal cognition. *Animal Cognition 21*, 21–35. https://doi.org/10.1007/s10071-017-1152-0

Kabadayi, C., Krasheninnikova, A., O'Neill, L., van de Weijer, J., Osvath, M., & von Bayern, A. M. (2017). Are parrots poor at motor self-regulation or is the cylinder task poor at measuring it? *Animal Cognition, 20*, 1137–1146. https://doi.org/10.1007/s10071-017-1131-5

Kabadayi, C., Taylor, L. A., von Bayern, A. M., & Osvath, M. (2016). Ravens, New Caledonian crows and jackdaws parallel great apes in motor self-regulation despite smaller brains. *Royal Society Open Science, 3*, 160104. https://doi.org/10.1098/rsos.160104

Kahneman, D., & Tversky, A. (1984). Choices, values, and frames. *American Psychologist, 39*, 341–350. https://doi.org/10.1037/0003-066X.39.4.341

Kirkpatrick, K., Marshall, A. T., & Smith, A. P. (2015). Mechanisms of individual differences in impulsive and risky choice in rats. *Comparative Cognition & Behavior Reviews, 10*, 45. https://doi.org/10.3819/ccbr.2015.100003

Koepke, A. E., Gray, S. L., & Pepperberg, I. M. (2015). Delayed gratification: A Grey parrot (*Psittacus erithacus*) will wait for a better reward. *Journal of Comparative Psychology, 129*, 339–346. https://doi.org/10.1037/a0039553

Köhler, W. (1925). *The mentality of apes*. Kegan Paul, Trench, Trubner & Co, Ltd.

Kralik, J. D. (2005). Inhibitory control and response selection in problem solving: How cotton-top tamarins (*Saguinas oedipus*) overcome a bias for selecting the larger quantity of food. *Journal of Comparative Psychology, 119*, 78–89. https://doi.org/10.1037/0735-7036.119.1.78

Lempert, K. M., & Phelps, E. A. (2016). The malleability of intertemporal choice. *Trends in Cognitive Sciences, 20*, 64–74. https://doi.org/10.1016/j.tics.2015.09.005

Leonardi, R. J., Vick, S. J., & Dufour, V. (2012). Waiting for more: The performance of domestic dogs (*Canis familiaris*) on exchange tasks. *Animal Cognition, 15*, 107–120. https://doi.org/10.1007/s10071-011-0437-y

Logue, A. W. (1988). Research on self-control: An integrating framework. *Behavioral and Brain Sciences, 11*, 665–679. https://doi.org/10.1017/S0140525X00053978

MacLean, E. L., Hare, B., Nunn, C. L., Addessi, E., Amici, F., Anderson, R. C., . . . & Boogert, N. J. (2014). The evolution of self-control. *Proceedings of the National Academy of Sciences, 111*, E2140–E2148. https://doi.org/10.1073/pnas.1323533111

Madden, G. J., & Bickel, W. K. (Eds.) (2010). *Impulsivity: The behavioral and neurological science of discounting*. American Psychological Association.

Mischel, W. (2014). *The marshmallow test: Mastering self-control*. Little, Brown.

Mulcahy, N. J., & Call, J. (2006). Apes save tools for future use. *Science, 312*, 1038–1040. https://doi.org/10.1126/science.1125456

Murray, E. A., Kralik, J. D., & Wise, S. P. (2005). Learning to inhibit prepotent responses: successful performance by rhesus macaques, Macaca mulatta, on the reversed-contingency task. *Animal Behaviour, 69*(4), 991–998. https://doi.org/10.1016/j.anbehav .2004.06.034Osvath, M., & Osvath, H. (2008). Chimpanzee (*Pan troglodytes*) and orangutan (*Pongo abelii*) forethought: Self-control and pre-experience in the face of future tool use. *Animal Cognition, 11*, 661–674. https://doi.org/10.1007/s10071-008-0157-0

Paglieri, F. (2013). The costs of delay: Waiting versus postponing in intertemporal choice. *Journal of the Experimental Analysis of Behavior, 99*, 362–377. https://doi.org/10.1002/ jeab.18

Paglieri, F., Addessi, E., Sbaffi, A., Tasselli, M. I., & Delfino, A. (2015). Is it patience or motivation? On motivational confounds in intertemporal choice tasks. *Journal of the Experimental Analysis of Behavior, 103,* 196–217. https://doi.org/10.1002/jeab.118

Parrish, A. E., James, B. T., Rossettie, M. S., Smith, T., Otalora-Garcia, A., & Beran, M. J. (2018). Investigating the depletion effect: Self-control does not waiver in capuchin monkeys. *Animal Behavior and Cognition, 5,* 118–138. https://doi.org/10.1002/jeab.118

Parrish, A. E., Otalora-Garcia, A., & Beran, M. J. (2017). Dealing with interference: Chimpanzees respond to conflicting cues in a food-choice memory task. *Journal of Experimental Psychology: Animal Learning and Cognition, 43,* 366–376. https://doi.org/10.1037/xan0000151

Parrish, A. E., Perdue, B. M., Stromberg, E. E., Bania, A. E., Evans, T. A., & Beran, M. J. (2014). Delay of gratification by orangutans (*Pongo pygmaeus*) in the accumulation task. *Journal of Comparative Psychology, 128,* 209–214. https://doi.org/10.1037/a0035660

Pelé, M., Dufour, V., Micheletta, J., & Thierry, B. (2010). Long-tailed macaques display unexpected waiting abilities in exchange tasks. *Animal Cognition, 13,* 263–271. https://doi.org/10.1007/s10071-009-0264-6

Perdue, B. M., Bramlett, J. L., Evans, T. A., & Beran, M. J. (2015). Waiting for what comes later: Capuchin monkeys show self-control even for nonvisible delayed rewards. *Animal Cognition, 18,* 1105–1112. https://doi.org/10.1007/s10071-015-0878-9

Rachlin, H. (2000). *The science of self-control.* Harvard University Press.

Rachlin, H., & Green, L. (1972). Commitment, choice, and self-control. *Journal of the Experimental Analysis of Behavior, 17,* 15–22. https://doi.org/10.1901/jeab.1972.17-15

Seed, A., & Byrne, R. (2010). Animal tool-use. *Current Biology, 20,* R1032–R1039. https://doi.org/10.1016/j.cub.2010.09.042

Shifferman, E. M. (2009). Its own reward: Lessons to be drawn from the reversed-reward contingency paradigm. *Animal Cognition, 12,* 547–558. https://doi.org/10.1007/s10071-009-0215-2

Shumaker, R. W., Walkup, K. R., & Beck, B. B. (2011). *Animal tool behavior: the use and manufacture of tools by animals.* Johns Hopkins University Press.

Silberberg, A., & Fujita, K. (1996). Pointing at smaller food amounts in an analogue of Boysen and Berntson's procedure. *Journal of the Experimental Analysis of Behavior, 66,* 143–147. https://doi.org/10.1901/jeab.1996.66-143

Simon, H. A. (1975). The functional equivalence of problem-solving skills. *Cognitive Psychology, 7,* 268–288. https://doi.org/10.1016/0010-0285(75)90012-2

Stevens, J. R., Hallinan, E. V., & Hauser, M. D. (2005). The ecology and evolution of patience in two New World monkeys. *Biology Letters, 1,* 223–226. https://doi.org/10.1098/rsbl.2004.0285

Stevens, J. R., & Mühlhoff, N. (2012). Intertemporal choice in lemurs. *Behavioural Processes, 89,* 121–127. https://doi.org/10.1016/j.beproc.2011.10.002

Stevens, J. R., Rosati, A. G., Heilbronner, S. R., & Mühlhoff, N. (2011). Waiting for grapes: Expectancy and delayed gratification in bonobos. *International Journal of Comparative Psychology, 24,* 99–111. https://escholarship.org/uc/item/4km2r37j

Stevens, J. R., Rosati, A. G., Ross, K. R., & Hauser, M. D. (2005). Will travel for food: Spatial discounting in two New World monkeys. *Current Biology, 15,* 1855–1860. https://doi.org/10.1016/j.cub.2005.09.016

Stevens, J., & Stephens, D. (2010). The adaptive nature of impulsivity. In G. Madden & W. Bickel (Eds.), *Impulsivity: The behavioral and neural science of discounting* (pp. 361–387). American Psychological Association. https://doi.org/10.1037/12069-013

Strickland, J. C., & Johnson, M. W. (2020). Rejecting impulsivity as a psychological construct: A theoretical, empirical, and sociocultural argument. *Psychological Review.* Advance online publication. http://dx.doi.org/10.1037/rev0000263

Stroop, J. R. (1935). Studies of interference in serial verbal reactions. *Journal of Experimental Psychology, 18,* 643–662. https://doi.org/10.1037/h0054651

Takahashi, T. (2005). Loss of self-control in intertemporal choice may be attributable to logarithmic time-perception. *Medical Hypotheses, 65,* 691–693. https://doi.org/10.1016/j.mehy.2005.04.040

Thorndike, E. L. (1911). *Animal intelligence: Experimental studies.* Macmillan.

Tobin, H., Chelonis, J. J., & Logue, A. W. (1993). Choice in self-control paradigms using rats. *The Psychological Record, 43,* 441–454.

Tobin, H., & Logue, A. W. (1994). Self-control across species (*Columba livia, Homo sapiens,* and *Rattus norvegicus*). *Journal of Comparative Psychology, 108,* 126–133. https://doi.org/10.1037/0735-7036.108.2.126

Tobin, H., Logue, A. W., Chelonis, J. J., Ackerman, K. T., & May, J. G. (1996). Self-control in the monkey *Macaca fascicularis. Animal Learning and Behavior, 24,* 168–174. https://doi.org/10.3758/BF03198964

Toner, I. J., Lewis, B. C., & Gribble, C. M. (1979). Evaluative verbalization and delay maintenance behavior in children. *Journal of Experimental Child Psychology, 28,* 205–210. https://doi.org/10.1016/0022-0965(79)90084-5

Toner, I. J., & Smith, R. A. (1977). Age and overt verbalization in delay-maintenance behavior in children. *Journal of Experimental Child Psychology, 24,* 123–128. https://doi.org/10.1016/0022-0965(77)90025-X

Tversky, A., & Kahneman, D. (1981). The framing of decisions and the psychology of choice. *Science, 211,* 453–458. https://doi.org/10.1126/science.7455683

Uher, J., & Call, J. (2008). How the great apes (*Pan troglodytes, Pongo pygmaeus, Pan paniscus, Gorilla gorilla*) perform on the reversed reward contingency task II: Transfer to new quantities, long-term retention, and the impact of quantity ratios. *Journal of Comparative Psychology, 122,* 204–212. https://doi.org/10.1037/0735-7036.122.2.204

Vanderveldt, A., Oliveira, L., & Green, L. (2016). Delay discounting: Pigeon, rat, human – Does it matter? *Journal of Experimental Psychology: Animal Learning and Cognition, 42,* 141–162. https://doi.org/10.1037/xan0000097

Vernouillet, A., Anderson, J., Clary, D., & Kelly, D. M. (2016). Inhibition in Clark's nutcrackers (*Nucifraga columbiana*): results of a detour reaching test. *Animal Cognition, 19,* 661–665. https://doi.org/10.1007/s10071-016-0952-y

Vick, S. J., Bovet, D., & Anderson, J. R. (2010). How do African grey parrots (*Psittacus erithacus*) perform on a delay of gratification task? *Animal Cognition, 13,* 351–358. https://doi.org/10.1007/s10071-009-0284-2

Vlamings, P. H., Hare, B., & Call, J. (2010). Reaching around barriers: The performance of the great apes and 3–5-year-old children. *Animal Cognition, 13,* 273–285. https://doi.org/10.1007/s10071-009-0265-5

Vlamings, P. H., Uher, J., & Call, J. (2006). How the great apes (*Pan troglodytes, Pongo pygmaeus, Pan paniscus,* and *Gorilla gorilla*) perform on a reversed contingency task: The effects of food quantity and food visibility. *Journal of Experimental Psychology: Animal Behavior Processes, 32,* 60–70. https://doi.org/10.1037/0097-7403.32.1.60

Washburn, D. A. (1994). Stroop-like effects for monkeys and humans: Processing speed or strength of association? *Psychological Science, 5,* 375–379. https://doi.org/10.1111/j.1467-9280.1994.tb00288.x

Zhang, H. H., Zhang, J., & Kornblum, S. (1999). A parallel distributed processing model of stimulus–stimulus and stimulus–response compatibility. *Cognitive Psychology, 38,* 386–432. https://doi.org/10.1006/cogp.1998.0703

Zucca, P., Antonelli, F., & Vallortigara, G. (2005). Detour behaviour in three species of birds: quails (*Coturnix* sp.), herring gulls (*Larus cachinnans*) and canaries (*Serinus canaria*). *Animal Cognition, 8,* 122–128. https://doi.org/10.1007/s10071-004-0243-x

22

METACOGNITIVE MONITORING AND CONTROL IN MONKEYS

Robert R. Hampton

Imagine you are getting in the car to drive to a friend's new house you have visited only once, several weeks ago. You try to imagine the route you will take but cannot bring all the turns to mind. So, you enter the address into your phone's map application before you start driving. This simple imaginary experience illustrates that metacognition, or thinking about thinking, has both monitoring and control components. When you tried to bring all the needed turns to mind, you found you could not. This ability to detect that you do not know something, or are failing to remember it, illustrates the monitoring component of metacognition. You then took steps to correct your lack of knowledge by activating your map application. This corrective action illustrates the control aspect of metacognition. As a result of monitoring your memory failure, you took steps to correct the problem by seeking the needed information. This behavior is such a common experience for humans that we have difficulty imagining the alternative. The alternative is that you do not introspect about whether or not you remember the way, and you either set out blindly (and in this case get lost), or you depend indefinitely and redundantly on the map application, no matter how well you know the way.

The behavior of patients with dense amnesia helps illustrate what is lost, and what is spared, when one cannot introspect about one's own cognition. It is not the case that amnesic people are incapable of introspection. The problem is that amnesic people are unable to create the kind of memories about which we can introspect. In a groundbreaking study, Barbara Milner (1962; later replicated in other amnesics by Gabrieli et al., 1993) dissociated knowing *how* from knowing *that*. She found that while the famous amnesic H.M. could learn the difficult task of tracing a complex shape guided only by the reversed view of his hand in a mirror, he could not remember one day to the next that he had ever done it. Thus, when he came back for a second day of testing, he would claim he did not know how to do the mirror tracing task, but when he tried it, to his surprise he was quite good! H.M. learned *how* to

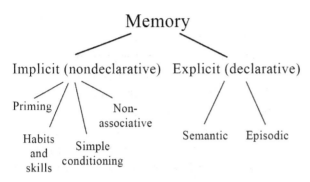

FIGURE 22.1. Taxonomy of human memory systems. Implicit memory affects behavior without awareness. In contrast, humans are consciously aware of explicit memories (Squire & Zola-Morgan, 1991). In other words, explicit memories are accessible to cognitive monitoring, but implicit memories are not. We can potentially use this difference in accessibility of metacognitive monitoring to classify nonhuman primate cognitive systems as implicit or explicit, despite the absence of language.

do mirror-guided tracing, but he never learned *that* he knew how to do it. This is a man who could not remember what year it was, who current political leaders were, or what he ate for breakfast. Since this early study, an enormous literature has developed showing that amnesics like H.M. retain a wide range of cognitive abilities, including the acquisition of many skills, most types of conditioning, and even such complex processes as learning grammar (Squire et al., 1993). The kinds of memories that remain intact in amnesics have become known as implicit or nondeclarative, contrasting with those kinds of memories that we can introspect about, which are known as explicit or declarative (Figure 22.1).

Further work with intact humans shows clearly that the kinds of memories that remain intact in amnesics are implicit in normal people too. Grammar is a good example. We often know how to form a grammatical sentence implicitly, without knowing an explicit rule that justifies or guides our behavior. Much, maybe most, of what our nervous systems accomplish is done without introspection or metacognition. We digest food, we regulate our metabolism, we control our heart rate, we make grammatical sentences, we walk and run and chew and ride bicycles and grasp tools and know very little about *how* we do these things. The types of nervous system activity of which we are explicitly aware are likely the tiny tip of a giant iceberg of cognitive activity. Explicit, conscious cognition seems so prevalent to us precisely because it is the kind of cognition we are aware of in ourselves. Meanwhile, a vast machinery of implicit cognition, critical for our function and survival, chugs along dutifully, without supervision, outside our awareness (see Church, Jackson, and Smith, Chapter 13).

The fact that amnesic people retain so many complex cognitive capacities, and that healthy human brains acquire many skills without introspective awareness, admits the possibility that nonhuman animals could potentially carry out the fullness of their complicated lives without explicit cognition and metacognition. That fact raises the question of why explicit memory and metacognition would ever evolve. And it motivates research in the comparative study of metacognition, where we ask whether other animals share our capacity, limited as it may be, for introspection, explicit memory, and metacognition. In this chapter I summarize evidence for metacognition in rhesus monkeys, the species on which most studies of nonhuman metacognition have been conducted. I make some references to other species, but our knowledge of the status of metacognition in other species remains very limited. I also offer some suggestions for beginning to think about why metacognition might have evolved.

22.1 EVIDENCE FOR METACOGNITIVE MONITORING IN MONKEYS

Rhesus monkeys sometimes monitor their own cognition. This ability means that they can sometimes tell whether they remember or forget, or whether a decision is difficult or easy to make. These capacities were not empirically documented until investigators began offering monkeys a "decline test response" that allowed them to avoid difficult laboratory tests. Up to that point we had learned a great deal about what monkeys know by evaluating their performance in all sorts of tests that required knowledge of the difference between stimuli, which stimulus had been reinforced in the past, or which one of a set of pictures or objects they had seen recently. These tests were always presented as forced choices, where animals had to choose a test response each time to advance through a day's testing. This kind of work is extraordinarily valuable in teaching us about the cognitive abilities of animals, but for all we knew, monkeys were like H.M., capable of doing various tasks but not aware of that fact. Beginning in 1997, some monkeys were offered a choice between completing a test and skipping the test in one way or another. This procedural addition brought our understanding of monkey minds from the purely cognitive realm into the metacognitive realm. Monkeys had the opportunity to show both *what* they knew and *that* they knew it (or did not know it; Shields et al., 1997). Now monkeys showed us not only which tests were difficult, as evident in low accuracy, but also which tests *they thought* were difficult, which was evident in their avoidance of particular tests by use of the decline test response. The earliest work in this area found that monkeys were more likely to use a decline test response when presented with a difficult visual discrimination than when presented with an easy one. Similar techniques were applied in the memory domain, and we learned that monkeys avoided tests when they had forgotten (Figure 22.2; Basile et al., 2015; Hampton, 2001; Smith et al., 1998; Templer & Hampton, 2012).

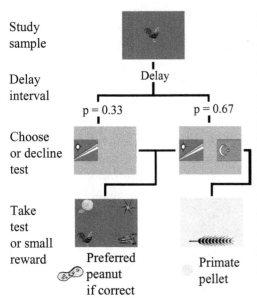

Study
sample

Delay
interval

Delay

p = 0.33   p = 0.67

Choose
or decline
test

Take
test
or small
reward

Preferred
peanut
if correct

Primate
pellet

Study Phase: At the start of each trial the monkey studied an image.

Delay interval: A delay period of seconds to several minutes followed over which the monkey often forgot the image.

Choice Phase: On 67% of trials, the monkey then chose between taking a memory test (near panel, leftmost stimulus) and declining the test (rightmost stimulus). On the remaining 33% of trials, the monkey was required to take the memory test; only the option leading to the test was offered (far left panel).

Test Phase: Monkeys received a preferred peanut after correct responses or a less-preferred pellet after declining tests. Monkeys got no reward for incorrect choices. To maximize reward they should therefore take the test when they remember and decline the test when they have forgotten.

Conclusion: Better average performance on freely chosen tests compared to forced tests indicates memory monitoring. The animal knows when it remembers and declines to take tests when it does not. Note that the choice to decline the memory test was offered *before the monkey saw the memory test. Thus, the decision to decline tests was based on memory, rather than on a reaction to the test display.*

FIGURE 22.2. A memory-monitoring paradigm for detecting explicit memory in monkeys. Each panel depicts what the monkey saw on a touch-sensitive computer monitor at different stages in a trial.

Many variations of the decline test paradigm have been used across studies, and together these studies have built a strong case that metacognitive monitoring is a real phenomenon in monkeys (Basile et al., 2015; Hampton et al., 2020; Smith et al., 2014). Figure 22.2 illustrates the general logic used with the decline test response. A test of metacognition using the decline test response requires two general components. First, subjects perform a primary cognitive task in which accuracy can be varied systematically. Systematic variation of accuracy might take the form of manipulating the similarity of stimuli that must be discriminated (Shields et al., 1997), the delay interval in a memory test (Hampton, 2001), or the degree to which a task has been learned to perfection (Kornell et al., 2007). This systematic variation in accuracy creates the opportunity for subjects to discriminate between easy and difficult trials in the second component of these tasks. The second component consists of a response by which subjects choose either to proceed immediately to a test or to avoid or delay that test. In some cases, subjects are able to entirely skip a particular test, settling for a smaller reward than could be earned by a correct response in the primary cognitive task, or simply skipping to the next trial. In other cases, also called tests of information seeking, the decline test response may allow subjects to acquire more information to facilitate an accurate response (Basile et al., 2015; Beran & Smith, 2011; Tu et al., 2015; see Beran and Parrish, Chapter 21). In all cases, the inference that monkeys metacognitively monitor the difficulty of the primary cognitive task is supported when the probability that they use the decline test response tracks difficulty. Monkeys that selectively decline difficult tests while accepting easy tests appear to "know that they know."

By some definitions, selectively declining difficult tests alone confirms metacognition (Flavell, 1979; Hampton, 2009). Nonetheless, much of the research effort in this field has been devoted to determining whether or not the metacognitive performance of monkeys is due to *introspective* metacognitive monitoring. Introspective metacognitive monitoring implies attending to some internal cognitive state to determine whether or not a test is difficult. This ability contrasts with attending to external, or public sources of information that can also accurately predict difficulty (Hampton, 2009). To illustrate, think about whether you know the capitals of France and Gambia. You likely readily remembered "Paris" and felt very confident, but you may have had more difficulty coming up with "Banjul," either drawing a complete blank, or feeling uncertain that you had the correct capital name in mind. These experiences illustrate introspective metacognition. Contrast this task with being given the choice between answering 10 quiz questions of different types for a cash award. You can either answer 10 introductory-level questions about your field of specialization, or 10 questions on advanced quantum theory. Presumably you would find the 10 questions in your field of specialization easier and would select those. You can make this judgment without knowing the specific questions you will be asked, and you do not need to introspect about whether or not you know the specific answers. You know, on the basis of public information, just about as well as I would know about you, that you will do better, on average, answering questions in your field of specialization. You arguably can behave metacognitively, and certainly adaptively, without introspection. Nonetheless, we know that both humans and, at least some, primates are introspectively metacognitive.

22.2 TESTS THAT RULE OUT NONINTROSPECTIVE METACOGNITION

Converging evidence indicates that in at least some circumstances monkeys introspect about their own cognitive processes. If the choice to decline tests is controlled by a central sense of uncertainty rather than by public stimuli specific to particular cognitive tests, then use of a metacognitive choice should transfer between tasks. Monkeys transferred use of both a retrospective confidence judgment (Kornell et al., 2007) and a decline test response (Brown et al., 2017) from perceptual tasks to memory tasks. Such transfer suggests that the same internal "sense of uncertainty" mediated metacognitive choices across the different tasks. In a rare application of transcranial magnetic stimulation (TMS) with nonhuman primates, Washburn et al. (2010) "magnetically erased" memory for the sample image needed to complete a memory test. The single monkey studied used the decline test response more when his memory had been erased than he did when exposed to similar TMS that did not disrupt his memory. Apparently it was the presence or absence of the memory, not any other cue, that controlled his use of the decline test response. In another study, monkeys were given tests that required them to indicate which of a pair of test images had occurred first in lists of five images. Monkeys were more accurate when many images appeared between the two test images, compared to when the images had been adjacent in the study list, the so-called *symbolic distance effect*. Monkeys used a decline test response more on difficult than easy trials (Templer et al., 2018). It is difficult to imagine what aspect of the test display could indicate difficulty here – the "distance" between the stimuli is something that is only represented in the subjects' memory. Using variations of a task that required memory for the location of a recently seen dot, Basile et al. (2015) ruled out seven alternative hypotheses to introspective metacognition. Although studies that rule out alternatives can never prove positively that some metacognition in monkeys is introspective, the failure of so many alternatives to account for the behavior of the monkeys makes a strong case for introspective metacognition.

Two other features of some of the metacognitive performances observed in monkeys point to a specific, metacognitive, introspective process. Metacognition is mentally taxing, increasing the total cognitive load experienced by subjects. It consumes cognitive resources that could otherwise be used for other mental work. In a clever experiment, Smith et al. (2013) imposed a concurrent cognitive load in the form of a memory test on monkeys that were making metacognitive judgments about the difficulty of perceptual tests. Addition of the concurrent cognitive load had a large negative impact on metacognitive judgements about the difficulty of the perceptual task. This concurrent cognitive load had comparatively little effect on the quality of the perceptual judgments themselves. This finding suggests that the metacognitive process is of a different, more fragile kind than is the primary cognitive process controlling the discrimination itself. Lastly, monkeys sometimes appear to show metacognition spontaneously without training (Rosati & Santos, 2016). One monkey was observed to "slap," rather than touch, a computer screen when making responses in a memory test that were going to be incorrect, compared to those that would be correct. These responses occurred before the monkey had gotten feedback about whether the response was correct or not, suggesting that he spontaneously introspected about the status of his own memory and knew when he was likely to be wrong (Hampton & Hampstead, 2006).

Together, the results briefly reviewed here indicate that monkeys sometimes introspect about the quality of their ongoing cognition. They appear to attend to a generalizable signal that reflects whether they know how to respond. These findings embody an important parallel between some components of monkey cognition and human explicit, conscious cognition. The strong evidence from these artificial testing situations shows that the capacity for introspective metacognition exists in monkeys. But these experiments provide little traction on the problem of why this ability would evolve. Of what value is it to remember whether or not you remember or can complete a particular discrimination?

22.3 WHY WOULD METACOGNITION EVOLVE?

The fact that accurate metacognitive monitoring can occur by attending to either public cues or introspective cues has implications for how to think about the evolution of metacognition. Your choice to select questions in your field of specialization in the imaginary example given earlier is equally adaptive in terms of the prize money you will win, whether you make that judgment on the basis of an introspective assessment of your own knowledge state or on the basis of external public information. It only matters that the judgment about which questions you can answer is accurate. Similarly, nonhuman animals could avoid dangerous situations and approach rewarding situations without metacognitive monitoring. They could make adaptive decisions about whether they can handle particular prey, jump a given gap, see a predator down the trail, or defeat a competitor, all on the basis of external, publicly available information. They could avoid prey with large claws, jump only narrow gaps, take a different path whenever there is the hint of a predator, and yield to large competitors. There may not be many situations in which using introspection to make such judgments would be necessary or even helpful. If this is true, why would metacognition ever evolve, in monkeys or any other animal?

One possible answer is that metacognitive monitoring did not evolve to serve "one off" decisions like those modeled in the decline test experiments described earlier, even though these studies do reveal the capacity. In these experiments, the action monkeys took was to choose dichotomously between proceeding with a test or avoiding it. It can be useful to avoid a situation in which you do not have needed information or cannot make a decision. But perhaps of more value would be to take corrective action when you do not know or cannot decide. Such action could potentially expand the repertoire of successful behavior dramatically. So-called "information-seeking" studies begin to address this question. In information-seeking studies, the choice to use the equivalent of the decline test response does not merely result in escape from the test. Instead the decline test response results in presentation of more information that might aid in completing the test correctly. In some of these tests, the information-seeking response can be used repeatedly, until such time as the monkey determines that it can make a successful test response. This iterative cycle of monitoring a cognitive state, taking corrective action, and monitoring again until success is achieved is sometimes called cognitive control.

Effective cognitive control depends on cognitive monitoring, which can provide updated information about the status of ongoing cognition. Monkeys categorizing images as birds, fish, flowers, or people sought information until they could accurately identify each image (Brady & Hampton, 2021; Tu et al., 2015). In these studies, images either started out dark or covered by a gray square. Making an information-seeking response caused the image to brighten or to be revealed incrementally (Figure 22.3). Monkeys made more information-seeking responses when more information was needed, showing that they monitored their evolving categorization decision. Similar findings exist in the domain of memory. Monkeys "requested" to see the sample image in matching to sample tests that began without one, but did not do so when the sample was already available (Beran & Smith, 2011).

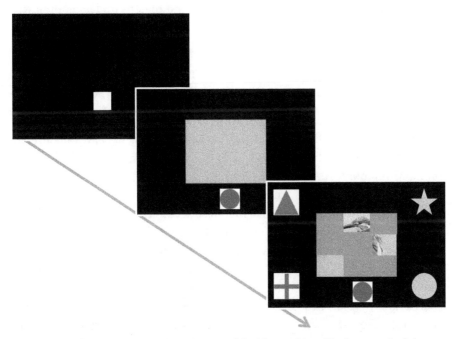

FIGURE 22.3. Dynamic cognitive monitoring of decision-making. Monkeys touched the square in the leftmost panel to start the trial. When the grey plaque appeared, monkeys could touch the round button to gradually reveal the image. They were free to identify the image as a bird, fish, person, or flower at any time by contacting the choice stimuli in the corners of the screen. Monkeys adaptively regulated how much of the image they revealed, pressing the button more times when each button press revealed only a small part of the image, and pressing fewer times when each press revealed a large part of the image.

Cognitive control can also be evident during retention of information in memory. Maintaining information in working memory is often thought to involve ongoing, active cognitive control (Baddeley, 1992; Basile & Hampton, 2013; Brady & Hampton, 2018; Unsworth & Engle, 2007). When we don't use active working memory, we can sometimes still detect that we have seen something previously because it feels familiar when we see it a second time. Monkeys used both cognitively controlled working memory and passive familiarity to identify previously seen images in memory tests. Requiring monkeys to do a cognitively taxing categorization task during the memory interval caused a dramatic decrease in accuracy when monkeys actively held images in working memory. In contrast, when monkeys identified images on the basis of passive familiarity, the requirement to categorize during the memory interval had little or no effect on accuracy (Basile & Hampton, 2013; Brady & Hampton, 2018). Perhaps the clearest demonstration of active cognitive control of working memory comes from studies of "directed forgetting," which found that monkeys followed instructions, in the form of distinctive visual cues, that indicated that they should remember or forget (Brown & Hampton, 2020; Tu & Hampton, 2014). Together these studies demonstrate a role for metacognitive monitoring in optimizing metacognitive control, and may take us one step along the road to understanding why metacognitive monitoring would evolve.

22.4 METACOGNITION AND THE EVOLUTION OF MEMORY SYSTEMS

As shown in Figure 22.1, human memory is understood to consist of separate systems that have different functional properties and depend on different parts of the brain (Squire et al., 1993). Nonhuman brains also include multiple memory systems. The diversity of functionally distinct memory systems in both humans and nonhumans likely evolved in response to divergent selection pressures that manifest as "functional incompatibilities" in the way memories are acquired or retrieved (Sherry, 2006; Sherry & Schacter, 1987). For example, a cortico-striatal habit memory system facilitates the gradual learning of an indefinite number of habits and skills that are stable over long intervals and are not accessible to cognitive monitoring (Bachevalier, 1990; Gasbarri et al., 2014; Hay & Jacoby, 1996; Malamut et al., 1984; Squire et al., 1993). By contrast, working memory facilitates the rapid acquisition and relatively brief retention of a limited amount of information (Baddeley, 1992; Shettleworth, 2010; Squire et al., 1993). In humans, and in at least some nonhumans, the contents of working memory are actively maintained and accessible to cognitive monitoring (Basile & Hampton, 2013; Basile et al., 2015; Brady & Hampton, 2018; Cowan, 2008; Hampton, 2001; Smith et al., 1998; Tu & Hampton, 2014). In a third system, familiarity signals code for whether or not a percept has been experienced previously. The familiarity signal is automatic and does not require cognitive control during retention (Brown & Hampton, 2020; Kelley & Jacoby, 2000; Yonelinas, 2002), but is subject to metacognition when activated (Brown et al., 2019). These and other memory systems can act in parallel, simultaneously and seamlessly contributing to learning and behavior, and greatly contributing to the range of situations in which memory is functional (Poldrack & Packard, 2003). These systems are revealed to be distinct only when they are isolated by brain damage, focused behavioral manipulations, or measures such as whether or not they are subject to metacognition.

Although metacognitive monitoring reflects a functional parallel to human explicit cognition, it does not by itself evince other qualities often associated with explicit cognition in humans, such as consciousness, self-awareness, or theory of mind (e.g., Hampton, 2001). Studies of metacognition are the best tools we have available for contrasting implicit and explicit cognition in nonhumans. Like other forms of learning and cognition, metacognition is likely present in at least rudimentary form in some animals other than humans. Information about the extent to which metacognition occurs in animals other than humans informs our understanding about the evolution of memory systems and provides an opportunity to determine the extent to which the distinction between implicit and explicit cognition, so fundamental to human cognitive neuroscience, is evident in nonhumans.

In contrast with the robust evidence of memory monitoring in rhesus monkeys, the current pattern of results from other species is variable and puzzling. Strikingly, New World tufted capuchin monkeys (*Cebus apella*) are much less likely than are rhesus monkeys to evidence memory monitoring, or metacognition generally (Basile et al., 2009; Beran et al., 2009; Fujita, 2009; Paukner et al., 2006; Smith et al., 2018). Capuchin monkeys failed to show behavior consistent with metacognition even though they were tested using the same procedures that had been used with rhesus monkeys (Basile et al., 2009; Smith et al., 2018). Evidence for metacognition in pigeons and dogs is also comparatively weak (Belger & Bräuer, 2018; Brauer et al., 2004; Inman & Shettleworth, 1999; McMahon et al., 2010; Roberts et al., 2009; Sutton & Shettleworth, 2008). Perhaps surprisingly, given their phylogenetic distance from humans, there seems to be comparatively strong, but limited, evidence for metacognition in rats (Foote & Crystal, 2007; Templer et al., 2017). It is too early to state whether this pattern reflects true species differences, or is the result of differences in techniques or research effort. Better addressing this question of species differences is an exciting part of current comparative work, which may tell us whether metacognition evolved in response to specific ecological or social selection pressures, or represents a general cognitive capacity shared by many species.

Comparative studies so far have drawn many parallels between human and nonhuman primate metacognitive abilities. Monkeys show metamemory, or the ability to monitor the presence or absence of a memory (Brown et al., 2017, 2019; Hampton, 2001; Templer et al., 2019). Monkeys and apes both seek information when they do not know where a valued item is hidden (Basile et al., 2015; Call & Carpenter, 2001; Hampton et al., 2004). Rhesus monkeys seek information in a memory test (Beran & Smith, 2011; Roberts et al., 2009) and monkeys spontaneously show memory monitoring without training (Hampton & Hampstead, 2006; Rosati & Santos, 2016). Furthermore, monkeys are subject to metacognitive illusions, that is, false estimates about how confident they should be in their memory, similar to humans (Ferrigno et al., 2017). Recent work has demonstrated an iterative feedback loop between cognitive monitoring and cognitive control allowing for adaptive information-seeking behavior (Brady & Hampton, 2021; Tu et al., 2015). Taken together, these findings suggest that the cognitive capacities necessary for metacognition evolved in primates at least 32 million years ago, when rhesus monkeys and humans most recently shared a common ancestor (Finstermeier et al., 2013). Of course, metacognition could be much older and much more widespread. Although there are tantalizing hints that some other species are less adept at metacognition than rhesus monkeys, we just do not have much information on metacognition in more distant relatives of humans.

Finally, we should recognize that the occurrence of metacognition in laboratory studies of nonhuman primates does not mean that the metacognitive skills shown by these monkeys are quantitatively representative of those of a primate ancestor, or even of extant monkeys. It is possible that experience with cognitive testing in laboratories has enhanced expression of these skills based on ancient cognitive foundations. The extent to which metacognitive skill can be enhanced through training in monkeys is another fascinating question that should be investigated. Whatever we learn about that, monkeys do sometimes know that they know, and we are coming to know more about that.

REFERENCES

Bachevalier, J. (1990). Ontogenic development of habit and memory formation in primates. *Annals of the New York Academy of Sciences, 608,* 457–484. https://doi.org/10.1111/j .1749-6632.1990.tb48906.x

Baddeley, A. (1992). Working memory. *Science, 255*(5044), 556–559. www.jstor.org/stable/ 2876819

Basile, B. M., & Hampton, R. R. (2013). Dissociation of active working memory and passive recognition in rhesus monkeys. *Cognition, 126*(3), 391–396. https://doi.org/10.1016/j .cognition.2012.10.012

Basile, B. M., Hampton, R. R., Suomi, S. J., & Murray, E. A. (2009). An assessment of memory awareness in tufted capuchin monkeys (*Cebus apella*). *Animal Cognition, 12*(1), 169–180. https://doi.org/10.1007/s10071-008-0180-1

Basile, B. M., Schroeder, G. R., Brown, E. K., Templer, V. L., & Hampton, R. R. (2015). Evaluation of seven hypotheses for metamemory performance in rhesus monkeys. *Journal of Experimental Psychology: General, 144*(1), 85–102. https://doi.org/10.1037/xge0000031

Belger, J., & Bräuer, J. (2018). Metacognition in dogs: Do dogs know they could be wrong?. *Learning & Behavior, 46*(4), 398–413. https://doi.org/10.3758/s13420-018-0367-5

Beran, M. J., & Smith, J. D. (2011). Information seeking by rhesus monkeys (*Macaca mulatta*) and capuchin monkeys (*Cebus apella*). *Cognition, 120*(1), 90–105. https://doi.org/10.1016/j.cognition.2011.02.016

Beran, M. J., Smith, J. D., Coutinho, M. V. C., Couchman, J. J., & Boomer, J. (2009). The psychological organization of "uncertainty" responses and "middle" responses: A dissociation in capuchin monkeys (*Cebus apella*). *Journal of Experimental Psychology: Animal Behavior Processes, 35*(3), 371–381. https://doi.org/10.1037/a0014626

Brady, R. J., & Hampton, R. R. (2018). Nonverbal working memory for novel images in rhesus monkeys. *Current Biology, 28*(24), 3903–3910.e3. https://doi.org/10.1016/j.cub.2018.10.025

(2021). Rhesus monkeys (*Macaca mulatta*) monitor evolving decisions to control adaptive information seeking. *Animal Cognition, 24*(4), 777–785. https://doi.org/10.1007/s10071-021-01477-5

Brauer, J., Call, J., & Tomasello, M. (2004). Visual perspective taking in dogs (*Canis familiaris*) in the presence of barriers. *Applied Animal Behaviour Science, 88*(3–4), 299–317. https://doi.org/10.1016/j.applanim.2004.03.004

Brown, E. K., Basile, B. M., Templer, V. L., & Hampton, R. R. (2019). Dissociation of memory signals for metamemory in rhesus monkeys (*Macaca mulatta*). *Animal Cognition, 22*(3), 331–341. https://doi.org/10.1007/s10071-019-01246-5

Brown, E. K., & Hampton, R. R. (2020). Cognitive control of working memory but not familiarity in rhesus monkeys (*Macaca mulatta*). *Learning & Behavior, 48*(4), 444–452. https://doi.org/10.3758/s13420-020-00432-7

Brown, E. K., Templer, V. L., & Hampton, R. R. (2017). An assessment of domain-general metacognitive responding in rhesus monkeys. *Behavioural Processes, 135*, 132–144. https://doi.org/10.1016/j.beproc.2016.12.004

Call, J., & Carpenter, M. (2001). Do apes and children know what they have seen? *Animal Cognition, 4*, 207–220. https://doi.org/10.1007/s100710100078

Cowan, N. (2008). What are the differences between long-term, short-term, and working memory? In W. S. Sossin, J. C. Lacaille, V. F. Castellucci, & S. Belleville (Eds.), *Essence of memory* (vol. 169, pp. 323–338). Elsevier Science Bv. https://doi.org/10.1016/s0079-6123(07)00020-9

Ferrigno, S., Kornell, N., & Cantlon, J. F. (2017). A metacognitive illusion in monkeys. *Proceedings of the Royal Society B: Biological Sciences, 284*(1862), 6, Article 20171541. https://doi.org/10.1098/rspb.2017.1541

Finstermeier, K., Dietmar, Z., Brameier, M., Meyer, M., Kreuz, E., Hofreiter, M., & Roos, C. (2013). A mitogenomic phylogeny of living primates. *PLOS ONE, 8*(7), e69504. https://doi.org/10.1371/journal.pone.0069504

Flavell, J. H. (1979). Metacognition and cognitive monitoring: A new area of cognitive-developmental inquiry. *American Psychologist, 34*, 906–911. https://psycnet.apa.org/doi/10.1037/0003-066X.34.10.906

Foote, A. L., & Crystal, J. D. (2007). Metacognition in the rat. *Current Biology, 17*(6), 551–555. https://doi.org/10.1016/j.cub.2007.01.061

Fujita, K. (2009). Metamemory in tufted capuchin monkeys (*Cebus apella*). *Animal Cognition, 12*(4), 575–585. https://doi.org/10.1007/s10071-009-0217-0

Gabrieli, J. D. E., Corkin, S., Mickel, S. F., & Growdon, J. H. (1993). Intact acquisition and long-term retention of mirror-tracing skill in Alzheimer's disease and in global amnesia. *Behavioral Neuroscience, 107*(6), 899–910. https://psycnet.apa.org/doi/10.1037/0735-7044.107.6.899

Gasbarri, A., Pompili, A., Packard, M. G., & Tomaz, C. (2014). Habit learning and memory in mammals: Behavioral and neural characteristics. *Neurobiology of Learning and Memory, 114*, 198–208. https://doi.org/10.1016/j.nlm.2014.06.010

Hampton, R. R. (2001). Rhesus monkeys know when they remember. *Proceedings of the National Academy of Sciences of the United States of America, 98*(9), 5359–5362. https://doi.org/10.1073/pnas.071600998

(2009). Multiple demonstrations of metacognition in nonhumans: Converging evidence or multiple mechanisms? *Comparative Cognition and Behavior Reviews, 4*, 17–28.

Hampton, R. R., Engelberg, J. W., & Brady, R. J. (2020). Explicit memory and cognition in monkeys. *Neuropsychologia, 138*, 107326. https://doi.org/10.1016/j.neuropsychologia.2019.107326

Hampton, R. R., & Hampstead, B. M. (2006). Spontaneous behavior of a rhesus monkey (*Macaca mulatta*) during memory tests suggests memory awareness. *Behavioral Processes, 72*, 184–189.

Hay, J. F., & Jacoby, L. L. (1996). Separating habit and recollection: Memory slips, process dissociations, and probability matching. *Journal of Experimental Psychology: Learning, Memory, and Cognition, 22*(6), 1323–1335. https://psycnet.apa.org/doi/10.1037/0278-7393.22.6.1323

Inman, A., & Shettleworth, S. J. (1999). Detecting metamemory in nonverbal subjects: A test with pigeons. *Journal of Experimental Psychology: Animal Behavior Processes, 25*(3), 389–395. https://psycnet.apa.org/doi/10.1037/0097-7403.25.3.389

Kelley, C. M., & Jacoby, L. L. (2000). Recollection and familiarity. In E. Tulving & C. I. M. Fergus (Eds.), *The Oxford handbook of memory* (pp. 215–228). Oxford University Press.

Kornell, N., Son, L. K., & Terrace, H. S. (2007). Transfer of metacognitive skills and hint seeking in monkeys. *Psychological Science, 18*(1), 64–71. https://doi.org/10.1111%2Fj.1467-9280.2007.01850.x

Malamut, B. L., Saunders, R. C., & Mishkin, M. (1984). Monkeys with combined amygdalo-hippocampal lesions succeed in object discrimination-learning despite 24-hour inter-tribal intervals. *Behavioral Neuroscience, 98*, 759–769. https://doi.org/10.1037/0735-7044.98.5.759

McMahon, S., Macpherson, K., & Roberts, W. A. (2010). Dogs choose a human informant: Metacognition in canines. *Behavioral Processes, 85*(3), 293–298. https://doi.org/10.1016/j.beproc.2010.07.014

Milner, B. (1962). Les troubles de la memoire accompagnant deslesions hippocampiques bilaterales [Memory impairment accompanying bilateral hippocampal lesions]. In *Psychologie de l'hippocampe.Paris: Centre National de la Recherche Scientifique* (pp. 257–272).

Paukner, A., Anderson, J., & Fujita, K. (2006). Redundant food searches by capuchin monkeys (*Cebus apella*): A failure of metacognition? *Animal Cognition, 9*(2), 110–117. www.springerlink.com/openurl.asp?genre=article&id=doi:10.1007/s10071-005-0007-2

Poldrack, R. A., & Packard, M. G. (2003). Competition among multiple memory systems: Converging evidence from animal and human brain studies. *Neuropsychologia, 41*, 245–251. https://doi.org/10.1016/S0028-3932(02)00157-4

Roberts, W. A., Feeney, M. C., McMillan, N., MacPherson, K., Musolino, E., & Petter, M. (2009). Do pigeons (*Columba livia*) study for a test? *Journal of Experimental Psychology: Animal Behavior Processes, 35*(2), 129–142. https://doi.org/10.1037/a0013722

Rosati, A. G., & Santos, L. R. (2016). Spontaneous metacognition in rhesus monkeys. *Psychological Science, 27*(9), 1181–1191. https://doi.org/10.1177/0956797616653737

Sherry, D. F. (2006). Neuroecology. *Annual Review of Psychology, 57*, 167–197. https://doi.org/10.1146/annurev.psych.56.091103.070324

Sherry, D. F., & Schacter, D. L. (1987). The evolution of multiple memory-systems. *Psychological Review, 94*(4), 439–454.

Shettleworth, S. J. (2010). *Cognition, evolution, and behavior* (2nd ed.). Oxford University Press.

Shields, W. E., Smith, J. D., & Washburn, D. A. (1997). Uncertain responses by humans and rhesus monkeys (*Macaca mulatta*) in a psychophysical same-different task. *Journal of Experimental Psychology: General, 126*(2), 147–164. https://psycnet.apa.org/doi/10.1037/0096-3445.126.2.147

Smith, J. D., Couchman, J. J., & Beran, M. J. (2014). Animal metacognition: A tale of two comparative psychologies. *Journal of Comparative Psychology, 128*(2), 115–131. https://doi.org/10.1037/a0033105

Smith, J. D., Coutinho, M. V. C., Church, B. A., & Beran, M. J. (2013). Executive-attentional uncertainty responses by rhesus macaques (*Macaca mulatta*). *Journal of Experimental Psychology: General, 142*(2), 458–475. https://doi.org/10.1037/a0029601

Smith, J. D., Shields, W. E., & Washburn, D. A. (1998). Memory monitoring by animals and humans. *Journal of Experimental Psychology: General, 127*(3), 227–250. https://psycnet.apa.org/doi/10.1037/0096-3445.127.3.227

Smith, T. R., Smith, J. D., & Beran, M. (2018). Not knowing what one knows: A meaningful failure of metacognition in capuchin monkeys. *Animal Behavior and Cognition, 5*(1), 55–67. https://doi.org/10.26451/abc.05.01.05.2018

Squire, L. R., Knowlton, B., & Musen, G. (1993). The structure and organization of memory. *Annual Review of Psychology, 44*, 453–495.

Squire, L. R., & Zola-Morgan, S. (1991). The medial temporal-lobe memory system. *Science, 253*(5026), 1380–1386. https://doi.org/10.1126/science.1896849

Sutton, J. E., & Shettleworth, S. J. (2008). Memory without awareness: Pigeons do not show metamemory in delayed matching to sample. *Journal of Experimental Psychology-Animal Behavior Processes, 34*(2), 266–282.

Templer, V. L., Brown, E. K., & Hampton, R. R. (2018). Rhesus monkeys metacognitively monitor memories of the order of events. *Scientific Reports, 8*(1), 11541. https://doi.org/10.1038/s41598-018-30001-y

Templer, V. L., & Hampton, R. R. (2012). Rhesus monkeys (*Macaca mulatta*) show robust evidence for memory awareness across multiple generalization tests. *Animal Cognition, 15*(3), 409–419. https://doi.org/10.1007/s10071-011-0468-4

Templer, V. L., Lee, K. A., & Preston, A. J. (2017). Rats know when they remember: Transfer of metacognitive responding across odor-based delayed match-to-sample tests. *Animal Cognition, 20*(5), 891–906. https://doi.org/10.1007/s10071-017-1109-3

Tu, H.-W., & Hampton, R. R. (2014). Control of working memory in rhesus monkeys (*Macaca mulatta*). *Journal of Experimental Psychology: Animal Learning and Cognition, 40*(4), 467–476. https://doi.org/10.1037/xan0000030

Tu, H. W., Pani, A., & Hampton, R. R. (2015). Rhesus monkeys (*Macaca mulatta*) adaptively adjust information seeking in response to information accumulated. *Journal of Comparative Psychology, 129*, 347–355. https://psycnet.apa.org/doi/10.1037/a0039595

Unsworth, N., & Engle, R. W. (2007). The nature of individual differences in working memory capacity: Active maintenance in primary memory and controlled search from secondary memory. *Psychological Review, 114*(1), 104–132. https://doi.org/10.1037/0033-295x.114.1.104

Washburn, D. A., Gulledge, J. P., Beran, M. J., & Smith, J. D. (2010). With his memory magnetically erased, a monkey knows he is uncertain. *Biology Letters, 6*(2), 160–162. https://doi.org/10.1098/rsbl.2009.0737

Yonelinas, A. P. (2002). The nature of recollection and familiarity: A review of 30 years of research. *Journal of Memory and Language, 46*, 441–517. https://doi.org/10.1006/jmla.2002.2864

23

ADAPTIVE MEMORY

Fitness-Relevant Tunings in Human Memory

James S. Nairne and Michelle E. Coverdale

Human memory scholars have been reluctant to consider the evolutionary origins of mnemonic processes. There is wide agreement that the capacity to remember is the product of an extended period of evolution, guided by natural selection, but neither the criterion used to shape memory's development (the enhancement of fitness) nor the selection pressures potentially involved (e.g., remembering the location of food or predators) have significantly influenced theory development. In the biological sciences, such an omission would be unimaginable, as would the belief that a trait's structure can be understood without some consideration of its function. Biological systems evolve because they solve particular adaptive problems, and their operating characteristics often reflect the problems that they evolved to solve. If we want to understand memory, then, arguably we need to know something about what memory is designed to do (Klein et al., 2002; Nairne, 2005; Sherry & Schacter, 1987).

We have speculated elsewhere about the reasons for neglecting evolution in cognitive research (e.g., Nairne, 2015). In the case of human memory, the reason is partly historical. When Ebbinghaus began the scientific study of remembering in the 1870s (Ebbinghaus, 1885/1964), his strategy was completely data driven. He was mainly concerned with how different variables affect the acquisition and retention of information. To Ebbinghaus, memory was a "black box" that could be understood simply by testing the scope and limits of remembering (see Slamecka, 1985). Ebbinghaus's approach produced a number of empirical regularities, such as the shape of the retention function, and memory researchers have spent the last century and a half following his strategy and attempting to account for the obtained patterns.

However, if your goal is to understand the empirical "stuff" of retention – forgetting curves, spacing effects, and serial position functions – then evolutionary accounts can appear hopelessly *post hoc*. Attempting to determine the selection pressures that led to negatively accelerated forgetting curves encourages the generation of speculative "just-so stories" that have little or no grounding in empirical fact. Moreover, there are no fossilized memory traces, and the selection pressures that were present in ancestral environments, shaping memory's development, are open to debate (e.g., Buller, 2005; Richardson, 2007). Thus, in the psychological sciences we may lack sufficient evidence to test evolutionary accounts, even though remembering almost certainly reflects the output of an evolved adaptation.

For over the past decade, our laboratory has been using an alternative approach, one that does not involve post hoc analysis of existing retention data. Instead, through the technique of forward engineering, we have derived empirical predictions about remembering *a priori* by focusing on the main criteria that drive natural selection. Memory systems must have evolved because they enhanced fitness – i.e., survival and reproduction – so we reasoned that memory's operating characteristics likely show sensitivity to fitness dimensions. As we review in this chapter, this strategy has led to the discovery of a number of novel phenomena, some of which turn out to be among the most potent memory-enhancing techniques known in the memory field. Perhaps not surprisingly, the interpretation of these new phenomena remains controversial among memory researchers.

We begin our brief overview of this work with a discussion of the *survival processing paradigm*, an encoding procedure designed to test whether processing information in a survival context improves retention (Nairne et al., 2007). We then consider whether items with properties that are inherently related to fitness likewise show a retention benefit; as a case in point, we and others have demonstrated that living or animate things are remembered better than nonliving or inanimate things (Bonin et al., 2014; Nairne et al., 2013). In fact, animacy turns out to be one of the most important predictors of whether or not an item will be remembered. We end our review by considering other important (but less well-studied) fitness dimensions – reproduction and contamination. We also comment on the nature of evolutionary arguments as they pertain to the interpretation of mnemonic and other cognitive phenomena.

23.1 THE MNEMONIC VALUE OF SURVIVAL PROCESSING

It seems certain that human memory systems evolved to help us remember certain kinds of information better than others. From a fitness perspective, not all stimuli are created equal. On average, it is more important to remember the appearance of a predator or the location of food than it is to remember the details of a wall hanging. Consequently, we expected to find enhanced retention of information when it occurs in, or is relevant to, a survival context. Anecdotal evidence certainly supports this view. When survival-relevant events occur, such as escaping from an approaching car or encountering a predator while hiking, we are likely to remember those events well.

However, the concept of "survival-relevance" is tricky and almost certainly context dependent. As Nairne and Pandeirada (2008) noted: "food is survival relevant, but more so at the beginning of a meal than at its completion" (p. 240); similarly, a fur coat has high survival value at the North Pole, but low at the Equator. This means that survival relevance cannot be defined in an absolute or fixed way; instead, it must rely on an attribution process that requires processing both stimulus properties (e.g., bared teeth) and context. A similar process drives our reaction to threat more generally. The fight-or-flight response is an automatic response to threat, but what constitutes a "threat" relies on appraisal of the situation. A car doesn't initiate a characteristic stress response unless you are directly in its path; a lion at the zoo produces a very different reaction from one encountered in the grasslands. Our strategy was to induce people to process neutral stimuli in a survival context, to force the attribution of survival relevance, and then assess the effects on later retention. We chose to focus on survival *processing* for a methodological reason as well. It is possible to compare a natural predator, such as a lion with bared teeth, to a neutral control animal, such as a sheep, but lions and sheep differ in many ways, which makes it hard to isolate the factors that control performance. In our case, we asked people to process and remember exactly the same target stimuli, but either in a survival or control context.

SURVIVAL PROCESSING PARADIGM

In the survival processing paradigm, people are presented with sets of words or pictures of objects, which they are required to rate through one of several orienting tasks. In the critical condition, people are asked to imagine themselves stranded in the grasslands of a foreign land, where they must find steady supplies of food and water, and avoid predators. The participant is asked to determine the relevance of each stimulus to this survival scenario – for example, on a scale from one (irrelevant) to five (extremely relevant), how relevant is "stone" or "book" to surviving in this situation? As a control, standard deep processing tasks are commonly used (such as rating words for pleasantness or forming a visual image) along with equally complex but fitness-irrelevant scenarios (e.g., such as going on vacation). After a slight delay, the participant is given a surprise retention test for the rated words (i.e., free recall and/or recognition).

As Figure 23.1 shows, processing items with respect to the survival scenario typically produces robust retention (Nairne et al., 2007, 2008). In fact, a few seconds of survival processing produces better retention than a veritable "who's who" of classic encoding procedures, such as forming visual images, self-generation of items, and intentional learning. This "survival processing effect" has now been replicated hundreds of times in laboratories across the world (for recent meta-analyses, see Scofield et al., 2017).

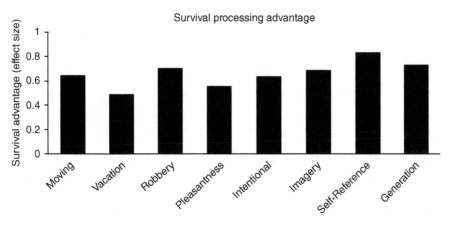

FIGURE 23.1. Cohen's d effect sizes for survival processing advantage relative to a variety of control conditions. Each bar represents the size of the survival processing advantage relative to the condition listed below it such that larger bars represent a larger memory advantage for survival processing relative to the corresponding control condition. The first three bars represent scenarios in which the participant imagines moving to a new land, going on vacation, and being involved in a bank robbery. The remaining bars represent classically effective encoding tasks.

It remains robust in both between- and within-subject designs, after short and long delays, for the elderly and preschool children, and when a variety of survival-based and control scenarios are used. Survival processing enhances other forms of memory as well, such as source memory, which refers to the characteristics that generally accompany an item's presentation – for example, spatial position or whether the item occurred in a survival context or not (Kroneisen & Bell, 2018; Nairne et al., 2012; Misirlisoy et al., 2019).

The main concern, of course, is whether fitness-based processing is responsible for the benefit. There could be differences between the typical survival and control scenarios that remain uncontrolled. For example, perhaps rating the relevance of items to a survival scenario is inherently more unusual, effortful, arousing, or emotional than the standard control tasks. Researchers have tried to equate the survival and control scenarios along these dimensions (e.g., emotionality, effort, or distinctiveness) and the survival processing advantage generally remains robust (see Kazanas & Altarriba, 2015; Nairne, Pandeirada et al., 2017). Plus, as noted earlier, many different versions of survival and control scenarios have been tested in the literature. For example, survival benefits have been detected against control scenarios such as participating in a bank robbery, winning the lottery, organizing a picnic, and exploring the relevance of words to the afterlife. In addition, Nairne et al. (2009) crafted experiments in which people rated the relevance of items to *exactly the same activities*, but in a context that was either fitness-relevant or not. In one experiment, people rated the relevance of words to a hunting scenario, one in which they were required to hunt big

Hunting for Survival:
In this task, please imagine that you are living long ago in the grasslands of a foreign land. As a part of a small group, you are in charge of contributing meat to feed your tribe. You will need to hunt big game, trap small animals, or even fish in a nearby lake or river. Hunters often have to travel great distances, pursue animals through unfamiliar terrain, and successfully return home. Whatever the conditions, you must hunt successfully to feed your tribe. We are going to show you a list of words, and we would like you to rate how relevant each of these words would be in your attempt to hunt successfully for food. Some of the words may be relevant and others may not – it's up to you to decide.

Hunting for Contest:
In this task, please imagine that you have been invited to participate in a hunting contest. As a part of a team, you are in charge of contributing captured game to the team effort. You will need to hunt big game, trap small animals, or even fish in a nearby lake or river. Members of the team often have to travel great distances, pursue animals through unfamiliar terrain, and successfully return to the contest center. Whatever the conditions, you must hunt successfully to help your team win the contest. We are going to show you a list of words, and we would like you to rate how relevant each of these words would be in your attempt to hunt successfully. Some of the words may be relevant and others may not – it's up to you to decide.

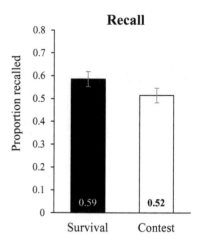

FIGURE 23.2. Instructions and subsequent recall for two matched hunting scenarios (from Nairne et al., 2009) that differ only in the context of the hunting activity (either for survival or for a contest). Error bars represent 95% confidence intervals.

game, trap small animals, and fish, but either to survive or to win a hunting contest. Both scenarios required tracking and hunting for food, in exactly the same way, but only the survival-based version was designed to induce fitness-relevant processing. Significantly better recall performance was found in the survival-based hunting condition (see Figure 23.2). It appears, then, that fitness-based processing is primarily responsible for the mnemonic benefit.

The survival processing advantage also does not depend on rating items to a fixed survival scenario; in fact, the effect remains robust in the absence of any defined scenario. Klein (2013) found a significant survival processing advantage when participants were simply asked to "imagine that you are trying to stay alive" (p. 52). More recently, Nairne et al. (2019) reported robust retention advantages when people were asked to generate their own survival situations rather than react to an experimenter-provided scenario. No constraints were placed on the generation process other than that it needed to be survival related and refer to a target stimulus. For example, when given the word DOOR, a participant might respond with "my house is on fire and I can escape through the DOOR." One advantage of the generation procedure is that it decouples survival processing from any particular ancestral scenario (e.g., the grasslands) and it provides more flexibility in the use of control tasks (see Nairne et al., 2019).

Collectively, research on the survival processing effect strongly suggests that it is not an artifact of specific procedural details, such as rating the relevance of words to a particular ancestral scenario. The effect is quite general and not likely caused by some spurious processing confound such as interest, self-relevance, effort, or emotional arousal. There is something about activating a survival context that uniquely benefits retention, producing retention levels that match or exceed the best-known encoding techniques. Such a finding is consistent with our original evolutionary hypothesis. Memory systems could only have evolved by promoting survival and reproduction and, consequently, are likely biased or tuned to the retention of fitness-relevant events.

PROXIMATE MECHANISMS

The evolutionary hypothesis predicts that people should remember fitness-relevant events particularly well, but it does not specify the mechanisms involved. In our original work (Nairne et al., 2007), we did not attempt to characterize a survival "module" or a particular mnemonic adaptation of any type. Rather, we simply concluded that the main criterion of natural selection – namely, that evolved traits or mechanisms must advance reproductive fitness – likely left its mark on memory and its efficiencies. Exactly how this tuning was accomplished is an important question, but it is not one that we actively pursued.

In keeping with the Ebbinghaus tradition, however, other researchers have tried to "explain" adaptive memory effects by dipping into the standard toolkit of the memory researcher. If traditional memory mechanisms can handle the survival processing benefit, then, some have argued, appeals to special evolutionary "tunings" are not necessary (see Erdfelder & Kroneisen, 2014; see Kroneisen, Chapter 24). Nearly a dozen mechanisms have been proposed to account for the survival advantage, including semantic or "deep" processing, self-referential encoding, and individual-item and relational processing, among others. The most popular account appeals to "richness of encoding," which assumes that the survival context simply induces participants to generate an especially large number of highly distinctive and rich ideas during encoding. Richly encoded items lead to memory representations that are easy to access because lots of retrieval cues are potentially available to aid retrieval. Rich or elaborative encodings are often used *post hoc* to explain retention differences among encoding techniques. For example, pictures are more likely to be remembered than words because mental images are thought to contain richer and more complex representations than printed words.

In fact, considerable evidence now links elaborative or rich encoding and survival processing. Röer et al. (2013) recorded the number of ideas that people generated during survival and standard control scenarios. Across several experiments, people generated more ideas when rating items for survival than they did for controls, and the number of ideas generated tracked how well the rated items were later recalled. In addition, a number of studies have shown that people sometimes recall items after survival processing that were not actually rated, a finding that is also consistent with an elaborative or richness of encoding account (Howe & Derbish, 2010). Some neurological work, using event-related potentials, has detected the neurological signatures for enhanced elaborative encoding after survival processing as well (e.g., Fellner et al., 2013; Forester et al., 2019; Zhang et al., 2020). Thus, there is support for the claim that survival processing generally leads to elaborate and richly encoded memory traces.

Additional evidence comes from "boundary conditions," cases where the survival processing advantage fails to emerge. Butler et al. (2009) found that when word lists were highly relevant or irrelevant to the scenario, and thus not requiring any kind of elaborative processing, survival advantages disappeared. Kroneisen and Erdfelder (2011) showed that when the survival scenario was narrowed to a single activity – finding potable water – the survival advantage was eliminated as well, at least when compared with the standard "moving" control. The survival advantage is also sometimes absent when people are required to perform a demanding secondary task while rating the words (Kroneisen et al., 2014; Stillman et al., 2014). Other boundary conditions include a failure to find significant survival advantages for abstract words (Bell et al., 2013), faces (Savine et al., 2011), stories (Seamon et al., 2012), and possibly for certain retrieval situations such as cued recall or when the retrieval environment is implicit (McBride et al., 2013; Tse & Altarriba, 2010). What is significant about these findings is the failure to find retention benefits even though the processing itself remains fitness relevant.

Importantly, though, this evidence merely supports the involvement of a particular proximate mechanism – i.e., elaborative encoding – when survival processing is engaged. Some researchers have argued that the evidence for elaboration negates the power of the evolutionary argument because: (1) there is no need to appeal to speculative evolutionary tunings and (2) cognitive adaptations should show evidence of special design, meaning their operating characteristics should be uniquely tailored to handle fitness-based input rather than retention in general. However, as we discuss below, neither of these arguments is particularly compelling when the nature of evolutionary arguments and adaptations are considered in detail.

ULTIMATE VERSUS PROXIMATE ACCOUNTS

If we stipulate that a domain-general mechanism (elaborative encoding) is primarily responsible for the survival processing benefit, an important question remains unanswered: *Why* do survival situations engage such a powerful form of encoding? As we have discussed elsewhere (e.g., Nairne, 2014; Nairne & Pandeirada, 2016), evolutionary accounts typically are concerned with exactly this kind of question. Evolutionary accounts focus on *ultimate explanations* of traits, meaning the reasons "why" traits are selected during an evolutionary process. Natural selection is governed by a criterion, enhancing fitness, so ultimate explanations appeal to (and are judged by) this criterion. *Proximate explanations* focus on the mechanisms that produce the trait – i.e., they are statements about "how" the trait works and the conditions under which the trait is likely to be expressed. For example, crying increases a baby's chances of gaining the care and comfort it needs for survival; an ultimate explanation of crying focuses on its fitness effects and why the trait likely gained traction in the population over generations. Alternatively, we can study the biological mechanisms that induce and control crying, such as how glands secrete lachrymal fluid, along with the triggering conditions that produce the behavior (e.g., separation from the caretaker). The latter constitutes an investigation of the proximate mechanisms that drive the behavior (Nairne, 2014).

Both ultimate and proximate explanations are necessary for a full accounting of an evolved trait (Tinbergen, 1963). But proximate mechanisms do not generally provide answers to ultimate questions, which focus on how traits affect fitness. From an evolutionary perspective, we have not "explained" crying by pointing to the production of lachrymal fluid. The evolutionary theorist seeks to identify possible selection pressures in our ancestral past that reinforced the development of a mechanism that produces tears, and characteristic facial expressions, in fitness-relevant situations. Similarly, the fact that survival situations might engage mechanisms that are possibly domain-general, such as elaboration, certainly does not "rule out" Nairne et al.'s (2007) hypothesis about evolutionary tunings – it simply suggests a possible way in which the fitness-relevant tuning may be realized.

Moreover, if we accept the argument that "special design" is a useful criterion for identifying biological or cognitive adaptations (Williams, 1966), then the relevant proximate mechanisms need not be encapsulated or unique. In fact, evolved adaptations often co-opt other evolved mechanisms to achieve their intended effect. The immune system is an adaptation, but it co-opted the circulatory system to function. Flying is an adaptation in birds, but it relies on feathers that likely evolved for thermoregulation or sexual display (cf. Nairne & Pandeirada, 2016, p. 498). We are not suggesting that the immune system is "just another example of the circulatory system," that flying is "just feathers," or that the presence of either completely explains the phenomenon. Adaptations often recruit basic processes as part of their normal response repertoire. In fact, the coordination of co-opted mechanisms is often the central feature of an evolved adaptation (e.g., the fight-or-flight response). Nairne and Pandeirada (2016) suggested that mnemonic tunings for survival-related events may be part of a more general survival optimization system designed to envisage, predict, and simulate future scenarios.

Moreover, proximate mechanisms need an ultimate account as well – why would nature craft a retention system that is tuned to elaboration, "deep" (i.e., meaning-based) processing, or self-relevance? If elaboration is the mechanism, then we need to specify the selection pressures that reinforced its evolution. Elaboration has no inherent fitness value unless it is selectively activated by conditions that improve an organism's fitness. Survival processing leads to good retention because it is important for people to remember survival-relevant information, not because it engenders a form of elaboration (or some other form of mnemonic process). In line with nature's criterion, memory-enhancing processes must have evolved in the service of benefiting survival-relevant information, not the other way around. Selection pressures favored a memory system that retained fitness-relevant information, and elaboration could have evolved to meet that goal. The fact that we can remember generally must be a by-product of a system that evolved to meet the needs of survival and reproduction. From this perspective, it is not surprising that memory systems work particularly well when dealing with fitness-relevant information.

23.2 MNEMONIC VALUE OF ANIMACY

The core prediction of the adaptive memory framework is that things that are inherently fitness-relevant should receive processing priority and be remembered well. Animacy represents another key dimension: Animate beings can be predators, prey, competitors for resources, and prospective mating partners. Consequently, we might expect an adaptive memory system to be "tuned" to the animate characteristics of stimuli because living things are apt to be more fitness-relevant than nonliving things. In fact, there is considerable evidence suggesting that animacy plays a central role in many cognitive processes, including language, cognitive development, the organization of semantic knowledge, and visual perception and attention (see Nairne, Van Arsdall et al., 2017).

To provide an initial test of this idea, our laboratory created two pools of words – one animate and the other inanimate – and matched them on 10 different dimensions: age of acquisition, category size, category typicality, concreteness, familiarity, imagery, frequency, meaningfulness, word length, and semantic relatedness. Animate and inanimate words were intermixed in lists that participants were asked to study for a retention test. As shown in Figure 23.3, a later free recall test revealed an animacy advantage (Nairne et al., 2013). In subsequent analyses, using existing recall norms, animacy was discovered to be one of the strongest predictors of recall – superior to such well-known dimensions as frequency of use, meaningfulness, and even concreteness (see VanArsdall, 2016). Similar animacy advantages have now been reported in other laboratories, using different word pools, and the advantage remains robust for pictures of animate entities, on recognition and some cued-recall tests, in between-list designs, and when an additional memory load is required during encoding (e.g., Bonin et al., 2014, 2015; Popp & Serra, 2016). People also remember the locations of animate items better than that of inanimate items (van Buren & Scholl, 2017) and learn novel words easier if the definitions refer to animate things (Laurino & Kaczer, 2019).

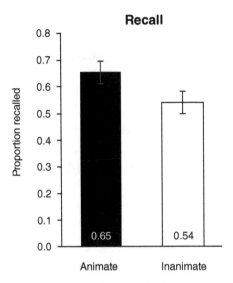

FIGURE 23.3. Recall of matched animate and inanimate words (from Nairne et al., 2013). Error represents 95% confidence intervals.

We can only briefly tap the rapidly growing literature on animacy and memory. But as with survival processing, researchers have focused most of their energy on identifying possible proximate mechanisms. It is possible that the memory advantage can be reduced to enhanced attentional focus because animate items tend to capture attention. Other work suggests that similar to survival, processing animate items leads to richer or more elaborate encodings. It turns out that people generate more ideas in response to animate, compared to inanimate, items and the number of ideas generated predicts later recall (Meinhardt et al., 2020). Others have suggested that animate items produce more emotional arousal, although animacy effects remain robust when arousal levels are carefully controlled (e.g., Popp & Serra, 2018). Regardless of the mechanisms involved, the effect itself is highly replicable and stands as another success of the forward engineering strategy: We generated an *a priori* prediction – animate items should be remembered well – based on an analysis of nature's main criterion, the enhancement of fitness.

23.3 MNEMONIC VALUE OF CONTAMINATION

Survival-relevance appears in many forms – avoiding predators, gathering food, securing necessary shelter. Our laboratory has also been interested in the mnemonic consequences of potential contamination from disease. Evolutionary psychologists have been keenly interested in *disgust*, an emotion that plays a critical role in helping us avoid ingesting and interacting with potential sources of contamination (see Tybur et al., 2013). The experience of disgust is thought to be part of a broader system, known as the behavioral immune system (Schaller & Park, 2011), that helps us avoid initial contact with potential sources of contamination and disease. Perhaps not surprisingly, people tend to remember disgusting objects particularly well, compared to neutral objects, although item-selection concerns remain a problem (Chapman et al., 2013).

In our work, we were interested in whether people would be better at remembering objects that had been touched by people suffering from a potentially communicable disease than objects touched by healthy people (Fernandes et al., 2017). People were shown pictures of everyday objects along with a short description of the health status of a person who had just touched the object. For example, a picture of a cup might be presented along with the statement "person with a runny nose" (sick condition) or the statement "person with brown hair" (healthy condition). After every third item, an immediate memory test followed in which the three preceding objects were presented again and people were asked to identify whether each had been touched by a sick or a healthy person. (Performance on this task allowed us to ensure that participants were relating the descriptor to the object and to confirm that the sentences were being correctly interpreted as descriptive of a sick or a healthy person.) After a series of these trials, and a short distractor period, participants were given a surprise free recall test for the objects. Participants performed close to perfect on the immediate memory task with no differences between the sick and healthy conditions. However, on the final test they recalled significantly more of the objects paired with descriptions of sick people than those paired with descriptions of healthy people—in other words, they remembered more of the potentially contaminated objects, which is clearly adaptive in the sense that remembering contaminated items can help us avoid those items in future interactions.

We have replicated these results using different stimuli and descriptors – e.g., faces with disease-related facial cues – and other laboratories have reported similar results (Bonin et al., 2019). There is now a growing literature on contamination effects and memory which can be seen as a natural extension of our work on adaptive memory.

23.4 MNEMONIC VALUE OF MATING-RELATED PROCESSING

Nature's criterion, the enhancement of fitness, ultimately rests on the ability to secure passage of one's genetic record to future generations. Traits that improve survival, such as remembering information relevant to animates or survival-relevant events, are likely to improve the chances of reproduction as well. However, our retention systems should also be tuned to reproduction itself, particularly to events that are relevant to securing a high-value mating partner. Indeed, there is considerable evidence to support this prediction.

The presence of physical characteristics that signal the mate value of individuals has been shown to influence retention. For instance, target items spoken by male voices with lower pitches, pitch level being one indicator of reproductive success, are remembered better than items spoken by males with less masculinized voices (Smith et al., 2012). People also tend to remember more personal and physical information about women when their physical characteristics, such as waist-to-hip ratio, signal health and fitness (e.g., Fitzgerald et al., 2016). Women also remember more about the physical characteristics of men when they are first told to consider the man as a potential short-term mate (Horgan et al., 2016).

Work using the relevance rating paradigm of Nairne et al. (2007), however, has produced more equivocal results. Sandry et al. (2013) used a variety of mate-selection scenarios in which people were asked to rate the relevance of words to searching for a partner who would satisfy them sexually or, in a different condition, would serve as an effective mating partner. No recall advantage was found relative to control conditions. Similarly, Klein (2013) tested a "mate choice" scenario in which participants rated the relevance of words to selecting a mate. Again, no memory advantage was found in this condition compared to a pleasantness-rating control. Derringer et al. (2017) and Seitz et al. (2018) employed a similar research strategy and, again, found no evidence for a mnemonic tuning based on mating-related processing. One notable exception is Pandeirada et al. (2017), who found that women had better memory for the faces of men when they were first asked to consider how desirable the men would be as long-term mating partners compared to long-term work partners.

The relevance-rating paradigm has also been used to explore the effect of kinship on long-term retention. Krause et al. (2019) had people rate the relevance of words to several survival scenarios that depicted people who were either close family members, nonkin relations (e.g., friends), or strangers. The survival scenarios produced enhanced recall relative to control conditions, but the degree of kinship had no effect on performance. Seitz et al. (2018) conducted experiments along similar lines and found that an imagined parenting scenario, one that required providing care and nourishment for your child, produced recall levels comparable to those found after survival processing. They also found that manipulating the biological relatedness of the child (adopted versus biological) affected performance in the expected direction (larger memory advantages for the biological child; see Seitz et al., 2019, 2020; see Blaisdell and Seitz, Chapter 26). Bonin et al. (2020) reported a similar finding – a survival scenario based on caring for one's own biological child produced better retention than a scenario involving an adopted child.

Overall, though, it is surprising that mating-related scenarios fail to produce consistent memory enhancement effects. It is almost certainly adaptive to remember information that helps to secure an effective mating partner, yet the existing evidence remains equivocal at this point. The failure to find consistent memory advantages with mating-related scenarios has been used to argue against an evolutionary account of adaptive memory effects (e.g., Schwartz, 2019), but the null result is troubling for standard "nonevolutionary" accounts as well. Mating-related scenarios are generally regarded as more interesting, arousing, emotional, and self-relevant than control scenarios, so many of the same mechanisms that have been proposed to account for survival processing advantages fail to produce a similar advantage for mating scenarios.

23.5 CONCLUDING COMMENTS

If nature "tuned" our memory systems to process and remember fitness-relevant information, then our ancestors likely possessed an improved ability to survive and propagate their genetic record. This is an evolutionary argument, one that generates an *a priori* empirical prediction: People should be particularly good at remembering information that is inherently fitness relevant, or is processed in a fitness context. The survival processing effect, among the other phenomena reviewed here, supports this prediction.

At the same time, one might reasonably question the application of adaptationist logic to these particular phenomena, especially given the unspecified nature of the relevant mnemonic adaptation(s). Many of the defining features of adaptations championed by evolutionary psychologists, such as evidence for "special design" (e.g., Schmitt & Pilcher, 2004), have yet to be specified for the mnemonic "tunings" discussed here. We can make no claims about heritability, nor can we offer any insight into whether unique tunings might have evolved for the different adaptive problems discussed here – i.e., survival based, animacy, mate related, or contamination. Elsewhere we have argued that adaptive memory tunings might be part of larger systems designed to enhance fitness, such as survival optimization or, in the case of contamination, the behavioral immune system, but these ideas remain speculative. Moreover, no direct connection has yet been made between the enhanced retention engendered by the forms of survival processing studied here and a direct or indirect boost to survival or reproduction.

However, the idea that retention is "tuned" to fitness relevance is not without precedent in simple learning contexts (e.g., Shettleworth, 2010). Both Pavlovian and operant conditioning depend on the presentation of reinforcing events, which in practice are fitness-relevant events. In traditional Pavlovian conditioning, the organism learns that a neutral stimulus (the conditioned stimulus) predicts the occurrence of a second event, called the unconditioned stimulus. Unconditioned stimuli are ingrained stimuli that automatically produce responses in the absence of any initial training (e.g., withdrawing from shock). It is easy for an organism to learn that a flashing light predicts the occurrence of food or shock, but difficult to learn that a conditioned stimulus predicts something neutral, such as a flower or a black square. Humans and other animals can learn to associate neutral events, and not all theories of reinforcement rely on ecologically significant events (Premack, 1959), but it is widely accepted that nature supplied us with "crib sheets" specifying the kinds of stimuli that are important to learn about. Moreover, important work with nonhuman species has established that learning about some ecologically relevant events, such as cues that predict predators or mate availability, can improve later reproductive success (see Krause & Domjan, 2017).

We can all agree that the capacity to remember is the product of an extended process of evolution, guided by natural selection. Organisms learn, remember, and forget because these processes are adaptive, ultimately improving reproductive fitness. It is conceivable that memory storage originally evolved in the service of another evolved process, such as perceptual processing, but the capacity of humans and other animals to retrieve and use prior experience in the absence of an originating stimulus is almost certainly a biological adaptation of some kind. As with any biological adaptation, then, its operating characteristics are likely to bear the imprint of the selection pressures that drove its evolution. To understand remembering properly, as a consequence, it is imperative to ask functional questions about its purpose and to seek out the adaptive problems that it is ultimately designed to solve. Functional questions have great heuristic value as well, often leading to hypothesis that may not be suggested by more traditional methods of understanding memory.

REFERENCES

Bell, R., Röer, J. P., & Buchner, A. (2013). Adaptive memory: The survival-processing memory advantage is not due to negativity or mortality salience. *Memory & Cognition*, 41(4), 490–502. https://doi.org/10.3758/s13421-012-0290-5

Bonin, P., Gelin, M., & Bugaiska, A. (2014). Animates are better remembered than inanimates: Further evidence from word and picture stimuli. *Memory & Cognition*, 42(3), 370–382. https://doi.org/10.3758/s13421-013-0368-8

Bonin, P., Gelin, M., Laroche, B., Méot, A., & Bugaiska, A. (2015). The "how" of animacy effects in episodic memory. *Experimental Psychology*, 62, 371–384. https://doi.org/10.1027/1618-3169/a000308

Bonin, P., Gelin, M., Laroche, B. et al. (2020). "Survival Processing of the Selfish Gene?": Adaptive memory and inclusive fitness. *Evolutionary Psychological Science*, 6, 155–165. https://doi.org/10.1007/s40806-019-00220-1

Bonin, P., Thiebaut, G., Witt, A., & Méot, A. (2019). Contamination is "good" for your memory! Further evidence for the adaptive view of memory. *Evolutionary Psychological Science*, 5, 300–316. https://doi.org/10.1007/s40806-019-00188-y

Buller, D. J. (2005). *Adapting minds: Evolutionary psychology and the persistent quest for human nature*. MIT Press.

Butler, A. C., Kang, S. H. K., & Roediger III, H. L. (2009). Congruity effects between materials and processing tasks in the survival processing paradigm. *Journal of Experimental Psychology: Learning, Memory, and Cognition, 35*, 1477–1486. https://doi.org/10.1037/a0017024

Chapman, H. A., Johannes, K., Poppenk, J. L., Moscovitch, M., & Anderson, A. K. (2013). Evidence for the differential salience of disgust and fear in episodic memory. *Journal of Experimental Psychology: General, 142*(4), 1100–1112. https://doi.org/10.1037/a0030503

Derringer, C. J., Scofield, J. E., & Kostic, B. (2017). Investigations of a reproductive processing advantage in memory. *Memory & Cognition, 45*(6), 983–1001. https://doi.org/10.3758/s13421-017-0709-0

Ebbinghaus, H. (1885/1964). *Memory: A contribution to experimental psychology.* Dover, (Originally published 1885; translated 1913.) https://doi.org/10.1037/10011-001

Erdfelder, E., & Kroneisen, M. (2014). Proximate cognitive mechanisms underlying the survival processing effect. In B. Schwartz, M. Howe, M. Toglia, & H. Otgaar (Eds.), *What is adaptive about adaptive memory?* (pp. 172–198). Oxford University Press. https://doi.org/10.1093/acprof:oso/9780199928057.003.0010

Fellner, M.-C., Bäuml, K.-H. T., & Hanslmayr, S. (2013). Brain oscillatory subsequent memory effects differ in power and long-range synchronization between semantic and survival. *NeuroImage, 79*, 361–370. https://doi.org/10.1016/j.neuroimage.2013.04.121

Fernandes, N. L., Pandeirada, J. N. S., Soares, S., & Nairne, J. S. (2017). Adaptive memory: The mnemonic value of contamination. *Evolution and Human Behavior, 38*, 451–460. https://doi.org/10.1016/j.evolhumbehav.2017.04.003

Fitzgerald, C. J., Horgan, T. G., & Himes, S. M. (2016). Shaping men's memory: The effects of a female's waist-to-hip ratio on men's memory for her appearance and biographical information. *Evolution and Human Behavior, 37*, 510–516. https://doi.org/10.1016/j.evolhumbehav.2016.05.004

Forester, G., Kroneisen, M., Erdferlder, E., & Kamp, S.-M. (2019). On the role of retrieval processes in the survival processing effect: Evidence from ROC and ERP analyses. *Neurobiology of Learning and Memory, 166*, 107083. https://doi.org/10.1016/j.nlm.2019.107083

Horgan, T. G., Broadbent, J., McKibbin, W. F., & Duehring, A. J. (2016). Show versus tell? The effects of mating context on women's memory for a man's physical features and verbal statements. *Journal of Social and Personal Relationships, 33*, 733–750. https://doi.org/10.1177/0265407515590279

Howe, M. L., & Derbish, M. H. (2010). On the susceptibility of adaptive memory to false memory illusions. *Cognition, 115*, 252–267. https://doi.org/10.1016/j.cognition.2009.12.016

Kazanas, S. A., & Altarriba, J. (2015). The survival advantage: Underlying mechanisms and extant limitations. *Evolutionary Psychology, 13*, 360–396. https://doi.org/10.1177%2F147470491501300204

Klein, S. B. (2013). Does optimal recall in the adaptive memory paradigm require the encoding context to encourage thoughts about the environment of evolutionary adaptation? *Memory & Cognition, 41*, 49–59. https://doi.org/10.3758/s13421-012-0239-8

Klein, S. B., Cosmides, L., Tooby, J., & Chance, S. (2002). Decisions and the evolution of memory: Multiple systems, multiple functions. *Psychological Review, 109*, 306–329.

Krause, M. A., & Domjan, M. (2017). Ethological and evolutionary perspectives on Pavlovian conditioning. In J. Call, G. M. Burghardt, I. M. Pepperberg, C. T. Snowdon, & T. Zentall (Eds.), *APA handbook of comparative psychology: Perception, learning, and cognition* (pp. 247–266). American Psychological Association. https://doi.org/10.1037/0000012-012

Krause, M. A., Trevino, S., Cripps, A., Chilton, K., Sower, E., & Taylor, J. P. (2019). Inclusive fitness does not impact the survival processing effect. *Animal Behavior and Cognition, 6*, 13–31. https://doi.org/10.26451/abc.06.01.02.2019

Kroneisen, M., & Bell, R. (2018). Remembering the place with the tiger: Survival processing can enhance source memory. *Psychonomic Bulletin & Review, 25*, 667–673. https://doi.org/10.3758/s13423-018-1431-z

Kroneisen, M., & Erdfelder, E. (2011). On the plasticity of the survival processing effect. *Journal of Experimental Psychology: Learning, Memory, and Cognition, 37*, 1553–1562. https://doi.org/10.1037/a0024493

Kroneisen, M., Rummel, J., & Erdfelder, E. (2014). Working memory load eliminates the survival processing effect. *Memory, 22*, 92–102. https://doi.org/10.1080/09658211.2013.815217

Laurino, J., & Kaczer, L. (2019). Animacy as a memory enhancer during novel word learning: evidence from orthographic and semantic memory tasks. *Memory, 27*, 820–828. https://doi.org/10.1080/09658211.2019.1572195

McBride, D. M., Thomas, B. J., & Zimmerman, C. (2013). A test of the survival processing advantage in implicit and explicit memory tests. *Memory and Cognition, 41*, 862–871. https://doi.org/10.3758/s13421-013-0304-y

Meinhardt, M. J., Bell, R., Buchner, S., & Röer, J. P. (2020). Adaptive memory: Is the animacy effect on memory due to richness of encoding? *Journal of Experimental Psychology: Learning, Memory, and Cognition, 46*, 416–426. https://doi.org/10.1037/xlm0000733

Misirlisoy, M., Tanyas, H., & Atalay, N. B. (2019). Does survival context enhance memory for source? A within-subjects comparison. *Memory, 27*, 780–791. https://doi.org/10.1080/09658211.2019.1566928

Nairne, J. S. (2005). The functionalist agenda in memory research. In A. F. Healy (Ed.), *Experimental cognitive psychology and its applications: Festschrift in honor of Lyle Bourne, Walter Kintsch, and Thomas Landauer* (pp. 115–126). American Psychological Association. https://doi.org/10.1037/10895-009

(2014). Adaptive memory: Controversies and future directions. In B. L. Schwartz, M. L. Howe, M. P. Toglia, & H. Otgaar (Eds.). *What is adaptive about adaptive memory?* (pp. 308–321). Oxford University Press. https://doi.org/10.1093/acprof:oso/9780199928057.001.0001

(2015). Adaptive memory: Novel findings acquired through forward engineering. In D. S. Lindsay, C. M. Kelley, A. P. Yonelinas, & Roediger, H. L., III (Eds.), *Remembering: Attributions, processes, and control in human memory: Papers in honor of Larry L. Jacoby* (pp. 3–14). Psychology Press. https://doi.org/10.4324/9781315752808

Nairne, J. S., Coverdale, M. E., & Pandeirada, J. N. S. (2019). Adaptive memory: The mnemonic power of survival-based generation. *Journal of Experimental Psychology: Learning, Memory, and Cognition, 45*, 1970–1982. https://doi.org/10.1037/xlm0000687

Nairne, J. S., & Pandeirada, J. N. S. (2008). Adaptive memory: Remembering with a stone-age brain. *Current Directions in Psychological Science, 17*, 239–243. https://doi.org/10.1111%2Fj.1467-8721.2008.00582.x

(2016). Adaptive memory: The evolutionary significance of survival processing. *Perspectives on Psychological Science, 11*, 496–511. https://doi.org/10.1177%2F1745691616635613

Nairne, J. S., Pandeirada, J. N. S., & Fernandes, N. L. (2017). Adaptive memory. In J. H. Byrne (Ed.), *Learning and memory: A comprehensive reference* (2nd ed., vol. 2) (pp. 279–293). Elsevier. https://doi.org/10.1016/B978-0-12-809324-5.21060-2

Nairne, J. S., Pandeirada, J. N. S., Gregory, K. J., & VanArsdall, J. E. (2009). Adaptive memory: Fitness-relevance and the hunter-gatherer mind. *Psychological Science, 20*, 740–746. https://doi.org/10.1111/j.1467-9280.2009.02356.x

Nairne, J. S., Pandeirada, J. N. S., & Thompson, S. R. (2008). Adaptive memory: The comparative value of survival processing. *Psychological Science, 19*, 176–180. https://doi.org/10.1111/j.1467-9280.2008.02064.x

Nairne, J. S., Thompson, S. R., & Pandeirada, J. N. S. (2007). Adaptive memory: Survival processing enhances retention. *Journal of Experimental Psychology: Learning, Memory, & Cognition, 33*, 263–273. https://doi.org/10.1037/0278-7393.33.2.263

Nairne, J. S., VanArsdall, J. E., & Cogdill, M. (2017). Remembering the living: Episodic memory is tuned to animacy. *Current Directions in Psychological Science, 26*, 22–27. https://doi.org/10.1177%2F0963721416667711

Nairne, J. S., VanArsdall, J. E., Pandeirada, J. N. S., & Blunt, J. R. (2012). Adaptive memory: Enhanced location memory after survival processing. *Journal of Experimental Psychology: Learning, Memory, and Cognition, 38*, 495–501. https://doi.org/10.1037/a0025728

Nairne, J. S., VanArsdall, J. E., Pandeirada, J. N. S., Cogdill, M., & LeBreton, J. M. (2013). Adaptive memory: The mnemonic value of animacy. *Psychological Science, 24,* 2099–2105. https://doi.org/10.1177/0956797613480803

Pandeirada, J. N. S., Fernandes, N. L., Vasconcelos, M., & Nairne, J. S. (2017). Adaptive memory: Remembering potential mates. *Evolutionary Psychology, 15,* 1–11. https://doi.org/10.1177%2F1474704917742807

Popp, E. Y., & Serra, M. J. (2016). Adaptive memory: Animacy enhances free recall but impairs cued recall. *Journal of Experimental Psychology: Learning, Memory, and Cognition, 42,* 186–201. https://doi.org/10.1037/e528942014-958

(2018). The animacy advantage for free-recall performance is not attributable to greater mental arousal. *Memory, 26,* 89–95. https://doi.org/10.1080/09658211.2017.1326507

Premack, D. (1959). Toward empirical behavior laws: 1. Positive reinforcement. *Psychological Review, 66,* 219–233. https://doi.org/10.1037/h0040891

Richardson, R. C. (2007). *Evolutionary psychology as maladapted psychology.* MIT Press. https://doi.org/10.7551/mitpress/7464.001.0001

Röer, J., Bell, R., & Buchner, A. (2013). Is the survival-processing memory advantage due to richness of encoding? *Journal of Experimental Psychology: Learning, Memory, and Cognition, 39,* 1294–1302. https://doi.org/10.1037/a0031214

Sandry, J., Trafimow, D., Marks, M. J., & Rice, S. (2013). Adaptive memory: Evaluating alternative forms of fitness-relevant processing in the survival processing paradigm. *PLoS ONE., 8*(4) E60868. https://doi.org/10.1371/journal.pone.0060868

Savine, A. C., Scullin, M. K., & Roediger H. L., III. (2011). Survival processing of faces. *Memory & Cognition, 39,* 1359–1373. https://doi.org/10.3758/s13421-011-0121-0

Schaller, M., & Park, J. H. (2011). The behavioral immune system (and why it matters). *Current Directions in Psychological Science, 20,* 99–103. https://doi.org/10.1177%2F0963721411402596

Schmitt, D. P., & Pilcher, J. J. (2004). Evaluating evidence of psychological adaptation: How do we know one when we see one? *Psychological Science, 15,* 642–649. https://doi.org/10.1111/j.0956-7976.2004.00734.x

Schwartz, B. L. (2019). Using natural ecology to predict higher cognition in human and non-human primates. *Animal Behavior and Cognition, 6,* 344–354. https://doi.org/10.26451/abc.06.04.13.2019

Scofield, J. E., Buchanan, E. M., & Kostic, B. (2017). A meta-analysis of the survival-processing advantage in memory. *Psychonomic Bulletin & Review, 25,* 997–1012. https://doi.org/10.3758/s13423-017-1346-0

Seamon, J. G., Bohn, J. M., Coddington, I. E., Ebling, M. C., Grund, E. M., Haring, C. T., Jang, S.-J., Kim, D., Liong, C., Paley, F. M., Pang, L. K., & Siddique, A. H. (2012). Can survival processing enhance story memory? Testing the generalizability of the adaptive memory framework. *Journal of Experimental Psychology: Learning, Memory, and Cognition, 38,* 1045–1056. https://doi.org/10.1037/a0027090

Seitz, B. M., Blaisdell, B. M., Polack, C. P., & Miller, R. R. (2019). The role of biological significance in human learning and memory. *International Journal of Comparative Psychology, 32.* Retrieved from https://escholarship.org/uc/item/67k6ron9

Seitz, B. M., Polack, C. P., & Miller, R. R. (2018). Adaptive memory: Is there a reproduction-processing effect? *Journal of Experimental Psychology: Learning, Memory, and Cognition, 44,* 1167–1179. https://doi.org/10.1037%2Fxlm0000513

(2020). Adaptive memory: Generality of the parent processing effect and effects of biological relatedness on recall. *Evolutionary Psychological Science, 6,* 246–260. (https://doi.org/10.1007/s40806-020-00233-1

Sherry, D. F., & Schacter, D. L. (1987). The evolution of multiple memory systems. *Psychological Review, 94,* 439–454. https://doi.org/10.1037/0033-295X.94.4.439

Shettleworth, S. J. (2010). *Cognition, evolution, and behavior* (2nd ed.). Oxford University Press.

Slamecka, N. J. (1985). Ebbinghaus: Some associations. *Journal of Experimental Psychology: Learning, Memory, & Cognition, 11,* 414–435. https://doi.org/10.1037/0278-7393.11.3.414

Smith, D. S., Jones, B. C., Feinberg, D. R., & Allan, K. (2012). A modulatory effect of male voice pitch on long-term memory in women: Evidence of adaptation for mate choice? *Memory and Cognition, 40,* 135–144. https://doi.org/10.3758/s13421-011-0136-6

Stillman, C. M., Coane, J. H., Profaci, C. P., Howard, J. H., & Howard, D. V. (2014). The effects of healthy aging on the mnemonic benefit of survival processing. *Memory & Cognition, 42,* 175–185. https://doi.org/10.3758/s13421-013-0353-2 https://doi.org/10.3758/s13421-013-0353-2

Tinbergen, N. (1963) On the methods and aims of ethology. *Ethology, 20,* 410–433. https://doi.org/10.1111/j.1439-0310.1963.tb01161.x

Tse, C.-S., & Altarriba, J. (2010). Does survival processing enhance implicit memory? *Memory and Cognition, 38,* 1110–1121. https://doi.org/10.3758/MC.38.8.1110

Tybur, J. M., Lieberman, D., Kurzban, R., & DiScioli, P. (2013). Disgust: Evolved function and structure. *Psychological Review, 120,* 65–84. https://doi.org./10.1037/a0030778

VanArsdall, J. E. (2016). Exploring animacy as a mnemonic dimension. *Open Access Dissertations.* https://docs.lib.purdue.edu/open_access_dissertations/873

Van Buren, B., & Scholl, B. J. (2017). Minds in motion in memory: Enhanced spatial memory driven by the perceived animacy of simple shapes. *Cognition, 163,* 87–92. https://doi.org/10.1016/j.cognition.2017.02.006

Williams, G. C. (1966). *Adaptation and natural selection: A critique of some current evolutionary thought.* Princeton University Press. https://doi.org/10.1515/9780691185507

Zhang, J., Li, X., & Guo, C. (2020). The neurocognitive features in survival processing: An ERP study. *International Journal of Psychophysiology, 149,* 35–47. https://doi.org/10.1016/j.ijpsycho.2019.10.012

24

REMEMBERING CHEATERS

The Influence of Social Relevance on Source Memory

Meike Kroneisen

When we think about the evolutionary history of humankind, it seems unlikely that humans were directly selected to process, store, or learn abstract information. It seems more likely that our memory systems evolved to prepare us for future events (Klein, 2013; Nairne & Pandeirada, 2016; see Nairne and Coverdale, Chapter 23). Nevertheless, most memory researchers focus on questions of *how* we remember. Specific memory effects are explained by assuming a set of general principles or processes which underlie human thought and behavior. These general principles should hold regardless of the type of material used in this kind of studies. For example, when analyzing factors influencing storage and retrieval, researchers often study people's performance on highly artificial tasks, such as learning word pairs. However, this approach toward understanding the human mind has been criticized by evolutionary psychologists. What if our cognitive processes have been shaped by natural selection? What if the functional properties of memory mirror selection pressures from our ancestral past? If memory indeed evolved, shaped by the process of natural selection, then its structural properties should reflect their functionality (Tooby & Cosmides, 1992). Selection pressures, which are essentially adaptive problems that have to be solved, constrain how and why a structure develops, and also the form it takes. Based on these ideas, one core assumption of evolutionary psychology is that the human mind consists of a large number of highly specialized cognitive mechanisms, also called modules (Tooby & Cosmides, 1992, 2005). An evolved module is a particular set of techniques within the organism specially designed to process a particular piece of information and transform that information into an output that helps to solve an adaptive problem that arose during our ancestral past.

However, what are the adaptive problems human episodic memory was designed to solve? Nairne et al. (2007; see Nairne and Coverdale, Chapter 23) discovered that evaluating the survival relevance of verbal material leads to exceptionally good memory for this material. This finding, called the survival processing effect, has led to a discussion about the ultimate function of human episodic memory (Erdfelder & Kroneisen, 2014). The survival processing effect suggests that episodic memory evolved to enable encoding, storage, and retrieval of fitness-relevant information in general and survival-relevant information in particular. Are other cognitive processes likewise fine-tuned to meet evolutionarily relevant challenges? In this chapter, literature concerning another aspect of the adaptive memory question is reviewed in more detail. More precisely, this chapter attempts to answer the question of whether we have better memory for information relevant for social exchange in comparison to irrelevant information.

24.1 ENHANCED MEMORY FOR CHEATERS?

According to Dunbar (2003), selection pressures exerted by living in complexly bonded social groups have been important factors in human evolution. Therefore, evolutionary psychologists have proposed that humans possess cognitive modules for social exchange like speech, face processing, and cooperation (Barclay, 2008; Bell & Buchner, 2012). Specifically, social contract theory (Cosmides, 1989; Tooby & Cosmides, 1992, 2005) postulates cognitive modules specialized in the detection of cheaters. If a situation involves some kind of social contract, then a cheater detection algorithm is activated. This algorithm can quickly and easily draw inferences about whether someone has cheated in prior exchanges or is about to cheat in future interactions. Therefore, with the help of this module, social cooperation is possible.

At first, cooperation among unrelated individuals seems puzzling from an evolutionary standpoint. Obviously, individuals can increase their fitness by cooperating with each other (Axelrod & Hamilton, 1981; Trivers, 1971). However, social cooperation usually implies some kind of fitness costs for the acting individual and is therefore risky (Trivers, 1971). One solution to this problem is the concept of reciprocity, which suggests that cooperation between unrelated individuals should occur only when there is the possibility that the favor of the helping individual is returned later on (Axelrod, 1984; Axelrod & Hamilton, 1981; Trivers, 1971). However, reciprocity can be a stable behavior only when cooperators have the ability to recognize and remember who has been cooperative and who has not (Barclay, 2008; Trivers, 1971). Otherwise, cheaters could infiltrate groups and exploit cooperators. In line with these ideas, it has been shown that cooperation is not stable when there is no possibility to identify or punish cheaters (Fehr & Gächter, 2000; Janssen, 2008). As mentioned above, Tooby and Cosmides (1992, 2005) concluded that humans are equipped with a cheater detection module that helps with the successful detection and memorizing of cheaters. In line with this, Mealey et al. (1996) showed that old–new recognition for faces differed depending on whether the people were described as cheaters, as trustworthy, or as neutral on these two dimensions.

For faces associated with low-status professions, old–new discrimination was better for faces of cheaters than for faces of people described as trustworthy. This effect was not found for faces associated with high-status professions. Nevertheless, these results were interpreted in favor of the social contract theory (e.g., Buss, 2004; Mealey et al., 1996). Moreover, other studies have been unable to replicate these findings (Barclay & Lalumière, 2006; Mehl & Buchner, 2008). However, the question arises if this is really a problem for social contract theory. Indeed, recognizing a face as old (item memory) is not enough for a successful reciprocal social exchange. If I want to avoid being exploited by cheaters, I should not only remember the face, I should remember that a face was associated with a history of cheating (source memory; Buchner et al., 2009).

How can one test this? Social cooperation depends fundamentally on expectations about other people's behaviors (Mieth et al., 2016). It is possible to form expectations of opponents by (a) third-hand information (description paradigm) or (b) first-hand impressions (involvement paradigm). Both ways were used to test if individuals have better source memory for cheaters. Forming third-hand expectations is usually done by presenting participants with pictures of faces paired with short statements describing the pictured persons as cheaters, cooperative, or neutral (see Table 24.1 for example descriptions). Subsequently, in a surprise source memory test, old and new faces are presented together and participants have to indicate which faces they recognized from the initial learning phase. If they categorize a face as old, they have to remember the behavior that was used in the description accompanying that face in the learning phase. Thus, this procedure is often referred to as description paradigm. First-hand impressions as another method to form expectations can be built using an involvement paradigm in which participants interact directly with their opponents. Bell et al. (2010) let their participants play a trust game during the encoding phase. In the trust game, participants saw a picture of their opponent on the screen. They first had to decide whether they wanted to invest 15, 30, 45, or 60 cents. After they

TABLE 24.1. *Example behavior descriptions from Buchner et al. (2009)*

Condition	Description
Cheater	K. S. is a secondhand-car dealer. Regularly, he sells restored crash cars as supposedly accident-free and conceals serious defects from the customers.
Cooperator	N. G. is a mechanic. He is always eager to provide spare parts as cheap as possible for his clients and to fulfill his jobs efficiently.
Neutral/ Irrelevant	J. L. is a gardener. He is extremely interested in orchids and owns a collection of some very rare and expensive exemplars.

decided this, the opponent's investment was shown to them. A cooperator always invested the same amount of money as the participant. A cheater invested much less than the participant. After the decisions, a profit was added and the total sum was split up between the participant and the opponent. Therefore, the participant would gain money when the opponent was cooperative but would lose money when the opponent was a cheater. When the opponent was a neutral person, the participant got back exactly what they had invested (without any profit). Again, the encoding phase was followed by a surprise source memory test. This method is often referred to as an involvement paradigm.

Consistent with social contract theory, a source memory advantage for cheaters in comparison to cooperators and neutral people can be found for both designs: the description paradigm (e.g., Bell & Buchner, 2009, 2010; Buchner et al., 2009; Kroneisen, 2018) and the involvement paradigm (e.g., Bell et al., 2010, 2012b). Figure 24.1 shows the typical pattern of data that emerged in these kinds of experiments: A clear source memory advantage for cheaters can be seen.

These results could be taken as evidence for the existence of a highly specific cognitive module to detect and remember only cheaters (but see Bell et al., 2010, 2016; Schaper et al., 2019, for different results). Several evolutionary psychologists have argued that proper evolutionary theories must focus on such domain-specific proximate explanations, mainly because more general mechanisms serving several adaptive goals simultaneously are unlikely to evolve (e.g., Buss, 2004; Tooby & Cosmides, 1992, 2005). However, not everyone shares this view. Alternative perspectives deny the idea of domain-specific proximate explanations (e.g., Buller, 2005a, 2005b; Over, 2003). There are reasons to expect more general cognitive systems, rather

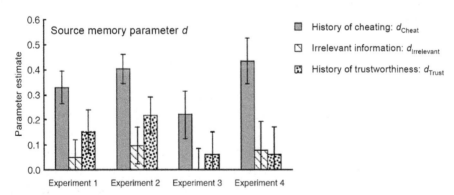

FIGURE 24.1. Source memory as a function of the context in which the face was encountered (cheater, neutral, cooperator) across four experiments.
Figure adapted from "No enhanced recognition memory, but better source memory for faces of cheaters." by Buchner, A., Bell, R., Mehl, B., and Musch, J. (2009). *Evolution and Human Behavior, 30*, 217. Adapted with permission of the publisher.

than systems that focus specifically on only one problem (see Blaisdell and Seitz, Chapter 26). Buller (2005c) explained this perspective nicely:

> Evolutionary psychologists argue that distinct adaptive problems throughout our evolutionary history would have required distinct solutions, and they conclude that these distinct solutions must be distinct cognitive mechanisms. But all that follows is that distinct adaptive problems would have required distinct *behavioral solutions*, not that they would have required distinct modules. Indeed, domain-general cognitive mechanisms could operate on domain-specific inputs, and make use of information "specific to" those inputs, in order to generate domain-specific behavioral solutions to the problems they encounter. The need for behavioral solutions specific to adaptive problems in our evolutionary history wouldn't have necessarily selected for modules.
>
> (p. 884)

Therefore, it could be argued that the assumption of an existing cheater avoidance module can be made only when its cheater specificity finds empirical evidence (Bell & Buchner, 2012). However, if this source memory advantage generalizes to a wider set of variables and can therefore be explained with more general tendencies, such an explanation would be disconfirmed.

The following sections will focus on the question of whether there is a specific cheater-avoidance module or if the source memory advantage can be attributed to more general cognitive systems such as the "influence of emotion on memory" or "expectancy violation."

24.2 THE INFLUENCE OF EMOTION ON MEMORY

Negative information is more readily attended to than neutral and positive information, at least for young adults (e.g., Buchner et al., 2004, 2006). Furthermore, emotion, especially negative emotion, can enhance information processing (for a review, see Baumeister et al., 2001). There are many studies showing that memory is better for emotional information compared to neutral information (e.g., D'Argembeau & Van der Linden, 2004; Doerksen & Shimamura, 2001; Kensinger & Corkin, 2003). Bell and Buchner (2010) made the assumption that cheating behavior elicits negative emotions, which in turn stimulate attentional resources and, therefore, the encoding and retrieval of information. This leads to the hypothesis that the source-memory advantage for cheaters can be attributed to negativity rather than to a domain-specific module. Indeed, Bell and Buchner (2010) demonstrated that the source-memory advantage generalizes to threatening information that is irrelevant for social exchange: disgusting information (e.g., "J.F. is a shop assistant. He never has a handkerchief, so he always wipes his nose with his shirt sleeve, which is already stained and sticky."). Moreover, when comparing memory for cheating and disgusting contexts directly, no difference could be found (Bell et al., 2012c). In line with this, Bell and Buchner (2011) showed that the source memory advantage for cheaters abolishes when the cheating was of low – and the trustworthy behavior was of high – valence and arousal. Here, both types of behavior elicited similarly strong emotional reactions toward the stimulus face. Kroneisen et al. (2015) demonstrated that the effect can also be found for other negative but social-exchange-relevant behavior, like aggressive information (e.g., "Q.P. is a fanatical soccer fan. He often meets his friends to provoke a fight with other soccer fans.").

However, is the conclusion that source memory is generally enhanced for negative information supported by other evidence? This seems not to be the case. Bell and Buchner (2011), for example, found no source memory advantage for victims ("e.g., T.M. is a glazier. He gave a friend a large sum of money to invest it, but he gambled it away.") in comparison to perpetrators ("e.g., T.M. is a glazier. A friend gave him a large sum of money to invest it, but he gambled it away.") despite the fact that the behavior descriptions were equal in negativity and arousal. In line with that, Bell et al. (2012c) found better memory for persons associated with aggressive behavior toward others in comparison to persons associated with self-directed aggressive behavior (also despite the fact that both behaviors were comparable in negativity and arousal). Furthermore, Bell et al. (2014) showed that personal benefits or costs influence memory for cheaters. More precisely, their participants remembered faces showing immoral behavior well when they were associated with personal costs (e.g., "He lied to you to sell you the useless products of another person.") but poorly when associated with personal benefits (e.g., "He lied to another person to sell that person your useless products."). Interestingly, no difference in memory depending on personal benefits or costs for faces associated with moral behavior could be detected. It seems to be that motivational factors also influence source memory. Based on this, Kroneisen (2018) demonstrated that personal relevance as a motivational factor influences memory for cheaters. She tested the hypothesis that behavior of others with immediate relevance to ourselves influences one's memory of these persons. Indeed, there was better source memory for faces of cheaters associated with a high relevance for a student population (e.g., "P.L. sneaks into student parties and pours knockout drops into the drinks of other party guests.") in comparison to faces of cheaters associated with a low relevance for a student population (e.g., "P.O. fulfills his military service. Because he has free access to the armory, he steals ammunition and sells it on the black market."). For faces associated with trustworthy behavior, no difference in memory depending on high or low relevance could be found.

All these findings suggest that it is not negativity per se that enhances source memory. Apparently, the information has to be associated with a social component (i.e., negative or threatening consequences for oneself). However, there is no general source memory advantage for behaviors implying a norm violation. This indicates that motivational factors also influence source memory.

To summarize, evolutionary theories focus on cognitive modules designed to react to specific information like cheater avoidance. The empirical evidence discussed above suggest a more general cognitive system. Nonetheless, there is still the possibility that human information processing is characterized by a general tendency to prioritize the processing of threatening social information, even when this is mediated by motivational factors. However, a fixation on the mere negative aspects of a situation can be seen as maladaptive. A general negativity bias would not allow a person to adapt to the demands of a changing situation (Rothermund, 2011). Furthermore, a fixation on only negative aspects would mean being trapped in a negative motivational-emotional state (Rothermund et al., 2008; Wentura et al., 2009). This could lead to a general withdrawal from any social interaction because the individual would only focus on the dangers (Bell et al., 2012a). Therefore, it seems reasonable to predict mechanisms that ensure that social cooperation is maintained, even after negative social experiences.

24.3 EXPECTANCY VIOLATION: THE INCONGRUITY HYPOTHESIS

A flexible organism should be able to react to a given situation. When confronted with a situation in which cooperation is the rule and cheating is the exception, it seems reasonable to remember the smaller population group, that is, the cheaters. Conversely, in a situation in which cooperating is the exception and cheating the rule, the best strategy would be to restrict cooperation to the few cooperators and to avoid social exchange with everyone else. In such a situation, finding cooperators is extremely valuable. It would be very important to remember other cooperators instead of cheaters (Aktipis, 2006; Barclay, 2008; Bell et al., 2012a; Volstorf et al., 2011). Such a system could be more powerful than a system that always focuses on cheaters because it would demand fewer cognitive resources (Barclay, 2008). By focusing on expectancy violations, it is possible to remember only the exception, independent of the character of a person. Overall, a general and flexible expectation-incongruity mechanism can be seen as an efficient strategy. Furthermore, remembering unexpected information is important because this type of information characterizes situations in which the currently dominant behavior pattern (approach or avoidance) is maladaptive. By remembering the incongruent behavior of an opponent, one's own behavior strategies can be adjusted and wrong decisions can be avoided. In contrast, remembering expected information is less important. Here, existing mental models can lead social decisions.

Recent studies are in line with this argument. People seem to focus on information that violates their positive or negative expectations. Barclay (2008), Bell et al. (2010), and Volstorf et al. (2011) were able to demonstrate this kind of incongruity detection. All studies showed that rarity of behavior strategies within an experiment modulated memory. When playing cooperation games in which most opponents acted cooperatively, cheaters were remembered best. However, when the majority of the interaction partners cheated, the memory pattern was reversed. Cook et al. (2003) discovered an impact of social expectancies on memory. Their participants were better at assigning valenced statements to a source (Geoff vs. Mark) when these statements were incongruent with the description of the person (college professor, enjoyed drinking wine with friends, etc., vs. blue-collar employee, enjoyed drinking beer at a bar, etc.). Similarly, Ehrenberg and Klauer (2005) showed that stereotype-inconsistent information influences source memory. However, this effect was only discovered when the retrieval was delayed and an additional cognitive load task had to be accomplished during encoding. These findings could be extended to memory for social exchange partners. Suzuki and Suga (2010) found a source memory advantage for faces of trustworthy looking cheaters. This effect was replicated by Bell et al. (2012a) in a description paradigm. Furthermore, Bell et al. (2012b) demonstrated a source memory advantage for likeable cheaters as well as unlikeable cooperators, and a source memory advantage for smiling cheaters in an involvement paradigm. The assumption that source memory for social exchange partners could be generally enhanced by emotional incongruent information is further supported by Kroneisen and Bell (2013). They found a source memory advantage for women described as cheaters or disgusting persons in comparison to cheating or disgusting men. They explained these findings in terms of a stereotype effect: Cheating and disgusting behaviors in women are seen as uncommon in our everyday life and are therefore unexpected. However, no source memory advantage for trustworthy men could be found. Kroneisen et al. (2015) tried to manipulate expectancies more directly. They compared two different groups. Group 1 had to accomplish the typical description paradigm in which participants were confronted with faces combined with aggressive, prosocial, and neutral behavior descriptions. No additional information was given. In contrast, Group 2 was told that they would see persons described as very aggressive and unsocial. However, in the later learning phase, both groups saw exactly the same information. Results showed a source memory advantage for aggressive persons in Group 1, but comparable source memory for aggressive and prosocial persons in Group 2. Again, these effects were interpreted in terms of expectancies: People have a general person positivity bias (Sears, 1983), which usually leads to positive expectations toward others. In general, people do not expect others to behave aggressively, therefore, a source memory advantage for Group 1 was found.

However, when expectations were explicitly manipulated, source memory for persons showing prosocial behavior increased. Interestingly, memory for aggressive persons was still very high.

These results lead to another important point: Is the weighting of positive and negative expectancy violation symmetrical or asymmetrical? Although source memory was superior for both positive and negative incongruent information in most experiments (Barclay, 2008; Bell et al., 2010; Volstorf et al., 2011), results from other experiments were consistent with the assumption that the weighting of expectancy violations is asymmetrical (Bell et al., 2012b; Kroneisen & Bell, 2013; Kroneisen et al., 2015; Mieth et al., 2016; Suzuki & Suga, 2010). Furthermore, while Bell et al. (2010) showed that rarity could modulate source memory, they only found a memory advantage when the differences between the base rates for cooperators and cheaters were extreme. They could demonstrate an effect of rarity when there were either 80% cooperators or 80% cheaters in a sample. However, they did not find an effect of rarity when there were 60% cooperators or cheaters in a sample. Overall, positive information that violates negative expectations is remembered less than negative information that violates positive expectations. Thus, this asymmetrical weighting of positive and negative expectancy violations should be integrated in the assumed underlying mechanism.

Interestingly, Mieth et al. (2016) demonstrated that cognitive load has no influence on the expectancy-violation effect. In their experiments, trustworthy-looking cheaters were remembered best, regardless of whether a secondary task had to be accomplished during encoding. They concluded that remembering reputational information has to be an automatic process and used the schema-copy-plus-tag model to explain their results. According to this model, unexpected (i.e., schema-atypical) information is encoded in the form of unelaborated tags. This form of encoding does not need many processing resources and should therefore be unaffected by cognitive load (Graesser & Nakamura, 1982, Mieth et al., 2016). However, this also means that the remembered information about cheaters is not very specific, but should instead be a very rough classification. This is indeed in line with a finding from Bell et al. (2012a). The authors showed that the source memory advantage for cheaters was not always accompanied by recollection of specific details. More precisely, their participants could roughly remember if a face was associated with general cheating behavior but they could not remember details about the behavior description.

How general is the effect of expectancy violation? Bell et al. (2015) tried to answer this question. More precisely, they wanted to know if this is an effect limited to information relevant for social exchange. Furthermore, they also wanted to answer the question if this effect is especially pronounced for emotional information (to trigger approach or avoidance tendencies). The authors tried to answer these questions in four experiments. In Experiments

1 and 2, they combined a priori pleasant- and disgusting-looking faces with pleasant and disgusting behavior descriptions to test if the source memory advantage generalizes beyond social-exchange relevant information. Results showed that behaviors that violated expectations were remembered better than behaviors that confirmed expectations. In Experiment 3, a priori intelligent- and unintelligent-looking faces were combined with intelligent and unintelligent behavioral descriptions. Again, a strong source memory advantage for behavior that violated appearance-based expectations could be detected. This shows that the effect generalizes to information not relevant for approach and avoidance tendencies. Finally, in Experiment 4, faces were a priori categorized as "typical farmer" or "typical lawyer" faces and combined with farmer or lawyer behavioral descriptions. In line with the other experiments, source memory was enhanced for behavior contrary to appearance-based expectations. Therefore, it can be concluded that the source memory benefit for incongruent information can be generalized beyond exchange-relevant and emotional information. However, it has to be noted that the experiments from Bell et al. (2015) still manipulated social expectations. The question remains if the mechanisms determining memory performance also hold for information not related to a social area.

The research discussed is again inconsistent with the notion that memory is biased toward remembering only cheaters. In contrast, a more general mechanism that is sensitive to incongruent social information seems like an efficient way to optimize fast information processing in a changing environment.

24.4 SOURCE MEMORY AND DECISION-MAKING

One critical assumption behind the adaptive memory discussion is the idea that memory helps us to survive by informing our decisions in the present and in the future. Two questions arise here: First, how persistent is this source memory advantage for social information? Second, can we find confirmation of adaptive decision-making based on this source memory advantage? Buchner et al. (2009) addressed the first question: They found a stable memory advantage for cheaters even after one week between learning and testing. Interestingly, Suzuki et al. (2013) showed that the memory of bad lenders persisted even after verbal extinction compared to the memory of good lenders. Murty et al. (2016) addressed the second question. Indeed, they showed that source memory performance is linked to adaptive decision-making. Besides having better memory for opponents making less fair offers in a Dictator game, participants were more likely to reengage with old opponents in a later decision task if these opponents made more favorable offers during the preceding Dictator game. These results were confirmed by Schaper et al. (2019), who found evidence that the willingness of their participants to cooperate in a Prisoner's Dilemma game was determined by the behavior of opponents in previous rounds.

24.5 CONCLUSION

Cooperation among individuals is often seen as puzzling from an evolutionary standpoint. Persons invest time and/or other resources but they are always in danger of being exploited by cheaters. Hence, cooperation can be a stable behavior only when it is reciprocal (Trivers, 1971). According to Barclay (2008), this requires specific cognitive abilities, like remembering who showed cooperative behavior and who did not. In line with this argument, a number of experiments found enhanced source memory for cheaters. At first, these findings were interpreted in terms of the existence of a highly specialized cheater detection and avoidance algorithm. However, such a strong hypothesis cannot be accepted unless it can be shown that this effect can be found only for negative behaviors in social exchange situations. The research discussed in this chapter leads to the conclusion that general memory mechanisms are more suited to explain the current findings. Thus, if we want to speculate about the evolutionary selection pressures that may have influenced our human memory systems, it seems more appropriate to hypothesize that these selection pressures led to mechanisms that generally allow humans to efficiently use their limited memory resources. Remembering, for example, especially incongruent information may represent a simple and efficient way to optimize information processing during a social exchange situation. Overall, this could help in finding a balance between scarce cognitive resources and optimal behavior.

REFERENCES

Aktipis, C. A. (2006). Recognition memory and the evolution of cooperation: How simple strategies succeed in an agent-based world. *Adaptive Behavior, 14,* 239–247. https://doi .org/10.1177/105971230601400301

Axelrod, R. (1984). *The evolution of cooperation.* Basic Books.

Axelrod, R., & Hamilton, W. (1981). The evolution of cooperation. *Science, 211,* 1390–1396. https://doi.org/10.1126/science.7466396

Barclay, P. (2008). Enhanced recognition of defectors depends on their rarity. *Cognition, 107,* 817–828. https://doi.org/10.1016/j.cognition.2007.11.013

Barclay, P., & Lalumière, M. L. (2006). Do people differentially remember cheaters? *Human Nature, 17,* 98–113. https://doi.org/10.1007/s12110-006-1022-y

Baumeister, R. F., Bratslavsky, E., Finkenauer, C., & Vohs, K. D. (2001). Bad is stronger than good. *Review of General Psychology, 5,* 323–370. https://doi.org/10.1037/1089-2680.5.4 .323

Bell, R., & Buchner, A. (2009). Enhanced source memory for names of cheaters. *Evolutionary Psychology, 7,* 317–330. https://doi.org/10.1177/147470490900700213

(2010). Valence modulates source memory for faces. *Memory & Cognition, 38,* 29–41. https://doi.org/10.3758/MC.38.1.29

(2011). Source memory for faces is determined by their emotional evaluation. *Emotion, 11*, 249–261. https://doi.org/10.1037/a0022597

(2012). How adaptive is memory for cheaters? *Current Directions in Psychological Science, 21*, 403–408. https://doi.org/10.1177/0963721412458525

Bell, R., Buchner, A., Erdfelder, E., Giang, T., Schain, C., & Riether, N. (2012a). How specific is source memory for faces of cheaters? Evidence for categorical emotional tagging. *Journal of Experimental Psychology: Learning, Memory, and Cognition, 38*, 457–472. https://doi.org/10.1037/a0026017

Bell, R., Buchner, A., Kroneisen, M., & Giang, T. (2012b). On the flexibility of social source memory: A test of the emotional incongruity hypothesis. *Journal of Experimental Psychology: Learning, Memory, & Cognition, 38*, 1512–1529. https://doi.org/10.1037/a0028219

Bell, R., Buchner, A., & Musch, J. (2010). Enhanced old-new recognition and source memory for faces of cooperators and defectors in a social-dilemma game. *Cognition, 117*, 261–275. https://doi.org/10.1016/j.cognition.2010.08.020

Bell, R., Giang, T., & Buchner, A. (2012c). Partial and specific source memory for faces associated to other- and self-relevant negative contexts. *Cognition and Emotion, 26*, 1036–1055. https://doi.org/10.1080/02699931.2011.633988

Bell, R., Mieth, L., & Buchner, A. (2015). Appearance-based first impressions and person memory. *Journal of Experimental Psychology: Learning, Memory, & Cognition, 41*, 456–472. https://doi.org/10.1037/xlm0000034

Bell, R., Sasse, J., Möller, M., Czernochowski, D., Mayr, S., & Buchner, A. (2016). Event-related potentials in response to cheating and cooperation in a social dilemma game. *Psychophysiology, 53*, 216–228. https://dx.doi.org/10.1111/psyp.12561

Bell, R., Schain, C., & Echterhoff, G. (2014). How selfish is memory for cheaters? Evidence for moral and egoistic biases. *Cognition, 132*, 437–442. https://doi.org/10.1016/j.cognition.2014.05.001

Buchner, A., Bell, R., Mehl, B., & Musch, J. (2009). No enhanced recognition memory, but better source memory for faces of cheaters. *Evolution and Human Behavior, 30*, 212–224. https://doi.org/10.1016/j.evolhumbehav.2009.01.004

Buchner, A., Mehl, B., Rothermund, K., & Wentura, D. (2006). Artificially induced valence of distractor words increases the effects of irrelevant speech on serial recall. *Memory & Cognition, 34*, 1055–1062. https://doi.org/10.3758/BF03193252

Buchner, A., Rothermund, K., Wentura, D., & Mehl, B. (2004). Valence of distractor words increases the effects of irrelevant speech on serial recall. *Memory & Cognition, 32*, 722–731. https://doi.org/10.3758/BF03195862

Buller, D. J. (2005a). *Adapting minds: Evolutionary psychology and the persistent quest for human nature*. MIT Press.

(2005b). Evolutionary psychology: The emperor's new paradigm. *Trends in Cognitive Sciences, 9*, 277–283. https://doi.org/10.1016/j.tics.2005.04.003

(2005c). Get over: Massive modularity. *Biology and Philosophy, 20*, 881–891.

Buss, D. M. (2004). *Evolutionary psychology: The new science of the mind*. Allyn & Bacon.

Cook, G. I., Marsh, R. L., & Hicks, J. L. (2003). Halo and devil effects demonstrate valenced-based influences on source-monitoring decisions. *Consciousness and Cognition: An International Journal, 12*, 257–278. https://doi.org/10.1016/S1053-8100(02)00073-9

Cosmides, L. (1989). The logic of social exchange: Has natural selection shaped how humans reason? Studies with the Wason selection task. *Cognition, 31*, 187–276. https://doi.org/10.1016/0010-0277(89)90023-1

D'Argembeau, A., & Van der Linden, M. (2004). Influence of affective meaning on memory for contextual information. *Emotion, 4*, 173–188. https://doi.org/10.1037/1528-3542.4.2.173

Doerksen, S., & Shimamura, A. P. (2001). Source memory enhancement for emotional words. *Emotion, 1*, 5–11. https://doi.org/10.1037/1528-3542.1.1.5

Dunbar, R. I. M. (2003). The social brain: Mind, language, and society in evolutionary perspective. *Annual Review of Anthropology, 32*, 163–181. https://doi.org/10.1146/annurev.anthro.32.061002.093158

Ehrenberg, K., & Klauer, K. C. (2005). Flexible use of source information: Processing components of the inconsistency effect in person memory. *Journal of Experimental Social Psychology, 41*, 369–387. https://doi.org/10.1016/j.jesp.2004.08.001

Erdfelder, E., & Kroneisen, M. (2014). Proximate cognitive mechanisms underlying the survival processing effect. In B. L. Schwartz, M. Howe, M. Toglia, & H. Otgaar (Eds.), *What is adaptive about adaptive memory?* (pp. 172–198). Oxford University Press.

Fehr, E., & Gächter, S. (2000). Cooperation and punishment in public goods experiments. *American Economic Review, 90*, 980–994. https://doi.org/10.1257/aer.90.4.980

Graesser, A. C., & Nakamura, G. V. (1982). The impact of a schema on comprehension and memory. In G. H. Bower (Ed.), *The psychology of learning and motivation* (vol. 16, pp. 59–109). Academic Press.

Janssen, M. A. (2008). Evolution of cooperation in a one-shot prisoner's dilemma based on recognition of trustworthy and untrustworthy agents. *Journal of Economic Behavior & Organization, 65*, 458–471. https://doi.org/10.1016/j.jebo.2006.02.004

Kensinger, E. A., & Corkin, S. (2003). Memory enhancement for emotional words: Are emotional words more vividly remembered than neutral words? *Memory & Cognition, 31*, 1169–1180. https://doi.org/10.3758/BF03195800

Klein, S. B. (2013). The temporal orientation of memory: It's time for a change of direction. *Journal of Applied Research in Memory and Cognition, 2*, 222–234. https://doi.org/10.1016/j.jarmac.2013.08.001

Kroneisen, M. (2018). Is he important to me? Source memory advantage for personally relevant cheaters. *Psychonomic Bulletin & Review, 25*, 1129–1137. https://doi.org/10.3758/s13423-017-1345-1

Kroneisen, M., & Bell, R. (2013). Sex, cheating, and disgust: Enhanced source memory for trait information that violates gender stereotypes. *Memory, 21*, 167–181. https://doi.org/10.1080/09658211.2012.713971

Kroneisen, M., Woehe, L., & Rausch, L. S. (2015). Expectancy effects in source memory: How moving to a bad neighborhood can change your memory. *Psychonomic Bulletin & Review, 22*, 179–189. https://doi.org/10.3758/s13423-014-0655-9

Mealey, L., Daood, C., & Krage, M. (1996). Enhanced memory for faces of cheaters. *Ethology & Sociobiology, 17*, 119–128. https://doi.org/10.1016/0162-3095(95)00131-X

Mehl, B., & Buchner, A. (2008). No enhanced memory for faces of cheaters. *Evolution and Human Behavior, 29*, 35–41. https://doi.org/10.1016/j.evolhumbehav.2007.08.001

Mieth, L., Bell, R., & Buchner, A. (2016). Cognitive load does not affect the behavioral and cognitive foundations of social cooperation. *Frontiers in Psychology, 7*, 1312. https://doi.org/10.3389/fpsyg.201601312

Murty, V. P., FeldmanHall, O., Hunter, L. E., Phelps, E. A., & Davachi, L. (2016). Episodic memories predict adaptive value-based decision-making. *Journal of Experimental Psychology: General, 145*, 548–558. https://doi.org/10.1037/xge0000158

Nairne, J. S., & Pandeirada, J. N. S. (2016). Adaptive memory: The evolutionary significance of survival processing. *Perspectives on Psychological Science, 11*, 496–511. https://doi.org/10.1177/1745691616635613

Nairne, J. S., Thompson, S. R., & Pandeirada, J. N. S. (2007). Adaptive memory: Survival processing enhances retention. *Journal of Experimental Psychology: Learning, Memory, and Cognition, 33*, 263–273. https://doi.org/10.1037/0278-7393.33.2.263 UID 2007-02740-001

Over, D. E. (Ed.) (2003). *Evolution and the psychology of thinking: The debate.* Psychology Press.

Rothermund, K. (2011). Counter-regulation and control-dependency: Affective processing biases in the service of action regulation. *Social Psychology, 42*, 56–66. https://doi.org/10.1027/1864-9335/a000043

Rothermund, K., Voss, A., & Wentura, D. (2008). Counter-regulation in affective attentional biases: A basic mechanism that warrants flexibility in emotion and motivation. *Emotion, 8*, 34–46. https://doi.org/10.1037/1528-3542.8.1.34

Schaper, M. L., Mieth, L., & Bell, R. (2019). Adaptive memory: Source memory is positively associated with adaptive social decision making. *Cognition, 186*, 7–14. https://dx.doi.org/10.1016/j.cognition.2019.01.014

Sears, D. O. (1983). The person-positivity bias. *Journal of Personality and Social Psychology, 44*, 233–250. https://doi.org/10.1037/0022-3514.44.2.233

Suzuki, A., & Suga, S. (2010). Enhanced memory for the wolf in sheep's clothing: Facial trustworthiness modulates face–trait associative memory. *Cognition, 117*, 224–229. https://doi.org/10.1016/j.cognition.2010.08.004

Suzuki, A., Honma, Y., & Suga, S. (2013). Indelible distrust: Memory bias toward cheaters revealed as high persistence against extinction. *Journal of Experimental Psychology: Learning, Memory, & Cognition, 39*, 1901–1913. https://doi.org/10.1037/a0033335

Tooby, J., & Cosmides, L. (1992). The psychological foundations of culture. In J. Barkow, L. Cosmides, & J. Tooby (Eds.), *The adapted mind: Evolutionary psychology and the generation of culture* (pp. 19–136). Oxford University Press.

(2005). Conceptual foundations of evolutionary psychology. In D. M. Buss (Ed.), *The handbook of evolutionary psychology* (pp. 5–67). John Wiley & Sons.

Trivers, R. (1971). The evolution of reciprocal altruism. *Quarterly Review of Biology, 46*, 35–57. https://doi.org/10.1086/406755

Volstorf, J., Rieskamp, J., & Stevens, J. R. (2011). The good, the bad, and the rare: Memory for partners in social interactions. *PLoS ONE, 6*(4), e18945. www.plosone.org/article/info: doi/10.1371/journal.pone.0018945

Wentura, D., Voss, A., & Rothermund, K. (2009). Playing TETRIS for science counter-regulatory affective processing in a motivationally "hot" context. *Acta Psychologica, 131*, 171–177. https://doi.org/10.1016/j.actpsy.2009.05.008

25

DEVELOPMENT OF MEMORY CIRCUITS UNDER EPIGENETIC REGULATION

Ji-Song Guan

Memory is an essential ability to quickly adapt to the environment. The nervous system stores information efficiently and retrieves it in a flexible way. Such an amazing capacity is the result of successful changes at two distinct time scales. At a long time scale, as memory systems become increasingly complex, functional neuronal structures, such as the hippocampus and amygdala emerged during evolution, facilitating the processing of information. These evolved structures in advanced species are developed during embryonic life under the control of genetic and epigenetic programs. While the precise developmental programs that generate memory circuits develop at the long time scale, individual memories of experiences are encoded by the quick development of naïve neural circuits at a much faster pace. The experience-dependent remodeling of neural circuits is full of "trial-and-error" dynamics and is tightly regulated by long-lasting molecular mechanisms, including epigenetic regulation.

25.1 STRUCTURE OF THE MEMORY SYSTEM TO RETAIN SPECIFIC INFORMATION

In mammalian brains, neural circuits in the neocortex and hippocampus are responsible for the encoding and retrieval of environmental information. Among the large number of neurons in the mammalian neocortex (10^{10}) and hippocampus (10^7), only a small fraction of the population shows specificity for a given context or context-dependent memory (Liu et al., 2012, Tonegawa et al., 2015, Xie et al., 2014). Although these memory-related neurons are sparsely distributed in many parts of the brain, they are located in specialized microcircuit structures, such as the dentate gyrus in the hippocampus (Liu et al., 2012) and layer 2 of the neocortex (Li et al., 2019; Wang et al., 2019; Xie et al., 2014). As cellular representations of stored information, these neurons are known as memory engrams (Tonegawa et al., 2015).

Engrams are specialized neurons in neural networks underlying the context-specific storage of experience. Distinct features highlight the structure and function of engram networks. A highly specified small network of less than 5% of the neurons in the neocortex is involved in the network that encodes memories (Xie et al., 2014). However, inhibition or excitation of the engram network alters brain activity and affects the behavioral output of memory retrieval. Therefore, engram ensembles are highly efficient associative networks that engage neural representations of memories in the entire brain. Although engram activities are closely coupled with acquired memories, they are allocated to specific neuronal populations via intrinsic gene expression. For example, the preactivation of CREB, a transcription factor (see Glossary at the end of this chapter), attracts memories to activated neural ensembles, whereas various brain states could alter global patterns of activated ensembles to modulate memory encoding and retrieval (Han et al., 2007; Jiang et al., 2018). In fact, the development of naive memory circuits not only is determined by external stimuli and the experience of the individual, but also is tightly regulated by intrinsic factors, such as genetic and epigenetic mechanisms. Nonetheless, the engram circuit is the biological substrate for memory representation. The organization and structure of such neural circuits underlie the architecture of memory storage and are regulated by experience-activated epigenetic mechanisms.

At the subcellular level, the formation of new memories is associated with the structural and functional remodeling of synapses, which is also driven by molecular regulatory mechanisms. For example, synaptic plasticity, especially that occurring in the engram circuit, is required for the formation of context-dependent memories (Ryan et al., 2015). The encoding of the information is likely achieved by the long-lasting reduction or enhancement of synaptic strength, known as long-term depression (LTD) and long-term potentiation (LTP), in response to a specific pattern of neuronal activity. Cellular and synaptic plasticity is regulated by molecular events: Neuronal activation triggers the modification, trafficking, and synthesis of new proteins of memory-related molecules through intracellular signaling cascades (Dash et al., 2007), gene transcription, and protein synthesis (Barondes & Jarvik, 1964; Davis & Squire, 1984).

Daily life experience changes the memory circuit via activity-dependent synaptic plasticity that incorporates, modifies, and maintains the information in the brain. The development of these networks depends on structural deformation and reformation driven by external and internal signals. For example, motor learning continuously prunes many synapses in the motor cortex and newly formed spines are subjected to extensive competition for survival (Xu et al., 2009). In contrast to external stimuli, adult newborn neurons in the hippocampus bring internal deviation signals to cortical memory networks that facilitate extinction learning of contextual fear memory (Wang et al., 2019). Such intrinsic and extrinsic forces continuously drive the development of memory networks. It is quite amazing that specific information can be stored in such a developing system, in which some memories can be stored and retrieved even across the life span.

Besides potential network dynamic and stabilization features based on its structure, such as the attractor, which is a specific pattern of activity of the network that is invariant under dynamics, in response to stimuli, epigenetic regulation has also been recently recognized as an intrinsic force that regulates memory stability. Epigenetic regulation has been widely recognized as a memory mechanism (see Kriete and Hollis, Chapter 3) that maintains developmental stages and is involved in heritable phenomena that require cellular memory (Levenson & Sweatt, 2005; Lipsky, 2013; Ringrose & Paro, 2004). Importantly, epigenetic regulation modulates synaptic plasticity and memory (Guan et al., 2009; Kaas et al., 2013; Liu et al., 2009; Lubin et al., 2008; Rudenko et al., 2013; Stefanko et al., 2009; Sui et al., 2012; Yu et al., 2011). During learning, different epigenetic regulators work in concert to converge on upstream cascade signals that influence downstream gene transcription (Ding et al., 2017) and maintain the effects for a long time to guide the direction of network change. Epigenetic regulation has two functions in the development of memory circuits: As a "gating" mechanism that enables changes in gene expression that are important for adding and modifying information to the circuits, and as a "stabilizing" mechanism important for memory preservation. Such dual roles of epigenetic regulation allow cellular memory to retain stable information in the memory circuit, where information regarding different properties is stored in discrete neuronal ensembles (Xie et al., 2014).

25.2 EPIGENETIC MODIFICATIONS IN MEMORY FORMATION

Nucleosomes, the basic units used by eukaryotic chromatin to pack huge genomes into the cell nucleus, contain an octamer of histone proteins, which are two pairs of the core histones H2A, H2B, H3, and H4 surrounded by 147 bp of DNA. The protruding N-terminal tails of the histone proteins undergo posttranslational modifications to regulate gene transcription (Jiang et al., 2008). For example, histone acetylation releases compacted DNA to be accessible to the transcription machinery, facilitating transcriptional initiation and elongation (Shahbazian & Grunstein, 2007). The addition and removal of the acetyl group is catalyzed by histone acetyltransferases (HATs) and histone deacetylases (HDACs). In addition, histone phosphorylation, which is tightly associated with histone acetylation, affects transcription in a histone microenvironment-dependent manner (Banerjee & Chakravarti, 2011; Chwang et al., 2006).

A variety of studies have revealed essential epigenetic regulators that are involved in memory circuit modifications (Table 25.1). While HDAC inhibitors (HDACi) enhance long-term memory, genetic disruption of HATs impairs the formation of long-term memory (Alarcon et al., 2004; Barrett et al., 2011; Vecsey et al., 2007; Yeh et al., 2004). HDAC2 is one of the major regulators. Specifically, mice overexpressing HDAC2 show impaired LTP and memory, while HDAC2-knockout mice show enhanced synaptic plasticity (Guan et al., 2009) that facilitates memory formation. HDAC2 is also involved in memory stabilization by regulating the alternative splicing choices of synaptic proteins (Ding et al., 2017). Besides HDAC2, the inhibition of HDAC3 enhances behavior during fear-memory formation and the extinction of drug-seeking behavior (Malvaez et al., 2013; McQuown et al., 2011; Rogge et al., 2013). Brain-specific knockout of HDAC4 leads to significant memory deficits (Kim et al., 2012). Importantly, the disruptions of those epigenetic regulators are associated with the pathogenesis of Alzheimer's disease (Graff et al., 2012) and neuropsychological diseases, such as Tourette's syndrome (Liu et al., 2019).

Other histone modifications are involved in learning and memory. Forebrain-specific histone methyltransferase myeloid/lymphoid or mixed-lineage leukemia 2 (mll2/kmt2b) gene, which specifically regulates H3K4 di- and tri-methylation, impairs learning (Kerimoglu et al., 2013). Suv39h1 maintains the inhibitory marker H3K9me3 around the selectively expressed exons of Nrxns to suppress the synaptic formation of activated engram neurons, thereby preserving existing memories (Ding et al., 2017). Ash1L, modulating H3K36me2, allows the activity-dependent elimination of synapses (Zhu et al., 2016) and is also involved in neurodevelopmental diseases, such as Tourette's syndrome (Liu et al. 2019). Additionally, the inhibition of the G9a/GLP complex in the hippocampus affects long-term memory formation in mice, while the inhibition of G9a in the entorhinal cortex interferes with memory consolidation (Gupta-Agarwal et al., 2012).

Besides histone modifications, inhibition of DNA methyltransferases results in memory suppression and impaired memory consolidation (Lubin et al., 2008; Miller et al., 2008; Miller & Sweatt, 2007). Importantly, DNA methylation undergoes activity-dependent dynamics in the hippocampus of adult mice (Guo et al., 2011). The overexpression of TET1, a DNA methylation regulator, in the hippocampus impaired memory formation (Kaas et al., 2013), whereas TET1 knockout mice showed only abnormal memory extinction, with no memory formation deficits (Rudenko et al., 2013).

Interestingly, neuronal activation itself triggers changes in many epigenetic markers that differ across time and brain regions in a specific manner during memory tasks. For example, acetylation of histone H3 is enhanced after several hippocampal-dependent behavioral paradigms, such as contextual fear conditioning and water-maze learning (Alarcon et al., 2004;

TABLE 25.1. *Major category of epigenetic regulators and their specific roles in learning and memory*

Classification	Regulator	Effect
HATS	CBP/P300	Knockout of CBP in dorsal CA1 or p300 in superficial layers of the cortex and CA1 impairs long-term potentiation and long-term memory for contextual fear and object recognition. Intra-LA inhibition of CBP/P300 activity impairs fear memory consolidation and reconsolidation in the LA.
	PCAF (p300/CBP associated factor)	PCAF-KO mice show impaired learning and memory.
HDACs	HDAC1	Overexpression of HDAC1 in the hippocampus affects the extinction of contextual fear memories.
	HDAC2	Neuron-specific overexpression of HDAC2 decreased dendritic spine density, synapse number, synaptic plasticity, and memory formation; loss of HDAC2 increases synapse number, improves associative learning and extinction rate of conditioned fear responses.
	HDAC3	Genetic deletions and pharmacologic inhibition of Hdac3 in area CA1 of the dorsal hippocampus enhanced long-term memory; Hdac3 deletion in nucleus accumbens enhance CPP acquisition. In aged animals, the HDAC3 inhibitor RGFP966 reestablished synaptic tagging and capture and restored L-LTP.
	HDAC4	Selective deletion of Hdac4 in brain impairs long-term synaptic plasticity and hippocampal-dependent learning and memory.
	SIRT1	Loss of function of SIRT1 impairs memory and synaptic plasticity; knockout of SIRT1 affects both short- and long-term hippocampus-dependent memory.
HMTs	EHMT	Both short- and long-term courtship memories are impaired in EHMT mutant flies EHMT1 haplo-insufficient mice exhibit intellectual disabilities and autistic phenotype.
	G9a/GLP	Inhibition of G9a/GLP in the EC enhances contextual fear conditioning. Knockdown of GLP–G9a leads to derepression of genes expressed in adult neurons and leads to deficits in learning.
	Mll	Knockout of mll2/kmt2b gene in forebrain impairs hippocampus-dependent memory formation. Loss of Kmt2a partially reflects memory deficits in a model for Alzheimer's disease.
	Suv39H1	Systemic administration of an inhibitor of the histone methyltransferase SUV39H1 improved memory performance in aged mice. Suv39h1 is required for the preservation of old memories.
DNMTs	DNMT1/DNMT3a	Dnmt1 and Dnmt3a double knockout mice show abnormal long-term plasticity in CA1 region and impaired learning and memory.
	Dnmt3a2	Cognitive decline associated with aging is concomitant with a reduction in DNA methyltransferase Dnmt3a2 expression in the hippocampus.

TABLE 25.1. (*cont.*)

Classification	Regulator	Effect
DNA demethylation	Tet	Expression of TET1 catalytically inactive mutant impairs contextual fear memory; Tet1KO mice exhibited abnormal hippocampal long-term depression and impaired extinction memory.
	Gadd45b	Gadd45bKO mice show selective enhancements in hippocampal-dependent memory and synaptic plasticity.
Nucleosome remodeling	H3.3	Knocking down H3.3 expression reduced the density of hippocampal dendritic spines and impaired memory.
	H2AZ	Neuronal activity incorporates H2AZ into the nucleosome to regulate formation of fear memory.
	BRG1-associated factor (BAF)	Cultured Baf53b−/− hippocampal neurons showed impairments in activity-dependent dendritic outgrowth, leading to impairments in both long-term memory and long-lasting forms of synaptic plasticity.
Others	Bromodomain-containing protein (BRD4)	BRD4 regulates activity-dependent expression of immediate-early genes, and BRD4 inhibitor impairs novel object recognition.

Bousiges et al., 2013; Korzus et al., 2004; Levenson et al., 2004). By contrast, histone H4, but not H3, shows significant enhancement in acetylation during latent inhibition (Levenson et al., 2004).

25.3 "GATING" MECHANISM OF MEMORY FORMATION UNDER EPIGENETIC REGULATION

It has been known for decades that new protein synthesis is required for long-term memory formation (Davis & Squire, 1984). Because gene transcription is governed by epigenetics, epigenetic regulation might act as a "gating" mechanism allowing long-term changes of memory circuits in response to stimuli. This process primes circuits to be available for new information storage. Sensory stimuli trigger signal cascades, starting from the activation of N-methyl-D-aspartate acid (NMDA) receptors. Several signaling pathways, such as the mitogen-activated protein kinase/extracellular signal-regulated kinase (MAPK/ERK), the AMPK pathway, and the PKA pathway transduce the activation signal to the nucleus. Essential factors, such as the CRE-binding protein (CREB), activate the transcription of key memory-related genes (Loebrich & Nedivi, 2009). The status of chromatin conformation before and during training is critical to gate activity-dependent gene expression (Guan et al., 2009). Histone modifications, which increase or dampen activity-dependent gene expression, modulate the amount of protein expression essential for neuronal circuit modification to facilitate or block stimulus-induced changes in the activated neuron.

Such regulation is gene specific. For instance, HDAC2 is significantly enhanced at the promoters of genes related to synaptic plasticity. HDAC2-knockout mice show increased acetylation of histones H3 and H4 at the promoter regions of bdnf (brain-derived neurotrophic factor), zif268, fos, and glur1 (Guan et al., 2009). Tet1 knockout mice have robust reductions in the expression levels of activity-regulated genes, such as npas4, arc, and c-fos (Rudenko et al., 2013). A lack of HDAC3 prolongs the learning-induced expression of c-fos and Nr4a2 (McQuown et al., 2011). Both HDAC2- and HDAC3-deficient mice show alterations of memory formation.

In addition, beside the native state of the chromatin, neuronal activation triggers modifications of epigenetic markers that reprogram learning-induced gene expression. For example, contextual fear conditioning induces histone H3 acetylation and phosphorylation of BDNF promoters. Evidence shows that such activity-dependent epigenetic remodeling is induced by upstream classic signal cascades, such as NMDA receptor inhibitors or ERK inhibitors, which impair the formation of new memories, preventing learning-induced epigenetic changes (Levenson et al., 2004). Similar to histone acetylation, learning also induces the expression of DNMT3a, a DNA methylation regulator. The learning-induced expression of DNMT3a is suppressed by the inhibition of NMDA receptors and ERK (Monsey et al., 2011). In addition to the NMDA-ERK pathway, other memory-related signaling pathways are involved in epigenetic regulation: In response to learning, the CREB co-activator CBP/P300, a histone acetyltransferase, is phosphorylated through the Ca^{2+}/calmodulin-dependent kinase-IV (CamK IV), ribosomal protein S6 kinase-2 (RSK2), and mitogen-activated protein kinase (MAPK) pathways. The learning-induced activation of L-type Ca^{2+} channels and cAMP-dependent protein kinase A is sufficient to induce acetylation in histone H3 (J. Li et al., 2004). The coupling between epigenetic changes and activity-dependent pathway activation may amplify the initial signal. For instance, BDNF is a well-known neurotrophin involved in neuroplasticity and in learning and memory (Choi et al., 2010; Park & Poo, 2012; Psotta et al., 2013). It has been reported that the promoter of BDNF undergoes dynamic chromatin remodeling. Interestingly, the activation of the Trk receptor by BDNF depolarizes the neuron and increases the phosphorylation of NMDA receptors (Figurov et al., 1996). At the same time, BDNF activation leads to the dissociation of HDAC2 from the chromatin by nitrosylation on cysteine 262 and 274 of HDAC2 (Nott et al., 2008). Both of these effects result in increased histone acetylation of the promoter regions of the BDNF gene and other plasticity-related genes to largely increase gene expression by forming a positive feedback loop, thus maximizing circuit changes during memory formation. Therefore, neuronal activation, as the trigger of new memory formation, is tightly associated with gene transcription and posttranscriptional regulation of epigenetic regulators. Preventing such changes in the epigenetic markers and gene expression leads to deficits in circuit modification and memory formation.

Importantly, such epigenetic regulation of memory occurs during a specific time window. Histone H3 only shows increased acetylation one hour after contextual fear conditioning, but not 24 hours later. A similar phenomenon has been reported for H3K9me2 (Gupta-Agarwal et al., 2012; Levenson et al., 2004). Such precise timing of epigenetic regulation during learning appears to be critical for memory formation. The inhibition of DMNT impairs fear memory only if infused immediately after training. The HDACi only improves memory retrieval at Day 30 if applied during early exposure (Lesburgueres et al., 2011; Lubin et al., 2008; Miller et al., 2008). Similarly, the effect of DNMT inhibition and HDACi on memory consolidation is observed only if infusion is conducted one hour, but not six hours, after memory reactivation (Maddox & Schafe, 2011). In general, epigenetic changes are required at specific time points to encode or modify memory traces, introducing a constraint on the experience-dependent development of memory circuits.

25.4 "STABILIZATION" MECHANISM OF LONG-TERM MEMORY UNDER EPIGENETIC REGULATION

Learning-induced protein synthesis is transient, while memories stored in our brain usually last for months or even years. Owing to the rapid turnover of proteins, newly synthesized proteins might not be responsible for the long-lasting character of long-term memory. In fact, epigenetic regulation might also take on the role of "stabilization" of long-term memory, according to which specific epigenetic markers maintain gene expression changes that are important for memory consolidation. The markers that play a role in memory "stabilization" are different from those that perform the role of "gating." Different epigenetic regulatory mechanisms and marker dynamics are employed. For example, contextual fear conditioning induces rapid and transient increases in DNMT expression in the hippocampus within 24 hours of training (Gupta et al., 2010; Miller et al., 2008). Surprisingly, a long-lasting increase of DNA methylation in the specific gene promoter region in the medial prefrontal cortex (mPFC) has been observed 30 days after fear conditioning. Furthermore, the administration of a DNMT inhibitor in the mPFC on day 30 after training impairs memory recall (Miller et al., 2010). DNA demethylation is required for memory extinction. TET1 knockout mice show impaired memory extinction and the lack of TET1 in the hippocampus blocks memory recall (Rudenko et al., 2013). Keeping the marker for changes in DNA methylation could be essential for the proper recall of long-term memory.

In addition to DNA methylation, histone modifications might also be involved in the maintenance of long-term memory. DNA methylation and histone markers show intensive cross talk to maintain memory status. The administration of a DNMT inhibitor, which prevents the reinstatement of old memories before extinction (Lattal et al., 2007; Maddox & Schafe, 2011; Wang et al., 2010), affects not only DNA methylation but also the decrease of H3 and H4 acetylation (Sui et al., 2012). Similarly, histone deacetylase inhibitors (HDACis) can also prevent the reinstatement of past memories when administered before extinction. HDACis not only increase histone acetylation, but also reduce DNMT1 expression through the suppression of the ERK pathway (Sarkar et al., 2011). Consistently, HDACis rescue the impairment of memory reconsolidation and retrieval-induced H3 acetylation by inhibiting the expression of DNMT (Maddox & Schafe, 2011). The various modifications on the histone tail show intensive cross talk as well. The administration of HDACi in the hippocampus leads to an increase in H3K4me3, but a decrease in H3K9me2 (Gupta et al., 2010). Such cross talk between various epigenetic modifications suggests that the epigenetic machinery might require different enzymes working in concert to achieve memory consolidation and maintenance.

Studies have illustrated the importance of the cross talk between various epigenetic regulators. PP1, a memory suppressor gene (Koshibu et al., 2010), is responsible for histone H3 S10 dephosphorylation. It interacts with and regulates the activities of other epigenetic regulators (Koshibu et al., 2009), such as HDACs and histone demethylases. HDACi abolishes the interaction between PP1 and HDACs (Brush et al., 2004). However, the inhibition of DNMT by inhibitors increases PP1 expression (Miller & Sweatt, 2007). In addition, activity-dependent histone methylation is found to be regulated by HDAC2 and Suv39h1 after activation of the AMPK pathway; therefore, HDAC2 activity is essential for the effects of Suv39h1 on the long-term regulation of Nrxn1 alternative splicing (Ding et al., 2017).

Furthermore, long-term memory requires epigenetic tagging in cortical circuits – part of the "stabilization" role of epigenetic regulation. Neuron tagging (a post-acquisition process, which is required for long-term memory consolidation) is observed in the hippocampus only at an early stage, but it persists in the neocortex (Lesburgueres et al., 2011). While neural activity in the neocortex in the early post-acquisition period is essential for the tagging process, histone acetylation of histone H3 is elevated. Interestingly, HDACi treatment in the early tagging phase strongly enhances the remote memory, indicating that epigenetic tagging is critical for long-term memory. Such neural activity-associated epigenetic regulations are not limited to the early phase of learning. S-nitrosylation of HDAC2 and histone acetylation have been found during recent memory recall, which enables the expression of c-fos and genes related to neural plasticity. Neural activity triggers deposition of epigenetic regulators, such as HDAC2, Ash1L, and suv39h1 on specific gene loci, regulating neural gene expression (Figure 25.1). Such epigenetic

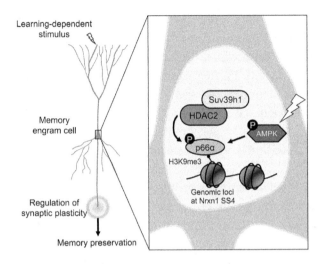

Learning-dependent
stimulus

Memory
engram cell

Regulation of
synaptic plasticity

Memory preservation

Suv39h1

HDAC2

AMPK

p66α

H3K9me3

Genomic loci
at Nrxn1 SS4

FIGURE 25.1. Epigenetic mechanisms that regulate the development of memory circuits in the brain.

regulations occur in specific neuronal populations that are related to memory to limit the expression or control the selectivity of synaptic protein expression. In this way, neural ensembles and synaptic maps are stabilized by tagging mechanisms (Ding et al., 2017). Memory persistence is regulated by the stabilization of the memory engram, which is regulated by neural genes. Further intervention of the epigenetic tagging by HDACi during the reconsolidation phase allows for the attenuation of the remote memory (Graff et al., 2014). In addition to fear conditioning, the administration of HDACi converts short-term memory into long-term memory in object-recognition tasks (Stefanko et al., 2009). Therefore, although the molecular mechanisms underlying the maintenance of long-term memory are unclear, evidence supports the role of epigenetic regulation in "stabilizing" parts of the developing neural circuit to ensure the persistence of long-term memories.

25.5 SUMMARY AND OUTLOOK

Taken together, the epigenetic "gating" mechanism modulates the speed of the stimulus-driven developmental process in naïve neural circuits. This gating allows the selection of significant events to be embedded into a brain circuit or the selection of a specific time window for information storage. On the other hand, the epigenetic "stabilization" mechanism slows down the development of the circuit that stores information. This process allows for the maintenance of long-term memory integrity within the brain circuit. In a population of neurons, such dual roles of epigenetic regulation might facilitate learning in the early period of life under the "gating" mechanism and secure learned information in adults under the "stabilization" mechanism. The transition from the "gating" mechanism to the "stabilization" mechanism remains to be discovered. Meanwhile, the regulation of the network is firmly controlled by specific signals. Further exploration of novel epigenetic factors and processes would definitely broaden our understanding of the control and development of memory circuits, and our understanding of the capacity and flexibility of memory in the brain. In fact, such epigenetic regulations on temporal precision and regional selectivity have put new challenges on top of the plasticity-memory theorem, where the physiology features of synaptic plasticity allow neural activity-engaged modifications in the neural network to store information, requiring more complex modeling to describe the whole picture of the development of experience-dependent memory networks.

In addition to the role of epigenetics in developing the memory circuit, potential impacts of epigenetics may also take effects on the transgenerational regulation of learning and memory. Via imposing DNA methylation and specific histone markers in germline after dramatic environmental changes, the development of memory circuits may adapt to the epigenetically regulated genome environment to build the memory circuit in a generation-specific manner. In this sense, the memory circuit and its development are evolving via epigenetic regulation.

GLOSSARY OF TERMS AND ACRONYMS

Attractor   A stable network activity pattern or trajectory, toward which neighboring states in a given basin of attraction asymptotically approach in the course of dynamic development.

bp   Base pair, the basic unit of double-strained DNA

CREB   Cyclic adenosine monophosphate response-binding protein – a transcription factor involved in gene expression.

DNA methylation   Adding a methyl group to DNA that can block transcription of the corresponding gene.

Exon   A sequence of DNA that is expressed into RNA. Adjacent exons may be separated by an intron, a noncoding DNA sequence, which is later removed from the RNA transcript via a splicing mechanism.

Histone   A group of alkaline proteins occurring in cell nuclei, combined ionically with DNA to form nucleoproteins.

Nrxns   Neurexins are membrane proteins that can form stoichiometric complex, the complex with the exact proportions of compounds, with dystroglycan and neuroligins. They are critical for synaptogenesis.

N-terminal tails Peptide on one end of the protein, which has an amine group on the alpha carbon.

REFERENCES

Alarcon, J. M., Malleret, G., Touzani, K., Vronskaya, S., Ishii, S., Kandel, E. R., & Barco, A. (2004). Chromatin acetylation, memory, and LTP are impaired in CBP+/− mice: A model for the cognitive deficit in Rubinstein-Taybi syndrome and its amelioration. *Neuron, 42*, 947–959. https://doi.org/10.1016/j.neuron.2004.05.021

Banerjee, T., & Chakravarti, D. (2011). A peek into the complex realm of histone phosphorylation. *Molecular & Cell Biology, 31*, 4858–4873. https://doi.org/10.1128/MCB.05631-11

Barondes, S. H., & Jarvik, M. E. (1964). The influence of actinomycin-D on brain RNA synthesis and on memory. *Journal of Neurochemistry, 11*, 187–195. https://doi.org/10.1111/j.1471-4159.1964.tb06128.x

Barrett, R. M., Malvaez, M., Kramar, E., Matheos, D. P., Arrizon, A., Cabrera, S. M., Lynch, G., Greene, R. W., & Wood, M. A. (2011). Hippocampal focal knockout of CBP affects specific histone modifications, long-term potentiation, and long-term memory. *Neuropsychopharmacology, 36*, 1545–1556. https://doi.org/10.1038/npp.2011.61

Bousiges, O., Neidl, R., Majchrzak, M., Muller, M. A., Barbelivien, A., Pereira de Vasconcelos, A., Schneider, A., Loeffler, J. P., Cassel, J. C., & Boutillier, A. L. (2013). Detection of histone acetylation levels in the dorsal hippocampus reveals early tagging on specific residues of H2B and H4 histones in response to learning. *PLOS ONE, 8*, e57816. https://doi.org/10.1371/journal.pone.0057816

Brush, M. H., Guardiola, A., Connor, J. H., Yao, T. P., & Shenolikar, S. (2004). Deactylase inhibitors disrupt cellular complexes containing protein phosphatases and deacetylases. *Journal of Biological Chemistry, 279*, 7685–7691. https://doi.org/10.1074/jbc.M310997200

Choi, D. C., Maguschak, K. A., Ye, K., Jang, S. W., Myers, K. M., & Ressler, K. J. (2010). Prelimbic cortical BDNF is required for memory of learned fear but not extinction or innate fear. *Proceedings of the National Academy of Sciences USA, 107*, 2675–2680. https://doi.org/10.1073/pnas.0909359107

Chwang, W. B., O'Riordan, K. J., Levenson, J. M., & Sweatt, J. D. (2006). ERK/MAPK regulates hippocampal histone phosphorylation following contextual fear conditioning. *Learning & Memory, 13*, 322–328. https://doi.org/10.1101/lm.152906

Dash, P. K., Moore, A. N., Kobori, N., & Runyan, J. D. (2007). Molecular activity underlying working memory. *Learning & Memory, 14*, 554–563. https://doi.org/10.1101/lm.558707

Davis, H. P., & Squire, L. R. (1984). Protein synthesis and memory: A review. *Psychological Bulletin, 96*, 518–559. https://doi.org/10.1037/0033-2909.96.3.518

Ding, X., Liu, S., Tian, M., Zhang, W., Zhu, T., Li, D., Wu, J., Deng, H., Jia, Y., Xie, W., & Guan, J. S. (2017). Activity-induced histone modifications govern neurexin-1 mRNA splicing and memory preservation. *Nature Neuroscience, 20*, 690–699. https://doi.org/10.1038/nn.4536

Figurov, A., Pozzo-Miller, L. D., Olafsson, P., Wang, T., & Lu, B. (1996). Regulation of synaptic responses to high-frequency stimulation and LTP by neurotrophins in the hippocampus. *Nature, 381*, 706–709. https://doi.org/10.1038/381706a0

Graff, J., Joseph, N. F., Horn, M. E., Samiei, A., Meng, J., Seo, J., Rei, D., Bero, A. W., Phan, T. X., Wagner, F., & Tsai, L. H. (2014). Epigenetic priming of memory updating during reconsolidation to attenuate remote fear memories. *Cell, 156*, 261–276. https://doi.org/10.1016/j.cell.2013.12.020)

Graff, J., Rei, D., Guan, J. S., Wang, W. Y., Seo, J., Hennig, K. M., Nieland, T. J., Fass, D. M., Kao, P. F., Kahn, M., & Tsai, L. H. (2012). An epigenetic blockade of cognitive functions in the neurodegenerating brain. *Nature, 483*, 222–226. https://doi.org/10.1038/nature10849

Guan, J. S., Haggarty, S. J., Giacometti, E., Dannenberg, J. H., Joseph, N., Gao, J., Nieland, T. J., Zhou, Y., Wang, X., Mazitschek, R., & Tsai, L. H. (2009). HDAC2 negatively regulates memory formation and synaptic plasticity. *Nature, 459*, 55–60. https://doi.org/10.1038/nature07925

Guo, J. U., Su, Y., Zhong, C., Ming, G. L., & Song, H. (2011). Hydroxylation of 5-methylcytosine by TET1 promotes active DNA demethylation in the adult brain. *Cell, 145,* 423–434. https://doi.org/10.1016/j.cell.2011.03.022

Gupta, S., Kim, S. Y., Artis, S., Molfese, D. L., Schumacher, A., Sweatt, J. D., Paylor, R. E., and Lubin, F. D. (2010). Histone methylation regulates memory formation. *Journal of Neuroscience, 30,* 3589–3599. https://doi.org/10.1523/JNEUROSCI.3732-09.2010

Gupta-Agarwal, S., Franklin, A. V., Deramus, T., Wheelock, M., Davis, R. L., McMahon, L. L., & Lubin, F. D. (2012). G9a/GLP histone lysine dimethyltransferase complex activity in the hippocampus and the entorhinal cortex is required for gene activation and silencing during memory consolidation. *Journal of Neuroscience, 32,* 5440–5453. https://doi.org/10.1523/JNEUROSCI.0147-12.2012

Han, J. H., Kushner, S. A., Yiu, A. P., Cole, C. J., Matynia, A., Brown, R. A., Neve, R. L., Guzowski, J. F., Silva, A. J., and Josselyn, S. A. (2007). Neuronal competition and selection during memory formation. *Science, 316,* 457–460. https://doi.org/10.1126/science.1139438

Jiang, J., Wang, G. Y., Luo, W., Xie, H., & Guan, J. S. (2018). Mammillary body regulates state-dependent fear by alternating cortical oscillations. *Science Reports, 8,* 13471. https://doi.org/10.1038/s41598-018-31622-z

Jiang, Y., Langley, B., Lubin, F. D., Renthal, W., Wood, M. A., Yasui, D. H., Kumar, A., Nestler, E. J., Akbarian, S., & Beckel-Mitchener, A. C. (2008). Epigenetics in the nervous system. *Journal of Neuroscience, 28,* 11753–11759. https://doi.org/10.1523/JNEUROSCI.3797-08.2008

Kaas, G. A., Zhong, C., Eason, D. E., Ross, D. L., Vachhani, R. V., Ming, G. L., King, J. R., Song, H., & Sweatt, J. D. (2013). TET1 controls CNS 5-methylcytosine hydroxylation, active DNA demethylation, gene transcription, and memory formation. *Neuron, 79,* 1086–1093. https://doi.org/10.1016/j.neuron.2013.08.032

Kerimoglu, C., Agis-Balboa, R. C., Kranz, A., Stilling, R., Bahari-Javan, S., Benito-Garagorri, E., Halder, R., Burkhardt, S., Stewart, A. F., & Fischer, A. (2013). Histone-methyltransferase MLL2 (KMT2B) is required for memory formation in mice. *Journal of Neuroscience, 33,* 3452–3464. https://doi.org/10.1523/JNEUROSCI.3356-12.2013

Kim, M. S., Akhtar, M. W., Adachi, M., Mahgoub, M., Bassel-Duby, R., Kavalali, E. T., Olson, E. N., and Monteggia, L. M. (2012). An essential role for histone deacetylase 4 in synaptic plasticity and memory formation. *Journal of Neuroscience, 32,* 10879–10886. https://doi.org/10.1523/JNEUROSCI.2089-12.2012

Korzus, E., Rosenfeld, M. G., & Mayford, M. (2004). CBP histone acetyltransferase activity is a critical component of memory consolidation. *Neuron, 42,* 961–972. https://doi.org/10.1016/j.neuron.2004.06.002

Koshibu, K., Graff, J., Beullens, M., Heitz, F. D., Berchtold, D., Russig, H., Farinelli, M., Bollen, M., & Mansuy, I. M. (2009). Protein phosphatase 1 regulates the histone code for long-term memory. *Journal of Neuroscience, 29,* 13079–13089. https://doi.org/10.1523/JNEUROSCI.3610-09.2009

Koshibu, K., Graff, J., & Mansuy, I. M. (2010). Nuclear protein phosphatase-1: An epigenetic regulator of fear memory and amygdala long-term potentiation. *Neuroscience, 173,* 30–36. https://doi.org/10.1016/j.neuroscience.2010.11.023

Lattal, K. M., Barrett, R. M., & Wood, M. A. (2007). Systemic or intrahippocampal delivery of histone deacetylase inhibitors facilitates fear extinction. *Behavioral Neuroscience, 121,* 1125–1131. https://doi.org/10.1037/0735-7044.121.5.1125

Lesburgueres, E., Gobbo, O. L., Alaux-Cantin, S., Hambucken, A., Trifilieff, P., & Bontempi, B. (2011). Early tagging of cortical networks is required for the formation of enduring associative memory. *Science, 331,* 924–928. https://doi.org/10.1126/science.1196164

Levenson, J. M., O'Riordan, K. J., Brown, K. D., Trinh, M. A., Molfese, D. L., & Sweatt, J. D. (2004). Regulation of histone acetylation during memory formation in the hippocampus. *Journal of Biological Chemistry, 279,* 40545–40559. https://doi.org/10.1074/jbc.M402229200

Levenson, J. M., & Sweatt, J. D. (2005). Epigenetic mechanisms in memory formation. *Nature Reviews Neuroscience, 6*, 108–118. https://doi.org/10.1038/nrn1604

Li, D., Wang, G., Xie, H., Hu, Y., Guan, J. S., & Hilgetag, C. C. (2019). Multimodal memory components and their long-term dynamics identified in cortical layers II/III but not layer V. *Frontiers in Integrative Neuroscience, 13*, 54. https://doi.org/10.3389/fnint.2019.00054

Li, J., Guo, Y., Schroeder, F. A., Youngs, R. M., Schmidt, T. W., Ferris, C., Konradi, C., & Akbarian, S. (2004). Dopamine D2-like antagonists induce chromatin remodeling in striatal neurons through cyclic AMP-protein kinase A and NMDA receptor signaling. *Journal of Neurochemistry, 90*, 1117–1131. https://doi.org/10.1111/j.1471-4159.2004.02569.x

Lipsky, R. H. (2013). Epigenetic mechanisms regulating learning and long-term memory. *International* Journal of Developmental Neuroscience, *31*, 353–358. https://doi.org/10.1016/j.ijdevneu.2012.10.110

Liu, L., van Groen, T., Kadish, I., & Tollefsbol, T. O. (2009). DNA methylation impacts on learning and memory in aging. *Neurobiology of Aging, 30*, 549–560. https://doi.org/10.1016/j.neurobiolaging.2007.07.020

Liu, S., Tian, M., He, F., Li, J., Xie, H., Liu, W., Zhang, Y., Zhang, R., Yi, M., Che, F., & Guan, J. S. (2019). Mutations in ASH1L confer susceptibility to Tourette syndrome. *Molecular Psychiatry, 25*, 476–490. https://doi.org/10.1038/s41380-019-0560-8

Liu, X., Ramirez, S., Pang, P. T., Puryear, C. B., Govindarajan, A., Deisseroth, K., & Tonegawa, S. (2012). Optogenetic stimulation of a hippocampal engram activates fear memory recall. *Nature, 484*, 381–385. https://doi.org/10.1038/nature11028

Loebrich, S., & Nedivi, E. (2009). The function of activity-regulated genes in the nervous system. *Physiological Review, 89*, 1079–1103. https://doi.org/10.1152/physrev.00013.2009

Lubin, F. D., Roth, T. L., & Sweatt, J. D. (2008). Epigenetic regulation of BDNF gene transcription in the consolidation of fear memory. *Journal of Neuroscience, 28*, 10576–10586. https://doi.org/10.1523/JNEUROSCI.1786-08.2008

Maddox, S. A., & Schafe, G. E. (2011). Epigenetic alterations in the lateral amygdala are required for reconsolidation of a Pavlovian fear memory. *Learning & Memory, 18*, 579–593. https://doi.org/10.1101/lm.2243411

Malvaez, M., McQuown, S. C., Rogge, G. A., Astarabadi, M., Jacques, V., Carreiro, S., Rusche, J. R., & Wood, M. A. (2013). HDAC3-selective inhibitor enhances extinction of cocaine-seeking behavior in a persistent manner. *Proceedings of the National Academy of Sciences USA, 110*, 2647–2652. https://doi.org/10.1073/pnas.1213364110

McQuown, S. C., Barrett, R. M., Matheos, D. P., Post, R. J., Rogge, G. A., Alenghat, T., Mullican, S. E., Jones, S., Rusche, J. R., Lazar, M. A., & Wood, M. A. (2011). HDAC3 is a critical negative regulator of long-term memory formation. *Journal of Neuroscience, 31*, 764–774. https://doi.org/10.1523/JNEUROSCI.5052-10.2011

Miller, C. A., Campbell, S. L., & Sweatt, J. D. (2008). DNA methylation and histone acetylation work in concert to regulate memory formation and synaptic plasticity. *Neurobiology of Learning & Memory, 89*, 599–603. https://doi.org/10.1016/j.nlm.2007.07.016

Miller, C. A., Gavin, C. F., White, J. A., Parrish, R. R., Honasoge, A., Yancey, C. R., Rivera, I. M., Rubio, M. D., Rumbaugh, G., & Sweatt, J. D. (2010). Cortical DNA methylation maintains remote memory. *Nature Neuroscience, 13*, 664–666. https://doi.org/10.1038/nn.2560

Miller, C. A., & Sweatt, J. D. (2007). Covalent modification of DNA regulates memory formation. *Neuron, 53*, 857–869. https://doi.org/10.1016/j.neuron.2007.02.022

Monsey, M. S., Ota, K. T., Akingbade, I. F., Hong, E. S., & Schafe, G. E. (2011). Epigenetic alterations are critical for fear memory consolidation and synaptic plasticity in the lateral amygdala. *PLOS ONE, 6*, e19958. https://doi.org/10.1371/journal.pone.0019958

Nott, A., Watson, P. M., Robinson, J. D., Crepaldi, L., & Riccio, A. (2008). S-Nitrosylation of histone deacetylase 2 induces chromatin remodelling in neurons. *Nature, 455*, 411–415. https://doi.org/10.1038/nature07238

Park, H., & Poo, M. M. (2012). Neurotrophin regulation of neural circuit development and function. *Nature Reviews Neuroscience, 14*, 7–23. https://doi.org/10.1038/nrn3379

Psotta, L., Lessmann, V., & Endres, T. (2013). Impaired fear extinction learning in adult heterozygous BDNF knock-out mice. *Neurobiology of Learning & Memory, 103*, 34–38. https://doi.org/10.1016/j.nlm.2013.03.003

Ringrose, L., & Paro, R. (2004). Epigenetic regulation of cellular memory by the Polycomb and Trithorax group proteins. *Annual Reviews of Genetics, 38*, 413–443. https://doi.org/10.1146/annurev.genet.38.072902.091907

Rogge, G. A., Singh, H., Dang, R., & Wood, M. A. (2013). HDAC3 is a negative regulator of cocaine-context-associated memory formation. *Journal of Neuroscience, 33*, 6623–6632. https://doi.org/10.1523/JNEUROSCI.4472-12.2013

Rudenko, A., Dawlaty, M. M., Seo, J., Cheng, A. W., Meng, J., Le, T., Faull, K. F., Jaenisch, R., & Tsai, L. H. (2013). Tet1 is critical for neuronal activity-regulated gene expression and memory extinction. *Neuron, 79*, 1109–1122. https://doi.org/10.1016/j.neuron.2013.08.003

Ryan, T. J., Roy, D. S., Pignatelli, M., Arons, A., & Tonegawa, S. (2015). Memory. Engram cells retain memory under retrograde amnesia. *Science, 348*, 1007–1013. https://doi.org/10.1126/science.aaa5542

Sarkar, S., Abujamra, A. L., Loew, J. E., Forman, L. W., Perrine, S. P., & Faller, D. V. (2011). Histone deacetylase inhibitors reverse CpG methylation by regulating DNMT1 through ERK signaling. *Anticancer Research, 31*, 2723–2732. https://doi.org/10.3390/ma8105358

Shahbazian, M. D., & Grunstein, M. (2007). Functions of site-specific histone acetylation and deacetylation. *Annual Reviews of Biochemistry, 76*, 75–100. https://doi.org/10.1146/annurev.biochem.76.052705.162114

Stefanko, D. P., Barrett, R. M., Ly, A. R., Reolon, G. K., & Wood, M. A. (2009). Modulation of long-term memory for object recognition via HDAC inhibition. *Proceedings of the National Academy of Sciences USA, 106*, 9447–9452. https://doi.org/10.1073/pnas.0903964106

Sui, L., Wang, Y., Ju, L. H., & Chen, M. (2012). Epigenetic regulation of reelin and brain-derived neurotrophic factor genes in long-term potentiation in rat medial prefrontal cortex. *Neurobiology of Learning & Memory, 97*, 425–440. https://doi.org/10.1016/j.nlm.2012.03.007

Tonegawa, S., Liu, X., Ramirez, S., & Redondo, R. (2015). Memory engram cells have come of age. *Neuron, 87*, 918–931. https://doi.org/10.1016/j.neuron.2015.08.002

Vecsey, C. G., Hawk, J. D., Lattal, K. M., Stein, J. M., Fabian, S. A., Attner, M. A., Cabrera, S. M., McDonough, C. B., Brindle, P. K., Abel, T., & Wood, M. A. (2007). Histone deacetylase inhibitors enhance memory and synaptic plasticity via CREB:CBP-dependent transcriptional activation. *Journal of Neuroscience, 27*, 6128–6140. https://doi.org/10.1523/JNEUROSCI.0296-07.2007

Wang, G., Xie, H., Wang, L., Luo, W., Wang, Y., Jiang, J., Xiao, C., Xing, F., & Guan, J. S. (2019). Switching from fear to no fear by different neural ensembles in mouse retrosplenial cortex. *Cerebral Cortex, 29*, 5085–5097. https://doi.org/10.1093/cercor/bhz050

Wang, L., Lv, Z., Hu, Z., Sheng, J., Hui, B., Sun, J., & Ma, L. (2010). Chronic cocaine-induced H3 acetylation and transcriptional activation of CaMKIIalpha in the nucleus accumbens is critical for motivation for drug reinforcement. *Neuropsychopharmacology, 35*, 913–928. https://doi.org/10.1038/npp.2009.193

Xie, H., Liu, Y., Zhu, Y., Ding, X., Yang, Y., & Guan, J. S. (2014). In vivo imaging of immediate early gene expression reveals layer-specific memory traces in the mammalian brain. *Proceedings of the National Academy of Sciences USA, 111*, 2788–2793. https://doi.org/10.1073/pnas.1316808111

Xu, T., Yu, X., Perlik, A. J., Tobin, W. F., Zweig, J. A., Tennant, K., Tennant, K., Jones, T., & Zuo, Y. (2009). Rapid formation and selective stabilization of synapses for enduring motor memories. *Nature, 462*, 915–919. https://doi.org/10.1038/nature08389

Yeh, S. H., Lin, C. H., & Gean, P. W. (2004). Acetylation of nuclear factor-kappaB in rat amygdala improves long-term but not short-term retention of fear memory. *Molecular Pharmacology, 65,* 1286–1292. https://doi.org/10.1124/mol.65.5.1286

Yu, N. K., Baek, S. H., & Kaang, B. K. (2011). DNA methylation-mediated control of learning and memory. *Molecular Brain, 4,* 5. https://doi.org/10.1186/1756-6606-4-5

Zhu, T., Liang, C., Li, D., Tian, M., Liu, S., Gao, G., & Guan, J. S. (2016). Histone methyl-transferase Ash1L mediates activity-dependent repression of neurexin-1α. *Scientific Report, 6,* 26597. https://doi.org/10.1038/srep26597

26

CONSTRAINTS ON LEARNING AND MEMORY

A Resolution

Aaron P. Blaisdell and Benjamin M. Seitz

Selective pressures have endowed organisms with remarkable specialized abilities to navigate their environments. But environments are dynamic; thus, learning and memory mechanisms are adaptive for those aspects of the environment that are dynamic and may, thereby, render species-typical behaviors unsuitable. Learning processes allow an individual to learn about and remember past experiences to successfully exploit resources and avoid predation. The extent to which specialized cognitive abilities versus general learning mechanisms govern behavior has been a topic of debate over the past century. Some have advocated for adaptive specializations in learning that are specific to narrow ecological contexts, while others have advocated for a general process approach to learning and memory. Here, we suggest these two approaches to understanding behavior do not conflict, but rather are facets of the interplay between proximate and ultimate level explanations of behavior. In this chapter, we focus on the interaction between these perspectives in associative learning and memory.

The history of associative learning has largely been in search for general laws (Escobar & Miller, 2004; Miller & Escobar, 2002). Thorndike's (1898) extensive dissertation research documenting empirical evidence for instrumental learning in animals led to his formulation of the Law of Effect (Thorndike, 1911). This was followed by many attempts at formulating general models of, and the processes that govern, instrumental and Pavlovian learning, including Hull (1943), Bush and Mostellar (1955), and Rescorla and Wagner (1972), to name a few.

Despite his formulation of the Law of Effect, even Thorndike (1911) recognized that not all behaviors could be equally shaped by reinforcement. When trying to train a cat to escape from a puzzle box, for example, he noted that not all responses could equally serve as escape responses. Responses directed at the environment, such as pushing and pulling on objects such as doors, levers, and string, were easily strengthened through reinforcement (escape from the box and acquiring food). Self-directed behaviors, such as grooming and yawning, however, proved difficult or impossible to strengthen through reinforcement. Thus, Thorndike was the first not only to formulate general laws of associative learning, but also to demonstrate constraints on associative learning, whereby certain responses naturally "belong with" the reinforcer due to the evolutionary history of the animal.

Since Thorndike's initial discovery of *belongingness*, other examples of constraints on learning have emerged (see Silva and Silva, Chapter 12). While training a wide variety of animals, the Brelands (Breland & Breland, 1961) occasionally found that after an animal had learned some sort of instrumental response, instinctual behaviors would drift back into the animal's repertoire, consequently preventing the animal from performing the correct response to obtain reward. This phenomenon of *instinctive drift* is often put forth as an example of how evolved specializations prevent, or at least interfere with, general learning processes.

Shettleworth (1975) extended Thorndike's (1911) observations of response-reinforcer belongingness with studies of the golden hamster. She demonstrated how the periodic delivery of food increases certain unconditioned behaviors (e.g., digging, scrabbling, and rearing) while decreasing others (e.g., face washing and scratching). She proposed that reinforcers activate specific behavior systems, with food reinforcement activating the feeding behavior system. Each behavior system is a functional collection of behaviors that has been shaped by evolution to meet the needs of the organism. For example, because hamsters are seed-eaters, the feeding behavior system of the hamster includes behaviors that ensure the finding and consuming of seeds. Unlike seed-eaters, predators such as cats have a different set of behaviors in their behavior system that includes looking for moving prey (e.g., hamsters and mice), sitting and waiting for prey to come within striking distance, and chasing and capturing prey. The concept of behavior systems has been further developed by Timberlake and Lucas (1989) and Domjan (1997) (see Silva et al., 2019), and is also found in Pavlovian conditioning research, starting with the classic demonstration of selective CS-US associations by Garcia and Koelling (1966). Garcia and Koelling suggested that natural selection shaped the mechanisms that associate which types of initially neutral stimuli become associated with specific unconditioned stimuli (more on this below). Seligman (1970) would later introduce the term *preparedness* to illustrate how animals come into the world prepared to learn some associations better than others.

Many additional demonstrations of selective associations, constraints on learning, belongingness, etc., have been reported, but we will not elaborate on them here (see Akins et al., 1994; Foree & LoLordo, 1973; Öhman & Mineka, 2001; Staddon & Simmelhag, 1971 for a few examples, and for a review, see Domjan & Krause, 2017).

26.1 EVIDENCE FOR GENERAL PROCESSES OF LEARNING

Learned taste aversions inspired much research in the 1970s because they could be observed with few pairings of flavor and illness and with large temporal delays (Garcia et al., 1955, 1966), which challenged traditional conceptions of learning processes. Nevertheless, Logue (1979) fit this seeming uniqueness of taste aversion learning within a general process framework (see also Domjan, 1983), concluding that, "In virtually all cases the same principles are sufficient for describing taste aversion and traditional learning data" (Logue, 1979, p. 289). She posited that even large differences in the particulars of learning across species, task, and behavioral system likely reflect quantitative rather than qualitative differences. Quantitative differences are shaped by natural selection by environmental situations to which the learned behaviors are adapted. For example, applying this reasoning to the example of CS-US belongingness by Garcia and Koelling (1966), natural selection could have reduced the effectiveness of the learning process to associatively connect audiovisual cues and gastric illness, and enhanced the effectiveness of the learning process to acquire taste-illness associations. Likewise, the process of natural selection could lead to enhanced learning of audiovisual cue-shock learning, and reduced the ability to form associations between taste cues and shock. A similar quantitative tweaking of learning processes to fit specific ecological situations is provided in the example described below, discussing optimal interstimulus intervals (ISIs) found in different conditioning preparations. Indeed, there is much evidence for the operation of general processes in many forms of learning and across many species. A few examples will illustrate.

In a review of evidence that temporal contiguity plays a fundamental role in Pavlovian conditioning, Rescorla (1988) describes the different CS-US delays in several Pavlovian procedures involving different species, CSs, USs, and response systems (Figure 26.1). Despite the different optimal delays particular to each case, he noted the common functional relation of temporal contiguity by which the success of conditioning followed a nonmonotonic function of the amount of time between CS and US presentation. The common functional pattern shown across all procedures suggests a fundamental principle (or law) with quantitative differences reflecting adaptation to optimal functional ISIs. It is highly plausible that the same learning process supports each learning situation, but that the optimal time for an anticipatory eye blink to protect the eye from harm is on the order of milliseconds, whereas the optimal time to associate a flavor with gastric illness follows the amount of time it takes for an ingested toxin to bring on its effects.

A similar example comes from the study of list learning and short-term memory. A. A. Wright et al. (1985) presented pigeons, rhesus monkeys, and

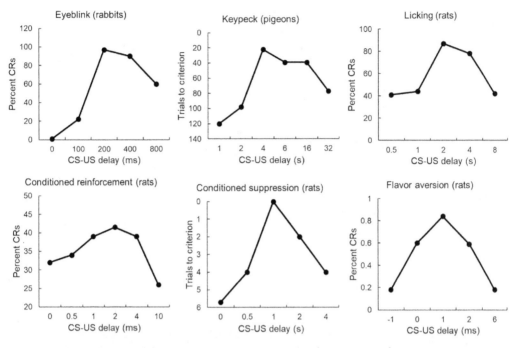

FIGURE 26.1. CS-US interval functions in various Pavlovian conditioning procedures (adapted from Rescorla, 1988).

human participants with lists of four visual stimuli presented sequentially. Following some of these four-item lists, the participant was presented with test items and was rewarded for identifying the item as one from the list. The test item was sometimes presented immediately and other times after various delays. Figure 26.2 shows that all three species exhibited the following patterns: (1) a recency effect of strongest performance on the last list item when tested immediately after the last item on the list, (2) a reduction in the recency effect at increasing test delays, and (3) an increase in a primacy effect of strong performance on the first list item as an increasing function of test delay. The three species differed in the timing of the transition from only a recency effect, to showing both recency and primacy effects, to finally showing only a primacy effect as delay length increased. For instance, delay between encoding and test necessary to induce a primacy effect was 10 seconds in humans and 1 second in rhesus monkeys and pigeons, while the recency effect disappeared by 100 seconds in humans, 20 seconds in rhesus monkeys, and 6 seconds in pigeons. Nevertheless, despite the absolute differences in accuracy transition times, the same underlying pattern emerged, suggesting that short-term memory in all three species is governed by a common set of processes. Had the researchers decided only to test primacy and recency effects at a fixed delay between encoding and test, they would have arrived at a different conclusion regarding the mnemonic capabilities of these animals. For example, if they had chosen just a 6-second

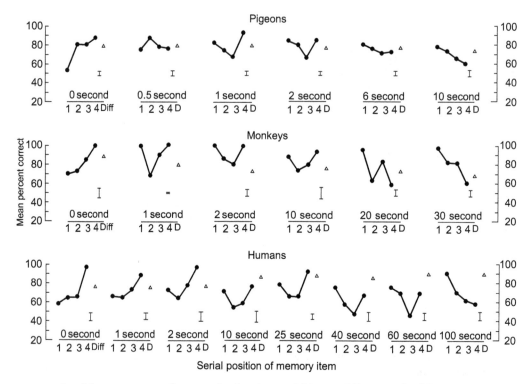

FIGURE 26.2. Mean memory performance for four-item serial lists at different probe delays (retention intervals), the interval between the last item (labeled 4) and the probe test item. The bar shown for each serial-position function is the average standard error of the mean for the four serial positions ("same" trials). Open triangles show performance on "different" trials where the probe item matched none of the four list items.

From Wright, A. A., Santiago, H. C., Sands, S. F., Kendrick, D. F., and Cook, R. G. (1985). Memory processing of serial lists by pigeons, monkeys, and people. *Science.* https://doi.org/10.1126/science.9304205. Reprinted with permission from AAAS.

delay, both primacy and recency effects would have been demonstrated in primates (monkeys and humans) but only a primacy effect would have been shown in pigeons. This would have given a misleading impression of class differences (i.e., mammals versus birds) in working memory processes, rather than quantitative differences in the qualitatively same underlying memory dynamics. This provides an important lesson for those interested in comparative cognition and constraints on learning. What might appear as a simple species difference, or constraint on learning, or separate psychological processes, may in fact be an artifact of the experimental parameters or procedures (Bitterman, 1975).

As a third example, Bitterman (1996) reviewed the experimental studies of learning in the honeybee. Learning in the honeybee has been investigated with a wide variety of procedures as are typically employed in the study of learning in the rat – one of the most common laboratory vertebrates in learning research. Despite the distant evolutionary relationship between insects (see Kriete and Hollis, Chapter 3) (phylum Arthropoda) and vertebrates (~550 million years ago), Bitterman (1996) concluded that none of the species differences found suggest differences in their learning processes. Rather, he noted striking similarities in learning phenomena in honeybees and vertebrates, including forward and backward blocking, overshadowing, latent inhibition, conditioned inhibition, probability matching, second-order conditioning, context conditioning, conditional discrimination, extinction, and spontaneous recovery from extinction, to name but a few. Organisms in other nonvertebrate phyla also show evidence for basic learning phenomena, including mollusks such as sea slugs (*Aplysia*, Hawkins et al., 1998) and snails (Loy et al., 2017), nematodes such as *C. elegans* (Wen et al., 1997), flatworms such as planaria (Shomrat & Levin, 2013), cnidarians such as the sea anemone (Haralson et al., 1975), and potentially even plants (Mittelbach et al., 2019).

26.2 MEMORY PROCESSES

While learning theorists have grappled with and debated over the extent to which constraints on learning challenge general theories of learning, similar debates have not occurred in the field of human memory. At present, general process memory models dominate introductory textbooks, and little consideration is given to how intrinsic differences between stimuli may affect their memorability. Nevertheless, there is extensive evidence for great variability in memory performance that is, to some extent, modulated by characteristics of the stimulus and its perception. For example, it is well documented that pictures are better remembered than words (Shepard, 1967). In memory for words, more frequently spoken words tend to be more memorable than less frequent words (Scarborough et al., 1977), and words for animate objects are better remembered than words for inanimate objects (Gelin et al., 2018; Nairne et al., 2013, 2017). Despite these findings, why such differences in memory are observed at the level of stimulus variations is not considered in dominant models of memory, such as the Multi-Store Model (Atkinson & Shiffrin, 1968), Parallel Distributed Processing (Rumelhart & Mcclelland, 1986), Levels of Processing (Craik & Lockhart, 1972), or Baddeley's Working Memory Model (Baddeley, 1992). In the following section, we document a number of biases to the human memory system that appear to reflect evolutionary pressures. Specifically, stimuli that are perceived to be of greater evolutionary fitness value tend to be better remembered than similar stimuli that are perceived to be of lesser fitness value.

26.3 CONSTRAINTS ON MEMORY

Recently, a number of researchers have begun to discover mnemonic biases that appear similar to biological constraints on learning. Nairne et al. (2007;

see Nairne and Coverdale, Chapter 23) demonstrated that words encoded based on their relevancy to an imagined survival scenario were better remembered than those same words encoded based on their relevancy to a similarly worded, but non-survival-relevant scenario (moving to a foreign land) and others (e.g., Kang et al., 2008) have shown the survival scenario enhances recall better than other arousing and novel tasks, such as imagining oneself performing a bank heist (Kang et al., 2008). Nairne and colleagues interpreted these results as suggesting that the human memory system performs optimally when remembering information relevant to one's evolutionary fitness. This "survival processing effect" resembles the preparedness for developing a fear of snakes in humans and monkeys (Öhman & Mineka, 2001), in that both demonstrate that learning/memory processes are biased toward fitness-relevant information. Studies demonstrating selective associations in 1-day-old rat pups (Gemberling & Domjan, 1982) and in which the survival processing effect has been observed in young children 4–12 years old (Aslan & Bäuml, 2012; Howe & Otgaar, 2013; Otgaar & Smeets, 2010) suggests that these learning/memory predispositions develop early.

Many mnemonic biases that appear to reflect evolutionary pressures have now been identified. For instance, Seitz et al. (2018) showed that information encoded based on its relevance to an imagined parenting scenario resulted in a similar benefit to retrieval as the survival processing effect. Furthermore, memory for information described as relevant to one's biological child is better remembered than that same information described as relevant to one's adopted child (Bonin et al.,2020; Seitz, Polack et al., 2020, but see Krause et al., 2019). Memory is also enhanced for information relevant to finding a mate (Pandeirada et al., 2017) and for potential sources of contamination (Bonin et al., 2019; Fernandes et al., 2017). New et al. (2007) demonstrated that memory for the location of food stands is related to the caloric density of the food item sold at the stand, with high-calorie-food stands better remembered than low-calorie-food stands. Similarly, Seitz, Blaisdell et al. (2021) showed that eating behaviors are better recalled than nearly identical procedural behaviors that do not involve eating. Taken together it has been argued that these results indicate evidence of constraints on general memory processes (Nairne, 2010; Nairne & Pandeirada, 2008; Seitz et al., 2019).

Thus, memory researchers should consider how these mnemonic biases impact existing models of memory, especially because the vast majority of memory models are silent about how characteristics of the stimuli affect memorability. While it is possible that these enhancements in memory for fitness-relevant stimuli may reflect unique memory processes specific to the encoding, storage, and retrieval of fitness-relevant information, we feel this is unlikely. As we will discuss further here in the context of learning processes, it appears more likely that the same general memory processes underlie all of the described examples of adaptive memory, but that perceiving information to be fitness relevant somehow triggers the increased efficacy or strength of these processes. If so, then computational models of memory should consider the perceived fitness relevance of the information encoded. Seitz et al. (2019) proposed a computational parameter, *Omega*, to quantify the perceived fitness value, between 0 and 1, of encoded information. This value can be added to existing learning and memory models to scale the memorability of information. Regardless of the model (e.g., Rescorla-Wagner, Multi-Store Model) used in conjunction with this parameter, a linear relationship between the perceived fitness relevance of information and its potential to be remembered is predicted. Assuming researchers can make reasonable decisions about the perceived fitness relevance of a stimulus, they can make *a priori* predictions about how different types of information will be remembered. For instance, assuming the consumption of calories is an important component of survival, the Omega scaling factor predicts that eating higher-calorie foods will be better remembered than eating lower-calorie foods. We tested this hypothesis and found that eating 30 M&Ms or 30 peanuts (5 kcal per unit) was better remembered than eating 30 pieces of popcorn (1 kcal per unit) (Seitz, Blaisdell et al., 2021 and see Seitz, Tomiyama et al., 2021 for further discussion). Further studies of this kind are necessary to validate or challenge this parameter, but it does well in modeling the observed constraints to human memory and predicting novel mnemonic predispositions.

26.4 CONSTRAINTS ON LEARNING: A RESOLUTION

How can we reconcile the preponderance of evidence for general processes of learning and memory – across a wide range of species, tasks, behavioral systems, etc. – on the one hand, with the well-documented cases of what we may collectively refer to as "constraints on learning" on the other hand? There are two answers that resolve this conflict (Papini, 2002, 2020).

The first part of the resolution arises from considering learning at different levels of analysis. Let's start with an analogy to how proteins are made within cells. With only a few exceptions (e.g., mature red blood cells and germ cells), each cell contains the entire DNA blueprint needed to create all of the proteins for any particular species. Each lung, liver, skin, or brain cell in a human, for example, contains the complete instructions for making all of the proteins that are made anywhere in the body, such as lung, liver, skin, brain, etc. If each cell in a given species contains the complete instructions for making any product of any cell in the body for that given species, how is the specificity of the actual proteins made by each cell achieved? Why does a brain cell only make brain cell proteins and not liver cell proteins for which it also carries the instruction code? This specificity is the result of developmental processes, such as asymmetric cell division (Knoblich, 2008), that guide the ultimate expression of the entire contents of each cell's DNA when transitioning from a stem cell to a tissue-specific cell. During liver development, for example, liver cells lose the ability to express all of the non-liver-cell proteins, such that at maturity it is only capable of producing liver cell proteins. One can view this as a *constraint* on the proteins that the liver cell can make. Yet, the processes by which any cell – liver, heart, lung, brain, etc. – makes its specific proteins are the same in every cell. That is, protein expression follows a *general* process that is the same in any cell, no matter what specific (specialized) proteins it makes. These are the general processes of transcription and translation that turn DNA into RNA, and then RNA into codon sequences that self-assemble into three-dimensional proteins that carry out their various and sundry functions. Thus, a biologist can choose to study how individual cells make their particular proteins, or they can study the general process of transcription and translation, identifying the general laws that govern gene expression regardless of which proteins are made and what functions those proteins play in the organism. There are certainly "adaptive specializations" for each organ system. Epithelial cells must regenerate constantly, as do many types of immune cell and red blood cells. Once neurogenesis is complete, however, no new neurons are created except in certain brain structures like the hippocampus and olfactory bulb (Gould, 2007). Would the biologist conclude from these differences that general laws or principles of genetics do not exist? Of course not. They exist in support of the various adaptive ways different tissues and organ systems have been designed to function via evolutionary processes such as natural selection.

We can apply this analogy to the study of learning and memory. Learning and memory researchers who focus on constraints on learning and memory or adaptive specializations in learning and memory are like the biologists studying the specific aspects of how liver cells make liver proteins, or the genetic nuances of immune system function. Learning researchers who focus on general processes (or laws) of learning are like the biologists seeking to understand the general processes of transcription and translation that operate for any type of cell. Indeed, there may be differences in when and where transcription and translation happen in epithelial tissue versus immune cells versus brain cells, as discussed earlier, because each of these tissue and organ systems serves different needs. But how these processes operate is bound by common principles, and differences are better thought of as quantitative rather than qualitative. This is the insight we wish to bring to the debate about adaptive specializations versus general processes in learning and memory. Taste aversion learning, for example, can occur at full strength after a single learning event and with an extremely long interval between the flavor CS and the gastric illness US (Garcia et al., 1955). Eye blink conditioning, however, can rarely bridge a CS-US interval longer than one second (Smith et al., 1969). These systems were shaped by evolution to operate at optimal time scales for the biological functions they serve (see Rescorla, 1988).

Nevertheless, the general processes that govern these types of associative learning could very well be the same, just as transcription and translational processes are the same whether they produce a constant overturning of epithelial cells in the skin or gut lining, neurotransmitters and receptors in neurons, or immune cells in the bone marrow.

Given this new perspective, it would be odd indeed if there were not differences in how learning occurs in different functional systems. Likewise, Pavlovian learning can occur at various circuits and neural centers in the brain of a human, rat, pigeon, or honeybee. The coincidence detectors (i.e., neural circuits that link the occurrence of contiguously occurring events) responsible for eye blink conditioning in the vertebrate, for example, appear to be located in the cerebellum (Thompson, 1986), while the coincidence detector responsible for fear conditioning in the vertebrate appears to be located in the amygdala (Sigurdsson et al., 2007). Appetitive conditioning in vertebrates also appears to take place in the amygdala among other places (Everitt et al., 2003), while in insects, aversive and appetitive conditioning involves the mushroom bodies (Perisse et al., 2016). Whereas the neural basis of error correction in appetitive conditioning is thought to be modulated by dopamine (Hollerman & Schultz, 1998; Waelti et al., 2001), fear conditioning appears to involve different circuitry performing similar computational error correction processes. For instance, Bolles and Fanselow (1980) suggested that a conditioned analgesic response could minimize the error between expected and experienced pain, resulting in smaller prediction error and thus less learning over trials. Supportive of this, Zelikowsky and Fanselow (2010) administered an opioid antagonist to rats which then formed a fear response to a light in a noise-light compound that typically results in overshadowing to the light. Importantly though, the reliance on coincidence detectors, reinforcement, error reduction, and feedback loops to modulate learning and behavior remains consistent across species and procedures.

The second part of the resolution comes from understanding how similarities in behavioral phenomena can arise. Just like morphology, anatomy, and physiology, behavior is a phenotype, that is, a measurable trait of the organism. Phenotypes can be similar across species either (1) if those species share a common ancestor from which they inherited that phenotype or (2) if those species exhibit convergent evolution to the same trait from different evolutionary starting points (Hall, 2013). Traits shared through common ancestry are called homologies. Humans, apes, and monkeys have five fingers on each hand because the ancestral primate had five fingers. Humans, rats, and rabbits all show eye blink conditioning, a form of Pavlovian conditioning, and cerebellar circuits mediate this learning in all three species, presumably because the common ancestor of all three species exhibited a cerebellar-mediated eye blink conditioning. Thus, this trait is a shared ancestral trait (in cladistic terms, a *symplesiomorphy*). Other behaviors, such as language, are unique to some taxa, such as humans, but not in closely related taxa, such as apes and monkeys. Human language is a unique derived trait (in cladistic terms, an autapomorphy).

Similarity due to convergent evolution is called homoplasy. The fusiform body of sharks and dolphins independently evolved due to its optimal design for movement through water. The wings of bats and birds is another example of homoplasy. In terms of behavioral processes such as learning, appetitive conditioning in insects and vertebrates is homoplastic at the level of neural circuitry. In insects, appetitive conditioning involves the mushroom bodies, whereas in vertebrates it involves the amygdala. Nevertheless, explanations at lower levels of analysis, such as cell-molecular explanations reveal that appetitive conditioning in insects (see Kriete and Hollis, Chapter 3) and vertebrates are homologies involving the same transcriptional factors, such as cAMP response-element binding protein (CREB) (Keifer & Summers, 2016).

Even closely related species can often present a mixture of homologous and homoplastic psychological traits. An illustrative example concerns the phylogenetic distribution of neural processes that underlie nonassociative learning processes in the sea snail (Wright et al., 1996; see Wright, Chapter 2). Figure 26.3 presents the cladogram of the species investigated, including the mollusk *Aplysia*. The intracellular processes of spike broadening and increased excitability that underlie sensitization and dishabituation, respectively, were assessed in each species. The story that

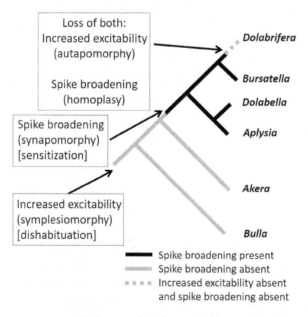

FIGURE 26.3. Cladogram of phylogenetic relationships of six marine mollusks and physiological traits underlying simple learning
(based on Wright et al., 1996).

emerged was of independent evolution of each of these processes. Beginning with *Bulla* and *Akera*, the two most distantly related species of the group, only increased excitability is present. Thus, this is the ancestral condition and indicates this neural trait had already evolved prior to the emergence of the hypothetical common ancestor to all of the species under study. Spike broadening appears to have evolved after the last common ancestor of *Bulla* and *Akera* on the one hand and the remaining mollusks on the other hand. Thus, spike broadening is a shared derived trait among three of these species. What is remarkable is that sometime after the last common ancestor of *Bursatella* and *Dolabrifera*, the ancestors of *Dolabrifera* lost both neuro-modulatory processes. The loss of increased excitability is therefore a unique derived trait while the loss of spike broadening resulted in homoplasy in that the lack of this process is shared with *Bulla* and *Akera* due to convergent evolution. This example serves as an important lesson as to how tricky it can be to tease apart the evolutionary history of phenotypic characteristics, and how confusing it can be to distinguish similarity due to homology versus homoplasy.

There exist many deep homologies in disparate taxa, such as vertebrates and arthropods. Shared genes and proteins (including neurotransmitters and neuromodulators) are responsible for similarities in circadian rhythm function in humans and fruit flies (Reaume & Sokolowski, 2011), exploratory behavior in humans and honeybees (Liang et al., 2012), and anxiety-like behavior in humans, rodents, and fruit flies (Mohammad et al., 2016). Likewise, homologous neural circuits appear to underlie many aspects of avian and mammalian cognition (Güntürkün & Bugnyar, 2016).

These resolutions, namely, (a) consideration for the level of analysis at which a behavior is being explained and (b) determination of whether similarities in behavioral processes across species at each particular level of analysis are homologous or homoplastic, unite psychological explanations of behavior with the rest of biology. Advances in the techniques and knowledge acquired in the study of neuroscience, developmental biology, evolutionary biology, and genetics can be marshalled to build a richer and more nuanced understanding of psychological processes, such as learning and memory.

26.5 CONCLUSION

This perspective provides insight into the hierarchical framework, by which learning phenomena can be analyzed at multiple mechanistic levels. For example, the processes of transcription and translation inside the nucleus of a cell are deep homologies shared by lifeforms on Earth, and can therefore be described by general process models. The functioning of different organ systems, however, can be quite divergent both within the individual and across species, and reflect their adaptive history of selection. Likewise, deep homologies likely exist in the cell-molecular level of neural mechanisms that contribute to learning phenomena (Keifer & Summers, 2016), while adaptive specializations exist at the circuit level for both behavior systems within an individual (e.g., eye blink conditioning involving the cerebellum and fear conditioning involving the amygdala), as well as across species (e.g., pigeons learn taste aversions to visual cues, Foree & LoLordo, 1973, while rats, Garcia & Koelling, 1966, and humans, Logue, 1985, learn them to flavors). Different neural mechanisms can produce the same psychological processes, thus showing the importance of convergent evolution on shaping processes of learning, memory, and cognition. For example, many conditioning phenomena are found in different species, from human to honeybee. Various behavioral phenomena of learning have been documented in honeybees, including Pavlovian conditioning, instrumental conditioning, blocking, overshadowing, conditioned inhibition, and discrimination learning. So, too, have various memory phenomena, such as working memory used in a radial-maze-like task, and stimulus-response chain learning in navigating complex mazes. Finally, some higher-level cognitive processes, such as relational learning as evidenced by oddity and nonoddity learning (Muszynski & Couvillon, 2015) and Same-Difference concept learning (Muszynski, 2018), have been demonstrated in honeybees. These striking similarities in psychological processes in highly divergent species with independently evolved neural circuits suggest that environments and perhaps biological mechanisms of neural circuits themselves provide powerful constraints on achieving processes of information encoding, storage, retrieval, and decision-making.

Likewise, the perspective we provide makes clear contact with the different levels of analysis proposed by Marr (1982), in which different, independently evolved mechanisms may support similar algorithmic level processes. It could be the case for reasons of optimal computational function, that independently evolved neural circuits for coincidence detection could all instantiate the same algorithmic principle as described by learning models, such as that of Rescorla and Wagner (1972) for Pavlovian conditioning, and Thorndike (1911) or our own modification of the Law of Effect (Blaisdell et al., 2016) for instrumental learning.

Our perspective also provides insight into the learning/performance distinction. While preparedness of learning suggests different learning mechanisms adapted to each unique functional role (e.g., taste aversion, fear conditioning, food preferences, eye blink conditioning, etc.), these differences could reflect processes that govern behavioral output and expression rather than learning and encoding. For example, Holland (1981) presented rats with a compound of a tone and a flavor. Rats were subsequently presented with the tone followed by injection of LiCl, which normally produces a conditioned taste aversion when it is paired with flavor. Rats that received these treatments drank less of the flavor that had been paired with the tone than did control rats that did not receive both treatments. Thus, while rats may not show evidence of learning a tone-illness association directly when tested on the tone, a tone-illness association must have been acquired for the tone to mediate conditioning of aversion to the flavor. Examples of latent learning, such as this, exemplifies the delicate nature of deriving inferences about learning from subject performance, since many processes determine performance, with learning being merely one of those processes. Holland's demonstration of latent tone-illness association, for example, is perfectly consistent with the view that general processes of learning, such as contiguity, operate along with adaptive specializations for the expression of that learning into performance. Similarly, while we have outlined a number of phenomena that appear to reflect constraints on human memory performance, we know of no evidence that these constraints represent distinct mnemonic processes for particular situations in which optimal memory performance is observed. Instead, evidence of adaptive memory phenomenon are more likely to reflect basic memory processes that are heightened because fitness-relevant information has been detected (Seitz et al., 2019).

Even long-held, dogmatic views about the cellular mechanisms of learning are receiving new critical analysis. For many decades, long-term potentiation (LTP) has been thought to be the mechanism of encoding memories by strengthening connections between presynaptic and postsynaptic neurons. This has been called into question by recent experiments, suggesting that new synaptic connections are not the locus of newly encoded memories, but instead may reflect the process by which those memories are expressed into behavior. Instead, memories may be stored in the cell nucleus through epigenetic mechanisms acting on the nuclear DNA, rather than the synthesis of new or upregulated synaptic connections (Abraham et al., 2019). For example, methylation of DNA during exposure to shock appears to be necessary for long-term sensitization in *Aplysia*. Evidence for this comes from inhibiting DNA methyltransferase, the mechanism by which DNA methylation occurs, which in turn blocks consolidation of long-term memory of the sensitization event (Pearce et al., 2017). This ties in nicely with the learning-performance distinction. Learning could be encoded through epigenetic tags (e.g., methylation), and expression of that learning could in part be mediated through synaptic plasticity. Only a general-process view of learning and performance can account for how the same cell-molecular memory mechanism could underlie the various types of learning expressed in the behavior of the organism, regardless of the boundary conditions and other specific features of the various types of learning. Throughout this chapter, we have argued for such a general process view of learning, which we feel is capable of uniting psychology with the rest of biology, and psychology is certainly grounded in biology. It would be fitting, though quite a surprise, if the fundamental mechanisms of learning and memory that capture the ontogenetic history of the organism turn out to be intertwined with the fundamental processes of genetics that capture the evolutionary history of the organism.

REFERENCES

Abraham, W. C., Jones, O. D., & Glanzman, D. L. (2019). Is plasticity of synapses the mechanism of long-term memory storage? *Npj Science of Learning, 4*, 9. https://doi .org/10.1038/s41539-019-0048-y

Akins, C. K., Domjan, M., & Gutiérrez, G. (1994). Topography of sexually conditioned behavior in male Japanese quail (*Coturnix japonica*) depends on the CS-US interval. *Journal of Experimental Psychology: Animal Behavior Processes 20*(2), 199–209. https:// doi.org/10.1037/0097-7403.20.2.199

Aslan, A., & Bäuml, K.-H. T. (2012). Adaptive memory: Young children show enhanced retention of fitness-related information. *Cognition, 122*(1), 118–122. https://doi.org/10 .1016/j.cognition.2011.10.001

Atkinson, R. C., & Shiffrin, R. M. (1968). Human memory: A proposed system and its control processes. In K. W. Spence & J. T. Spence (Eds.), *Psychology of learning and motivation: Advances in research and theory* (Vol. 2, pp. 89–195). Academic Press. http://dx.doi.org/ 10.1016/s0079-7421(08)60422-3

Baddeley, A. (1992). Working memory. *Science, 255*(5044), 556–559. https://doi.org/10.1126/ SCIENCE.1736359

Bitterman, M. E. (1975). The comparative analysis of learning. *Science, 188*(4189), 699–709. www.jstor.org/stable/1741035

  (1996). Comparative analysis of learning in honeybees. *Animal Learning and Behavior, 24*, 123–141 https://doi.org/10.3758/BF03198961

Blaisdell, A. P., Stolyarova, A., & Stahlman, W. D. (2016). The law of expect or a modified law of effect? Outcome expectation and variation in learned behavior. *Conductual, 4*(2), 61–90. https://doi.org/ISSN: 2340-0242

Bolles, R. C., & Fanselow, M. S. (1980). A perceptual-defensive-recuperative model of fear and pain. *Behavioral and Brain Sciences, 3*(2), 291–301. https://doi.org/10.1017/ S0140525X0000491X

Bonin, P., Gelin, M., Laroche, B. et al. (2020) "Survival processing of the selfish gene?": Adaptive memory and inclusive fitness. *Evolutionary Psychological Science, 6*, 155–165. https://doi.org/10.1007/s40806-019-00220-1

Bonin, P., Thiebaut, G., Witt, A., & Méot, A. (2019). Contamination is "good" for your memory! Further evidence for the adaptive view of memory. *Evolutionary Psychological Science, 5*, 300–316. https://doi.org/10.1007/s40806-019-00188-y

Breland, K., & Breland, M. (1961). The misbehavior of organisms. *American Psychologist, 16* (11), 681–684. https://doi.org/10.1037/h0040090

Bush, R. R., & Mostellar, F. (1955). *Stochastic models for learning*. John Wiley & Sons.

Craik, F. I. M., & Lockhart, R. S. (1972). Levels of processing: A framework for memory research. *Journal of Verbal Learning and Verbal Behavior, 11*(6), 671–684. https://doi .org/10.1016/S0022-5371(72)80001-X

Domjan, M. (1983). Biological constraints on instrumental and classical conditioning: Implications for general process theory. *Psychology of Learning and Motivation, 17*, 215–277. https://doi.org/10.1016/S0079-7421(08)60100-0

  (1997). Behavior systems and the demise of equipotentiality: Historical antecedents and evidence from sexual conditioning. In M. E. Bouton & M. S. Fanselow (Eds.), *Learning, motivation, and cognition: The functional behaviorism of Robert C. Bolles* (pp. 31–51). American Psychological Association.

Domjan, M., & Krause, M. (2017). Generality of the laws of learning: From biological constraints to ecological perspectives. In J. H. Byrne (Ed.), *Learning and Memory: A Comprehensive Reference* (pp. 189–201). Academic Press. https://doi.org/10.1016/b978-0-12-809324-5.21012-2

Escobar, M., & Miller, R. R. (2004). A review of the empirical laws of basic learning in Pavlovian conditioning. *International Journal of Comparative Psychology, 17*, 279–303.

Everitt, B. J., Cardinal, R. N., Parkinson, J. A., & Robbins, T. W. (2003). Appetitive behavior: Impact of amygdala-dependent mechanisms of emotional learning. *Annals of the New York Academy of Sciences, 985*, 233–250. https://doi.org/10.1111/j.1749-6632.2003.tb07085.x

Fernandes, N. L., Pandeirada, J. N. S., Soares, S. C., & Nairne, J. S. (2017). Adaptive memory: The mnemonic value of contamination. *Evolution and Human Behavior, 38*, 451–460 https://doi.org/10.1016/j.evolhumbehav.2017.04.003

Foree, D. D., & LoLordo, V. M. (1973). Attention in the pigeon: Differential effects of food-getting versus shock-avoidance procedures. *Journal of Comparative and Physiological Psychology, 85*(3), 551–558. https://doi.org/10.1037/h0035300

Garcia, J., Ervin, F. R., & Koelling, R. A. (1966). Learning with prolonged delay of reinforcement. *Psychonomic Science, 5*(3), 121–122. https://doi.org/10.3758/BF03328311

Garcia, J., Kimeldorf, D. J., & Koelling, R. A. (1955). Conditioned aversion to saccharin resulting from exposure to gamma radiation. *Science, 122*, 157–158. https://doi.org/10.1126/SCIENCE.122.3160.157

Garcia, J., & Koelling, R. A. (1966). Relation of cue to consequence in avoidance learning. *Psychonomic Science, 4*(1), 123–124. https://doi.org/10.3758/BF03342209

Gelin, M., Bonin, P., Méot, A., & Bugaiska, A. (2018). Do animacy effects persist in memory for context? *Quarterly Journal of Experimental Psychology, 71*(4), 965–974. https://doi.org/10.1080/17470218.2017.1307866

Gemberling, G. A., & Domjan, M. (1982). Selective associations in one-day-old rats: Taste-toxicosis and texture-shock aversion learning. *Journal of Comparative and Physiological Psychology, 96*(1), 105–113. https://doi.org/10.1037/h0077855

Gould, E. (2007). How widespread is adult neurogenesis in mammals? *Nature Reviews Neuroscience, 8*(6), 481–488. https://doi.org/10.1038/nrn2147

Güntürkün, O., & Bugnyar, T. (2016). Cognition without cortex. *Trends in Cognitive Sciences, 20*, 291–303. https://doi.org/10.1016/j.tics.2016.02.001

Hall, B. K. (2013). Homology, homoplasy, novelty, and behavior. *Developmental Psychobiolog, 55*, 4–12. https://doi.org/10.1002/dev.21039

Haralson, J. V., Groff, C. I., & Haralson, S. J. (1975). Classical conditioning in the sea anemone, *Cribrina xanthogrammica. Physiology and Behavior, 15*, 455–460. https://doi.org/10.1016/0031-9384(75)90259-0

Hawkins, R. D., Greene, W., & Kandel, E. R. (1998). Classical conditioning, differential conditioning, and second-order conditioning of the *Aplysia* gill-withdrawal reflex in a simplified mantle organ preparation. *Behavioral Neuroscience, 112*, 636–645. https://doi.org/10.1037/0735-7044.112.3.636

Holland, P. C. (1981). Acquisition of representation-mediated conditioned food aversions. *Learning and Motivation, 12*, 1–18. https://doi.org/10.1016/0023-9690(81)90022-9

Hollerman, J. R., & Schultz, W. (1998). Dopamine neurons report an error in the temporal prediction of reward during learning. *Nature Neuroscience, 1*, 304–309. https://doi.org/10.1038/1124

Howe, M. L., & Otgaar, H. (2013). Proximate mechanisms and the development of adaptive memory. *Current Directions in Psychological Science, 22*(1), 16–22. https://doi.org/10.1177/0963721412469397

Hull, C. L. (1943). *Principles of behavior: An introduction to behavior theory.* Appleton-Century-Crofts.

Kang, S. H. K., McDermott, K. B., & Cohen, S. M. (2008). The mnemonic advantage of processing fitness-relevant information. *Memory & Cognition, 36,* 1151–1156. https://doi .org/10.3758/MC.36.6.1151

Keifer, J., & Summers, C. H. (2016). Putting the "biology" back into "neurobiology": The strength of diversity in animal model systems for neuroscience research. *Frontiers in Systems Neuroscience, 10,* 1–9. https://doi.org/10.3389/fnsys.2016.00069

Knoblich, J. A. (2008). Mechanisms of asymmetric stem cell division. *Cell, 132,* 583–597. https://doi.org/10.1016/j.cell.2008.02.007

Krause, M. A., Trevino, S., Cripps, A., Chilton, K., Sower, E., & Taylor, J. P. (2019). Inclusive fitness does not impact the survival processing effect. *Animal Behavior and Cognition, 6,* 13–31. https://doi.org/10.26451/abc.06.01.02.2019

Liang, Z. S., Nguyen, T., Mattila, H. R., Rodriguez-Zas, S. L., Seeley, T. D., & Robinson, G. E. (2012). Molecular determinants of scouting behavior in honey bees. *Science, 335,* 1225–1228. https://doi.org/10.1126/science.1213962

Logue, A. W. (1979). Taste aversion and the generality of the laws of learning. *Psychological Bulletin, 86,* 276–296. https://doi.org/10.1037/0033-2909.86.2.276

   (1985). Conditioned food aversion learning in humans. *Annals of the New York Academy of Sciences, 443,* 316–329. https://doi.org/10.1111/j.1749-6632.1985.tb27082.x

Loy, I., Álvarez, B., Strempler-Rubio, E. C., & Rodríguez, M. (2017). Coordinating associative and ecological accounts of learning in the garden snail *Cornu aspersum. Behavioural Processes, 129,* 26–32. https://doi.org/10.1016/j.beproc.2017.03.004

Marr, D. (1982). *Vision: A computational investigation into the human representation and processing of visual information.* W. H. Freeman.

Miller, R. R., & Escobar, M. (2002). Learning: Laws and models of basic conditioning. In H. Pashler & R. Gallistel (Eds.), *Stevens' handbook of experimental psychology* (pp. 47–102). John Wiley & Sons.

Mittelbach, M., Kolbaia, S., Weigend, M., & Henning, T. (2019). Flowers anticipate revisits of pollinators by learning from previously experienced visitation intervals. *Plant Signaling and Behavior, 14,* 6. https://doi.org/10.1080/15592324.2019.1595320

Mohammad, F., Aryal, S., Ho, J. et al. (2016). Ancient anxiety pathways influence *Drosophila* defense behaviors. *Current Biology, 26,* 981–986. https://doi.org/10.1016/j.cub.2016.02.031

Muszynski, N. M. (2018). *Same/Different concept learning and category discrimination in honeybees.* University of Hawai'i at Manoa. http://hdl.handle.net/10125/62751

Muszynski, N. M., & Couvillon, P. A. (2015). Relational learning in honeybees (*Apis mellifera*): Oddity and nonoddity discrimination. *Behavioural Processes, 115,* 81–93. https:// doi.org/10.1016/j.beproc.2015.03.001

Nairne, J. S. (2010). Adaptive memory: Evolutionary constraints on remembering. *Psychology of Learning and Motivation, 53,* 1–32. https://doi.org/10.1016/S0079-7421(10)53001-9

Nairne, J. S., & Pandeirada, J. N. S. (2008). Adaptive memory: Is survival processing special? *Journal of Memory and Language, 59,* 377–385. https://doi.org/10.1016/J.JML.2008.06.001

Nairne, J. S., Thompson, S. R., & Pandeirada, J. N. S. (2007). Adaptive memory: Survival processing enhances retention. *Journal of Experimental Psychology: Learning, Memory, and Cognition, 33,* 263–273. https://doi.org/10.1037/0278-7393.33.2.263

Nairne, J. S., VanArsdall, J. E., & Cogdill, M. (2017). Remembering the Living. *Current Directions in Psychological Science, 26,* 22–27. https://doi.org/10.1177/0963721416667711

Nairne, J. S., VanArsdall, J. E., Pandeirada, J. N. S., Cogdill, M., & LeBreton, J. M. (2013). Remembering the living: Episodic memory is tuned to animacy. *Psychological Science, 24,* 2099–2105. https://doi.org/10.1177/0956797613480803

New, J., Krasnow, M. M., Truxaw, D., & Gaulin, S. J. (2007). Spatial adaptations for plant foraging: women excel and calories count. *Proceedings of the Royal Society B: Biological Sciences, 274,* 2679–2684. https://doi.org/10.1098/rspb.2007.0826

Öhman, A., & Mineka, S. (2001). Fears, phobias, and preparedness: Toward an evolved module of fear and fear learning. *Psychological Review, 108,* 483–522. https://doi.org/10 .1037/0033-295X.108.3.483

Otgaar, H., & Smeets, T. (2010). Adaptive memory: Survival processing increases both true and false memory in adults and children. *Journal of Experimental Psychology: Learning, Memory, and Cognition, 36*, 1010–1016. https://doi.org/10.1037/a0019402

Pandeirada, J. N. S., Fernandes, N. L., Vasconcelos, M., & Nairne, J. S. (2017). Adaptive memory: Remembering potential mates. *Evolutionary Psychology, 15*, 147470491774280. https://doi.org/10.1177/1474704917742807

Papini, M. R. (2002). Pattern and process in the evolution of learning. *Psychological review, 109*, 186–201. https://doi.org/10.1037//0033-295X.109.1.186

(2020). *Comparative psychology: Evolution and development of brain and behavior.* Taylor & Francis. https://doi.org/10.4324/9781003080701

Pearce, K., Cai, D., Roberts, A. C., & Glanzman, D. L. (2017). Role of protein synthesis and DNA methylation in the consolidation and maintenance of long-term memory in *Aplysia. Elife, 6*, e18299. https://doi.org/10.1016/j.tins.2018.10.005

Perisse, E., Owald, D., Barnstedt, O., Talbot, C. B. B., Huetteroth, W., & Waddell, S. (2016). Aversive learning and appetitive motivation toggle feed-forward inhibition in the *Drosophila* mushroom body. *Neuron, 90*, 1086–1089. https://doi.org/10.1016/j.neuron.2016.04.034

Reaume, C. J., & Sokolowski, M. B. (2011). Conservation of gene function in behaviour. *Philosophical Transactions of the Royal Society B: Biological Sciences, 366*, 2100–2110. https://doi.org/10.1098/rstb.2011.0028

Rescorla, R. (1988). Behavioral studies of Pavlovian conditioning. *Annual Review of Neuroscience, 11*, 329–352. https://doi.org/10.1146/annurev.neuro.11.1.329

Rescorla, R. A., & Wagner, A. R. (1972). A theory of Pavlovian conditioning: Variations in the effectiveness of reinforcement and nonreinforcement. In A. H. Black & W. F. Prokasy (Eds.), *Classical conditioning II: Current research and theory* (pp. 64–99). https://pdfs.semanticscholar.org/afaf/65883ff75cc19926f61f181a687927789ad1.pdf

Rumelhart, D. E., & Mcclelland, J. L. (1986). *Parallel distributed processing: Explorations in the microstructure of cognition. Volume 1: Foundations.* MIT Press. https://pdfs.semanticscholar.org/ff2c/2e3e83d1e8828695484728393c76ee07a101.pdf

Scarborough, D. L., Cortese, C., & Scarborough, H. S. (1977). Frequency and repetition effects in lexical memory. *Journal of Experimental Psychology: Human Perception and Performance, 3*, 1–17. https://doi.org/10.1037/0096-1523.3.1.1

Seitz, B. M., Blaisdell, A. P., Polack, C. W., & Miller, R. R. (2019). The role of biological significance in human learning and memory. *International Journal of Comparative Psychology, 32*, 1–20.

Seitz, B. M., Blaisdell, A., & Tomiyama, A. J. (2021). Calories count: Memory of eating is evolutionarily special. *Journal of Memory and Language, 117*, https://doi.org/10.1016/j.jml.2020.104192

Seitz, B. M., Polack, C. W., & Miller, R. R. (2018). Adaptive memory: Is there a reproduction-processing effect? *Journal of Experimental Psychology: Learning, Memory, and Cognition, 44*, 1167–1179. https://doi.org/10.1037/xlm0000513https://doi.org/10.1037/xlm0000513

(2020). Adaptive memory: Generality of the parent 44 processing effect and effects of biological relatedness on recall. *Evolutionary Psychological Science, 6*, 246–260. https://doi.org/10.1007/s40806-020-00233-1

Seitz, B. M., Tomiyama, A. J., & Blaisdell, A. P. (2021). Eating behavior as a new frontier in memory research. *Neuroscience & Biobehavioral Reviews, 127*, 795–807. https://doi.org/10.1016/j.neubiorev.2021.05.024

Seligman, M. E. (1970). On the generality of the laws of learning. *Psychological Review, 77*, 406–418. https://doi.org/10.1037/h0029790

Shepard, R. N. (1967). Recognition memory for words, sentences, and pictures. *Journal of Verbal Learning and Verbal Behavior, 6*, 156–163. https://doi.org/10.1016/S0022-5371(67)80067-7

Shettleworth, S. J. (1975). Reinforcement and the organization of behavior in golden hamsters: Hunger, environment, and food reinforcement. *Journal of Experimental Psychology: Animal Behavior Processes, 1*, 56–87. https://doi.org/10.1037/0097-7403.1.1.56

Shomrat, T., & Levin, M. (2013). An automated training paradigm reveals long-term memory in planarians and its persistence through head regeneration. *Journal of Experimental Biology, 216,* 3799–3810. https://doi.org/10.1242/jeb.087809

Sigurdsson, T., Doyère, V., Cain, C. K., & LeDoux, J. E. (2007). Long-term potentiation in the amygdala: A cellular mechanism of fear learning and memory. *Neuropharmacology, 52,* 215–227. https://doi.org/10.1016/j.neuropharm.2006.06.022

Silva, K. M., Silva, F. J., & Machado, A. (2019). The evolution of the behavior systems framework and its connection to interbehavioral psychology. *Behavioural Processes, 158,* 117–125. https://doi.org/10.1016/j.beproc.2018.11.001

Smith, M. C., Coleman, S. R., & Gormezano, I. (1969). Classical conditioning of the rabbit's nictitating membrane response at backward, simultaneous, and forward CS-US intervals. *Journal of Comparative and Physiological Psychology, 69,* 226–231. https://doi.org/10.1037/h0028212

Staddon, J. E., & Simmelhag, V. L. (1971). The "supersitition" experiment: A reexamination of its implications for the principles of adaptive behavior. *Psychological Review, 78,* 3–43. https://doi.org/10.1037/h0030305

Thompson, R. F. (1986). The neurobiology of learning and memory. *Science, 233,* 941–947. https://doi.org/10.1126/science.3738519

Thorndike, E. L. (1898). *Animal intelligence: An experimental study of the associative processes in animals.* Columbia University Press. https://doi.org/10.1037/10780-000

(1911). *Animal intelligence: Experimental studies.* Macmillan.

Timberlake, W., & Lucas, G. A. (1989). Behavior systems and learning: From misbehavior to general principles. In S. B. Klein & R. R. Mowrer (Eds.), *Contemporary learning theories: Instrumental conditioning and the impact of biological constraints on learning* (pp. 237–275). Erlbaum.

Waelti, P., Dickinson, A., & Schultz, W. (2001). Dopamine responses comply with basic assumptions of formal learning theory. *Nature, 412,* 43–48. https://doi.org/10.1038/35083500

Wen, J. Y. M., Kumar, N., Morrison, G., Rambaldini, G., Runciman, S., Rousseau, J., & Van Der Kooy, D. (1997). Mutations that prevent associative learning in *C. elegans. Behavioral Neuroscience, 111,* 354–368. https://doi.org/10.1037/0735-7044.111.2.354

Wright, A. A., Santiago, H. C., Sands, S. F., Kendrick, D. F., & Cook, R. G. (1985). Memory processing of serial lists by pigeons, monkeys, and people. *Science, 229* (4710), 287–289. https://doi.org/10.1126/science.9304205

Wright, W. G., Kirschman, D., Rozen, D., & Maynard, B. (1996). Phylogenetic analysis of learning-related neuromodulation in molluscan mechanosensory neurons. *Evolution, 50,* 2248–2263. https://doi.org/10.2307/2410695

Zelikowsky, M., & Fanselow, M. S. (2010). Opioid regulation of Pavlovian overshadowing in fear conditioning. *Behavioral Neuroscience, 124,* 510–519. https://doi.org/10.1037/a0020083

INDEX

absolute reward value
 defined, 177–180
 learning mechanisms for, 176–177
 strengthening-weakening (S/W) learning
  principle and, 178–180
ACCg brain region, social learning and,
 255–257
accumulation test, delay of gratification and,
 380
actinopterygians
 hippocampal pallium in, 164–168
 research on, 6
 spatial memory in, 160–164
actions, in behavior systems framework,
 210–214
adaptation. *See also* prepared learning
 bottom-up research approach to, 37–44
 complex cognition and, 319–320
 co-opted mechanisms for, 412–414
 ecological hypotheses in, 40–41
 forgetting and, 83
 generalist sources for specialization in, 45–47
 implicit and explicit learning and, 234–235
 learning and memory and, 2–4
 mnemonic value of animacy and, 414–415
 model lineage in research on, 33–47
 Pavlovian conditioning and, 133–139
 predator-induced phenotypic change in
  prey and, 145–146
 proximate mechanisms in, 411–412
 social learning and, 266–268
 source memory and, 433–434
 top-down research approach to, 44–47
adaptive bias, reinforcement learning and,
 273–275
adaptive degradation, phenotypic variation
 and, 45

adaptive information seeking, memory
 evolution and, 402
adaptive memory
 constraints on, 461
 contamination and, 415–416
 evolution and, 7–8
 fitness-relevant tunings and, 406–419,
  466–467
 mnemonic value of animacy and, 414–415
adaptive specialization
 evolution and, 6–9
 generalist ancestry and, 45–47
 genetics and, 461–465
adaptive value
 cognitive mapping and, 109
 conditioned stimulus and, 199–200
 of learning ability, 98–99
 multi-stimulus interactions in, 73–74
 of sensitization, 40–41
Adkins–Regan, E., 130–131
Adler, K., 109–110
AESOP model
 behavior systems theory and, 217–218
 conditioned inhibition and backward
  conditioning in, 218–221
AFD thermosensory neurons, thermosensory
 learning in *C. elegans* and, 24–25
aging, habituation and, 17
Águila, Tamara del, 159–170
alcohol consumption, allele creation and,
 271–272
allelic differences
 genetic variation in learning ability and, 92–94
 prepared learning research and, 84–85
allocentric strategies, teleost hippocampal
 pallium structure and spatial mapping
 in, 164–168

CPSIA information can be obtained
at www.ICGtesting.com
Printed in the USA
LVHW020906250522
719703LV00005B/134

9 781108 738316